Taiwanese Grammar

a concise reference

Philip T. Lin

First published 2015 by Greenhorn Media

To find out more about all of our publications or mobile apps, please visit:

www.gogreenhorn.com

© 2015 Philip T. Lin

Typeset in Tinos in accordance with the terms of the Apache License, version 2.0. Typeset in Noto Sans SJK published under the SIL Open Font License, version 1.1.

All rights reserved. No part of this book may be reprinted or reproduced or utilized in any form by any electronic, mechanical, or other means, now known or hereafter invented, including photocopying and recording, or in any information storage or retrieval system, without permission in writing from the publisher.

ISBN13: 978-0-9963982-0-6 (pbk)
ISBN13: 978-0-9963982-1-3 (ebk)

2015080422

Contents

Preface   xxiii
  Acknowledgements   xxiv
  About the author   xxiv
Usage notes   xxv
  The inclusion of Mandarin   xxv
  Conventions used in this text   xxvi
    Character spacing   xxvi
    Location names   xxvi
    Use of characters   xxvi
    Use of Romanization   xxviii
    Context for example sentences   xxix
  A few caveats to the student   xxx
    Varying usage of the language   xxxi
    Notions of grammar   xxxi

1 Introduction   1
1.1 Defining the Taiwanese language   1
  1.1.1 Other names   1
  1.1.2 Within the Sinitic language family   2
  1.1.3 Local differences within Taiwan   4
1.2 Comparing Taiwanese and Mandarin   7
  1.2.1 Origins and development of Chinese languages   7
    1.2.1.1 Min language development   8
    1.2.1.2 Literary and colloquial register   8
  1.2.2 Distinguishing linguistic features   10
    1.2.2.1 Pronunciation differences with Mandarin   10
    1.2.2.2 Vocabulary   13
    1.2.2.3 Grammar   14
1.3 Taiwan linguistic history   17
  1.3.1 Brief linguistic history of Taiwan   17
  1.3.2 Mandarin as an official language   19

1.4 Standardization of Taiwanese	20
1.4.1 Characters	20
1.4.1.1 Special Taiwanese characters	21
1.4.1.2 Taiwanese Ministry of Education characters	23
1.4.2 Romanization schemes	24
1.4.2.1 白話字 Pe̍h-ōe-jī (POJ)	24
1.4.2.2 Taiwanese Language Phonetic Alphabet (TLPA)	25
1.4.2.3 台羅 Tâi-lô (TL)	26
1.4.2.4 Differences between POJ and TL	26
1.4.3 Contemporary approaches to reading Taiwanese	27

2 Pronunciation   30

2.1 Initials	30
2.1.1 Aspiration	30
2.1.2 Voicing	31
2.1.3 Palatalization	32
2.1.4 Comparisons to Mandarin initials	33
2.2 Finals	35
2.2.1 Nasals	36
2.2.1.1 Nasal vowels	36
2.2.1.2 Nasal consonants	36
2.2.1.3 Syllabic nasal consonants	37
2.2.2 Stops	37
2.2.3 Letters o and o˙	39
2.2.4 Finals -ek, -eng	40
2.2.5 Comparison to Mandarin finals	40
2.3 Sound changes	43
2.3.1 Contractions	43
2.3.2 Liaision with suffix 仔 -á	43
2.3.3 Other sound changes	44
2.4 Regional variation	44
2.5 Tones	45
2.5.1 Original tones	46
2.5.2 Placement of tone diacritics	51
2.5.3 Tone changes	52
2.6 Tone change rules	58
2.6.1 The guiding principle of tone changes	59

     2.6.2 The neutral tone and tone changes 61
     2.6.3 Part of speech based rules 61
          2.6.3.1 Nouns 61
          2.6.3.2 Pronouns 63
          2.6.3.3 Verbs 64
          2.6.3.4 Aspect markers 65
          2.6.3.5 Verb complements 68
          2.6.3.6 Adverbs 72
          2.6.3.7 Question words 72
          2.6.3.8 Location participles 73
          2.6.3.9 Numbers 74
          2.6.3.10 Other parts of speech 75
     2.6.4 Word-specific rules 76
          2.6.4.1 Suffix 仔 -á 76
          2.6.4.2 Names and titles 78
          2.6.4.3 遮 chia 'here' and 遐 hia 'there' 79

3 Numbers 80
  3.1 Counting numbers 80
     3.1.1 Numbers 0-10 80
     3.1.2 Literary reading for numbers 81
     3.1.3 Numbers 11-99 82
     3.1.4 Numbers 100 and greater 83
     3.1.5 Interior zeroes 85
  3.2 Ordinal numbers 86
  3.3 Partial numbers 87
     3.3.1 Fractions 87
     3.3.2 Rates 88
     3.3.3 Percentages 89
     3.3.4 Discounts 90
     3.3.5 Decimals 91
     3.3.6 Multiples 92
     3.3.7 Arithmetic 93
  3.4 Approximations 95
     3.4.1 Range 95
     3.4.2 Estimates 95
     3.4.3 More than 97

3.4.4 Less than	99
3.5 Money	100

4 Nouns — 103

4.1 Noun suffix 仔 -á	103
4.2 Plural and singular	104
4.3 Measure words	104
4.3.1 Numbers with measure word forms	106
4.3.2 Cognates between Taiwanese and Mandarin measure words	106
4.3.3 Differences between Taiwanese and Mandarin measure words	107
4.4 Plural marked by group measure words	108
4.5 Plural marked by 幾 kúi 'several'	109
4.6 Demonstratives	110
4.6.1 Demonstrative adjectives – singular	110
4.6.2 Demonstrative adjectives – plural specified number	111
4.6.3 Demonstrative adjectives – plural unspecified number	112
4.7 Omitting the noun	113
4.8 Possessive	113
4.8.1 Using the possessive marker 的 ê	114
4.8.2 Implied possession with close personal relations or titles	115
4.8.3 Implied possession before demonstrative adjectives	116
4.9 Definite and indefinite nouns	117

5 Pronouns — 119

5.1 Personal pronouns	119
5.1.1 Subject and object personal pronouns	119
5.1.2 Exclusive and inclusive 'we'	120
5.1.3 Plural personal pronouns	120
5.1.4 Gender in personal pronouns	121
5.1.5 Honorific personal pronouns	121
5.2 Reflexive pronouns	122
5.2.1 Subject receives the action	122
5.2.2 Subject performs action alone	123
5.3 Possessive pronouns	123
5.3.1 Using the possessive marker 的 ê	124
5.3.2 Plural personal pronouns marking possession	125
5.3.3 Possession by using demonstrative adjectives	126

5.4 Demonstrative pronouns	127
5.4.1 Singular demonstrative pronouns	128
5.4.2 Plural demonstrative pronouns	129
5.4.3 Unspecified demonstrative pronouns	130
5.5 Indefinite pronouns	131
5.5.1 Expressing 'any-', 'every-', or '-ever'	131
5.5.2 Expressing 'no-' or 'not any'	132
5.5.3 Expressing 'some-'	133

6 Adjectives   135

6.1 Intensifiers	136
6.1.1 Common intensifiers	136
6.1.2 Placeholder intensifier	137
6.2 Absolute adjectives	138
6.3 Comparisons	140
6.3.1 Comparisons using 比 pí ... 較 khah 'compared with…more than'	140
6.3.2 Comparisions using 比較 pí-kàu 'to compare'	141
6.3.3 Implicit comparisons	142
6.3.4 Specifying how much difference in a comparison	143
6.3.5 Comparing actions	143
6.3.6 Negating a comparison	144
6.3.7 Comparisons expressing inferiority	144
6.3.8 Comparisons expressing equality	145
6.3.9 Comparative degree	146
6.3.10 Superlative degree	147
6.4 Desirable and undesirable adjectives	147
6.4.1 Adjective structure based on desirability	147
6.4.2 Verb choice based on adjective desirability	149
6.4.3 Negation based on adjective desirability	150
6.5 Adjectives with verb characteristics	152
6.5.1 Change-of-state particle 矣 --ah	153
6.5.2 Describing conditions that have worsened 去 --khì	153
6.6 Noun phrases and the modifying particle 的 ê	154
6.6.1 Adjectives with modifying particle 的 ê	155
6.6.2 Nouns, verbs, and phrases that modify with 的 ê	157
6.6.3 Nouns that modify without 的 ê	159
6.6.4 Omitting the head noun (nominalization)	159

6.6.5 Multiple modifiers in sequence	161
6.6.5.1 Modifiers (background)	161
6.6.5.2 Modifiers (properties)	163
6.6.5.3 Co-occurring modifiers	165
6.7 Repetition	167
6.7.1 Reduplication with single-syllable adjectives	167
6.7.2 Reduplication with two-syllable adjectives	167
6.7.3 Exceeding suffix	169
6.8 Expressions with adjectives describing change	171
6.8.1 Changes over time	171
6.8.2 Changes that cause other changes	172

7 Action verbs   173

7.1 Open-ended action verbs	173
7.1.1 Specifying the duration	175
7.1.2 Specifying the frequency	175
7.1.3 Specifying the endpoint	176
7.1.4 Default objects	178
7.1.5 Including both objects and duration	179
7.1.6 Including both objects and frequency	181
7.2 Change-of-state action verbs	181
7.2.1 Change-of-state verbs in the continuous aspect	182
7.2.2 Change-of-state verbs doubling as stative verbs	183

8 Aspect   185

8.1 Perfective aspect	187
8.1.1 Perfective aspect with 有 ū	188
8.1.2 Perfective aspect with phase complements	190
8.2 Continuous aspect	191
8.2.1 Dynamic continuous aspect	192
8.2.1.1 Dynamic continuous aspect marker 咧 teh	192
8.2.1.2 Emphasizing the immediacy of an action	193
8.2.2 Static continuous aspect	194
8.2.2.1 Describing a manner of existence	194
8.2.2.2 Describing a continued posture	195
8.2.2.3 Describing repetitive movements	196
8.2.3 Verbs exhibiting both dynamic and static aspects	197

8.3 Experiential aspect	197
8.3.1 Experiential aspect with 捌 bat	198
8.3.2 Experiential aspect with 過 -kòe	198
8.3.3 Experiential aspect with both 捌 bat and 過 -kòe	199
8.4 Anterior aspect	200
8.4.1 Anterior aspect particle 矣 --ah	200
8.4.2 Anterior with other aspects	201
8.5 Habitual aspect	203
8.5.1 Habitual actions in the present	203
8.5.2 Habitual actions in the past	204
8.6 Tentative aspect	205
8.6.1 Reduplicating the verb	205
8.6.2 Adding the phrase 一下 --chit-ē	206
8.6.3 Adding the phrase 看覓 khòaⁿ-māi	207
8.6.4 Attaching verbs to 試 chhì	208
8.7 Summary of aspect	210

9 Stative Verbs   211

9.1 Common stative verbs	211
9.2 Stative verbs and intensifiers	212
9.3 Stative verbs and continuous aspect	213
9.4 Stative verbs in the past	214

10 Special verbs   216

10.1 是 sī	216
10.1.1 是 sī as a linking verb	216
10.1.2 是 sī in the focusing construction	217
10.1.3 是 sī marking the passive voice	218
10.1.4 是 sī expressing existence	219
10.2 有 ū	220
10.2.1 有 ū expressing possession	220
10.2.2 有 ū expressing existence	221
10.2.3 有 ū as a perfective aspect maker	222
10.2.4 有 ū as an emphasis marker	222
10.2.5 有 ū as a habitual aspect marker	224
10.2.6 有 ū with verb complements	225
10.2.6.1 Phase complements with 有 ū	225

        10.2.6.2 Potential complements with 有 ū 226
    10.2.7 有 ū with desirable adjectives 227
 10.3 佇 tī 228
    10.3.1 佇 tī expressing existence at a specific location 228
    10.3.2 佇 tī as a preposition 228
    10.3.3 佇咧 tī-leh as a continuous aspect marker 229

11 Verb complements   231

11.1 Phase complements 231
    11.1.1 Phase complements indicating completion 231
    11.1.2 Phase complements indicating achievement 233
    11.1.3 Phase complements indicating potential 234
    11.1.4 Phase complements and objects 235
        11.1.4.1 Phase complements indicating completion with objects 236
        11.1.4.2 Phase complements indicating achievement and potential with objects 237
11.2 Resultative complements 239
    11.2.1 Resultative complements from adjectives 239
    11.2.2 Resultative complements with objects 242
        11.2.2.1 Indefinite objects 242
        11.2.2.2 Definite objects 243
11.3 Directional complements 245
    11.3.1 Directional complements indicating speaker perspective 246
    11.3.2 Double-directional complements 246
    11.3.3 Directional complements and objects 249
        11.3.3.1 Object comes before the verb compound 249
        11.3.3.2 Object comes after the verb compound 250
        11.3.3.3 Object comes in the middle of the verb compound 251
11.4 Potential complements 253
    11.4.1 Actualized potential complements 253
    11.4.2 Unrealized potential complements 255
    11.4.3 Potential complement with suffix 得 -tit 258
    11.4.4 Potential complements and objects 260
11.5 Complements with question marker 敢 kám 261
11.6 Manner complements 262
    11.6.1 Manner complements describing habitual actions 262
    11.6.2 Manner complements describing specific instances 263

11.6.3 Manner complements with objects	264
11.7 Extent complements	265
11.7.1 Extent complements with 甲 kah	265
11.7.2 Extent complements with 予 hō͘	266
11.7.3 Extent complements with objects	267
11.8 Duration and absolute frequency complements	268
11.8.1 Duration and absolute frequency complement placement	268
11.8.2 Duration and absolute frequency complements with objects	269
11.8.3 Duration and absolute frequency complements with negated verbs	271
11.9 Summary for object placement	274
11.10 Summary of verb complements	275

12 Modal verbs   277

12.1 Possibility	277
12.1.1 Modal verb 會 ē 'will'	278
12.1.2 Modal verb 欲 beh 'to be going to'	278
12.1.3 Emphasizing that an action is 'going to happen soon'	280
12.2 Desire	281
12.2.1 Modal verb 欲 beh 'to want'	281
12.2.2 Modal verb 愛 ài 'to want'	282
12.2.3 Modal verbs 想欲 siūⁿ-beh and 想愛 siūⁿ-ài 'would like, thinking of'	283
12.2.4 Expressing desire for nouns	285
12.3 Ability	285
12.3.1 Modal verb 會曉 ē-hiáu 'can'	286
12.3.2 Modal verb 會當 ē-tàng 'can'	287
12.4 Permission	287
12.4.1 Modal verb 會使(得) ē-sái(-tit) 'may'	288
12.4.2 Modal verb 通(好) thang(-hó) 'may'	289
12.5 Obligation	289
12.5.1 Modal verb 愛 ài 'to need'	290
12.5.2 Degree of obligation	291
12.6 Prohibition	293
12.6.1 Modal verb 莫 mài 'do not'	293
12.6.2 Modal verb 毋通 m̄-thang 'do not'	294
12.6.3 Modal verb 毋好 m̄-hó 'do not'	295
12.7 Summary of modal verbs	295

13 Negation — 297

- 13.1 Negative 毋 m̄ — 298
  - 13.1.1 Pure negative 毋 m̄ 'not' — 299
  - 13.1.2 Volitional 毋 m̄ 'not want' — 300
  - 13.1.3 毋 m̄ in questions — 301
    - 13.1.3.1 Affirmative-negative questions (X-not-X format) — 301
    - 13.1.3.2 Tag questions with negatives — 302
  - 13.1.4 毋 m̄ in prohibitions — 305
  - 13.1.5 Negating the experiential aspect marker 捌 bat — 306
- 13.2 Negative 無 bô — 306
  - 13.2.1 無 bô negating possession and existence — 307
  - 13.2.2 無 bô in the perfective aspect — 308
  - 13.2.3 無 bô negating the experiential aspect suffix 過 -kòe — 308
  - 13.2.4 無 bô in the habitual aspect — 308
  - 13.2.5 無 bô as an emphasis marker — 309
  - 13.2.6 無 bô in verb complements — 309
  - 13.2.7 無 --bô in questions — 310
    - 13.2.7.1 無 --bô as a general-purpose question tag — 310
    - 13.2.7.2 無 --bô as perfective aspect question particle — 310
    - 13.2.7.3 無 --bô as a universal question particle — 311
  - 13.2.8 無 bô negating desirable adjectives — 311
- 13.3 Negative 袂 bē — 311
  - 13.3.1 袂 bē as a modal verb — 312
    - 13.3.1.1 袂 bē negating possibility — 312
    - 13.3.1.2 袂 bē negating ability — 312
    - 13.3.1.3 袂 bē negating permission — 313
  - 13.3.2 袂 bē as question particle — 313
  - 13.3.3 袂 bē in verb complements — 314
  - 13.3.4 袂 bē negating undesirable adjectives — 314
- 13.4 Negative 未 bōe — 315
  - 13.4.1 未 bōe in the anterior aspect — 315
  - 13.4.2 未 bōe as question particle — 315
- 13.5 Negative 免 bián — 316
  - 13.5.1 免 bián negating obligation — 316
  - 13.5.2 免 bián as question particle — 317
- 13.6 Summary of negation — 317

14 Adverbs   319
  14.1 Sentence-level adverbs   320
    14.1.1 Attitude adverbs   320
    14.1.2 Time adverbs   322
    14.1.3 Confidence adverbs   325
    14.1.4 Co-occurring sentence-level adverbs   326
  14.2 Verb-level adverbs   327
    14.2.1 Reference adverbs   328
      14.2.1.1 Inclusion   329
        14.2.1.1.1 All, both   329
        14.2.1.1.2 Also   330
        14.2.1.1.3 Sentences with both 嘛 mā and 攏 lóng   331
      14.2.1.2 Repetition   331
      14.2.1.3 Continuation   332
      14.2.1.4 Exclusivity   333
      14.2.1.5 Promptness   334
        14.2.1.5.1 Only, only after   334
        14.2.1.5.2 Precisely, just   335
        14.2.1.5.3 Following time expressions   336
        14.2.1.5.4 Two clauses (sequence)   336
    14.2.2 Relative frequency adverbs   337
    14.2.3 Manner adverbs   339
      14.2.3.1 Short one-syllable adjectives   339
      14.2.3.2 Multi-syllable adverbs   341
      14.2.3.3 Manner adverbs in commands   342
    14.2.4 Co-occurring verb-level adverbs   343
  14.3 Adverbs with other grammatical elements   343
    14.3.1 Negation and adverbs   344
    14.3.2 Modal verbs and adverbs   347
    14.3.3 Prepositional phrases and adverbs   348
  14.4 Summary of word order for adverbs   351

15 Prepositions   352
  15.1 Prepositions of movement   353
  15.2 Prepositions of orientation   354
  15.3 Prepositions of location   355
  15.4 Prepositions of time   356

15.5 Prepositions of accompaniment and interaction ... 357
15.6 Prepositions of manner ... 358
15.7 Prepositions for benefactives ... 359
15.8 Prepositions with grammatical function ... 360
    15.8.1 予 hō͘ marking indirect objects ... 360
    15.8.2 共 kā marking direct objects ... 360
    15.8.3 予 hō͘ marking passive voice constructions ... 361
15.9 Prepositions doubling as verbs ... 362

16 Location and directional expressions ... 363

16.1 Prepositions for location expressions ... 363
16.2 Location participles ... 364
    16.2.1 Common location participles ... 365
    16.2.2 Location participles with noun suffixes 面 -bīn and 頭 -thâu ... 366
    16.2.3 Cardinal directions ... 368
16.3 Placement of location expressions ... 369
    16.3.1 Placement between the subject and verb ... 369
        16.3.1.1 Single prepositional phrase ... 369
        16.3.1.2 Location expressions with other prepositional phrases ... 370
    16.3.2 Placement before the subject ... 371
    16.3.3 Placement after the verb ... 372
        16.3.3.1 Displacement verbs ... 373
        16.3.3.2 Placement verbs ... 374
        16.3.3.3 Appearance verbs ... 376
        16.3.3.4 Posture verbs ... 377
16.4 Directional expressions ... 379
    16.4.1 Destination verbs ... 379
    16.4.2 Speaker perspective with directional expressions ... 380

17 Direct objects ... 383

17.1 Pre-posed objects ... 385
17.2 Topicalized objects ... 385
17.3 Verb copying ... 386
17.4 共 kā construction ... 387
    17.4.1 Setting up the 共 kā construction ... 387
    17.4.2 Comparisons to the Mandarin 把 bǎ construction ... 388
    17.4.3 Traditional usage of 共 kā and 將 chiong ... 389

17.4.4 Placement with other grammatical elements	390
17.4.5 共 kā construction in commands	392

18 Indirect objects 393

18.1 Using 予 hōˈ to mark indirect objects	393
18.2 Dative verbs	394
18.2.1 Dative verbs that require 予 hōˈ	394
18.2.2 Dative verbs that optionally use 予 hōˈ	396
18.2.3 Dative verbs that cannot use 予 hōˈ	399
18.2.4 Dual-direction dative verbs	400
18.3 Benefactives	403
18.3.1 Prepositions marking benefactives	403
18.3.2 Benefactive and indirect object phrases	405

19 Passive voice 408

19.1 Passive marker 予 hōˈ	409
19.2 Stating the agent	410
19.3 The use of 共 kā in the passive voice	411
19.4 Causative verbs	412

20 Questions 415

20.1 敢 kám question marker	416
20.1.1 敢 kám placement restrictions	417
20.1.2 敢 kám in verb compounds	418
20.1.3 Responding to 敢 kám questions	418
20.2 Tag questions	419
20.2.1 General-purpose tag 是著無 sī tio̍h--bô 'is that right?'	420
20.2.2 Responding to the general-purpose tag 是著無 sī tio̍h--bô?	420
20.2.3 Affirmative tags	422
20.2.4 Pure negative 毋 m̄ tags	422
20.3 Particle questions	424
20.3.1 Negative question particles	424
20.3.2 無 --bô as a universal question particle	427
20.4 Disjunctive questions	429
20.4.1 The conjunction 抑是 ia̍h-sī 'or'	429
20.4.2 Affirmative-negative disjunctive question (X-or-not-X)	430
20.4.3 Affirmative-negative questions (X-not-X)	432

20.5 Question words	433
20.5.1 What	434
20.5.2 Who	435
20.5.3 Where	436
20.5.4 When	437
20.5.5 Which	438
20.5.6 Why	439
20.5.7 How	441
20.5.8 How much / how many	442
20.5.9 How long / how big	443
20.5.10 Whose	444
20.5.11 Summary of question words	445

21 Requests and commands — 447

21.1 Particle 咧 --leh	447
21.2 Using 去 khì 'to go' in commands	448
21.3 Using the tentative aspect	449
21.3.1 Verb reduplication	449
21.3.2 Adding the phrase 一下 --chi̍t-ē 'a little bit'	451
21.4 Polite words and phrases	452
21.4.1 請 chhiáⁿ 'please'	452
21.4.2 麻煩你 Mâ-hôan lí 'May I trouble you'	453
21.4.3 拜託 pài-thok 'please'	454
21.4.4 歹勢 pháiⁿ-sè 'apologies'	455
21.5 Modal verbs in requests	456
21.6 Group proposals	457
21.7 Negative commands	457
21.8 Using causative verbs in commands	459
21.9 Using the 共 kā construction in commands	460

22 Particles — 461

22.1 End-of-sentence particles	461
22.1.1 Single particles	461
22.1.2 Double particles	465
22.2 Exclamatory particles	466

23 Terms of address — 470

- 23.1 Social niceties — 470
  - 23.1.1 Greetings — 471
  - 23.1.2 Giving thanks — 471
  - 23.1.3 Apologies — 472
  - 23.1.4 Salutations — 473
- 23.2 Introductions — 473
  - 23.2.1 Surnames — 473
  - 23.2.2 Given names — 475
  - 23.2.3 Titles — 477
  - 23.2.4 Adding the suffix 姓 --sèⁿ to a surname — 479
  - 23.2.5 Adding the suffix 的 --ê to a surname — 480
  - 23.2.6 Adding the suffix 仔 --á to a surname — 480
  - 23.2.7 Adding the prefix 阿 A- to mark endearment — 481
  - 23.2.8 Referencing a family with the suffix 家 --ka — 481
- 23.3 Kinship terms — 482
  - 23.3.1 Immediate family — 483
  - 23.3.2 Paternal side — 485
  - 23.3.3 Maternal side — 487
  - 23.3.4 In-laws — 488
  - 23.3.5 Children of relatives — 491
  - 23.3.6 Multiple siblings — 492
  - 23.3.7 Group kinship terms — 493
  - 23.3.8 Friends and colleagues within the same generation — 494

24 Time — 495

- 24.1 Duration — 495
  - 24.1.1 Exact duration — 495
  - 24.1.2 Approximate duration — 496
    - 24.1.2.1 More than — 496
    - 24.1.2.2 Less than — 497
    - 24.1.2.3 Within and between — 499
- 24.2 Clock time — 500
  - 24.2.1 Telling time — 500
  - 24.2.2 Clock-time expressions — 501
    - 24.2.2.1 Half-hour increments — 501
    - 24.2.2.2 Past the hour — 502

xviii   Taiwanese Grammar: A Concise Reference

24.2.2.3 Before the hour	503
24.3 Parts of the day	504
24.3.1 Period of the day	504
24.3.2 Parts of the day relative to the present	507
24.3.3 Referring to habitual occurrences	508

25 Calendar   509

25.1 Years	509
25.1.1 Relative references to a year	509
25.1.2 Specifying a year	510
25.2 Months	510
25.2.1 Relative references to a month	511
25.2.2 Approximate duration	512
25.2.3 Months of the year	512
25.3 Weeks	513
25.4 Days	514
25.4.1 Relative references to a day	515
25.4.2 Days of the week	515
25.4.3 Days of the month	516
25.5 Specifying dates	516
25.6 Seasons	517

26 Present   518

26.1 Present tense from context	518
26.2 Time expressions and time adverbs indicating the present	519
26.3 Ongoing actions	520
26.3.1 Emphasizing that an action is in progress using 咧 teh	520
26.3.2 Emphasizing the immediacy of an action in progress	521
26.3.3 Including manner with ongoing actions	522
26.3.4 Describing an ongoing state using verb suffix 咧 --leh	523
26.4 Habitual actions in the present	524
26.4.1 Habitual actions in the present	524
26.4.2 Using time adverbs to indicate habitual actions	526
26.4.3 Using relative frequency adverbs to indicate habitual actions	526
26.5 Indicating past events relevant to the present using 矣 --ah	527

27 Past — 529

27.1 Time expressions and time adverbs indicating the past — 529
27.2 Completed actions in the past — 530
    27.2.1 Expressing a completed action with 有 ū — 530
    27.2.2 Expressing a completed action with a phase complement — 532
    27.2.3 Emphasizing a completed action in the past with 有 ū — 532
    27.2.4 Expressing an action that did not occur — 533
    27.2.5 Expressing actions that have not yet occurred using 猶未 iáu-bōe — 535
27.3 Habitual actions in the past — 535
27.4 Expressing a repeated event in the past with 閣(再) koh(-chài) — 537
27.5 Expressing the recent past with 頭拄仔 thâu-tú-á — 537
27.6 Past experiences — 538
    27.6.1 Expressing past experiences using 捌 bat and 過 -kòe — 538
    27.6.2 Expressing not having had an experience — 540

28 Future — 542

28.1 Time expressions and time adverbs indicating the future — 542
28.2 Indicating the future with possibility modal verbs — 543
    28.2.1 Expressing possibility using 會 ē — 543
    28.2.2 Expressing possibility using 欲 beh — 544
28.3 Describing events that are just about to happen — 545
28.4 Indicating the future with desire modal verbs — 546
    28.4.1 'Wanting to' perform an action — 546
    28.4.2 'Would like to' perform an action — 547

29 Changes — 548

29.1 Words expressing change — 548
    29.1.1 Changes that occur with no object — 548
        29.1.1.1 Changes in characteristics — 548
        29.1.1.2 To transform — 549
        29.1.1.3 To become something — 550
    29.1.2 Changing an object — 550
        29.1.2.1 To correct, edit, or fix — 550
        29.1.2.2 To exchange, switch — 550
        29.1.2.3 To improve — 551
29.2 Resultative complements indicating change — 553
    29.2.1 Changing into with resultative 做 -chò — 553

29.2.2 Successfully achieving with resultative 成 -sêng ... 554
29.3 Expressing a new situation with end-of-sentence particles ... 555
    29.3.1 Indicating a change of state with adjectives and particle 矣 --ah ... 555
    29.3.2 Emphasizing a new situation with the end-of-sentence particle --啦 lah ... 556
29.4 Describing a condition that has gotten worse using 去 --khì ... 557
29.5 Emphasizing a change in the immediate future ... 558
29.6 Expressing changes over time ... 559
    29.6.1 Changes over time 'more and more' ... 559
    29.6.2 Changes over time 'less and less' ... 560
    29.6.3 Changes caused by another action ... 561

30 Additions   562

30.1 Expanding the subject or object ... 562
30.2 Providing additional information about the subject ... 563
    30.2.1 Adding descriptions in a subsequent sentence ... 563
    30.2.2 Describing two qualities within a sentence ... 564
    30.2.3 Expressing surprise at having two qualities ... 565
30.3 Describing a subject performing multiple actions ... 566
    30.3.1 Multiple actions of equal standing ... 566
    30.3.2 Multiple actions contrary to expectation ... 566
30.4 Introducing related information to the previous statement ... 567
    30.4.1 Moreover, furthermore ... 567
    30.4.2 In addition, also, one other thing ... 568
    30.4.3 Besides, except for ... 569
        30.4.3.1 Inclusive 除了 tû-liáu ... 569
        30.4.3.2 Exclusive 除了 tû-liáu ... 570

31 Contrasts   571

31.1 Conjunctions indicating contrast ... 571
    31.1.1 Simple contrasts ... 573
    31.1.2 Emphasizing contrasts ... 573
31.2 Offering a concession in an argument ... 574
    31.2.1 Concessions with simple contrasts ... 574
    31.2.2 Emphasizing contrasts between clauses with a concession ... 575

32 Sequence — 576

- 32.1 Chronological sequence — 576
  - 32.1.1 Expressing sequence through consecutive verbs — 576
  - 32.1.2 Adverbs in sequences — 576
    - 32.1.2.1 Describing an event occurring prior to another event — 576
    - 32.1.2.2 Describing an event occurring after another event — 577
  - 32.1.3 Reference adverbs 就 tō and 才 chiah — 580
    - 32.1.3.1 就 tō 'then' — 580
    - 32.1.3.2 才 chiah 'then' — 581
    - 32.1.3.3 才 chiah 'only then' — 582
  - 32.1.4 Describing an event occurring as soon as another event occurs — 582
- 32.2 Cause and effect — 583
  - 32.2.1 Using 因為 in-ūi 'because' and 所以 só-í 'therefore' for cause and effect — 583
  - 32.2.2 Using 既然 kì-jiân 'since' to express cause — 585
  - 32.2.3 Using 毋才 m̄-chiah 'therefore' to express effect — 586

33 Purpose — 587

- 33.1 Expressing purpose through consecutive verbs — 587
- 33.2 Using 來 lâi 'come' and 去 khì 'go' to indicate purpose — 588
- 33.3 Expressing a goal or purpose of action with 為著 ūi-tio̍h — 589
- 33.4 Expressing actions taken to avoid an outcome — 590
- 33.5 Expressing for whom an action is performed — 590

34 Simultaneous actions — 592

- 34.1 Describing two actions occurring at the same time — 592
  - 34.1.1 When each activity receives attention independently — 592
  - 34.1.2 When two activities are performed at once 像時 siāng-sî — 593
  - 34.1.3 When multiple subjects perform an activity together at once — 594
  - 34.1.4 Performing actions together — 594
- 34.2 Giving priority to one action over another — 595
  - 34.2.1 Indicating a constant state with verb suffix 咧 --leh — 596
  - 34.2.2 Indicating a state or action already occurring in the background — 596
  - 34.2.3 Habitual occurrences — 597

35 Conditionals — 598

35.1 Conditionals without special conjunctions — 599
35.2 If-then clauses — 599
35.3 Other types of conditional clauses — 601
    35.3.1 In the event, just in case — 601
    35.3.2 Unless, only if — 602
    35.3.3 Even if — 603
    35.3.4 If not for, if it weren't for — 604
    35.3.5 As long as, provided that, if only — 604
    35.3.6 Regardless, no matter, whether or not, in any case — 605
35.4 Implying possible consequences 'otherwise, or else, if not' — 606

References — 607
Index — 611

Preface

The inspiration for this text arose from the marked lack of reference and study materials available in English for Taiwanese (or other Southern Min languages). In particular, resources providing clear and comprehensive treatments of Taiwanese grammar were practically non-existent or inaccessible to learners residing outside of Taiwan.

Given the resurgence of Taiwanese usage in the public sphere and the nascent programs in native language education (Taiwanese, Hakka, and aboriginal languages) in elementary schools, the opportunity to use the Taiwanese language is ever more imaginable in contemporary Taiwan. Nevertheless, the expansion of this language's usage occurs at a unique stage in Taiwan's demographic development. Currently, the oldest generations, educated in Japanese or only partially in Mandarin, prefer to communicate in Taiwanese. In contrast, the younger generations tend to prefer communication with peers in Mandarin reserving Taiwanese only for older family members. As such, today Taiwanese functions as a lingua franca across generations but will soon face challenges as a viable language if younger generations no longer continue to share this legacy with future generations.

Along with the growing public presence of spoken Taiwanese, the past decade has given rise to a wave of new scholarship within the field of Chinese linguistics focusing on previously neglected Chinese 'dialects'. While attention to phonology and lexicon has been the traditional domain of Chinese dialectology, recent research has investigated topics in grammar, unveiling a new understanding of the linguistic complexity found in non-Mandarin Chinese languages.

For the student of Taiwanese many challenges exist not the least of which are the lack of recognition as an official language and its consideration by many as only a spoken language. Without official status, independent efforts to standardize the language often go unheeded by the majority of speakers resulting in a wide variety of pronunciations and usages. Indeed the lack of official recognition extends to a perception by many that the language is merely a patois without a grammatical structure and spoken only informally among family and friends. In actuality, if taken in comparison with Mandarin, the Taiwanese language is imbued with a great deal of grammatical complexity, a sizable phonological structure with an elaborate tonal system, and a vocabulary rich with ancient Chinese and foreign origins.

The aim of this text is to provide a grammatical framework on which the student of Taiwanese can affix the vocabulary and sayings gathered from everyday conversations and other contexts. For many native speakers of Taiwanese, grammar of the language has never been learned formally or even considered as part of the language. As such, this text was conceived as a reference for those seeking a deeper grammatical understanding of the language and as part of a broader program of study. To be sure, this text focuses on grammar and students of Taiwanese would likely benefit from supplementing their studies with other materials covering topics such as vocabulary acquisition, refining pronunciation, and listening comprehension.

Acknowledgements

The completion of this text would not be possible without the assistance and support of many people to whom I am deeply indebted for their tremendous amount of patience and enthusiasm.

First and foremost, I would like to thank my parents who provided my first exposure to this fascinating language and have always offered unwavering support in all my endeavors.

I am also extremely grateful to Casey Alt for his extensive assistance in proofreading, design consultation, and technical expertise. I have benefited immeasurably by his continued encouragement and enthusiasm for this project.

Special thanks must also be extended to Wenjun Lin for her tireless help in proofreading examples and consulting on local usages.

Finally, I am deeply indebted to the many native Taiwanese speakers with whom I have consulted on this work. Their knowledge and experience have revealed to me the breadth of which Taiwanese has continued to evolve and develop. And, without their assistance the realization of this text would not be possible. I offer my sincerest gratitude to Renton Hu, Chiting Huang, Luke Cheng, Jimmy Cheng, Mars Chen, Knut Huang, Edwin Hsieh, Chien-yu Yu, Chien-ying Lee, Rainbow Liu, Agnes Yen, and Ching-wei Liu. To all of them I am enormously grateful.

I alone am responsible for all errors made in this text.

Philip T. Lin, 2015

About the author

Philip T. Lin currently resides in Taiwan and has a broad background in the areas of education, design, and finance. He is a graduate of Stanford University and additionally holds advanced degrees from Columbia University and the London School of Economics and Political Science.

Usage notes

This text is primarily organized by parts of speech, grammatical topics, and special topics. It should be noted that traditional Chinese grammar categories and terms do not always map easily onto English grammatical structures. However, with the ease of learning for the English speaker in mind, this text utilizes English grammatical concepts whenever possible and only introduces less familiar terms (e.g. aspect, stative verbs, directional expressions, etc.) when necessary to fully understand the overall structure of Taiwanese grammar.

The inclusion of Mandarin

The inclusion of Mandarin as a supplementary language in this text is an acknowledgement that many students of Taiwanese will have had some level of exposure to Mandarin Chinese. While Taiwanese and Mandarin can be considered distinct languages due to their non-mutual intelligibility, they do share enough similarities in grammar, vocabulary, and pronunciation to allow students of Taiwanese to take advantage of any prior knowledge of Mandarin.

The Mandarin glosses in this book are based on the *Standard Mandarin* (**國語 Guóyǔ** 'the national language') as spoken and taught in Taiwan. While there is a degree of variance in vocabulary between this standard and that of China (**普通話 Pǔtōnghuà** 'the common speech'), the difference in grammar is minimal and pointed out in the text when necessary. At the same time, many speakers of Mandarin in Taiwan use a more informal style of Mandarin that sometimes borrows grammatical structures from Taiwanese. In this text, the term *Taiwan Mandarin* will be used to refer to this more colloquial form of spoken Mandarin. In contrast, the term *Standard Mandarin* will be used to refer to that which is considered the official standard in Taiwan, China, and other Mandarin-speaking areas.

Additionally, in all example sentences, the Mandarin glosses (note that if unmarked in this text, Mandarin glosses are rendered in gray) seek to capture both a similar overall tone and grammatical structure to those found in the Taiwanese sentences. In some instances, accomplishing both objectives is not so easily achieved. When this is the case, the Mandarin glosses in this text favor a closer correspondence to the Taiwanese grammatical structure. While these Mandarin translations may not necessarily be the most common way to express an idea in Mandarin, they are still considered acceptable to the Mandarin ear, as there is generally more than one way to express an idea within the confines of a language. By prioritizing likeness in grammar over tone and popular usage, the hope is to facilitate the learning process for those who already have some command of Mandarin.

Furthermore, the English glosses provided in this text are by no means exhaustive and for reference only. While Taiwanese words can have multiple meanings especially when read in isolation, the English glosses given provide the most common meaning or one that is relevant to the particular chapter.

Conventions used in this text

Character spacing

While Chinese written in characters generally does not contain spaces between words, this text leaves spaces in example sentences as a visual aid, allowing students to more easily see the correspondence between characters and the Romanization. Moreover, particles and the overall grammatical structure may become more visible when spaces help to isolate these elements. That being said, the notion of what constitutes a word is less clearly defined in Chinese than in English (e.g. verbs and their default objects), and the reader may come across a differing demarcation of words used in this text compared to others. The spacing convention used has been chosen to be consistent with how grammatical structures are explained in this text.

Location names

Names of geographic locations in example sentences such as cities and countries are rendered in Taiwanese pronunciations. However, note that the usage of Taiwanese pronunciations for locations often depends on the speaker's own familiarity with the Taiwanese reading. For many, particularly younger speakers, Mandarin readings are used instead for locations and proper nouns.

Use of characters

While written Taiwanese does not have an official standard, the Taiwanese Ministry of Education (MOE) has put forth a selection of Chinese characters in an effort to standardize the content used in educational materials *(see 4.1 Characters)*. Although it remains to be seen if the MOE promulgated set of characters for Taiwanese takes hold among a large number of users, the characters (as an internally consistent set of characters) remain useful for instructional purposes. This text uses both this set of Taiwanese characters and Romanized text because the combination is particularly helpful for students who might need help disambiguating the many homophones (or at least similar sounding words) in Taiwanese. Even for students that cannot necessarily read characters, the difference in pictorial representation may help to reduce ambiguity.

Note that a few MOE characters fall outside the character set of the fonts used in the digital and print versions of this text. For example, the third person plural pronoun 'they' should be rendered with a character composed of 亻 + 因. In these cases, this text makes use of alternate characters that have been recognized by the MOE, such as 怹 for 'they'.

Below are some example sentences with common, frequent, and similar sounding words. To the ear still unfamiliar with tones and proper context, differentiating among the sounds can be a challenge.

TAIWANESE	MEANING
一 chit	one
這 chit	this

一个無夠，你看，這个已經破去矣。
<u>Chit</u> ê bô kàu, lí khòaⁿ, <u>chit</u> ê í-keng phòa--khì--ah.
一個不夠，你看，這個已經破了。
Yī gè bù gòu, nǐ kàn, zhège yǐjīng pòle.
One of them is not enough. Look! This one is already broken.

TAIWANESE	MEANING
的 ê	modifying particle
个 ê	general measure word
會 ē	will

伊的佮彼个濫做伙敢會予插雜？
I--<u>ê</u> kah hit--<u>ê</u> lām chò-hóe kám <u>ē</u> hō͘ chhap-cha̍p?
他的和那個混一起會不會被雜亂無章？
Tā de hé nàge hùn yīqǐ huìbùhuì bèi záluànwúzhāng?
Will mixing his together with that one cause confusion?

TAIWANESE	MEANING
阿 a-	endearment prefix
矣 --ah	anterior aspect marker
仔 -á	noun suffix

阿姨 共 狗<u>仔</u> 洗 了 <u>矣</u>，所以 伊 這馬 較 芳 <u>矣</u>。
A-î kā káu-<u>á</u> sé liáu--<u>ah</u>, só-í i chit-má khah phang--<u>ah</u>.
阿姨 把 狗 洗完 了，所以 牠 現在 變 香 了。
Āyí bǎ gǒu xǐwán le, suǒyǐ tā xiànzài biàn xiāng le.
Auntie has washed the dog, so it smells better now.

Aside from the combined use of characters and Romanized text to help early students of Taiwanese disambiguate among the many homophones, the use of characters helps to tie together the range in pronunciations that might appear among the local and generational variation occurring among Taiwanese speakers.

For example, both **欲 beh / boeh** 'going to, to want' and **買 bé / bóe** 'to buy' have alternate pronunciations that vary by local and individual preferences. While both words can be differentiated by context and pronunciation (tone and glottal stop), for the beginner student these distinctions can be difficult to discern.

伊 欲 買 菜。
I <u>beh</u> <u>bé</u> chhài.
I <u>beh</u> <u>bóe</u> chhài.
I <u>boeh</u> <u>bé</u> chhài.
I <u>boeh</u> <u>bóe</u> chhài.

他 要 買 菜。
Tā yāo mǎi cài.
He is going to buy vegetables.

Because the origins of the Taiwanese language stem from different regions in southern China with distinct accents, both the vocabulary and pronunciation of words vary significantly throughout different localities in Taiwan. Without standardization, many differences in pronunciation persist. This text uses the more common pronunciations while also providing frequently heard alternate pronunciations.

Use of Romanization

This text uses the *Pe̍h-ōe-jī* (POJ) Romanization system for transcribing Taiwanese. While the Taiwanese Ministry of Education currently promotes a revised version of POJ called *Tâi-lô* (TL) for usage in its educational materials, this text has chosen to use the POJ Romanization system. Because the bulk of Taiwanese literature has been written in POJ, familiarity with this Romanization system offers access to a corpus of literature dating back to the mid-nineteenth century. This legacy has allowed POJ to persist amid a large number of Romanization systems that have been proposed over the years. Today it remains the most popular system among online users and among those who remain unsure of the viability of other Romanization systems. As many current Romanization schemes are based off of POJ, learning POJ and then making adjustments to learn another POJ-based system such as TL is fairly manageable *(see 4.2.4 Differences between POJ and TL)*.

This text uses the *Hànyǔ Pīnyīn* Romanization system for transcribing Mandarin.

It should be noted that tone changes have not been transcribed. This includes changes made to two consecutive syllables with the third tone, the negative 不 **bù** 'no, not' before syllables in the fourth tone, and the number 一 **yī** 'one' before any syllable when used to describe a quantity.

WRITTEN IN TEXT	ACTUAL PRONUNCIATION	MEANING
THIRD TONES		
Nǐ hǎo	Ní hǎo	你好 'Hello'
shuǐjiǎo	shuíjiǎo	水餃 'dumpling'
BÙ 不 'NO, NOT'		
bù duì	bú duì	不對 'incorrect'
bù chòu	bú chòu	不臭 'not stinky'
YĪ 一 'ONE'		
yī kuài	yí kuài	一塊 'one piece'
yī běn shū	yì běn shū	一本書 'one book'
yī tiáo lù	yì tiáo lù	一條路 'one road'
yī fēng xìn	yì fēng xìn	一封信 'one letter'

The neutral tone is left unmarked in this text.

Context for example sentences

Taiwanese is much more contextually based than English. As a result, example sentences in isolation face the challenge of not being understood in their full context. In example sentences where differentiating between two interpretations of a sentence is necessary, additional context has been provided in parentheses. However, note that most example sentences have not been provided the full context in which the sentence could occur. The reader is encouraged to broadly consider all possible contexts for each example sentence. Moreover, because the goal of this text is to showcase the full possibilities of what Taiwanese grammar can accomplish, in some instances it may be necessary to consider contexts beyond the most common situation to highlight a less used grammatical structure.

A few caveats to the student

While consulting and practicing with native speakers of Taiwanese will likely provide a significant resource in the student's language studies, one should be aware of some potential challenges when studying Taiwanese. Because Taiwanese remains an unofficial language and has not undergone standardization, this consequently produces conflicting views among native speakers of what should be deemed acceptable speech.

Varying usage of the language

With regards to choice in vocabulary and pronunciation, differences may occur due to a speaker's locality, generation, and/or individual preference. In addition, because the language in the past has been restricted to particular domains (i.e. not in education, government, or in most public settings), each native speaker has a different scope of what sounds acceptable depending on his or her accustomed environment for using the language. For example, some of the language informants for this text used Taiwanese exclusively with grandparents, while others had a more diverse engagement that included peers, neighbors, and colleagues. In general, the language is most commonly used with family members or close friends, which in turn tends to bias a speaker's exposure to the Taiwanese spoken in a certain locality.

The hope of this text is to capture what is grammatically possible and acceptable for some speakers (and not necessarily all speakers). As a result, some grammatical structures, vocabulary, and pronunciations presented in this book may not always be familiar to a particular native speaker.

Notions of grammar

Aside from the challenges of conflicting and differing usages of a non-standardized language, the student of Taiwanese may encounter difficulties when inquiring of native speakers about grammatical usage.

Because grammar for Mandarin is generally not explicitly taught within the education system in Taiwan, most native speakers are not even aware that Chinese languages have any grammar. It is not uncommon in Taiwan to hear in response to a question about Mandarin grammar, 'Chinese has grammar?' For many in Taiwan, grammar is equated to verb inflections or noun gender agreement found in other languages.

For the Taiwanese language, the perception is exacerbated by the fact that many consider Taiwanese only to be a 'spoken language' and thereby informal and incapable of having a systematized grammar. The lack of standardization, the great degree of local variation, and restriction of its usage to less formal contexts in the past century have contributed to this overall sense among many that Taiwanese is not a full, complex language imbued with a complex grammar.

Aside from the Taiwan-specific issue of little to no formal grammar instruction in the education system, the student of Taiwanese should also be aware that a native speaker's individual awareness of his or her mother tongue's grammar and usage can vary significantly. For example, for many native speakers of English, the correct usage of tense or case is not always used in accordance with English grammar standards. However, due to an individual's language experience and environment, the ungrammatical usage may actually sound more natural.

UNGRAMMATICAL USAGE

I wish I was rich.

Who are you calling?

GRAMMATICAL USAGE

I wish I were rich.

Whom are you calling?

In the examples above, the ungrammatical versions are widely used among many native speakers of English.

That being said, grammar itself is less a prescriptive set of rules than a description of how a living and constantly evolving language is used by the majority of its speakers. For languages that have not undergone standardization or a major overhaul, this is even more so the case. In fact, the Southern Min language had already accumulated four distinct layers of vocabulary from various migrations of people in China before arriving in Taiwan where additional influences by aboriginal languages, Japanese, and Mandarin continued to change the language *(see 1.2.2 Min language development)*. Even among the many language informants for this text, acceptability of some grammatical structures varied quite widely, reflecting not only differences in local, generational, and individual usage but also a language that is continually in flux.

1 Introduction

Taiwan (officially known as the Republic of China) is an island nation of 23 million inhabitants off the southeastern coast of China (officially known as the People's Republic of China). While the official language on Taiwan is Mandarin Chinese, approximately 70% of the population speak Taiwanese, 12% Hakka, and 2% aboriginal (Austronesian) languages[1]. 'Taiwanese' (台灣話 Tâi-ôan-ōe or 台語 Tâi-gí) refers to the most commonly used term by locals when designating this variant of Southern Min Chinese[2].

While acknowledging there is some controversy over the term 'Taiwanese' due to the implication that other languages spoken on the island are not considered 'Taiwanese' languages, this text uses 'Taiwanese' in deference to the most recognizable term in English by both locals and those abroad when referring to Taiwanese Southern Min.

1.1 Defining the Taiwanese language

1.1.1 Other names

Taiwanese is one among many Chinese languages and originates from the modern southern Chinese province of Fujian. Due to famine and conflicts throughout the period spanning from the 17th to the mid-20th century, waves of emigrants from this region of China spread the language to Taiwan and various parts of Southeast Asia, including Singapore, Malaysia, Indonesia, Vietnam, Thailand, the Philippines, and overseas Chinese communities on other continents throughout the world.

Because speakers live across many regions, the language has evolved over time into several variants as well as taken on a number of different names.

---

[1] Klöter, Henning. (2004). Language Policy in the KMT and DPP Eras. *China Perspectives 56*. Retrieved from: http://chinaperspectives.revues.org/442
[2] Ota, Katsuhiro J. (2005). *An Investigation of Written Taiwanese*. Masters thesis. University of Hawaii at Manoa. Retrieved from ScholarSpace: http://scholarspace.manoa.hawaii.edu/

ENGLISH	CHARACTERS	TAIWANESE (Pe̍h-ōe-jī)	MANDARIN (Hànyǔ Pīnyīn)	MEANING
Taiwanese	台灣話	Tâi-ôan-ōe	Táiwān huà	Taiwan speech
	台語	Tâi-gí	Táiyǔ	Taiwan language
Hokkien (Fookien)	福建	Hok-kiàn	Fújiàn	Fujian province
Hokkienese (Fukienese)	福建話	Hok-kiàn-ōe	Fújiàn huà	Fujian speech
Hoklo	福佬	Hok-ló	Fúlǎo	Fujian folk
Holo	河洛	Hô-lo̍k	Héluò	Yellow and Luo Rivers
	鶴佬	Ho̍h-ló	Hèlǎo	Crane folk
Amoy	廈門	Ē-mn̂g	Xiàmén	Xiamen
Lang-nang-oe	咱人話	Lán-lâng-ōe	Zán rén huà	Our people's speech
Min Nan (Minnanyu)	閩南語	Bân-lâm-gí	Mǐnnán yǔ	Southern Min language

The names given to the language generally stem from geographic references to areas from which the language originated or is spoken. Usage of terms varies according to region. For example, the term Lang-nang-oe (**咱人話 Zán rén huà**) 'our people's speech' originates from the minority ethnic Chinese population in the Philippines where the majority of this group speaks a variant of Southern Min.

1.1.2 Within the Sinitic language family

Taiwanese comes from a larger Chinese linguistic grouping called Southern Min, which in turn belongs to even larger groupings of Chinese languages. Most linguists classify Chinese languages as part of the Sino-Tibetan language family, a large category comprising more than 400 separate languages spoken by about one-fifth of the world population.

Below is a chart outlining the classification of Taiwanese as a variant within the broader Sino-Tibetan language family[3].

LANGUAGE FAMILY

Sino-Tibetan	Indo-European	Niger-Congo	Afroasiatic	Austronesian	Dravidian	Altaic	Austroasiatic	Tai-Kadai

BRANCH

Sinitic	Tibetan

DIALECTS

Min	Mandarin	Wu	Yue	Hakka	Gan	Xiang

SUB-DIALECTS

Southern Min	Northern Min	Central Min	Puxian Min

VERNACULAR

Hokkien	Teochew	Hainanese

ACCENT

Zhangzhou	Quanzhou

VARIANT

Taiwanese	Amoy	Singaporean Hokkien	Penang Hokkien	Medan Hokkien	Philippine Hokkien

Hokkien can further be subdivided into accents from Quanzhou (**泉州 Quánzhōu**) and Zhangzhou (**漳州 Zhāngzhōu**), two neighboring regions within Fujian province with distinct pronunciations and vocabulary. All Hokkien variants (including Taiwanese) are derived from a mixture of these two regional accents.

VARIANT	LOCATION	COMPOSITION OF REGIONAL ACCENT
Taiwanese	Taiwan	generally equal mix
Amoy	China	generally equal mix
Singaporean Hokkien	Singapore	slightly more Quanzhou
Penang Hokkien	Indonesia	more Zhangzhou
Medan Hokkien	Indonesia	more Zhangzhou
Philippine Hokkien	the Philippines	more Quanzhou

---

3 Norman, Jerry. (1991). The Mǐn dialects in historical perspective. In William S.Y. Wang (Ed.). *Languages and dialects of China*. Berkeley: Journal of Chinese Linguistics Monograph Series 3, 325-360.

Amoy (**廈門 Xiàmén**) is the port city nestled in between the Quanzhou and Zhangzhou regions. As a result of commerce and geography, the Amoy variant emerged as a mixture of both Quanzhou and Zhangzhou accents. The importance of Amoy as a trading port in the late nineteenth century made the Amoy variant one of the most popular Chinese languages to learn during that period.

Because Taiwan was settled by migrants from both Zhangzhou and Quanzhou regions, a mixture of both accents also developed on the island. Without standardization many local differences arose within Taiwanese from continued internal migrations resulting in the patchwork of accents that exist today *(see 1.1.3 Local differences within Taiwan)*.

1.1.3 Local differences within Taiwan

As both Quanzhou and Zhangzhou sit along the Taiwan Strait, migrants from both regions traveled to Taiwan beginning in the 17th century. Because of this, the Taiwanese language has evolved from a mixture of both Quanzhou and Zhangzhou accents. While migrants from each region initially settled in a particular locality in Taiwan, four hundred years of internal movement as well as a lack of standardization of the language has resulted in local accents in Taiwan that are less attributed to the Quanzhou/Zhangzhou divide than to the geographic differences within the island of Taiwan. Recent scholarship within the field of Taiwanese sociolinguistics has found distinctions to classify Taiwanese into five local accents: seaport (**海口 hǎikǒu**), coastal (**篇海 piānhǎi**), inner plains (**內埔 nèibù**), interior (**偏內 piānnèi**), and the common (**通行 tōngxíng**), which represents most of the the larger urban centers[4]. The common accent is further subdivided into North (Taipei, Hsinchu) and South (Tainan, Kaoshiung, Taitung).

---

4 Klöter, Henning. (2005). *Written Taiwanese*. Wiesbaden: Otto Harrassowitz.

FIGURE 1 Map of local accents

City names are listed per official Taiwanese spelling.

Distribution data provided by the Taiwanese Ministry of Education (MOE)[5]

---

5 *Zhōnghuá Mínguó Jiàoyùbù* (中華民國教育部) [ROC Ministry of Education]. (2011). Retrieved from: http://twblg.dict.edu.tw/holodict_new/index.html

LOCAL ACCENT	REPRESENTATIVE CITIES	EXAMPLE WORDS							
		卵 'egg'	二 'two'	毛 'hair'	姊 'sister'	水雞 'frog'	先生 'sir, Mr.'	生 'to be born'	好 'good'
	Quanzhou								
Seaport	Lukang	nn̂g	lī	mn̂g	chí	súi-koe	sian-si^n	si^n	hó
Coastal	Penghu, Nanliao, Taihsi	nn̂g	lī	mn̂g	ché	súi-koe	sian-si^n	si^n	hó
Common (North)	Taipei, Hsinchu	nn̂g	lī	mn̂g	ché / chí	chúi-koe / súi-koe	sian-si^n	si^n	hó
Common (South)	Tainan, Kaoshiung, Taitung	nn̂g	jī	moˋ / mn̂g	ché / chí	chúi-ke / súi-ke	sian-si^n / sian-se^n	se^n	hór
Interior	Taichung, Chiayi, Changhua	nn̂g	jī	mn̂g	ché	chúi-ke	sin-se^n	se^n	hó
Inner Plains	Yilan	nūi	jī	moˋ	chí	chúi-ke	sin-se^n	se^n	hó
	Zhangzhou								

As can seen from this table, the variation in pronunciation by local accent is not entirely consistent with the Quanzhou and Zhangzhou division. Some words such as 卵 **nn̂g** 'egg' have been adopted by most Taiwanese speakers using the Quanzhou accent. In contrast, other words such as those for 'two' 二 **lī/jī** and 'hair' 毛 **mn̂g/mo**ˋ are more evenly distributed between Quanzhou and Zhangzhou accents across all localities in Taiwan.

Moreover, given the degree of mobility in contemporary Taiwanese society and the influence of Taiwanese language media, the accents of the larger urban centers, as represented by the Common dialects, appear to be gravitating towards one another. For example, the word for 水雞 'frog', which is pronounced **súi-koe** in the Quanzhou accent and **chúi-ke** in the Zhangzhou accent, appears to be currently unstable within the Common dialects in which alternate pronunciations **chúi-koe** and **súi-ke** have also emerged. With all four permutations of the two-syllable word present in the Common dialects, this instability suggests an additional axis of division resulting from the urban/rural divide.

Additionally, in some cases, a new pronunciation is emerging from urban centers irrespective of the traditional Quanzhou and Zhangzhou division. The pronunciation of the 'o' in **hó** 好 'good' similar to the 'a' in the English word 'sof<u>a</u>' is found primarily only in the larger southern cities of Tainan, Kaoshiung, and Taitung. Currently in other localities, the 'o' in **hó** 好 'good' is similar to the 'o' in the English word 'w<u>o</u>ke'.

Nonetheless, a few words are difficult to align with either the Quanzhou/Zhangzhou or urban/rural axes. The word for 'older sister' 姊 appears to have the pronunciation of both **ché** and **chí** in defiance of these orientations. In Taiwan's bilingual society, it is possible that there is interference from the Mandarin term for 'older sister' 姐 **jiě**. The Mandarin term itself 姐 **jiě** appears to be now used almost interchangeably in Taiwan with the character 姊, which in other Mandarin-speaking areas has the pronunciation 姊 **zǐ**.

Despite the complexity of how local accents differ in Taiwan, many local Taiwanese prefer to use a simplified north/south division to explain the variation in their speech.

1.2 Comparing Taiwanese and Mandarin

While the term 'Chinese' often refers to Mandarin Chinese in common parlance, Chinese is actually a large family of languages. For many, Mandarin is regarded as the 'standard language', while other Chinese languages are simply considered 'dialects'.

However, the degree of linguistic difference found among Chinese languages can roughly be compared to that found among Romance languages (i.e. Portuguese and French vs. Mandarin and Cantonese). The distinction between 'language' and 'dialect' is more often made for political reasons than linguistic ones. Within traditional Chinese linguistics, 方言 fāngyán 'regional speech' is a broader and more inclusive term than the more common English translation 'dialect'. For this reason, many prefer to use the term 'variety' or 'language' instead of 'dialect'.

1.2.1 Origins and development of Chinese languages

The origins of the various Chinese languages that exist today are difficult to pinpoint. Some scholars suggest that differentiation among Chinese languages began around the end of the Zhou Dynasty (~250 BC)[6]. For comparison purposes, Latin began to evolve into the Romance languages beginning in the sixth century after the fall of the Roman Empire in AD 476.

Despite centuries of independent evolution among the different Chinese languages, a writing system that was divorced from pronunciation and spoken grammar provided a unifying element for the disparate Chinese languages. The origin of the pictorial-based Chinese character writing system dates back to artifacts from 1200 BC documenting Old Chinese written in 'oracle bone script'.

More than half a millennium later, Classical Chinese literature emerged during the beginning of the Spring and Autumn period of the Zhou Dynasty (~500 BC) documenting the teachings of Confucius, Mencius and Laozi. By the end of the Han Dynasty (AD 220), a revised writing style based on Classical Chinese called Literary Chinese became the primary form of written Chinese. This style of writing would continue on until the early twentieth century. Over the centuries, the grammar and vocabulary of written Chinese diverged significantly with all varieties of spoken Chinese. However, as the primary visual representation of the language, written Literary Chinese bound the spoken languages together under the rubric of Chinese.

---
6 Chen, Ping. (2004). *Modern Chinese: History and Sociolinguistics*, 7. Cambridge: Cambridge University Press.

1.2.1.1 Min language development

With regards to the Min languages, most scholars describe their development in four distinct linguistic layers. The oldest layer is from the non-Sinitic Min-Yue (閩越 **Mǐn Yuè**) people who occupied the Fujian region since before the arrival of the Han Chinese around 110 BC. Some scholars suggest that the language spoken by these people belonged to the Austronesian or Tai-Kadai language family[7].

The first Han Chinese imperial armies came into southern China during the Qin-Han Dynasty (221 BC-AD 220). The language from this influx of people is thought to have contributed significantly to the colloquial base of Southern Min.

About half a millennia later, more arrivals from northern China came during the Northern and Southern Dynasties (AD 420-550) period. As those that came during this period were part of the aristocracy, more elevated language was introduced into Southern Min.

The final layer was introduced during the Tang Dynasty (AD 618-907) when the bulk of the literary register was added to the Southern Min vocabulary.

Below is a comparison of how the word for 'stone' entered the Southern Min language at three distinct moments, occupying different layers within the language.

QIN-HAN	NORTHERN AND SOUTHERN	TANG
(221 BC - AD 220)	(AD 420-550)	(AD 618-907)
chio̍h	*siȧh*	*se̍k*
石頭 chio̍h-thâu	石榴 siȧh-liû	藥石 io̍k-se̍k
'stone'	'pomegranate'	'stone acupuncture'

These three layers in addition to the pre-Sinitic layer constituted the base of the Southern Min language before subsequent influences from colonial and neighboring powers in the 19th and 20th centuries introduced additional vocabulary to the variants of Hokkien *(see 1.2.2.2 Vocabulary)*.

1.2.1.2 Literary and colloquial register

Like most Chinese languages, Taiwanese has both literary and colloquial readings for characters. *Literary readings* arose from the Middle Chinese pronunciation of words used in formal settings during the Tang Dynasty (AD 618-907). These newer pronunciations allowed officials from all regions of China to more easily understand each other when conducting official business in the capital city of Chang'an (Xi'an). As a result, the contemporary reader will find that the Taiwanese in the literary register bears

---
[7] Norman, Jerry. (1979). Chronological strata in the Min dialects. *Fāngyán* 方言 (4), 268-273.

a closer resemblance phonetically to Mandarin. For Taiwanese and other Min languages, *colloquial readings* are older pronunciations originating from Old Chinese during the Qin-Han Dynasties (221 BC-AD 220) and the time of the Northern and Southern Dynasties (AD 420-550).

In general, literary readings are more commonly found in place names, proverbs, surnames, literature, and higher-level concepts. In contrast, colloquial readings tend to be used for terms found in everyday speech. However, for Taiwanese this distinction between literary and colloquial readings is less severe than this bifurcation may suggest. Many Taiwanese words used in everyday speech actually incorporate literary readings. Even so, these literary readings tend to be in *bound form*, only appearing in combination with another syllable. Colloquial readings, in contrast, are more likely to function as stand-alone syllables.

	LIT.		COLL.	
西 'west'	se	西裝 se-chong 'suit'	sai	西爿 sai-pêng 'west side'
轉 'turn'	chóan	運轉 ūn-chóan 'to revolve'	tńg	轉 tńg 'to return'
人 'people'	jîn	人事 jîn-sū 'personnel'	lâng	人客 lâng-kheh 'guest'
學 'learn'	ha̍k	學生 ha̍k-seng 'student'	o̍h	學 o̍h 'to learn'

Mandarin does have some words with both colloquial and literary readings as well. However, there are far fewer of these since the Mandarin dialects have historically shared a closer pronunciation to the language used in official settings, **官話 guānhuà** 'official speech'.

	LIT.		COLL.	
薄 'thin'	bó	薄膜 bómó 'membrane'	báo	薄餅 báobǐng 'pancake'
血 'blood'	xiě	血緣 xiěyuán 'bloodline'	xuè	流血 liúxuè 'to bleed'
露 'drop'	lù	露點 lùdiǎn 'dewpoint'	lòu	露底 lòudǐ 'to leak secrets'
削 'peel'	xuē	削減 xuējiǎn 'to reduce'	xiāo	削尖 xiāojiān 'to sharpen'

Furthermore, the use of colloquial and literary registers within Hokkien dialects varies as well. In some regions, the colloquial terms are used while in others the literary ones. For example, the term **大學** 'university' follows a literary reading **tāi-ha̍k** in Taiwanese but a colloquial reading **tōa-o̍h** in Penang Hokkien. Taiwanese appears to use more literary readings in its vocabulary than other variants of Hokkien[8].

---

8 Ota, Katsuhiro J. (2005). *An Investigation of Written Taiwanese*. Masters thesis. University of Hawaii at Manoa, 13. Retrieved from ScholarSpace: http://scholarspace.manoa.hawaii.edu/

	LITERARY	COLLOQUIAL
大 'big'	tāi	tōa
學 'learn'	ha̍k	o̍h

	TAIWANESE	PENANG HOKKIEN
大學 'university'	tāi-ha̍k	tōa-o̍h

In some cases, the choice in pronunciation between literary and colloquial registers is still in flux. For example, the multi-syllabic expression 放假 'to go on vacation, holiday' has not settled on a reading within the Taiwanese and the Penang Hokkien dialects. In fact, a mixed-register reading **pàng-ká** appears in both dialects.

	LITERARY	COLLOQUIAL
放 'release'	hòng	pàng
假 'vacation, holiday'	kà	ké

	TAIWANESE	PENANG HOKKIEN
放假 'to go on vacation'	hòng-ká	pàng-ké
	pàng-ká	pàng-ká

1.2.2 Distinguishing linguistic features

In comparison to Mandarin, many distinctions exist with Taiwanese pronunciation, vocabulary, and grammar. This section briefly highlights some of the more salient differences between these two languages. For more detail exploring these differences, see the specified chapters.

1.2.2.1 Pronunciation differences with Mandarin

Taiwanese maintains many sounds and tones that were used in Middle Chinese but no longer exist in Standard Mandarin. Some of these include nasal sounds, stopped endings, and additional tones *(see 2 Pronunciation)*. At the same time, Mandarin possesses a few phonological features that are not present in Taiwanese such as rounded vowels and retroflex sounds.

Nasal sounds

Taiwanese has a larger catalog of nasal sounds including nasal vowels, nasal consonants, and syllabic nasal consonants *(see 2.2.1 Nasal sounds)*. Mandarin does not have nasal vowels, although vowels followed by nasal consonants can take on a nasal quality. Nor does Mandarin have syllabic nasal consonants.

TAIWANESE	MANDARIN	MEANING
NASAL VOWELS		
saⁿ	sān	三 'three'
pêⁿ	píng	平 'flat'
NASAL CONSONANTS		
lâm	nân	南 'south'
nn̄g	liǎng	兩 'two'
SYLLABIC NASAL CONSONANTS		
m̄	--	毋 'no, not'
n̂g	huáng	黃 'yellow'

Stops

Taiwanese possesses stopped endings, which occur when the flow of air is halted by a glottal stop or consonant ending '-p', '-t', or '-k'. While still part of Middle Chinese, this trait has since disappeared from Mandarin *(see 2.2.2 Stops)*.

TAIWANESE	MANDARIN	MEANING
sek	sè	色 'color'
chiap	jiē	接 'to receive'

Rounded vowels

Taiwanese lacks the rounded vowels **ü [y]** and **üe [yɛ]** that occur in Mandarin *(see 2.2.5 Comparison to Mandarin finals)*.

TAIWANESE	MANDARIN	MEANING
lú	nǚ	女 'female'
seh	xuě	雪 'snow'

Retroflex consonants

Taiwanese lacks retroflex consonants, which are formed by the upward curl of the tongue *(see 2.1.4 Comparisons to Mandarin initials)*.

TAIWANESE	MANDARIN	MEANING
sī	shì	是 'to be'
chí	zhǐ	只 'only'

Additional tones

Taiwanese retains seven of the original eight Middle Chinese tones. The sixth tone has merged with the second tone. Additionally, the fourth and eighth tones are only used for syllables with stopped endings *(see 2.5.1 Original tones)*.

TONE	TAIWANESE	MANDARIN
1	high flat	high flat
2	high falling	rising
3	low falling	dipping
4	low stopped	high falling
5	rising	--
6	--	--
7	low flat	--
8	high stopped	--

Extensive tone changes

While Mandarin undergoes tone changes with consecutive syllables in the third tone or in different combinations with 一 **yī** 'one' and 不 **bù** 'no, not', Taiwanese has an extensive system of changing tones. Every tone maps to a different tone under circumstances dependent on phrasing, grammar, and vocabulary *(see 2.5.3 Tone changes, 2.6 Tone change rules)*.

ORIGINAL TONE		CHANGED TONE	
1	high flat	7	low flat
2	high falling	1	high flat
3	low falling	2	high falling
4 (-h)	low stopped	2	high falling
4 (-p, -t, -k)	low stopped	8	high stopped
5	rising	7	low flat *(South)*
		3	low falling *(North)*
6	--	--	--
7	low flat	3	low falling
8 (-h)	high stopped	3	low falling
8 (-p, -t, -k)	high stopped	4	low stopped

1.2.2.2 Vocabulary

Only about 85% of the lexicon, or vocabulary, of Taiwanese have cognates with Mandarin[9]. The remaining vocabulary appears to have originated from the oldest non-Sinitic layer of Southern Min or come from more recent loanwords such as from Japanese.

Pre-sinitic words

Some words only found in Min dialects are thought to have originated from this pre-Sinitic layer, which some scholars hypothesize was an Austronesian language[10].

TAIWANESE	MANDARIN	MEANING
囝 kiá^n	孩子 háizi	child
糜 môe	粥 zhōu	rice porridge
刣 thâi	殺 shā	to kill
睏 khùn	睡 shuì	to sleep

Archaic Sinitic words

A number of archaic Chinese words are still preserved within Taiwanese. Many scholars believe this resulted from Min languages splitting from Old Chinese (1200-220 BC) earlier than other Chinese varieties.

TAIWANESE	MANDARIN	MEANING
鼎 tiá^n	鍋 guō	pot
目睭 ba̍k-chiu	眼睛 yǎnjīng	eye
箸 tī	筷子 kuàizi	chopsticks
冊 chheh	書 shū	book

Loanwords from Japanese

During the fifty-year Japanese colonial period, many words related to technology, medicine, and western cultural products were imported from Japanese into Taiwanese. A good number of these terms had previously been borrowed into Japanese from English.

At least 172 loanwords with foreign or native Japanese origin have been incorporated into the Taiwanese Ministry of Education (MOE) official Taiwanese language dictionary loanword appendix[11]. The MOE has not suggested replacement characters but leaves them

---

9 Lin, Alvin. (1999). Writing Taiwanese: The Development of Modern Written Taiwanese. *Sino-Platonic Papers (89)*. Philadelphia: Department of Asian and Middle Eastern Studies, University of Pennsylvania.
10 Blust, Robert. (1999). Subgrouping, circularity and extinction: some issues in Austronesian comparative linguistics. In E. Zeitoun & P.J.K Li (Eds.) *Selected papers from the Eighth International Conference on Austronesian Linguistics*, 31–94. Taipei: Academia Sinica.
11 *Zhōnghuá Mínguó Jiàoyùbù* (中華民國教育部) [ROC Ministry of Education]. (2011). *Wàilái cí* 外來詞 [loanwords]. Retrieved from: http://twblg.dict.edu.tw/holodict_new/index/fulu_wailaici.jsp

as Romanized loanwords with the original Japanese kana script annotating its origin.

TAIWANESE POJ	JAPANESE KANA	RŌMAJI	MEANING
chiō͘-ko͘-lé-to͘	チョコレート	chokorēto	chocolate
pháng	パン	pan	bread
ō͘-to͘-bái	オートバイ	ōtobai	motorcycle
siat-chuh	シャツ	shatsu	dress shirt
bí-lu	ビール	bīru	beer
ō͘-ba-sáng	おばさん	obasan	auntie, older woman
ō͘-ji-sáng	おじさん	ojisan	uncle, older man
khā-la-o͘-khe	カラオケ	karaoke	karaoke

However, Taiwanese additionally has many Japanese loanwords with Sinitic origins that are not included in this appendix. Instead, they are included in the dictionary and listed according to their respective Chinese characters.

TAIWANESE CHARACTERS	POJ	JAPANESE KANA	RŌMAJI	MEANING
便所	piān-só͘	べんじょ	benjo	lavatory, toilet
病院	pēⁿ-īⁿ	びょういん	byōin	hospital
注射	chù-siā	ちゅうしゃ	chūsha	shot, syringe
郵便局	iû-piān-kiȯk	ゆうびんきょく	yūbin kyoku	post office
都合	to-hȧp	つごう	tsugō	circumstances
紺色	khóng-sek	こんいろ	kon-iro	blue

1.2.2.3 Grammar

While the bulk of grammar between Taiwanese and Mandarin is similar, there are several areas where significant differences exist.

Extensive negation

Negation in Mandarin is generally split between the two negative particles 沒 **méi** and 不 **bù** according to mood and aspect. In contrast, Taiwanese negation involves five negative particles with usage determined by a more complex combination of these two factors *(see 13 Negation)*.

TAIWANESE	MOOD	ASPECT
無 bô	—	Perfective, Experiential, Habitual
毋 m̄	Desire, Prohibition	Experiential
袂 bē	Possibility, Ability, Permission	—
未 bōe	—	Anterior
免 bián	Obligation	—

With adjectives, the use of negative particles **無 bô** or **袂 bē** depends on whether an adjective is considered desirable or undesirable by the speaker *(see 6.4 Desirable and undesirable adjectives)*.

DESIRABLE 無 BÔ	UNDESIRABLE 袂 BĒ
西瓜 無 甜。	茶 袂 甜。
Si-koe bô tiⁿ.	Tê bē tiⁿ.
西瓜 不 甜。	茶 不 甜。
Xīguā bù tián.	Chá bù tián.
The watermelon is not sweet *(sweetness is desirable)*.	The tea is not sweet *(sweetness is undesirable)*.

Additional particles for potential, manner, and extent complements

With additional grammatical particles, Taiwanese offers more specificity in the use of verbal complements *(see 11.4 Potential complements, 11.6 Manner complements, 11.7 Extent complements)*.

TAIWANESE	MANDARIN	MEANING
POTENTIAL COMPLEMENTS		
ACTUALIZED		
看有完 khòaⁿ-ū-ôan	看得完 kàndewán	was able to finish seeing
UNREALIZED		
看會完 khòaⁿ-ē-ôan	看得完 kàndewán	is/will be able to finish seeing
MANNER COMPLEMENTS		
HABITUAL		
寫著 真 媠	寫 得 很 漂亮	writes beautifully
siá-tio̍h chin súi	xiě de hěn piàoliang	
SINGLE OCCASION		
寫 了 真 媠	寫 得 很 漂亮	wrote beautifully
siá liáu chin súi	xiě de hěn piàoliang	

TAIWANESE	MANDARIN	MEANING
EXTENT COMPLEMENTS		
哭 甲 目睭 紅紅	哭 得 眼睛 紅紅	
khàu kah ba̍k-chiu âng-âng	kū de yǎnjīng hónghóng	cried until eyes are red
哭 予 目睭 紅紅	哭 得 眼睛 紅紅	
khàu hō· ba̍k-chiu âng-âng	kū de yǎnjīng hónghóng	cry until eyes are red

Preference for pre-verbal objects

Because of restrictions on object placement after verb compounds, Taiwanese tends to place objects before the verb more often than Mandarin does.

阿爸 這 張 報紙 看 了 矣。
A-pa chit tiuⁿ pò-chóa khóaⁿ liáu--ah.
爸爸 看完 這 張 報紙 了。
Bàba kànwán zhè zhāng bàozhǐ le.
Dad has read this newspaper.

Pre-verbal aspect markers

Taiwanese has markers for the experiential and perfective aspects that can occur before the verb. Most other Chinese languages including Mandarin mark aspect through the use of suffixes or particles that can only be placed after the verb. That being said, Taiwanese also has markers for experiential and perfective aspects that can occur after the verb. This may be an indication of an area of linguistic change (*see 8.1.1 Perfective aspect with* 有 *ū, 8.3 Experiential aspect*).

EXPERIENTIAL ASPECT WITH PRE-VERBAL 捌 BAT
伊 捌 去 美國。
I bat khì Bí-kok.
他 去過 美國。
Tā qùguò Měiguó.
He has gone to America before.

PERFECTIVE ASPECT WITH PRE-VERBAL 有 Ū
伊 有 買 牛仔褲。
I ū bé gû-á-khò·.
她 買了 牛仔褲。
Tā mǎile niúzǎikù.
She bought jeans.

Question marker 敢 *kám*

While the additional negative particles in Taiwanese allows for an increased number of end-of-sentence question particles, the question marker **敢 kám** is quite distinct without a direct equivalent in Mandarin *(see 20.1 敢 kám question marker)*. The question marker **敢 kám** is positioned immediately before any word under question as long as placement occurs before the main verb.

FOCUS ON WITH WHOM

你 昨昏 敢 和 朋友 去 看 電影？

Lí cha-hng <u>kám</u> hām pêng-iú khì khòaⁿ tiān-iáⁿ?

你 昨天 是 和 朋友 去 看 電影 嗎？

Nǐ zuótiān shì hé péngyǒu qù kàn diànyǐng ma?

Did you go with a friend to see a movie yesterday?

FOCUS ON WHEN

你 敢 昨昏 和 朋友 去 看 電影？

Lí <u>kám</u> cha-hng hām pêng-iú khì khòaⁿ tiān-iáⁿ?

你 是 昨天 和 朋友 去 看 電影 嗎？

Nǐ shì zuótiān hé péngyǒu qù kàn diànyǐng ma?

Was it yesterday that you went with a friend to see a movie?

1.3 Taiwan linguistic history

1.3.1 Brief linguistic history of Taiwan

First inhabited by aborigines around 8000 years ago, the island of Taiwan once supported 24 aboriginal languages (only 14 are still spoken), which belong to the Austronesian language family[12]. Due to the rich linguistic diversity found among the aboriginal languages on the island, many scholars believe that Taiwan was indeed the birthplace of the Austronesian language family, which has modern-day descendants from Madagascar to Easter Island and includes languages such as Malay, Hawaiian, and Tagalog[13].

It was not until the 17th century that European explorers came to the island to establish trading posts. In 1622 Dutch merchants began forming settlements in the southern part of

---

12 Li, Paul Jen-kuei. (2000). *Formosan languages: The state of the art*. In David Blundell (Ed.), 45-67.

13 Blust, Robert. (1999). Subgrouping, circularity and extinction: some issues in Austronesian comparative linguistics. In E. Zeitoun & P.J.K Li (Eds.) *Selected papers from the Eighth International Conference on Austronesian Linguistics*, 31–94. Taipei: Academia Sinica.

the island near Tainan (台南 **Táinán**) while Spanish traders occupied the northern ports of Tamshui (淡水 **Dànshuǐ**) and Keelung (基隆 **Jīlóng**) beginning in 1626. Seventeen years later in 1642, Dutch forces took over the small Spanish settlements and gained full control of the island. During this period, agricultural laborers from Fujian province were brought over in large numbers to develop the land. These workers brought with them the Hokkien and Hakka languages.

After 38 years of ruling the island, the Dutch were defeated in 1662 by a renegade Ming Dynasty commander, Koxinga (國姓爺 **Guóxìngyé**), who established a base on Taiwan from which to retake the throne from the Qing Dynasty. In addition to the military forces that had arrived on the island, waves of Han Chinese continued to arrive from southeastern China, primarily from Fujian and eastern Guangdong provinces. Eventually in 1683, Qing Dynasty military forces landed on Taiwan and took control. The new administrators instituted a ban on migration to Taiwan until 1874.

In 1895, the defeat of the Qing Dynasty by Japan in the First Sino-Japanese War led to the ceding of Taiwan to Japan. The Japanese occupied Taiwan as a colony for fifty years until 1945. Initially, the Japanese allowed the use of the Taiwanese language as part of a gradual process of assimilation into Japanese culture. However, by 1912 the Japanese administrators switched to a Japanese-only education policy. By 1944, approximately 70% of the local population had attained proficiency in Japanese[14]. During this colonial period, many Japanese loanwords were imported into the Taiwanese vocabulary particularly those in areas concerning medicine, technology, and foreign goods.

Following Japan's surrender at the end of World War II in 1945, the Allied Forces allowed the Republic of China to administer Taiwan. For a brief period, usage of Taiwanese by the local population was encouraged by the Nationalist government as a means to ease the linguistic transition to Mandarin. Once defeated by Communists, the Nationalists fled China in 1949 and established their government in Taiwan. Language policies as well as other aspects of life during this period grew more oppressive. From 1950-1980, laws were passed that restricted the usage of Taiwanese or any other non-Mandarin language in the government, schools, and media.

With the lifting of martial law in 1987, the Taiwanese language reappeared in the public realm. The Taiwanese language movement grew rapidly in the 1990s and 2000s, giving rise to language revival groups, popular media, and literature. At the same time, experimentation with local languages classes in various school districts began. In 2001, local language education (Taiwanese, Hakka, or aboriginal languages) became a compulsory subject in elementary schools. Given that language policy is a charged political issue in Taiwan, further legislation promoting language equality has not progressed beyond draft resolutions within the legislature in recent years.

---

14 Chen, Ping. (2004). *Modern Chinese: History and Sociolinguistics*, 31. Cambridge: Cambridge University Press.

1.3.2 Mandarin as an official language

Seeking a single standardized language that could be spoken by all Han Chinese would not become a central concern until the twentieth century when newly formed nation-states used standardized languages as tools for nation-building. Before then, only civil servants who were part of the Chinese empire and officials serving in the imperial court had the need to speak a common tongue. This lingua franca was referred to as **官話 guānhuà** 'official speech' beginning in the Ming Dynasty (1368-1644). Around this time, the Portuguese term *mandarim* for 'official', which arrived via Malay for the Sanskrit term for 'counselor' *mantrin*, was imported into English as 'Mandarin' to refer to this 'official speech'. However, it would be a few centuries later before a more formalized form of this language took shape.

Not until the fall of the Qing Dynasty and the birth of the Republic of China in 1912 did a strong desire arise for a shared standardized language to be spoken by all common people. A commission of linguists representing all regions and dialects spoken in China was assembled to go about the task of developing a standardized language in pronunciation, grammar, vocabulary, and writing. Ultimately, the result was **國語 Guóyǔ** 'national language', which was based heavily on the pronunciation and grammar of the Beijing dialect. Dialect-specific traits such as syllables rarely found in other dialects, the retroflex 'r', and the preponderance of weak stress (neutral tones) were either diminished or removed. Attempts at promoting this new standardized language in China continued over the next three decades intermittently until the invasion of Japanese forces in 1937.

After the end of World War II, the civil war between Communist and Nationalist forces prevented any further national efforts at promotion of a standard language. Once the Nationalists fled to Taiwan in 1949, they gradually began enforcing **國語 Guóyǔ** as the official and only language acceptable in the public sphere.

Meanwhile in China, after two conferences for language reform were held in 1955, the communist government changed the name of **國語 Guóyǔ** 'national language' to **普通話 Pǔtōnghuà** 'common speech' and refined what constituted this new standardized language with regards to pronunciation, grammar, and vocabulary. Additionally efforts continued to promote **普通話 Pǔtōnghuà** as the language of education, media, and government across the land. Moreover, in 1956 simplified characters were introduced as a tool to increase literacy among adults. Two years later, **漢語拼音 Hànyǔ Pīnyīn** was introduced both in schools and to the general public to replace **注音符號 Zhùyīn Fúhào**, a character-based phonetic alphabet, as a means to teach pronunciation. **注音符號 Zhùyīn Fúhào** continues to be used as a means of notating pronunciation in Taiwan.

In both Taiwan and China, Mandarin has now become a language that is understood and used by a sizeable majority. In China, Mandarin usage has now reached about 70% of the population, which is about 840 million people. In Taiwan, the percentage is higher at 80%, covering about 19 million people[15].

1.4 Standardization of Taiwanese

Because Southern Min does not have status as an official language in any country, standardization has been a challenging task. Only in Taiwan with the recent semi-official status as a 'local language' to be taught in public primary schools has a government become more involved with the standardization of the language. Aside from the usual challenges of educating a user population with new practices, Taiwanese poses some particular linguistic issues.

With regards to pronunciation, within Taiwan there is still quite a wide variety of pronunciation differences as a result of the original emigrants from China hailing from different regions in Fujian province, each having its own regional accent, Zhangzhou and Quanzhou. After hundreds of years of internal migration and mixing of populations within Taiwan, a new patchwork of accents has arisen *(see 1.1.3 Local differences within Taiwan)*.

In addition to variation within pronunciation, the writing of Taiwanese faces a number of challenges in standardization. Approximately 15% of Taiwanese words do not have a readily apparent cognate with Mandarin characters *(see 1.4.1.1 Special Taiwanese characters)*. In addition, many polysyllabic loanwords from Japanese and English lack character representation. While not insurmountable, additional challenges to a character-based system for Taiwanese are the large number of contractions and words with colloquial and literary readings[16].

1.4.1 Characters

Until the early 20th century, all written Chinese (regardless of the spoken variety) since the end of the Han Dynasty (AD 220) used the grammar and vocabulary of Literary Chinese, a reformed writing style of Classical Chinese *(see 1.2.1 Origins and development of Chinese languages)*.

Spoken Chinese, which scholars believe already began to evolve into a variety of 'dialects' beginning in the late Zhou Dynasty (~250 BC), had long not been written down in the way people actually spoke it. Only after the fall of Imperial China and the beginning of the Republic of China in 1912 more than two thousand years later did significant efforts take place to form a written standard based on the vernacular speech. Most of these efforts

15 Ethnologue. (2009). Chinese, Min Nan. Retrieved from: http://www.ethnologue.com/language/nan
16 Cheng, Robert L. (鄭良偉). (1990). *Yǎnbiàn zhōng de Táiwān shèhuì yǔwén: Duō yǔ shèhuì jí shuāngyǔ jiàoyù* (演變中的台灣社會語文：多語社會及雙語教育) [Essays on sociolinguistic problems of Taiwan], 222-24. Taipei: *Zìlì wǎnbào shè wénhuà chūbǎn bù* (自立晚報社文化出版部).

went towards the reform and promotion of Mandarin as a standard language by virtue of its status as the language spoken in the capital and by a majority of Han Chinese *(see 1.3.2 Mandarin as an official language)*. The selection of and focus on Mandarin as the standard language limited developments in the vernacular writing of non-Mandarin varieties such as Southern Min, Cantonese, Hakka, or Wu.

All varieties of Chinese face challenges of representing grammatical particles that are not included in the writing of Literary Chinese. Some varieties such as Cantonese, Wu, and Southern Min took on this issue through the creation of new characters or the borrowing of archaic characters.

1.4.1.1 Special Taiwanese characters

While the movement to promote a written Chinese script representing spoken Chinese did not fully take hold until the early twentieth century, there had been earlier attempts in the past by individuals and private groups to write in the vernacular speech.

For Southern Min, a Ming Dynasty play published in 1566 by the name of **荔境記 Lìjìng jì** 'Romance of the Litchi mirror' marks the earliest surviving document written in the vernacular speech of Southern Min. Aside from plays, other written materials in the form of rime books, songbooks, and Christian missionary texts also made use of characters to transcribe the Southern Min language.

Many of these early authors borrowed obsolete or rarely used archaic characters from Classical Chinese or invented new characters. Because there was no standardization in these practices, a great number of special Taiwanese characters arose.

Archaic character borrowing

For many words an etymological root can be traced back to archaic characters found in Classical Chinese. Some of these have been resurrected to write Taiwanese. In a few cases, the characters have taken on a slightly different meaning in modern Mandarin.

	TAIWANESE	MANDARIN
走	cháu 'run'	zǒu 'walk'
喙	chhùi 'mouth'	huì 'beak'
食	chiàh 'to eat'	shí 'food'
懸	kôan 'tall'	xuán 'to hang'

Sometimes it is not possible to determine a direct etymological link to a Classical Chinese character. When this is the case, one option is to borrow an obsolete or rarely used archaic character with a similar meaning.

TAIWANESE	MANDARIN	MEANING
佇 tī	在 zài	at
囥 khǹg	放 fàng	to place, to put
吼 háu	哭 kū	to cry
媠 súi	美 měi	pretty

Newly created characters

Some special Taiwanese characters were inventions that arose from two traditional methods of character creation: meaning aggregation and phonetic borrowing.

Meaning aggregation

Characters constructed from meaning aggregation are an assembly of *radicals*, which are the semantic components of a character. The new combination of individual meanings represented by each radical forms a composite idea that matches the Taiwanese word.

RADICAL COMPONENTS				TAIWANESE SPECIAL CHARACTER
走	+	坐	=	趖 sô
'walk'	+	'sit'	=	'crawl'

The new character for the verb 趖 **sô** 'crawl' clearly stems from an action somewhat in between 坐 'sitting' and 走 'walking'.

RADICAL COMPONENTS				TAIWANESE SPECIAL CHARACTER
毛	+	灬	=	毳 chhōa
'feather'	+	'fire'	=	'to guide, take care'

However, the new character 毳 **chhōa** 'to guide' perhaps requires an additional degree of interpretation. The 毛 'feather' represents a mother hen, while the 灬 'fire' radical depicts four baby chicks. Together the pictorial combination of a mother hen with four chicks below her suggest 'to guide' or 'to take care of'.

RADICAL COMPONENTS				TAIWANESE SPECIAL CHARACTER
辶	+	日	=	迌 chhit
'road'		'day'	=	
辶	+	月	=	迌 thô
'road'		'moon'	=	
迌 chhit	+	迌 thô	=	迌迌 chhit-thô
'--'	+	'--'	=	'to play'

The new characters for 廸迌 **chhit-thô** 'to play' only exist bound together. One possible interpretation is the combination of radicals for 辶 'road', 日 'day', and 月 'moon' suggests the idea of being outside both day and night to 'play'.

Phonetic borrowing

Another method of character creation involves combining one semantic component with one phonetic component. The phonetic component is borrowed from another character of which the meaning is discarded but the sound preserved. Note that in some cases the phonetic component does not share the same pronunciation but merely rhymes or possesses a similar initial sound.

SEMANTIC		PHONETIC		NEW CHARACTER
刂	+	台	=	刣
'blade'	+	tâi 'pedestal'	=	thâi 'to kill'

In the preceding example, the character 刣 **thâi** 'to kill' is composed of the semantic component 'blade' and the phonetic component of the character for 'pedestal'. The meaning of phonetic component is disregarded and only borrowed for its approximate pronunciation.

SEMANTIC		PHONETIC		NEW CHARACTER
口	+	舍	=	啥
'mouth'		siá 'residence'		siá^n 'what'

In the preceding example, the character 啥 **siá^n** 'what' combines the semantic component 'mouth' with the phonetic component 'siá'. Note that the actual pronunciation of 啥 **siá^n** 'what' is slightly different. Additionally, the semantic component 口 'mouth' radical is used to signal that the character is purely a phonetic borrowing. This practice of using the 口 'mouth' radical to denote a phonetically borrowed character is also commonly found in special characters for Cantonese.

1.4.1.2 Taiwanese Ministry of Education characters

While in the past there have been a variety of approaches to represent Taiwanese through Chinese characters, the lack of standardization has limited the use of a consistent writing system among a large number of users.

The passage of a local languages education act in 2001 required primary schools to begin offering language courses in Taiwanese, Hakka, and aboriginal languages. This move created a need to have some degree of language standardization for consistent teacher training and textbook production.

During the years 2007-2009, the Taiwanese Ministry of Education (MOE) took another step towards standardization of Taiwanese by promulgating the use of 700 characters to be used for unique Taiwanese words without an immediate cognate in Mandarin. Some of these chosen characters include special Taiwanese characters (both archaic borrowings and newly created characters) that have already gained some degree of familiarity among the general population *(see 1.4.1.1 Special Taiwanese characters)*. A few words that have historical roots to archaic characters but are not easily recognizable or overly complex were instead assigned a Mandarin character with a similar meaning despite the lack of an etymological relation. Additionally, some words that did not have a clear candidate were assigned a character by the MOE as a pure phonetic borrowing.

Note that because the lack of standardization often generated multiple characters to represent Taiwanese words, not all contemporary readers of Taiwanese will be familiar with the newly selected set of standardized characters.

The characters used in this text to write Taiwanese are based on those put forth by the Taiwanese Ministry of Education. However, due to font restrictions, some characters have been replaced by alternate characters that are still recognized by the MOE.

1.4.2 Romanization schemes

Aside from a character-based orthography for Taiwanese, there is an established history of writing Southern Min with the Latin script. Initially devised by missionaries to transcribe the speech of local populations, several Romanization schemes for Taiwanese have been developed both for use as full-fledged orthographies and as transcription systems for reading characters.

The earliest documented attempts at Romanizing the Southern Min language appear to have occurred in the late sixteenth century by Dominican missionaries in the Philippines[17]. However, it was not until the late 1800s before Presbyterian missionaries began using the Latin script for the Southern Min variant in Taiwan.

1.4.2.1 白話字 Pe̍h-ōe-jī (POJ)

白話字 Pe̍h-ōe-jī (POJ) 'vernacular writing' is the oldest and most commonly used Romanization system for transcribing variants of Southern Min. Its origins can be traced to Presbyterian missionaries working in Fujian province and Southeast Asia in the mid-nineteenth century. As a result, this system is sometimes referred to as Missionary Romanization or Church Romanization.

---

17 Klöter, Henning (2005). *Written Taiwanese*. Wiesbaden: Otto Harrassowitz.

In the late nineteenth century, missionaries brought the system to Taiwan where it flourished as a method to spread church teachings as well as document the locally spoken language in letters, newspapers, and books. As a result, POJ currently enjoys the largest body of historical documents and literature of all the Romanization systems put forth for Southern Min.

After martial law was lifted in Taiwan in 1987, a revival of Taiwanese gradually took place in the 1990s. Some promoters of the language not affiliated with any religious organizations adopted this Romanization scheme as orthography for Taiwanese. Conversely, during this period the Presbyterian Church began to use Chinese characters to represent Taiwanese.

Today, POJ still appears to be the most popular Romanization scheme for rendering Southern Min in the English-language media. Despite its popularity, other systems based on POJ have been devised to deal with some perceived shortcomings including the need for special characters (**o͘ , ⁿ**), diacritics for tone markings (**ó, ò, ô, ō, o̍**), and initial confusion or difficulty in reading some letter combinations **(chh-, -oe, -oa, -ek, -eng)**.

EXAMPLE IN POJ

遮的 衫褲，你 閣 愛 捅 無？

Chiah-ê saⁿ-khò͘, lí koh ài tih--bô?

這 些 衣服，你 還 要 嗎？

Zhè xiē yīfú, nǐ hái yào ma?

Do you still want these clothes?

1.4.2.2 Taiwanese Language Phonetic Alphabet (TLPA)

The Taiwanese Language Phonetic Alphabet (TLPA) is a Romanization scheme devised in the late 1990s by the Linguistic Society of Taiwan and briefly adopted by the Taiwan Ministry of Education as an official Romanization scheme for Taiwanese from 1998 until 2006. The advantages of this scheme include not requiring any special characters (**o͘ , ⁿ**) or tone marks, allowing all sounds to be represented without the need for a special font. Instead, the 'o dot above right' or '**-o͘**' is represented with the combination of letters ' **oo** ' while the superscript ' **-ⁿ** ' for nasal sounds is similarly replaced by a doubled ' **nn** '. Tones are also denoted using numbers instead of diacritics. In addition, some letter combinations have been altered to help reflect more accurately the proper pronunciation (such as **tsh-, -ue, -ua, -ik, -ing**). As a result of these modifications, this scheme has the benefit of being an efficient way of quickly typing Romanized Taiwanese.

EXAMPLE IN TLPA

遮的 衫褲，你 閣 愛 挃 無？

Tsiah4-e5 sann1-khoo3, li2 koh4 ai3 tih8 bo5?

這 些 衣服，你 還 要 嗎？

Zhè xiē yīfú, nǐ hái yào ma?

Do you still want these clothes?

1.4.2.3 台羅 Tâi-lô (TL)

Tâi-uân Lô-má-jī Phing-im or *Tâi-lô* (TL) for short is a combination of the POJ and TLPA Romanization schemes and was put forth by the MOE in 2006.

Because of the ongoing popularity of POJ, *Tâi-lô* was created as a compromise between TLPA and POJ. The result is essentially a scheme that does not use any special characters (**o͘**, **ⁿ**) but does retain tone marks (although diacritic placement differs). In addition, changes in letter combinations for TLPA were retained as well. Since 2006, all official Taiwanese educational materials use this Romanization scheme.

EXAMPLE IN TL

遮的 衫褲，你 閣 愛 挃 無？

Tsiah-ê sann-khòo, lí koh ài ti̍h--bô?

這 些 衣服，你 還 要 嗎？

Zhè xiē yīfú, nǐ hái yào ma?

Do you still want these clothes?

1.4.2.4 Differences between POJ and TL

Because *Tâi-lô* (TL) is based on the *Pe̍h-ōe-jī* (POJ) Romanization scheme, the two systems are fairly similar. Below is a table highlighting key differences.

INITIALS

PE̍H-ŌE-JĪ (POJ)		*TÂI-LÔ (TL)*		*MEANING*
ch-	chú	**ts-**	tsú	煮 'to cook'
chh-	chheh	**tsh-**	tsheh	冊 'book'

FINALS

PĖH-ŌE-JĪ (POJ)		TÂI-LÔ (TL)		MEANING
-aⁿ	saⁿ	-ann	sann	衫 'clothes'
-aiⁿ	pháiⁿ	-ainn	pháinn	歹 'bad'
-ek	sek	-ik	sik	色 'color'
-eⁿ	pêⁿ	-enn	pênn	平 'flat'
-eng	bêng	-ing	bîng	明 'bright, clear'
-iaⁿ	thiaⁿ	-iann	thiann	聽 'to listen, hear'
-iⁿ	chîⁿ	-inn	tsînn	錢 'money'
-iuⁿ	siūⁿ	-iunn	siūnn	想 'to think'
-o͘	hō͘	-oo	hōo	予 'to give'
-oa	tōa	-ua	tuā	大 'big'
-oah	joa̍h	-uah	jua̍h	熱 'hot'
-oai	koai	-uai	kuai	乖 'well-behaved'
-oaiⁿ	koaiⁿ	-uainn	kuainn	關 'to close'
-oaⁿ	pòaⁿ	-uann	puànn	半 'half'
-oan	chóan	-uan	tsuán	賺 'to earn'
-oat	hoat	-uat	huat	發 'to emit, to send out'
-oe	poe	-ue	pue	飛 'to fly'
-oeh	boeh	-ueh	bueh	欲 'to want, going to'
-oⁿ	hoⁿ	-onn	honn	齁 'to snore'

1.4.3 Contemporary approaches to reading Taiwanese

Outside of certain social circles of language enthusiasts, writers, poets, and religious groups, most contemporary Taiwanese speakers are not familiar or able to employ many of the different Romanization systems developed to write Taiwanese. Because the recent standardization of characters for Taiwanese has only just begun for learners in primary school, the current approaches for most casual readers or writers of Taiwanese involve writing in Mandarin but reading in Taiwanese, borrowing Mandarin characters purely for their phonetic value, or using a hybrid of characters and Latin script.

Real-time translation

As the majority of native speakers of Taiwanese are fully bilingual in Mandarin, many are able to rely on their understanding of the meaning of Chinese characters written in Mandarin sentences and directly translate in real time the appropriate Taiwanese word.

MANDARIN-BASED CHARACTERS

你 在 吃 什麼？我 肚子 餓 了。

TAIWANESE PRONUNCIATION

Lí teh chiàh siáⁿ-mih? Góa pak-tó˙teh iau.

MANDARIN PRONUNCIATION

Nǐ zài chī shénme? Wǒ dùzi è le.

What are you eating? I'm hungry.

Phonetic borrowing

Another common method is to borrow a character for its phonetic value regardless of the character's meaning. By seeing that a character does not fit semantically with its neighbors, the reader can immediately detect that the sentence is not written in Mandarin but in Taiwanese. Despite only having a phonetic cue, context and familiarity with the language generally allows the reader to figure out the meaning.

TAIWANESE WRITTEN WITH BORROWED MANDARIN CHARACTERS

哩 賀！挖 系 台南 郎。

Lí hó! Góa sī Tâi-lâm lâng.

MANDARIN PRONUNCIATIONS AND MEANINGS OF BORROWED CHARACTERS

哩	賀	挖	系	台南	郎
lī	hè	wā	xì	Táinán	láng
'mile'	'congratulate'	'dig'	'system'	'Tainan'	'youth'

MANDARIN TRANSLATION

你 好！我 是 台南 人。

Nǐ hǎo! Wǒ shì Táinán rén

ENGLISH TRANSLATION

Hello! I'm from Tainan.

Hybrid script 漢羅 *Hàn-lô*

Another popular method used to write Taiwanese is a mixed script method known as **漢羅 Hàn-lô**. This approach was developed in the 1960s and uses characters for those words with immediate Mandarin cognates and Latin script for the remaining 15% of Taiwanese words which do not have easily recognizable characters.

HYBRID SCRIPT

聽--leh！我 kā 你 ê 錢 khǹg tī hia。

MOE   TAIWANESE CHARACTERS

聽咧！我 共 你 的 錢 囥 佇 遐。

POJ

Thiaⁿ--leh! Góa kā lí ê chîⁿ khǹg tī hia.

MANDARIN

聽著！我 把 你 的 錢 放 在 那裡。
Tīngzhě! Wǒ bǎ nǐ de qián fàng zài nàlǐ.

Listen! I put your money over there.

2 Pronunciation

Taiwanese syllables are made up of three components: initial, final, and tone. The *initial* is a consonant sound, though not always present. The *final*, which is required, is generally a vowel sound that can have nasal, glottal stops, or consonant endings. Finally, the *tone*, or pitch contour, is also a required component that impacts the entire syllable.

[*(initial)* + *final*]

TONE

The following chapter describes the Taiwanese sound system by using the *Pėh-ōe-jī* (POJ) Romanization system *(see 1.4.2.1 白話字 Pėh-ōe-jī (POJ))*. English approximations and International Phonetic Alphabet (IPA) transcriptions are also provided for reference in some sections.

2.1 Initials

Initials are consonant sounds that form the beginning of Taiwanese syllables. Note that some syllables begin with a vowel and do not have an initial consonant or consist only of a syllabic consonant. In all, there are 17 initials in Taiwanese represented by the following letters or letter combinations:

b ch chh g h j k kh l m n ng p ph s t th

Most initials are quite similar to their English counterparts. However, a few differences do exist and will be explored more in the following sections.

2.1.1 Aspiration

Several letter combinations include the letter '**h**' (**chh-, kh-, ph-, th-**). The '-h' indicates aspiration and is considered part of the 'letter' or sound. *Aspiration* is the puff of air that comes from the mouth when pronouncing certain letters. Note that in the *Pėh-ōe-jī* (POJ) Romanization system, the letter '**ch-**' is a non-aspirated sound, but '**chh-**' is the aspirated version. In English, aspiration can be felt by placing the hand in front of the mouth and noticing the difference between the following pairings:

	ASPIRATED	NON-ASPIRATED
p	park	spell
t	time	stop
k	kiss	sky
ts	tsunami	eats

As the English examples indicate, the non-aspirated versions of the letters '**p**', '**t**', and '**k**' only appear in English words when following a consonant. In Taiwanese, these non-aspirated versions can begin words and (to the English ear) may appear to sound like 'softer' or 'quieter' versions of their aspirated counterparts.

	ASPIRATED		NON-ASPIRATED
ph	膨 phòng 'swollen'	p	碰 pōng 'bump into'
th	討 thó 'to beg'	t	倒 tò 'to topple over'
kh	看 khòaⁿ 'to see'	k	寒 kôaⁿ 'cold'
chh	請 chhiáⁿ 'please'	ch	正 chiaⁿ 'right'

While some English speakers may be tempted to equate non-aspirated '**p**', '**t**', '**k**' to their voiced counterparts '**b**', '**d**', '**g**', respectively, Taiwanese also has separate letters for the voiced letters '**b**', '**d**', '**g**' *(see 2.1.2 Voicing)*. Perhaps it can be helpful to think of the non-aspirated letters as a sound in between their aspirated and voiced counterparts.

2.1.2 Voicing

Voiced letters create sounds that vibrate the vocal chords when spoken. If the hand is placed on the throat covering the vocal chords, a light vibration can be felt when pronouncing the sound. In English, there are several consonants that are voiced. Below are just a few pairings that indicate this contrast:

	VOICED		NON-VOICED
z	zap	s	sap
v	very	f	fairy
th	though	th	thought
b	bell	p	spell
d	dock	t	stock
g	girl	k	skid

Taiwanese has several voiced initials '**b-**', '**g-**', '**j-**', '**l-**', '**m-**', '**n-**', '**ng-**'. Four of them have direct non-voiced counterparts.

	VOICED			NON-VOICED	
b	欲	beh 'to want'	p	白	pe̍h 'white'
g	牛	gû 'cow'	k	舊	kū 'old'
j	如	jû 'if'	ch	煮	chú 'to cook'
ji	日	jit 'day'	chi	一	chit 'one'
l	啉	lim 'to drink'			--
m	罵	mē 'to scold'			--
n	藍	nâ 'blue'			--
ng	夾	ngeh 'to pinch'			--

The letter combination '**ng**' can be both an initial (扭 **ngiú** 'to twist') and a final (冷 **léng** 'cold'). In English, words cannot begin with the '**ng**' sound. A close approximation is the sound from the '**n**' in the English word 'u<u>n</u>cle'. The hard '**c**' sound influences the ending of the '**n**' creating a '**ng**' nasal sound that is close to the Taiwanese initial '**ng-**'.

The initial '**j-**' also does not have a precise equivalent in English. A close approximation is the '**ds**' found at the end of the English word 'ki<u>ds</u>'. When the Taiwanese '**j-**' is followed by the letter '**-i**' (二 **jī** 'two') there is a slight adjustment in the sound that pushes the tongue farther back in the mouth called palatalization *(see 2.1.3 Palatalization)*. The '**j-**' sound is relatively rare within Taiwanese, and for many speakers the sound is replaced by the '**l-**' sound.

2.1.3 Palatalization

Palatalization is the backward shift in the placement of the tongue to the palate, which is the roof of the mouth. In Taiwanese, this adjustment impacts the initials '**ch-**', '**chh-**', '**s-**' and '**j-**' whenever these initials are followed by '**-i-**', '**-ek**', or '**-eng**'. Technically, '**chi-**', '**chhi-**', '**si-**', '**ji-**' are phonetically different consonant sounds, but the POJ Romanization system treats them only as a special case of the initials '**ch-**', '**chh-**', '**s-**' and '**j-**'.

Below is a comparison between palatalized and non-palatalized sounds within English words.

	NON-PALATALIZED		PALATALIZED
-ts	eat<u>s</u>	**g-**	<u>g</u>ym
ts-	<u>ts</u>unami	**ch-**	<u>ch</u>eap
s-	<u>s</u>oap	**sh-**	<u>sh</u>eep
g-	bei<u>g</u>e	**j-**	<u>j</u>eans

Below is a comparison between palatalized and non-palatalized initials within Taiwanese.

	NON-PALATALIZED		PALATALIZED
ch-	chá 早 'early'	chi-	chîⁿ 錢 'money'
chh-	chhù 厝 'house'	chhi-	chhiú 手 'hand'
s-	sé 洗 'to wash'	si-	sek 色 'color'
j-	jû 如 'if'	ji-	jip 入 'to enter'

2.1.4 Comparisons to Mandarin initials

While Taiwanese and Mandarin initials share a large number of the same sounds, there are still a few which differ.

The table below compares the initials in both Taiwanese and Mandarin. Initials that have the same phonetic sound are highlighted by the cognate chosen as an example in both languages. While these cognates may differ in finals, tone, and Romanization spelling, the sound of the initial is actually equivalent. English approximations and International Phonetic Alphabet (IPA) transcriptions are also provided for reference.

TAIWANESE (Pe̍h-ōe-jī)		MANDARIN (Hànyǔ Pīnyīn)		MEANING	ENGLISH APPROX	IPA
b	bah	--	--	肉 'meat'	bat	[b]
p	pau	b	bāo	包 'to wrap'	spell	[p]
ph	phiò	p	piào	票 'ticket'	park	[pʰ]
t	tōa	d	dà	大 'big'	stop	[t]
th	thng	t	tāng	湯 'soup'	time	[tʰ]
g	gû	--	--	牛 'cow'	gift	[g]
k	kái	g	gài	改 'to alter'	sky	[k]
kh	khàu	k	kū	哭 'to cry'	kiss	[kʰ]
ch	chē	z	zuò	坐 'to sit'	eats	[ts]
chi	chiap	j	jiē	接 'to receive'	gym	[tɕ]
(incl. chek, cheng)						
chh	chhài	c	cài	菜 'vegetable'	tsunami	[tsʰ]
chhi	chhiáⁿ	q	qǐng	請 'please'	cheap	[tɕʰ]
(incl. chhek, chheng)						
h	hó	--	--	好 'good'	help	[h]
--	--	h	hǎo	好 'good'	loch	[x]
j	joa̍h	--	--	熱 'hot'	roads	[dz]

TAIWANESE (Pe̍h-ōe-jī)		MANDARIN (Hànyǔ Pīnyīn)		MEANING	ENGLISH APPROX	IPA
ji	ji̍t	--	--	日 'day'	pu<u>dg</u>y	[dz]
l	lâi	l	lái	來 'to come'	<u>l</u>ake	[l]
s	saⁿ	s	san	三 'three'	<u>s</u>it	[s]
si	sin	x	xīn	新 'new'	<u>sh</u>eep	[ɕ]
(incl. sek, seng)						
m	mē	m	mà	罵 'to scold'	<u>m</u>ap	[m]
n	niáu	n	niǎo	鳥 'bird'	<u>n</u>ight	[n]
ng	ngeh	--	--	夾 'to pinch'	u<u>n</u>cle	[ŋ]
--	--	r	rén	人 'people'	plea<u>s</u>ure	[ʐ]
--	--	ch	chī	吃 'to eat'	<u>ch</u>urn	[tʂʰ]
--	--	sh	shàng	上 'above'	<u>sh</u>irt	[ʂ]
--	--	zh	zhōng	中 'middle'	<u>g</u>erm	[tʂ]
--	--	f	fēi	飛 'to fly'	<u>f</u>at	[f]

Taiwanese 'h'

While the Mandarin initial '**h-**' varies somewhat regionally among speakers, the standard Mandarin '**h-**' occurs farther back in the mouth than the Taiwanese '**h-**' and can often have a rougher quality similar to the '**ch**' of the Scottish 'lo<u>ch</u>'. Also note that Taiwanese does not have an '**f**' sound as in the Mandarin word 服務 <u>f</u>úwù 'service'. Instead, Taiwanese cognates tend to have an '**h**' sound such as in the Taiwanese word 服務 <u>h</u>o̍k-bū 'service'.

Aspiration and voicing

Note that Mandarin does not have the voiced initials **[b]** or **[g]** that are found in both Taiwanese (肉 <u>b</u>ah 'meat', 牛 <u>g</u>û 'cow') and English (<u>b</u>at, <u>g</u>ift). As a result, the devisers of the Mandarin *Hànyǔ Pīnyīn* Romanization system used the Latin letters '**b**' and '**g**' to represent the non-aspirated **[p]** and **[k]**. Because Taiwanese has all three sounds (aspirated, non-aspirated/non-voiced, voiced) while Mandarin and English only have two out of the three sounds for initials, learners may have a hard time at first distinguishing among the three types of sounds. Below is a comparison of the three sounds within Taiwanese.

ASPIRATED	NON-ASPIRATED / NON-VOICED	VOICED
<u>p</u>hah 拍 'to hit'	<u>p</u>ah 百 'hundred'	<u>b</u>ah 肉 'meat'
<u>k</u>hùn 睏 'to sleep'	<u>k</u>ún 滾 'to boil'	<u>g</u>ún 阮 'we'
<u>ch</u>hoah 掣 'to tremble'	<u>ch</u>oah 泏 'to splash out'	<u>j</u>oah 熱 'hot'
<u>ch</u>hit 七 'seven'	<u>ch</u>it 一 'one'	<u>j</u>it 日 'day'

Palatalization

Both Taiwanese and Mandarin have sounds that become palatalized (the tongue placement occurs farther back on the roof of the mouth). However, the Mandarin *Hànyǔ Pīnyīn* Romanization indicates this with different letters while the Taiwanese *Pe̍h-ōe-jī* Romanization relies on this change in articulation by using certain finals (**-i-**, **-ek**, **-eng**).

	NON-PALATALIZED		PALATALIZED
	做 'to do'		煎 'fry'
ch-	chò	**chi-**	chian
z-	zuò	j-	jiān
	冊 'book, volume'		清 'to clean'
chh-	chheh	**chhi-**	chheng
c-	cè	q-	qīng
	送 'to send'		先 'first'
s-	sàng	**si-**	sian
s-	sòng	x-	xiān
	如 'if'		字 'character'
j-	jû	**ji-**	jī
--	--	--	--

Retroflexes

Additionally, Taiwanese lacks the curled tongue sounds (*retroflexes*) that are present in the Mandarin initials '**r-**', '**ch-**', '**sh-**', and '**zh-**'.

2.2 Finals

Finals form the ending component of every Taiwanese syllable. In general, they are vowel sounds that can have nasal or stopped consonant endings. In addition, two syllabic nasal consonants ('**m**' and '**ng**') can function as finals without a vowel.

2.2.1 Nasals

Nasals are formed when air leaves from both the nose and the mouth. Taiwanese has a large number of nasal sounds which help gives the language its unique character.

2.2.1.1 Nasal vowels

There are four pure vowel nasals and five vowel nasals that are diphthongs, or vowel clusters. English does not have distinct nasal vowels even though some vowel sounds become slightly nasalized when occurring next to nasal consonants. Mandarin similarly does not have explicit nasal vowels but also has nasal consonants that impact the preceding vowel sounds. The *Pėh-ōe-jī* (POJ) Romanization indicates nasal vowels by placing a superscript ' -ⁿ ' after the vowel(s).

In the table below, English approximations are provided by using vowels adjacent to nasal consonants. Note that Taiwanese nasal vowels are even more enunciated than these English approximations.

	ENG APPROX	IPA	EXAMPLE
-aⁿ	n<u>o</u>nsense (*nasalized*)	[ã]	s<u>a</u>ⁿ 衫 'clothes'
-eⁿ	m<u>e</u>nd (*nasalized*)	[ẽ]	p<u>ê</u>ⁿ 平 'flat'
-iⁿ	m<u>ea</u>n (*nasalized*)	[ĩ]	t<u>i</u>ⁿ 甜 'sweet'
-oⁿ	m<u>oa</u>n (*nasalized*)	[ɔ̃]	<u>o</u>ⁿ 嗚 'buzz'
-aiⁿ	m<u>i</u>ning (*nasalized*)	[aĩ]	ph<u>ái</u>ⁿ 歹 'bad'
-iaⁿ	insomn<u>ia</u> (*nasalized*)	[iã]	th<u>ia</u>ⁿ 聽 'to hear'
-iuⁿ	n<u>ew</u> (*nasalized*)	[iũ]	s<u>iu</u>ⁿ 傷 'too much'
-oaⁿ	ig<u>ua</u>na (*nasalized*)	[uã]	p<u>oa</u>ⁿ 搬 'to move'
-oaiⁿ	wh<u>i</u>ning (*nasalized*)	[uaĩ]	k<u>oai</u>ⁿ 關 'to close'

2.2.1.2 Nasal consonants

Aside from nasal vowels, Taiwanese also has nasal consonants finals (**-m**, **-n**, **-ng**), which can form the ending of a syllable. As mentioned earlier, vowels that precede nasal consonants become nasalized but not to the same degree as nasal vowels. In Taiwanese, the difference between nasal vowels and nasal consonants marks a distinction between words.

NASAL VOWEL	NASAL CONSONANTS		
-ⁿ	-n	-ng	-m
saⁿ 三	sán 瘦	sang 鬆	sàm 搧
'three'	'skinny'	'loose'	'to slap'
kìⁿ 見	kín 緊	kéng 揀	kim 金
'to meet'	'fast'	'to select'	'gold'
siaⁿ 聲	sian 先	siang 雙	siám 閃
'sound'	'first'	'pair'	'to hide'

2.2.1.3 Syllabic nasal consonants

The two nasal consonants '**m**' and '**ng**' can form complete syllables without a vowel sound. Because of this, they are considered *syllabic consonants*.

	ENG APPROX	IPA	EXAMPLE
m	pri<u>sm</u>	[m̩]	m̄ 毋 'not, not want'
ng	to<u>ngue</u>	[ŋ̍]	n̂g 黃 'yellow'

The '**ng**' can stand alone as a syllabic consonant (as in **n̂g** 黃 'yellow') or combine with an initial (as in 糖 **thn̂g** 'sugar'). Additionally, the '**ng-**' can also begin a syllable as an initial (as in **ngeh** 夾 to pinch).

The nasal consonant '**m**' cannot combine with an initial and only forms the syllabic '**m**' (as in **m̄** 毋 'not, not want').

2.2.2 Stops

Taiwanese finals also can end in stops, which block the flow of air by ending the syllable with consonant endings '**-p**', '**-t**', '**-k**' or a glottal stop '**-h**'. Unlike Mandarin, Taiwanese (as well as other southern Chinese languages such as Cantonese and Hakka) has retained stops that were present in Middle Chinese.

The hard consonant endings '**-p**', '**-t**', '**-k**' differ from their English counterparts in that they do not release air at the end of the sound. In English, a similar phenomenon occurs in the middle of words with doubled consonants.

	ENG APPROX	IPA	EXAMPLE
p	po<u>p</u>ped	[p]	ka<u>p</u> 蓋 'to cover'
t	co<u>t</u>ton	[t]	ba<u>t</u> 捌 'familiar with'
k	o<u>c</u>cupy	[k]	tà<u>k</u> 逐 'every'

Words ending in '**-h**' have what is referred to as a *glottal stop*, an obstruction in the airflow (caused by closure of the vocal chords) thereby abruptly stopping any sound. In English, this can also be observed between doubled consonants such as the *pause* between the '**tt**' in the English word 'bi<u>tt</u>en' or like the space represented by the hyphen in the English utterance 'uh-oh!'

	ENG APPROX	IPA	EXAMPLE
h	uh-oh!	[ʔ]	ba<u>h</u> 肉 'meat'

It should also be noted that there is a historical connection between tones and stopped endings *(see 2.5.3 Tone changes)*. In Middle Chinese, syllables that ended in stops belonged to separate tone classes (4th and 8th tones). As a result, in Taiwanese, when a syllable ends in '**-p**', '**-t**', '**-k**', or '**h**', the tone must be either in the 4th or 8th tone. It may also be helpful to group words that end in the glottal stop '**-h**' separately from those that end in '**-p**', '**-t**', '**-k**'. With regards to tone changes, these two groups follow different rules.

Furthermore, the stops '**-p**', '**-t**', '**-k**' are actually counterparts to the nasal consonant finals '**-m**', '**-n**', '**-ng**', respectively, from other tone classes. The correspondence is mapped in the table below.

	NASALS						STOPS	
TONES	1	2	3	5	7		4	8
-m	籠 lam 'to cage'	荏 lám 'weak'	湳 làm 'mud'	男 lâm 'male'	濫 lām 'mix in'	**-p**	塌 lap 'collapse'	納 la̍p 'hand in'
-n	薰 hun 'smoke'	粉 hún 'powder'	楦 hùn 'expand'	雲 hûn 'cloud'	份 hūn 'portion'	**-t**	囫 hut 'devour'	核 hu̍t 'core'
-ng	先 seng 'first'	省 séng 'save'	性 sèng 'quality'	成 sêng 'succeed'	盛 sēng 'glorious'	**-k**	色 sek 'color'	熟 se̍k 'ripe'

Moreover, due to a lack of standardization among some speakers, the distinction between words with a final '**-h**' and those words without may not always be made clearly, if at all. For example, for some speakers there is no phonetic distinction made between the prepositions 佮 **kah** 'with, and' and 共 **kā** 'to, facing'. As a result, the two words are often conflated.

伊 佮 我 欲 去 看 電影。
I kah góa beh khì khòaⁿ tiān-iáⁿ.
他 和 我 要 去 看 電影。
Tā hé wǒ yào qù kàn diànyǐng.
He and I are going to see a movie.

伊 共 我 講 笑話。
I kā góa kóng chhiò-ōe.
他 跟 我 講 笑話。
Tā gēn wǒ jiǎng xiàohuà.
He told me a joke.

2.2.3 Letters o and o·

In Taiwanese, letters **o** and **o·** represent distinct vowel sounds. The *Pe̍h-ōe-jī* (POJ) Romanization has a special character '**o·**' referred to as the 'o with a raised dot', which sounds similar to the 'aw' in the English word 'p<u>aw</u>'.

	ENG APPROX	IPA	EXAMPLE
o	sof<u>a</u> (*South*)	[ɤ]	h<u>ó</u> 好 'good, well'
	sp<u>o</u>ke (*North*)	[o]	
o·	p<u>aw</u>	[ɔ]	h<u>ō</u>· 予 'to give'

The final '**-o**' (as in **hó** 好 'good') has two regional pronunciations. In the accent representative of Southern Taiwan, the pronunciation sounds like the 'a' in the English word 'sof<u>a</u>'. In the accent representative of Northern Taiwan, the final '**-o**' sounds like the 'o' in the English word 'sp<u>o</u>ke'.

2.2.4 Finals -ek, -eng

In the *Pe̍h-ōe-jī* (POJ) Romanization, the finals '**-eng**' and '**-ek**' deviate in pronunciation from the other finals that contain '**-e-**'. The actual vowel sound is similar to that in the finals '**-ip**', '**-it**', and '**-ih**'.

		ENG APPROX	IPA	EXAMPLE
-e		f<u>e</u>llow	[ɛ]	坐 ch<u>ē</u> 'to sit'
-eh		h<u>eh</u>	[ɛʔ]	提 t<u>eh</u> 'to take'
-ip		whi<u>pp</u>ed	[ɪp]	翕 h<u>ip</u> 'stuffy'
-it		ki<u>tt</u>en	[ɪt]	這 ch<u>it</u> 'this'
-ek		hi<u>cc</u>up	[ɪk]	叔 ch<u>ek</u> 'uncle'
-ih		p<u>ea</u>pod	[iʔ]	滴 t<u>ih</u> 'to drip'
-eng		ki<u>ng</u>	[ɪŋ]	揀 k<u>éng</u> 'to select'

Also note that both '**-ek**' and '**-eng**' follow the same sound changes as other finals beginning with '**-i-**'. For example, the intial '**s-**' changes to a sound like 'sh' in the English '<u>sh</u>eep' when occurring before finals beginning with '**-i-**'.

	EXAMPLES WITH INITIAL 'S-'	MEANING	ENG APPROX
-e	sé	洗 'to wash'	<u>s</u>ell
-eh	seh	雪 'snow'	<u>s</u>even
-ip	sip	濕 'moist'	<u>sh</u>ip
-it	sit	失 'to lose'	<u>sh</u>it *(vul.)*
-ek	sek	色 'color'	<u>sh</u>iksa
-ih	sih	蝕 'to erode'	<u>ch</u>ic
-eng	seng	先 'first'	pu<u>sh</u>ing

2.2.5 Comparison to Mandarin finals

The table below compares the finals in both Taiwanese and Mandarin. Finals that have the same phonetic sound are highlighted by the cognate chosen as an example in both languages. While these cognates may differ in initials, tone, and Romanization spelling, the sound of the final is actually equivalent. English approximations and International Phonetic Alphabet (IPA) are also provided for reference.

TAIWANESE (Pe̍h-ōe-jī)		MANDARIN (Hànyǔ Pīnyīn)		MEANING	ENGLISH APPROX	IPA
a	chh<u>â</u>	**a**	ch<u>á</u>	差 'to check'	f<u>a</u>ther	[a]
ah	b<u>ah</u>	--	--	肉 'meat'	bl<u>ah</u>	[aʔ]
ai	<u>ài</u>	**ai**	<u>ài</u>	愛 'love'	<u>eye</u>	[aɪ]
aiⁿ	ph<u>ái</u>ⁿ	--	--	歹 'bad'	m<u>i</u>ning *(nasalized)*	[aĩ]

TAIWANESE (Pe̍h-ōe-jī)		MANDARIN (Hànyǔ Pīnyīn)		MEANING	ENGLISH APPROX	IPA
ak	s<u>ak</u>	--	--	揀 'push'	<u>o</u>ccupy	[ak]
am	h<u>ām</u>	--	--	和 'with'	b<u>om</u>b	[am]
an	p<u>an</u>	an	b<u>ān</u>	班 'class'	f<u>aw</u>n	[an]
aⁿ	t<u>àⁿ</u>	--	--	擔 'vendor'	n<u>o</u>nsense (nasalized)	[ã]
ang	k<u>áng</u>	ang	g<u>ǎng</u>	港 'harbor'	s<u>ong</u>	[ɑŋ]
ap	k<u>ap</u>	--	--	敆 'connect'	p<u>op</u>ped	[ap]
at	b<u>at</u>	--	--	捌 'to know'	c<u>ot</u>ton	[at]
au	l<u>āu</u>	ao	l<u>ǎo</u>	老 'old'	c<u>ow</u>	[aʊ]
e	b<u>é</u>	--	--	馬 'horse'	f<u>e</u>llow	[ɛ]
eh	p<u>e̍h</u>	--	--	白 'white'	h<u>eh</u>	[ɛʔ]
--	--	ei	b<u>ēi</u>	杯 'cup'	cl<u>ay</u>	[eɪ]
ek	s<u>ek</u>	--	--	色 'color'	h<u>ic</u>cup	[ɪk]
--	--	en	h<u>ěn</u>	很 'very'	f<u>u</u>n	[ən]
eⁿ	p<u>êⁿ</u>	--	--	平 'flat'	m<u>e</u>nd (nasalized)	[ɛ̃]
eng	p<u>eng</u>	ing	b<u>īng</u>	冰 'ice'	k<u>ing</u>	[iŋ]
--	--	eng	l<u>ěng</u>	冷 'cold'	l<u>ung</u>	[əŋ]
--	--	er	<u>èr</u>	二 'two'	<u>ur</u>n	[ɻ]
i	l<u>í</u>	i	n<u>ǐ</u>	你 'you'	s<u>ee</u>	[i]
ia	kh<u>ia</u>	ia	j<u>iā</u>	迦 (phonetic)	pap<u>aya</u>	[ɪa]
iah	l<u>ia̍h</u>	--	--	掠 'catch'	<u>ya</u>cht	[ɪaʔ]
iam	l<u>iâm</u>	--	--	鹽 'salt'	<u>yum</u>my	[ɪam]
ian	p<u>iàn</u>	ian	b<u>iàn</u>	變 'to change'	civil<u>ian</u>	[ɪɛn]
iaⁿ	s<u>iaⁿ</u>	--	--	聲 'sound'	insom<u>nia</u> (nasalized)	[ɪã]
iang	l<u>iâng</u>	iang	l<u>iáng</u>	涼 'cool'	B<u>ia</u>nca	[jɑŋ]
iap	ch<u>iap</u>	--	--	接 'to receive'	<u>yup</u>	[ɪap]
iat	l<u>ia̍t</u>	--	--	烈 'intense'	<u>get</u>	[ɪɛt]
iau	th<u>iàu</u>	iao	t<u>iào</u>	跳 'to jump'	m<u>eow</u>	[ɪaʊ]
--	--	ie	j<u>iē</u>	街 'street'	<u>ye</u>llow	[jɛ]
ih	m<u>ih</u>	--	--	物 'thing'	p<u>ea</u>pod	[iʔ]
im	s<u>im</u>	--	--	心 'heart'	d<u>im</u>	[ɪm]
in	s<u>in</u>	in	x<u>īn</u>	新 'new'	gr<u>een</u>	[in]
iⁿ	t<u>iⁿ</u>	--	--	甜 'sweet'	m<u>ea</u>n (nasalized)	[ĩ]
io	s<u>io</u>	--	--	燒 'warm'	<u>year</u>n (with pursed lips)	[ɪo]
ioh	t<u>io̍h</u>	--	--	著 'correct'	<u>jer</u>k	[ɪoʔ]
iok	ch<u>iok</u>	--	--	足 'very'	<u>yolk</u>	[ɪok]
iong	h<u>iông</u>	iong	x<u>ióng</u>	雄 'mighty'	w<u>e own g</u>old	[ɪoŋ]
ip	j<u>ip</u>	--	--	入 'enter'	wh<u>ip</u>ped	[ɪp]

TAIWANESE (Pe̍h-ōe-jī)		MANDARIN (Hànyǔ Pīnyīn)		MEANING	ENGLISH APPROX	IPA
it	ch**it**	--	--	一 'one'	k**i**tten	[ɪt]
iu	k**iû**	--	--	球 'ball'	**you**	[iu]
--	--	iu	l**iù**	六 'six'	**yo**gurt	[jəʊ]
iuⁿ	s**iūⁿ**	--	--	想 'to think'	n**ew** (nasalized)	[iũ]
m	m̄	--	--	毋 'not'	pris**m**	[m̩]
ng	th**ng**	--	--	湯 'soup'	to**ng**ue	[ŋ̍]
o (S)	kh**ò**	e	k**è**	課 'lesson'	sof**a**	[ɤ]
o (N)	p**ô**	o	p**ó**	婆 'grandmother'	sp**o**ke	[o]
o·	h**ō·**	--	--	雨 'rain'	p**aw**	[ɔ]
--	--	ou	t**óu**	頭 'head'	t**oe**	[əʊ]
oa	k**òa**	ua	g**uà**	掛 'to hang'	**aqua**	[ua]
oah	kh**oah**	--	--	闊 'broad'	m**uah** (kiss)	[uaʔ]
oai	k**oai**	uai	g**uāi**	乘 'well-behaved'	q**ui**et	[uai]
oaiⁿ	k**oai**ⁿ	--	--	關 'to close'	**whi**ning (nasalized)	[uaĩ]
oaⁿ	s**oa**ⁿ	--	--	山 'mountain'	**igua**na (nasalized)	[uã]
oan	ch**óan**	uan	zh**uàn**	轉 'to turn'	q**uan**tity	[uan]
--	--	uang	g**uàng**	逛 'to stroll'	w**on**k	[waŋ]
oat	h**oat**	--	--	法 'law'	kil**owatt**	[uat]
oe	**ōe**	--	--	話 'speech'	w**ay**	[ue]
oeh	h**oeh**	--	--	血 'blood'	w**eigh**	[ueʔ]
oh	t**oh**	--	--	卓 'table'	d**ough**	[oʔ]
ok	k**ok**	--	--	國 'country'	c**aulk**	[ɔk]
om	**om**	--	--	掩 'to conceal'	**om**elet	[ɔm]
ong	t**ông**	ong	t**óng**	同 'same'	**own** goal	[ɔŋ]
u	h**ù**	u	f**ù**	付 'to pay'	f**oo**d	[u]
--	--	ü	n**ǚ**	女 'female'	v**i**ew (with pursed lips)	[y]
--	--	ue	y**uè**	月 'moon'	d**ue**t (with pursed lips)	[yɛ]
uh	t**u̍h**	--	--	揬 'poke'	p**oo**h	[uʔ]
ui	k**ùi**	--	--	貴 'expensive'	q**uee**n	[ui]
un	k**ún**	un	g**ǔn**	滾 'to boil'	**Owen**	[wən]
ut	k**ut**	--	--	骨 'bone'	p**ut**	[ut]
--	--	ui	t**uī**	推 'push'	qu**ai**l	[weɪ]
--	--	uo	z**uò**	坐 'to sit'	w**o**ke	[wo]
--	--	weng	w**ēng**	翁 'old man'	s**wung**	[wəŋ]

As is evident, Taiwanese has a much greater number of finals than Mandarin. The majority of the difference arises from Taiwanese having additional nasal vowels (**-a^n**, **-ai^n**, **-e^n**, **-i^n**, **-ia^n**, **-iu^n**, **-oa^n**, **-oai^n**), the nasal consonant (**-m**), consonant stops (**-p**, **-t**, **-k**), and the glottal stop (**-h**).

In contrast, Taiwanese lacks several sounds found in Mandarin including rounded vowels with the 'ü' sound (including **-üe** and the finals **-u**, **-un** after **j-**, **x-**, or **y-**).

2.3 Sound changes

2.3.1 Contractions

Often in rapid spoken speech multiple syllables are contracted into fewer syllables or a particular sound is omitted. Below are a few common examples.

ORIGINAL	CONTRACTION	MEANING
e-hng-àm	eng-àm	下昏暗 'tonight'
phàng-m̄-kì^n	phàng-kì^n	拍毋見 'missing'
siá^n-lâng	siâng	啥人 'who, whom'
chit-má	chím-á	這馬 'now'
kā lâng	kâng	共人 'to, for someone'
hō˙lâng	hông	予人 'to allow someone'
kā góa	kā-á	共我 'to, for me'
hō˙góa	hō-á	予我 'to, give me'

2.3.2 Liaision with suffix 仔 -á

With some nouns that end in the suffix 仔 **-á**, a phenomenon similar to the French *liaision* occurs. For Taiwanese nouns that end in a consonant sound (**-p**, **-t**, **-k**) or nasal (**-m**, **-n**, **-ng**, **-^{n}**), the consonant or nasal sound is carried over to the beginning of the following syllable 仔 **-á**. If the final consonant is unvoiced, then it becomes voiced at the beginning of the next syllable.

ORIGINAL	ALTERED VERSION	MEANING
a̍p-á	a̍p-bá	盒仔 'small box'
chha̍t-á	chha̍t-lá	賊仔 'thief'

ORIGINAL	ALTERED VERSION	MEANING
chhȧk-á	chhȧk-gá	鑿仔 'chisel'
chiam-á	chiam-má	尖仔 'needle'
kin-á	kin-ná	巾仔 'towel'
hāng-á	hāng-ngá	巷仔 'alley'
piⁿ-á	piⁿ-ná	邊仔 'side'

2.3.3 Other sound changes

In some words, note that some speakers may add or alter certain consonant sounds to make them easier to pronounce.

ORIGINAL	ALTERED VERSION	MEANING
chōng-hóng	chōng-khóng	狀況 'situation'
khí-lâi	khit-lâi	起來 'to rise'
sàn-pō͘	sàm-pō͘	散步 'to go for a walk'

2.4 Regional variation

There is a great deal of regional variation in pronunciation within Taiwan. Most localities have some mixture of accents from Quanzhou and Zhangzhou, the two provinces in China from which most speakers of Hokkien originated. However, over four hundred years of population movements within the island have led to local accents that are difficult to align along the Quanzhou/Zhangzhou divide *(see 1.1.3 Local differences within Taiwan)*. Nevertheless, some of the pronunciation differences encountered in Taiwanese can be attributed to this distinction.

Below are some more common pronunciation differences that occur between the two originating accents.

INITIALS		
ZHANGZHOU	*QUANZHOU*	*MEANING*
l- / g-	**j-**	
liáu / giáu	jiáu	爪 'claws'
lip / gip	jip	入 'to enter'

ZHANGZHOU	QUANZHOU	MEANING
b-	**m-**	
bîn-á-chài	miâ-á-chài	明仔載 'tomorrow'
bîn-chhn̂g	mn̂g-chhn̂g	眠床 'bed'

FINALS

ZHANGZHOU	QUANZHOU	MEANING
-i	**-u**	
gí	gú	語 'language'
ti	tu	豬 'pig'
-eⁿ	**-iⁿ**	
sèⁿ	sìⁿ	姓 'to be surnamed'
pēⁿ	pīⁿ	病 'sick'
-e	**-oe**	
ê	ôe	鞋 'shoes'
beh	boeh	欲 'to want, going to'

Some of the more common variations in pronunciation have been noted throughout this text.

2.5 Tones

Tones are a component of every Taiwanese syllable. A tone indicates that the syllable should be spoken at a particular pitch that can be sustained, rising, falling, stopped, or a combination thereof.

Because Chinese languages tend to have many homophones, the tone is a critical part of pronunciation. Along with context, the tones help to disambiguate between otherwise similar sounding syllables. And, while context does help to indicate the correct meaning, some situations plausibly allow for confusion if correct tones are not used. For example, the word 買 **bé** 'buy' is pronounced with a second tone while the word 賣 **bē** 'sell' is said with a seventh tone.

Tones in Chinese languages are thought to have evolved from Middle Chinese (~AD 600), which originally had eight classes of tones. However, over the centuries most of the different varieties of Chinese have both split and merged tones into different classes. Taiwanese still maintains seven distinct tones with the 2nd and 6th tones having merged. This explains the 'missing' 6th tone. In contrast, Mandarin only has four tones while

Cantonese has six to seven tones depending on region.

2.5.1 Original tones

Each syllable has an original tone that can be indicated on the syllable using the Pe̍h-ōe-jī (POJ) Romanization scheme.

Tones are relative to one's vocal register. If the range of tones were graphed onto a scale measuring from pitch 1 (lowest) to 5 (highest) of one's vocal register, the middle line 3 (middle) would represent the pitch of one's voice at its most relaxed.

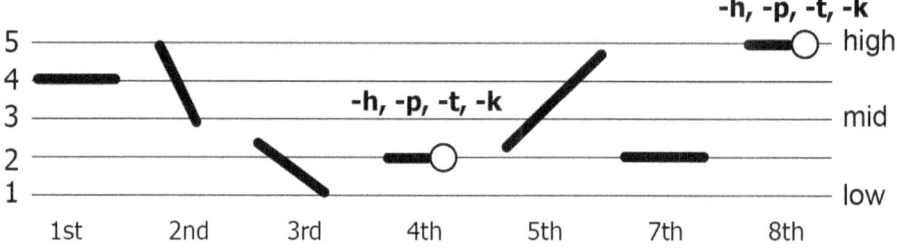

FIGURE 2.1 Original tones for Southern Taiwan

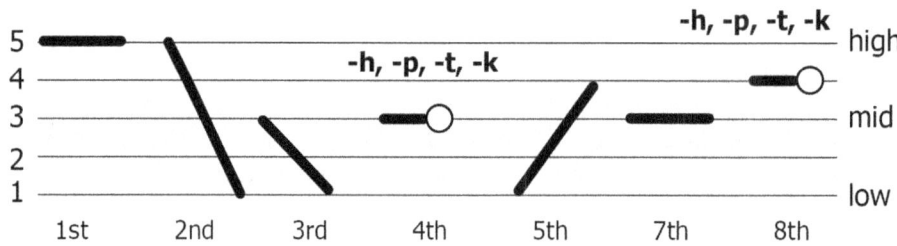

FIGURE 2.2 Original tones for Northern Taiwan

As with pronunciation and vocabulary, there is a certain degree of regional variation in tone usage. This section will use overall tone descriptions that capture the general differences in pitch contour for the majority of Taiwanese accents. More specific differences in beginning and ending pitch are provided in the images, which indicate specific pitch and contour information for the two major Common accents spoken in southern Taiwan (as represented by Tainan, Kaoshiung, and Taitung) and northern Taiwan (as represented by Taipei and Hsinchu) *(see 1.1.3 Local differences within Taiwan).*

First tone *(High flat)*

The first tone (high flat) starts at a high pitch and is held at the same pitch throughout the syllable. Plain, unmarked syllables that do not end in '**-p**', '**-t**', '**-k**', and '**-h**', are in the first tone.

EXAMPLES

si 詩 'poetry'   to 刀 'knife'   hong 風 'wind'

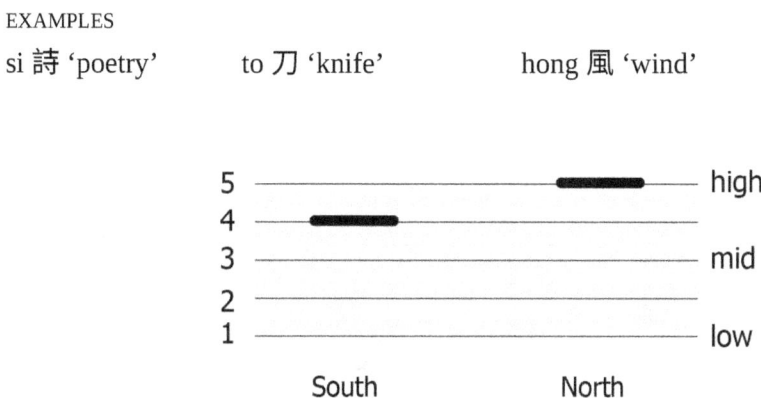

FIGURE 2.3 First tone

The Taiwanese first tone is similar to the Mandarin flat first tone. Note that Mandarin marks the first tone with a macron accent (¯), but Taiwanese uses no diacritic.

Second tone *(High falling)*

The second tone (high falling) starts high and rapidly drops. An acute accent (´) placed over the syllable indicates the second tone.

EXAMPLES

sí 死 'to die'   tó 倒 'to fall over'   hóng 仿 'to imitate'

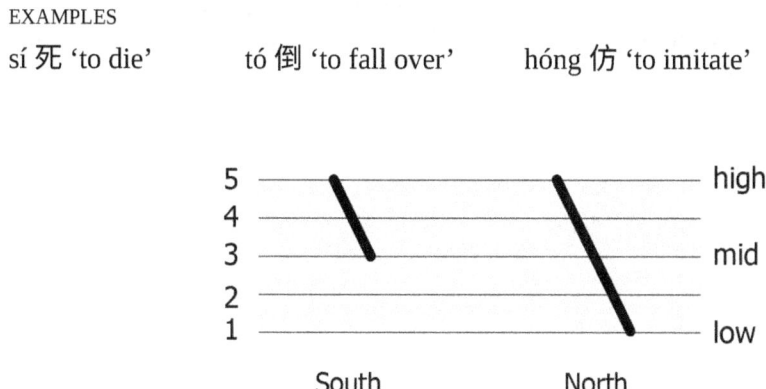

FIGURE 2.4 Second tone

The Taiwanese second tone is similar to the Mandarin falling fourth tone. However, note that the accent mark is written in the reverse direction.

Third tone *(Low falling)*

The third tone (low falling) starts in the middle of one's register and drops slightly lower. A grave accent (`) placed over the syllable indicates the third tone.

EXAMPLES

sì 四 'four'   tò 倒 'to pour'   hòng 放 'to release'

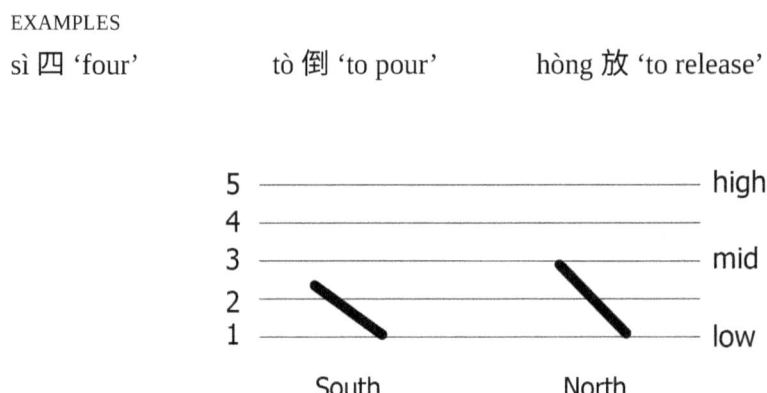

FIGURE 2.5 Third tone

The Taiwanese third tone is similar to the Mandarin half-third tone, a dipping tone that does not rise again. Note that the accent mark differs.

Fourth tone *(Mid stopped)*

The fourth tone (mid stopped) starts at the middle of one's register and then stops abruptly. Note that this tone only occurs when the syllable ends with '**-p**', '**-t**', '**-k**', or '**-h**'. No accent mark is written on syllables in the fourth tone, but the syllables are distinguished from those in the first tone by the presence of any of the four stopped endings (**-p, -t, -k, -h**).

EXAMPLES

sih 熾 'bright'   toh 桌 'table'   hok 福 'fortune'

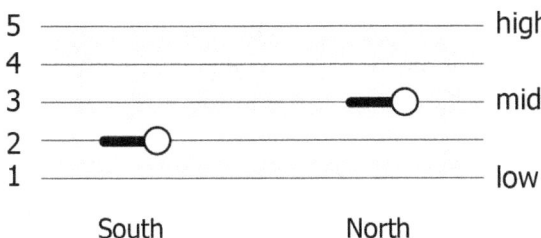

FIGURE 2.6 Fourth tone

Mandarin does not have syllables with stopped endings.

Fifth tone *(Rising)*

The fifth tone (rising) starts at the lower end of one's register and rises quickly. A circumflex accent (ˆ) placed over the syllable indicates the fifth tone.

EXAMPLES

sî 時 'time'   tô 逃 'to flee'   hông 防 'to defend'

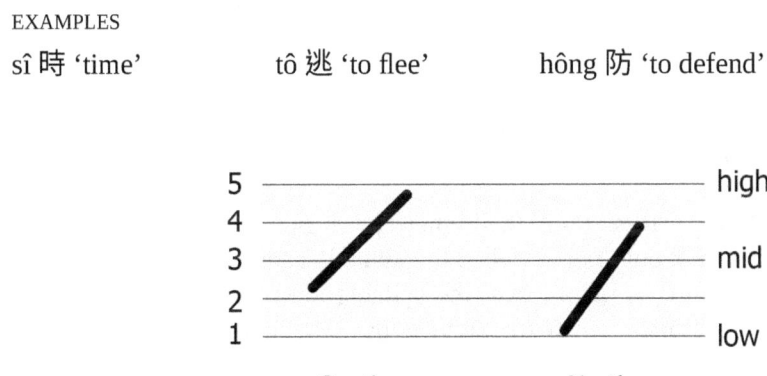

FIGURE 2.7 Fifth tone

The Taiwanese fifth tone is similar to the Mandarin rising second tone. Note that the accent mark differs.

Sixth tone = Same as Second tone

In Taiwanese, the sixth tone has merged with the second tone.

Seventh tone *(Low flat)*

The seventh tone (low flat) starts in the middle to lower end of one's register and is held at the same pitch throughout the syllable. A macron accent (¯) placed over the syllable indicates the seventh tone.

EXAMPLES

sī 是 'to be'   tō 就 'just'   hōng 鳳 'phoenix'

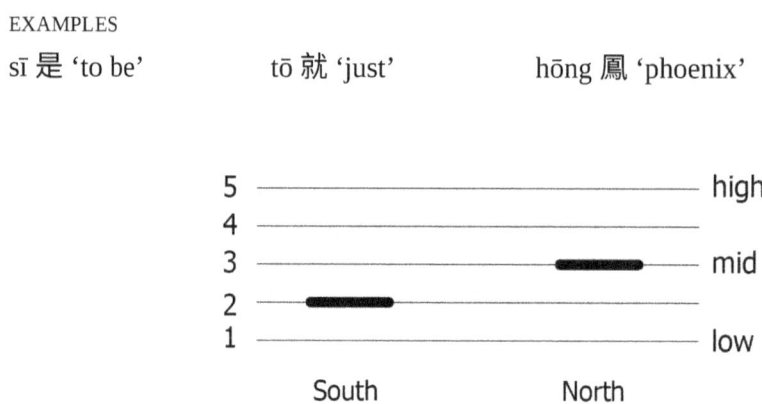

FIGURE 2.8 Seventh tone

Mandarin does not have an equivalent to the Taiwanese low flat tone.

Eighth tone *(High stopped)*

The eighth tone (high stopped) starts at the higher end of one's register and then stops abruptly. Note that this tone only occurs when the syllable ends with '**-p**', '**-t**', '**-k**', or '**-h**'. A vertical line accent (˙) placed over the syllable indicates the eighth tone and distinguishes the syllable from a fourth tone (mid stopped) syllable.

EXAMPLES

si̍h 蝕 'to erode'   to̍h 著 'to light'   ho̍k 復 'again'

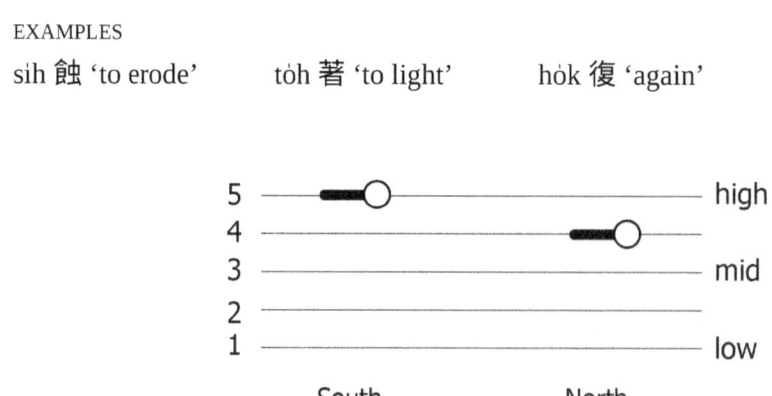

FIGURE 2.9 Eighth tone

Mandarin does not have stopped syllables.

Neutral tone

The neutral tone in Taiwanese is generally light, mid-register and can be thought of as similar to the third tone (low falling). POJ marks the neutral tones by preceding the syllable with a double hyphen. Neutral tones tend to be applied to suffixes or particles occurring at the end of a clause or sentence.

EXAMPLES

--bô 無 *question particle*   --chit-ē 一下 'a little bit'

Note that there is a degree of inconsistency in usage with hyphens. In theory, hyphens connect syllables that form a cohesive unit of meaning. This can play a useful role when deciding on tone changes. For example, for multi-syllable nouns the final syllable does not change tone. For other parts of speech, the use of a hyphen is negligible and has no impact on tone changes. In some of these areas, there can be some inconsistency among users of the POJ or TL Romanization systems *(see 1.4.2.4 Differences between POJ and TL)*.

2.5.2 Placement of tone diacritics

Tone markings are placed over vowels within a syllable, or nasal consonants if no vowel is present. Below are general guidelines for accent placement according to the *Pe̍h-ōe-jī* (POJ) Romanization scheme. Note that some software input editors and users of POJ do not always adhere to these guidelines.

1) If the syllable has a single vowel, place the tone mark over the vowel.

khì 去 'to go'
gû 牛 'cow'

2) If there is no vowel, place the tone mark over the nasal consonant.

m̄ 毋 'no, not'
thn̂g 糖 'sugar'

3) Because the letters '**i**' and '**u**' are considered *semi-vowels* (also known as glides), they are subordinate to the vowels '**a**', '**e**', and '**o**'. As a result, if a syllable contains '**i**' and/or '**u**', place the tone mark over the other vowel.

pháiⁿ 歹 'bad'

cháu 走 'run'

thiàu 跳 'to jump'

4) If there are two vowels in a syllable that contains both '**i**' and '**u**', place the tone mark over the '**u**'.

kiû 球 'ball'

súi 媠 'pretty'

5) If '**o**' co-occurs with '**a**' or '**e**', place the tone mark over the '**o**'.

hôai 懷 'to cherish'

hòe 歲 'years old'

2.5.3 Tone changes

Similar to other Chinese languages, Taiwanese syllables can change tones. While Mandarin only has a few tone changes (e.g. consecutive third tones or changes to **bù** 不 'not' or **yī** 一 'one' before certain tones), Taiwanese has relatively extensive tone change rules *(see 2.6 Tone change rules)*.

While there are many rules for when tone changes occur, for the purposes of introducing the pattern of tone changes, one rule will be introduced here: a two-syllable noun will have the first syllable change tone, while the last syllable remains in the original tone.

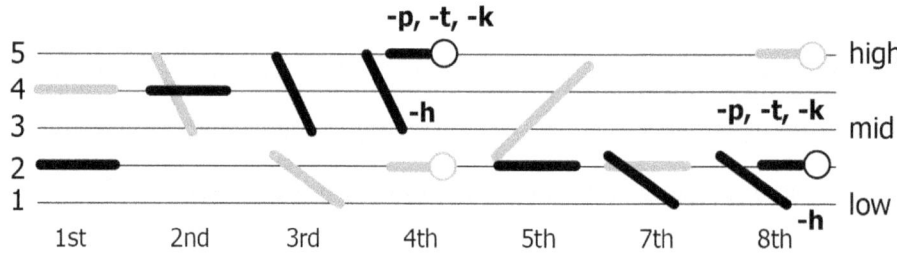

FIGURE 2.10 Changed tones for Southern Taiwan

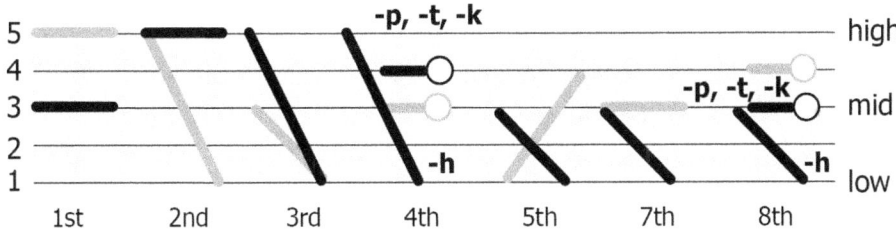

FIGURE 2.11 Changed tones for Northern Taiwan

The convention in the *Pe̍h-ōe-jī* (POJ) Romanization is to only annotate the original tone leaving it up to the reader to know when to pronounce the syllables with the changed tone.

First tone (High flat)

First tone (High flat) → Seventh tone (Low flat)

The high flat tone changes to a low flat tone. For example, for the two-syllable noun 身軀 **seng-khu** 'body', the first syllable '**seng-**' should be read in the seventh tone as if it were marked '**sēng-**'. The last syllable '**-khu**' remains in the first tone.

ORIGINAL TONES	CHANGED TONES (IF MARKED)	MEANING
seng-khu	sēng-khu	身軀 'body'

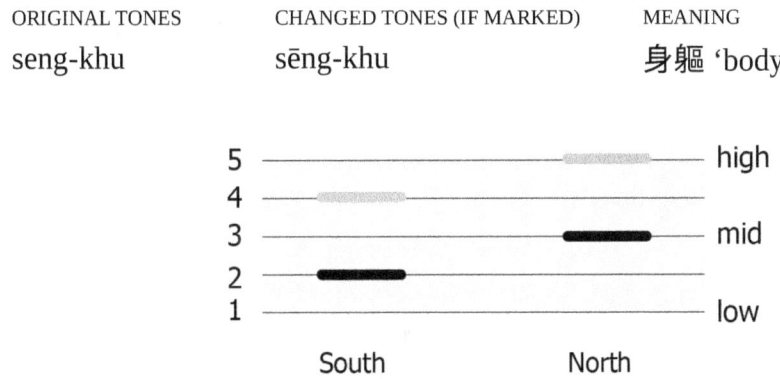

FIGURE 2.12 Changed first tone

Second tone (High falling)

Second tone (High falling) → First tone (High flat)

The high falling tone changes to a high flat tone. For example, for the two-syllable noun

果子 **kóe-chí** 'fruit', the first syllable '**kóe-**' should be read in the first tone as if it were marked '**koe-**'. The last syllable '**-chí**' remains in the second tone.

ORIGINAL TONES	CHANGED TONES (IF MARKED)	MEANING
kóe-chí	koe-chí	果子 'fruit'

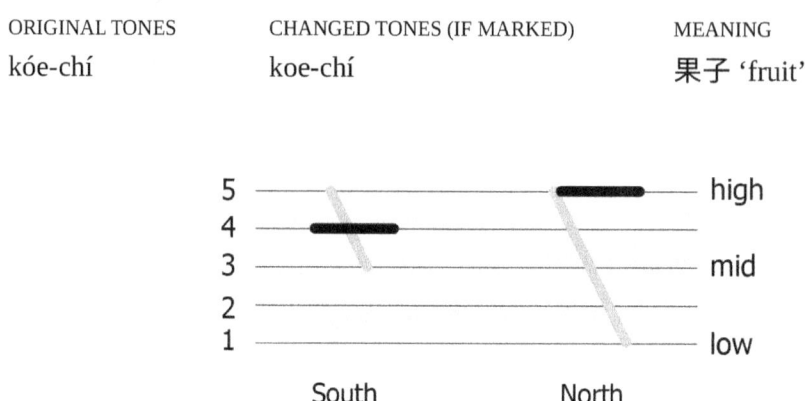

FIGURE 2.13 Changed second tone

Third tone (Low falling)

Third tone (Low falling) → Second tone (High falling)

The low falling tone changes to a high falling tone. For example, for the two-syllable noun 太太 **thài-thài** 'Mrs., wife', the first syllable '**thài-**' should be read in the first tone as if it were marked '**thái-**'. The last syllable '**-thài**' remains in the third tone.

ORIGINAL TONES	CHANGED TONES (IF MARKED)	MEANING
thài-thài	thái-thài	太太 'Mrs., wife'

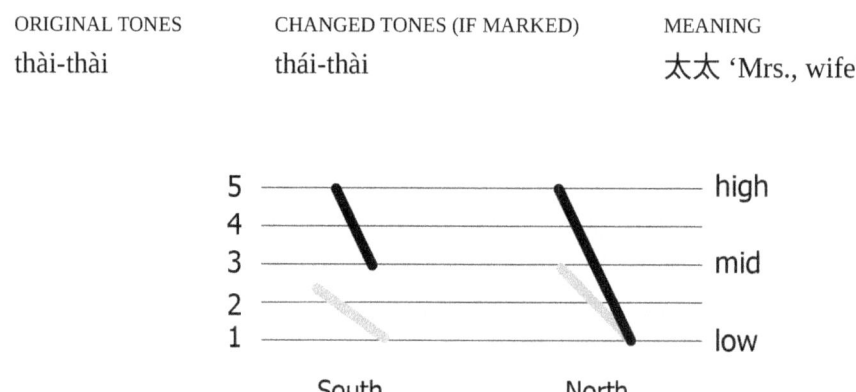

FIGURE 2.14 Changed third tone

Fourth tone (Mid stopped)

Fourth tone ends in -h (Mid stopped) → Second tone (High falling)

The mid stopped tone changes to a high falling tone if the syllable ends in '**-h**'. For example, for the two-syllable noun 客廳 **kheh-thiaⁿ** 'living room', the first syllable '**kheh-**' should be read in the eighth tone as if it were marked '**khé-**'. The last syllable '**-thiaⁿ**' remains in the first tone. Also, notice that along with the tone change, the syllable loses the '**-h**' and now flows from the first to the second syllable without a glottal stop.

ORIGINAL TONES	CHANGED TONES (IF MARKED)	MEANING
kheh-thiaⁿ	khé-thiaⁿ	客廳 'living room'

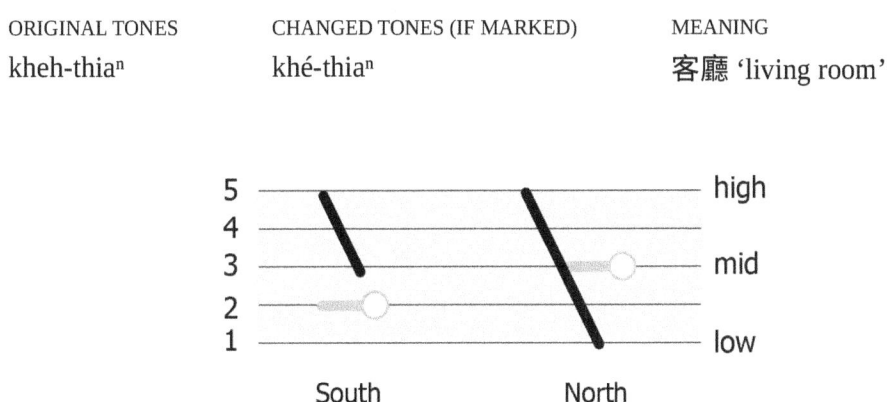

FIGURE 2.15 Changed fourth tone ending in -h

Fourth tone ends in -p, -t, -k (Mid stopped) → Eighth tone (high Stopped)

The mid stopped tone flips to a high stopped tone if the syllable ends in '**-p**', '**-t**', '**-k**'. For example, for the two-syllable noun 腹肚 **pak-tó** 'stomach', the first syllable '**pak-**' should be read in the eighth tone as if it were marked '**pa̍k-**'. The last syllable ' **-tó** ' remains in the second tone.

ORIGINAL TONES	CHANGED TONES (IF MARKED)	MEANING
pak-tó˙	pa̍k-tó˙	腹肚 'stomach'

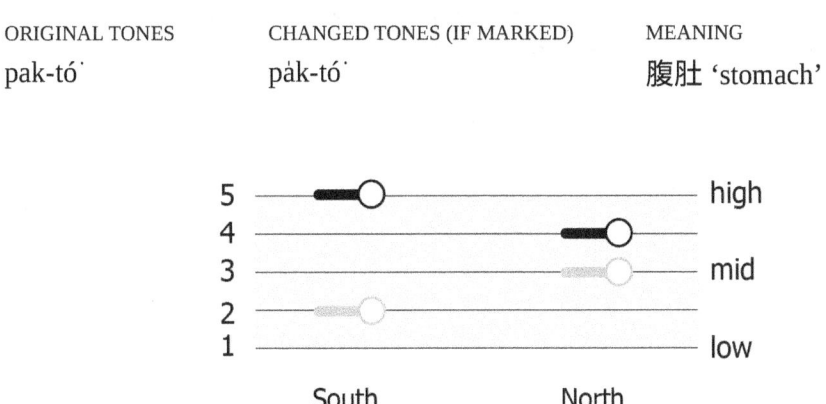

FIGURE 2.16 Changed fourth tone ending in -p, -t, -k

Fifth tone (Rising)

Fifth tone (Rising) → Seventh tone (Low flat) - Southern Taiwan

Fifth tone (Rising) → Third tone (Low falling) - Northern Taiwan

The rising tone changes to a low flat tone (southern Taiwan) or a low falling tone (northern Taiwan). For example, for the two-syllable noun 台灣 **Tâi-ôan** 'Taiwan', the first syllable '**Tâi-**' should be read in the seventh tone as if it were marked '**Tāi-**' (in southern Taiwan) or in the third tone as it were marked '**Tài-**' (in northern Taiwan). The last syllable '**-ôan**' remains in the fifth tone.

ORIGINAL TONES	CHANGED TONES (IF MARKED)	MEANING
Tâi-ôan	Tāi-ôan (S) / Tài-ôan (N)	台灣 'Taiwan'

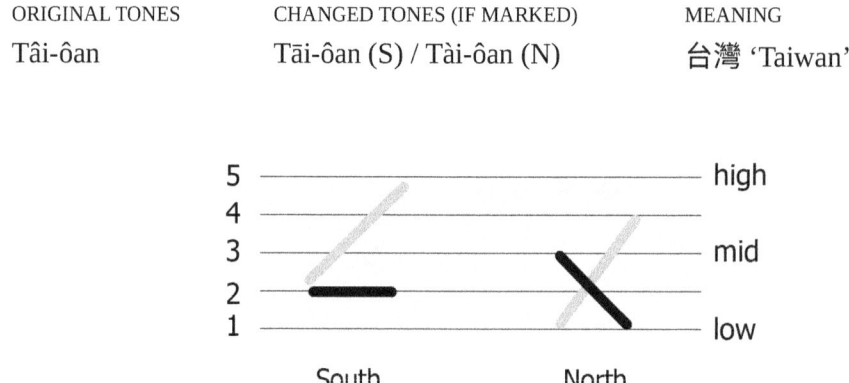

FIGURE 2.17 Changed fifth tone

Seventh tone (Low flat)

Seventh tone (Low flat) → Third tone (Low falling)

The low flat tone changes to a low falling tone. For example, for the two-syllable noun 護士 **hō-sū** 'nurse', the first syllable '**hō-**' should be read in the third tone as if it were marked '**hò-**'. The last syllable '**-sū**' remains in the seventh tone.

ORIGINAL TONES	CHANGED TONES (IF MARKED)	MEANING
hō-sū	hò-sū	護士 'nurse'

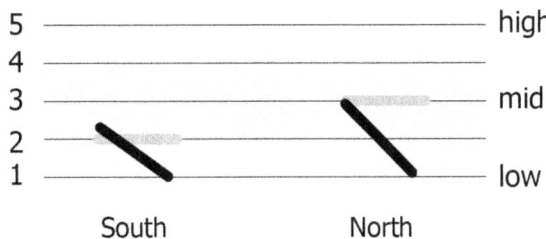

FIGURE 2.18 Changed seventh tone

Eighth tone (High Stopped)

Eighth tone ends in -h (High stopped) → Third tone (Low falling)

The high stopped tone changes to a low falling tone if the syllable ends in '**-h**'. For example, for the two-syllable noun 物件 **mih-kiāⁿ** 'thing', the first syllable '**mih-**' should be read in the third tone as if it were marked '**mi-**'. The last syllable '**-kiāⁿ**' remains in the seventh tone. Also, notice that along with the tone change, the syllable loses the '**-h**' and now flows from the first to the second syllable without a glottal stop.

ORIGINAL TONES	CHANGED TONES (IF MARKED)	MEANING
mih-kiāⁿ	mi-kiāⁿ	物件 'thing'

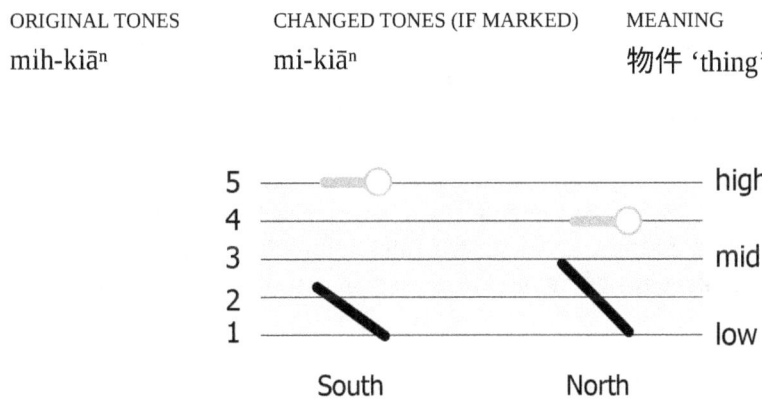

FIGURE 2.19 Changed eighth tone ending in -h

Eighth tone ends in -p, -t, -k (High stopped) → Fourth tone (Mid stopped)

The high stopped tone flips to a mid stopped tone if the syllable ends in '**-p**', '**-t**', '**-k**'. For example, for the two-syllable noun 雪文 **sap-bûn** 'soap', the first syllable '**sap**' should be read in the fourth tone as if it were marked '**sap-**'. The last syllable '**-bûn**' remains in the fifth tone.

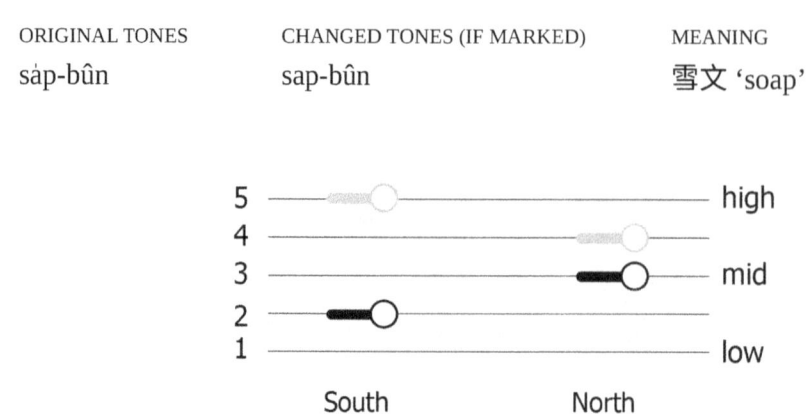

FIGURE 2.20 Changed eighth tone ending in -p, -t, -k

2.6 Tone change rules

Taiwanese and its Southern Min cousins have some of the most extensive systems of changing tones *(tone sandhi)* among Chinese languages. In fact, most syllables in a sentence are read in the changed tone rather than the original tone.

Unlike Mandarin, which has tone changes primarily due to phonetic reasons (such as consecutive third tones **很好 hěn hǎo** 'very good' or fourth tones **不大 bù dà** 'not big'), Taiwanese tone changes are driven more by grammatical reasons. In general, tone changes in Taiwanese help to group ideas within a sentence and indicate emphasis.

More specifically, the overarching guiding principle is to change the tones of all syllables except for the final syllables before the end of a clause or sentence—thereby marking borders between thoughts and ideas. Additional rules refine this grouping by allowing other syllables within to keep their original tone based on part of speech or word-specific reasons.

Another layer of refinement at the word and phrase level comes from placing some syllables in the neutral tone, allowing emphasis to fall on the preceding syllable, which generally does not change tone.

Essentially, places of emphasis occur on syllables that do not change tone. From this observation, it can be seen that borders between thoughts and ideas as well as the demarcation of nouns (the primary actors within a sentence) receive the most attention. Other parts of speech or specific words may also receive stress by keeping their original tone. Additionally, it is possible to use these points of emphasis as a way to pace one's speech and give sentences the natural cadence of Taiwanese.

Note to the student: For many students of Taiwanese, the number of tone changes and rules governing their usage can be intimidating and overwhelming. Moreover, the prospect of processing every one of these rules and tone changes in real-time speech is even more daunting. Native speakers, of course, do not go through this process when they speak, but perhaps recall how they have heard certain words and phrases spoken in the past. For learners, perhaps this can be instructive as to focus attention on remembering how phrases or words 'sound' in order to achieve a more authentic pronunciation. The tone change rules can be applied during study as an aid to help accurately read aloud and hear the proper tones. Ideally, hearing oneself pronounce correct tones will also help refine one's 'sense' of proper tones.

2.6.1 The guiding principle of tone changes

The guiding principle for tone changes in Taiwanese is to change the tone of all syllables except for the final syllable before the end of a clause or sentence. In other words, syllables at the end of a clause or sentence stay in their original tones

Guiding principle: *syllables at the end of a clause or sentence stay in their original tones.*

This general rule applies regardless of the final syllable's part of speech. The only exception to this rule is if the final syllable(s) is in the neutral tone in which case the preceding non-neutral tone syllable becomes the one that stays in the original tone.

Punctuation such as commas, periods, semi-colons, and question marks helps to delineate the borders of clauses and sentences. However, in light of a scarcity of written material in Taiwanese using Romanization, one can think of these borders as occurring where the speaker might naturally pause for a breath (such as to emphasize the preceding content or prior to moving on to a new thought or idea).

In fact, as places of emphasis, syllables that keep their original tones can be considered interim destinations for one's speech. These original-tone syllables form stopping points during an utterance and are often slightly elongated with brief pauses (or long pauses for rhetorical effect) following immediately after. The pauses give emphasis to the preceding idea or to mark the end of a thought.

In the examples below, the ***bolded italicized*** syllables stay in their original tone while all other syllables change. Note that characters will not be italicized.

我 會 曉 講 台灣**話**。
Góa ē-hiáu kóng Tâi-ôan-***ōe***.
我 會 講 台語。
Wǒ huì jiǎng Táiyǔ
I can speak Taiwanese.

我 的 **筆** 借 予 **你**，但是 一定 愛 還 **我**。
Góa ê *pit* chioh hō *lí,* tān-sī it-tēng ài hêng *góa.*
我 的 筆 借 給 你，但是 一定 要 還 我。
Wǒ de bǐ jiè gěi nǐ, dànshì yīdìng yào huán wǒ.
I will lend you my pen, but you must return it to me.

你 敢 買 了 矣？
Lí kám bé *liáu*--ah?
你 買完 了 沒有？
Nǐ mǎiwán le méiyǒu?
Did you buy it?

你 **看**，有 **人** 咧 排**隊**，咱 應該 較 早 **來**。
Lí *khòaⁿ,* ū *lâng* teh pâi-*tūi,* lán eng-kai khah chá *lâi.*
你 看，有 人 在 排隊，我們 應該 早 一 點 來。
Nǐ kàn, yǒu rén zài páiduì, wǒmen yīnggāi zǎo yīdiǎn lái.
Look! There are people lining up. We should have come earlier.

Note that Taiwanese is less stringent with comma placement than English is.

2.6.2 The neutral tone and tone changes

The neutral tone, essentially a third tone (low falling), is lighter and softer to de-emphasize the syllable. The use of the neutral tone also has the effect of emphasizing the preceding syllable by usually allowing it to stay in the original tone. With consecutive syllables in the neutral tone, the syllable before the first neutral tone syllable stays in the original tone. Note that neutral tones can occur both at the end of a clause or sentence and mid-clause. The neutral tone is written with double hyphens when occurring at the end of a clause or sentence.

伊 佇 膨**椅** **坐** 咧。
I tī phòng-*í chē*--leh.
她 在 沙發 坐著。
Tā zài shāfā zuòzhe.
She is sitting on the sofa.

張 太太 共 阮 趕出去 矣。

Tiuⁿ thài-*thài* kā gún *kóaⁿ*--chhut-khì--ah.

張 太太 把 我們 趕出去。

Zhāng tàitài bǎ wǒmen gǎnchūqù.

Mrs. Tiunn has shooed us away.

2.6.3 Part of speech based rules

Aside from the general rule of tone changes, additional rules based on part of speech further refine tone changes that occur mid-clause.

In the following sections, **bolded italicized** syllables denote all syllables that keep their original tone. That is to say, all other syllables will change tone. <u>Underlined</u> syllables highlight examples of the specific rule discussed in each section. Note that characters will not be italicized.

2.6.3.1 Nouns

The last syllable of multi-syllable nouns does not change tone regardless of position within a sentence *(see 4 Nouns)*. Single-syllable nouns also do not change tone.

彼 台 跤踏車 已經 歹去 矣。

Hit tâi kha-ta̍h-*chhia* í-keng *pháiⁿ*--khì--ah.

那 台 腳踏車 已經 壞掉 了。

Nà tái jiǎotàchē yǐjīng huàidiào le.

That bicycle is already broken.

明仔載 你 一定 愛 共 冊 還 圖書館。

Bîn-á-*chài* lí it-tēng ài kā *chheh* hêng tô͘-su-*koán.*

明天 你 一定 要 把 書 還 圖書館。

Míngtiān nǐ yīdìng yào bǎ shū huán túshūguǎn.

Tomorrow, you definitely have to return the book to the library.

If a noun or location is modified by another noun, all syllables of any modifying noun will change tone *(see 6.6.3 Nouns that modify without 的 ê)*. Only the final syllable of the head noun will keep its original tone.

台北 動物<u>園</u>

Tâi-pak tōng-bu̍t-hn̂g

台北 動物園

Táiběi dòngwùyuán

Taipei zoo

韓國 同<u>事</u>

Hân-kok tông-<u>sū</u>

韓國 同事

Hánguó tóngshì

Korean colleague

If a noun is modified by a phrase with the modifying particle 的 ê, then the final syllable before the modifier ê does not change tone *(see 6.6 Noun phrases and the modifying particle 的 ê)*. Note that the particle 的 ê itself does change tone and the head noun following adheres to regular tone change rules.

伊 穿去 我 上 <u>愛</u> 的 膨紗<u>衫</u>。

I chhēng-khì góa siōng <u>*ài*</u> ê phòng-se-*sa*ⁿ.

她 穿走 我 最愛 的 毛衣。

Tā chuānzǒu wǒ zuì'ài de máoyī.

She wore my favorite sweater.

However, if the head noun is omitted, then the modifying particle 的 ê is put in the neutral tone *(see 6.6.4 Omitting the head noun - nominalization)*.

伊 穿去 我 上 <u>愛</u> <u>的</u>。

I chhēng-khì góa siōng *<u>ài--ê</u>*.

她 穿走 我 最愛 的。

Tā chuānzǒu wǒ zuì'ài de.

She wore my favorite one.

If a noun is omitted (and implied) after a measure word, the measure word does not change tone *(see 4.7 Omitting the noun)*.

三 <u>隻</u> *(*鳥鼠仔*)* 攏 <u>死</u>去 矣。

Saⁿ <u>***chiah***</u> *(niáu-chhí-á)* lóng *sí*--khì--ah.

三 隻 *(*老鼠*)* 都 死掉 了。

Sān zhī *(lǎo shǔ)* dōu sǐdiào le.

All three *(mice)* died.

2.6.3.2 Pronouns

Pronouns generally change tone *(see 5 Pronouns)*. However, if pronouns appear at the end of a clause or sentence, they can be either placed in the neutral tone or kept in the original tone depending on emphasis. A neutral tone reading places emphasis on the preceding word, while a reading in the original tone focuses on the pronoun itself.

阮 老師 罵 **我**。

Gún lāu-*su* mē ***góa***.

我 的 老師 罵 我。

Wǒ de lǎoshī mà wǒ.

My teacher scolded <u>me</u> (*surprised at being the target of anger*).

阮 老師 **罵** 我。

Gún lāu-*su* ***mē***--góa.

我 的 老師 罵 我。

Wǒ de lǎoshī mà wǒ.

My teacher <u>scolded</u> me (*surprised at the teacher's behavior*).

The demonstrative pronouns 這 **che** 'this' and 彼 **he** 'that' do not change tone in any position.

這 是 阮 **兜** 的 車。

Che sī gún ***tau*** ê ***chhia***.

這 是 我 家 的 車。

Zhè shì wǒ jiā de chē.

This is my family's car.

彼 敢 是 你 的 電腦?

He kám sī lí ê tiān-***náu***?

那 是 不 是 你 的 電腦?

Nà shìbùshì nǐ de diànnǎo?

Is that your computer?

2.6.3.3 Verbs

In general, verbs follow regular tone change rules. When occurring mid-clause, all syllables undergo tone changes. If occurring at the end of a clause or sentence, only the final syllable keeps its original tone.

阮 男 朋**友** 共 我 <u>介紹</u> 予 恁 爸**母**。
Gún lâm pêng-*iú* kā góa <u>kài-siāu</u> hōˈin pē-*bú*.
我 的 男 朋友 把 我 介紹 給 他 的 父母。
Wǒ de nán péngyǒu bǎ wǒ jièshào gěi tā de fùmǔ.
My boyfriend introduced me to his parents.

伊 的 表**兄** 共 阮 介**紹**。
I ê piáu-*hiaⁿ* kā gún <u>**kài-siāu.**</u>
她 的 表哥 介紹 我們 認識。
Tā de biǎogē jièshào wǒmen rènshi.
Her cousin introduced us.

Some Taiwanese verbs take default objects *(see 7.1.4 Default objects)*. In these cases, the verb and object components follow the tone change rules for their respective parts of speech: the verb changes tone according to the rule for verbs stated above, and the default object follows the rules for nouns.

你 當**時** 欲 <u>食</u> **飯**?
Lí tang-*sî* beh <u>chia̍h</u> <u>***pn̄g***</u>?
你 何時 要 吃 飯?
Nǐ héshí yào chīfàn?
When do you want to eat?

2.6.3.4 Aspect markers

For the perfective aspect, the pre-verbal marker 有 **ū** follows normal tone change rules for verbs *(see 8.1 Perfective aspect)*. Phase complements used to mark the perfective aspect (了 **liáu**, 好 **hó**, 完 **ôan**, 煞 **soah**) do not undergo tone changes regardless of position within a sentence.

> 恁 阿**母** 講 <u>了</u> 有 道**理**。
> Lín a-***bú*** kóng <u>***liáu***</u> ū tō-***lí***.
> 你 媽媽 說 的 有 道理。
> Nǐ māmā shuō de yǒu dàolǐ.
> What your mom said is reasonable.

For the continuous aspect, the pre-verbal dynamic continuous aspect marker 咧 **teh** always occurs mid-clause and changes tone *(see 8.2 Continuous aspect)*. The static continuous aspect marker 咧 **--leh** remains in the neutral tone regardless of position. However, note that the preceding verb will change tone mid-clause but keep its original tone at the end.

> 哪 恁 無 <u>咧</u> 照顧 囡仔？
> Ná lín bô <u>teh</u> chiàu-kò˙gín-***á***?
> 為甚麼 你們 沒有 在 照顧 小孩？
> Wèishènme nǐmen méiyǒu zài zhàogù xiǎohái?
> Why aren't you taking care of the children?

> 伊 倒<u>咧</u> 佇 眠床**頂**。
> I tó<u>--leh</u> tī mn̂g-chhn̂g-***téng***.
> 她 在 床上 躺著。
> Tā zài chuángshàng tǎngzhe.
> She is lying on the bed.

> 我 的 珠**寶** 攏 **包** 咧。
> Góa ê chu-***pó*** lóng ***pau*<u>--leh</u>***.
> 我 的 飾品 都 包著。
> Wǒ de shìpǐn dōu bāozhe.
> All of my jewelry is wrapped.

For the experiential aspect, the pre-verbal marker **捌 bat** follows normal tone change rules for verbs *(see 8.3 Experiential aspect)*. When mid-clause, the verb suffix **過 -kòe** does not change tone, but the preceding verb does change tone. However, at the end of a clause or sentence, the verb suffix **過 -kòe** is neutralized with the preceding verb keeping its original tone.

我 捌 食過 臭 豆腐。

Góa <u>bat</u> chiáh-***kòe*** chhàu tāu-***hū.***

我 吃過 臭 豆腐。

Wǒ chīguò chòu dòufu.

I have eaten stinky tofu before.

德國，我 已經 去過。

Tek-***kok,*** góa í-keng ***khì***--<u>kòe</u>.

德國，我 已經 去過。

Déguó, wǒ yǐjīng qùguò.

I've already gone to Germany.

For the anterior aspect, the end-of-sentence particle **矣 --ah** is always placed in the neutral tone *(see 8.4 Anterior aspect)*.

外口 天 暗 矣。

Gōa-***kháu* thi**ⁿ ***àm***--<u>ah.</u>

外面 天 黑 了。

Wàimiàn tiān hēi le.

Outside the sky has gotten dark.

For the habitual aspect, the pre-verbal marker **有咧 ū teh** only occurs mid-clause and changes tone on both syllables.

暗頓 食 了，我 有 咧 啉 茶。

Àm-***tǹg*** chiáh ***liáu***, góa <u>ū teh</u> lim ***tê.***

晚餐 吃 完，我 經常 喝 茶。

Wǎncān chī wán, wǒ jīngcháng hē chá.

I drink tea after dinner.

For the tentative aspect, if the verb is repeated, the first verb changes tone regardless of position within the sentence, while the second verb keeps the original tone *(see 8.6 Tentative aspect)*.

替我共塗跤掃掃。
Thè góa kā thô͘-*kha* sàu-*sàu.*
替我把地板掃一掃。
Tì wǒ bǎ dìbǎn sǎoyisǎo.
Clean the floor a little for me.

先哺哺才吞落去。
Seng pō͘-*pō͘* chiah ***thun*** --lȯh-khì.
先嚼嚼再吞下去。
Xiān juéjué zài tūn xiàqù.
First chew then swallow.

When used to indicate the tentative aspect, the phrase 一下 --**chit-ē** is always placed in the neutral tone regardless of position.

咱來公園行一下。
Lán lâi kong-*hn̂g* kiâⁿ--chit-ē.
我們來走一下吧。
Wǒmen lái zǒu yīxià ba.
After we eat, let's go walk a little.

With the phrase 看覓 **khòaⁿ-māi** the final syllable 覓 -**māi** keeps its original tone, while 看 **khòaⁿ** and the preceding verb undergo tone changes.

咱來去新公園行看覓。
Lán lâi khì sin kong-*hn̂g* kiâⁿ khòaⁿ-*māi*.
我們去新公園走走看吧。
Wǒmen qù xīn gōngyuán zǒuzǒukàn ba.
Let's go for a walk and check out the new park.

If 試 **chhì**- precedes a verb to mark the tentative aspect, the 試 **chhì**- undergoes a tone change, while the following verb keeps its original tone.

試啉這甌麥仔酒。
Chhì-*lim* chit au bėh-á-*chiú.*
呵呵看這杯啤酒。
Hēhēkàn zhè bēi píjiǔ.
Try this glass of beer.

2.6.3.5 Verb complements

Verb complements vary in tone changes according to type of complement and position within the sentence.

Phase complements indicating completion (**了 liáu**, **完 ôan**, **煞 soah**, **好 hó**) keep their original tone even mid-clause *(see 11.1.1 Phase complements indicating completion).*

阿母 熨 **了** 這 領 **褲**。
A-bú ut ***liáu*** chit niá ***khò͘***.
媽媽 燙了 這 件 褲子。
Māmā tàngle zhè jiàn kùzi.
Mom ironed these pants.

學生 的 考試單仔 改 **好** 矣。
Ha̍k-***seng*** ê khó-chhì-toaⁿ-***á*** kái ***hó***--ah.
學生 的 考卷 改好 了。
Xuéshēng de kǎojuàn gǎihǎo le.
The students' tests are graded.

Phase complements of achievement and potential (**著** -tio̍h, **有** ū) differ in their tone changes. While both **著** -tio̍h and **有** ū undergo regular tone changes mid-clause, **著** -tio̍h is neutralized, and **有** ū keeps its original tone at the end of clauses and sentences *(see 11.1.2 Phase complements indicating achievement, 11.1.3 Phase complements indicating potential).*

伊 揣 **有** 鎖匙 的 **時**, 共 我 **講**。
I chhōe ***ū*** só-***sî*** ê ***sî***, kā góa ***kóng***.
他 找到 鑰匙 的 時候, 跟 我 講。
Tā zhǎodào yàoshi de shíhòu, gēn wǒ jiǎng.
When he finds his keys, tell me.

你 的 臭 衫 **味**, 我 攏 鼻 **有** 矣。
Lí ê chhàu saⁿ ***bī***, góa lóng phīⁿ ***ū***--ah.
你 的 衣服 臭 味道, 我 都 聞到 了。
Nǐ de yīfú chòu wèidào, wǒ dōu wéndàole.
I can smell all of your dirty clothes.

我 昨昏**暗** 拄著 恁 小**弟**。

Góa cha-hng-***àm*** tú-tio̍h lín sió-***tī***.

我 昨晚 碰到 你 弟弟。

Wǒ zuówǎn pèngdào nǐ dìdì.

I bumped into your younger brother last night.

恁 後**生** 的 畫圖，我 無 看著。

In hāu-***seⁿ*** ê ōe-***tô***, góa bô ***khòaⁿ--tio̍h.***

他們 兒子 的 圖畫，我 沒 看到。

Tāmen érzi de túhuà, wǒ méi kàndào.

I didn't see their son's drawing.

Resultative complements mid-clause undergo tone changes, while those at the end of a clause or sentence keep their original tone *(see 11.2 Resultative complements)*. The verb preceding the complement changes tone.

你 無 關牢 窗仔，所以 內底 才 有 蠓仔。

Lí bô koaiⁿ-***tiâu*** thang-***á***, só-í lāi-***té*** chiah ū báng-***á.***

你 沒有 關好 窗戶，所以 裡面 才 有 蚊子。

Nǐ méiyǒu guān hǎo chuānghù, suǒyǐ lǐmiàn cái yǒu wénzi.

You didn't close the window tightly, so inside there are mosquitoes.

這 張 **批** 可能 愛 用 刀**仔** 割**開**。

Chit tiuⁿ ***phoe*** khó-lêng ài ēng to-***á*** koah-***khui.***

這 封 信 可能 需要 用 刀子 割開。

Zhè fēng xìn kěnéng xūyào yòng dāozi gēkāi.

You probably need a knife to open up this letter.

Directional complements mid-clause undergo tone changes but are placed in the neutral tone at the end of clauses and sentences *(see 11.3 Directional complements)*. Note that with double-directional complements at the end of clauses and sentences both directional complements are neutralized, and the verb keeps its original tone.

楊 先生 共 **報告** 提<u>過去</u> 顧**客** 的 辦公**室**。

Iûⁿ sian-siⁿ kā pò-***kò*** theh-<u>kòe-khì</u> kò͘-***kheh*** ê pān-kong-***sek***.

楊 先生 把 報告 帶過去 顧客 的 辦公室。

Yáng xiānshēng bǎ bàogào dàiguòqù gùkè de bàngōngshì.

Mr. Iunn took the report over to his client's office.

莫 拖 椅**仔**, 用 兩 枝 **手 夯**起來。

Mài thoa í-***á***, ēng nñg ki ***chhiú giâ***--khí-lâi.

不要 拖 椅子, 用 兩 隻 手 抬起來。

Bùyào tuō yǐzi, yòng liǎng zhī shǒu táiqǐlái.

Don't drag the chairs. Use both hands to lift them up.

Because of their length, potential complements generally do not appear mid-clause *(see 11.4 Potential complements)*. At the end of a clause or sentence, the verb and potential infix undergo tone changes, while the complement stays in the original tone. If a speaker perspective directional complement is added, this is put in the neutral tone.

到 尾**仔**, 伊 的 答**案** 講<u>有</u><u>**出**</u>來。

Kàu boé-***á***, i ê tap-***àn*** kóng-ū-***chhut***--lâi.

到 最後, 他 的 答案 說出來 了。

Dào zuìhòu, tā de dá'àn shuōchūlái le.

Finally he was able to give his answer.

遐爾 大 的 藥**丸**, 伊 絕對 吞<u>袂</u><u>**落**</u>去。

Hiah-nī tōa ê io̍h-***ôan***, i choat-tùi thun-bē-***lo̍h***--khì.

那麼 大 的 藥丸, 他 絕對 吞不下去。

Nàme dà de yàowán, tā juéduì tūnbuxiàqù.

He absolutely can't swallow that large of a pill.

阮 朋友 的 鋼琴 演奏會，我 看無著。
Gún pêng-*iú* ê kǹg-khîm ián-chàu-*hōe*, góa khòaⁿ-bô-*tio̍h*.
我 的 朋友 的 鋼琴 演奏會，我 看不到。
Wǒ de péngyǒu de gāngqín yǎnzòuhuì, wǒ kànbudào.
I wasn't able to see my friend's piano recital.

Manner complements (著 **tio̍h** and 了 **liáu**) only occur mid-clause since they are always followed by a description of the manner *(see 11.6 Manner complements)*. However, even though they appear mid-clause, manner complements keep their original tone.

阮 阿姊 拍 籃球 拍著 足 好。
Gún a-*chí* phah nâ-*kiû* phah-*tio̍h* chiok **hó**.
我 姊姊 打 籃球 打得 很 好。
Wǒ jiějie dǎ lánqiú dǎ de hěn hǎo.
My older sister plays basketball really well.

伊 食 了 真 緊。
I chia̍h *liáu* chin *kín*.
他 吃得 很 快。
Tā chī de hěn kuài.
He ate really fast.

Extent complements (甲 **kah** and 予 **hō·**) also only occur mid-clause because they are always followed by a description of extent or degree *(see 11.7 Extent complements)*. While 甲 **kah** undergoes tone changes, 予 **hō·** keeps its original tone.

學生 讀 冊 讀 甲 目睭 攏 紅紅。
Ha̍k-*seng* tha̍k *chheh* tha̍k *kah* ba̍k-*chiu* lóng âng-*âng*.
學生 讀書 讀得 眼睛 都 紅紅。
Xuéshēng dú shū dú de yǎnjīng dōu hónghóng.
The students studied so much that their eyes were all red.

咖啡 共 我 斟 予 滇。
Ka-*pi* kā góa thîn *hō·tīⁿ*.
咖啡 幫 我 倒滿。
Kāfēi bāng wǒ dào mǎn.
Fill my coffee to the brim.

2.6.3.6 Adverbs

Multi-syllable time expressions ('tomorrow', 'next week') keep the original tone on the final syllable *(see 14.1.2 Time adverbs)*.

郭 小**姐** 明仔**暗** 會 去 台**中**。
Koeh sió-*chiá* bîn-á-*àm* ē khì Tâi-*tiong*.
郭 小姐 明晚 會 去 台中。
Guō xiǎojiě míngwǎn huì qù Táizhōng.
Ms. Koeh will go to Taichung tomorrow evening.

All other single and multi-syllable adverbs undergo tone changes on all syllables.

<u>好佳哉</u> 恁 朋**友** 有 紮 三 枝 雨**傘**。
<u>Hó-ka-chài</u> lín pêng-*iú* ū chah saⁿ ki hō͘-*sòaⁿ*.
幸虧 你 的 朋友 有 帶 三 枝 雨傘。
Xìngkuī nǐ de péngyǒu yǒu dài sān zhī yǔsǎn.
Fortunately, your friend brought three umbrellas.

2.6.3.7 Question words

Question words follow the regular tone change rule of changing tones mid-clause and keeping original tones at the end of a clause or sentence *(see 20.5 Question words)*. However, some question words have nouns as part of the question word (**啥貨 siáⁿ-hòe** 'what', **啥人 siáⁿ-lâng** 'who, whom', **按怎樣 án-chóaⁿ-iūⁿ** 'how was it', etc.). The noun components follow the normal tone change rules for nouns.

啥人 講 我 袂使 **去**?
<u>Siáⁿ-**lâng**</u> kóng góa bē-sái ***khì***?
誰 說 我 不 可以 去?
Shéi shuō wǒ bù kěyǐ qù?
Who said I couldn't go?

啥**貨** 遐爾 **臭**？

<u>Siáⁿ-*hòe*</u> hiah-nī *chhàu*?

什麼 東西 那麼 臭？

Shénme dōngxī nàme chòu?

What smells so bad?

你 欲 愛 **啥**？

Lí beh ài <u>***siáⁿ***</u>?

你 要 什麼？

Nǐ yào shénme?

What do you want?

伊 **怎樣** 買 三 台 **車**？

I <u>chóaⁿ-***iūⁿ***</u> bé saⁿ tâi *chhia*?

他 怎樣 買 三 台 車？

Tā zěnyàng mǎi sān tái chē?

How did he buy three cars?

2.6.3.8 Location participles

Location participles keep their original tone whether they are mid-clause or at the end of a clause or sentence *(see 16.2 Location participles)*.

佇 桌仔**頂** 已經 有 四 盤 **菜**。

Tī toh-á-<u>*téng*</u> í-keng ū sì pôaⁿ *chhài*.

在 桌子 上 已經 有 四 盤 菜。

Zài zhuōzi shàng yǐjīng yǒu sì pán cài.

There are already four dishes on the table.

你 的 舊 鞋仔 攏 囥 佇 眠床**跤**。

Lí ê kū ê-*á* lóng khǹg tī bîn-chn̂g-<u>***kha.***</u>

你 的 舊 鞋子 都 放 在 床下。

Nǐ de jiù xiézi dōu fàng zài chuángxià.

Your old shoes are all placed underneath your bed.

2.6.3.9 Numbers

Numbers read in isolation change tones on each syllable except for the final syllable *(see 3 Numbers)*. Single-syllable numbers also do not change tone.

4	四	**sì**
	四	sì
17	十**七**	chȧp-***chhit***
	十七	shíqī
205	兩百空**五**	nñg-pah khòng ***gō·***
	兩百零五	liǎng bǎi líng wǔ

If numbers modify a noun, tone changes apply to all syllables. The modified noun follows regular tone change rules for nouns.

4 people	四个**人**	sì ê ***lâng***
	四個人	sì gè rén
17 chairs	十七 條 椅**仔**	chȧp-chhit liâu ***í-á***
	十七 把 椅子	shíqī bǎ yǐzi
205 dollars	兩百空五 **箍**	nñg-pah khòng gō· ***kho·***
	兩百零五 塊	liǎng bǎi líng wǔ kuài

The numerical measure words 千 **chheng** 'thousand', 萬 **bān** 'ten thousand', 億 **ek** 'hundred million', and higher all keep their original tones in all positions unless the number is part of a modifying phrase. 百 **pah** 'hundred' is an exception and changes tone unless it is the final syllable.

1004	一**千**空**四**	chit-***chheng*** khòng ***sì***
	一千零四	yī qiān líng sì
2500	兩**千**五**百**	nñg-***chheng*** gō·-***pah***
	兩千五百	liǎng qiān wǔ bǎi
15, 000	一**萬**五**千**	chhit-***bān*** go·-***chheng***
	一萬五千	yī wàn wǔ qiān
20, 500	兩**萬**空五**百**	nñg-***chheng*** khòng gō·-***pah***
	兩萬零五百	liǎng wàn líng wǔ bǎi

If numbers with numerical measure words modify a noun, tone changes will also apply to the measure words. The modified noun follows regular tone change rules for nouns.

1004 students	一千空四个 學生	chit-<u>chheng</u> khòng sì ê ha̍k-**seng**
	一千零四個 學生	yī qiān líng sì gè xuéshēng
2500 dollars	兩千五百 箍	nn̄g-<u>chheng</u> gō͘-pah **kho͘**
	兩千五百 塊	liǎng qiān wǔ bǎi kuài
20, 500 houses	兩萬空五百 間 厝	nn̄g-<u>chheng</u> khòng gō͘-pah keng **chhù**
	兩萬零五百 間 房屋	liǎng wàn líng wǔ bǎi jiān fángwū

2.6.3.10 Other parts of speech

Other parts of speech such as negation, adjectives, prepositions, conjunctions, and measure words all follow regular tone change rules. Mid-clause these parts of speech change tone on each syllable. At the end of a clause or sentence, the final syllable keeps the original tone.

NEGATION

這 个 冊包 毋是 我 的。
Chit ê chheh-***pau*** <u>m̄</u>-sī ***góa***--ê.
這個 書包 不是 我 的。
Zhège shūbāo bùshì wǒ de.
This book bag is not mine.

ADJECTIVE

莫 共 垃圾 衫仔褲 囥 踮 塗跤。
Mài kā <u>lah-sap</u> saⁿ-á-***khò͘*** khǹg tàm thô͘-***kha.***
不要 把 髒 衣服 放 在 地上。
Bùyào bǎ zāng yīfú fàng zài dìshàng.
Don't put your dirty clothes on the floor.

PREPOSITION

阮 小**妹** 和 我 去 博物**館**。

Gún sió-***mōe*** h<u>ām</u> góa khì phok-bu̍t-***kóan.***

我 妹妹 和 我 去 博物館。

Wǒ mèimei hé wǒ qù bówùguǎn.

My younger sister went with me to the museum.

CONJUNCTIONS

因為 我 袂記得 鎖 **門**，所以 阮 阿**爸** 受**氣** 矣。

In-ūi góa bē-kì-tit só ***mn̂g***, s<u>ó-í</u> gún a-***pa*** siū-***khì***--ah.

因為 我 忘記 鎖 門，所以 我 爸爸 生氣 了。

Yīnwèi wǒ wàngjì suǒ mén, suǒyǐ wǒ bàba shēngqì le.

Because I forgot to lock the door, my dad became angry.

MEASURE WORDS

伊 欲 買 彼 枝 錶**仔**，毋是 這 **枝**。

I beh bé hit <u>ki</u> pió-***á***, m̄-sī chit ***<u>ki.</u>***

他 要 買 那 枝 手錶，不是 這 枝。

Tā yào mǎi nà zhī shǒubiǎo, bùshì zhè zhī.

He wants to buy that watch, not this one.

2.6.4 Word-specific rules

Some tone changing rules apply to specific words in particular contexts. Below are some of the more common cases.

2.6.4.1 Suffix 仔 -á

As part of a noun suffix, the normal rules for a multi-syllable noun apply. In other words, the final syllable, which is '**仔 -á**', does not change while the preceding syllables do change *(see 4.1 Noun suffix 仔 -á)*.

手錶**仔**
chhiú-pió-*á*
手錶
shǒubiǎo
wristwatch

湯匙**仔**
thng-sî-*á*
湯匙
tāngchí
soup spoon

When **仔** --á is part of a manner adverb expression, it is placed in the neutral tone, and the preceding syllable does not change tone *(see 14.2.3 Manner adverbs)*.

彼 个 查埔 囡仔 直直仔 行 轉去。
Hit ê cha-po‧gín-*á* tit-*tit*--á **kiâ**ⁿ--tńg-khì.
那個 男孩子 直直 地 走回去。
Nàge nán háizi zhízhí de zǒuhuíqù.
The boy is walking home in a straight line.

When **仔** -á- is in the middle of a multi-syllable word, it changes tone. Only the final syllable of the word keeps the original tone.

今仔日
kin-á-***jit***
今天
jīntiān
today

牛仔褲
gû-á-***khò***‧
牛仔褲
niúzǎikù
jeans

2.6.4.2 Names and titles

Among terms of address only 先生 **sian-si^n** 'Mr.' follows special tone change rules. When following a surname, 先生 **sian-si^n** is placed in the neutral tone, while the surname retains the original tone. If 先生 **sian-si^n** is not preceded by a surname including when used to mean 'sir', 'doctor', or 'teacher', the first syllable changes tone, while the second syllable keeps the original tone *(see 23.2.3 Titles)*.

李 先生，請 等 一下。
Lí--sian-si^n, chhiá^n ***tán***--chit-ē.
李 先生，請 等 一下。
Lǐ xiānshēng, qǐng děng yīxià.
Mr. Li, please wait a moment.

先生，請 等 一下。
Sian-*si^n*, chhiá^n ***tán***--chit-ē.
先生，請 等 一下。
Xiānshēng, qǐng děng yīxià.
Sir, please wait a moment.

Other forms of address and titles such as 小姐 **sió-chiá** 'Ms., madam', 老師 **lāu-su** 'teacher', 醫師 **i-su** 'doctor', etc. are not put in the neutral tone but follow the regular tone rules for nouns. In addition, the surname itself changes tone when followed by these titles.

謝 小姐	林 教授	黃 醫師
Siā sió-*chiá*	Lîm kàu-*siū*	Ñg i-*su*
謝 小姐	林 教授	黃 醫師
Xiè xiǎojiě	Lín jiàoshòu	Huáng yīshī
Ms. Sia	Professor Lim	Dr. Ng

When someone's full name is provided, only the final syllable of the given name keeps the original tone.

王 瑩偉
Ông Êng-*úi*
王 瑩偉
Wáng Yíngwěi
Eng-ui Ong

2.6.4.3 遮 chia 'here' and 遐 hia 'there'

The location expressions **遮 chia** 'here' and **遐 hia** 'there' do not change tone in any position.

我 园 衫仔褲 佇 遮 敢 會 使？
Góa khǹg saⁿ-á-*khò* tī *chia* kám ē-*sái*?
我 放 衣服 在 這裡 可不可以？
Wǒ fàng yīfú zài zhèlǐ kěbukěyǐ?
May I put my clothes here?

遐 是 上 好 的 田地。
Hia sī siōng hó ê chhân-*tē.*
那裡 是 最 好 的 田地。
Nàlǐ shì zuì hǎo de tiándì.
Over there is the best farmland.

3 Numbers

3.1 Counting numbers

3.1.1 Numbers 0-10

		TAIWANESE	MANDARIN
0	空	khòng	--
	零	lân / lêng	líng
1	一	it / chi̍t	yī
2	二 / 兩	jī / nn̄g	èr / liǎng
3	三	saⁿ	sān
4	四	sì	sì
5	五	gō͘	wǔ
6	六	la̍k	liù
7	七	chhit	qī
8	八	peh	bā
9	九	káu	jiǔ
10	十	cha̍p	shí

In Taiwanese 空 **khòng** is the primary counting number used for 'zero'. 零 **lân / lêng** 'zero' is used only in specific expressions.

	TAIWANESE	MANDARIN
pocket change	零星錢 lân-san-chîⁿ	零錢 língqián
parts, components	零件 lêng-kiāⁿ	零件 língjiàn

The Taiwanese numbers 一 **chit** 'one' and 兩 **nňg** 'two' are forms used before measure words *(see 4.3 Measure words)*.

	TAIWANESE	MANDARIN
one book	一本冊 <u>chit</u> pún chheh	一本書 <u>yī</u> běn shū
two pens	兩枝筆 <u>nňg</u> ki pit	兩枝筆 <u>liǎng</u> zhī bǐ

Additionally, it is also common to use these readings when counting from 1 to 10. However, after 10, only 一 **it** 'one' and 二 **jī** 'two' are used in the ones digit.

	TAIWANESE	MANDARIN
eleven	十一 cha̍p-it	十一 shíyī
twenty-two	二十二 jī-cha̍p-jī	二十二 èrshí'èr

Unlike Mandarin where colloquial readings allow for 二百 **èr bǎi** or 二千 **èr qiān**, Taiwanese must use 兩 **nňg** before measure words.

	TAIWANESE	MANDARIN
two hundred	兩百 nňg pah	兩百 liǎng bǎi / 二百 èr bǎi
two thousand	兩千 nňg chheng	兩千 liǎng qiān / 二千 èr qiān

3.1.2 Literary reading for numbers

The literary reading for numbers is rarely used nowadays except for reading aloud individual digits *(see 1.2.1.2 literary and colloquial register)*. Some uses include reciting telephone numbers, years, or numbers within set expressions.

0	空	khòng
1	一	it
2	二	jī
3	三	sam
4	四	sù
5	五	ngó͘
6	六	lio̍k
7	七	chhit
8	八	pat
9	九	kiú
10	十	sip

Note that Standard Mandarin does not use a separate set of literary readings for numbers.

Telephone numbers

我 的 電話 是 空 二 三 五 四 八 九 一 六 七。
Góa ê tiān-ōe sī khòng – jī – sam – ngó͘ – sù – pat – kiú – it – liȯk – chhit.
我 的 電話 是 ○ 二 三 五 四 八 九 一 六 七。
Wǒ de diànhuà shì líng – èr – sān – wǔ – sì – bā – jiǔ – yī – liù – qī.
My telephone number is 0-2-3-5-4-8-9-1-6-7.

Years

伊 1-9-8-3 年 出世。
I it – kiú – pat – sam nî chhut-sì.
他 1-9-8-3 年 出生。
Tā yī – jiǔ – bā – sān nián chūshēng.
He was born in 1983.

Set expressions

四季
sù-kùi
四季
sìjì
four seasons

3.1.3 Numbers 11-99

Numbers between 11-99 use a combination of a multiple of 十 **chȧp** 'tens' with digits from 一 **it** 'one' to 九 **káu** 'nine'.

		TAIWANESE	MANDARIN
11	十一	chȧp-it	shíyī
12	十二	chȧp-jī	shíèr
13	十三	chȧp-saⁿ	shísān
14	十四	chȧp-sì	shísì
15	十五	chȧp-gō͘	shíwǔ
16	十六	chȧp-lȧk	shíliù

		TAIWANESE	MANDARIN
17	十七	chȧp-chhit	shíqī
18	十八	chȧp-peh	shíbā
19	十九	chȧp-káu	shíjiǔ
20	二十	jī-chȧp	èrshí
21	二十一	jī-chȧp-it	èrshíyī
22	二十二	jī-chȧp-jī	èrshíèr
:	:	:	:
:	:	:	:
30	三十	saⁿ-chȧp	sānshí
40	四十	sì-chȧp	sìshí
50	五十	gō͘-chȧp	wǔshí
60	六十	lȧk-chȧp	liùshí
70	七十	chhit-chȧp	qīshí
80	八十	peh-chȧp	bāshí
90	九十	káu-chȧp	jiǔshí

Numbers from 11-19 do not use 一 **it** 'one' before the 十 **chȧp** 'ten'. Note that unlike Mandarin this does not change even in larger numbers.

	TAIWANESE	MANDARIN
114	一百十四	一百一十四
	chit pah chȧp-sì	yī bǎi yīshísì
219	兩百十九	兩百一十九
	nn̄g pah chȧp-káu	liǎng bǎi yīshíjiǔ

3.1.4 Numbers 100 and greater

Numbers 100 and above use measure words to represent the following increments.

		TAIWANESE	MANDARIN
hundreds	百	pah	bǎi
thousands	千	chheng	qiān
ten thousands	萬	bān	wàn
hundred millions	億	ek	yì

Numbers larger than 10,000 are broken down by how many 'ten thousands' (every 4 digits) they contain. The measure word forms of 一 **chit** 'one' and 兩 **nn̄g** 'two' are used when preceding these numerical measure words.

		TAIWANESE	MANDARIN
100	一百	chit pah	yī bǎi
1000	一千	chit chheng	yī qiān
10,000	一萬	chit bān	yī wàn
100,000	十萬	cha̍p bān	shí wàn
1,000,000	一百萬	chit pah bān	yī bǎi wàn
10,000,000	一千萬	chit chheng bān	yī qiān wàn
100,000,000	一意	chit ek	yī yì
1,000,000,000	十意	cha̍p ek	shí yì

Below is an example comparing the structure of a number in both the English and Chinese numerical systems.

219,743,526

ENGLISH

2 hundred 19 million | 7 hundred 43 thousand | 5 hundred 26

TAIWANESE / MANDARIN

2 hundred-millions | 1 thousand 9 hundred 74 ten-thousands | 3 thousand 5 hundred 26

兩 意 | 一 千 九 百 七十四 萬 | 三 千 五 百 二十六

nn̄g ek | chit chheng káu pah chhit-cha̍p-sì bān | saⁿ chheng gō͘ pah jī-cha̍p-la̍k

liǎng yì | yī qiān jiǔ bǎi qīshísì wàn | sān qiān wǔ bǎi èrshíliù

Below are more examples of numbers following the Chinese numerical system.

258	兩 百 五十八
	nn̄g pah gō͘-cha̍p-peh
	liǎng bǎi wǔshíbā

1533	一 千 五 百 三十三
	chit chheng gō͘ pah saⁿ-cha̍p-saⁿ
	yī qiān wǔ bǎi sānshísān

Numbers 85

48,230	四萬八千兩百三十
	sì bān peh chheng nn̄g pah saⁿ-chȧp
	sì wàn bā qiān liǎng bǎi sanshí
362,400	三十六萬兩千四百
	saⁿ-chȧp-lȧk bān nn̄g chheng sì pah
	sānshíliù wàn liǎng qiān sì bǎi
5,793,000	五百七十九萬三千
	gō͘ pah chhit-chȧp-káu bān saⁿ chheng
	wǔ bǎi qīshíjiǔ wàn sān qiān
68,240,000	六千八百二十四萬
	lȧk chheng peh pah jī-chȧp-sì bān
	liù qiān bā bǎi èrshísì wàn
219,700,000	兩億一千九百七十萬
	nn̄g ek chit chheng káu pah chhit-chȧp bān
	liǎng yì yī qiān jiǔ bǎi qīshí wàn

3.1.5 Interior zeroes

When a zero occurs two between two numerals, **空 khòng** 'zero' serves as a placeholder when the number is read aloud. If there are consecutive zeroes, only a single **空 khòng** 'zero' needs to be stated.

2<u>0</u>2	兩百空二
	nn̄g pah <u>khòng</u> jī
	兩百零二
	liǎng bǎi <u>líng</u> èr
2<u>0</u>42	兩千空四十二
	nn̄g chheng <u>khòng</u> sì-chȧp-jī
	兩千零四十二
	liǎng qiān <u>líng</u> sìshí'èr

2402	兩千四百空二
	nňg chheng sì pah khòng jī
	兩千四百零二
	liǎng qiān sì bǎi líng èr

2002	兩千空二
	nňg chheng khòng jī
	兩千零二
	liǎng qiān líng èr

20, 402	兩萬空四百空二
	nňg bān khòng sì pah khòng jī
	兩萬零四百零二
	liǎng wàn líng sì bǎi líng èr

2, 040, 002	兩百空四萬空二
	nňg pah khòng sì bān khòng jī
	兩百零四萬零二
	liǎng bǎi líng sì wàn líng èr

3.2 Ordinal numbers

Ordinal numbers are formed by placing **第 tē** as a prefix before a counting number.

		TAIWANESE	MANDARIN
first	第一	tē-it	dìyī
second	第二	tē-jī	dìèr
third	第三	tē-san	dìsān
:	:	:	:
:	:	:	:
tenth	第十	tē-cha̍p	dìshí
:	:	:	:
:	:	:	:
fifteenth	第十五	tē-cha̍p-gō·	dìshíwǔ

3.3 Partial numbers

3.3.1 Fractions

Fractions in Taiwanese are expressed by first stating the 'whole' followed by 'part of the whole'. The two parts are joined together by the phrase 分之 **hun chi**. Note that this is the reverse of how fractions are expressed in English.

whole + 分之 + *part of the whole*

whole + hun chi + *part of the whole*

'part of the whole / whole'

1/3	三分之一	sa^n hun chi it
		sān fēn zhī yī
4/5	五分之四	gō˙ hun chi sì
		wǔ fēn zhī sì

Improper fractions, which have a larger numerator than denominator, follow the same format.

7/5	五分之七	gō˙ hun chi chhit
		wǔ fēn zhī qī

The common fractional value 'half' is expressed by 半 **pòa^n**.

½	半	pòa^n
		bàn

When used before a noun, 半 **pòaⁿ** 'half' comes *before* the measure word and noun.

| half an hour | 半點鐘 | pòaⁿ tiám-cheng |
| | 半個小時 | bàn gè xiǎoshí |

| half a year | 半年 | pòaⁿ-nî |
| | | bàn nián |

| half a cake | 半个雞卵糕 | pòaⁿ ê ke-nn̄g-ko |
| | 半個蛋糕 | bàn gè dàngāo |

When a half is added to an existing number, the 半 **pòaⁿ** 'half' comes after the measure word but before the noun.

| one and a half hours | 一點半鐘 | chit tiám pòaⁿ cheng |
| | 一個半小時 | yī gè bàn xiǎoshí |

| two and a half months | 兩個半月 | nn̄g kò pòaⁿ goeh |
| | | liǎng gè bàn yùe |

| two and a half cakes | 兩塊半雞卵糕 | nn̄g tè pòaⁿ ke-nn̄g-ko |
| | 兩塊半蛋糕 | liǎng kuài bàn dàngāo |

| five and a half pages | 五頁半 | gō iah pòaⁿ |
| | | wǔ yè bàn |

Note that some measure words such as 頁 **iah** 'page' also function as nouns and do not require a noun to follow 半 **pòaⁿ** 'half'.

3.3.2 Rates

In English, a rate is often expressed by specifying a quantity followed by the preposition 'per' and a singular noun.

four books per person
700 dollars per night
two cars per family

Taiwanese does the reverse order of English by placing the singular noun before the specified quantity. No special preposition is used.

一 + *measure word* + *(singular noun)* + *number* + *measure word* + *(noun)*

chi̍t + *measure word* + *(singular noun)* + *number* + *measure word* + *(noun)*

'*number* + *noun* per *singular noun*'

一个人 四 本
chi̍t ê lâng sì pún
一個人 四 本
yī gè rén sì běn
four books per person

一 暗 七 百 箍
chi̍t àm chhit pah kho·
一 夜 七 百 塊
yī yè qī bǎi kuài
seven hundred dollars per night

一 戶 兩 台 車
chi̍t hō· nn̄g tâi chhia
一 戶 兩 台 車
yī hù liǎng tái chē
two cars per household

3.3.3 Percentages

Percentages follow the same form as fractions with the 'whole' always stated as 百 **pah** '100' followed by the 'part of the whole'. The two parts are again linked by the phrase 分之 **hun chi**.

百 + 分之 + *number*

pah + hun chi + *number*

'*number* %'

| 25% | 百分之二十五 | pah hun chi jī-cha̍p-gō͘ |
| | | bǎi fēn zhī èrshíwǔ |

| 42% | 百分之四十二 | pah hun chi sì-cha̍p-jī |
| | | bǎi fēn zhī sìshí'èr |

| 100% | 百分之百 | pah hun chi pah |
| | | bǎi fēn zhī bǎi |

3.3.4 Discounts

Discounts are often expressed as the percentage to be paid on the original price rather than the percentage taken off the price. For example, '10% off' is instead marked as '90% of the original price'.

The verb phrase 拍折 **phah chiat** 'to offer a discount' is used with a number between 0-10 placed before 折 **chiat** 'discount'. The percentage derived is based on the number out of ten (2/10 = 20%, 5/10 = 50%).

拍 ＋ *number between 0-10* ＋ 折

phah ＋ *number between 0-10* ＋ chiat

| 20% off | 拍8折 | phah peh chiat |
| | 打8折 | dǎ bā zhé |

| 50% off | 拍5折 | phah gō͘ chiat |
| | 打5折 | dǎ wǔ zhé |

Numbers that are not multiples of ten are recited as individual digits.

| 5% off | 拍9, 5折 | phah káu gō͘ chiat |
| | 打9, 5折 | dǎ jiǔ wǔ zhé |

| 75% off | 拍2, 5折 | phah jī gō͘ chiat |
| | 打2, 5折 | dǎ èr wǔ zhé |

When discussing absolute amounts for discounts, use **扣 khàu** 'to deduct, to take off'.

頭家 講 伊 欲 <u>扣掉</u> 五十 箍。
Thâu-ke kóng i beh <u>khàu</u>-tiāu gō͘-cha̍p kho͘.
老闆 說 他 要 <u>扣掉</u> 五十 塊。
Lǎobǎn shuō tā yào <u>kòu</u>diào wǔshí kuài.
The owner said he would <u>take off</u> 50 dollars.

Shorthand for percentages which are multiples of ten may use **成 siân** as a measure word.

| 40% | 四成 | sì <u>siân</u> |
| | | sì <u>chéng</u> |

| 70% | 七成 | chhit <u>siân</u> |
| | | qī <u>chéng</u> |

Additionally, some speakers will use the Japanese imported term **phâ-sián-to͘** (パーセント) 'percent'.

| 25% | jī-cha̍p-gō͘ <u>phâ-sián-to͘</u> |
| | èrshíwǔ <u>pā</u> |

| 60% | la̍k-cha̍p <u>phâ-sián-to͘</u> |
| | liùshí <u>pā</u> |

Taiwan Mandarin also uses the term **趴 pā** as a shorthand for 'percent'.

3.3.5 Decimals

The decimal point is expressed as **點 tiám** 'point'. Numbers that come before the decimal may either be read as a single number or broken down into individual digits. After the decimal point, numbers are always recited as individual digits. Interior zeroes after the decimal point must each be read aloud.

number + 點 + *digit, digit, digit…*
number + tiám + *digit, digit, digit…*
'*number* + . + *digit, digit, digit…*'

0.7	(空) 點七	(khòng) tiám chhit
	零點七	líng diǎn qī
2.5	二 / 兩點五	jī/nńg tiám gō·
	二點五	èr diǎn wǔ
6.41	六點四一	la̍k tiám sì it
		liù diǎn sì yī
9.005	九點空空五	káu tiám khòng khòng gō·
	九點零零五	jiǔ diǎn líng líng wǔ
12.38	十二點三八 / 一二點三八	cha̍p-jī tiám saⁿ peh / it jī tiám saⁿ peh
		shí'èr diǎn sān bā / yī èr diǎn sān bā
39.04	三十九點空四 / 三九點空四	saⁿ-cha̍p-káu tiám khòng sì / saⁿ káu tiám khòng sì
	三十九點零四 / 三九點零四	sānshíjiǔ diǎn líng sì / sān jiǔ diǎn líng sì

3.3.6 Multiples

To indicate multiples of a number (twice, five times as much/many, etc.) the measure word **倍 pōe** (also pronounced **pòe**) '-fold' is placed after the number.

number + 倍
number + pōe
'*number* times as much/many'

onceover (doubled)	一倍	chi̍t pōe
		yī bèi
twice as much/many	兩倍	nńg pōe
		liǎng bèi

| three times as much | 三倍 | saⁿ pōe |
| | | sān bèi |

| ten times as much/many | 十倍 | cha̍p pōe |
| | | shí bèi |

Another common way to state an amount has increased onceover is to use **加倍 ka-pōe** 'to double'.

我 毋 信 票價 已經 加倍 矣。
Góa m̄ sìn phiò-kè í-keng ka-pōe--ah.
我 不 相信 票價 已經 加倍 了。
Wǒ bù xiāngxìn piàojià yǐjīng jiābèi le.
I don't believe the ticket price has already doubled.

If a half value is included, then **半 pòaⁿ 'half'** comes after the measure word **倍 pōe** '-fold'.

| one and a half times as much | 一倍半 | chit pōe pòaⁿ |
| | | yī bèi bàn |

| two and a half times as much | 兩倍半 | nn̄g pōe pòaⁿ |
| | | liǎng bèi bàn |

3.3.7 Arithmetic

add (plus)	加	ka	1 加 3 等於 偌濟？
			Chit ka saⁿ téng-î gōa-chē?
		jiā	1 加 3 等於 多少？
			Yī jiā sān děngyú duōshǎo?
			1 + 3 = ?

subtract (minus)	減	kiám	5 減 2 等於 偌濟？
			Gō͘ kiám jī téng-î gōa-chē?
		jiǎn	5 減 2 等於 多少？
			Wǔ jiǎn èr děngyú duōshǎo?
			5 - 2 = ?

multiply (times)	乘以	sêng-í	4 乘以 7 等於 偌濟？ Sì sêng-í chhit téng-î gōa-chē?
		chéngyǐ	4 乘以 7 等於 多少？ Sì chéngyǐ qī děngyú duōshǎo? 4 x 7 = ?
divided by	除以	tû-í	10 除以 5 等於 偌濟？ Cha̍p tû-í gō͘ téng-î gōa-chē?
		chúyǐ	10 除以 5 等於 多少？ Shí chúyǐ wǔ děngyú duōshǎo? 10 ÷ 5 = ?
divided into	除	tû	5 除 10 等於 偌濟？ Gō͘ tû cha̍p téng-î gōa-chē?
		chú	5 除 10 等於 多少？ Wǔ chú shí děngyú duōshǎo? 5 divided into 10 = ?
equals	等於	téng-î	8 減 6 等於 2。 Peh kiám la̍k téng-î jī.
		děngyú	8 減 6 等於 2。 Bā jiǎn liù děngyú èr. 8 minus 6 equals 2.
leaves	賰	chhun	8 減 6 賰 2。 Peh kiám la̍k chhun jī.
	剩下	shèng xià	8 減 6 剩下 2。 Bā jiǎn liù shèngxià èr. 8 less 6 leaves 2.
answer	答案	tap-àn	答案 是 五。 Tap-àn sī gō͘.
		dá'àn	答案 是 五。 Dá'àn shì wǔ. The answer is 5.

3.4 Approximations

3.4.1 Range

To offer a rough approximation within a given range, state the two numbers that provide the extents of the range.

2-3 dollars	兩三箍	nn̄g-saⁿ kho˙
	兩三塊	liǎng sān kuài
10-20 minutes	一二十分鐘	it-jī-cha̍p hun-cheng
		yī èrshí fēnzhōng
16-17 years old	十六七歲	cha̍p-la̍k chhit hòe
		shíliù qī suì
200-300 people	兩三百个人	nn̄g-saⁿ pah ê lâng
	兩三百個人	liǎng sān bǎi gè rén

Note that when stating the range 10-20, the numeral 一 **it** 'one' is used and attributed to the following 十 **cha̍p** 'ten'.

3.4.2 Estimates

To express that a value is an estimate, use the phrase 差不多 **chha-put-to** 'nearly', 左右 **chó-iū** 'more or less', or 成 **chiâⁿ** 'almost'.

差不多 **chha-put-to** 'nearly' or 'almost' used before a number indicates an amount that just falls short of the number.

> 差不多 + *number* + *measure word* + *(noun)*
> chha-put-to + *number* + *measure word* + *(noun)*
> 'almost *number*'

差不多 一 點鐘
chha-put-to chit tiám-cheng
差不多 一 個 小時
chàbùduō yī gè xiǎoshí
nearly an hour

差不多 一 千 人
chha-put-to chit chheng lâng
差不多 一 千 人
chàbùduō yī qiān rén
almost a thousand people

左右 chó-iū 'more or less' can be placed after a number to indicate that the actual value is slightly above or below the target number.

number + measure word + (noun) + 左右

number + measure word + (noun) + chó-iū

'more or less *number*'

兩 點鐘 左右
nn̄g tiám-cheng chó-iū
兩 個 小時 左右
liǎng gè xiǎoshí zuǒyòu
two hours more or less

五 百 个 人 左右
gōˑpah ê lâng chó-iū
五 百 個 人 左右
wǔ bǎi gè rén zuǒyòu
around 500 people

Numbers 97

成 chiâⁿ 'almost' is also placed before a number to express that the actual value is close to a target number but falls short. This usage tends to be more old-fashioned.

成 + *number* + *measure word* + *(noun)*

chiâⁿ + *number* + *measure word* + *(noun)*

'almost or nearly a *number*'

成 五十 个 人客
chiâⁿ gō·-cha̍p ê lâng-kheh
接近 五十 個 客人
jiējìn wǔshí gè kèrén
nearly 50 guests

3.4.3 More than

To express that a figure is actually greater than the stated number, attach 外 -gōa 'more' after the number.

number + 外

number + -gōa

'more than *number*'

over 50	五十外	gō·-cha̍p-gōa
	五十多	wǔshí duō
more than 2000	兩千外	nn̄g chheng-gōa
	兩千多	liǎng qiān duō
greater than 86,000	八萬六千外	peh bān la̍k chheng-gōa
	八萬六千多	bā wàn liù qiān duō

If the measure word and noun are included, **外 gōa** 'more' comes *before* the measure word and noun.

number ＋ 外 + *measure word* + *(noun)*
number ＋ -gōa + *measure word* + *(noun)*
'more than *number* + *noun*'

| more than 20 people | 二十外个人 | jī-cha̍p-gōa ê lâng |
| | 二十多個人 | èrshí duō gè rén |

| greater than 700 books | 七百外本冊 | chhit pah-gōa pún chheh |
| | 七百多本書 | qī bǎi duō běn shū |

| over 10,000 applications | 一萬外份申請 | chit bān-gōa hun sin-chhéng |
| | 一萬多份申請 | yī wàn duō fèn shēnqǐng |

幾 **kúi** 'several, few' can also be used to express an approximate value that is similar to the English suffix '-some' or '-odd'. If the measure and noun are included, 幾 **kúi** comes *before* the measure word and noun

number ＋ 幾 + *measure word* + *(noun)*
number ＋ -kúi + *measure word* + *(noun)*
'*number*-some/odd *noun*'

| sixty-some pounds | 六十幾磅 | la̍k-cha̍p-kúi pōng |
| | | liùshí jǐ bàng |

| twenty-odd students | 二十幾个學生 | jī-cha̍p-kúi ê ha̍k-seng |
| | 二十幾個學生 | èrshí jǐ gè xuéshēng |

To express that the stated value is *equal to or more than* the actual value, place 以上 **í-siōng** after the number. If a measure word is used, the placement is between the number and 以上 **í-siōng**.

number + *(measure word)* + *(noun)* + 以上

number + *(measure word)* + *(noun)* + í-siōng

'*number* + *noun* or more'

60 or more	六十以上	la̍k-cha̍p í-siōng
		liùshí yǐshàng
10,000 or more soldiers	一萬个兵以上	chit-bān ê peng í-siōng
	一萬個兵以上	yī wàn gè bīng yǐshàng

3.4.4 Less than

To express that the stated value is *equal to or less than* the actual value, place 以下 **í-hā** after the number. If a measure word and noun is used, the placement is between the number and 以下 **í-hā**.

number + *(measure word)* + *(noun)* + 以下

number + *(measure word)* + *(noun)* + í-hā

'*number* + *noun* or less'

less than 25	二十五以下	jī-cha̍p-gō͘ í-hā
	二十五以下	èrshíwǔ yǐxià
less than 200 flowers	兩百蕊花以下	nn̄g pah lúi hoe í-hā
	兩百朵花以下	liǎng bǎi duǒ huā yǐxià

Another common way to express 'less than' emphasizes that the actual value has not reached the stated number. Place 無到 bô kàu 'not even' before the number.

無到 + number + (measure word) + (noun)

bô kàu + number + (measure word) + (noun)

'not even number + noun'

not even 25	無到二十五	bô kàu jī-cha̍p-gō͘
	不到二十五	bù dào èrshíwǔ
not even 200 flowers	無到兩百蕊花	bô kàu nñg pah lúi hoe
	不到兩百朵花	bù dào liǎng bǎi duǒ huā

3.5 Money

Money in Taiwanese is expressed through measure words for specific denominations of a currency. The term 錢 chîⁿ 'money' can optionally follow.

number + monetary measure word + (錢)

number + monetary measure word + (chîⁿ)

	TAIWANESE	MANDARIN
dollar	箍 kho͘	塊 kuài
dime	角 kak	毛 máo
cent	仙 sián	分 fēn

The smallest commonly used denomination of currency in Taiwan is 一箍 chi̍t-kho͘ 'one dollar' (1 NTD = New Taiwanese dollar). However, smaller denominations can be found in the financial industry for products such as stocks or currencies. Additionally, usage of Taiwanese in other countries that have currencies with smaller subdivisions can use the traditional terms 角 kak 'dime' and 仙 sián 'cent'. 仙 sián 'cent' itself is a borrowed term from the English 'cent'.

連 一 <u>仙</u> 錢，我 攏 無 啦。
Liân chit <u>sián</u> chîⁿ, góa lóng bô--lah.
連 一 <u>分</u> 錢，我 都 沒有 啦。
Lián yī <u>fēn</u> qián, wǒ doū méiyǒu la.
I don't even have a <u>cent</u>.

Below are some examples demonstrating how to express monetary amounts.

$30.25	三十箍	兩角	五仙	(錢)
	saⁿ-cha̍p khoˑ	nn̄g kak	gō˙sián	(chîⁿ)
	三十塊	兩/二毛	五分	(錢)
	sānshí kuài	liǎng/èr máo	wǔ fēn	(qián)
$209.61	兩百空九箍	六角	一仙	(錢)
	nn̄g pah khòng káu khoˑ	la̍k kak	chit sián	(chîⁿ)
	兩百零九塊	六毛	一分	(錢)
	liǎng bǎi líng jiǔ kuài	liù máo	yī fēn	(qián)

Additionally, 一 **chit** 'one' can be omitted before measure words when expressing monetary amounts. This occurs when the first digit is 1 and the second digit is a value between 1-9. If the remaining digits have a non-zero value, then 一 **chit** 'one' cannot be omitted and the full number is stated.

$1.60	(一)箍六	(chit) khoˑ-la̍k
	一塊六	yī kuài liù
$1.62	一箍六角二仙	chit khoˑ la̍k kak jī sián
	一快六毛二分	yī kuài liù máo èr fēn
$140	(一)百四箍	(chit) pah sì khoˑ
	一百四塊	yī bǎi sì kuài
$145	一百四十五箍	chit pah sì-cha̍p-gō˙khoˑ
	一百四十五塊	yī bǎi sìshíwǔ kuài
$1,800	(一)千八箍	(chit) chheng peh khoˑ
	一千八塊	yī qiān bā kuài

$1,850	一千八百五十箍	chit chheng peh pah gō͘-cha̍p kho͘
	一千八百五十塊	yī qiān bā bǎi wǔshí kuài
$10,500	一萬空五百箍	chit bān khòng gō͘ pah kho͘
	一萬零五百塊	yī wàn líng wǔ bǎi kuài
$15,000	(一)萬五箍	(chit) bān gō͘ kho͘
	一萬五塊	yī wàn wǔ kuài

Mandarin cannot omit the leading 一 **yī** 'one'.

4 Nouns

Taiwanese nouns generally do not reflect number (singular or plural), gender (masculine or feminine), or case (accusative, nominative, genitive, etc.).

4.1 Noun suffix 仔 -á

Most Taiwanese nouns do not have a special marker to differentiate them from other parts of speech. However, the suffix **仔 -á** 'small thing' that originally served as a diminutive has now become a noun marker. These days, the suffix **仔 -á** does not necessarily imply smallness. Additionally, its usage is optional for many words and is often added purely for euphony.

NOUN	NOUN WITH SUFFIX	MEANING
鼻 phīⁿ	鼻仔 phīⁿ-á 鼻子 bízi	nose
狗 káu	狗仔 káu-á 狗 gǒu	dog
賊 chha̍t	賊仔 chha̍t-á (chha̍t-lá) 小偷 xiǎotōu	thief

With nouns that end in a consonant sound (**-p**, **-t**, **-k**, **-m**, **-n**, **-ng**, **-ⁿ**), the sound is often carried over to the beginning of the following syllable **仔 -á**. In the examples above, **賊仔 chha̍t-á** 'thief' sounds more like **chha̍t-lá** because of the glide *(see 2.3.2 Liaision with 仔 -á)*.

Note the Taiwanese **仔 -á** is equivalent to the Mandarin noun suffix **子 -zi**. However, not all cognates shared between Mandarin and Taiwanese will use the noun suffix.

TAIWANESE	MANDARIN	MEANING
帽仔 bō-á	帽子 màozi	hat
藥仔 io̍h-á	藥 yào	medicine
鏡 kiàⁿ	鏡子 jìngzi	mirror

4.2 Plural and singular

In general there is no distinction between the singular and plural form of nouns. To indicate that a noun is single or that there are multiple, the *number* of items must be specified. Between the number and the noun, a *measure word*, a word that is added to help make the noun countable, is always used.

number + measure word + noun

SINGULAR	PLURAL
一本冊 chit pún chheh	三本冊 saⁿ pún chheh
一本書 yī běn shū	三本書 sān běn shū
<u>one</u> book	<u>three</u> books

In Mandarin, the suffix 們 -men is sometimes added to mark the plural forms of some nouns involving people (such as 朋友們 **péngyǒumen** 'friends' and 孩子們 **háizimen** 'children') or personal pronouns (such as 我們 **women** 'we, us' and 他們 **tāmen** 'they'). However, in Taiwanese there is no direct equivalent for this personal pronoun suffix *(see 5.1.3 Plural personal pronouns).*

4.3 Measure words

Taiwanese nouns cannot be directly counted as in English (three birds, four stones, etc.). Instead, every noun must use a specific measure word. These measure words are sometimes referred to as 'counter words' or 'classifiers'.

In English, there are instances where measure words are used to isolate individual parts of a collective noun (a <u>piece</u> of paper, a <u>pair</u> of pants, a <u>drop</u> of water). However, in Taiwanese every noun, collective or not, has a specific measure word associated with it.

Most nouns fall into broad categories of measure words that are distinguished by whether they specify a quantity (value, duration, weight) or physical property (shape, container shape, size) of the noun.

磅 PONG (POUND)

三 磅 蘋果

saⁿ pong phōng-kó

三 磅 蘋果

sān bàng píngguǒ

three pounds of apples

枝 KI (LONG THIN OBJECTS)

一 枝 筆

chit ki pit

一 枝 筆

yī zhī bǐ

one pen

條 TIÂU (LONG THIN OBJECTS THAT CAN BE BENT)

這 條 路

chit tiâu lō͘

這 條 路

zhè tiáo lù

this road

In Taiwanese, the general measure word 个 ê can be used for both people and things. If unfamiliar with a specific measure word associated with a noun, the general measure word 个 ê can usually be substituted. Note that in Taiwanese the pronunciations for the general measure word 个 ê and for the possessive and modifying particle 的 ê are the same.

這 个 是 我 的。

Chit ê sī góa--ê.

這 個 是 我 的。

Zhège shì wǒ de.

This (one) is mine.

4.3.1 Numbers with measure word forms

In Taiwanese the numbers 'one' and 'two' have two forms. One version is for counting and the other is used before measure words.

	COUNTING FORM		MEASURE WORD FORM	
one	一	it / yī	一	chit / yī
two	二	jī / èr	兩	nn̄g / liǎng

Note that Mandarin does not have a separate measure word form for 一 yī 'one'.

TAIWANESE COUNTING FORM	MANDARIN	MEANING
十一 chȧp-it	十一 shíyī	eleven
二十 jī-chȧp	二十 èrshí	twenty
MEASURE WORD FORM		
一个人 chit ê lâng	一個人 yī gè rén	one person
兩本冊 nn̄g pún chheh	兩本書 liǎng běn shū	two books

Higher numbers will often use both counting and measure word forms within a single number because higher units of value such as 百 **pah** 'hundreds', 千 **chheng** 'thousands', 萬 **bān** 'ten thousands', and 億 **ek** 'hundred millions' are all measure words.

101	一百空一	chit pah khòng it
	一百零一	yī bǎi líng yī
2222	兩千兩百二十二	nn̄g chheng nn̄g pah jī-chȧp-jī
		liǎng qiān liǎng bǎi èrshí'èr

4.3.2 Cognates between Taiwanese and Mandarin measure words

For the most part, Taiwanese shares with Mandarin many of the same measure words, although often with a slight adjustment in pronunciation. See the table below for a list of common measure words that are cognates between Taiwanese and Mandarin.

MEASURE WORD	TAIWANESE	MANDARIN	CATEGORIES OF NOUNS
本	pún	běn	books, periodicals, files
枝	ki	zhī	rods, branches, pens
條	tiâu	tiáo	roads, rivers, belts
雙	siang	shuāng	pair
間	keng	jiān	rooms, houses, apartments
樓	lâu	lóu	floors (building)
段	tōaⁿ	duán	paragraphs, stories, time
台	tâi	tái	electronics, machines, cars
句	kù	jù	words, phrases, sentences
歲	hòe	suì	years of age
位	ūi	wèi	people (polite)
班	pan	bān	groups, classes, flights

Note that for some nouns multiple measure words may be considered acceptable.

4.3.3 Differences between Taiwanese and Mandarin measure words

While Taiwanese and Mandarin have many measure words that are cognates, their usage may differ within each language.

In some cases, multiple Taiwanese measure words representing different concepts correspond to a single measure word used in Mandarin.

TAIWANESE	MANDARIN	CATEGORIES OF NOUNS
隻 chiah	隻 zhī	animals
跤 kha	隻 zhī	single (one of a pair)
領 niá	件 jiàn	pieces of clothing
項 hāng	件 jiàn	affairs, matters
個 kò	個 gè	months
个 ê	個 gè	people, *general counter*

Based on the characters selected by the Ministry of Education in Taiwan to represent Taiwanese, the general measure word 个 **ê** is differentiated from 個 **kò**, which serves as a counter for months in Taiwanese as in 兩個月 **nn̄g kò goe̍h** 'two months'. Note that in Mandarin, the general measure word 個 **gè** is used in both of these circumstances and the character 个 **gè** is just the simplified character form of 個 gè.

Conversely, there are cases where a single Taiwanese measure word corresponds to multiple measure words in Mandarin.

TAIWANESE	MANDARIN	CATEGORIES OF NOUNS
塊 tè	塊 kuài	chunks, bite-sized pieces
塊 tè	張 zhāng	tables, charis
塊 tè	首 shǒu	songs
罐 kòan	罐 guàn	cans, jars, jugs
罐 kòan	瓶 píng	bottles

There are also some measure words that are not cognates. That is to say, different measure words are used to express the same concept.

TAIWANESE	MANDARIN	CATEGORIES OF NOUNS
齣 chhut	部 bù	movies
欉 châng	棵 kē	plants, trees
莢 ngeh	根 gēn	bananas
逝 chōa	趟 tàng	trips
尾 bóe	條 tiáo	fish

4.4 Plural marked by group measure words

Besides specifying the number of items to mark a noun as plural (**五塊椅仔 gō͘ tè í-á** 'five chairs'), an indefinite group measure word can be used to indicate multiple items. The most general of these group measure words is **寡 kóa** 'several, few'. The phrase 一寡 **chit-kóa** is equivalent in usage to the English indefinite plural 'some'.

寡 KÓA (SEVERAL, FEW)
一寡 朋友
<u>chit-kóa</u> pêng-iú
一些 朋友
<u>yīxiē</u> péngyǒu
<u>some</u> friends

Note that group measure words generally are preceded by 一 **chit** 'one' unless indicating multiple groupings, in which case a plural number may precede the measure word.

Below are some other common group measure words.

堆 TUI (A MESSY, UNSORTED GROUPING)

一 堆 人

chit <u>tui</u> lâng

一 堆 人

yī <u>duī</u> rén

a <u>heap</u> of people

群 KÛN (GROUPS OF ANIMALS, PEOPLES, OR INSECTS)

兩 群 人

nn̄g <u>kûn</u> lâng

兩 群 人

liǎng <u>qún</u> rén

two <u>groups</u> of people

垺 PÛ (A HEAP OF ITEMS OR A SINGLE MASS)

三 垺 衫仔褲

saⁿ <u>pû</u> saⁿ-á-khò͘

三 堆 衣服

sān <u>duī</u> yīfú

three <u>piles</u> of clothes

4.5 Plural marked by 幾 kúi 'several'

The plural can also be marked by using **幾 kúi** 'several' to indicate an unknown quantity less than ten. **幾 kúi** is placed before the measure word.

幾 + *measure word* + *noun*

kúi + *measure word* + *noun*

'several noun'

幾 个 朋友

<u>kúi</u> ê pêng-iú

幾 個 朋友

<u>jǐ</u> gè péngyǒu

<u>several</u> friends

幾 **kúi** can also be used as a question word to ask how many *(see 20.5.8 How many)*.

伊有幾个囝?
I ū <u>kúi</u> ê kiáⁿ?
他有幾個孩子?
Tā yǒu jǐ gè háizi?
<u>How many</u> children does he have?

4.6 Demonstratives

Demonstratives are words that show where an object is in relationship to the speaker. In English, the demonstratives 'this/these' indicate objects that are closer to the speaker, while 'that/those' refer to objects that are farther away.

CLOSE TO THE SPEAKER	AWAY FROM THE SPEAKER
<u>This</u> car	<u>That</u> car
<u>These</u> shirts	<u>Those</u> shirts

In a way, demonstratives can function like adjectives by describing the noun that follows. Note that *demonstrative adjectives* differ from demonstratives that work like pronouns (<u>This</u> is mine. <u>Those</u> are dirty), which are further discussed in the chapter on pronouns *(see 5.4 Demonstrative pronouns)*.

4.6.1 Demonstrative adjectives – singular

In Taiwanese, the demonstratives 這 **chit** 'this' and 那 **hit** 'that' can be placed before a measure word and noun to indicate where the noun is in relationship to the speaker. While nouns themselves have no plural marker, the use of singular demonstrative adjectives 這 **chit** 'this' and 那 **hit** 'that' can indicate that the nouns that follow are singular.

CLOSE TO SPEAKER	AWAY FROM SPEAKER
這 + *measure word* + *noun*	那 + *measure word* + *noun*
chit + *measure word* + *noun*	hit + *measure word* + *noun*
'this *noun*'	'that *noun*'

這 个 查某 囡仔
chit ê cha-bó͘ gín-á
這個 女 孩子
zhège nǚ háizi
this girl

彼 个 查某 囡仔
hit ê cha-bó͘ gín-á
那個 女 孩子
nàge nǚ háizi
that girl

這 枝 筆
chit ki pit
這 枝 筆
zhè zhī bǐ
this pen

彼 枝 筆
hit ki pit
那 枝 筆
nà zhī bǐ
that pen

In Mandarin, if the general measure word 個 **gè** is attached to the demonstrative 這 **zhè** 'this' or 那 **nà** 'that', the measure word 個 **gè** is suffixed and neutralized in tone to form 這個 **zhège** and 那個 **nàge**.

4.6.2 Demonstrative adjectives – plural specified number

To express the plural form of demonstrative adjectives 'these' and 'those' with a specific quantity (these two books, those three girls), the Taiwanese singular demonstrative adjective 這 **chit** 'this' or 那 **hit** 'that' is followed by a number greater than one, measure word, and noun.

CLOSE TO SPEAKER

這 + *number* + *measure word* + *noun*
chit + *number* + *measure word* + *noun*
'these *number noun*'

AWAY FROM SPEAKER

那 + *number* + *measure word* + *noun*
hit + *number* + *measure word* + *noun*
'those *number noun*'

這 兩 个 人客
chit nn̄g ê lâng-kheh
這 兩 個 客人
zhè liǎng gè kèrén
these two guests

彼 四 塊 眠床
hit sì tè mn̂g-chn̂g
那 四 張 床
nà sì zhāng chuáng
those four beds

4.6.3 Demonstrative adjectives – plural unspecified number

To express the plural form of demonstrative adjectives 'these' and 'those' but without a specific number in mind, the location expression 遮 **chia** 'here' or 遐 **hia** 'there' is followed by the possessive marker 的 **-ê** and the noun.

CLOSE TO SPEAKER	AWAY FROM SPEAKER
遮 + 的 + *noun*	遐 + 的 + *noun*
chia + -ê + *noun*	hia + -ê + *noun*
'these *noun*'	'those *noun*'
遮的 查某 囡仔	遐的 查某 囡仔
chia-ê cha-bó͘ gín-á	hia-ê cha-bó͘ gín-á
這些 女 孩子	那些 女 孩子
zhè xiē nǚ háizi	nà xiē nǚ háizi
these girls	those girls

Note that this construction for the plural demonstrative adjectives differs from Mandarin. The plural form in Mandarin continues to use the singular demonstrative adjectives 這 **zhè** 'this' or 那 **nà** 'that' but then adds the group measure word 些 **xiē** 'some, few'.

Demonstratives can also act like pronouns and replace nouns (This works. These taste great!). In Taiwanese there are two versions of singular demonstrative pronouns 這 **che** 'this' and 彼 **he** 'that' or 這个 **chit--ê** 'this' and 彼个 **hit--ê** 'that' *(see 5.4 Demonstrative pronouns)*.

DEMONSTRATIVE ADJECTIVE	DEMONSTRATIVE PRONOUN
這 本 冊 真 重。	這 / 這个 真 重。
Chit pún chheh chin tāng.	Che / chit--ê chin tāng.
這 本 書 很 重。	這 很 重。
Zhè běn shū hěn zhòng.	Zhè hěn zhòng.
This book is heavy.	This (one) is heavy.

4.7 Omitting the noun

Because measure words help to identify what kind of object a noun might be, the noun can be omitted if proper context has been established.

> *number + measure word + (noun)*

這兩隻真古錐。
Chit nn̄g chiah chin kó͘-chui.
這兩隻很可愛。
Zhè liǎng zhī hěn kě'ài.
These two are cute *(some type of animal)*.

三本攏真重。
Saⁿ pún lóng chin tāng.
三本都很重。
Sān běn dōu hěn zhòng.
All three are heavy *(books, periodicals, or files)*.

4.8 Possessive

In English, possessive is indicated by adding an apostrophe 's' (John's, the girl's, mother's), adding the preposition 'of' (the book of John, the dress of the girl, the right of the mother), or by using a possessive pronoun (my, his, our, their).

APOSTROPHE 'S'

Steven's book

girl's dress

parents' right

OF

book of Steven

dress of the girl

right of the parents

POSSESSIVE PRONOUN
<u>his</u> book
<u>her</u> dress
<u>their</u> rights

4.8.1 Using the possessive marker 的 ê

Taiwanese uses the possessive marker 的 ê to indicate possession. The possessive marker 的 ê joins the possessor and the object in a way similar to the English use of the apostrophe 's'.

> *owner* + 的 + *object*
> *owner* + ê + *object*
> '*owner*'s *object*'

頭家 的 車
thâu-ke ê chhia
老闆 的 車
lǎobǎn de chē
the boss'<u>s</u> car

囡仔 的 早頓
gín-á ê chá-tǹg
孩子 的 早餐
háizi de zǎocān
the children'<u>s</u> breakfast

我 的 班幾
góa ê pan-ki
我 的 航班
wǒ de hángbān
<u>my</u> flight

While there are no separate possessive pronouns in Taiwanese, personal pronouns followed by the possessive marker 的 ê can serve this function.

personal pronoun + 的 + *noun*
personal pronoun + ê + *noun*
'*personal pronoun (his, my, our, etc.) noun*'

伊 的 頭毛
<u>i ê</u> thâu-mo͘
她 的 頭髮
<u>tā de</u> tóufa
<u>her</u> hair

阮 的 衫
<u>gún ê</u> san
我們 的 衣服
<u>wǒmen de</u> yīfú
<u>our</u> clothes

4.8.2 Implied possession with close personal relations or titles

Additionally, possession can be implied without use of the possessive marker 的 ê. If expressing a close personal relationship or connection to someone with a title, the plural personal pronoun can be used in place of a singular personal pronoun with possessive marker 的 ê *(see 5.3.2 Plural personal pronouns marking possession)*. Context typically makes clear whether the possessor is singular or plural. For additional emphasis, the possessive marker 的 ê can still be used with plural pronouns.

阮 (的) 查某囝
<u>gún (ê)</u> cha-bó͘-kiá^n
我 / 我們 (的) 女兒
<u>wǒ / wǒmen (de)</u> nǚ'ér
<u>my / our</u> daughter

怹 翁
in ang

她 先生
tā xiānshēng

her husband

恁 醫生
lín i-seng

你 / 你們 的 醫生
nǐ / nǐmen de yīshēng

 your *(singular / plural)* doctor

In Mandarin the possessive marker **的 de** can be omitted when expressing possession with a close personal relationship. However, usage of the plural personal pronoun to indicate possession does not occur in Mandarin.

4.8.3 Implied possession before demonstrative adjectives

Placing a personal pronoun before a demonstrative adjective can also imply possession *(see 5.3.3 Possession by using demonstrative adjectives)*.

personal pronoun + demonstrative adjective + measure word + noun

怹 彼 台 車
in hit tâi chhia

他們 那 台 車
tāmen nà tái chē

their car

我 這 篇 文章
góa chit phiⁿ bûn-chiong

我 這 篇 文章
wǒ zhè piān wénzhāng

my essay

4.9 Definite and indefinite nouns

When referring to a noun, the reference can be considered *definite* or *indefinite*.

Definite nouns refer to nouns that are already known to the listener. In English, these nouns are often marked by a demonstrative adjective (<u>this</u> cat, <u>those</u> dresses) or by the article 'the' (<u>the</u> boy, <u>the</u> fork).

In contrast, *indefinite nouns* refer to a noun that is not known to the listener. These nouns are often preceded by a number (<u>one</u> tree, <u>seven</u> cookies) or the article 'a(n)' (<u>a</u> restaurant, <u>an</u> author).

Taiwanese has both demonstrative adjectives (**這 chit** 'this', **遐的 hiah-ê** 'those) and numbers (**七个 chhit ê** 'seven items', **十本 chȧp pún** 'ten books') but does not have distinct articles such as 'a(n)' or 'the'.

DEFINITE NOUN	INDEFINITE NOUN
彼 枝 雨傘	三 隻 狗仔
<u>hit</u> ki hō͘-sòaⁿ	<u>saⁿ</u> chiah káu-á
那 枝 雨傘	三 隻 狗
<u>nà</u> zhī yǔsǎn	<u>sān</u> zhī gǒu
<u>that</u> umbrella	<u>three</u> dogs

When demonstrative adjectives or numbers are not present, Taiwanese uses the position of the noun relative to the main verb as well as context to help determine definiteness.

In general, when nouns are placed before the main verb without any particular marker, the noun is considered *definite*. If the noun is unmarked and placed after the verb, the noun is generally considered *indefinite*. This also follows the general reasoning within Taiwanese sentences that usually information known to the listener is presented first, while new information for the listener is presented last.

DEFINITE	INDEFINITE
伊 錶仔 欲 買。	伊 欲 買 錶仔。
I pió-á beh bé.	I beh bé pió-á.
他 手錶 要 買。	他 要 買 手錶。
Tā shǒubiǎo yào mǎi.	Tā yào mǎi shǒubiǎo.
He wants to buy <u>the</u> watch.	He wants to buy <u>a</u> watch.

Note that if the noun is the subject, Mandarin allows for placement before or after the verb indicating definite or indefinite reference. Taiwanese, however, does not accept placing the subject after a verb marked with the perfective aspect marker 矣 --**ah**. To express an indefinite noun as the subject in this situation, the noun must be placed before the verb and marked with a number to render it indefinite.

DEFINITE

公車 來 矣。
Kong-chhia lâi--ah.
公車 來 了。
Gōngchē lái le.
The bus has come.

INDEFINITE

一 台 公車 來 矣。
<u>chit</u> tâi kong-chhia lâi--ah.
來 了 公車。
Lái le gōngchē.
<u>A</u> bus has come.

If a marker is used to explicitly indicate that a noun is indefinite (number) or definite (demonstrative adjective), then the position of the noun relative to the verb no longer signals the definiteness.

DEFINITE

伊 欲 買 彼 枝 錶仔。
I beh bé <u>hit</u> ki pió-á.
他 要 買 那 枝 手錶。
Tā yào mǎi <u>nà</u> zhī shǒubiǎo.
He wants to buy <u>that</u> watch.

INDEFINITE

伊 兩 枝 錶仔 欲 買。
I <u>nn̄g</u> ki pió-á beh bé.
他 兩 枝 手錶 要 買。
Tā <u>liǎng</u> zhī shǒubiǎo yào mǎi.
He wants to buy <u>two</u> watches

A noun following the preposition 共 **kā** as part of the 共 kā construction is always *definite* if left unmarked *(see 17.4 共 kā construction).*

DEFINITE

我 共 麥仔酒 囥 踮 外口。
Góa kā beh-a-chiú khǹg tàm gōa-kháu.
我 把 啤酒 放 在 外面。
Wǒ bǎ píjiǔ fàng zài wàimiàn.
I put <u>the</u> beer outside.

INDEFINITE

我 共 一 罐 麥仔酒 囥 踮 外口。
Góa kā <u>chit</u> kòan beh-á-chiú khǹg tàm gōa-kháu.
我 把 一 瓶 啤酒 放 在 外面。
wǒ bǎ <u>yī</u> píng píjiǔ fàng zài wàimiàn.
I put <u>a</u> beer outside.

5 Pronouns

Pronouns are words used to replace nouns or other pronouns that have been previously mentioned. There are several types of pronouns that will be discussed in the following chapter.

Uncle is coming tomorrow, but <u>he</u> will be late *(personal pronoun)*.

I will clean my room by <u>myself</u> *(reflexive pronoun)*.

The green pants are <u>mine</u> *(possessive pronoun)*.

<u>Those</u> are not good to eat *(demonstrative pronoun)*.

<u>Nobody</u> has heard of that film *(indefinite pronoun)*.

5.1 Personal pronouns

Personal pronouns refer to a specific person(s). Unlike English, Taiwanese does not differentiate between subject pronouns (I, he, we) and object pronouns (me, him, us). The same personal pronouns are used in both cases.

5.1.1 Subject and object personal pronouns

TAIWANESE	MANDARIN	MEANING
我 góa	我 wǒ	I, me
你 lí	你, 妳 nǐ	you *(singular)*
伊 i	他, 她 tā	he, she
阮 gún (góan)	我們 wǒmen	we, us *(exclusive)*
咱 lán	咱們 zánmen	we, us *(inclusive)*
恁 lín	你們 nǐmen	you *(plural)*
悠 in	他們, 她們 tāmen	they, them

5.1.2 Exclusive and inclusive 'we'

The first person plural pronoun 'we' has two forms. The exclusive form 阮 **gún** (also pronounced **góan**) indicates that the speaker and listener are in different groups. The inclusive form 咱 **lán** indicates that the speaker and listener are part of the same group.

阮 無 欲 和 你 做伙 泅 水。
Gún bô beh hām lí chò-hóe siû chúi.
我們 並 不 要 跟 你 一起 游泳。
Wǒmen bìng bù yào gēn nǐ yīqǐ yóuyǒng.
We (*exclusive*) are not going to swim with you.

咱 來 去 公園。
Lán lâi khì kong-hn̂g.
咱們 來 去 公園 吧。
Zánmen lái qù gōngyuán ba.
Let's (*inclusive*) go to the park.

Note that in Mandarin, the inclusive first person plural 咱們 **zánmen** 'we (*inclusive*)' is limited to usage in the area around Beijing and in some northern Mandarin dialects. For other Mandarin speakers, 我們 **wǒmen** 'we, us' is used for all cases without distinction.

5.1.3 Plural personal pronouns

To indicate plural forms of the personal pronouns, Taiwanese phonetically attaches '-n' to the end of singular forms. Because '-n' itself is not an independent syllable, a different character is used to represent the new phonetically combined syllable.

SINGULAR	PLURAL
'I, ME'	'WE, US'
我 góa	阮 gún (góan)
我 wǒ	我們 wǒmen
'YOU'	'YOU (PLURAL)'
你 lí	恁 lín
你 nǐ	你們 nǐmen

SINGULAR	PLURAL
'HE, SHE'	'THEY, THEM'
伊 i	悠 in
他/她 tā	他們/她們 tāmen

Note that Mandarin personal pronouns can add the suffix marker **們 -men** to indicate the plural. The usage of **們 -men** in Mandarin to indicate plural for nouns involving people such as **朋友們 péngyǒumen** 'friends' or **孩子們 háizimen** 'children' does not occur in Taiwanese.

5.1.4 Gender in personal pronouns

Taiwanese does not distinguish gender with its personal pronouns in either the written or spoken form.

TAIWANESE	MANDARIN			MEANING
	MASCULINE	NEUTER/MIX	FEMININE	
你 lí	你 nǐ	--	妳 nǐ	you (*singular*)
伊 i	他 tā	它 tā	她 tā	he, she, it
恁 lín	你們 nǐmen	你們 nǐmen	妳們 nǐmen	you (*plural*)
悠 in	他們 tāmen	它們 tāmen	她們 tāmen	they, them

While Mandarin also does not differentiate gender in speech, the written language does reflect gender differences through the use of gender-specific characters in the second and third person personal pronouns.

5.1.5 Honorific personal pronouns

Taiwanese does not have a specific pronoun to politely address strangers or superiors, but traditionally uses **咱 lán** 'we (*inclusive*)' in place of **你 lí** 'you' in order to express politeness. While this usage is more common among older generations, the use of **咱 lán** 'we (*inclusive*)' suggests that the listener and speaker relationship is more familial and less formal *(see 23.1 Social niceties)*.

TAIWANESE	MANDARIN
請問 咱 貴姓?	請問 您 貴姓?
Chhiá^n-mñg lán kùi-sè^n?	Qǐngwèn nín guìxìng?

May I ask what is your surname? *(polite)*

In contrast, Mandarin does have a polite form in the second person 您 **nǐn** 'you (*singular polite*)' and 您們 **nǐnmen** 'you (*plural polite*)'.

5.2 Reflexive pronouns

Reflexive pronouns are used when the subject is also the object of an action or when there is a desire to emphasize that the subject is alone in performing an action. In English, the pronouns all add the suffix '–self'.

> They washed <u>themselves</u> under the waterfall (*the subject and object is the same*).
>
> He looked at <u>himself</u> in the mirror (*the subject and object is the same*).
>
> I will do it <u>myself</u> (*the subject 'I' alone is emphasized*).

Taiwanese does not have specific reflexive pronouns, but uses the word 家己 **ka-tī** 'oneself' (also pronounced **ka-kī**) to give a reflexive meaning. Like English, Taiwanese uses the reflexive pronoun in cases when the subject is also the object of the action or to emphasize that the subject is alone in performing an action.

5.2.1 Subject receives the action

When 家己 **ka-tī** 'oneself' indicates that the subject receives the action (i.e. the subject is also the object of the action), the placement occurs after the verb. The appropriate personal pronoun may optionally be placed immediately before 家己 **ka-tī**.

> *subject* + *verb* + (*personal pronoun*) + 家己
>
> *subject* + *verb* + (*personal pronoun*) + ka-tī
>
> '*subject* doing *verb* on/to/at oneself'

> 伊 拍 家己。
> I phah <u>ka-tī</u>.
> 她 打 自己。
> Tā dǎ <u>zìjǐ</u>.
> She hit <u>herself</u>.

阮 笑 阮 家己。

Gún chhiò gún ka-tī.

我們 笑 我們 自己。

Wǒmen xiào wǒmen zìjǐ.

We laughed at ourselves.

5.2.2 Subject performs action alone

If the reflexive is used to emphasize that the subject performs an action alone, then 家己 **ka-tī** 'oneself' comes immediately after the subject.

subject + 家己 + *verb*

subject + ka-tī + *verb*

'*subject* doing *verb* by oneself'

我 家己 會 做。

Góa ka-tī ē chò.

我 自己 會 做。

Wǒ zìjǐ huì zuò.

I will do it myself.

伊 家己 駛車 去 庄跤。

I ka-tī sái-chhia khì chng-kha.

他 自己 開車 去 鄉下。

Tā zìjǐ kāichē qù xiāngxià.

He drove by himself to the countryside.

5.3 Possessive pronouns

Possessive pronouns are used to show who owns a particular object, person, or animal.

That bag is mine.

Ours is over by the bench.

Don't forget to bring yours on the trip.

5.3.1 Using the possessive marker 的 ê

Taiwanese does not have distinct words for possessive pronouns as in English (mine, yours, its, his, hers, ours, theirs). Instead, the personal pronouns are followed by the possessive marker 的 ê to convey possession.

personal pronoun + 的

personal pronoun + ê

'mine / yours / its / his / hers / ours / theirs'

紅 裙 是 我 的。
Âng kûn sī góa--ê.
紅 裙子 是 我 的。
Hóng qúnzi shì wǒ de.
The red dress is mine.

恁 的 是 白色 的 厝。
In--ê sī pe̍h-sek ê chhù.
他們 的 是 白色 的 房屋。
Tāmen de shì báisè de fángwū.
Theirs is the white house.

Note that the personal pronoun followed by the possessive marker 的 ê can be used to express both possessive adjectives (my, your, his, her, our, their) and possessive pronouns (mine, yours, his, hers, ours, theirs).

POSSESSIVE PRONOUN

土色 鞋仔 是 我 的。
Thô͘-sek ê-á sī góa--ê.
棕色 鞋子 是 我 的。
Zōngsè xiézi shì wǒ de.
The brown shoes are mine.

POSSESSIVE ADJECTIVE

我 的 鞋仔 佇 櫥仔內。
Góa ê ê-á tī tû-á-lāi.
我 的 鞋子 在 櫃子 裡。
Wǒ de xiézi zài guìzi lǐ.
My shoes are in the cupboard.

你 的 延誤 矣。
Lí--ê iân-gō͘--ah.
你 的 延誤 了。
Nǐ de yánwù le.
Yours is delayed.

你 的 班機 延誤 矣。
Lí ê pan-ki iân-gō͘--ah.
你 的 航班 延誤 了。
Nǐ de hángbān yánwù le.
Your flight is delayed.

Note that the possessive pronouns have two dashes between the personal pronoun and possessive marker 的 ê. This both indicates that the possessive marker 的 ê is read in the neutral tone and emphasizes the personal pronoun *(see 4.8.1 Using possessive marker* 的 *ê)*.

5.3.2 Plural personal pronouns marking possession

When expressing close personal relationships or connection to someone with a title, the plural personal pronoun can be used in place of a singular personal pronoun with possessive marker 的 ê *(see 4.8.2 Implied possession with close personal relations or titles)*. Context typically makes clear whether the possessor is singular or plural.

阮 後生 佇 遐。
Gún hāu-seⁿ tī hia.
我 兒子 在 那裡。
Wǒ érzi zài nàlǐ.
My son is over there.

恁 翁 欲 去 無?
Lín ang beh khì--bô?
你 先生 要 去 嗎?
Nǐ xiānshēng yào qù ma?
Is your husband going?

悠 老師 欲 過來。
In lāu-su beh kòe--lâi.
他 的 老師 要 過來。
Tā de lǎoshī yào guòlái.
His teacher will come over.

請 敲 電話 予 恁 醫生。
Chhiáⁿ khà tiān-ōe hō͘ lín i-seng.
請 打 電話 給 你 的 醫生。
Qǐng dǎ diànhuà gěi nǐ de yīshēng.
Please call your doctor.

阮 厝 佇 市區。
Gún chhù tī chhī-khu.
我 家 在 市區。
Wǒ jiā zài shìqū.
My house is in the downtown area.

In colloquial usage, the possessive marker 的 ê is also sometimes omitted with objects as well.

你 (的) 飯 緊 食食 咧！
Lí (ê) pn̄g kín chiȧh-chiȧh--leh!
你 (的) 飯 快 吃 啊！
Nǐ (de) fàn kuài chī a!
Hurry up and eat your food!

If the subject actually is plural, the plural pronoun is still used. The possessive marker 的 ê is optional and may be added for emphasis.

阮 (的) 厝 是 佇 遐。
Gún (ê) chhù sī tī hia.
我們 (的) 家 在 那裡。
Wǒmen (de) jiā zài nàlǐ.
Our house is over there.

恁 (的) 公車 咧欲 來 矣。
Lín (ê) kong-chhia teh-beh lâi--ah.
你們 (的) 公車 快要 來 了。
Nǐmen (de) gōngchē kuàiyào lái le.
Your *(plural)* bus is about to come.

In Mandarin the possessive marker 的 de can be omitted when expressing possession with a close personal relationship. However, usage of the plural personal pronoun to indicate possession does not occur in Mandarin.

5.3.3 Possession by using demonstrative adjectives

An alternative method to show personal possession is to combine the use of a personal pronoun with a demonstrative adjective followed by the appropriate measure word. The noun can be omitted if understood from context.

personal pronoun + demonstrative adjective + measure word + (noun)

伊 彼 領 褲
i hit niá khò͘
他 那 件 褲子
tā nà jiàn kùzi
his pants

我 這 个 皮包仔
góa chit ê phôe-pau-á
我 這個 錢包
Wǒ zhège qiánbāo
my wallet

伊 這 條 拔鍊
i chit tiâu phoa̍h-liān
她 這 條 項鍊
tā zhè tiáo xiàngliàn
her necklace

5.4 Demonstrative pronouns

Demonstratives are words that indicate a specific object or objects to which the speaker is referring. In English, the demonstratives 'this/these' indicate objects that are closer to the speaker, while 'that/those' refer to those objects that are further away. Demonstratives can also function like pronouns and replace nouns.

CLOSE TO THE SPEAKER	FAR FROM THE SPEAKER
I want this.	Don't give me that.
These are better.	Those are dirty.

Taiwanese has both singular and plural demonstrative pronouns. In addition, another set of demonstrative pronouns can be used to refer to an unspecified item or group of items.

	SINGULAR	PLURAL	NON-SPECIFIC
CLOSE TO SPEAKER	這个 chit--ê	遮的 chia--ê	這 che
	這個 zhège	這些 zhè xiē	這 zhè
	this (one)	these (ones)	this
FAR FROM SPEAKER	彼个 hit--ê	遐的 hia--ê	彼 he
	那個 nàge	那些 nà xiē	那 nà
	that (one)	those (ones)	that

Note that these *demonstrative pronouns* differ from demonstratives that function like adjectives (<u>this</u> car, <u>those</u> shirts) *(see 4.6 Demonstratives)*.

5.4.1 Singular demonstrative pronouns

Singular demonstrative pronouns are formed by joining the demonstratives 這 **chit** 'this' and 彼 **hit** 'that' with a measure word. Note that they are linked by a double-hyphen which neutralizes the tone on the measure word and places emphasis on the demonstrative 這 **chit** 'this' and 彼 **hit** 'that'. This slight difference in pronunciation and the lack of a noun following the measure word helps to distinguish between the demonstrative pronoun and demonstrative adjective.

DEMONSTRATIVE PRONOUN	DEMONSTRATIVE ADJECTIVE
這 + --*measure word*	這 + *measure word* + *noun*
chit + --*measure word*	chit + *measure word* + *noun*
'this (one)'	'this *noun*'

這个 有名。	這 个 人 有名。
Chit--ê ū-miâ.	Chit ê lâng ū-miâ.
這個 有名。	這個 人 有名。
Zhège yǒumíng.	Zhège rén yǒumíng.
<u>This (one)</u> is famous.	<u>This</u> person is famous.

DEMONSTRATIVE PRONOUN	DEMONSTRATIVE ADJECTIVE
彼 + --*measure word*	彼 + *measure word* + *noun*
hit + --*measure word*	hit + *measure word* + *noun*
'that (one)'	'that *noun*'

彼欉真懸。　　　　　　　彼欉樹仔真懸。
Hit--châng chin kôan.　　Hit châng chhiū-á chin kôan.
那棵很高。　　　　　　　那棵樹很高。
Nà kē hěn gāo.　　　　　Nà kē shù hěn gāo.
That (one) is tall.　　　　That tree is tall.

5.4.2 Plural demonstrative pronouns

The plural demonstrative pronouns are the same as the plural demonstrative adjectives for an unspecified number *(see 4.6.3 Demonstratives adjectives - plural unspecified number)*.

However, there is a slight difference in pronunciation marked by a double-hyphen before the possessive marker 的 **--ê**. This double-hyphen indicates that the possessive marker 的 **--ê** is in the neutral tone and gives more emphasis on the preceding syllable 遮 **chia** or 遐 **hia**. Note that the plural forms are not followed by a measure word.

DEMONSTRATIVE PRONOUN	DEMONSTRATIVE ADJECTIVE
遮的	遮的 + *noun*
chia--ê	chia-ê + *noun*
'these (ones)'	'these *noun*'

遮的上貴。　　　　　　　遮的錶仔上貴。
Chia--ê siōng kùi.　　　　Chia-ê pió-á siōng kùi.
這些最貴。　　　　　　　這些手錶最貴。
Zhè xiē zuì guì.　　　　　Zhè xiē shǒubiǎo zuì guì.
These (ones) are the most expensive.　　These watches are the most expensive.

DEMONSTRATIVE PRONOUN	DEMONSTRATIVE ADJECTIVE
遐的	遐的 + *noun*
hia--ê	hia-ê + *noun*
'those (ones)'	'those *noun*'

共遐的提轉去。　　　　　共遐的冊提轉去。
Kā hia--ê thẻh--tńg-khì.　　Kā hia-ê chheh thẻh--tńg-khì.
把那些拿回去。　　　　　把那些書拿回去。
Bǎ nà xiē ná huíqù.　　　Bǎ nà xiē shū ná huíqù.
Take those back home.　　Take those books back home.

Because the plural demonstrative pronouns and the plural demonstrative adjectives for an unspecified number are constructed from the words 遮 **chia** and 遐 **hia**, there is the risk of conflating them with 遮 **chia** 'here' and 遐 **hia** 'there' when used with the modifying particle 的 ê. In this usage, the emphasis is on that of an object 'belonging' to a specific location.

DEMONSTRATIVE PRONOUN	DEMONSTRATIVE ADJECTIVE	MODIFYING PARTICLE
遮的 chia--ê	遮的 chia-ê	遮 的 chia ê
遮的 chia--ê 這些 zhè xiē these (trees)	遮的 樹仔 chia-ê chhiū-á 這些 樹 zhè xiē shù these trees	遮 的 樹仔 chia ê chhiū-á 這裡 的 樹 zhèlǐ de shù trees from here
DEMONSTRATIVE PRONOUN	DEMONSTRATIVE ADJECTIVE	MODIFYING PARTICLE
遐的 hia--ê	遐的 hia-ê	遐 的 hia ê
遐的 hia--ê 那些 nà xiē those (trees)	遐的 樹仔 hia-ê chhiū-á 那些 樹 nà xiē shù those trees	遐 的 樹仔 hia ê chhiū-á 那裡 的 樹 nàlǐ de shù trees from there

5.4.3 Unspecified demonstrative pronouns

Taiwanese has another set of demonstrative pronouns that can be used when the number or category of items is unspecified. The demonstrative pronouns 這 **che** 'this' and 彼 **he** 'that' are used without measure words. They can be used both for abstract (ideas, concepts, etc.) and concrete (books, chairs, etc.) nouns.

Note that while the characters used for both singular and unspecified demonstrative pronouns are the same, the pronunciation differs.

UNSPECIFIED DEMONSTRATIVE PRONOUN	SINGULAR DEMONSTRATIVE PRONOUN
這 che 'this'	這 + --*measure word* chit + --*measure word* 'this (one)'

這 真 好食。
Che chin hó-chiah.
這 很 好吃。
Zhè hěn hàochī.
This is delicious.

這个 真 好食。
Chit--ê chin hó-chiah.
這個 很 好吃。
Zhège hěn hàochī.
This (one) is delicious.

While 這 **che** and 彼 **he** can refer to either a single or multiple number of objects, generally the reference is a singular entity, whether a single item or singular grouping of many items. In contrast, the use of the plural demonstrative pronoun emphasizes multiple items that are not considered as part of a collection.

UNSPECIFIED DEMONSTRATIVE PRONOUN	PLURAL DEMONSTRATIVE PRONOUN
彼	遐 + --*measure word*
he	hiah + --*measure word*
'those'	'those (ones)'

彼 攏 真 嬌。
He lóng chin súi.
那 都 很 漂亮。
Nà dōu hěn piàoliang.
Those *(a set of items)* are all pretty.

遐的 攏 真 嬌。
Hiah--ê lóng chin súi.
那 些 很 漂亮。
Nà xiē hěn piàoliang.
Those *(different items)* are all pretty.

5.5 Indefinite pronouns

Indefinite pronouns refer to unspecified people, objects, times, or places. In English, indefinite pronouns often begin with 'every-', 'any-', 'some-', or 'no-' (everyone, anything, someone, nobody, etc.) but can also include words such as 'all', 'several', or 'few'.

5.5.1 Expressing 'any-', 'every-', or '-ever'

In Taiwanese, indefinite pronouns beginning with 'any-' and 'every-' or ending in '-ever' are constructed by placing a question word before the adverb 攏 **lóng** 'both, all' or 嘛 **mā** 'also' *(see 20.5 Question words)*. A noun may optionally be placed immediately after the question word. Generally, these indefinite pronoun constructions occur before the main verb.

question word + *(noun)* + 攏 / 嘛 + *verb*

question word + *(noun)* + lóng / mā + *verb*

伊 啥物 攏 愛。

I siáⁿ-mih lóng ài.

他 什麼 都 喜歡。

Tā shénme dōu xǐhuān.

He likes everything/anything/whatever.

彼 隻 狗仔 啥人 嘛 會 吠。

Hit chiah káu-á siáⁿ-lâng mā ē pūi.

那 隻 狗 誰 也 會 吠。

Nà zhī gǒu shéi yě huì fèi.

That dog barks at anyone/everyone/whomever.

日本 啥物 所在 攏 有 便利 商店。

Jit-pún siáⁿ-mih só͘-chāi lóng ū piān-lī siong-tiàm.

日本 什麼 地方 都 有 便利 商店。

Rìběn shénme dìfāng dōu yǒu biànlì shāngdiàn.

Everywhere in Japan has a convenient store.

5.5.2 Expressing 'no-' or 'not any'

Indefinite pronouns beginning with 'no-' or 'not any' are constructed by placing the appropriate negation after the adverb **攏 lóng** 'both, all' or **嘛 mā** 'also'.

    question word + (noun) + 攏 / 嘛 + negation

    question word + (noun) + lóng / mā + negation

伊 啥物 攏 無 愛。

I siáⁿ-mih lóng bô ài.

他 什麼 都 不 喜歡。

Tā shénme dōu bù xǐhuan.

He likes nothing.

He doesn't like anything.

頭家 和 啥物 人 嘛 袂 講 話。
Thâu-ke hām siáⁿ-mih lâng mā bē kóng ōe.
老闆 跟 什麼人 也 不 會 講 話。
Lǎobǎn gēn shénme rén yě bù huì jiǎng huà.
The boss talks to nobody.
The boss doesn't talk to anybody.

啥物 所在 攏 無 便所。
Siáⁿ-mih só͘-chāi long bô piān-só͘.
什麼 地方 都 沒有 廁所。
Shénme dìfāng dōu méiyǒu cèsuǒ.
Nowhere are there bathrooms.
There are no bathrooms anywhere.

5.5.3 Expressing 'some-'

Indefinite pronouns 'some-' are constructed by placing 有 ū 'to exist' before a question word *(see 20.5 Question words)*.

有 + *question word* + *(noun)*

ū + *question word* + *(noun)*

有 啥物 人 阮 會當 問 無?
Ū siáⁿ-mih lâng gún ē-tàng mn̄g--bô?
有 誰 我們 能不能 問?
Yǒu shéi wǒmen néngbùnéng wèn?
Is there someone we can ask?

有 啥物 伊 愛 無?
Ū siáⁿ-mih i ài--bô?
有 什麼 他 喜歡 嗎?
Yǒu shénme tā xǐhuan ma?
Is there something he likes?

有 佗位 賣 冷氣機?
Ū tó-ūi bē léng-khì-ki?
有 哪裡 賣 冷氣機?
Yǒu nǎlǐ mài lěngqìjī?
Is there <u>somewhere</u> that sells air conditioners?

6 Adjectives

Adjectives are words that describe nouns. In English, adjectives generally appear *before* the noun they modify.

    the <u>new</u> car

An adjective can also appear *after* the noun it modifies if there is a linking verb joining the noun and adjective.

    The car is <u>new</u>.

In Taiwanese, most adjectives can similarly be placed *before* or *after* the nouns they modify.

When the adjective is placed *before* the noun, the group of words cannot stand alone as a complete sentence.

    這台新車
    chit tâi <u>sin</u> chhia
    這台新車
    zhè tái <u>xīn</u> chē
    this <u>new</u> car

However, when the adjective occurs *after* the noun, there is no need for a linking verb like in English. In this way, adjectives in Taiwanese are often described as capable of taking on characteristics of verbs. The linking verb 'to be' is already bound up in the adjective. When in this position, the noun-adjective phrase can form a complete stand-alone sentence.

    這台車真新。
    Chit tâi chhia chin <u>sin.</u>
    這台車很新。
    Zhè tái chē hěn <u>xīn.</u>
    This car <u>is new</u>.

However, when the adjective appears *after* the noun, an *intensifier* must come before the adjective. An *intensifier* is a type of adverb that specifies the degree of an adjective.

Below is a table of some common adjectives.

TAIWANESE	MANDARIN	MEANING
貴 kùi	貴 guì	expensive
懸 kôan	高 gāo	tall
清氣 chheng-khì	乾淨 gānjìng	clean
古錐 kó͘-chui	可愛 kě'ài	cute
忝 thiám	累 lèi	tired
燒 sio	溫暖 wēnnuǎn	warm/hot (*things*)
新 sin	新 xīn	new
媠 súi	漂亮 piàoliang	pretty

6.1 Intensifiers

Intensifiers are a type of adverb that modifies other adjectives or adverbs by specifying degree *(see 14 Adverbs)*.

This food is <u>very</u> good.

Your son is <u>truly</u> awful.

6.1.1 Common intensifiers

Taiwanese has a number of intensifiers that frequently (and in some cases *must*) appear before adjectives. Below is a table of some common intensifiers.

TAIWANESE	MANDARIN	MEANING
真 chin	很 hěn	very (*default*)
誠 chiâⁿ	真 zhēn	really, truly
足 chiok	非常 fēicháng	extremely
有夠 ū-kàu	非常 fēicháng	extremely
非常 hui-siông	非常 fēicháng	extremely
袂講得 bē-kóng-tit(eh)	得不得了 -debùdéliǎo	exceedingly
特別 tėk-piàt	特別 tèbié	particularly
尤其 iû-kî	尤其 yóuqí	especially

TAIWANESE	MANDARIN	MEANING
遮(爾)(仔) chiah(-nī)(-á)	這麼 zhème	so, so very much
遐(爾)(仔) hiah(-nī)(-á)	那麼 nàme	so, so very much
較 khah	比較 bǐjiào	rather, relatively
閣較 koh-khah	更 gèng	even more
愈較 jú-khah	更 gèng	even more
完全 ôan-chôan	完全 wánquán	completely
上 siōng	最 zuì	most
傷 siuⁿ	太 tài	too
無多 bô-gōa	不太 bùtài	not too
一點仔 chit-tiám-á	有點 yǒudiǎn	a bit, a little
一屑仔 chit-sut-á	有點 yǒudiǎn	a bit, a little
略仔 lioh-á	稍微 shāowēi	slightly

Note that Mandarin has a few intensifiers that can appear *after* the adjective such as 極了 **-jí le** 'exceedingly', 得不得了 **-de bùdéliǎo** 'extremely', or 得很 **-de hěn** 'very'. Taiwanese generally places all intensifiers *before* the adjective. In spite of this, Taiwanese does use extent complements *(see 11.7 Extent complements)*, which appear *after* the verb and are used more commonly than in Mandarin for superlative constructions.

歹 食 甲 欲 死
pháiⁿ chiah kah beh sì
難 吃 得 要 死
nán chī de yào sǐ
bad tasting (lit. 'bad tasting to the point of wanting to die')

6.1.2 Placeholder intensifier

When an adjective functions like a verb and comes *after* the noun, generally an intensifier or negative must be used with the adjective.

伊 的 裙 真 媠。
I ê kûn <u>chin súi.</u>
她 的 裙子 很 漂亮。
Tā de qúnzi <u>hěn piàoliang</u>.
Her skirt <u>is (very) pretty</u>.

伊 的 裙 無 媠。

I ê kûn bô súi.

她 的 裙子 不 漂亮。

Tā de qúnzi bù piàoliang.

Her skirt is not (very) pretty.

Unless emphasized, the intensifier 真 **chin** serves as a default placeholder and has no additional meaning of 'very'. This is equivalent in function to the Mandarin intensifier 很 **hěn**.

6.2 Absolute adjectives

There are some adjectives that cannot be modified by intensifiers because a degree cannot be specified. These *absolute adjectives* describe a particular property or characteristic that a noun either possesses or does not. Unlike other adjectives, absolute adjectives cannot take on verb characteristics such as direct negation or occur independently after the nouns they modify.

Below is a table of some common absolute adjectives.

TAIWANESE	MANDARIN	MEANING
空 khāng	空 kōng	empty
國際 kok-chè	國際 guójì	international
現代 hiān-tāi	現代 xiàndài	modern
無形 bô hêng	無形 wúxíng	invisible
假 kè	假 jiǎ	fake
女 lú	女 nǔ	female
天然 thian-jiân	天然 tiānrán	natural

When an absolute adjective comes before the noun it describes, the adjective behaves like other adjectives.

absolute adjective + (的) + *noun*

absolute adjective + (ê) + *noun*

我 的 <u>女</u> 朋友 徛 佇 遐。

Góa ê <u>lú</u> pêng-iú khiā tī hia.

我 的 <u>女</u> 朋友 站 在 那裡。

Wǒ de <u>nǚ</u> péngyǒu zhàn zài nàlǐ.

My <u>girl</u>friend is standing over there.

<u>現代</u> 的 機場 應該 有 網路，著無?

<u>Hiān-tāi</u> ê ki-tiûⁿ eng-kai ū bāng-lō͘, tio̍h--bô?

<u>現代</u> 的 機場 應該 有 網路，對不對?

<u>Xiàndài</u> de jīchǎng yīnggāi yǒu wǎnglù, duìbùduì?

<u>Modern</u> airports should have internet access, right?

However, when the adjective appears after the noun, the absolute adjective must be changed into a noun by adding the modifying particle **的** --ê *(see 6.6.4 Omitting the head noun (nominalization))*. Once the adjective has been changed into a noun, the linking verb 是 sī 'to be' may be used to join the two nouns together.

    noun + 是 + *absolute adjective* + 的

    noun + sī + *absolute adjective* + --ê

天頂 <u>是</u> <u>空</u> 的。

Thiⁿ-téng <u>sī khang</u>--ê.

天空 <u>是</u> <u>空</u> 的。

Tiānkōng <u>shì kōng de</u>.

The sky is <u>empty</u>.

遮的 護照 攏 <u>是</u> <u>假</u> 的。

Chiah-ê hō͘-chiàu lóng <u>sī ké</u>--ê.

這 些 護照 都 <u>是</u> <u>假 的</u>。

Zhè xiē hùzhào dōu <u>shì jiǎ de</u>.

These passports are <u>fakes</u>.

Additionally, absolute adjectives cannot be directly negated. Instead the linking verb 是 **sī** 'to be' is changed to the negative form 毋是 **m̄-sī** 'is not'.

天頂 毋是 空 的。
Thiⁿ-téng m̄-sī khāng--ê.
天空 不是 空 的。
Tiānkōng bùshì kōng de.
The sky is not empty.

遮的 護照 攏 毋是 假 的。
Chiah-ê hō·-chiàu lóng m̄-sī kè--ê.
這 些 護照 都 不是 假 的。
Zhè xiē hùzhào dōu bùshì jiǎ de.
These passports are not fakes.

6.3 Comparisons

In English, comparisons are generally made by adding the suffix '-er' to an adjective or by using the adverb 'more' before the adjective.

The cat is cleaner than the pig.

The cat is more clean than the pig.

The word 'than' indicates that the first item is 'more' compared to the second item.

Taiwanese creates comparisons with special constructions using 比 **pí** 'compared with'. Note that because absolute adjectives do not have degrees, they cannot be placed in comparison constructions.

6.3.1 Comparisons using 比 pí ... 較 khah 'compared with...more than'

Taiwanese places 比 **pí** 'compared with' between the two items to be compared. After introducing the subjects of the comparison, the adverb 較 **khah** 'more' and adjective follow.

item 1 + 比 + *item 2* + 較 + *adjective*

item 1 + pí + *item 2* + khah + *adjective*

'*item 1* is more *adjective* than *item 2*'

貓仔 比 豬仔 較 清氣。

Niau-á pí ti-á khah chheng-khì.

貓 比 豬 乾淨。

Māo bǐ zhū gānjìng.

Cats are cleaner than pigs.

Note that in Mandarin, there is no need for an additional 'more' before the adjective. However, in Taiwanese **較 khah** 'more' must precede the adjective.

Often repetitive elements may be omitted from the second item of the comparison.

對 你 來 講，這 張 報紙 比 彼 張 (報紙) 較 有 趣味。

Tùi lí lâi kóng, chit tiuⁿ pò-chóa pí hit tiuⁿ (pò-chóa) khah ū chhù-bī.

對 你 來 說，這 張 報紙 比 那 張 (報紙) 有 趣。

Duì nǐ lái shuō, zhè zhāng bàozhǐ bǐ nà zhāng (bàozhǐ) yǒu qù.

This newspaper will be more interesting for you than that (newspaper).

If the items for comparison are already understood from context, they do not need to be reintroduced.

這 領 較 好看。

Chit niá khah hó-khòaⁿ.

這 件 比較 好看。

Zhè jiàn bǐjiào hǎokàn.

This one looks better (*two items of clothing have already been discussed*).

6.3.2 Comparisions using 比較 pí-kàu 'to compare'

Another method to express comparisons in Taiwanese is to use **比較 pí-kàu** 'to compare' as a verb. To construct this comparison structure, the sentence is divided into two clauses. The first clause includes the subjects of comparison joined by a conjunction (such as **和 hām**, **佮 kah**, or **參 chham**) and then followed by the verb **比較 pí-kàu**. The second clause repeats the 'more than' or 'greater than' item and is followed by **較 khah** 'more' and the adjective. An alternate form is **比起來 pí--khí-lâi** instead of **比較 pí-kàu**.

item 1 + 和 + item 2 + 比較，item (*greater*) + 較 + *adjective*

item 1 + hām + item 2 + pí-kàu, item (*greater*) + khah + *adjective*

'Comparing item 1 and item 2, item (the 'greater') is more *adjective*'

新加坡 佮 台灣 比較，台灣 較 大。
Sin-ka-pho kah Tâi-oan pí-kàu, Tâi-ôan khah tōa.
新加坡 和 台灣 比，台灣 比較 大。
Xīnjiāpō hé Táiwān bǐ, Táiwān bǐjiào dà.
Comparing Singapore and Taiwan, Taiwan is bigger.

狗仔 和 貓仔 比起來，狗仔 較 忠誠。
Káu-á hām niau-á pí--khí-lâi, káu-á khah tiong-sêng.
狗 和 貓 比起來，狗 比較 忠誠。
Gǒu hé māo bǐqǐlái, gǒu bǐjiào zhōngchéng.
Between dogs and cats, dog are more loyal.

Note that the sentence pattern for comparisons using the cognate 比較 **pí-kàu** differs between Taiwanese and Mandarin. With Taiwanese, 比較 **pí-kàu** functions more like a verb meaning 'to compare'. The Mandarin 比較 **bǐjiào** functions more like an adverb to express 'relatively more'.

6.3.3 Implicit comparisons

較 **khah** 'more' can also be used to make hypothetical comparisons, even when no other items have been mentioned earlier.

> *subject* + 較 + *adjective*
> *subject* + khah + *adjective*
> '*subject* is relatively more *adjective*'

遮的 衫 較 貴。
Chiah-ê saⁿ khah kùi.
這 些 衣服 比較 貴。
Zhè xiē yīfú bǐjiào guì.
These clothes are more expensive (*no specific pieces of clothing have been referred to earlier. Only the overall sense of the average cost of clothes is being asssessed*).

這 个 百花 公司 的 便所 較 清氣。
Chit ê pah-hoè kong-si ê piān-só khah chheng-khì.
這個 百貨 公司 的 廁所 比較 乾淨。
Zhège bǎihuò gōngsī de cèsuǒ bǐjiào gānjìng.
This department store's restrooms are clean*er* (*relative to other department stores*).

6.3.4 Specifying how much difference in a comparison

Indicating how much the difference is between two items of comparison can be accomplished by placing the quantity or multiplier after the adjective.

>   *item 1* + 比 + *item 2* + 較 + *adjective* + *quantity/multiplier*
>   *item 1* + pí + *item 2* + khah + *adjective* + *quantity/multiplier*

伊 的 暗餐 比 我 的 較 貴 十 箍。
I ê àm-tng pí góa--ê khah kùi chȧp kho.
他 的 晚餐 比 我 的 貴 十 塊。
Tā de wǎncān bǐ wǒ de guì shí kuài.
His dinner is ten dollars more expensive than mine.

伊 比 恁 阿兄 肥 兩 倍。
I pí in a-hiaⁿ pûi nn̄g pōe.
他 比 他 哥哥 胖 兩 倍。
Tā bǐ tā gēgē pàng liǎng bèi.
He is twice as fat as his older brother.

6.3.5 Comparing actions

Items of comparison can also include verbs and verb phrases.

>   *verb 1* + 比 + *verb 2* + 較 + *adjective*
>   *verb 1* + pí + *verb 2* + khah + *adjective*

坐 計程車 比 坐 火車 較 緊。

Chē kè-thêng-chhia pí chē hóe-chhia khah kín.

坐 計程車 比 坐 火車 快。

Zuò jìchéngchē bǐ zuò huǒchē kuài.

Taking a taxi is faster than taking a train.

6.3.6 Negating a comparison

Comparisons can be negated by placing the negative **無 bô** 'not' or **袂 bē** 'will not' before **比 pí** 'compared with'.

    item 1 + 無 / 袂 + 比 + *item 2* + 較 + *adjective*

    item 1 + bô / bē + pí + *item 2* + khah + *adjective*

    '*item 1* is/will not be more *adjective* than *item 2*'

豬仔 無 比 貓仔 較 清氣。

Ti-á bô pí niau-á khah chheng-khì.

豬 不 比 貓 乾淨。

Zhū bù bǐ māo gānjìng.

Pigs are not cleaner than cats.

坐 計程車 袂 比 坐 火車 較 緊。

Chē kè-thêng-chhia bē pí chē hóe-chhia khah kín.

坐 計程車 不會 比 坐 火車 快。

Zuò jìchéngchē bù huì bǐ zuò huǒchē kuài.

Taking a taxi will not be faster than taking a train.

6.3.7 Comparisons expressing inferiority

An item can be shown to be 'less than' or 'not as much' as another item in some characteristic by placing the negative **無 bô** 'not have' between the items. After introducing the items, the intensifiers **遮爾仔 chiah-nī-á** or **遐爾仔 hiah-nī-á** 'so' can optionally be placed before the adjective.

> *item 1* + 無 + *item 2* + (遮爾仔 / 遐爾仔) + *adjective*
> *item 1* + bô + *item 2* + (chiah-nī-á / hiah-nī-á) + *adjective*
> '*item 1* is not as (so) *adjective* as *item 2*'

伊 無 你 遐爾仔 賢。
I bô lí hiah-nī-á gâu.
她 沒有 你 那麼 能幹。
Tā méiyǒu nǐ nàme nénggàn.
She is not as talented as you are.

阮 後生 無 恁 的 躼。
Gún hāu-seⁿ bô lín--ê lò.
我 的 兒子 沒有 你 的 高。
Wǒ de érzi méiyǒu nǐ de gāo.
My son is not as tall as yours.

6.3.8 Comparisons expressing equality

An item can be shown to be the 'same as' or 'identical to' another item by placing a conjunction (such as 和 **hām**, 佮 **kah**, or 參 **chham**) between the items followed by 仝款 **kāng-khóan** 'same type'.

Additionally, to specify what quality the two items share equally, an adjective describing this quality can be placed after 仝款 **kāng-khóan**. Alternative forms include 相仝 **sio-kāng** 'same, identical' or 平 **pêⁿ** 'equally'.

> *item 1* + 和 + *item 2* + 仝款 + (*adjective*)
> *item 1* + hām + *item 2* + kāng-khóan + (*adjective*)
> '*item 1* and *item 2* are the same (equally *adjective*)'

阿爸 佮 阿母 仝款 歹。
A-pa kah a-bú kāng-khóan pháiⁿ.
爸爸 和 媽媽 一樣 兇。
Bàba hé māmā yīyàng xiōng.
Dad and mom are equally mean.

這張相和彼張相仝。
Chit tiuⁿ siòng hām hit tiuⁿ sio-kāng.

這張照片和那張一樣。
Zhè zhāng zhàopiàn hé nà zhāng yīyàng.

This photograph is the same as that one.

昨昏暗的電影參下昏暗的平歹看。
Cha-hng-àm ê tiān-iáⁿ chham e-hng-àm--ê pêⁿ pháiⁿ-khòaⁿ.

昨晚的電影和今晚的一樣難看。
Zuówǎn de diànyǐng hé jīnwǎn de yīyàng nánkàn.

Last night's movie was as bad as tonight's.

6.3.9 Comparative degree

The comparative degree is used to express that an item is 'even more' in some quality than another item, which has already been mentioned. Place the intensifier **閣較 koh-khah** before the adjective. Alternative forms include **愈較 jú-khah** 'even more' and **猶閣較 iáu-koh khah** 'still more'.

item + 閣較 + *adjective*

item + koh-khah + *adjective*

'this *item* is even more *adjective*'

這棟大樓真懸。彼棟閣較懸。
Chit tòng tōa-lâu chin kôan. Hit tòng koh-khah kôan.

這棟大樓很高。那棟更高。
Zhè dòng dàlóu hěn gāo. Nà dòng gèng gāo.

This building is tall. That building is even taller.

這个紅嬰仔真古錐,但是你的猶閣較古錐。
Chit ê âng-eⁿ-á chin kó͘-chui, tān-sī lí--ê iáu-koh khah kó͘-chui.

這個嬰兒很可愛,但是你的還是更可愛。
Zhège yīng'ér hěn kě'ài, dànshì nǐ de háishì gèng kě'ài.

This baby is cute, but yours is still even cuter.

6.3.10 Superlative degree

The superlative degree is used in comparisons to express the 'most' out of three or more items. The exact number of items to be compared does not need to be specified. In English, the superlative form is generally created by adding the suffix '-est' to an adjective or by using the adverb 'most' before the adjective. In Taiwanese, 上 **siōng** 'most' is placed before the adjective.

> 上 + *adjective*
> siōng + *adjective*
> 'most *adjective*'

上 俗 的 位 佇 後面。
<u>Siōng</u> siok ê ūi tī āu-bīn.
最 便宜 的 位子 在 後面。
<u>Zuì</u> piányí de wèizi zài hòumiàn.
The cheap<u>est</u> seats are in the back.

我 是 這 班 泅水 泅 甲 上 慢 的。
Góa sī chit pan siû chúi siû kah <u>siōng</u> bān--ê.
我 是 這 班 游泳 游 得 <u>最</u> 慢 的。
Wǒ shì zhè bān yóuyǒng yóu de <u>zuì</u> màn de.
I am the slow<u>est</u> swimmer in this class.

6.4 Desirable and undesirable adjectives

The desirability of an adjective can have an impact on word structure, choice of verb, and negation. Generally, what is deemed desirable comes from the speaker's perspective.

6.4.1 Adjective structure based on desirability

Some adjectives can be formed by adding 好 **hó** to an action verb. The effect is to create an adjective indicating that it is 'easy to' do the action verb. This adjective structure is generally reserved for desirable qualities.

好 + *action verb*

hó + *action verb*

'easy to *action verb*'

這 塊 餅 真 <u>好</u>食。

Chit tè piáⁿ chin <u>hó</u>-chia̍h.

這 塊 餅乾 很 <u>好</u>吃。

Zhè kuài bǐnggān hěn <u>hào</u>chī.

This cookie is delicious.

In contrast, **歹 pháiⁿ** 'difficult to' can equally be used to create adjectives for undesirable qualities.

歹 + *action verb*

pháiⁿ + *action verb*

'difficult to *action verb*'

這 塊 餅 真 <u>歹</u>食。

Chit tè piáⁿ chin <u>pháiⁿ</u>-chia̍h.

這 塊 餅乾 很 <u>難</u>吃。

Zhè kuài bǐnggān hěn <u>nán</u>chī.

This cookie tastes bad.

Some combinations have become so commonplace that they are now joined by a hyphen and form part of the lexicon.

ACTION VERB	ADJECTIVE (DESIRABLE) 有 ū / 無 bô	ADJECTIVE (UNDESIRABLE) 會 ē / 袂 bē
食 chia̍h	好食 hó-chia̍h	歹食 pháiⁿ-chia̍h
吃 chī	好吃 hǎochī	難吃 nánchī
to eat	delicious	bad tasting
看 khòaⁿ	好看 hó-khòaⁿ	歹看 pháiⁿ-khòaⁿ
看 kàn	好看 hǎokàn	難看 nánkàn
to see	attractive	ugly

ACTION VERB	ADJECTIVE (DESIRABLE)	ADJECTIVE (UNDESIRABLE)
聽 thiaⁿ	好聽 hó-thiaⁿ	歹聽 pháiⁿ-thiaⁿ
聽 tīng	好聽 hǎotīng	難聽 nántīng
to hear	nice sounding	bad sounding
坐 chē	好坐 hó chē	歹坐 pháiⁿ chē
坐 zuò	好坐 hǎozuò	難坐 nánzuò
to sit	easy to sit	difficult to sit
捾 kōaⁿ	好捾 hó kōaⁿ	歹捾 pháiⁿ kōaⁿ
提 tí	好提 hǎotí	難提 nántí
to carry	easy to carry	difficult to carry

6.4.2 Verb choice based on adjective desirability

The choice of verb before an adjective also depends on the desirability of the adjective. Generally, the verbs 有 ū / 無 bô are used with adjectives connoting desirable qualities. What constitutes desirability depends on the speaker's viewpoint. Additionally, the use of verb 有 ū can be used in past, present, or future descriptions.

有 / 無 + *adjectives (desirable)*

ū / bô + *adjectives (desirable)*

這个 歌手 的 上新 的 唱片 有 好聽。
Chit ê koa-chhiú ê siōng sin ê chhiùⁿ-phìⁿ ū hó-thiaⁿ.
這個 歌手 的 最新 的 唱片 好聽。
Zhège gēshǒu de zuì xīn de chàngpiàn hǎotīng.
This singer's latest album <u>sounds</u> good.

我 的 冊包 有 好 攑。
Góa ê chheh-pau ū hó giȧh.
我 的 書包 很 好 背。
Wǒ de shūbāo hěn hǎo bèi.
My backpack <u>is</u> easy to carry.

In contrast, the verbs 會 ē / 袂 bē are used with adjectives connoting undesirable qualities. Again, what constitutes undesirability depends on the speaker's viewpoint. Additionally, the use of verb 會 ē can be used in past, present, or future descriptions.

> 會 / 袂 + *adjectives (undesirable)*
>
> ē / bē + *adjectives (undesirable)*

> 你 會 感覺 遮的 窗也布 真 歹看 袂？
> Lí ē kám-kak chia-ê thang-á-pò͘ chin pháiⁿ-khòaⁿ--bē?
> 你 會 覺得 這 些 簾子 難看 嗎？
> Nǐ huì juéde zhè xiē liánzi nánkàn ma?
> Do you think these curtains <u>are</u> ugly?

> 這 條 椅仔，坐 傷 久 會 歹 坐。
> Chit liâu í-á, chē siuⁿ kú <u>ē</u> pháiⁿ chē.
> 這 把 椅子，坐 太 久 會 難 坐。
> Zhè bǎ yǐzi, zuò tài jiǔ <u>huì</u> nán zuò.
> This chair <u>is</u> hard to sit in for very long.

6.4.3 Negation based on adjective desirability

The choice of negation for adjectives also depends on desirability of the adjective. For adjectives deemed to be desirable by the speaker, the negative used is 無 **bô**. In contrast, undesirable qualities are preceded by the negative 袂 **bē**.

While in other grammatical contexts these two negatives (無 **bô** and 袂 **bē**) differ according to aspect *(see 8 Aspect),* when occurring before adjectives the choice between the two negatives 無 **bô** and 袂 **bē** is based only on desirability of the adjective. Additionally, it should be noted that it is possible that the same adjective may be seen as desirable in one context and undesirable for another context.

> 無 + *adjective (desirable quality)*
>
> bô + *adjective (desirable quality)*
>
> 'not *adjective (desirable quality)*'

下昏暗 的 節目 無 好笑。

E-hng-àm ê chiat-bȯk bô hó-chhiò.

今晚 的 節目 不 好笑。

Jīnwǎn de jiémù bù hǎoxiào.

Tonight's program will not be funny.

這 个 西瓜 無 甜。

Chit ê si-koe bô tiⁿ.

這個 西瓜 不 甜。

Zhège xīguā bù tián.

This watermelon is not sweet.

彼 間 店 的 臭 豆腐 無 臭。

Hit keng tiàm ê chhàu tāu-hū bô chhàu.

那 家 店 的 臭 豆腐 不 臭。

Nà jiā diàn de chòu dòufu bù chòu.

That restaurant's stinky tofu is not stinky *(it should be stinky)*.

袂 + *adjective (undesirable quality)*

bē + *adjective (undesirable quality)*

'not *adjective (undesirable quality)*'

咱 昨昏 食 的 王梨 袂 酸。

Lán cha-hng chiȧh ê ông-lâi bē sng.

我們 昨天 吃 的 鳳梨 不 酸。

Wǒmen zuótiān chī de fènglí bù suān.

The pineapple we ate yesterday wasn't sour *(sour is undesirable)*.

彼 隻 狗 真 乖, 袂 吵。

Hit chiah káu chin koai, bē chhá.

那 隻 狗 很 乖, 不 吵。

Nà zhī gǒu hěn guāi, bù chǎo.

That dog is very well behaved; it isn't noisy.

車頭 的 便所 袂 垃圾。

Chhia-thâu ê piān-só͘ bē lah-sap.

車站 的 廁所 不 髒。

Chēzhàn de cèsuǒ bù zāng.

The bathrooms in the train station aren't dirty.

There are a few exceptions in which the adjectives are not negated by 無 bô and 袂 bē. Some adjectives must take the negation 毋 m̄ 'not' *(see 13.1 Negative particle 毋 m̄)* regardless of the adjective's desirability.

One common adjective that may be negated by both 毋 m̄ and 無 bô is 好 hó 'good'. However, each form of negation offers a slight difference in meaning.

無好 bô hó indicates 'not good' with regards to quality.

彼 齣 電影 無 好。

Hit chhut tiān-iáⁿ bô hó.

那 部 電影 不 好。

Nà bù diànyǐng bù hǎo.

That movie isn't good *(the storyline, acting, special effects, etc. are not good)*.

毋好 m̄-hó means 'not good' because of a sense of moral disapproval.

彼 齣 電影 毋好。

Hit chhut tiān-iáⁿ m̄-hó.

那 部 電影 不 好。

Nà bù diànyǐng bù hǎo.

The movie isn't good to watch *(there is objectionable or offensive content in the film)*.

Note that some native speakers of Taiwanese are not particular about the usage of 無好 bô hó and 毋好 m̄-hó and use them interchangeably. Mandarin uses 不好 bù hǎo in both contexts and leaves the meaning up to interpretation.

6.5 Adjectives with verb characteristics

Most adjectives (excluding absolute adjectives) can take on the properties of verbs such as aspect and direct negation.

6.5.1 Change-of-state particle 矣 --ah

Changes in state are often indicated by the end-of-sentence particle 矣 --ah, which signals the anterior aspect *(see 8.4 Anterior aspect)*.

天暗矣。
Thiⁿ àm--ah.
天空暗了。
Tiānkōng àn le.
The sky has darkened.

伊規熱天運動，所以這馬較勇矣。
I kui joah-thiⁿ ūn-tōng, só-í chit-má khah ióng--ah.
他整個夏天運動，所以現在比較壯了。
Tā zhěng gè xiàtiān yùndòng, suǒyǐ xiànzài bǐjiào zhuàng le.
He worked out all summer, so now he has become stronger.

二點鐘以後，湯的味有較重矣。
Nn̄g tiám-cheng í-āu, thng ê bī ū khah tāng--ah.
兩個小時之後，湯的味道更濃了。
Liǎng gè xiǎoshí zhīhòu, tāng de wèidào gèng nóng le.
After two hours, the flavor of the soup is stronger.

Mandarin often uses the end-of-sentence particle 了 -le to signal a change of state with adjectives.

6.5.2 Describing conditions that have worsened 去 --khì

When describing a condition that has gotten worse, the suffix 去 --khì is often added to adjectives. Additionally, the end-of-sentence particle 矣 --ah marking a change of state may be added.

adjective + 去 + (矣)

adjective + --khì + (--ah)

我 無 紮 雨傘，所以 西裝 澹 去 矣。
Góa bô chah hō͘-sòaⁿ, só͘-í se-chong tâm--khì--ah.
我 沒有 帶 雨傘，所以 西裝 濕 了。
Wǒ méiyǒu dài yǔsǎn, suǒyǐ xīzhuāng shī le.
I didn't bring an umbrella so my suit got wet.

恁 若 無 穿 鞋仔，跤 會 垃圾 去。
Lín nā bô chhēng ê-á, kha ē lah-sap--khì.
你們 要不是 穿 鞋子，腳 會 髒掉。
Nǐmen yàobùshì chuān xiézi, jiǎo huì zāngdiào.
If you don't wear shoes, your feet will get dirty.

One notable exception is **好去 hó--khì** which conveys that a condition related to one's health has improved.

歇睏 幾 工 了後，感冒 攏 好 去 矣。
Hioh-khùn kúi kang liáu-āu, kám-mō͘ lóng hó--khì--ah.
休息 幾 天 之後，感冒 都 好 了。
Xiūxí jǐ tiān zhīhòu, gǎnmào dōu hǎo le.
After resting a few days, my cold has completely gotten better.

6.6 Noun phrases and the modifying particle 的 ê

The modifying particle **的 ê** allows adjectives, nouns, verbs, and even whole phrases to modify nouns. The noun that becomes modified is often referred to as the *head noun*. Everything that helps to modify the head noun including the head noun itself is referred to as a *noun phrase*. Generally, all modifiers appear before the nouns that they modify. The modifying particle **的 ê** is placed between the modifier and the head noun.

   adjective / noun / verb / phrase + 的 + *head noun*

   adjective / noun / verb / phrase + ê + *head noun*

古錐 的 紅嬰仔
kó͘-chui ê âng-eⁿ-á
可愛 的 嬰兒
kě'ài de yīng'ér
cute baby

In the example above, **紅嬰仔 âng-eⁿ-á** 'baby' is the head noun and **古錐 的 紅嬰仔 kó͘-chui ê âng-eⁿ-á** 'cute baby' is the entire noun phrase.

6.6.1 Adjectives with modifying particle 的 ê

When an adjective comes before the noun and is more than one-syllable, a modifying particle **的 ê** is generally placed between the adjective and noun. Single-syllable adjectives often do not include **的 ê**.

single-syllable adjective + (的) + *head noun*
single-syllable adjective + (ê) + *head noun*

貴 手機
kùi chhiú-ki
贵 手机
guì shǒujī
expensive mobile phone

臭 的 襪仔
chhàu ê bo̍eh-á
臭 的 襪子
chòu de wàzi
smelly socks

multi-syllable adjective + 的 + *head noun*
multi-syllable adjective + ê + *head noun*

好 坐 的 膨椅
hó chē ê phòng-í
舒服 的 沙發
shūfu de shāfā
comfortable sofa

清氣 的 桌仔
chheng-khì ê toh-á
乾淨 的 桌子
gānjìng de zhuōzi
clean table

One-syllable adjectives preceded by an intensifier use the modifying particle 的 ê.

> *intensifier + one-syllable adjective + 的 + head noun*
> *intensifier + one-syllable adjective + ê + head noun*

> ONE-SYLLABLE ADJECTIVE
> 歹 囡仔
> pháiⁿ gín-á
> 壞 孩子
> huài háizi
> bad kid

> ONE-SYLLABLE ADJECTIVE WITH INTENSIFIER
> 真 歹 的 囡仔
> chin pháiⁿ ê gín-á
> 很 壞 的 孩子
> hěn huài de háizi
> very bad kid

However, if the adjective functions like a verb and appears after the noun, there is no need for the modifying particle 的 ê.

> *head noun + (intensifier) + adjective*

膨椅 真 好 坐。
Phòng-í chin hó chē.
沙發 很 舒服。
Shāfā hěn shūfu.
The sofa is comfortable.

桌仔 真 清氣。
Toh-á chin chheng-khì.
桌子 很 乾淨。
Zhuōzi hěn gānjìng.
The table is clean.

彼 个 囡仔 真 歹。
Hit ê gín-á chin pháiⁿ.
那個 孩子 很 壞。
Nàge háizi hěn huài.
That kid is very bad.

6.6.2 Nouns, verbs, and phrases that modify with 的 ê

Nouns, verbs, and also entire phrases can modify nouns when joined with the modifying particle 的 ê.

noun / verb / phrase + 的 + *head noun*
noun / verb / phrase + ê + *head noun*

MODIFYING NOUN
學校 的 運動埕
ha̍k-hāu ê ūn-tōng-tiâⁿ
學校 的 操場
xuéxiào de cāochǎng
school's athletic field

餐廳 的 停車場
chhan-thiaⁿ ê thêng-chhia-tiûⁿ
餐廳 的 停車場
cāntīng de tíngchēchǎng
restaurant parking lot

MODIFYING VERB

行 路 的 人客
kiâⁿ lō͘ ê lâng-kheh
走 路 的 客人
zǒu lù de kèrén
guests who walked

跳舞 的 查某
thiàu-bú ê cha-bó͘
跳舞 的 女人
tiàowǔ de nǚrén
ladies who danced

MODIFYING PHRASE

昨暗 做 暗餐 的 阿姨
cha-àm chò àm-tng ê a-î
昨晚 做 晚飯 的 阿姨
zuówǎn zuò wǎnfàn de āyí
the aunt who cooked dinner last night

會曉 講 韓國話 的 學生
ē-hiáu kóng Hân-kok-ōe ê ha̍k-seng
會 講 韓國話 的 學生
huì jiǎng Hánguóhuà de xuéshēng
the student who can speak Korean

As can be seen in the glosses above, Taiwanese does not have relative clauses, which are descriptive phrases that come after the noun and begin with 'who', 'whom', 'which', etc. Instead, Taiwanese places the entire descriptive phrase before the noun and adds the modifying particle **的 ê**.

6.6.3 Nouns that modify without 的 ê

There are a few occasions when nouns can modify other nouns without using the modifying particle 的 ê. If the modifying noun is closely associated with the head noun, the 的 ê may be omitted.

中國 (的) 人
Tiong-kok (ê) lâng
中國 (的) 人
Zhōngguó (de) rén
Chinese person

If the modifying noun has a close personal relationship with the head noun, the 的 ê may also be omitted.

朋友 (的) 阿姊
pêng-iú (ê) a-chí
朋友 (的) 姐姐
péngyǒu (de) jiějiě
friend's older sister

6.6.4 Omitting the head noun (nominalization)

In a noun phrase, the head noun itself can be omitted if understood from context.

adjective / noun / verb / phrase + 的 + *(head noun)*
adjective / noun / verb / phrase + ê + *(head noun)*

辦公室 的 咧 修理。
Pān-kong-sek--ê teh siu-lí.
辦公室 的 修理中。
Bàngōngshì de xiūlízhōng.
The office's (bathrooms) are out of service.

Omitting the head noun actually has the effect of changing the modifying adjective, verb, or phrase into a noun. This change is called *nominalization*, which is the process of changing other parts of speech into nouns. These nominalized adjectives, verbs, or phrases can be roughly translated into English as 'one(s) that *adjective/verb/phrase*'.

adjective / verb / phrase + 的

adjective / verb / phrase + --ê

'one(s) that *adjective / verb / phrase*'

ADJECTIVE

這 台 烏色的 是 阮 的。

Chit tâi o͘-sek--ê sī gún--ê.

這 台 黑色的 是 我們 的。

Zhè tái hēisè de shì wǒmen de.

This black one is ours *(car)*.

共 上 輕的, 攑來 予 我。

Kā siōng khin--ê, gia̍h-lâi hó͘ góa.

把 最 輕的, 拿來 給 我。

Bǎ zuì qīng de, nálái gěi wǒ.

Give me the one that is the lightest *(luggage)*.

VERB

掩咯雞的 佇 佗位?

Ng-ko̍k-ke--ê tī tó-ūi?

捉迷藏的 在 哪裡？

Zhuōmícáng de zài nǎlǐ?

Where is the one who is playing hide-and-seek *(child)*?

PHRASE

彼个 無 戴 帽仔的 是 上 緣投。

Hit ê bô tì bō-á--ê sī siōng iân-tâu.

那個 沒有 戴 帽子的 是 最 英俊。

Nàge méiyǒu dài màozi de shì zuì yīngjùn.

The one not wearing a hat is the most handsome *(man)*.

6.6.5 Multiple modifiers in sequence

It is possible for multiple modifiers to co-occur and describe a single noun. In general, a particular order is followed based on the meaning of the modifier.

The *number + measure word* can be seen as a dividing line of which some modifiers occur before, while others occur afterwards. Broadly speaking, modifiers which give a background context to the head noun come before the *number + measure word*, while the modifiers that describe properties of the head noun come after. Note that this ordering is not necessarily fixed and there can be some degree of flexibility depending on emphasis.

> **modifiers (background)** + number + measure word + **modifers (properties)** + head noun

6.6.5.1 Modifiers (background)

Modifiers which offer background context to help situate the noun are placed before the *number + measure word + head noun*. Background modifiers include possession, location, time, and scope. If more than one background modifier co-occurs then the ordering generally follows that as presented in the previous sentence.

> **modifiers (background)** + number + measure word + head noun

POSSESSION

林小姐的 一 隻 狗
Lîm sió-chiá ê chı̍t chiah káu

林小姐的 一 隻 狗
Lín xiǎojiě de yī zhī gǒu

Ms. Lim's dog

你的 二 台 電腦
lí ê nn̄g tâi tiān-náu

你的 兩 台 電腦
nǐ de liǎng tái diànnǎo

your two computers

LOCATION

銀行內 的 兩 个 警衛
gîn-hâng-lāi ê nñg ê kéng-ōe
銀行 裡 的 兩 個 警衛
yínháng lǐ de liǎng ge jǐngwèi
the two security guards <u>in the bank</u>

公園內 的 三 塊 椅條
kong-hn̂g-lāi ê saⁿ tè í-liâu
公園 裡 的 三 張 長板凳
gōngyuán lǐ de sān zhāng chángbǎndèng
three benches <u>in the park</u>

TIME

後 禮拜 的 一 个 班
āu lé-pài ê chit ê pan
下 禮拜 的 一 個 班
xià lǐbài de yī gè bān
a class <u>next week</u>

下早 的 一 杯 咖啡
e-chái ê chit poe ka-pi
早上 的 一 杯 咖啡
zǎoshang de yī bēi kāfēi
a cup of coffee <u>from this morning</u>

SCOPE

別的 三 个 故事
pat-ê saⁿ ê kò·-sū
別的 三 個 故事
biéde sān gè gùshì
three <u>other</u> stories

彼 寡 機會
hit kóa ki-hōe
那 些 機會
nà xiē jīhuì
those few opportunities

6.6.5.2 Modifiers (properties)

Modifiers which offer information on the properties of the head noun are placed after the *number + measure word* but before the head noun. Property modifiers include activity, characteristics, shape, color, material, and function. If more than one property modifier co-occurs then the ordering generally follows that as presented in the previous sentence.

*number + measure word + **modifiers (properties)** + head noun*

ACTIVITY
一 个 煮食 課
chit ê chú-chiah khò
一 堂 烹飪 課
yī táng pēngrèn kè
a cooking class

彼 寡 劉先生 寫 的 報告
hit kóa Lâu--sian-siⁿ siá ê pò-kò
那 些 劉先生 寫 的 報告
nà xiē Liú xiānshēng xiě de bàogào
the reports Mr. Lau wrote

CHARACTERISTICS
這 个 滑滑 的 塗跤
chit ê kut-kut ê thô·-kha
這個 滑滑 的 地板
zhège huáhuá de dìbǎn
this slippery floor

一 个 <u>巧</u> 賊仔
chit ê <u>khiáu</u> chha̍t-á

一 個 <u>聰明 的</u> 小偷
yī gè <u>cōngmíng de</u> xiǎotōu

a <u>clever</u> thief

SHAPE

一 塊 <u>圓圓 的</u> 桌仔
chit tè <u>îⁿ-îⁿ ê</u> toh-á

一 張 <u>圓圓 的</u> 桌子
yī zhāng <u>yuányuán de</u> zhuōzi

a <u>circular</u> table

一 个 <u>有 角 的</u> 面
chit ê <u>ū kak ê</u> bīn

一 個 <u>方形 的</u> 臉
yī gè <u>fāngxíng de</u> liǎn

an <u>angular</u> face

COLOR

一 點 <u>紅</u> 血
chit tiám <u>âng</u> hoeh

一 點 <u>紅</u> 血
yī diǎn <u>hóng</u> xuè

a drop of <u>red</u> blood

三 个 <u>青</u> 葉仔
saⁿ ê <u>chheⁿ</u> hio̍h-á

三 個 <u>青</u> 葉子
sān gè <u>qīng</u> yèzi

three <u>green</u> leaves

MATERIAL

一个 玻璃 的 罐仔
chi̍t ê po-lê ê kòan-á
一個 玻璃 的 瓶子
yī gè bōlí de píngzi
a glass bottle

十个 絲仔 圍巾
cha̍p ê si-á ûi-kin
十個 絲圍巾
shí gè sīwéijīn
ten silk scarves

FUNCTION

一 領 雨幔
chi̍t niá hō͘-moa
一 件 雨衣
yī jiàn yǔyī
a raincoat

一 雙 拳擊 用 的 手套
chi̍t siang kûn-kek iōng ê chhiú-thò
一 雙 拳擊 用 的 手套
yī shuāng quánjí yòng de shǒutào
a pair of boxing gloves

6.6.5.3 Co-occurring modifiers

If more than one category of modifier co-occurs, the ordering of modifiers roughly follows the list below.

possession + *location* + *time* + *scope* + **measure word** + *activity* + *characteristics* + *shape* + *color* + *material* + *function* + **noun**

我 的 眠床頂 昨昏 彼 領 垃圾去 新 的 長 烏色 棉布 的 出外 褲,是 你 提 去 無?

Góa ê bîn-chhn̂g-téng cha-hng hit niá lah-sap--khì sin ê tn̂g o·-sek mî-pò·ê chhut-gōa khò·, sī lí thėh--khì--bô?

我 的 床上 昨天 那 件 髒了 新 的 長 黑色 棉布 的 出外 褲子,是 你 拿走 嗎?

Wǒ de chuángshàng zuótiān nà jiàn zāngle xīn de cháng hēisè miánbù de chūwài kùzi, shì nǐ názǒu ma?

Did you take my pair of dirtied, new, long, black, cotton, going-out *(fancy)* pants that was on my bed yesterday?

NOUN WITH MULTIPLE MODIFIERS

possession	我的	góa ê	my
location	眠床頂	bîn-chhn̂g-téng	on the bed
time	昨昏	cha-hng	yesterday
scope	彼	hit	that
measure word	領	niá	pair *(measure word for clothing)*
activity	垃圾去	lah-sap--khì	dirtied
characteristics	新	sin	new
shape	長	tn̂g	long
color	烏色	o·-sek	black
material	棉布的	mî-pò·ê	cotton
function	出外	chhut-gōa	going out *(fancy)*
head noun	褲	khò·	pants

REMAINING ELEMENTS

focusing particle	是	sī	it was
subject	你	lí	you
verb phrase	提去	thėh--khì	take away
question particle	無	--bô	right?

In the example above, the object is topicalized and moved to the front of the sentence. Complicated and longer objects tend to be placed before the verb. The ordering of these modifiers is not rigid as there is some flexibility depending on emphasis and personal preference. Additionally, the example sentence provided above is intended to demonstrate the relative ordering of modifiers depending on attribute and what is grammatically possible. Nonetheless, Taiwanese speakers generally prefer multiple shorter sentences to a single longer sentence.

6.7 Repetition

Certain single-syllable adjectives that are physically descriptive or sensory in nature can be repeated or given special suffixes to express different intensities. Not all adjectives are a capable of this feature, but a few more commonly used adjectives do exhibit this property. Note that this only occurs when adjectives function like verbs and appear *after* the noun.

6.7.1 Reduplication with single-syllable adjectives

When single-syllable adjectives are doubled, this has the effect of lessening the intensity of the adjective suggesting a 'little' or 'bit'. Often the particle 仔 **-á** is added to the reduplicated adjective for euphony.

> *adjective* + *adjective* + (仔)
>
> *adjective* + *adjective* + (-á)

啉 一 杯 葡萄酒 了後，伊 的 面 就 紅紅。
Lim chit poe phû-tô-chiú liáu-āu, i ê bīn tō âng-âng.
喝 一 杯 葡萄酒 之後，他 的 臉 就 紅紅 的。
Hē yī bēi pútáojiǔ zhīhòu, tā de liǎn jiù hónghóng de.
After one sip of wine, his face becomes a little red.

這 隻 狗仔 戇戇仔，伊 一直 追 家己 的 尾仔 走。
Chit chiah káu-á gōng-gōng-á, i it-tit tui ka-tī ê bóe-á cháu.
這 隻 小狗 笨笨 的，牠 一直 追 自己 的 尾巴 跑。
Zhè zhī xiǎo gǒu bènbèn de, tā yīzhí zhuī zìjǐ de wěibā pǎo.
This puppy is a little stupid. It keeps chasing its own tail.

Note that in Mandarin, that the possessive marker 的 **de** must appear after the reduplicated adjective.

6.7.2 Reduplication with two-syllable adjectives

With two-syllable adjectives, doubling allows for the meaning to intensify. There are two methods to double two-syllable adjectives.

Split doubling method

The split doubling method doubles the first-syllable of the adjective and then doubles the second-syllable to follow an X-X-Y-Y format. This is the more common method of two-syllable adjective reduplication.

SPLIT DOUBLING WITH TWO-SYLLABLE ADJECTIVE X-Y

$X + X + Y + Y$

老老實實
láu-láu-sit-sit
老老實實
lǎolǎoshíshí
very honest

嚴嚴重重
giâm-giâm-tiōng-tiōng
嚴嚴重重
yányánchóngchóng
very serious

貧貧惰惰
pîn-pîn-tōaⁿ-tōaⁿ
懶懶惰惰
lǎnlǎnduòduò
very lazy

Repeated doubling method

The repeated doubling method repeats the entire two-syllable adjective to follow an X-Y-X-Y format. Fewer adjectives can use this method of reduplication. Unfortunately, adjectives that can accept this format must be learned on a case-by-case basis.

REPEATED DOUBLING WITH TWO-SYLLABLE ADJECTIVE X-Y

$X + Y + X + Y$

老實老實
láu-sit-láu-sit
老實老實
lǎoshílǎoshí
very honest

垃圾垃圾
lah-sap-lah-sap
非常髒
fēicháng zāng
very dirty

簡單簡單
kán-tan-kán-tan
簡單簡單
jiǎndānjiǎndān
very simple

6.7.3 Exceeding suffix

To express that the intensity of the adjective has exceeded a level of comfort, an *exceeding suffix* can be added to the adjective.

adjective + exceeding suffix

'exceedingly adjective'

This *exceeding suffix* is constructed from a reduplicated syllable that is a descriptive word or an onomatopoetic word representing a sound that evokes a more colorful description of the adjective's intensity.

DESCRIPTIVE WORD EXCEEDING SUFFIX

ADJECTIVE	RELATED WORD	ADJ WITH EXCEEDING SUFFIX
澹	漉漉	澹漉漉
tâm	lok-lok	tâm-lok-lok
wet	filter, sieve	soaked, dripping wet

In some cases the reduplicated syllable is derived from a descriptive word that together with the adjective depicts an image that expresses the intensity of the adjective. For example, 澹漉漉 **tâm-lok-lok** 'soaked' is composed of the single syllable adjective 澹 **tâm** 'wet' and a doubling of the word 漉 **lok** 'strain, filter'. This combination of meaning perhaps visually evokes being so wet that it is as if water is passing through a filter or sieve.

ONOMATOPOETIC WORD EXCEEDING SUFFIX

ADJECTIVE	ONOMATOPOETIC WORD	ADJ WITH EXCEEDING SUFFIX
冷	吱吱	冷吱吱
léng	ki-ki	léng-ki-ki
cold	chirping, squeaking	frosty, chillingly cold

In other cases the suffix provides an onomatopoetic quality to describe the experience of the adjective. For example, 冷吱吱 **léng-ki-ki** 'freezing' is composed of the single syllable adjective 冷 **léng** 'cold' and a doubling of the onomatopoetic word 吱 **ki** 'chirping, squeaking'. This combination perhaps suggests being so cold that the noises made from one's trembling or teeth chattering sound like a chirping bird or squeaking mouse.

ADJECTIVE	REDUPLICATED SYLLABLE	ADJ WITH EXCEEDING SUFFIX	MANDARIN
暗	摸摸	暗摸摸	黑壓壓
àm	mo͘-mo͘	àm-mo͘-mo͘	hēiyāyā
dark	to grope, to touch	pitch black	
紅	記記	紅記記	紅咚咚
âng	kì-kì	âng-kì-kì	hóngdōngdōng
red	to remember, to note	bright red	
膨	獅獅	膨獅獅	氣鼓鼓
phòng	sai-sai	phòng-sai-sai	qìgǔgǔ
swollen	lion	seething in anger	
澹	漉漉	澹漉漉	濕漉漉
tâm	lok-lok	tâm-lok-lok	shīlùlù
wet	filter, sieve	soaked, dripping wet	
冷	吱吱	冷吱吱	冷冰冰
léng	ki-ki	léng-ki-ki	lěngbīngbīng
cold	chirping, squeaking	fosty, chillingly cold	

緊 轉來，外面 已經 暗摸摸 矣。
Kín tńg--lâi, gōa-bīn í-keng àm-mo͘-mo͘--ah.

快 回家，天空 已經 黑壓壓 了。
Kuài huí jiā, tiānkōng yǐjīng hēiyāyā le.

Hurry and come home. It's already <u>pitch dark</u> outside.

哎喲喂! 你 的 面 攏 紅記記!
Ai-iō-ôe! Lí ê bīn lóng âng-kì-kì!

哎喲喂! 你 的 臉 紅咚咚 的!
Āiyōwèi! Nǐ de liǎn dōu hóngdōngdōng de!

Oh my! Your face is <u>all bright red</u>!

While Mandarin also has a number of adjectives with these exceeding suffixes, the usage is much more common in Taiwanese.

6.8 Expressions with adjectives describing change

A few common expressions using **愈 jú** (also pronounced **lú**) 'the more…' describe changes with adjectives over time or as a result of other changes.

6.8.1 Changes over time

To convey a gradual change over time, the expression **愈來愈 jú lâi jú** 'more and more' can be placed before an adjective *(see 29.6 Expressing changes over time)*.

愈 來 愈 + *adjective*

jú lâi jú + *adjective*

'more and more *adjective*'

天 愈來愈 暗。
Thiⁿ <u>jú lâi jú</u> àm.

天空 越來越 暗。
Tiānkōng <u>yuè lái yuè</u> àn.

The sky is <u>getting more and more</u> dark.

阿公 愈 來 愈 歹。

A-kong jú lâi jú pháiⁿ.

爺爺 越 來 越 兇。

Yéyé yuè lái yuè xiōng.

Grandpa is <u>becoming more and more</u> mean.

6.8.2 Changes that cause other changes

To convey that the change of an action verb directly impacts another change, **愈** **jú** can be placed before the action verb followed by repeating **愈** **jú** before an adjective *(see 29.6.3 Changes caused by another action).*

愈 + *action verb* + 愈 + *adjective*

jú + *action verb* + jú + *adjective*

'the more *action verb* the more *adjective*'

伊 愈 食 愈 肥。

I <u>jú</u> chia̍h <u>jú</u> pûi.

他 越 吃 越 胖。

Tā <u>yuè</u> chī <u>yuè</u> pàng.

The <u>more</u> he eats, the fatt<u>er</u> he gets.

阮 愈 讀 冊 愈 愛睏。

Gún <u>jú</u> tha̍k chheh <u>jú</u> ài-khùn.

我們 越 看 書 越 想 睡。

Wǒmen <u>yuè</u> kàn shū <u>yuè</u> xiǎng shuì.

The <u>more</u> we read, the sleepi<u>er</u> we become.

7 Action verbs

Action verbs involve movement and physical engagement (such as running, singing, reading). Moreover, action verbs can be further subdivided into those that are open-ended with duration and those that involve a change-of-state.

7.1 Open-ended action verbs

Open-ended action verbs represent an action that is continuous in nature over time. The extent of the action may be left unspecified or may be indicated as a duration (fixed amount of time), a frequency (fixed number of repetitions), an end location, or an end time. Thus, the term *open-ended* does not mean that the specified action never ends, but rather that the action will happen in a continuous fashion for as long as is designated.

For example, the verb 走 **cháu** 'to run' indicates continuous running movement unless otherwise specified.

> 我 走。
> Góa cháu.
> 我 跑。
> Wǒ pǎo.
> I am running (*the movement of running continues*).
>
> DURATION (FIXED AMOUNT OF TIME)
> 我 走 四十 分鍾。
> Góa cháu sí-chàp hun-cheng.
> 我 跑 四十 分鐘。
> Wǒ pǎo sìshí fēnzhōng.
> I ran for 40 minutes (*the movement occurred only for a period of time*).

FREQUENCY (FIXED NUMBER OF REPETITIONS)

我 走 五 輾。

Góa cháu gō˙liàn.

我 跑 五 圈。

Wǒ pǎo wǔ quān.

I ran five laps *(the movement occurred for a specified number of times)*.

ENDPOINT (LOCATION)

我 走 到 公園。

Góa cháu kàu kong-hn̂g.

我 跑 到 公園。

Wǒ pǎo dào gōngyuán.

I ran until I reached the park *(the movement occurred until a destination)*.

ENDPOINT (TIME)

我 走 到 三點。

Góa cháu kàu saⁿ tiám.

我 跑 到 三點。

Wǒ pǎo dào sān diǎn.

I ran until it was three o'clock *(the movement occurred until a specific time)*.

Below is a table of some common open-ended action verbs.

TAIWANESE	MANDARIN	MEANING
睏 khún	睡 shuì	to sleep
看 khòaⁿ	看 kàn	to see, to look
聽 thiaⁿ	聽 tīng	to hear, to listen
講 kóng	說 shuō	to talk
走 cháu	跑 pǎo	to run
寫 siá	寫 xiě	to write
買 bé	買 mǎi	to buy
讀 thak̇	讀 dú	to read, to study
食 chiah̍	吃 chī	to eat
耍 sńg	玩 wán	to play
啉 lim	喝 hē	to drink
唱 chhiùⁿ	唱 chàng	to sing
畫 ōe	畫 huà	to draw

7.1.1 Specifying the duration

To specify the duration of an open-ended action verb, place the period of time after the verb. Often 久 **kú** 'long *(time)*' is added after the duration expression for emphasis.

> *action verb* + *duration* + (久)
> *action verb* + *duration* + (kú)
> '*action verb* for *duration*'

我 昨暗 睏 十點鐘 久。
Góa cha-àm khùn <u>cha̍p tiám-cheng kú</u>.
我 昨晚 睡了 十個 小時。
Wǒ zuówǎn shuìle <u>shí gè xiǎoshí</u>.
Last night I slept <u>for ten hours</u>.

怹 泅 十五 分鐘。
In siû <u>cha̍p-gō͘-hun-cheng</u>.
他們 游泳 十五 分鐘。
Tāmen yóuyǒng <u>shíwǔ fēnzhōng</u>.
They swam <u>for 15 minutes</u>.

Note that Mandarin does not add 久 **jiǔ** 'long *(time)*' for emphasis.

7.1.2 Specifying the frequency

To specify the frequency of an open-ended action verb, place the frequency after the verb. Taiwanese can use the generic terms 擺 **pái**, 改 **kái**, and 遍 **piàn** to express completed 'times'. Measure words that implicitly convey frequency for specific actions (such as 輾 **liàn** 'laps', 逝 **chōa** 'trips', 輪 **lûn** 'rounds') are also used.

> *action verb* + *frequency*
> '*action verb for frequency*'

伊 的 名，伊 寫 五十 擺。

I ê miâ, i siá gō·-cha̍p pái.

他 的 名字，他 寫 五十 次。

Tā de míngzì, tā xiě wǔshí cì.

He wrote his name fifty times.

吳 先生 已經 離婚過 三 改。

Gô·-sian-siⁿ í-keng lī-hun-kòe saⁿ kái.

吳 先生 已經 離婚過 三 遍。

Wú xiānshēng yǐjīng líhūnguò sān biàn.

Mr. Gou has already divorced three times.

阮 阿叔 有 去過 中國 五 遍。

Gún a-chek ū khì-kòe Tiong-kok gō· piàn.

我 叔叔 去過 中國 五 遍。

Wǒ shūshu qùguò Zhōngguó wǔ biàn.

My uncle has traveled to China five times.

7.1.3 Specifying the endpoint

To specify an endpoint of an open-ended action verb, place an endpoint based on time or location after the verb. Generally, the preposition **到 kàu** 'up to' is placed before the endpoint.

action verb + 到 + *endpoint (location)*

action verb + kàu + *endpoint (location)*

我 欲 行 到 郵局。

Góa beh kiâⁿ kàu iû-kio̍k.

我 要 走 到 郵局。

Wǒ yào zǒu dào yóujú.

I will walk to the post office.

恁 應該 讀 到 五十 頁。
Lín eng-kai tha̍k kàu gō·-cha̍p ia̍h.
你們 應該 讀 到 五十 頁。
Nǐmen yīnggāi dú dào wǔshí yè.
You all should read to page 50.

  action verb + 到 + *endpoint (time)*
  action verb + kàu + *endpoint (time)*

恁 會使 踮 外口 耍 到 暗時。
Lín ē-sái tàm gōa-kháu sńg kàu àm-sî.
你們 可以 在 戶外 玩 到 傍晚。
Nǐmen kěyǐ zài hùwài wán dào bàngwǎn.
You can play outside until dark.

我 欲 睏 到 明仔載 中晝。
Góa beh khùn kàu bîn-á-chài tiong-tàu.
我 要 睡 到 明天 中午。
Wǒ yào shuì dào míngtiān zhōngwǔ.
I want to sleep until noon tomorrow.

The directional complements indicating speaker perspective (**去** -**khì** 'away from the speaker' and **來** -**lâi** 'towards the speaker) can also be used in place of a preposition to indicate a geographic endpoint *(see 11.3.1 Directional complements indicating speaker perspective)*.

  action verb + 去 / 來 + *endpoint (location)*
  action verb + -khì / -lâi + *endpoint (location)*

咱 泅去 彼 板 橋。
Lán siû-khì hit pán kiô.
我們 游泳 去 那 座 橋 吧。
Wǒmen yóuyǒng qù nà zuò qiáo ba.
Let's swim to that bridge.

下班 了後，駛來 阮 兜。
Hā-pan liáu-āu, sái-lâi gún tau.

下班 之後，開來 我 家。
Xiàbān zhīhòu, kāilái wǒ jiā.

Drive to my house when you finish work.

7.1.4 Default objects

Some open-ended action verbs can take a direct object. A direct object receives the action of a verb.

    My dad threw the ball.

In the example above, 'the ball' is the direct object of the action 'throwing'.

While many action verbs in Taiwanese can take a direct object, some take what is known as a *default object*. These verbs always use the default object unless a more specific direct object replaces it. Generally the default object does not get translated into English.

阮 咧 食 飯。
Gún teh chiảh pn̄g.

我們 在 吃 飯。
Wǒmen zài chī fàn.

We are eating.

In the example above, **飯 pn̄g** 'rice' is the default object for the verb **食 chiảh** 'to eat'. The phrase **食飯 chiảh pn̄g** needs only be translated as 'to eat'.

If a more specific object is required, the default object is simply replaced by the more specific object.

阮 咧 食 麵。
Gún teh chiảh mī.

我們 在 吃 麵。
Wǒmen zài chī miàn.

We are eating noodles.

Note that a verb and its object are not bound together and may be separated by other grammatical elements.

Below is a table of some common action verbs with default objects.

TAIWANESE	MANDARIN	LITERAL TRANSLATION	MEANING
看冊 khòaⁿ chheh	看書 kàn shū	'see' 'book'	to read
讀冊 thàk chheh	讀書 dú shū	'study' 'book'	to study
講話 kóng ōe	說話 shuō huà	'talk' 'speech'	to speak
食飯 chiàh pn̄g	吃飯 chī fàn	'eat' 'rice'	to eat
唱歌 chhiùⁿ koa	唱歌 chàng gē	'sing' 'song'	to sing
寫字 siá jī	寫字 xiě zì	'write' 'character'	to write
行路 kiâⁿ lō·	走路 zǒu lù	'walk' 'road'	to walk

Generally, Mandarin and Taiwanese share similar default objects for action verbs. However, a few common verbs used in Taiwanese differ from their Mandarin counterparts in that they do not require default objects.

TAIWANESE	MANDARIN	LITERAL TRANSLATION (MANDARIN)	MEANING
睏 khùn	睡覺 shuì jiào	'sleep' 'nap'	to sleep
走 cháu	跑步 pǎo bù	'run' 'step'	to run
泅 siû	游泳 yóu yǒng	'swim' 'dive'	to swim

7.1.5 Including both objects and duration

When both the object and the duration are included with an action verb, there are two possible sentence patterns.

Pattern 1 - Making the duration a modifier

The duration can be turned into a modifier by adding the modifying particle **的 ê**. As a modifier, the duration can be placed between the verb and the object. **久 kú** can follow the duration for emphasis.

PATTERN 1

verb + ***duration*** + (久) + 的 + *object*

verb + ***duration*** + (kú) + ê + *object*

阿爸 講 <u>四十 分鐘 久 的</u> 話。

A-pa kóng <u>sì-cha̍p hun-cheng kú ê</u> ōe.

爸爸 說 <u>四十 分鐘 的</u> 話。

Bàba shuō <u>sìshí fēnzhōng de huà</u>.

Dad spoke <u>for forty minutes</u>.

阮 會 唱 <u>五 分鐘 的</u> 歌。

Gún ē chhiùⁿ <u>gō͘ hun-cheng ê</u> koa.

我們 會 唱 <u>五 分鐘 的</u> 歌。

Wǒmen huì chàng <u>wǔ fēnzhōng de gē</u>.

We will sing <u>for five minutes</u>.

Pattern 2 - Verb copying

The verb can be repeated after the *verb + object* phrase and then followed by the duration *(see 17.3 Verb copying)*. 久 **kú** can follow the duration for emphasis.

PATTERN 2

verb + *object* + *verb* + **duration** + (久)

verb + *object* + *verb* + **duration** + (kú)

阿爸 講 話 講 <u>四十分鐘 久</u>。

A-pa kóng ōe kóng <u>sì-cha̍p-hun-cheng kú</u>.

爸爸 說 話 說 <u>四十 分鐘</u>。

Bàba shuō huà shuō <u>sìshí fēnzhōng</u>.

Dad spoke <u>for forty minutes</u>.

阮 會 唱 歌 唱 <u>五 分鐘</u>。

Gún ē chhiùⁿ koa chhiùⁿ <u>gō͘ hun-cheng</u>.

我們 會 唱 歌 唱 <u>五 分鐘</u>。

Wǒmen huì chàng gē chàng <u>wǔ fēnzhōng</u>.

We will sing <u>for five minutes</u>.

7.1.6 Including both objects and frequency

When both the object and the frequency are included with an action verb, only a verb copying sentence pattern is possible *(see 17.3 Verb copying)*. The verb is repeated after the *verb + object* phrase and then followed by the frequency.

*verb + object + verb + **frequency***

恁 已經 唱 歌 唱 三 擺!
Lín í-keng chhiùⁿ koa chhiùⁿ saⁿ pái!
你們 已經 唱 歌 唱 三 次!
Nǐmen yǐjīng chàng gē chàng sān cì!
You have already sung three times!

你 一定 一 工 讀 冊 讀 兩 改。
Lí it-tēng chi̍t kang tha̍k chheh tha̍k nn̄g kái.
你 一定 一 天 讀 書 讀 兩 次。
Nǐ yīdìng yī tiān dú shū dú liǎng cì.
You must study twice a day.

7.2 Change-of-state action verbs

Whereas open-ended action verbs represent continuous actions over time, change-of-state action verbs describe actions that change immediately from one state to another. For example, the verb 坐 **chē** 'to sit' is an action that describes the change from the state of 'standing' to the state of 'sitting'.

This grouping includes verbs that inherently describe some type of change such as verbs of displacement (跳 **thiàu** 'to jump'), changes in posture (徛 **khiā** 'to stand up'), changes in status (畢業 **pit-gia̍p** 'to graduate'), and changes in condition (懷胎 **hôai-thai** 'to be pregnant').

Below is a table of some common change-of-state action verbs.

TAIWANESE	MANDARIN	MEANING
DISPLACEMENT		
跳 thiàu	跳 tiào	to jump
來 lâi	來 lái	to come
開 khui	開 kāi	to open up
挂 kòa	挂 guà	to hang up
穿 chhēng	穿 chuān	to wear (to put on)
POSTURE		
徛 khiā	站 zhàn	to stand up
坐 chē	坐 zuò	to sit down
覆 phak	趴 pā	to lie on one's stomach
STATUS / CONDITION		
畢業 pit-giȧp	畢業 bìyè	to graduate
死 sí	死 sǐ	to die
懷胎 hôai-thai	懷孕 huáiyùn	to be pregnant

7.2.1 Change-of-state verbs in the continuous aspect

For the most part, change-of-state action verbs share many properties with open-ended action verbs. However, because there is no duration, change-of-state action verbs have a slightly different meaning when placed in the continuous aspect, which describes an ongoing activity *(see 8.2 Continuous aspect)*.

The dynamic continuous aspect indicates that an action is in the middle of occurring *(see 8.2.1 Dynamic continuous aspect)*. However, with change-of-state action verbs, there is no duration of action. The dynamic continuous aspect marker 咧 **teh** cannot be used with a change-of-state action verb.

To focus on the process of transitioning from one state to another, a directional complement needs to be added to the change-of-state verb.

change-of-state action verb + directional complement

阿公 慢慢 徛起來。
A-kong bān-bān khiā--khí-lâi.
爺爺 慢慢 站起來。
Yéyé mànman zhànqǐlái.
Grandpa is slowly standing up.

The static continuous aspect indicates that an action is in a constant or persistent state *(see 8.2.2 Static continuous aspect)*. With change-of-state action verbs, the static continuous aspect emphasizes that, after the change of state has occurred, the subject remains in a particular state or condition.

change-of-state action verb + 咧

action verb + --leh

阿母 坐咧 膨椅頂。
A-bú chē--leh phòng-í-téng.
媽媽 坐著 沙發 上。
Māma zuòzhě shāfā shàng.
Mom is sitting on the sofa.

窗仔 開咧，所以 這馬 較 冷。
Thang-á khui--leh, só-í chit-má khah léng.
窗戶 開著，所以 現在 比較 冷。
Chuānghù kāizhe, suǒyǐ xiànzài bǐjiào lěng.
The window is open, so now it's colder.

7.2.2 Change-of-state verbs doubling as stative verbs

When suffixed with the static continuous aspect marker 咧 **--leh**, some change-of-state verbs can be interpreted as stative verbs *(see 9 Stative verbs)*.

CHANGE-OF-STATE INTERPRETATION

你 徛起來 的 時陣，注意 頭殼 莫 去 予 硞著。

Lí khiā-khí-lâi ê sî-chūn, chù-ì thâu-khak mài khì hō͘ khók--tióh.

你 站起來 的 時候，注意 頭 不 會 被 撞到。

Nǐ zhànqǐlái de shíhòu, zhùyì tóu bù huì bèi zhuàngdào.

When you stand up, be careful not to hit your head.

STATIVE INTERPRETATION

你 若 佇 遐 徛咧，你 會 予 雨 沃著。

Lí nā tī hia khiā--leh, lí ē hō͘ hō͘ ak-tióh.

你 如果 在 那裡 站著，你 會 被 雨 淋到。

Nǐ rúguǒ zài nàlǐ zhànzhe, nǐ huì bèi yǔ líndào.

If you stand there, you will get wet from the rain.

8 Aspect

Unlike English, Taiwanese does not inflect verbs to indicate tense (past, present, and future). Instead, Taiwanese uses a combination of context, time adverb, time expressions, modal verbs, and aspect markers to help clarify when an action occurs.

In fact, the verb in the sentence below can refer to any point in time.

> 伊 清 房間。
> I <u>chheng</u> pâng-keng.
> 他 清 房間。
> Tā <u>qīng</u> fángjiān.
> He <u>cleaned</u> / <u>cleans</u> / <u>will clean</u> the room.

Generally, context will make clear when an action has occurred. However, if more clarification is required, a time adverb or time expression (e.g. 'January 30', 'last week', or '5 o'clock') can be provided *(see 14.1.2 Time adverbs)*.

> TIME ADVERB
> 伊 連鞭 清 房間。
> I <u>liâm-mi</u> chheng pâng-keng.
> 他 馬上 清 房間。
> Tā <u>mǎshàng</u> qīng fángjiān.
> He will clean the room <u>soon</u>.

> TIME EXPRESSION
> 伊 昨昏 清 房間。
> I <u>cha-hng</u> chheng pâng-keng.
> 他 昨天 清 房間。
> Tā <u>zuótiān</u> qīng fángjiān.
> He cleaned the room <u>yesterday</u>.

Besides context, time adverbs, and time expressions to help provide clues as to when an event occurs, Taiwanese makes use of modal verbs and aspect markers.

For example, the modal verb 會 ē 'will' can be placed before the verb to convey an action occurring in the future tense *(see 12 Modal verbs)*.

> MODAL VERB
> 伊會清房間。
> I ē chheng pâng-keng.
> 他會清房間。
> Tā huì qīng fángjiān.
> He will clean the room.

Additionally, aspect markers can be used to help understand when an action occurs. Aspect describes how a verb is understood with regards to the flow of time. That is to say, aspect provides further information such as whether an action was completed, continues, repeats, has relevance to the present, etc.

In English, aspect is often considered a type of tense. The four kinds of past tense below actually highlight different aspects for the past tense.

> SIMPLE PAST *(ACTION COMPLETED WITHIN A SET TIME FRAME)*
> I ate.
> PAST PERFECT SIMPLE *(ACTION COMPLETED BEFORE A SPECIFIC TIME IN THE PAST)*
> I had eaten.
> PAST PROGRESSIVE *(ACTION CONTINUOUS BEFORE INTERRUPTION)*
> I was eating.
> PAST PERFECT PROGRESSIVE *(ACTION CONTINUOUS FOR A DURATION OF TIME)*
> I had been eating.

While Taiwanese does not have tense markers, there are ways to mark aspect.

> PERFECTIVE ASPECT
> 伊有清房間。
> I ū chheng pâng-keng.
> 他清了房間。
> Tā qīngle fángjiān.
> He cleaned the room.

EXPERIENTIAL ASPECT

伊 清過 房間。

I chheng-kòe pâng-keng.

他 清過 房間。

Tā qīngguò fángjiān.

He has cleaned rooms before.

ANTERIOR ASPECT

伊 清 房間 矣。

I chheng pâng-keng--ah.

他 清 房間 了。

Tā qīng fángjiān le.

He has cleaned the room.

While the three examples above all occurred in the past tense, the use of different aspect markers allows the speaker to stress how the action of 'cleaning' can be understood. The perfective aspect stresses that 'the cleaning' occurred as a simple completed action with nothing more implied. The experiential aspect stresses the fact of having had the experience of 'cleaning' before. And, the anterior aspect stresses that the 'cleaning' was completed but also indicates that knowing this information is now relevant to listener.

This chapter explores six aspects in Taiwanese: perfective (bounded events), continuous (ongoing occurrences), experiential (past experiences), anterior (current relevance), habitual (routine actions), and tentative (brief actions/tests).

8.1 Perfective aspect

The *perfective aspect* describes an action that can be considered a completed action within a set time frame. More accurately, the action can be understood in its entirety (beginning, middle, and end). Nothing more is implied other than the action having begun, occurred, and then finished. Because of this, the perfective aspect is often used for events that have occurred in the past. This is similar to the simple past tense in English.

Taiwanese makes use of two methods to express the perfective aspect:

- placing 有 ū before the verb

- placing a phase complement 了 **liáu**, 完 **ôan**, 好 **hó**, 煞 **soah** after the verb *(see 11.1.1 Phase complements indicating completion)*.

Note that Mandarin generally puts a verb into the perfective aspect by adding the suffix 了 -le.

8.1.1 Perfective aspect with 有 ū

One approach to expressing the perfective aspect is to place 有 ū immediately before the verb. This method can only be used when describing events that have occurred in the past. The negative form is 無 bô.

> 有 + verb
>
> ū + verb

> 伊 下早 有 唱 歌。
> I e-chái ū chhiùⁿ koa.
> 他 早上 唱了 歌。
> Tā zǎoshang chàngle gē.
> He sang this morning.

> 阮 阿姐 有 生 雙生仔。
> Gún a-chí ū seⁿ siang-seⁿ-á.
> 我 姐姐 生了 雙胞胎。
> Wǒ jiějiě shēngle shuāngbāotāi.
> My older sister gave birth to twins.

> 謝 先生 無 共 我 借 錢。
> Siā--sian-siⁿ bô kā góa chioh chîⁿ.
> 謝 先生 沒有 跟 我 借 錢。
> Xiè xiānshēng méiyǒu gēn wǒ jiè qián.
> Mr. Sia didn't borrow money from me.

The perfective aspect may only be used with action verbs. Stative verbs, adjectives, and modal verbs are not easily understood as bound and completed actions. As a result, they cannot take a perfective marker. Instead, these types of verbs must use time expressions to describe occurrences in the past.

STATIVE VERB

我 舊年 知 愛 去 佗位。

Góa kū-nî chai ài khì tó-ūi.

我 去年 知道 要 去 哪裡。

Wǒ qùnián zhīdào yào qù nǎlǐ.

Last year, I knew where to go.

ADJECTIVE

伊 昨暗 真 忝。

I cha-àm chin thiám.

她 昨晚 很 累。

Tā zuówǎn hěn lèi.

Last night she was tired.

MODAL VERB

兩 禮拜前, 阮 會使 入去。

Nn̄g lé-pài-chêng, gún ē-sài jip-khì.

兩 個 禮拜 以前, 我們 可以 進去。

Liǎng gè lǐbài yǐqián, wǒmen kěyǐ jìnqù.

Two weeks ago, we were allowed to go inside.

Notice that Standard Mandarin does not employ the use of **有 yǒu** before verbs for the perfective aspect. However, some speakers of Taiwan Mandarin (due to the influence of Taiwanese), will include **有 yǒu** in their speech to mark the perfective aspect.

STANDARD MANDARIN

我 昨天 寫了 一 封 信。

Wǒ zuótiān xiěle yī fēng xìn.

TAIWAN MANDARIN

我 昨天 有 寫 一 封 信。

Wǒ zuótiān yǒu xiě yī fēng xìn.

Yesterday, I wrote a letter.

8.1.2 Perfective aspect with phase complements

A second approach to expressing the perfective aspect in Taiwanese is to use a phase complement (了 **liáu**, 完 **ôan**, 好 **hó**, 煞 **soah**) to indicate that the action of the verb has ended *(see 11.1.1 Phase complements indicating completion)*.

VERB + PHASE COMPLEMENT

伊 下早 歌 唱好。
I e-chái koa chhiùⁿ hó.
他 早上 唱了 歌。
Tā zǎoshang chàngle gē.
He sang this morning.

阮 阿姐 雙生仔 生了。
Gún a-chí siang-seⁿ-á seⁿ liáu.
我 姐姐 生了 雙胞胎。
Wǒ jiějiě shēngle shuāngbāotāi.
My older sister gave birth to twins.

In most contexts the usage of 有 **ū** or one of the phase complements to indicate the perfective aspect is interchangeable. However, because both 有 **ū** and some of the phase complements have different grammatical uses, there can also be different interpretations for the same sentence.

PERFECTIVE READING USING 有 Ū

我 有 啉 紅酒。
Góa ū lim âng-chiú.
我 喝了 紅酒。
Wǒ hēle hóngjiǔ.
I drank red wine.

PERFECTIVE READING USING PHASE COMPLEMENT

我 啉 了 紅酒。
Góa lim liáu âng-chiú.
我 喝了 紅酒。
Wǒ hēle hóngjiǔ.
I drank red wine.

EMPHATIC READING OF 有 Ū

我 <u>有 啉</u> 紅酒!

Góa <u>ū lim</u> âng-chiú!

我 有 喝 紅酒 啊!

Wǒ <u>yǒu hē</u> hóngjiǔ <u>a</u>!

I <u>*did* drink</u> red wine!

HABITUAL READING OF 有 Ū

我 <u>有 咧 啉</u> 紅酒。

Góa <u>ū teh lim</u> âng-chiú.

我 經常 喝 紅酒。

Wǒ <u>jīngcháng hē</u> hóngjiǔ.

I <u>do drink</u> red wine.

RESULTATIVE COMPLEMENT READING

我 紅酒 <u>啉 了</u> 矣。

Góa âng-chiú <u>lim liáu</u>--ah.

我 紅酒 喝 光 了。

Wǒ hóngjiǔ <u>hē guāng</u> le.

I <u>drank up all</u> the red wine.

Note that Mandarin must use an adverb such as **經常 jīngcháng** 'regularly' to indicate the habitual reading of its verbs.

8.2 Continuous aspect

The continuous aspect describes an activity that is ongoing. The term 'activity' is used here to include both physical movements described by action verbs (such as hitting or swimming) and active engagement described by some stative verbs (such as learning or explaining).

In some cases, the continuous aspect is similar to the English progressive tense, which adds the '-ing' suffix to a verb along with a form of 'to be' as a helping verb ('Julie <u>is talking</u>.').

In Taiwanese, this ongoing activity can be seen from two slightly different perspectives. A *dynamic perspective* examines an activity that is in the middle of happening ('She is waving her hand.'), while the *static perspective* describes a continuous condition ('The picture is hanging on the wall.'). Each perspective has a corresponding grammatical construction.

8.2.1 Dynamic continuous aspect

The dynamic version of the continuous aspect describes an activity that is already in progress.

8.2.1.1 Dynamic continuous aspect marker 咧 teh

Dynamic continuous aspect can be used with action verbs and stative verbs that involve active engagement.

A verb can be put into the dynamic continuous aspect, by placing 咧 **teh** before the verb (咧 may also be pronounced **leh**; however, the pronunciation **teh** is used in this text to help distinguish from the use of 咧 **--leh** as a static continuous aspect marker). Depending on emphasis, 咧 **teh** can also be separated from the main verb by other grammatical elements like adverbs or prepositions. The negative form places 無 **bô** before 咧 **teh**.

> 咧 + *verb*
>
> teh + *verb*

> 伊 敲 予 我 時，我 咧 食 飯。
> I khà hō͘ góa sî, góa teh chiàh pn̄g.
> 她 打 給 我 時，我 在 吃 飯。
> Tā dǎ gěi wǒ shí, wǒ zài chī fàn.
> I was eating when she called.

賴教授 咧 改 阮 的 文章。

Lōa kàu-siū teh kái gún ê bûn-chiong.

賴教授 在 改 我們 的 文章。

Lài jiàoshòu zài gǎi wǒmen de wénzhāng.

Professor Loa is grading our papers.

哪 恁 無 咧 照顧 囝仔？

Ná lín bô teh chiàu-kò͘ gín-á?

為甚麼 你們 沒有 在 照顧 小孩？

Wèishènme nǐmen méiyǒu zài zhàogù xiǎohái?

Why aren't you taking care of the children?

怹 咧 好好仔 準備 選舉。

In teh hó-hó-á chún-pī sóan-kí.

他們 在 好好 準備 選舉。

Tāmen zài hǎohǎo zhǔnbèi xuǎnjǔ.

They are preparing for the election.

8.2.1.2 Emphasizing the immediacy of an action

While the use of 咧 teh already stresses that an activity is in progress, the immediacy can be further emphasized by placing 當 tng- before 咧 teh to form 當咧 tng-teh. Alternate forms include 拄咧 tú-teh and 佇咧 tī-leh (note the slight change in pronunciation). These forms can only occur when referring to events in the present tense *(see 26.3 Ongoing actions)*.

當咧 + *verb*

tng-teh + *verb*

'to be *verb*-ing right now'

學生 當咧 考試，所以 請 恬恬 行 路。

Ha̍k-seng tng-teh khó-chhì, só-í chhiáⁿ tiām-tiām kiâⁿ lō͘.

學生 正在 考試，所以 請 悄悄 走 路。

Xuéshēng zhèngzài kǎoshì, suǒyǐ qǐng qiāoqiāo zǒu lù.

The students are taking a test, so please walk quietly.

阮 拄咧 做 餅，所以 較 緊 過來。

Gún tú-teh chò piáⁿ, só-í khah kín kòe-lâi.

我們 正在 做 餅乾，所以 快 過來。

Wǒmen zhèngzài zuò bǐnggān, suǒyǐ kuài guòlái.

We are making cookies so come over quickly.

陳 小姐 佇咧 和 人客 講 話，莫 鯁 伊。

Tân sió-chiá tī-leh hām lâng-kheh kóng ōe, mài chak i.

陳 小姐 正在 和 客人 說 話，不要 打擾 她。

Chén xiǎojiě zhèngzài hé kèrén shuō huà, bùyào dǎrǎo tā.

Ms. Tan is speaking with a client. Don't disturb her.

Note in Mandarin, the equivalent emphasis on immediacy can be expressed by placing 正 **zhèng** before 在 **zài** to form 正在 **zhèngzài**. However, note that Taiwanese does not have an equivalent end-of-sentence particle such as the Mandarin 呢 **ne** to emphasize the dynamic continuous aspect.

8.2.2 Static continuous aspect

The static version of the continuous aspect describes an action that is in a constant state. The verb can be describing a manner of existence (such as lights hanging from the ceiling), a persistent posture (such as lying on the grass), or repetitive motions without an implied ending (such as chewing gum).

8.2.2.1 Describing a manner of existence

The static continuous aspect marker 咧 **--leh** can be used to describe a manner of existence. When an action has been performed on an object, the object is considered to be in a continual state as a consequence of the verb (even when movement has ceased). By adding the suffix 咧 **--leh** to the verb, the current manner of existence is made clear.

verb + 咧

verb + --leh

一條長褲 囥咧 佇 椅仔頂。
Chit thiâu tn̂g-khò͘ khǹg--leh tī í-á-téng.
一條長褲 放 在 椅子 上。
Yī tiáo chángkù fàng zài yǐzi shàng.
A pair of pants is hanging on the chair.

我 的 珠寶 攏 包咧。
Góa ê chu-pó lóng pau--leh.
我 的 飾品 都 包著。
Wǒ de shìpǐn dōu bāozhe.
All of my jewelry is wrapped.

窗仔 愛 關咧 才 袂予 蠓仔 飛入去。
Thang-á ài koaiⁿ--leh chiah bē hō͘ báng-á poe--jip-khì.
窗戶 要 關起來 才 不會 讓 蚊子 飛進去。
Chuānghù yào guānqǐlái cái bù huì ràng wénzi fēijìnqù.
The windows need to be closed, so mosquitoes don't fly in.

Mandarin uses the suffix **著 -zhe** to indicate static continuous aspect. However, in some contexts, Taiwanese tends to use the static continuous aspect, while Mandarin prefers a resultative complement.

我 袂當 駛出去，因為 有 人 共 我 擋咧。
Góa bē-tàng sái--chhut-khì, in-ūi ū lâng kā góa tòng--leh.
我 不能 開出去，因為 有 人 把 我 攔住。
Wǒ bùnéng kāichūqù, yīnwèi yǒu rén bǎ wǒ lánzhù.
I can't drive out because someone is blocking me.

8.2.2.2 Describing a continued posture

A static situation also occurs with verbs of posture. Verbs that describe posture (such as sitting, kneeling, or lying down) can be suffixed with **咧 --leh** when the posture is maintained.

verb + 咧

verb + --leh

伊 倒咧 佇 眠床頂。

I tó--leh tī bîn-chhn̂g-téng.

她 在 床 上 躺著。

Tā zài chuáng shàng tǎngzhe.

She is lying on the bed.

彼 个 查埔 囡仔 跍咧 揣 水雞。

Hit ê cha-poˈ gín-á khû--leh chhōe chúi-ke.

那個 男孩子 蹲著 找 青蛙。

Nàge nánháizi dūnzhe zhǎo qīngwā.

The little boy is squatting by the creek looking for frogs.

Mandarin often uses the corresponding static continuous aspect marker **著 -zhe** to indicate a background action when two actions are occurring simultaneously. While Mandarin allows **著 -zhe** to be suffixed to a variety of verbs, Taiwanese can only attach **咧 --leh** to verbs of posture when signaling a background action *(see 34.2.1 Indicating a constant state with verb suffix 咧 --leh)*.

伊 規 晡 攏 徛咧 等 人客。

I kui poˈ lóng khiā--leh tán lâng-kheh.

他 整 個 下午 都 站著 等 客人。

Tā zhěng gè xiàwǔ dōu zhànzhe děng kèrén.

He has been standing all afternoon waiting for customers.

8.2.2.3 Describing repetitive movements

Continued movements with small repetitive motions (such as clapping, cutting, chewing) may also be suffixed with **咧 --leh**. Often the verb is reduplicated.

verb + *verb* + 咧

verb + *verb* + --leh

這 種 藥仔 愛 先 哺哺咧 才 會當 吞落去。
Chit chióng io̍h-á ài seng pō͘-pō͘--leh chiah ē-tàng thun--lo̍h-khì.
這 種 藥 得 先 嚼一嚼 才 能 吞下去。
Zhè zhǒng yào děi xiān juéyījué cái néng tūnxiàqù.
This kind of medicine needs to be chewed before swallowing.

共 這 隻 狗 掠 予 牢，我 欲 共 伊 的 毛 鉸鉸咧。
Kā chit chiah káu lia̍h hō͘ tiâu, góa beh kā i ê mn̂g ka-ka--leh.
把 這 隻 狗 抓著，我 要 把 牠 的 毛 剪一剪。
Bǎ zhè zhī gǒu zhuāzhe, wǒ yào bǎ tā de máo jiǎnyījiǎn.
Hold the dog tightly. I want to trim its fur.

8.2.3 Verbs exhibiting both dynamic and static aspects

With some verbs, both dynamic and static continuous aspects can be used. Note the difference in meaning between the dynamic and static forms.

DYNAMIC CONTINUOUS ASPECT
伊 咧 戴 安全帽。
I teh tì an-chôan-bō.
她 在 戴 安全帽。
Tā zài dài ānquánmào.
She is putting on a helmet.

STATIC CONTINUOUS ASPECT
伊 戴咧 安全帽。
I tì--leh an-chôan-bō.
她 戴著 安全帽。
Tā dàizhe ānquánmào.
She is wearing a helmet.

莫 齪 伊，伊 這馬 咧 記 路。
Mài chak i, i chit-má teh kì lō͘.
不要 打擾 他，他 正在 在 記 路。
Bùyào dǎrǎo tā, tā zhèngzài zài jì lù.
Don't bother him. He's memorizing the way.

毋免 煩惱，伊 路 已經 攏 記咧。
M̄-bián hôan-ló, i lō͘ í-keng lóng kì--leh.
不要 煩惱，他 已經 都 記住 路了。
Bùyào fánnǎo, tā yǐjīng dōu jìzhù lù le.
Don't worry. He's memorized the way.

8.3 Experiential aspect

The experiential aspect describes an action that has been experienced at some unspecified point in the past. Notice that non-repeatable actions (such as dying, graduating, or aging) cannot be placed in the experiential aspect.

Taiwanese has three methods to express the experiential aspect: placing **捌 bat** before the verb, placing **過 -kòe** after the verb, or using a combination of both **捌 bat** and **過 -kòe**. While all three methods are interchangeable, the tendency is to use the combination of both **捌 bat** and **過 -kòe** for longer utterances.

Mandarin can only indicate the experiential aspect by placing **過 -guò** after the verb.

8.3.1 Experiential aspect with 捌 bat

The aspect marker **捌 bat**, which is derived from the verb meaning 'to be familiar with', can be placed before a verb to indicate the experiential aspect. The negative form is **毋捌 m̄ bat**. When put in the negative form, **從來 chêng-lâi** 'from the beginning' or an adverb with a similar meaning is frequently added to lend the meaning of 'never'.

> 捌 + *verb*
>
> bat + *verb*

> 我 捌 食 臭 豆腐。
> Góa bat chiah chhàu tāu-hū.
> 我 吃過 臭 豆腐。
> Wǒ chīguò chòu dòufu.
> I have eaten stinky tofu before.

> 伊 從來 毋 捌 駛 車。
> I chêng-lâi m̄ bat sái chhia.
> 她 從來 沒 開過 車。
> Tā cónglái méi kāiguò chē.
> She has never driven a car before.

8.3.2 Experiential aspect with 過 -kòe

The suffix **過 -kòe** can be placed after the verb to indicate the experiential aspect. The character **過** literally means 'to cross, to go over' but can be used in a more figurative sense to have 'gone over' an experience. Often **有 ū** is added as an emphasis marker *(see 10.2.4 有 ū as an emphasis marker)*. The negative form of the **過 -kòe** construction is to place **無 bô** before the verb. When put in the negative form, **從來 chêng-lâi** 'from the beginning' or an adverb with a similar meaning is frequently added to lend the meaning of 'never'. Additionally, 過 --kòe is placed in the neutral tone at the end of clauses or sentences and preceded by a double-hyphen.

(有) + *verb* + 過

(ū) + *verb* + -kòe

我 有 食 過 臭 豆腐。
Góa ū chiah-kòe chhàu tāu-hū.
我 吃過 臭 豆腐。
Wǒ chīguò chòu dòufu.
I have eaten stinky tofu before.

伊 從來 無 駛過 車。
I chêng-lâi bô sái-kòe chhia.
她 從來 沒 開過 車。
Tā cónglái méi kāiguò chē.
She has never driven a car before.

8.3.3 Experiential aspect with both 捌 bat and 過 -kòe

The aspect marker 捌 **bat** and verb suffix 過 **-kòe** can be used in combination to indicate the experiential aspect.

捌 + *verb* + 過

bat + *verb* + -kòe

我 捌 食 過 臭 豆腐。
Góa bat chiah-kòe chhàu tāu-hū.
我 吃過 臭 豆腐。
Wǒ chīguò chòu dòufu.
I have eaten stinky tofu before.

伊 從來 毋 捌 駛過 車。

I chêng-lâi m̄ bat sái-kòe chhia.

她 從來 沒 開過 車。

Tā cónglái méi kāiguò chē.

She has never driven a car before.

8.4 Anterior aspect

The anterior aspect describes actions that started in the past but have continuing relevance in the present ('She has eaten (*no need to feed her*)', 'We have cleaned our room (*can we play now?*)'). In English, a tense that similarly accomplishes this is commonly referred to as the perfect tense, but this text will use 'anterior aspect' to prevent confusion with the 'perfective aspect' mentioned in *(see 8.1 Perfective aspect)*. The anterior aspect can also be used to mark a change in situation or relay new information to the listener.

Taiwanese marks the anterior aspect by placing the particle 矣 --ah at the end of a clause or sentence. This particle 矣 --ah is always in the neutral tone. The negation of the anterior aspect is 未 bōe (also pronounced bē) but is more commonly seen as part of the compound 猶未 iáu-bōe 'not yet'.

In Mandarin, the equivalent anterior aspect marker is the end-of-sentence particle 了 le.

TAIWANESE	MANDARIN	MEANING
AFFIRMATIVE		
矣 --ah	了 -le	'has / have + *verb*-ed'
NEGATIVE		
猶未 iáu-bōe	還沒 háiměi	'hasn't / haven't + *verb*-ed + yet'

8.4.1 Anterior aspect particle 矣 --ah

The anterior aspect particle 矣 --ah only occurs at the end of a clause or sentence and signals that there is relevance in the present arising from a change in situation or new information to the listener. This information can also be emphasized by optionally adding the adverb 已經 í-keng 'already'.

 (已經) + *verb* + …矣

 (í-keng) + *verb* + …--ah

 '(already) has/have *verb*'

咱 已經 唱過 這 條 歌 矣。
Lán í-keng chhiùⁿ-kòe chit tiâu koa--ah.
我們 已經 唱過 這 首 歌 了。
Wǒmen yǐjīng chàngguò zhè shǒu gē le.
We have already sung this song.

外口 天 暗 矣。
Gōa-kháu thiⁿ àm--ah.
外面 天 黑 了。
Wàimiàn tiān hēi le.
Outside the sky has gotten dark.

楊 先生 頭路 猶未 揣著。
Iûⁿ--sian-siⁿ thâu-lō͘ iáu-bōe chhōe--tio̍h.
楊 先生 還沒 找到 工作。
Yáng xiānshēng háiméi zhǎodào gōngzuò.
Mr. Iunn hasn't found a job yet.

The Taiwanese anterior aspect particle 矣 --ah is analogous to the Mandarin end-of-sentence particle 了 le.

8.4.2 Anterior with other aspects

The anterior aspect can co-occur with other aspects.

ANTERIOR AND CONTINUOUS ASPECTS

伊 這馬 咧 行 路 矣。
I chit-má teh kiâⁿ lō͘--ah.
他 現在 在 走 路 了。
Tā xiànzài zài zǒu lù le.
He is walking now (*as opposed to not before*).

ANTERIOR AND EXPERIENTIAL ASPECTS

伊 已經 捌 講過 矣。

I í-keng bat kóng--kòe--ah.

她 已經 說過 了。

Tā yǐjīng shuōguò le.

She has already said that before.

ANTERIOR AND TENTATIVE ASPECTS

恁 已經 共 塗跤 掃掃 矣。

In í-keng kā thô͘-kha sàu-sàu--ah.

他們 已經 把 地板 打掃 了。

Tāmen yǐjīng bǎ dìbǎn dǎsǎo le.

They have already cleaned the floor a little.

ANTERIOR AND HABITUAL ASPECTS

我 已經 有 咧 運動 矣。

Góa í-keng ū teh ūn-tōng--ah.

我 經常 運動 了。

Wǒ jīngcháng yùndòng le.

I have already been exercising (*regularly*).

ANTERIOR AND PERFECTIVE ASPECTS

阮 阿兄 大學 有 畢業 矣。

Gún a-hiaⁿ tāi-ha̍k ū pit-gia̍p--ah.

我 哥哥 是 大學 畢業 了。

Wǒ gēgē shì dàxué bìyè le.

My older brother has graduated college (*emphasizes he's a college graduate*).

While both the perfective and anterior aspects can refer to actions that happened in the past, the focus differs. The perfective aspect underscores the completion of an action while the anterior aspect looks at how an action (completed or not) has relevance to the present.

Because Mandarin uses the same character for both the perfective 了 -**le** and the end-of-sentence anterior aspect 了 **le**, there are instances where a sentence could end in 了 **le** and have either or both interpretations concurrently. This can occur when a verb is at the end of a sentence.

8.5 Habitual aspect

8.5.1 Habitual actions in the present

To indicate habitual actions in the present, **有 ū** combined with the dynamic continuous aspect marker **咧 teh** can be placed in front of the verb. Note that if a time expression is provided, the addition of **有咧 ū teh** before the verb is optional.

有 + 咧 + *verb*

ū + teh + *verb*

恁 拜六 有咧 騎 車 去 公園。

In pài-la̍k ū teh khiâ chhia khì kong-hn̂g.

他們 禮拜六 經常 騎 車 去 公園。

Tāmen lǐbàiliù jīngcháng qí chē qù gōngyuán.

They ride their bicycles to the park on Saturdays.

早起時 伊 做 瑜伽。

Chá-khí-sî i chò jû-ka.

早上 的 時候 他 做 瑜伽。

Zǎoshang de shíhòu tā zuò yújiā.

In the mornings he does yoga.

Note that Mandarin generally does not have a direct equivalent to mark the habitual aspect in the present. Instead, an adverb such as **經常 jīngcháng** 'regularly' can be used to convey a habitual action.

However, similar to Taiwanese, in Taiwan Mandarin **有在 yǒu zài** is used colloquially to express the habitual aspect.

TAIWAN MANDARIN

他們 禮拜六 有在 騎 車 去 公園。

Tāmen lǐbàiliù yǒu zài qí chē qù gōngyuán.

They ride their bicycles to the park on Saturdays.

8.5.2 Habitual actions in the past

To describe the habitual past ('I used to swim' or 'She used to sing'), a time expression can be added to emphasize that an action occurred regularly in the past.

> *time expression (past)* + 有 + 咧 + *verb*
>
> *time expression (past)* + ū + teh + *verb*
>
> 'used to *verb*'

我 五冬前 有 咧 啉 咖啡。
Góa gō·-tang-chêng ū teh lim ka-pi.
我 五 年 前 經常 喝 咖啡。
Wǒ wǔ nián qián jīngcháng hē kāfēi.
Five years ago, I used to drink coffee.

An alternate form to express habitual aspect in the past is to use a combination of time expressions, relative frequency adverbs, and the referential adverb 攏 **lóng**, which are all placed before the verb *(see 27.3 Habitual actions in the past)*.

> *time expression* + *relative frequency adverb* + 攏 + *verb*
>
> *time expression* + *relative frequency adverb* + lóng + *verb*
>
> '*time* ago, used to always *verb frequency*'

我 五冬前 逐日 攏 啉 咖啡。
Góa gō·-tang-chêng ta̍k-ji̍t lóng lim ka-pi.
我 五 年 前 每天 都 喝 咖啡。
Wǒ wǔ nián qián měitiān dōu hē kāfēi.
Five years ago, I used to always drink coffee everyday.

8.6 Tentative aspect

The tentative aspect looks at actions that are only performed 'for a little while' or 'to try out something'. Note that only action verbs can be placed in the tentative aspect. Taiwanese has four methods of expressing the tentative aspect: reduplication of the verb, adding the phrase 一下 **chit-ē**, adding the phrase 看覓 **khòaⁿ-māi**, and attaching the verb to 試 **chhì** 'to try'.

Similar to Taiwanese, Mandarin can express the tentative aspect with reduplication of the verb, the addition of the phrase 一下 **yīxià**, and verb reduplication with the suffix 看 **-kàn**. However, the Mandarin construction *verb* + 一 **yī** + *verb* (看一看 **kànyikàn**, 走一走 **zǒuyizǒu**) does not have an exact equivalent in Taiwanese.

8.6.1 Reduplicating the verb

Reduplicating a verb suggests that the action is performed for a short unspecified amount of time. The reason for performing an action in the tentative aspect is not made explicit, but the reason can range from not sufficient time to hesitancy.

verb + *verb*

食了了後，咱來公園 行行。
Chia̍h liáu liáu-āu, lán lâi kong-hn̂g kiâⁿ-kiâⁿ.
吃飯之後，我們來 走走 吧。
Chī fàn zhīhòu, wǒmen lái zǒuzǒu ba.
After we eat, let's go walk a little.

買這本冊進前，我欲先 看看。
Bé chit pún chheh chìn-chêng, góa beh seng khòaⁿ-khòaⁿ.
買這本書之前，我要先 看看。
Mǎi zhè běn shū zhīqián, wǒ yào xiān kànkàn.
I want to read this book a little before I buy it.

這 罐 牛奶 敢 有 歹去 矣? 共 我 鼻鼻 咧。
Chit kòan gû-leng kám ū pháiⁿ--khì--ah? Kā góa phīⁿ-phīⁿ--leh.

這 瓶 牛奶 壞了 沒 有? 幫 我 聞聞看。
Zhè píng niúnǎi huàile méi yǒu? Bāng wǒ wénwénkàn.

Can you sniff this milk for me to see if it's gone bad?

8.6.2 Adding the phrase 一下 --chit-ē

Placing the phrase 一下 **--chit-ē** 'a little bit' after the verb shortens the duration of the action and can indicate the tentative aspect. Note that the phrase 一下 **--chit-ē** is always in the neutral tone when suffixed to a verb.

   verb + 一下

   verb + --chit-ē

食 了 了後,咱 來 公園 行 一下。
Chiảh liáu liáu-āu, lán lâi kong-hñg kiâⁿ--chit-ē.

吃 飯 之後,我們 來 走 一下 吧。
Chī fàn zhīhòu, wǒmen lái zǒu yīxià ba.

After we eat, let's go walk a little.

買 這 本 冊 進前,我 欲 先 看 一下。
Bé chit pún chheh chìn-chêng, góa beh seng khòaⁿ--chit-ē.

買 這 本 書 之前,我 要 先 看 一下。
Mǎi zhè běn shū zhīqián, wǒ yào xiān kàn yīxià.

I want to read this book a little before I buy it.

這 罐 牛奶 敢 有 歹去 矣? 共 我 鼻 一下 看。
Chit kòan gû-leng kám ū pháiⁿ--khì--ah? Kā góa phīⁿ--chit-ē khòaⁿ?

這 瓶 牛奶 壞了 沒 有?幫 我 聞 一下 看。
Zhè píng niúnǎi huàile méi yǒu? Bāng wǒ wén yīxià kàn?

Can you sniff this milk for me to see if it's gone bad?

8.6.3 Adding the phrase 看覓 khòaⁿ-māi

Placing the phrase 看覓 khòaⁿ-māi after the verb can indicate the tentative aspect but only to express a desire 'to test out' or 'to try out'. Note if the main verb itself is 看 khòaⁿ 'to look, to read', only the suffix 覓 -māi needs to be added.

verb + 看覓

verb + khòaⁿ-māi

食了了後，咱來去新公園行看覓。
Chiàh liáu liáu-āu, lán lâi khì sin kong-hn̂g kiâⁿ khòaⁿ-māi.
吃飯之後，我們去新公園走走看吧。
Chī fàn zhīhòu, wǒmen qù xīn gōngyuán zǒuzǒu kàn ba.
After we eat, let's go for a walk and check out the new park.

買這本冊進前，我欲先看覓。
Bé chit pún chheh chìn-chêng, góa beh seng khòaⁿ-māi.
買這本書之前，我要先看看。
Mǎi zhè běn shū zhīqián, wǒ yào xiān kànkàn.
I want to read this book a little before I buy it.

這罐牛奶敢有歹去矣? 共我鼻看覓。
Chit kòan gû-leng kám ū pháiⁿ--khì--ah? Kā góa phīⁿ khòaⁿ-māi.
這瓶牛奶壞了沒有? 幫我聞聞看。
Zhè píng niúnǎi huàile méi yǒu? Bāng wǒ wénwénkàn.
Can you sniff this milk for me to see if it's gone bad?

8.6.4 Attaching verbs to 試 chhì

Placing 試 **chhì** 'to try' before a verb can also indicate the tentative aspect.

> 試 + *verb*
>
> chhì- + *verb*

我 若 無 <u>試啉</u>，我 按怎 知 這 罐 紅酒 有 好 啉？
Góa nā bô <u>chhì-lim</u>, góa án-nóa chai chit kòan âng-chiú ū hó lim?
如果 我 沒有 <u>喝喝看</u>，我 怎麼 知道 這 瓶 紅酒 好不好 喝？
Rúguǒ wǒ méiyǒu <u>hēhēkàn</u>, wǒ zěnme zhīdào zhè píng hóngjiǔ hǎobùhǎo hē?
If I don't <u>sip</u> any, how do I know if this bottle of red wine is any good?

你 先 <u>試穿</u> 這 領 褲，無 適合，我 閣 揣 一 領。
Lí seng <u>chhì-chhēng</u> chit niá khò, bô sek-hảp, góa koh chhōe chit niá.
你 先 <u>穿穿看</u> 這 件 褲子，不 適合 的 話，我 再 找 一 件。
Nǐ xiān <u>chuānchuānkàn</u> zhè jiàn kùzi, bù shìhé de huà, wǒ zài zhǎo yī jiàn.
First <u>try on</u> this pair of pants. If they don't suit you, then I'll find another pair.

試 **chhì** can also be followed by 一下 **--chit-ē** or 看覓 **khòaⁿ-māi** as a general phrase to express 'to try out' or 'to test out'.

我 拄才 煮 好 的 湯，你 敢 欲 <u>試一下</u>?
Góa tú-chiah chú hó ê thng, lí kám beh <u>chhì--chit-ē</u>?
我 剛才 煮完 的 湯，你 要不要 <u>喝喝看</u>？
Wǒ gāngcái zhǔwán de tāng, nǐ yàobùyào <u>hēhēkàn</u>?
Do you want <u>to try a little</u> of the soup I just finished making?

這 領 膨紗衫，<u>試 看覓</u>。
Chit niá phòng-se-saⁿ, <u>chhì khòaⁿ-māi</u>.
這 件 毛衣，<u>試試看</u>。
Zhè jiàn máoyī, <u>shìshìkàn</u>.
<u>Try on</u> this sweater.

Note that Taiwan Mandarin tends to use the structure *verb* + *verb* + 看 **kàn** to indicate the tentative aspect, while in Standard Mandarin the structure tends to be 試 **shì** ＋ 試 **shì** + *verb*.

TAIWAN MANDARIN	STANDARD MANDARIN
verb + *verb* + 看	試 ＋ 試 + *verb*
verb + *verb* + kàn	shì ＋ shì + *verb*
吃吃看	試試吃
chīchīkàn	shìshìchī

to try eating, to taste

8.7 Summary of aspect

PERFECTIVE
有 ū (無 bô) + *verb*
verb + 了 liáu
verb + 完 ôan
verb + 好 hó
verb + 煞 soah

CONTINUOUS
DYNAMIC
咧 teh + *verb*
STATIC
verb + 咧 --leh

EXPERIENTIAL
捌 bat + *verb*
verb + 過 -kòe
捌 bat + *verb* + 過 -kòe

ANTERIOR
verb + 矣 --ah

HABITUAL
PRESENT
有咧 ū teh + *verb*
PAST
time expression + 有咧 ū teh + *verb*
time expression + *relative frequency* + 攏 lóng + *verb*

TENTATIVE
verb + *verb*
verb + 一下 chit-ē
verb + 看覓 khòaⁿ-māi
試 chhì + *verb*

9 Stative Verbs

Stative verbs generally involve actions dealing with the mind, including cognition (to know, to remember, to understand), intentions (to plan, to prepare, to decide), emotions (to like or love, to fear, to be happy), and bodily sensations (to be hungry, to be thirsty, to be sore).

Because stative verbs in essence describe a 'state', they often share properties with adjectives. Similar to adjectives, stative verbs may be modified by intensifiers, used in comparison structures, and followed by extent structures. Unlike action verbs, stative verbs cannot be placed in the perfective or experiential aspects. Additionally, stative verbs cannot be followed by durational or frequency complements.

9.1 Common stative verbs

Below is a table of common stative verbs.

TAIWANESE	MANDARIN	MEANING
COGNITION		
知影 chai-iáⁿ	知道 zhīdào	to know
相信 siong-sìn	相信 xiāngxìn	to believe
會記得 ē-kì-tit	記得 jìde	to remember
袂記得 bē-kì-tit	忘記 wàngjì	to forget
了解 liáu-kái	了解 liǎojiě	to understand
INTENTIONS		
拍算 phah-sǹg	打算 dǎsuàn	to plan
希望 hi-bōng	希望 xīwàng	to hope
開始 khai-sí	開始 kāishǐ	to begin
準備 chún-pī	準備 zhǔnbèi	to prepare
學 o̍h	學 xué	to learn

TAIWANESE	MANDARIN	MEANING
EMOTIONS		
愛 ài	愛 ài, 喜歡 xǐhuān	to love, to like
佮意 kah-ì	喜歡 xǐhuān	to like
驚 kiaⁿ	怕 pà	to fear
歡喜 hoaⁿ-hí	高興 gāoxìng	to be happy
受氣 siū-khì	生氣 shēngqì	to be angry
煩惱 hoan-ló	煩惱 fánnǎo	to be worried
BODILY SENSATIONS		
枵 iau	餓 è	to be hungry
渴 khoah	渴 kě	to be thirsty
痠 sng	痠痛 suāntòng	to be sore
病 pēⁿ	病 bìng	to be sick
感覺 kám-kak	感到 gǎndào	to feel

9.2 Stative verbs and intensifiers

Like adjectives, stative verbs dealing with emotions can be modified by intensifiers *(see 6.1 Intensifiers)*. However, note that one-syllable stative verbs do not require a default placeholder intensifier. If 真 **chin** 'very' precedes a one-syllable stative verb, the meaning of 'very' does apply.

(intensifier) + one-syllable stative verb

伊 驚 狗。
I <u>kiaⁿ</u> káu.
她 怕 狗。
Tā <u>pà</u> gǒu.
She <u>is afraid</u> of dogs.

阮 阿兄 真 歡喜 提著 獎學金。
Gún a-hiaⁿ <u>chin hoaⁿ-hí</u> theh--tio̍h chióng-ha̍k-kim.
我 哥哥 很 高興 拿到 獎學金。
Wǒ gēgē <u>hěn gāoxìng</u> nádào jiǎngxuéjīn.
My brother was <u>very happy</u> to win a scholarship.

9.3 Stative verbs and continuous aspect

The dynamic continuous aspect emphasizes an activity in progress *(see 8.2 Continuous aspect)*. This activity does not necessarily have to be a physical movement (such as throwing or walking), but can be an active mental engagement. As a result, some stative verbs that imply active participation (such as explaining or appreciating) can take the dynamic continuous aspect marker 咧 **teh**, while more passive ones (such as fearing or knowing) cannot.

咧 + *active stative verb*

Because stative verbs inherently describe persistent states and mental conditions, generally the static continuous marker 咧 **--leh** is not necessary. Below is a table of some common stative verbs grouped according to active or passive engagement.

TAIWANESE	MANDARIN	MEANING
ACTIVE		
開始 khai-sí	開始 kāishǐ	to begin
準備 chún-pī	準備 zhǔnbèi	to prepare
解釋 kái-sek	解釋 jiěshì	to explain
學 o̍h	學 xué	to learn
欣賞 him-sióng	欣賞 xīnshǎng	to appreciate
PASSIVE		
愛 ài	愛 ài, 喜歡 xǐhuān	to love, to like
佮意 kah-ì	喜歡 xǐhuān	to like
知影 chai-iáⁿ	知道 zhīdào	to know
驚 kiaⁿ	怕 pà	to fear
相信 siong-sìn	相信 xiāngxìn	to believe
希望 hi-bōng	希望 xīwàng	to hope

阮 小妹 咧 學 芭蕾 舞。
Gún sió-mōe teh o̍h pa-lê bú.
我 妹妹 在 學 芭蕾 舞。
Wǒ mèimei zài xué bālěi wǔ.
My younger sister is learning ballet.

阮 目前 咧 決定 啥物 時陣 欲 搬厝。
Gún bo̍k-chêng teh koat-tēng siáⁿ-mih sî-chūn beh poaⁿ-chhù.
我們 目前 在 決定 什麼 時候 要 搬家。
Wǒmen mùqián zài juédìng shénme shíhòu yào bānjiā.
We are deciding on when we should move.

9.4 Stative verbs in the past

Stative verbs cannot be placed in the perfective or experiential aspects. To indicate that a stative verb has occurred in the past, a time expression or time adverb must be used *(see 27.1 Time expressions and time adverbs indicating the past)*. Compare the examples below using both stative and action verbs.

time expression / time adverb + stative verb

ACTION VERB WITH PERFECTIVE ASPECT
我 頂禮拜 這 份 報告 寫 了。
Góa téng lé-pài chit hūn pò-kò siá liáu.
我 上個禮拜 寫了 這 份 報告。
Wǒ shàng gè lǐbài xiěle zhè fèn bàogào.
I wrote this report last week.

STATIVE VERB WITH TIME EXPRESSION
我 頂禮拜 這 份 報告 準備。
Góa téng lé-pài chit hūn pò-kò chún-pī.
我 上個禮拜 準備 這 份 報告。
Wǒ shàng gè lǐbài zhǔnbèi zhè fèn bàogào.
I prepared this report last week.

ACTION VERB WITH EXPERIENTIAL ASPECT
林 小姐 已經 共 你 講過。
Lîm sió-chiá í-keng kā lí kóng--kòe.
林 小姐 已經 跟 你 說過。
Lín xiǎojiě yǐjīng gēn nǐ shuōguò.
Ms. Lim has already said this to you before.

STATIVE VERB WITH TIME ADVERB
林小姐 已經 共 你 解釋。
Lîm sió-chiá í-keng kā lí kái-sek.
林小姐 已經 跟 你 解釋。
Lín xiǎojiě yǐjīng gēn nǐ jiěshì.
Ms. Lim has already explained this to you before.

10 Special verbs

This chapter gives special treatment to three common verbs 是 **sī**, 有 **ū**, and 佇 **tī**, which all have several grammatical functions within Taiwanese.

10.1 是 sī

是 **sī** functions as a linking verb, a focusing marker, a passive voice marker, and also a verb indicating existence. The negative form of 是 **sī** is 毋是 **m̄-sī** in all cases.

10.1.1 是 sī as a linking verb

Linking verbs are used to 'equate' or 'link' two nouns. In English, a form of the verb 'to be' often accomplishes this task (such as 'She is the boss' or 'We are the winners').

伊 是 美國 人。
I <u>sī</u> Bí-kok lâng.
他 是 美國 人。
Tā <u>shì</u> Měiguó rén.
He <u>is</u> American (*He = American*).

我 是 王 先生。
Góa <u>sī</u> Ông--sian-siⁿ.
我 是 王 先生。
Wǒ <u>shì</u> Wáng xiānshēng.
I <u>am</u> Mr. Ong (*I = Mr. Ong*).

10.1.2 是 sī in the focusing construction

是 sī can be used to indicate emphasis whether by focusing attention or indicating contrast. Sometimes referred to as the 是 sī...的 --ê focusing construction, 是 sī is placed immediately before whichever element is under focus or to be given additional vocal emphasis. The particle 的 --ê is often omitted, but if used, 的 --ê must come at the end of the clause or sentence and be placed in the neutral tone. Additionally, 是 sī must occur before the main verb.

是 + *item for emphasis* + (的)

sī + *item for emphasis* + (--ê)

ORIGINAL SENTENCE

我 明仔載 和 阿媽 欲 去 機場。

Góa bîn-á-chài hām a-má beh khì ki-tiûⁿ.

我 明天 和 奶奶 要 去 機場。

Wǒ míngtiān hé nǎinai yào qù jīchǎng.

I will go with grandma to the airport tomorrow.

Bold indicates vocal stress in the examples below.

EMPHASIS ON WITH WHOM

我 明仔載 <u>是</u> **和 阿媽** 欲 去 機場 (的)。

Góa bîn-á-chài <u>sī</u> **hām a-má** beh khì ki-tiûⁿ (--ê).

我 明天 <u>是</u> **和 奶奶** 要 去 機場 (的)。

Wǒ míngtiān <u>shì</u> **hé nǎinai** yào qù jīchǎng (de).

<u>It is</u> **with grandma** with whom I will go to the airport tomorrow.

EMPHASIS ON WHEN

我 <u>是</u> **明仔**載 和 阿媽 欲 去 機場 (的)。

Góa <u>sī</u> **bîn-á-chài** hām a-má beh khì ki-tiûⁿ (--ê).

我 <u>是</u> **明天** 和 奶奶 要 去 機場 (的)。

Wǒ <u>shì</u> **míngtiān** hé nǎinai yào qù jīchǎng (de).

<u>It is</u> **tomorrow** that I will go with grandma to the airport.

EMPHASIS ON WHAT ACTIVITY

我 明仔載 和 阿媽 是 **欲 去 機場** (的)。

Góa bîn-á-chài hām a-má <u>sī</u> **beh khì ki-tiûⁿ** (--ê).

我 明天 和 奶奶 是 要 去 機場 (的)。

Wǒ míngtiān hé nǎinai <u>shì</u> **yào qù jīchǎng** (de).

It is **going to the airport** that I will do with grandma tomorrow.

Note that the emphasis conveyed with 是 sī is slightly different from that given by 有 ū *(see 10.2.4 有 ū as an emphasis marker)*.

是 SĪ INDICATING EMPHASIS

我 昨昏暗 是 食 兩 碗 飯。

Góa cha-hng-àm <u>sī</u> chia̍h nn̄g óaⁿ pn̄g.

我 昨晚 是 吃 兩 碗 飯。

Wǒ zuówǎn <u>shì</u> chī liǎng wǎn fàn.

I <u>ate two bowls of rice</u> last night *(as opposed to eating something else)*.

有 Ū INDICATING EMPHASIS

我 昨昏暗 有 食 兩 碗 飯。

Góa cha-hng-àm <u>ū</u> chia̍h nn̄g óaⁿ pn̄g.

我 昨晚 吃了 兩 碗 飯 啊。

Wǒ zuówǎn chīle liǎng wǎn fàn <u>a</u>.

I <u>did eat</u> two bowls of rice last night *(as opposed to not eating at all)*.

10.1.3 是 sī marking the passive voice

The 是 sī...的 --ê construction can also be used for passive voice sentences. In contrast to the 予 hō˙ construction, which can only be used for passive sentences in adverse circumstances *(see 19.1 Passive marker 予 hō˙)*, 是 sī...的 --ê can be used in neutral or positive contexts.

阮 阿母 是 入選 做 校長 的。

Gún a-bú <u>sī</u> jip-sóan chò hāu-tiúⁿ<u>--ê</u>.

我 媽媽 是 入選 為 校長 的。

Wǒ māmā <u>shì</u> rùxuǎn wèi xiàozhǎng <u>de</u>.

My mother <u>was</u> chosen to be principal.

這 張 批 是 阮 阿祖 寫 的。

Chit tiuⁿ phoe sī gún a-chó͘ siá--ê.

這 封 信 是 我 曾祖父 寫 的。

Zhè fēng xìn shì wǒ zēngzǔfù xiě de.

This letter is written by my great-grandfather.

10.1.4 是 sī expressing existence

是 sī can be used to express existence. Related to its use as a linking verb to equate two nouns, existence can be conveyed through a metaphorical connection between a location and a noun. By stating that a location 'is' another noun, the location is understood to be completely occupied by the noun.

> *location* + 是 + *noun*
>
> *location* + sī + *noun*

頭前 是 教室。

Thâu-chêng sī kàu-sek.

前面 是 教室。

Qiánmiàn shì jiàoshì.

The front is the classroom.

飯店 的 頂樓 是 游泳池。

Pn̄g-tiàm ê téng-lâu sī iû-éng-tî.

飯店 的 頂樓 是 游泳池。

Fàndiàn de dǐnglóu shì yóuyǒngchí.

On the hotel roof is a pool.

This usage differs slightly from how 有 ū expresses existence. 有 ū accounts for the nouns at a particular location but does not preclude the possibility of other items at that location (*see 10.2.2 有 ū expresses existence*). 是 sī, on the other hand, suggests that the noun is the only thing wholly existing at the location.

是 SĪ SHOWING EXISTENCE
第二 樓 是 健身房。
Tē-jī lâu sī kiān-sin-pâng.
第二 樓 是 健身房。
Dìèr lóu shì jiànshēnfáng.
The second floor is a gym.

有 Ū SHOWING EXISTENCE
第二 樓 有 健身房。
Tē-jī lâu ū kiān-sin-pâng.
第二 樓 有 健身房。
Dìèr lóu yǒu jiànshēnfáng.
The second floor has a gym.

是 SĪ SHOWING EXISTENCE
伊 的 塗跤 攏 是 衫。
I ê thô·-kha lóng sī saⁿ.
她 的 地板 上 都 是 衣服。
Tā de dìbǎn shàng dōu shì yīfú.
Her floor is just covered in clothes.

有 Ū SHOWING EXISTENCE
伊 的 塗跤 攏 有 衫。
I ê thô·-kha lóng ū saⁿ.
她 的 地板 上 都 有 衣服。
Tā de dìbǎn shàng dōu yǒu yīfú.
There are a lot of clothes on her floor.

10.2 有 ū

有 ū has many functions in Taiwanese as both a verb and grammatical particle. As a verb, 有 ū expresses possession and existence. As a grammatical particle, 有 ū can be used for the perfective aspect, for emphasis, for the habitual aspect, for verb complements, and for desirable adjectives. The negation of 有 ū in all these contexts is 無 bô.

10.2.1 有 ū expressing possession

有 ū can be used as a stative verb to express possession.

洪 小姐 有 兩 个 兄弟。
Âng sió-chiá ū nñg ê hiaⁿ-tī.
洪 小姐 有 兩 個 兄弟。
Hóng xiǎojiě yǒu liǎng gè xiōngdì.
Ms. Ang has two brothers.

這 間 套房 有 露台。
Chit keng thò-pâng ū lō·-tâi.
這 間 套房 有 陽台。
Zhè jiān tàofáng yǒu yángtái.
This apartment has a balcony.

10.2.2 有 ū expressing existence

When the subject is a time or location, 有 ū can express existence which often translates into English as 'there is/are'. The location or time may optionally be preceded by the preposition 佇 tī 'on, at, in'.

(佇) + *location / time* + 有

(tī) + *location / time* + ū

'there is/are…'

佇 公園內 有 游泳池。
Tī kong-hn̂g-lāi ū iû-êng-tî.
在 公園 有 游泳池。
Zài gōngyuán yǒu yóuyǒngchí.
There is a swimming pool in the park.

明仔早起 有 會議。
Bîn-á-chái-khí ū hōe-gī.
明天 早上 有 會議。
Míngtiān zǎoshang yǒu huìyì.
Tomorrow morning there is a meeting.

(遮) 有 車禍 無?
(Chia) ū chhia-hō--bô?
(這裡) 有 車禍 嗎?
(Zhèlǐ) yǒu chēhuò ma?
Was there a car accident (here)?

桌仔頂 無 碗箸。
Toh-á-téng bô óaⁿ-tī.
桌上 沒有 餐具。
Zhuōshàng méiyǒu cānjù.
There are no utensils or tableware on the table.

Note that some sentences with locations as the subject may translate 有 ū either as possession or existence depending on emphasis.

日本 有 真 濟 櫻花。

Jit-pún ū chin chē eng-hoe.

日本 有 很 多 櫻花。

Rìběn yǒu hěn duō yīnghuā.

Japan has many cherry trees.

There are many cherry trees in Japan.

10.2.3 有 ū as a perfective aspect maker

The perfective aspect describes actions that have been fully completed and generally describes events in the past *(see 8.1 Perfective aspect)*. While in Taiwanese there are several ways to put a verb in the perfective aspect, one approach places 有 ū before the verb.

王 老師 有 予 我 一 本 課本。

Ông lāu-su ū hō͘ góa chit pún khò-pún.

王 老師 給了 我 一 本 課本。

Wáng lǎoshī gěile wǒ yī běn kèběn.

Mr. Ong, our teacher, gave me a textbook.

阿母 有 替 阮 洗 衫。

A-bú ū thè gún sé saⁿ.

媽媽 幫 我們 洗了 衣服。

Māmā bāng wǒmen xǐle yīfú.

Mom washed our clothes for us.

Mandarin uses the verb suffix 了 -le to mark the perfective aspect.

10.2.4 有 ū as an emphasis marker

有 ū can be used to emphasize that an action is indeed occurring or did in fact occur in the past. When emphasizing that an action is occurring in the present, generally the dynamic continuous aspect marker 咧 **teh** is used in conjunction with 有 ū ('He is flying') *(see 8.2.1 Dynamic continuous aspect)*.

有 + 咧 + *verb*

ū + teh + *verb*

紅嬰仔 有 咧 講 話!
Âng-eⁿ-á ū teh kóng ōe!
嬰兒 在 說 話 啊!
Yīng'ér zài shuō huà a!
The baby *is* talking!

Note that in Standard Mandarin emphasis in the present is generally marked by the end-of-sentence particle 啊 **a**. However, in Taiwan Mandarin, some speakers may use 有 **yǒu** as an emphasis marker similar to that of Taiwanese.

TAIWAN MANDARIN

嬰兒 有 在 說 話!
Yīng'ér ū zài shuō huà!
The baby *is* talking!

The use of 有 **ū** as an emphasis marker in the past is similar to the English usage of 'did' in the past tense ('She did give me the keys'). Note the continuous aspect marker 咧 **teh** is dropped and only 有 **ū** is placed before the verb. Depending on context, the meaning of the sentence can be interpreted as a simple completed action in the perfective aspect or one which additionally has an emphasis marker. This ambiguity may occur when the 有 **ū** is used for indicating the perfective aspect *(see 8.1.1 Perfective aspect with 有 ū)*.

有 + *verb*

ū + *verb*

伊 有 敲 電話 予 朋友。
I ū khà tiān-ōe hō͘ pêng-iú.
她 有 打 電話 給 朋友 啊 / 她 打了 電話 給 朋友。
Tā yǒu dǎ diànhuà gěi péngyǒu a / Tā dǎle diànhuà gěi péngyǒu.
She *did* call her friend (*emphasis*) / She *called* her friend (*perfective aspect*).

If the sentence uses a phase complement to indicate the perfective aspect (了 **liáu**, 完 **ôan**, 好 **hó**, 煞 **soah**), 有 **ū** placed before a verb is unambiguously an emphasis marker *(see 8.1.2 Perfective aspect with phase complements)*.

有 + *verb* + *phase complement*

ū + *verb* + *phase complement*

伊 有 敲 了 予 朋友。

I ū khà liáu hō͘ pêng-iú.

她 有 打 電話 給 朋友 啊。

Tā yǒu dǎ diànhuà gěi péngyǒu a.

She *did call* her friend (*emphasis*).

10.2.5 有 ū as a habitual aspect marker

有 ū can be used to describe habitual actions in the present. In conjunction with the dynamic continuous aspect marker 咧 teh, 有 ū can be placed before a verb. Note that if a time expression is provided, the addition of 有咧 ū teh before the verb is optional *(see 8.5.1 Habitual actions in the present)*.

有 + 咧 + *verb*

ū + teh + *verb*

李 小姐 下早時仔 有 咧 泅 水。

Lí sió-chiá e-chái-sî-á ū teh siû chúi.

李 小姐 在 早上 經常 游泳。

Lǐ xiǎojiě zài zǎoshang jīngcháng yóuyǒng.

Ms. Li swims every morning.

For habitual actions in the past, a time expression or time adverb must be used to express that one 'used to' do an action in the past *(see 8.5.2 Habitual actions in the past)*.

time expression (past) + 有 + 咧 + *verb*

time expression (past) + ū + teh + *verb*

'used to *verb*'

彼 陣 阿公 有 咧 啉 酒。

Hit chūn a-kong ū teh lim chiú.

那 時候 爺爺 經常 喝 酒。

Nà shíhòu yéyě jīngcháng hē jiǔ.

At that time, grandpa used to drink alcohol.

Note that Standard Mandarin generally does not have a direct equivalent to mark the habitual aspect. Instead, an adverb such as **經常 jīngcháng** 'regularly' can be used to convey a habitual action. However, Taiwan Mandarin often places **有在 yǒu zài** before the verb, similar to Taiwanese.

TAIWAN MANDARIN

李 小姐 在 早上 <u>有 在</u> 游泳。

Lǐ xiǎojiě zài zǎoshang <u>yǒu zài</u> yóuyǒng.

Ms. Li <u>swims</u> every morning.

那 時候 爺爺 <u>有 在</u> 喝 酒。

<u>Nà shíhòu</u> yěyě <u>yǒu zài</u> hē jiǔ.

<u>At that time</u>, grandpa <u>used to</u> drink alcohol.

10.2.6 有 ū with verb complements

有 ū can appear in verb complement constructions for both phase complements and potential complements.

10.2.6.1 Phase complements with 有 ū

有 ū can be used in both phase complements indicating achievements and those indicating potential. Structurally, both types of complements are the same. However, the difference comes from the interpretation of the meaning. Phase complements indicating achievement state whether the action from the main verb has been achieved or completed. In contrast, phase complements indicating potential comment only on the *ability* of the main verb to complete the verb. Phase complements indicating potential only apply to verbs relating to the senses (see, hear, feel, taste, etc.).

main verb + 有

main verb + ū

PHASE COMPLEMENT INDICATING ACHIEVEMENT

門票 你 敢 買 有？

Mn̂g-phiò lí kám bé ū?

你 買到了 門票 嗎？

Nǐ mǎidàole ménpiào ma?

Did you buy the tickets?

PHASE COMPLEMENT INDICATING POTENTIAL

爵士樂 你 敢 聽 有？

Chiak-sū-gak lí kám thiaⁿ ū?

你 聽得懂 爵士 音樂 嗎？

Nǐ tīngdedǒng juéshì yīnyuè ma?

Do you understand jazz music?

10.2.6.2 Potential complements with 有 ū

有 ū can appear within potential verb complements constructions *(see 11.4 Potential complements)*. The 有 ū joins the verb to its complement and indicates whether the verb was *able* to achieve the complement. In potential verb complement constructions using 有 -ū-, the events have already occurred, making this construction past-oriented.

verb + 有 + *complement*

verb + -ū- + *complement*

'by doing *verb* was able to achieve *complement*'

睏 十 點鐘 應該 睏有飽。

Khùn chap tiám-cheng eng-kai khùn-ū-pá.

睡 十 個 小時 應該 睡得飽。

Shuì shí gè xiǎoshí yīnggāi shuìdebǎo.

Sleeping for 10 hours should be enough sleep.

坐 踮 遐 敢 <u>看有著</u>?
Chē tàm hia kám <u>khòaⁿ-ū-tio̍h</u>?

坐 在 那裡 <u>看得到</u> 嗎？
Zuò zài nàlǐ <u>kàndedào</u> ma？

<u>Were</u> you <u>able to see</u> by sitting there?

Mandarin does not have an exact equivalent to the actualized potential complement form. The distinction is not overtly made but left to interpretation of the context. At times, Mandarin translations will make use of the simple past tense form or the potential complement 得 **-de-**, which does not distinguish between an actualized or unrealized potential such as in Taiwanese *(see 11.4 Potential complements)*.

恁 這馬 <u>聽會著</u> 矣。
In chit-má <u>thiaⁿ-ē-tio̍h</u>--ah.

他們 現在 <u>聽得到</u> 了。
Tāmen xiànzài <u>tīngdedào</u> le.

They <u>are able to hear</u> it now.

10.2.7 有 **ū** with desirable adjectives

有 **ū** can be used before desirable adjectives including those that have been constructed with 好 **hó** 'good' combined with an action verb (好聽 **hó-thiaⁿ** 'good sounding', 好食 **hó-chia̍h** 'delicious'). Whether an adjective is considered desirable depends on the speaker as well as the noun that is described.

In contrast, 會 **ē** is used before undesirable adjectives including those formed by combining 歹 **pháiⁿ** 'bad' with action verbs (歹看 **pháiⁿ-khòaⁿ** 'ugly', 歹用 **pháiⁿ-ēng** 'hard to use') *(see 6.4 Desirable and undesirable adjectives)*.

這 台 機車 <u>有 好 駛</u>。
Chit tâi ki-chhia <u>ū hó sái</u>.

這 台 機車 <u>好 騎</u>。
Zhè tái jīchē <u>hǎo qí</u>.

This scooter is <u>easy to drive</u>.

這種茶有較好啉無？
Chit chióng tê ū khah hó lim bô?

這種茶比較好喝嗎？
Zhè zhǒng chá bǐjiào hǎo hē ma?

Does this tea taste better?

Note that in Mandarin, **有 yǒu** is generally not used before adjectives. Instead, the adjective stands alone or has an intensifier added.

10.3 佇 tī

佇 tī can be used as a verb to indicate existence at a specific location, a preposition specifying 'at', 'on', or 'in' a location, and a continuous aspect marker 佇咧 tī-leh.

10.3.1 佇 tī expressing existence at a specific location

佇 tī can be used as a verb to show existence at a specific location. The negative form is 無佇 bô tī.

阮囡仔佇學校。
Gún gín-á tī ha̍k-hāu.

我孩子在學校。
Wǒ háizi zài xuéxiào.

My children are at school.

棉被攏佇櫃仔。
Mî-phōe lóng tī kūi-á.

棉被都在櫃子。
Miánbèi dōu zài guìzi.

The blankets are all in the cabinet.

10.3.2 佇 tī as a preposition

佇 tī can also be used as a preposition indicating 'at', 'on', or 'in' a specific location or point in time. An alternate form of the preposition is 佇咧 tī-leh.

怹 佇 辦公室 食 中晝頓。

In tī pān-kong-sek chiah tiong-tàu-tǹg.

他們 在 辦公室 吃 午餐。

Tāmen zài bàngōngshì chī wǔcān.

They are eating lunch <u>at</u> the office.

我 佇 眠床頂 看 冊。

Góa tī bîn-chhn̂g-téng khòaⁿ chheh.

我 在 床上 看 書。

Wǒ zài chuángshàng kàn shū.

I am reading <u>in</u> bed.

你 的 貓仔 覆 佇 桌仔頂。

Lí ê niau-á phak tī toh-á-téng.

你 的 貓 趴 在 桌子上。

Nǐ de māo pā zài zhuōzi shàng.

Your cat is lying <u>on</u> the table.

咱 佇 下晡 已經 約 伊 去 看 電影。

Lán tī ē-po͘ í-keng iok i khì khòaⁿ tiān-iáⁿ.

我們 在 下午 已經 約 她 去 看 電影。

Wǒmen zài xiàwǔ yǐjīng yuē tā qù kàn diànyǐng.

We've already planned to watch a movie with her <u>in</u> the afternoon.

楊 老師 徛 佇咧 遐。

Iûⁿ lāu-su khiā tī-leh hia.

楊 老師 站著 那裡。

Yáng lǎoshī zhànzhe nàlǐ.

The teacher, Mr. Iunn, is standing over there.

10.3.3 佇咧 tī-leh as a continuous aspect marker

佇咧 tī-leh can be used as a dynamic continuous aspect marker, indicating that a verb is already in progress *(see 8.2.1 Dynamic continuous aspect)*. Compared to the basic form **咧 teh**, the use of **佇咧 tī-leh** emphasizes the immediacy of the action.

謝 小姐 佇咧 看 冊。

Siā sió-chiá tī-leh khòaⁿ chheh.

謝 小姐 正在 看 書。

Xiè xiǎojiě zhèngzài kàn shū.

Ms. Sia *is* reading a book (*right now*).

Additionally, when adding the static continuous aspect marker 咧 --**leh** after the verb 佇 **tī** 'to be located at', the meaning shifts slightly to an expression stating whether a person is present or absent.

恁 翁 這馬 無 佇咧。

In ang chit-má bô tī--leh.

她 的 先生 現在 不 在。

Tā de xiānshēng xiànzài bù zài.

Her husband *is* not home right now.

11 Verb complements

Verb complements are like extensions to the verb offering additional information about the action performed. Both Taiwanese and Mandarin use verb complements extensively to give more depth of information to verbs that do not inflect as they do in other languages.

In general, verbs and their complements form a cohesive unit and only in rare circumstances are they separable. Together they form a *verb compound*.

verb compound = verb + complement

Complements themselves range from verbs that can function independently in other settings to bound syllables that only appear within the verb compound structure.

11.1 Phase complements

Phase complements indicate the current 'phase', or stage, of action for a verb.

11.1.1 Phase complements indicating completion

Most phase complements indicate that the action of the main verb has completed or stopped occurring. While the action has stopped, no more is stated about whether the action was completed successfully or performed to a desired end. In contrast with resultative verb complements, which focus on the outcome of the verb, the focus of phase complements is on the action of the main verb itself *(see 11.2 Resultative complements)*.

The four primary phase complements indicating completion are in the table below.

TAIWANESE	MANDARIN	MEANING
了 liáu	完 -wán	to end
完 ôan	完 -wán	to end
煞 soah	完 -wán	to halt, to pause
好 hó	好 -hǎo	to complete sufficiently

verb + 了 / 完 / 煞 / 好

verb + liáu / ôan / soah / hó

我 這 本 冊 拄才 看了。
Góa chit pún chheh tú-chiah khòaⁿ liáu.
我 這 本 書 剛才 看完。
Wǒ zhè běn shū gāngcái kànwán.
I am done looking at this book (*may or may not have read the entire book*).

恁 的 運動 猶未 做完。
Lín ê ūn-tōng iáu-bōe chò ôan.
你們 的 運動 還沒 做完。
Nǐmen de yùndòng háiméi zuòwán.
You still didn't finish doing your exercises.

咱 先 講煞，就 食 飯。
Lán seng kóng soah, tō chiảh pn̄g.
我們 先 說完，就 吃 飯。
Wǒmen xiān shuōwán, jiù chī fàn.
Let's end our discussion and then eat (*we may begin again later*).

彼 張 申請表，你 敢 寫好？
Hit tiuⁿ sin-chéng-pió, lí kám siá hó?
那 張 申請表，你 寫好 嗎？
Nà zhāng shēnqǐngbiǎo, nǐ xiěhǎo ma?
Are you done filling out that application (*may or may not be filled out well*)?

Phase complements indicating completed actions can also be used to mark the perfective aspect, which describes actions that can be understood in their entirety (beginning, middle, and end) *(see 8.1.2 Perfective aspect with phase complements)*. Note that Taiwanese can also indicate the perfective aspect by placing 有 **ū** before verb.

伊 桌仔 拭 好。

I toh-á <u>chhit hó</u>.

她 桌子 擦了。

Tā zhuōzi <u>cā le</u>.

She <u>wiped</u> the table.

這 張 報紙，我 下早 看 煞。

Chit tiuⁿ pò-chóa, góa e-chái <u>khòaⁿ soah</u>.

這 張 報紙，我 早上 看了。

Zhè zhāng bàozhǐ, wǒ zǎoshang <u>kàn le</u>.

I <u>read</u> this newspaper in the morning.

In Mandarin, generally places an action into the perfective aspect by suffixing 了 **-le** to the main verb.

11.1.2 Phase complements indicating achievement

Some phase complements specifically indicate whether the action of the main verb has been achieved, or in other words, completed successfully. Verbs that can take this complement are typically those verb actions that can be evaluated by success or failure. For example, the verb 掠 **liảh** 'to catch' can only succeed if an object is caught.

TAIWANESE	MANDARIN	MEANING
著 -tiȯh	到 dào, 著 zháo	to attain, to achieve
有 ū	到 dào, 著 zháo	to obtain

At the end of a clause or sentence, 著 **--tiȯh** receives the neutral tone, while 有 **ū** keeps its original tone.

verb + 著 / 有

verb + -tiȯh / ū

伊 掠著 鳥鼠仔。
I liah-tioh niáu-chhí-á.
他 抓到 老鼠。
Tā zhuādào lǎoshǔ.
He caught the mouse.

新 餐廳，你 敢 揣 有？
Sin chhan-thiaⁿ, lí kám chhōe ū?
新 餐廳，你 找到 嗎？
Xīn cāntīng, nǐ zhǎodào ma?
Did you find the new restaurant?

狗 咧 吠 因為 伊 聽著 人 挵 門。
Káu teh pūi in-ūi i thiaⁿ-tioh lâng lòng mn̂g.
狗 在 吠 因為 牠 聽到 人 敲 門。
Gǒu zài fèi yīnwèi tā tīngdào rén qiāo mén.
The dog is barking because it heard a knock at the door.

這 个 好 主意，阮 頭拄仔 想著。
Chit ê hó chú-ì, gún thâu-tú-á siuⁿ--tioh.
這個 好 主意，我們 剛剛 想到。
Zhège hǎo zhǔyì, wǒmen gānggāng xiǎngdào.
We just thought of this good idea.

11.1.3 Phase complements indicating potential

In addition to indicating achievement, the phase complement 有 -ū can have the interpretation of indicating potential. This interpretation generally only applies to sensory verbs (see, hear, touch, feel, smell, etc.) and comments on the *subject's* ability to succeed or fail at achieving the verb. For example, the phrase **聽有 thiaⁿ ū** means that the subject is able to 'listen and understand'.

    verb + 有
    verb + ū

SENTENCE WITH TWO POSSIBLE INTERPRETATIONS

藝術館 的 現代 圖，你 敢 看 有？

Gē-sut-kóan ê hiān-tāi tô, lí kám khòaⁿ ū?

POTENTIAL READING

藝術館 的 現代 圖，你 看得懂 嗎？

Yìshùguǎn de xiàndài tú, nǐ kàndedǒng ma?

Were you <u>able to understand</u> the contemporary paintings in the art museum (*did you have the ability to appreciate them*)?

ACHIEVEMENT READING

藝術館 的 現代 圖，你 看到 了 嗎？

Yìshùguǎn de xiàndài tú, nǐ kàndào le ma?

<u>Did</u> you <u>see</u> the contemporary paintings in the art museum (*did you have a chance to see them before we left*)?

SENTENCE WITH TWO POSSIBLE INTERPRETATIONS

昨暗 的 紅酒，我 攏 啉 無。

Cha-àm ê âng-chiú, góa lóng lim bô.

POTENTIAL READING

昨晚 的 紅酒，我 喝不出 品質。

Zuó wǎn de hóngjiǔ, wǒ hēbùchū pǐnzhí.

I <u>couldn't taste</u> any differences among last night's red wines.

ACHIEVEMENT READING

昨晚 的 紅酒，我 都 喝不到。

Zuówǎn de hóngjiǔ, wǒ dōu hēbudào.

I <u>didn't get a chance to drink</u> any of last night's red wines (*wanted to but had no chance*).

11.1.4 Phase complements and objects

The verb and phase complement form a cohesive unit that generally cannot be separated called a *verb compound* (see exceptions in the following sections). When an object is introduced, the object must be placed before or after the verb compound (*main verb + phase complement*).

PATTERN 1
object + *verb* + *phase complement*

PATTERN 2
verb + *phase complement* + *object*

11.1.4.1 Phase complements indicating completion with objects

For phase complements indicating completed actions (了 **liáu**, 完 **ôan**, 煞 **soah**, 好 **hó**), objects are always placed *before* the verb compound. Objects may be placed after the subject or *topicalized* (i.e. put before the subject and set off by a comma) *(see 17.2 Topicalized objects)*.

object + *verb* + *phase complement (completion)*

彼 篇 論文, 伊 寫 了。
Hit phiⁿ lūn-bûn, i siá liáu.
那 篇 論文, 她 寫完。
Nà piān lùnwén, tā xiěwán.
She finished writing **that paper**.

阮 阿母 共 阮 的 衫 洗 好 矣。
Gún a-bú kā gún ê saⁿ sé hó--ah.
我們 的 媽媽 把 我們 的 衣服 洗好 了。
Wǒmen de māmā bǎ wǒmen de yīfú xǐhǎo le.
Our mom has finished washing **our clothes**.

Note that Mandarin has more flexibility in placing the object before or after the verb compound. The examples above can also be rewritten in Mandarin with the object *after* the verb compound.

MANDARIN SENTENCES WITH OBJECT AFTER VERB
她 寫完 那 篇 論文。
Tā xiěwán **nà piān lùnwén**.
She finished writing **that paper**.

我們 的 媽媽 洗好 我們 的 衣服 了。
Wǒmen de māmā xǐhǎo **wǒmen de yīfú** le.
Our mom finished washing **our clothes**.

11.1.4.2 Phase complements indicating achievement and potential with objects

For phase complements indicating achievement (**著 -tio̍h**, **有 ū**) or potential (**有 ū**), objects may be placed either *before* or *after* the verb compound.

   PATTERN 1

   object + verb + phase complement (achievement / potential)

伊 噴 的 芳水, 你 敢 <u>鼻 有</u>?
I phùn ê phang-chúi, lí kám <u>phīⁿ ū</u>?
她 噴 的 香水, 你 <u>聞到</u> 了 嗎?
Tā pēn de xiāngshuǐ, nǐ <u>wéndào</u> le ma?
<u>Did</u> you <u>smell</u> **the perfume she's wearing**?

我 好 朋友, 我 佇 市場 <u>拄著</u>。
Góa hó pêng-iú, góa tī chhī-tiûⁿ <u>tú--tio̍h</u>.
我 好 朋友, 我 在 市場 <u>遇到</u>。
Wǒ hǎo péngyǒu, wǒ zài shìchǎng <u>yùdào</u>.
I <u>bumped into</u> **my good friend** at the market.

教授 的 報告, 我 <u>聽 有</u>。
Kàu-siū ê pò-kò, góa <u>thiaⁿ ū</u>.
教授 的 報告, 我 <u>聽得懂</u>。
Jiàoshòu de bàogào, wǒ <u>tīngdedǒng</u>.
I <u>could understand</u> **the professor's lecture**.

   PATTERN 2

   *verb + phase complement (achievement / potential) + **object***

你 敢 <u>鼻 有</u> **伊 噴 的 芳水**?
Lí kám <u>phīⁿ ū</u> **i phùn ê phang-chúi**?
你 <u>聞到</u> 了 她 噴 的 香水 嗎?
Nǐ <u>wéndào</u> le tā pēn de xiāngshuǐ ma?
<u>Did</u> you <u>smell</u> **the perfume she's wearing**?

我佇市場拄著我好朋友。

Góa tī chhī-tiûⁿ tú-tio̍h góa hó pêng-iú.

我在市場遇到我好朋友。

Wǒ zài shìchǎng yùdào wǒ hǎo péngyǒu.

I bumped into **my good friend** at the market.

我聽有教授的報告。

Góa thiaⁿ ū kàu-siū ê pò-kò.

我聽得懂教授的報告。

Wǒ tīngdedǒng jiàoshòu de bàogào.

I could understand **the professor's lecture**.

While a verb and phase complement form a compound that generally cannot be separated, there are a few idiomatic expressions that allow an object (usually a pronoun) to split the main verb and phase complement.

放伊煞

pàng i soah

放過他

fàngguò tā

'to let someone to get away with something'

頭家掠著查某囝仔偷提物仔了後,伊放伊煞。

Thâu-ke lia̍h-tio̍h cha-bó͘ gín-á thau-the̍h mih-á liáu-āu, i pàng i soah.

老闆抓到女孩子偷拿東西之後,他放過她。

Lǎobǎn zhuādào nǚháizi tōuná dōngxī zhīhòu, tā fàngguò tā.

After the shopkeeper caught the little girl stealing, he let **her** go.

看伊有

khòaⁿ i ū

看得起他

kàndeqǐ tā

'to think highly of someone'

因為 阿公 家己 開店，所以 阮 攏 <u>看</u> **伊** <u>有</u>。
In-ūi a-kong ka-tī khui-tiàm, só-í gún lóng <u>khòaⁿ</u> **i** <u>ū</u>.
因為 爺爺 自己 開店，所以 我們 都 <u>看得起</u> 他。
Yīnwèi yéyě zìjǐ kāidiàn, suǒyǐ wǒmen dōu <u>kàndeqǐ</u> **tā**.
Because grandpa opened up his own shop, we all <u>think highly of</u> **him**.

11.2 Resultative complements

Resultative complements (resultatives) indicate a particular outcome as a 'result' of the action given by the verb. Often open-ended action verbs take on a resultative complement in order to conclude an action.

11.2.1 Resultative complements from adjectives

Because resultative complements generally describe an outcome, many are adjectives or stative verbs. This allows for a large number of possible resultatives.

RESULTATIVE	EXAMPLE	MEANING
飽 pá 'full'	食飽 chia̍h-pá 吃飽 chībǎo	to eat until full
牢 tiâu 'sticky'	食牢 chia̍h-tiâu 上癮 shàngyǐn	to become addicted
毋著 m̄-tio̍h 'incorrect'	食毋著 chia̍h-m̄-tio̍h 吃錯 chīcuò	to eat incorrectly

verb + resultative complement

狗仔 <u>食飽</u> 矣，毋通 閣 飼。
Káu-á <u>chia̍h-pá</u>--ah, m̄-thang koh chhī.
狗 <u>吃飽</u> 了，不要 再 餵。
Gǒu <u>chībǎo</u> le, bùyào zài wèi.
The dog is already <u>full</u>. Do not feed it more.

開始 食薰 真 簡單 食牢。
Khai-sí chiȧh-hun chin kan-tan chiȧh-tiâu.

開始 抽煙 很 容易 上癮。
Kāishǐ chōuyān hěn róngyì shàngyǐn.

If you start smoking it's very easy to become addicted.

While most resultatives are adjectives, some action verbs can also function as resultatives.

RESULTATIVE	EXAMPLES	MEANING
走 cháu 'to run'	提走 thėh-cháu	to take away
	拿走 názǒu	
死 sí 'to die'	枵死 iau-sí	to be dying of hunger
	餓死 èsǐ	
開 khui 'to open'	破開 phòa-khui	to crack something open
	剖開 pōukāi	

糞埽, 共 我 提走。
Pùn-sò, kā góa thėh-cháu.

垃圾, 幫 我 拿走。
Lèsè, bāng wǒ názǒu.

Help me take away the trash.

椰子 已經 破開 矣。
Iâ-chí í-keng phòa--khui--ah.

椰子 已經 剖開 了。
Yēzi yǐjīng pōukāi le.

The coconut is already split open.

Below is a table of some common resultative complements.

TAIWANESE	MANDARIN	MEANING
了(了) -liáu(-liáu)	光光 guāngguāng	to finish until nothing remains
完 -ôan	完 -wán	to finish completely
好 -hó	好 -hǎo	to do something well
走 -cháu	走 -zǒu	to remove or take away

TAIWANESE	MANDARIN	MEANING
掉 -tiāu	掉 -diào	to be fully removed
去 -khì, --khì	掉 -diào	to disappear from, to lose
牢 -tiâu	住 -zhù	to stick firmly
死 -sí	死 -sǐ	to die from
開 -khui, --khui	開 -kāi	to be open
飽 -pá	飽 -bào	to be full
醉 -chùi	醉 -zuì	to be drunk
毋著 -m̄-tio̍h	錯 -cuò	to do incorrectly
歹 -pháiⁿ	壞 -huài	to break, to ruin
破 -phòa	破 -pò	to break, to shatter
熟 -se̍k	熟 -shóu	to be ripe, fully cooked
滇 -tīⁿ	滿 -mǎn	to be full *(liquids)*
做 -chò	做 -zuò, 成 -chéng	to regard as *(mistakenly)*
成 -sêng	成 -chéng	to successfully complete

注意 你 坐 的 火車 的 時間，毋通 <u>坐毋著</u>。
Chù-ì lí chē ê hóe-chhia ê sî-kan, m̄-thang <u>chē-m̄-tio̍h</u>.
注意 你 坐 的 火車 的 時間，不要 <u>坐錯</u>。
Zhùyì nǐ zuò de huǒchē de shíjiān, bù yào <u>zuòcuò</u>.
Pay attention to the time of the train you're taking. Don't <u>take the wrong one</u>.

阮 舊 物仔，我 攏 想欲 <u>擲掉</u>。
Gún kū mi̍h-á, góa lóng siuⁿ-beh <u>tàn-tiāu</u>.
我 的 舊 東西，我 都 想要 <u>丟掉</u>。
Wǒ de jiù dōngxī, wǒ dōu xiǎngyào <u>diūdiào</u>.
I would like to <u>throw away</u> all my old things.

因為 伊 清彩 寫 字，所以 我 有 <u>看毋著</u> 地止。
In-ūi i chhìn-chhái siá jī, só͘-í góa ū <u>khòaⁿ-m̄-tio̍h</u> tē-chí.
因為 他 隨便 寫 字，所以 我 <u>看錯了</u> 地址。
Yīnwèi tā suíbiàn xiě zì, suǒyǐ wǒ <u>kàncuòle</u> dìzhǐ.
Because he wrote sloppily, I <u>misread</u> the address.

地動 了後，壁 攏 必開矣。

Tē-tāng liáu-āu, piah lóng pit--khui--ah.

地震 以後，牆壁 都 裂開 了。

Dìzhèn yǐhòu, qiángbì dōu lièkāi le.

After the earthquake, the walls all cracked open.

In the *Pe̍h-ōe-jī* (POJ) Romanization system, resultative complements are suffixed to the verb with a single hyphen. However, note that some resultative complements (such as 去 --khì and 開 --khui) are put in the neutral tone and written with double-hyphens when occurring at the end of a clause or sentence.

11.2.2 Resultative complements with objects

Generally, the verb and resultative complement form an indivisible unit that cannot be separated (see exceptions in the following sections) called the *verb compound*. When an object is introduced, the object must be placed *before* or *after* the verb compound. That said, not every type of object may be placed in either position.

> PATTERN 1
>
> **object** + verb + resultative complement

> PATTERN 2
>
> verb + resultative complement + **object**

11.2.2.1 Indefinite objects

Indefinite objects, which refer to objects that are not known to the listener (a book, two pencils, some chairs), are *always* placed *after* the verb compound *(see 4.9 Definite and indefinite nouns)*.

> verb + resultative complement + **indefinite object**

伊 挵破 一寡 杯仔。
I lóng-phòa chit-kóa poe-á.
他 弄破 一些 杯子。
Tā nòngpò yīxiē bēizi.
He broke **a few cups**.

總舖師 切開 兩 个 金瓜。
Chóng-phò·-sai chhiat-khui **nñg ê kim-koe**.
廚師 切開 兩 個 南瓜。
Chúshī qiēkāi liǎng gè nánguā.
The chef cut open **two pumpkins**.

11.2.2.2 Definite objects

With definite objects, which refer to objects known to the listener (the book, these pencils), the object can be placed in both positions: either *before* the main verb or *after* the verb complement *(see 4.8 Definite and indefinite nouns)*. However, note that individual preference may vary. When the object is moved before the main verb, the object can be *topicalized* (i.e. placed before the subject and set off by a comma) or introduced by the preposition 共 **kā** *(see 17.2 Topicalized objects, 17.4 共 kā construction)*.

PATTERN 1

definite object + *verb* + *resultative complement*

我 的 杯仔，伊 (共 恁) 挵破。
Góa ê poe-á, i (kā in) lóng-phòa.
我 的 杯子，他 弄破 了。
Wǒ de bēizi, tā nòngpò le.
He broke **my cups**.

總舖師 共 彼 个 金瓜 切開。
Chóng-phò·-sai kā **hit ê kim-koe** chhiat--khui.
廚師 把 那個 南瓜 切開。
Chúshī bǎ **nàge nánguā** qiēkāi.
The chef cut open **that pumpkin**.

PATTERN 2

*verb + resultative complement + **definite object***

伊 挵破 我 的 杯仔。
I lóng-phòa góa ê poe-á.
他 弄破 我 的 杯子。
Tā nòngpò wǒ de bēizi.
He broke my cups.

總舖師 切開 彼 个 金瓜。
Chóng-phò·-sai chhiat-khui hit ê kim-koe.
廚師 切開 那個 南瓜。
Chúshī qiēkāi nàge nánguā.
The chef cut open that pumpkin.

Additionally, if the definite object is a personal pronoun, then it must be placed *before* the verb with the use of the 共 kā construction.

共 + ***definite object (personal pronoun)*** *+ verb + resultative complement*

kā + ***definite object (personal pronoun)*** *+ verb + resultative complement*

阮 阿媽 共 恁 趕走。
Gún a-má kā in kóaⁿ-cháu.
我 的 奶奶 把 他們 趕走。
Wǒ de nǎinai bǎ tāmen gǎnzǒu.
My grandmother shooed them away.

恁 共 阮 驚死矣！
Lín kā gún kiaⁿ-sí--ah!
你們 把 我們 嚇死 了！
Nǐmen bǎ wǒmen xiàsǐ le!
You scared us to death!

There are a few exceptional expressions that allow the object to split the verb from the resultative complement. However, this placement is rather rare.

verb + **object** + resultative complement

食 飯 飽
chiảh pn̄g pá
吃飽 飯
chībǎo fàn
'to eat one's fill'

伊 食 **飯** 飽 未？
I chiảh **pn̄g** pá bōe?
他 吃飽 **飯** 了 沒有？
Tā chībǎo **fàn** le méiyǒu?
Has he eaten his fill yet?

啉 酒 醉
lim chiú chùi
喝醉 酒
hēzuì jiǔ
'to become drunk'

恁 啉 **酒** 醉 矣。
In lim **chiú** chùi--ah.
他們 喝醉 酒 了。
Tāmen hēzuì jiǔ le.
They have gotten drunk.

Note that Mandarin does not allow for a split between the main verb and the resultative complement.

11.3 Directional complements

Directional complements follow verbs that involve movement and provide further information about the direction of this movement.

11.3.1 Directional complements indicating speaker perspective

The directional complements 來 -lâi 'towards' and 去 -khì 'away' refer to the direction of movement with reference to the speaker.

verb + directional complement (speaker)

伊 明仔載 欲 搬來 美國。
I bîn-á-chài beh poaⁿ-lâi Bí-kok.
她 明天 要 搬來 美國。
Tā míngtiān yào bānlái Měiguó.
Tomorrow she will move to America (*the speaker is in America*).

伊 明仔載 欲 搬去 美國。
I bîn-á-chài beh poaⁿ-khì Bí-kok.
她 明天 要 搬去 美國。
Tā míngtiān yào bānqù Měiguó.
Tomorrow she will move to America (*the speaker is somewhere outside of America*).

In the *Pe̍h-ōe-jī* (POJ) Romanization system, directional complements are suffixed to the verb with a single hyphen. However, if the directional complements appear at the end of a clause or sentence, they are put in the neutral tone and written with double-hyphens. This signals that the directional complements essentially become third tones and the main verb keeps its original tone. When directional complements occur mid-clause they undergo tone changes.

11.3.2 Double-directional complements

In addition to the the speaker perspective directional complements, 來 -lâi 'towards' and 去 -khì 'away', there are six additional directional complements which further describe the direction of movement for an action verb.

TAIWANESE	MANDARIN	MEANING
起 -khí	起 qǐ, 上 shàng	upwards, up
落 -lo̍h	下 xià	downwards
入 -ji̍p	進 jìn, 入 rù	into, in
出 -chhut	出 chū	outwards, out

TAIWANESE	MANDARIN	MEANING
轉 -tńg	回 huí	backwards, return
過 -kòe	過 guò	over, through

These additional six directional complements must be combined with one of the two speaker referencing directional complements 來 **-lâi** 'towards' and 去 **-khì** 'away' to form a double-directional complement. With double-directionals, the movement of the main verb can be described by a combination of two directions.

The speaker referencing directional complements (來 **-lâi** 'towards' and 去 **-khì** 'away') are always placed at the end of the double-directional complement.

verb + directional complement + directional complement (speaker)

伊 好勢 的 時陣 就 <u>行過去</u>。
I hó-sè ê sî-chūn tō <u>kiâⁿ--kòe-khì</u>.
她 好了 的 時候 就 <u>走過去</u>。
Tā hǎole de shíhòu jiù <u>zǒuguòqù</u>.
When she's ready, <u>walk over</u> there.

However, in some cases, the double-directionals take on a more abstract or idiomatic meaning.

DIRECTIONALS	MEANING	EXAMPLES
起來 -khí-lâi	to go up	徛起來 khiā-khí-lâi 'to stand up'
		站起來 zhànqǐlái
	to initiate	冰起來 peng-khí-lâi 'to freeze'
		冷凍起來 lěngdòngqǐlái
落去 -lȯh-khì	to go down	倒落去 tó-lȯh-khì 'to fall over'
		倒下去 dàoxiàqù
	to continue	講落去 kóng-lȯh-khì 'to keep talking'
		說下去 shuōxiàqù

DIRECTIONALS	MEANING	EXAMPLES
出來 -chhut-lâi	to come out	提出來 thėh-chhut-lâi 'to take out'
		拿出來 náchūlái
	to realize	做出來 chò-chhut-lâi 'to produce'
		做出來 zuòchūlái

對 阮 阿媽 來 講，這 个 樓梯 真 歹 爬起來。
Tùi gún a-má lâi kóng, chit ê lâu-thui chin pháiⁿ peh--khí-lâi.
對 我 的 奶奶 來 說，這個 樓梯 很 難 爬上去。
Duì wǒ de nǎinǎi lái shuō, zhège lóutī hěn nán páshàngqù.
These stairs are difficult for my grandma to climb up.

這 包 糖仔，提轉去 予 恁 小妹。
Chit pau thn̂g-á, thėh-tńg-khì hō͘ lín sió-mōe.
這 包 糖果，拿回去 給 你 妹妹。
Zhè bāo tángguǒ, náhuíqù gěi nǐ mèimei.
Take this bag of candy back to your younger sister.

服務費 猶未 加入去。
Hȯk-bū-hùi iáu-bōe ka--jip-khì.
服務費 還沒 包含。
Fúwùfèi háiméi bāohán.
The service fee has not been included yet.

你 若 坐落去，椅仔 會 歹去。
Lí nā chē--lȯh-khì, í-á ē pháiⁿ--khì.
如果 你 坐下來，椅子 會 壞掉。
Rúguǒ nǐ zuòxiàlái, yǐzi huì huàidiào.
If you sit down, the chair will break.

Note that there is a Taiwanese verb **來去 lâi-khì** meaning 'to leave' or 'to proceed with some action'. It is not the verb **來 lâi** combined with the directional complement **去 khì**. Generally, **來去 lâi-khì** is used in the first person but not in the negative or past tense.

我 食飽 了後 先 來去 矣。

Góa chiàh-pá liáu-āu seng lâi-khì--ah.

我 吃飽 之後 先 離開 了。

Wǒ chībǎo zhīhòu xiān líkāi le.

I will leave after I'm full.

咱 下晡 來去 圖書館。

Lán ē-po͘ lâi-khì tô͘-su-kóan.

我們 下午 去 圖書館 吧。

Wǒmen xiàwǔ qù túshūguǎn ba.

Let's go to the library this afternoon.

Directional verb complements mid-clause undergo tone changes but are placed in the neutral tone at the end of clauses and sentences. Note that with double directional complements at the end of clauses and sentences, both directional complements are in the neutral tone, while the verb keeps its original tone.

11.3.3 Directional complements and objects

With directional complements and objects, there is much flexibility in the positioning of the object.

While there is a general tendency in Taiwanese to place the object *before* the main verb when there are directional complements, objects may also be placed *after* the complement or even *in between* the main verb and complement. However, not all types of objects have the same flexibility. Definite objects (the book, these pencils) can occur in all positions, but indefinite objects (a book, two pencils, some chairs) can only occur in the middle of the verb compound *(see 4.9 Definite and indefinite nouns)*.

11.3.3.1 Object comes before the verb compound

In Taiwanese there is a preference to place the object before the main verb. This may be done for both single and double-directional complements. In addition, the object may come before the subject as a topic set off by a comma or after the subject by employing the 共 **kā** construction *(see 17.2 Topicalized objects, 17.4 共 kā construction)*. However, note that only definite objects may occur in this position.

PATTERN 1

definite object + verb + directional complement(s)

恁 趁 的 錢，攏 提來。
Lín thàn ê chîⁿ, lóng thèh--lâi.
你們 賺 的 錢，都 拿來。
Nǐmen zhuàn de qián, dōu nálái.
Give me all **the money you've earned**.

你 共 **這 領 褲** 穿落去。
Lí kā **chit niá khò** chhēng--lòh-khì.
你 把 這 件 褲子 穿進去。
Nǐ bǎ zhè jiàn kùzi chuānjìnqù.
Put on **these pants**.

11.3.3.2 Object comes after the verb compound

Definite objects can be placed after the main verb and directional complement(s). However, this pattern is less common and does not sound natural for all verb and directional complement combinations. This placement of the object tends to be used when the object is also a location.

PATTERN 2

*verb + directional complement(s) + **definite object***

爬起來 **眠床**頂。
Peh-khí-lâi **bîn-chhn̂g**-téng.
爬上去 床 上。
Páshàngqù chuáng shàng.
Climb up onto **the bed**.

跳過去 **溪仔**。
Thiàu-kòe-khì **khe-á**.
跳過去 溪。
Tiàoguòqù xī.
Jump over **the creek**.

阿母 叫 我 提去 隔壁 這 兩 碗 菜。
A-bú kiò góa theh-khì keh-piah chit nng óaⁿ chhài.
媽媽 叫 我 帶去 鄰居 這 兩 碗 菜。
Māmā jiào wǒ dàiqù línjū zhè liǎng wǎn cài.

Mom asked me to take **these two dishes** over to the neighbor's house.

你 袂使 穿入去 彼 雙 淺拖仔。
Lí bē-sái chhēng-jip-khì **hit siang chhián-thoa-á**.
你 不 可以 穿進去 那 雙 拖鞋。
Nǐ bù kěyǐ chuānjìnqù **nà shuāng tuōxié**.

You aren't allowed to go inside wearing **those sandals**.

With directional complements, Mandarin has much more flexibility in positioning the object than Taiwanese. An object may be placed *before*, *after*, or *in between* the verb and directional, or even *in between* double-directional complements.

BEFORE VERB COMPOUND

兩 隻 狗, 他 帶回來 給 我。
Liǎng zhī gǒu, tā dàihuílái gěi wǒ.

AFTER VERB COMPOUND

他 帶回來 **兩 隻 狗** 給 我。
Tā dàihuílái **liǎng zhī gǒu** gěi wǒ.

BETWEEN VERB AND DIRECTIONALS

他 帶 **兩 隻 狗** 回來 給 我。
Tā dài **liǎng zhī gǒu** huílái gěi wǒ.

BEWEEN DIRECTIONALS

他 帶回 **兩 隻 狗** 來 給 我。
Tā dàihuí **liǎng zhī gǒu** lái gěi wǒ.

He brought back home **two dogs** for me.

11.3.3.3 Object comes in the middle of the verb compound

The object can also occur in the middle of the verb compound. If the object is indefinite, then it *must* be placed in this position between the main verb and the directional complement(s).

PATTERN 3

verb + **indefinite / definite object** + *directional complement(s)*

INDEFINITE

阿母 叫 我 提 兩 碗 菜 去 隔壁。

A-bú kiò góa <u>thèh</u> **nn̄g óaⁿ chhài** <u>khì</u> keh-piah.

媽媽 叫 我 帶 兩 碗 菜 去 隔壁。

Māmā jiào wǒ <u>dài</u> **liǎng wǎn cài** <u>qù</u> gébì.

Mom asked me <u>to take</u> **two dishes** <u>over to</u> the neighbor's house.

請 你 買 一寡 弓蕉 轉來。

Chhiáⁿ lí <u>bé</u> **chit-kóa keng-chio** <u>tńg--lâi</u>.

請 你 買 一些 香蕉 回來。

Qǐng nǐ <u>mǎi</u> **yīxiē xiāngjiāo** <u>huílái</u>.

Please <u>buy</u> **some bananas** <u>and bring them back</u>.

DEFINITE

阿母 叫 我 提 這 碗 菜 去 隔壁。

A-bú kiò góa <u>thèh</u> **chit óaⁿ chhài** <u>khì</u> keh-piah.

媽媽 叫 我 帶 這 碗 菜 去 隔壁。

Māmā jiào wǒ <u>dài</u> **zhè wǎn cài** <u>qù</u> gébì.

Mom asked me <u>to take</u> **this dish** <u>over to</u> the neighbor's house.

放 伊 去!

Pàng **i** <u>khì</u>!

放 她 去!

Fàng **tā** <u>qù</u>!

<u>Let</u> **her** <u>go</u>!

While definite objects can also occur in the middle of the verb compound, this is less common and does not sound natural with every verb and directional complement combination. In fact, there is some debate among linguists whether some of these expressions should be seen as two independent verbs in a series.

[Chinese characters] 恁 囡仔 出去。
<u>Chhōa</u> **gín-á** <u>chhut--khì</u>.
帶 孩子 出去。
<u>Dài</u> **háizi** <u>chūqù</u>.
<u>Take</u> **the kids** <u>out</u>.

From this perspective, the verbs 恁 **chhōa** 'to take' and 出去 **chhut-khì** 'to go out' in the example above are two separate verbs that form a sequence of actions.

11.4 Potential complements

Potential complements include an additional syllable called an *infix* that indicates whether the verb is *capable* of achieving the outcome stated in the complement. Phase, resultative, and directional complements may all be made into potential complements by adding the potential infix, which is similar to a suffix but appears 'inside' a word instead of at the end.

verb + potential infix + complement

Taiwanese has two types of potential complements. One type, *actualized potential complements*, focuses on the past and indicates whether the main verb was able to achieve the complement. The other type, *unrealized potential complements*, is more present and future-oriented, suggesting that the main verb can or will be able to achieve the complement.

Mandarin has only one form of potential complement that does not make a distinction between actualized or unrealized.

11.4.1 Actualized potential complements

The actualized potential complement describes whether the main verb already succeeded or failed at fulfilling the complement. As a result, these potential complements are used to describe past-oriented contexts. This type of potential complement is constructed by placing the infix 有 -ū- in between the main verb and the complement. 無 -bô- is the negative form.

verb + 有 + complement
verb + -ū- + complement

阮 碰無著。
Gún pōng-bô-tio̍h.
我們 碰不著。
Wǒmen pèngbuzháo.
We weren't able to touch it.

阿公 共 咱 講 的 故事，你 敢 記有牢？
A-kong kā lán kóng ê kò͘-sū, lí kám kì-ū-tiâu?
爺爺 告訴 我們 的 故事，你 記得住 嗎？
Yéyě gàosù wǒmen de gùshì, nǐ jìdezhù ma?
Were you able to memorize the story grandfather told us?

因為 落雨，阮 昨昏 的 比賽 拍無了。
In-ūi lo̍h-hō͘, gún cha-hng ê pí-sài phah-bô-liáu.
因為 下雨，我們 昨天 的 比賽 沒打完。
Yīnwèi xiàyǔ, wǒmen zuótiān de bǐsài méi dǎwán.
Because it rained, we couldn't finish playing yesterday's game.

Note that there is a distinction between the usage of the actualized potential complement and a phase, resultative, or directional complement placed in the perfective aspect.

POTENTIAL COMPLEMENT
伊 電影 看無著。
I tiān-iáⁿ khòaⁿ-bô-tio̍h.
他 看不到 電影。
Tā kànbudào diànyǐng.
He wasn't able to see the film (*he tried but failed*).

NON-POTENTIAL COMPLEMENT
伊 電影 無 看著。
I tiān-iáⁿ bô khòaⁿ-tio̍h.
他 沒 看到 電影。
Tā méi kàndào diànyǐng.
He didn't see the film (*nothing more implied*).

In the examples above, the implication with the potential complement is that 'he wasn't able to see the film'—perhaps the showing was sold out, perhaps he got there too late, or perhaps he sat in the theater, but the patron sitting in front blocked his view. The non-potential complement in the perfective aspect does not suggest anything more beyond the simple fact that 'he didn't see the film'.

Below are more examples comparing usage of potential and non-potential complements.

POTENTIAL COMPLEMENT
門 關無牢。
Mn̂g koaiⁿ-bô-tiâu.
門 關不住。
Mén guānbuzhù.
The door couldn't be closed (*perhaps the latch broke*).

NON-POTENTIAL COMPLEMENT
門 無 關牢。
Mn̂g bô koaiⁿ-tiâu.
門 沒 關住。
Mén méi guānzhù.
The door wasn't closed (*nothing more implied*).

阿公 咋昏 坐有起來。
A-kong cha-hng chē-ū-khí--lâi.
爺爺 昨天 坐得起來 了。
Yěyě zuótiān zuòdeqǐlái le.
Grandpa was able to sit up yesterday.

阿公 咋昏 有 坐起來。
A-kong cha-hng ū chē--khí-lâi.
爺爺 昨天 坐起來 了。
Yěyě zuótiān zuòqǐlái le.
Grandpa sat up yesterday.

11.4.2 Unrealized potential complements

The other type of potential complement focuses on the actions that are unrealized. These potential complements are present and future-oriented indicating whether the main verb is or will be able to achieve the complement. This type of potential complement is constructed by placing the infix 會 -ē- in between the main verb and the complement. 袂 -bē- is the negative form.

verb + 會 + *complement*

verb + -ē- + *complement*

用 餐巾 敢 拍會死？
Ēng chhan-kin kám phah-ē-sí?
用 餐巾 打得死 嗎？
Yòng cānjīn dǎdesǐ ma?
Can you kill it with a napkin?

阮 教授 真 愛 講 話，所以 講袂煞。
Gún kàu-siū chin ài kóng ōe, só-í kóng-bē-soah.
我們 的 教授 很 愛 說 話，所以 說個不停。
Wǒmen de jiàoshòu hěn ài shuō huà, suǒyǐ shuōgèbùtíng.
Our professor loves talking, so he just won't stop.

我 的 牛仔褲 傷 絚，錢袋仔 提袂出來。
Góa ê gû-á-khò˙ siuⁿ ân, chîⁿ-tē-á theh-bē-chhut--lâi.
我 的 牛仔褲 太 緊，錢包 拿不出來。
Wǒ de niúzǎikù tài jǐn, qiánbāo nábuchūlái.
My jeans are so tight that I can't take my wallet out.

Because Mandarin does not have separate potential complement forms for different tenses, Mandarin translations often use the generic potential complement infix **得 -de-** to express events occurring in the past, present, or future.

Also note that use of the potential complement has a slightly different focus than the modal verbs which express ability such as **會當 ē-tàng** or **會曉 ē-hiáu** *(see 12.3 Ability)*. Modal verbs focus more on whether the entire action can even begin. On the other hand, potential complements shift the focus to whether the result is achievable after the main verb has already begun.

POTENTIAL COMPLEMENT FORM

彼 條 椅仔 真 大，你 一 个 人 提會起來 無？
Hit liâu í-á chin tōa, lí chit ê lâng theh-ē-khí--lâi--bô?
那 把 椅子 很 大，你 一 個 人 拿得起來 嗎？
Nà bǎ yǐzi hěn dà, nǐ yī gè rén nádeqǐlái ma?
That chair is big. Are you able to lift it up by yourself (*once you start lifting will you be able to get it up*)?

MODAL VERB FORM

彼 條 椅仔 釘 佇 塗腳，會當 提起來 無？
Hit liâu í-á tèng tī thô˙-kha, ē-tàng theh--khí-lâi--bô?
那 把 椅子 釘 在 地板，能不能 拿起來？
Nà bǎ yǐzi dīng zài dìbǎn, néngbùnéng náqǐlái?
That chair is nailed to the ground. Can it be lifted off?

POTENTIAL COMPLEMENT FORM

這 條 小路 傷 長，咱 行袂了。
Chit tiâu sió-lō˙siuⁿ tn̂g, lán kiâⁿ-bē-liáu.
這 條 小道 太 長，我們 走不完。
Zhè tiáo xiǎodào tài cháng, wǒmen zǒubuwán.
This trail is too long. We can't reach the end of it (*perhaps they are too tired to keep going*).

MODAL VERB FORM

這 條 小路 的 路尾 無 開方，咱 袂當 行 了，所以 咱 來 行 別 條。
Chit tiâu sió-lō˙ê lō˙-bóe bô khai-hong, lán bē-tàng kiâⁿ liáu, só-í lán lâi kiâⁿ pa̍t tiâu.
這 條 小道 的 終端 不 開放 了，我們 不 能 走完，所以 我們 來 走 別 條 吧。
Zhè tiáo xiǎodào de zhōngduān bù kāifàng le, wǒmen bù néng zǒuwán, suǒyǐ wǒmen lái zǒu bié tiáo ba.
The end of this trail is closed (*discovered before hike begins*). We can't walk it, so let's take a different one.

Some complements when put into the potential form take on a slightly different meaning.

COMPLEMENT	POTENTIAL FORM	MEANING
來 -lâi 'to come'	verb + 會來 verb + ē-lâi	to know how to do
去 -khì 'to go'	verb + 會去 verb + ē-khì	to be able to finish completely
贏 -iâⁿ 'to win'	verb + 會贏 verb + ē-iâⁿ	to be able to succeed at

你 彼 工 共 我 講 的 笑話，我 講袂來。
Lí hit kang kā góa kóng ê chhiò-ōe, góa kóng-bē-lâi.
你 那 天 告訴 我 的 笑話，我 講不出來。
Nǐ nèitiān gàosù wǒ de xiàohuà, wǒ jiǎngbuchūlái.
That joke you told me the other day, I can't tell it like you do.

恁 著愛 加班 才 做會去。

In tio̍h-ài ka-pan chiah chò-ē-khì.

他們 得 加班 才 做得了。

Tāmen děi jiābān cái zuòdeliǎo.

They will have to work overtime <u>to be able to finish it completely</u>.

這 件 行李 傷 重，我 拖袂贏。

Chit kiāⁿ hêng-lí siuⁿ tāng, góa thoa-bē-iâⁿ.

這 件 行李 太 重，我 拖不動。

Zhè jiàn xínglǐ tài zhòng, wǒ tuōbudòng.

This suitcase is too heavy. I <u>can't pull</u> it.

11.4.3 Potential complement with suffix 得 -tit

An alternative construction for the unrealized potential complement is through the use of the suffix 得 -tit (also pronounced -eh). This construction is formed by putting 會 ē- before the verb and placing 得 -tit after the verb.

This construction indicates the possibility (likelihood) of the verb to occur, and in some contexts permission may also be included in the interpretation. It should be noted that this construction is less common and tends to be used with only a small number of verbs. Pronunciation of 得 -tit may reduce to -eh for some speakers. When appearing at the end of a clause or sentence, the final syllable 得 --tit becomes neutralized and the previous syllable (the main verb) does not change tone. The negative form replaces 會 ē- with 袂 bē-. This construction is similar to the Mandarin: verb + 得 dé and verb + 不得 bùdé.

Below is a table of the more common verbs using this construction.

TAIWANESE	MANDARIN	MEANING
會記得 ē-kì-tit	記得 jìdé	to remember
會行得 ē-kiâⁿ-tit	能走 néngzǒu	to be walkable
會認得 ē-jīn-tit	認得 rèndé	to be recognizable
會比得 ē-pí-tit	比得上 bǐdeshàng	to be comparable
會信得 ē-sìn-tit	能信 néngxìn	to be believable
會靠得 ē-khò-tit	靠得住 kàodezhù	to be reliable
會囥得 ē-khǹg-tit	能放 néngfàng	able to put or place
會磕得 ē-kha̍p-tit	能碰 néngpèng	to be touchable
會堪得 ē-kham-tit	受得了 shòudeliǎo	to be endurable

會 + *verb* + 得

ē- + *verb* + -tit

'*verb* can / will be able to occur'

這 兩 項 代誌 袂比得。
Chit nn̄g hāng tāi-chì bē-pí--tit.
這 兩 件 事情 比不得。
Zhè liǎng jiàn shìqíng bǐbudé.
These two issues aren't comparable.

我 愛 伊 這 个 人，因為 伊 會靠得。
Góa ài i chit ê lâng, in-ūi i ē-khò--tit.
我 喜歡 她 這個 人，因為 她 靠得住。
Wǒ xǐhuān tā zhège rén, yīnwèi tā kàodezhù.
I like her because she is reliable.

伊 的 名 我 煞 袂記得，請 你 閣 共 我 講 一 擺？
I ê miâ góa soah bē-kì--tit, chhiáⁿ lí koh kā góa kóng chi̍t pái?
他 的 名字 我 突然 忘記了，請 你 再 跟 我 說 一 次？
Tā de míngzì wǒ tūrán wàngjìle, qǐng nǐ zài gēn wǒ shuō yī cì?
I suddenly forgot his name. Can you please tell me again?

The verbs **會使得 ē-sài-tit** and **會用得 ē-ēng-tit** can also function as modal verbs expressing permission *(see 12.4 Permission)*.

TAIWANESE	MANDARIN	MEANING
會使得 ē-sài-tit	可行 kěxíng, 可以 kěyǐ	usable, allowed to use
會用得 ē-ēng-tit	可行 kěxíng, 可以 kěyǐ	usable, allowed to use

阮 踮 露台 烘 肉 敢 會使得？
Gún tàm lō͘-tâi hang bah kám ē-sái--tit?
我們 在 陽台 烤肉 行不行？
Wǒmen zài yángtái kǎo ròu xíngbùxíng?
Can we barbecue on the porch?

恁 上課 的 時 <u>會使得</u> 用 手機仔。

In siōng-khò ê sî <u>ē-sái-tit</u> ēng chhiú-ki-á.

他們 上課 時 <u>可以</u> 用 手機。

Tāmen shàngkè shí <u>kěyǐ</u> yòng shǒujī.

They <u>are allowed</u> to use mobile phones in class.

11.4.4 Potential complements and objects

With potential complements, objects may appear before, after, and in the middle of verb compounds. However, the most common placement of objects with potential complement verb structures is *before* the main verb.

> *object* + *verb* + 會 / 有 + *complement*
>
> *object* + *verb* + ē / ū + *complement*

這 領 褲,我 <u>穿袂入去</u>。
Chit niá khò, góa <u>chhēng-bē-jip--khì</u>.

這 件 褲子,我 <u>穿不進去</u>。
Zhè jiàn kùzi, wǒ <u>chuānbujìnqù</u>.

I <u>can't fit into</u> **these pants**.

彼 齣 電影,看 兩 點鐘 就 <u>看會了</u>。
Hit chhut tiān-iáⁿ, khòaⁿ nn̄g tiám-cheng tō <u>khòaⁿ-ē-liáu</u>.

那 部 電影,看 兩 個 小時 就 <u>看得完</u>。
Nà bù diànyǐng, kàn liǎng gè xiǎoshí jiù <u>kàndewán</u>.

That film <u>can be seen</u> in just two hours (*the film is capable of being completely watched in two hours*).

On occasion, the object can be placed *after* the complement. Note that linguistic research continues to be done in this area about what specific circumstances allow for the object to be placed in locations other than before the main verb.

> *verb* + 會 / 有 + *complement* + ***object***
>
> *verb* + ē / ū + *complement* + ***object***

服務員 敢 揣有著 你 的 目鏡？
Ho̍k-bū-ôan kám chōe-ū-tio̍h lí ê ba̍k-kiàⁿ?
服務員 找得到 你 的 眼鏡 嗎？
Fúwùyuán zhǎodedào nǐ de yǎnjìng ma?
Was the waiter able to find your glasses?

Additionally, there are exceptional cases (particularly when the objects are pronouns) in which the object occurs *in between* the main verb and potential infix.

verb + ***object (personal pronoun)*** + 會 / 有 + *complement*
verb + ***object (personal pronoun)*** + ē / ū + *complement*

四界 揣，我 揣 伊 無著。
Sì-kè chhōe, góa chhōe i bô-tio̍h.
到處 找，我 找不到 他。
Dàochù zhǎo, wǒ zhǎobudào tā.
I've looked everywhere and can't find him.

The Mandarin verb compound cannot be split by a pronoun except when the complement is a directional complement *(see 11.3.3 Directional complements and objects)*.

11.5 Complements with question marker 敢 kám

When verb complements are part of a 敢 kám-type question, the question marker 敢 kám may optionally be placed in between the main verb and complement *(see 20.1.2* 敢 *kám in verb compounds)*. In this construction, the action of the main verb has already begun and the achievement of the complement becomes the focus of the question.

verb + 敢 + *complement*
verb + kám + *complement*

伊 彼 張 批 寫敢好 矣？
I hit tiuⁿ phoe siá-kám-hó--ah?
她 那 封 信 寫好 了 嗎？
Tā nà fēng xìn xiěhǎo le ma?
Is she finished writing that letter?

佇 跤踏車頂 的 包裹 縛敢牢 矣？
Tī kha-tȧh-chhia-téng ê pau-kó pȧk-kám-tiâu--ah?

在 腳踏車 上 的 包裹 綁住 了 嗎？
Zài jiǎotàchē shàng de bāoguǒ bǎngzhù le ma?

Is the package on the bike <u>securely fastened</u>?

11.6 Manner complements

Manner complements describe how a verb is performed or appears to be carried out. Essentially, they are phrases that function like adverbs but appear after a verb.

11.6.1 Manner complements describing habitual actions

Manner complements are constructed by placing the grammatical particle 著 **-tiȯh** after the main verb and then adding an adjective. An intensifier can optionally be added before the adjective. Manner complements with 著 **-tiȯh** tend to be used to describe habitual actions. Note that 著 **-tiȯh** does not change tone *(see 2.6.3.5 Verb complements)*.

> *verb* + 著 + *(intensifier)* + *adjective*
> *verb* + -tiȯh + *(intensifier)* + *adjective*

頭家 罵著 誠 歹。
Thâu-ke <u>mē-tiȯh chiâⁿ pháiⁿ</u>.

老闆 罵 得 真 兇。
Lǎobǎn <u>mà de zhēn xiōng</u>.

The boss <u>scolds quite fiercely</u>.

恁 後生 學著 真 緊。
Lín hāu-seⁿ <u>ȯh-tiȯh chin kín</u>.

你 兒子 學 得 很 快。
Nǐ érzi <u>xué de hěn kuài</u>.

Your son learns <u>very quickly</u>.

Negation must come before the adjective but after the verb and grammatical particle 著 **tiȯh**.

> *verb* + 著 + *negation* + *adjective*
> *verb* + -tiȯh + *negation* + *adjective*

伊 駛著 無 緊。
I <u>sái-tiȯh bô kín</u>.
他 開 得 不 快。
Tā <u>kāi de bù kuài</u>.
He <u>doesn't drive fast</u>.

11.6.2 Manner complements describing specific instances

Manner complements can also be used to describe how a verb was performed in a particular instance. Note that the focus is the result of the action. This construction is created by placing the grammatical particle 了 **liáu** after the main verb and then adding an adjective. An intensifier can optionally be added before the adjective.

> *verb* + 了 + *(intensifier)* + *adjective*
> *verb* + liáu + *(intensifier)* + *adjective*

你 煮 了 真緊。
Lí <u>chú liáu chin kín</u>.
你 煮 得 很 快。
Nǐ <u>zhǔ de hěn kuài</u>.
You <u>cooked</u> it <u>very fast</u>.

阮 阿姨 唱 了 足 好聽。
Gún a-î <u>chhiùⁿ liáu chiok hó-thiaⁿ</u>.
我 阿姨 唱 得 非常 好聽。
Wǒ āyí <u>chàng de fēicháng hǎotīng</u>.
My aunt <u>sang very well</u>.

Negation must come before the adjective.

> verb + 了 + negation + adjective
>
> verb + liáu + negation + adjective

> 這 篇 報告，記者 寫 了 無 準確。
> Chit phiⁿ pò-kò, kì-chiá siá liáu bô chún-khak.
> 這 篇 報告，記者 寫 得 不 準確。
> Zhè piān bàogào, jìzhě xiě de bù zhǔnquè.
> The journalist didn't write this article accurately.

Similar to manner complements, manner adverbs also describe *how* an action of a verb is performed *(see 14.2.3 Manner adverbs)*. However, there are a few distinctions to be made.

Manner complements appear *after* the verb, while manner adverbs appear *before* the verb. Moreover, manner complements tend to be external observations, while manner adverbs tend to incorporate the subject's attitude towards the action. Finally, manner complements cannot be used in commands, while manner adverbs can.

> MANNER COMPLEMENTS
> 囡仔 坐 了 真 恬。
> Gín-á chē liáu chin tiām.
> 孩子 很 安靜 坐著。
> Háizi hěn ānjìng zuòzhe.
> The children sat quietly *(they appear to be this way)*.

> MANNER ADVERBS
> 囡仔 恬恬 坐。
> Gín-á tiām-tiām chē.
> 孩子 安安靜靜 地 坐。
> Háizi ānānjìngjìng de zuò.
> The children sat quietly *(they are making an effort)*.

11.6.3 Manner complements with objects

With manner complements, if an object follows the verb, the verb is repeated *(verb copying)* before adding the particle 著 **-tioh** / 了 **liáu** and adjective.

verb + **object** + *verb* + 著 / 了 + *(intensifier)* + *adjective*
verb + **object** + *verb* + -tio̍h / liáu + *(intensifier)* + *adjective*

伊 行 **路** 行 著 真 慢。
I kiâⁿ **lō͘** kiâⁿ-tio̍h chin bān.
他 走 **路** 走 得 很 慢。
Tā zǒu **lù** zǒu de hěn màn.
He walks slowly.

阮 阿母 煮 **飯** 煮著 足 好食。
Gún a-bú chú **pn̄g** chú-tio̍h chiok hó-chia̍h.
我 媽媽 煮 **飯** 煮 得 非常 好吃。
Wǒ māmā zhǔ **fàn** zhǔ de fēicháng hàochī.
My mom cooks really delicious **food**.

這 个 醫生 看 **我** 看 了 真 緊。
Chit ê i-seng khòaⁿ **góa** khòaⁿ liáu chin kín.
這個 醫生 看 **我** 看 得 很 快。
Zhège yīshēng kàn **wǒ** kàn de hěn kuài.
The doctor saw **me** quickly.

11.7 Extent complements

Extent complements can be used to describe a condition resulting from the main verb (similar to the function of resultative complements). They can also be used to describe the 'extent' or degree to which the main verb is carried out. This result or extent can be used to describe either the subject or the object.

11.7.1 Extent complements with 甲 kah

The particle **甲 kah** can be placed after the verb and introduce a result or extent. This result or extent can be a phase complement, resultative complement, adjective, or even a whole phrase.

verb + 甲 + *result or extent*

verb + kah + *result or extent*

'*verb* to the point of ....'

彼 規 支 排骨,伊 食 甲 了。

Hit kui ki pâi-kut, i chiah kah liáu.

那 整 個 排骨,他 吃 到 完。

Nà zhěng gè páigǔ, tā chī dào wán.

He ate up that entire pork chop.

我 讀 冊 讀 甲 欲 憨去 矣。

Góa thak chheh thak kah beh gōng--khì--ah.

我 讀 書 讀 到 變 笨 了。

Wǒ dú shū dú dào biàn bèn le.

I've been studying so much that I can't think anymore.

伊 走 甲 袂 喘氣 矣。

I cháu kah bē chhóan-khùi--ah.

她 跑 得 不能 呼吸 了。

Tā pǎo de bùnéng hūxī le.

She ran so much she couldn't breathe.

In Mandarin, generally 得 **de** is used as the extent complement. However, 到 **dào** can also be used in colloquial speech.

11.7.2 Extent complements with 予 hō·

予 **hō·** 'to allow' can also be used to introduce a result or extent. In contrast to 甲 **kah**, 予 **hō·** tends to be used in less extreme descriptions. Additionally, 予 **hō·** as a causative verb is generally used for actions that have not yet occurred, requests, and commands (*see 19.4 Causative verbs, 21.8 Using causative verbs in commands*).

verb + 予 + *result or extent*

verb + hō·+ *result or extent*

'*verb* to the point of ....'

食 予 袂枵 就 好 矣。
Chia̍h hó͘ bē-iáu tō hó--ah.

吃 到 不 會 餓 就 好 了。
Chī dào bù huì è jiù hǎo le.

Eating <u>until you aren't hungry</u> is enough.

外口 耍 了後，手 愛 洗 予 清氣。
Gōa-kháu sńg liáu-āu, chhiú ài sé hó͘ chheng-khì.

外面 玩 之後，手 要 洗乾淨。
Wàimiàn wán zhīhòu, shǒu yào xǐgānjìng.

After playing outside, you must <u>wash</u> your hands <u>until they're clean</u>.

雞肉 一定 愛 煮 予 熟。
Ke-bah it-tēng ài chú hō͘ se̍k.

雞肉 一定 要 煮熟。
Jīròu yīdìng yào zhǔshóu.

Chicken definitely needs to be <u>cooked fully</u>.

Taiwanese tends to use extent complements more often than Mandarin when indicating a resulting condition. As a result, in many circumstances Taiwanese prefers an extent complement, where Mandarin might use a resultative complement.

In addition, note that Mandarin uses **得 de** to express both manner and extent complements, while Taiwanese has a more explicit distinction between the two complements by using different particle markers (manner: **著 -tio̍h** / **了 liáu**, extent: **甲 kah** / **予 hō͘**).

11.7.3 Extent complements with objects

With extent complements, if an object follows the verb, the verb is repeated again *(verb copying)* before adding either the particles **甲 kah** or **予 hō͘** followed by an adjective or descriptive phrase.

   verb + ***object*** + *verb* + **甲** / **予** + *result or extent*

   verb + ***object*** + *verb* + kah / hō͘ + *result or extent*

阮**唱歌**唱甲嚨喉痛。

Gún chhiùⁿ **koa** chhiùⁿ kah nâ-âu thiàⁿ.

我們 唱 歌 唱 到 喉嚨 痛。

Wǒmen chàng gē chàng dào hóulóng tòng.

We sang until our throats were sore.

你 先 **講話** 講 予 了。

Lí seng kóng **ōe** kóng hó liáu.

你 先 把 話 講完。

Nǐ xiān bǎ huà jiǎngwán.

Go ahead and finish **what you want to say**.

11.8 Duration and absolute frequency complements

Duration and absolute frequency complements can be used to quantify the duration of the main verb or provide an absolute frequency of the number of times the main verb occurs.

Note that the absolute frequency expression (e.g. ten times, six laps, two rounds, etc.) differs from the relative frequency adverb (e.g. sometimes, often, never, etc.), which occurs before the main verb *(see 14.2.2 Relative frequency adverbs)*.

11.8.1 Duration and absolute frequency complement placement

Both the duration and absolute frequency expressions describe a specific measurable quantity and are generally placed immediately after the main verb or verb phrase. Typically the duration or absolute frequency expression includes a number, measure word, and noun. For duration, sometimes **久 kú** 'long *(time)*' is added at the end for emphasis.

number + measure word + noun + (久)

number + measure word + noun + (kú)

DURATION

伊 泅 水 四十 分鐘 久。
I siû chúi sì-cha̍p hun-cheng kú.
她 游了 四十 分鐘。
Tā yóule sìshí fēnzhōng.
She swam for 40 minutes.

ABSOLUTE FREQUENCY

伊 泅 水 八 輾。
I siû chúi peh liàn.
她 游了 八 圈。
Tā yóule bā quān.
She swam eight laps.

11.8.2 Duration and absolute frequency complements with objects

When an object is already present after the verb, there are several approaches to include duration or frequency.

One method is to topicalize the object phrase by moving it to the beginning of the sentence before the subject.

METHOD 1

object + *subject* + *verb* + *duration/frequency complement*

DURATION

這 本 冊，我 看 三 點鐘 久。
Chit pún chheh góa khòaⁿ saⁿ tiám-cheng kú.
這 本 書，我 看 三 個 小時。
Zhè běn shū, wǒ kàn sān gè xiǎoshí.
I read **this book** for three hours.

ABSOLUTE FREQUENCY

這本冊，我看兩擺。

Chit pún chheh, góa khòaⁿ nn̄g pái.

這本書，我看兩次。

Zhè běn shū, wǒ kàn liǎng cì.

I read **this book** two times.

Another method is to repeat the verb *(verb copying)* and follow it with the duration or frequency *(see 7.1.5 Including both objects and duration, 7.1.6 Including both objects and frequency)*.

METHOD 2

*verb + **object** + verb + duration / frequency*

DURATION

我看這本冊看三點鐘久。

Góa khòaⁿ **chit pún chheh** khòaⁿ saⁿ tiám-cheng kú.

我看這本書看三個小時。

Wǒ kàn zhè běn shū kàn sān gè xiǎoshí.

I read **this book** for three hours.

ABSOLUTE FREQUENCY

我看這本冊看兩擺。

Góa khòaⁿ **chit pún chheh** khòaⁿ nn̄g pái.

我看這本書看兩次。

Wǒ kàn zhè běn shū kàn liǎng cì.

I read **this book** two times.

An alternative format for verbs followed by both an object and duration is to construct a noun phrase by using the modifier 的 ê to join the duration and object *(see 6.7 Noun phrases and the modifying particle 的 ê)*. Note that this format cannot be used for absolute frequency.

METHOD 3

*verb + duration ＋ (久) + 的 + **noun***

*verb + duration ＋ (kú) + ê + **noun***

我 看 三 點鐘久 的 冊。
Góa khòaⁿ saⁿ tiám-cheng kú ê **chheh**.
我 看 三 個 小時 的 書。
Wǒ kàn sān gè xiǎoshí de shū.
I read **this book** for 3 hours.

11.8.3 Duration and absolute frequency complements with negated verbs

When a duration or absolute frequency complement occurs in sentences with negated verbs, the expression is placed before the negated verb.

duration / frequency + negative + verb

DURATION
兩 點鐘久 矣，伊 猶未 轉來。
Nn̄g tiám-cheng kú--ah, i iáu-bōe tńg--lâi.
兩 個 小時 了，他 還沒 回來。
Liǎng gè xiǎoshí le, tā hái méi huílái.
It's been two hours, and he hasn't returned yet.

阮 五 冬 無 去 美國 矣。
Gún gō͘ tang bô khì Bí-kok--ah.
我們 五 年 沒 去 美國 了。
Wǒmen wǔ nián méi qù Měiguó le.
We haven't gone to America in five years.

ABSOLUTE FREQUENCY
伊 考 三 擺 猶 考無著。
I khó saⁿ pái iáu khó-bô-tio̍h.
她 考 三 次 還 考不上。
Tā kǎo sān cì hái kǎobushàng.
After three times, she still hasn't passed the exam.

十 擺 去 動物園，阮 攏 無 看著 虎。
Cha̍p pái khì tōng-bu̍t-hn̂g, gún lóng bô khòaⁿ-tio̍h hó͘.
十 次 去 動物園，我們 都 沒 看到 老虎。
Shí cì qù dòngwùyuán, wǒmen dōu méi kàndào lǎohǔ.
All <u>ten times</u> we went to the zoo, we didn't see the tiger.

If the actual duration or absolute frequency complement itself is negated, then the placement remains in the default position after the verb.

*verb + negative + **duration / frequency***

DURATION

伊 轉來 猶未 兩 點鐘。
I tńg-lâi iáu-bōe nn̄g tiám-cheng.
他 回來 還 沒 兩 個 小時。
Tā huílái hái méi liǎng gè xiǎoshí.
He's returned, and it hasn't even been <u>two hours</u>.

阮 去 美國 猶未 五 冬。
Gún khì Bí-kok iáu-bōe gō͘ tang.
我們 去 美國 還 沒 五 年 了。
Wǒmen qù Měiguó hái méi wǔ nián.
We went to America, and it hasn't even been <u>five years</u> yet.

ABSOLUTE FREQUENCY

伊 考 猶未 三 擺。
I khò iáu-bōe saⁿ pái.
她 考 還 沒 三 次。
Tā kǎo hái méi sān cì.
She's taken the exam not even <u>three times</u> yet.

阮 看著 虎 攏總 猶未 十 擺。
Gún khòaⁿ-tio̍h hó͘ lóng-chóng iáu-bōe cha̍p pái.
我們 看到 老虎 一共 還 沒 十 次。
Wǒmen kàndào lǎohǔ yīgòng hái méi shí cì.
We've seen the tiger not even <u>ten times</u> altogether.

When a duration or absolute frequency complement is used with a negated verb, the complement moves to a position before the main verb. Among the adverbs in this space, the duration/frequency complement has a flexible position and can appear before sentence-level adverbs or after reference and relative frequency adverbs. However, depending on the context of the sentence, some positions sound more natural than others. The duration/frequency complement must appear before the negation of the main verb of the sentence *(see 14.3 Adverbs with other grammatical elements)*.

ORDER 1

subject + ***duration/absolute frequency complement (when used with negative verb)*** *+ sentence-level adverbs + reference/relative frequency adverbs + negative + modal verb + manner adverb + verb*

ORDER 2

subject + sentence-level adverbs + reference/relative frequency adverbs + ***duration/ absolute frequency complement (when used with negative verb)*** *+ negative + modal verb + manner adverb + verb*

DURATION

以前 伊 二 點鐘 閣 無 夠, 這馬 一 點鐘 就 好 矣。
Í-chêng i nn̄g tiám-cheng koh bô kàu, chit-má chit tiám-cheng tō hó--ah.
以前 他 兩 個 小時 還 不 夠 用, 現在 一 個 小時 就 好 了。
Yǐqián tā liǎng gè xiǎoshí hái bù gòu yòng, xiànzài yī gè xiǎoshí jiù hǎo le.
Before, two hours was never enough for him. Now, one hour is just right.

你 十五 分鐘 一定 看袂了。
Lí cha̍p-gō͘ hun-cheng it-tēng khòaⁿ-bē-liáu.
你 十五 分鐘 一定 看不完。
Nǐ shíwǔ fēnzhōng yīdìng kànbuwán.
You definitely won't finish watching it in fifteen minutes.

FREQUENCY

可能 一 個 月 兩 擺 猶閣 無 夠 予 厝 清氣。
Khó-lêng chit kò goe̍h nn̄g pái iáu-koh bô kàu hō͘ chhù chheng-khì.
可能 一 個 月 兩 次 還 不 夠 讓 房子 乾淨。
Kěnéng yī gè yuè liǎng cì hái bùgòu ràng fángzi gānjìng.
Maybe twice a month still won't be enough to keep the house clean.

伊 罕得 <u>三 遍</u> 攏 做無好。

I hán-tit <u>saⁿ piàn</u> lóng chò-bô-hó.

他 難得 <u>三 遍</u> 都 做不好。

Tā nándé <u>sān biàn</u> dōu zuòbuhǎo.

He rarely does not do it well <u>three times</u> in a row.

11.9 Summary for object placement

Below is a summary table for the placement of objects with regards to the verb compound.

Verb compound (VC) = verb + complement

	BEFORE *object* + VC	BETWEEN V + *object* + C	AFTER VC + *object*
PHASE COMPLEMENTS			
Completion	Yes	Rare	No
Achievement/Potential	Yes	Rare	Yes
RESULTATIVE COMPLEMENTS			
Indefinite	No	Rare	Yes
Definite	Yes	Rare	Yes
Pronouns	Yes	No	No
DIRECTIONAL COMPLEMENTS			
Indefinite	No	Yes	No
Definite	Yes	Rare	Rare (*locations*)
POTENTIAL COMPLEMENTS			
	Yes	Rare (*pronouns*)	No
MANNER COMPLEMENTS			
	Yes (*verb copying*)	No	No

	BEFORE *object* + VC	BETWEEN V + *object* + C	AFTER VC + *object*
EXTENT COMPLEMENTS	Yes *(verb copying)*	No	No
DURATION / ABSOLUTE FREQUENCY COMPLEMENTS	Yes *(verb copying/ topicalize)*	No	Yes *(noun phrase)*

11.10 Summary of verb complements

Below is a summary table for all verb complements presented in this chapter.

	TAIWANESE	MANDARIN
PHASE COMPLEMENTS		
Completion	了 liáu	完 wán, 了 le
	完 ôan	完 wán, 了 le
	煞 soah	完 wán, 了 le
	好 hó	好 hǎo, 了 le
Achievement	著 -tiȯh	到 dào, 著 zháo
	有 ū	到 dào, 著 zháo
Potential	有 ū	得 -de-
RESULTATIVE COMPLEMENTS		
	飽 -pá	飽 bǎo
	開 -khui, --khui	開 kāi
	牢 -tiâu	住 zhù
	破 -phòa	破 pò
	:	:
DIRECTIONAL COMPLEMENTS		
Speaker perspective	來 -lâi	來 lái
	去 -khì	去 qù
Double-directional	起來 -khí-lâi	起來 qǐlái
	起去 -khí-khì	—
	落來 -lȯh-lâi	下來 xiàlái
	落去 -lȯh-khì	下去 xiàqù

	TAIWANESE	MANDARIN
	入來 -jip-lâi	進來 jìnlái
	入去 -jip-khì	進去 jìnqù
	出來 -chhut-lâi	出來 chūlái
	出去 -chhut-khì	出去 chūqù
	轉來 -tńg-lâi	回來 huílái
	轉去 -tńg-khì	回去 huíqù
	過來 -kòe-lâi	過來 guòlái
	過去 -kòe-khì	過去 guòqù

POTENTIAL COMPLEMENTS

	TAIWANESE	MANDARIN
Actualized	有 -ū-	得 -de-
Unrealized	會 -ē-	得 -de-
	會 ē -*verb*- 得 tit	*verb* + 得 dé

MANNER COMPLEMENTS

	TAIWANESE	MANDARIN
	著 -tio̍h	得 de
	了 liáu	得 de

EXTENT COMPLEMENTS

	TAIWANESE	MANDARIN
	甲 kah	到 dào
	予 hō͘	到 dào

DURATION / ABOLUTE FREQUENCY COMPLEMENTS

	TAIWANESE	MANDARIN
	number + measure word + noun + (久 kú)	*number + measure word + noun*

12 Modal verbs

Modal verbs express the subject's mood, intention, inclination, or attitude towards an action. They are a type of helping verb used in conjunction with the main verb. More specifically, modal verbs are used to express possibility, ability, desire, permission, obligation, and prohibition.

>Tomorrow <u>might</u> snow heavily (*possibility*).
>
>I <u>can</u> climb trees with one hand (*ability*).
>
>We <u>want</u> to watch television (*desire*).
>
>You <u>may</u> stay until midnight (*permission*).
>
>They <u>must</u> take the test on Friday (*obligation*).
>
><u>Do not</u> dive here (*prohibition*).

12.1 Possibility

Possibility modal verbs express the likelihood of an action occurring in the future ('They will leave tomorrow' or 'I am going to sleep'). Because Taiwanese does not mark tense in its verbs, actions in the future are often preceded by the possibility modal verbs 會 **ē** 'will' or 欲 **beh** 'going to' (also pronounced **boeh**).

	TAIWANESE		MANDARIN	
	AFFIRM	*NEG*	*AFFIRM*	*NEG*
will	會 ē	袂 bē	會 huì	不會 bù huì
going to	欲 beh	未 bōe	要 yào	還沒 háiméi

12.1.1 Modal verb 會 ē 'will'

會 ē 'will' is placed before a verb to indicate that an event is very likely to occur. The feeling is generally neutral but describes an event that appears inevitable or beyond the control of the subject. The negative form is 袂 bē.

> 會 + *verb*
>
> ē + *verb*
>
> 'will *verb*'

> 明仔載 會 落雨。
> Bîn-á-chài ē lȯh-hō͘.
> 明天 會 下雨。
> Míngtiān huì xiàyǔ.
> Tomorrow it will rain.

> 我 春天 袂 畢業。
> Góa chhun-thiⁿ bē pit-gia̍p.
> 我 春天 不會 畢業。
> Wǒ chūntiān bù huì bìyè.
> I won't graduate in the spring (*the circumstances won't allow for it*).

12.1.2 Modal verb 欲 beh 'to be going to'

欲 **beh** (also pronounced **boeh**) 'to be going to' stresses the possibility that an event will likely occur in the immediate future. However, there is much overlap in usage between 會 ē and 欲 **beh**, and in many contexts they are interchangeable.

> 欲 + *verb*
>
> beh + *verb*
>
> 'to be going to *verb*'

阮 阿兄 欲 去 台北。

Gún a-hiaⁿ beh khì Tâi-pak.

我 哥哥 要 去 台北。

Wǒ gēgē yào qù Táiběi.

My older brother is going to go to Taipei (*near future*).

阮 阿兄 會 去 台北。

Gún a-hiaⁿ ē khì Tâi-pak.

我 哥哥 會 去 台北。

Wǒ gēgē huì qù Táiběi.

My older brother will go to Taipei (*distant future*).

Because **欲 beh** has another meaning 'to want', there is the possibility for ambiguity particularly when the subject is an animate being *(see 12.2.1 Modal verb 欲 beh 'to want')*.

伊 欲 去 法國。

I beh khì Hoat-kok.

她 要 去 法國。

Tā yào qù Fàguó.

She is going to go to France (*possibility*).

She wants to go to France (*desire*).

阿母 欲 去 市場 來 買 物件 矣。

A-bú beh khì chhī-tiûⁿ lâi bé mih-kiāⁿ--ah.

媽媽 要 去 市場 來 買 東西 了。

Māmā yào qù shìchǎng lái mǎi dōngxī le.

Mom is going to go to the market to buy a few things (*possibility*).

Mom wants to go to the market to buy a few things (*desire*).

If the subject is inanimate (objects, non-living things), **欲 beh** can only convey future possibility and not desire.

計程車 暗時 八 點 欲 來 矣。

Kè-thêng-chhia àm-sî peh tiám beh lâi--ah.

計程車 晚上 八 點 要 來 了。

Jìchéngchē wǎnshàng bā diǎn yào lái le.

The taxi is going to come at 8pm (*possibility*).

尪仔 欲 倒落去 矣,用 手 共 伊 扞。

Ang-á <u>beh</u> tó--lòh-khì--ah, ēng chhiú kā i hōaⁿ.

娃娃 要 倒下去 了,用 手 把 它 扶。

Wáwá <u>yào</u> dàoxiàqù le, yòng shǒu bǎ tā fú.

The doll <u>is about to</u> fall over. Use your hand to support it (*possibility*).

Additionally, because there is commonly a change in situation signaled to the listener when stating an event will happen in the immediate future, the anterior aspect marker 矣 **--ah** often appears at the end of the clause or sentence *(see 8.4 Anterior aspect)*.

The negative form for 欲 **beh** is (猶)未 **(iáu-)bōe** 'not yet' rather than 無欲 **bô beh** 'not want', which only negates 欲 **beh** when used in the sense of 'to want' *(desire) (see 12.2 Desire)*.

To indicate that an event will not occur at all in the future, 袂 **bē** 'will not' must be used.

伊 的 學生 猶未 清 教室。

I ê hàk-seng <u>iáu-bōe</u> chheng kàu-sek.

他 的 學生 還沒 清 教室。

Tā de xuéshēng <u>háiméi</u> qīng jiàoshì.

His students <u>have not</u> cleaned the classroom <u>yet</u>.

伊 的 學生 袂 清 教室。

I ê hàk-seng <u>bē</u> chheng kàu-sek.

他 的 學生 不會 清 教室。

Tā de xuéshēng <u>bù huì</u> qīng jiàoshì.

His students <u>will not</u> clean the classroom.

12.1.3 Emphasizing that an action is 'going to happen soon'

Placing the particle 咧 **teh** before 欲 **beh** forms 咧欲 **teh-beh** (also pronounced **tih-beh**) 'just about to', which stresses that an action is on the verge of occurring. An alternate form is 強欲 **kiōng-beh** (also pronounced **liong-beh**).

我 咧欲 出門。

Góa <u>teh-beh</u> chhut-mn̂g.

我 快要 出門。

Wǒ <u>kuàiyào</u> chūmén.

I'm <u>just about to</u> run out the door.

李 先生 列欲 睏去 矣。

Lí--sian-siⁿ teh-beh khùn--khì--ah.

李 先生 快要 睡覺 了。

Lǐ xiānshēng kuàiyào shuìjiào le.

Mr. Li is just about to fall asleep.

12.2 Desire

Desire modal verbs express 'wanting' to do an action ('He wants to run in the morning' or 'I would like to watch a movie').

	TAIWANESE		MANDARIN	
	AFFIRM	*NEG*	*AFFIRM*	*NEG*
want	欲 beh	毋 m̄, 無欲 bô beh	要 yào	不要 bùyào
	愛 ài	毋 m̄, 無愛 bô ài	要 yào	不要 bùyào
	欲愛 beh-ài	無欲愛 bô beh-ài	要 yào	不要 bùyào
	愛欲 ài-beh	無愛欲 bô ài-beh	要 yào	不要 bùyào
would like	想欲 siūⁿ-beh	無想欲 bô siūⁿ-beh	想要 xiǎngyào	不想要 bùxiǎngyào
	想愛 siūⁿ-ài	無想愛 bô siūⁿ-ài	想要 xiǎngyào	不想要 bùxiǎngyào

12.2.1 Modal verb 欲 beh 'to want'

To indicate 'wanting' to do an action, Taiwanese uses both modal verbs **欲 beh** and **愛 ài**. In general the two words are interchangeable when used as modal verbs, but there are some contexts in which one word is preferred over the other as well as differences in individual preference.

While **欲 beh** is a modal verb for desire, **欲 beh** also functions as a modal verb for future possibility *(see 12.1.2 Modal verb 欲 beh 'to be going to')*. The negative form can be either **毋 m̄** or **無欲 bô beh**. **毋 m̄** is currently declining in usage.

欲 + *verb*

beh + *verb*

'to want to *verb*'

我 食飽 了後，就 <u>欲</u> 睏。

Góa chiảh-pá liáu-āu, tō <u>beh</u> khùn.

我 吃飽 之後，就 <u>要</u> 睡覺。

Wǒ chībǎo zhīhòu, jiù <u>yào</u> shuìjiào.

After I have eaten, I <u>just want to</u> sleep.

這 隻 貓仔 <u>毋</u> 按 厝頂 落來。

Chit chiah niau-á <u>m̄</u> àn chhù-téng lòh--lâi.

這 隻 貓 <u>不要</u> 從 屋頂 下來。

Zhè zhī māo <u>bù yào</u> cóng wūdǐng xiàlái.

The cat <u>won't</u> come down from the roof.

阿公 <u>無欲</u> 去 購物 中心。

A-kong <u>bô beh</u> khì kò͘-bút tiong-sim.

爺爺 <u>不 要</u> 去 購物 中心。

Yěyě <u>bù yào</u> qù gòuwù zhōngxīn.

Grandpa <u>doesn't want</u> to go to the shopping center.

12.2.2 Modal verb 愛 ài 'to want'

The modal verb **愛 ài** 'to want' generally is preferred over **欲 beh** when there are different subjects or before adjectives. The negative form can be either **毋 m̄** or **無愛 bô ài**. **毋 m̄** is currently declining in usage.

愛 + *verb*

ài + *verb*

'to want to *verb*'

阮 阿爸 <u>愛</u> 我 做 醫生。

Gún a-pa <u>ài</u> góa chò i-seng.

我 爸爸 <u>要</u> 我 當 醫生。

Wǒ bàba <u>yào</u> wǒ dāng yīshēng.

My father <u>wants</u> me to be a doctor.

這个 查某 囝仔 愛 嬌。

Chit ê cha-bó͘ gín-á <u>ài</u> súi.

這個 女孩子 愛 漂亮。

Zhège nǚháizi <u>ài</u> piàoliang.

This little girl <u>wants</u> to be pretty.

遮的 衫褲，你 閣 愛 捏 無？

Chiah-ê saⁿ-khò͘, lí koh <u>ài</u> tih--bô?

這 些 衣服，你 還 要 嗎？

Zhè xiē yīfú, nǐ hái <u>yào</u> ma?

Do you still <u>want</u> these clothes?

捏 **tih** is originally a verb meaning 'to have'. However, 捏 **tih** is now commonly used to express 'wanting' of physical objects. 捏 **tih** is also commonly paired with 欲 **beh** and 愛 **ài** to form 欲捏 **beh tih** and 愛捏 **ài tih**.

12.2.3 Modal verbs 想欲 siūⁿ-beh and 想愛 siūⁿ-ài 'would like, thinking of'

想 **siūⁿ** 'to be thinking of' is often placed before 欲 **beh** to ensure that 欲 **beh** gets interpreted with its sense of 'to want' instead of its future-oriented sense of 'going to'. Because 想欲 **siūⁿ-beh** also retains some of the meaning from 想 **siūⁿ** 'to think', the feeling is also slightly more tentative and polite with a meaning similar to 'would like' or 'thinking of'. The negative form is 無 想欲 **bô siūⁿ-beh**.

想欲 + *verb*

siūⁿ-beh + *verb*

'would like to *verb*'

伊 想欲 去 夜市 來 食 飯。

I <u>siūⁿ-beh</u> khì iā-chhī lâi chia̍h pn̄g.

她 想 到 夜市 來 吃 飯。

Tā <u>xiǎng</u> dào yèshì lái chī fàn.

She <u>is thinking of</u> going to the night market to eat.

我 想欲 點 龍蝦。

Góa siūⁿ-beh tiám lêng-hê.

我 想要 點 龍蝦。

Wǒ xiǎngyào diǎn lóngxiā.

I would like to order the lobster.

劉 先生 無 想欲 出國。

Lâu--sian-siⁿ bô siūⁿ-beh chhut-kok.

劉 先生 不 想要 出國。

Liú xiānshēng bù xiǎngyào chūguó.

Mr. Lau is not thinking of leaving the country.

Note that in Mandarin, **想 xiǎng** by itself can suggest 'wanting' to do an action. However, **想 siūⁿ** in Taiwanese must be paired with **欲 beh** to express desire.

The modal verb **想愛 siūⁿ-ài** is also used but in fewer contexts than **想欲 siūⁿ-beh**. Because **愛 ài** has another reading ('to need'), placing **想 siūⁿ** before **愛 ài** helps to remove any ambiguity. The negative form is **無 想愛 bô siūⁿ-ài**.

想愛 + *verb*

siūⁿ-ài + *verb*

'would like to *verb*'

伊 無 想愛 食 西餐。

I bô siūⁿ-ài chia̍h se-chhan.

她 不 想 吃 西餐。

Tā bù xiǎng chī xīcān.

She would not like to eat western food.

囡仔 一直 想愛 迌。

Gín-á it-tit siūⁿ-ài chhit-thô.

孩子 一直 想要 玩。

Háizi yīzhí xiǎngyào wán.

Children always think of playing.

12.2.4 Expressing desire for nouns

The combination of **欲 beh** and **愛 ài** into **欲愛 beh ài** 'to want' is often not used as a modal verb but to indicate desire for a noun.

你 欲 愛 啥物 物件？
Lí <u>beh ài</u> siá`ⁿ`-mih mih-kiā`ⁿ`?
你 想要 什麼 東西？
Nǐ <u>xiǎngyào</u> shénme dōngxī?
What <u>would</u> you like?

Compared to the Mandarin **愛 ài**, the Taiwanese **愛 ài** covers a broader spectrum of meaning. While in both languages **愛 ài** can mean 'to love', Taiwanese also uses **愛 ài** to express the meanings of 'to like' (Mandarin typically uses **喜歡 xǐhuān**) and also as a modal verb expressing necessity *(see 12.5 Obligation)*.

逐家 愛 食 冰。
Ta̍k-ke <u>ài</u> chia̍h peng.
大家 喜歡 吃 冰淇淋。
Dàjiā <u>xǐhuān</u> chī bīngqílín.
Everyone <u>likes to</u> eat ice cream.

囡仔 愛 睏 上少 九 點鍾。
Gín-á <u>ài</u> khùn siōng-chió káu tiám-cheng.
小 孩子 需要 睡 至少 九 個 小時。
Xiǎo háizi <u>xūyào</u> shuì zhìshǎo jiǔ gè xiǎoshí.
Little children <u>need to</u> sleep at least 9 hours.

12.3 Ability

Ability modal verbs can express either one's personal skills ('She can really sing!' or 'He knows German') or the ability to complete a task given a set of circumstances ('We can meet you after work' or 'I can't fit into these clothes').

	TAIWANESE		MANDARIN	
	AFFIRM	*NEG*	*AFFIRM*	*NEG*
SKILLS				
can	會曉 ē-hiáu	袂曉 bē-hiáu	會 huì	不會 bùhuì
	會 ē	袂 bē	會 huì	不會 bùhuì
CIRCUMSTANCES				
can	會當 ē-tàng	袂當 bē-tàng	能 néng	不能 bùnéng

12.3.1 Modal verb 會曉 ē-hiáu 'can'

To express an ability that is an innate ability or an acquired skill through learning, use 會曉 ē-hiáu 'can'. The negative form is 袂曉 bē-hiáu. An alternate form is 會 ē. However, because 會 ē also has the future-oriented sense of 'will', 會曉 ē-hiáu is more commonly used.

會曉 + *verb*

ē-hiáu + *verb*

'can *verb*'

我 會曉 泅 水。
Góa ē-hiáu siû chúi.
我 會 游泳。
Wǒ huì yóuyǒng.
I can swim.

伊 袂曉 講 德文。
I bē-hiáu kóng Tik-bûn.
她 不 會 說 德文。
Tā bù huì shuō Déwén.
She cannot speak German.

伊 會 駛 車。
I ē sái chhia.
他 會 開 車。
Tā huì kāi chē.
He can drive (*ability*).
He will drive (*possibility*).

12.3.2 Modal verb 會當 ē-tàng 'can'

The modal verb 會當 ē-tàng is more often used to describe ability when external circumstances (physical or otherwise) allow an action to occur. The negative form is 袂當 bē-tàng.

會當 + *verb*

ē-tàng + *verb*

'can *verb*'

阮 五 个 人 攏 會當 坐 一 台 車 袂？
Gún gō͘ ê lâng lóng ē-tàng chē chit tâi chhia--bē?
我們 五 個 人 都 能 坐 一 台 車 嗎？
Wǒmen wǔ gè rén dōu néng zuò yī tái chē ma?
Can the five of us all fit into one car?

因為 落雨, 伊 袂當 外口 運動。
In-ūi lo̍h-hō͘, i bē-tàng gōa-kháu ūn-tōng.
因為 下雨, 他 不 能 外面 運動。
Yīnwèi xiàyǔ, tā bù néng wàimiàn yùndòng.
Because it's raining, he can't exercise outside.

12.4 Permission

Permission modal verbs grant or allow an action to be done ('You may eat first' or 'They are allowed to sit there').

	TAIWANESE		MANDARIN	
	AFFIRM	*NEG*	*AFFIRM*	*NEG*
GENERAL				
may	會使(得) ē-sái(-tit)	袂使(得) bē-sái(-tit)	可以 kěyǐ	不可以 bùkěyǐ
	會當 ē-tàng	袂當 bē-tàng	能 néng	不能 bùnéng
	會用得 ē-ēng-tit	袂用得 bē-ēng-tit	可以 kěyǐ	不可以 bùkěyǐ
POLITE				
may	通(好) thang(-hó)	--	--	--

12.4.1 Modal verb 會使(得) ē-sái(-tit) 'may'

The main modal verb to indicate permission to perform an action is 會使(得) ē-sái(-tit). In addition, other modal verbs are used including 會當 ē-tàng and 會用得 ē-ēng-tit. Note that for some speakers the 得 -tit suffix is also pronounced **-eh** (i.e. 會使得 ē-sái-eh, 會用得 ē-ēng-eh).

All of these modal verbs can be used interchangeably to express permission ('may' or 'to be allowed'). However, 會當 ē-tàng also carries the meaning of ability ('can'). In contrast, 會使(得) ē-sái(-tit) and 會用得 ē-ēng-tit only express permission.

The negative forms are 袂使(得) bē-sái(-tit), 袂當 bē-tàng, 袂用得 bē-ēng-tit.

會使 (得) + *verb*

ē-sái (-tit) + *verb*

'allowed to *verb*'

囡仔 <u>會使</u> 看 四 點鐘 的 電視。
Gín-á <u>ē-sái</u> khòaⁿ sì tiám-cheng ê tiān-sī.
孩子 <u>可以</u> 看 四 個 小時 的 電視。
Háizǐ <u>kěyǐ</u> kàn sì gè xiǎoshí de diànshì.
The children <u>may</u> watch television for four hours.

阿爸 講 阮 <u>會當</u> 飼 狗仔。
A-pa kóng gún <u>ē-tàng</u> chhī káu-á.
爸爸 說 我們 <u>能</u> 養 狗。
Bàba shuō wǒmen <u>néng</u> yǎng gǒu.
Dad says we <u>are allowed to</u> get a dog.

老師 共 學生 講 哺 樹奶糖 <u>袂用得</u>。
Lāu-su kā ha̍k-seng kóng pō͘ chhiū-leng-thn̂g <u>bē-ēng-tit</u>.
老師 跟 學生 說 嚼 口香糖 <u>不行</u>。
Lǎoshī gēn xuéshēng shuō jué kǒuxiāngtáng <u>bùxíng</u>.
The teacher told the students that chewing gum <u>is not permitted</u>.

12.4.2 Modal verb 通(好) thang(-hó) 'may'

The modal verb **通(好) thang(-hó)** 'may' can also be used to convey permission and is generally used as a polite form.

通(好) + *verb*

thang(-hó) + *verb*

'may *verb*'

阮 通好 坐 遮 無？

Gún <u>thang-hó</u> chē chiah--bô?

我們 可以 坐 這裡 嗎？

Wǒmen <u>kěyǐ</u> zuò zhèlǐ ma?

<u>May</u> we sit here?

Note that Mandarin does not have an exact equivalent for **通(好) thang(-hó)** 'may' when used as a more polite way to ask for permission.

The negative form of **通 thang** 'may' is **毋通 m̄-thang**. However, when used in the negative, the meaning shifts from one of permission to prohibition and can only be used in the second person.

恁 毋通 佇 內底 食 煙。

Lín <u>m̄-thang</u> tī lāi-té chiah hun.

你們 別 在 裡面 吸菸。

Nǐmen <u>bié</u> zài lǐmiàn xīyān.

<u>Do not</u> smoke inside.

12.5 Obligation

Obligation modal verbs can express needs from both an internal standpoint ('I need to eat') and an external standpoint ('You need to sit quietly'). Moreover, obligation can be understood in terms of degree. Weaker obligation comes from moral and ethical positions ('should' or 'supposed to'), while stronger obligation comes from the authority of rules and laws ('must' or 'have to').

	TAIWANESE		MANDARIN	
	AFFIRM	NEG	AFFIRM	NEG
GENERAL				
need	愛 ài	(毋)免 (m̄-)bián	要 yào	不用 bùyòng
	著愛 tio̍h-ài	(毋)免 (m̄-)bián	要 yào	不用 bùyòng
	著 tio̍h	(毋)免 (m̄-)bián	要 yào	不用 bùyòng
FORMAL				
need	需要 su-iàu	無需要 bô su-iàu	需要 xūyào	不需要 bùxūyào
ADVERBS				
should	應該 eng-kai	無應該 bô eng-kai	應該 yīnggāi	不應該 bùyīnggāi
must	一定 it-tēng	無一定 bô it-tēng	一定 yídìng	不一定 bùyídìng

12.5.1 Modal verb 愛 ài 'to need'

To indicate an obligation or necessity to do an action, Taiwanese uses the modal verb 愛 ài 'must' or 'need to'. However, because 愛 ài has other meanings such as 'to want' or 'to like/love', a two-syllable variation 著愛 tio̍h-ài can also be used to help ensure the necessity reading (著 tio̍h by itself may appear although this is less common).

The negative form is 免 bián, but 毋 m̄ is often added for emphasis to form 毋免 m̄-bián (also contracted to mián). Note that 無愛 bô ài can only be used to mean 'to not like/want' (*desire*).

(著)愛 + *verb*

(tio̍h-) ài + *verb*

'need to *verb*'

我 愛 煮 菜。
Góa <u>ài</u> chú chhài.
我 爱 煮 菜。
Wǒ <u>ài</u> zhǔ cài
I <u>must</u> cook (*necessity*).
I <u>love</u> cooking (*desire*).

吳小姐 著愛 借你的電腦。
Gô·sió-chiá tio̍h-ài chioh lí ê tiān-náu.

吳小姐 需要 借你的電腦。
Wú xiǎojiě xūyào jiè nǐ de diànnǎo.

Ms. Gou <u>needs to</u> borrow your computer.

咱 毋免 中晝 進前 到。
Lán m̄-bián tiong-tàu chìn-chêng kàu.

我們 不用 中午 之前 到。
Wǒmen bùyòng zhōngwǔ zhīqián dào.

We <u>don't need to</u> get there before noon.

需要 su-iàu in Taiwanese is more formal in tone and less common in daily speech than **愛 ài** or **著愛 tio̍h-ài**. The negative form is **無需要 bô su-iàu**.

需要 + *verb*

su-iàu + *verb*

'need to *verb*'

你 無 需要 簽名。
Lí bô su-iàu chhiam-miâ.

你 不 需要 簽名。
Nǐ bù xūyào qiānmíng.

You <u>do not have to</u> sign your name.

Note the Mandarin equivalent **需要 xūyào** 'to need' does not carry the same air of formality.

12.5.2 Degree of obligation

To distinguish between weaker obligation (*should*) and stronger obligation (*must*), Taiwanese makes use of adverbs for emphasis. Without the use of adverbs, the degree of obligation is left to interpretation and determined by context.

To emphasize weak obligation, place the adverb **應該 eng-kai** 'should' before the main verb. A modal verb can be included or omitted.

應該 + *(modal verb)* + *verb*

eng-kai + *(modal verb)* + *verb*

'should *(modal verb)* + *verb*'

阮 食 飯 進前，應該 洗 手。
Gún chiȧh pn̄g chìn-chêng, eng-kai sé chhiú.
我們 吃 飯 之前，應該 洗 手。
Wǒmen chī fàn zhīqián, yīnggāi xǐ shǒu.
We should wash our hands before we eat.

這 个 錯誤，你 應該 愛 共 恁 頭家 講 一下。
Chit ê chhò-gō͘, lí eng-kai ài kā lín thâu-ke kóng chi̍t-ē.
這個 錯誤，你 應該 要 跟 你的 老闆 說 一下。
Zhège cuòwù, nǐ yīnggāi yào gēn nǐ de lǎobǎn shuō yīxià.
You should tell your boss about this mistake.

To emphasize strong obligation, place the adverb **一定 it-tēng** 'definitely' before the main verb. A modal verb can be included or omitted.

一定 + *(modal verb)* + *verb*

it-tēng + *(modal verb)* + *verb*

'definitely *(modal verb)* + *verb*'

我 一定 愛 拜六 上班。
Góa it-tēng ài pài-la̍k siōng-pān.
我 得 禮拜六 上班。
Wǒ děi lǐbàiliù shàngbān.
I definitely must work on Saturdays.

入去 游泳池 進前，恁 一定 著愛 先 洗浴。
Ji̍p-khì iû-éng-tî chìn-chêng, in it-tēng tio̍h-ài seng sé-e̍k.
進入 游泳池 之前，他們 必須 先 洗澡。
Jìnrù yóuyǒngchí zhīqián, tāmen bìxū xiān xǐzǎo.
They have to shower before entering the pool.

Note that the Mandarin verbs 得 děi or 必須 bìxū 'must' already indicate strong obligation without having to add adverbs.

12.6 Prohibition

In the negative form, some modal verbs change meaning and can be used as prohibitions. Prohibitions are commands that warn or instruct not to do an action such as the English 'do not'.

	TAIWANESE		MANDARIN	
	AFFIRM	NEG	AFFIRM	NEG
do not	--	莫 mài	--	別 bié, 不要 bùyào
	--	毋通 m̄-thang	--	別 bié, 不要 bùyào
	--	毋好 m̄-hó	--	別 bié, 不要 bùyào

12.6.1 Modal verb 莫 mài 'do not'

When 愛 ài is used as a modal verb expressing 'to want' or 'to like', the negation formed by 無 bô and 愛 ài produces 無愛 bô ài meaning 'not to like' or 'not to want'.

伊無愛食魚。
I bô ài chia̍h hî.
他不喜歡吃魚。
Tā bù xǐhuan chī yú.
He doesn't like to eat fish.
He doesn't want to eat fish.

However, the combination of the negative 毋 m̄ and 愛 ài produces a phonetic combination 莫 mài which shifts the meaning to 'do not'. 莫 mài can only be used in the second person to prohibit or advise against an action.

莫 + verb

mài + verb

'do not verb'

莫 駛 傷 緊！

Mài sái siuⁿ kín!

不要 開 太 快！

Bùyào kāi tài kuài!

Don't drive too fast!

莫 關 門。

Mài koaiⁿ mn̂g.

別 關 門。

Bié guān mén.

Don't close the door.

In Mandarin the negation of the modal verb 要 **yào** 'to want' creates the prohibition 不要 **bùyào** (and its contraction 別 **bié**) to mean 'do not' when used in the second person.

12.6.2 Modal verb 毋通 m̄-thang 'do not'

The negative form of 通 **thang** 'to be allowed' can also be used as a modal verb for prohibition, 毋通 **m̄-thang** 'do not'. Note that 毋通 **m̄-thang** is less emphatic in tone than 莫 **mài**.

毋通 + *verb*

m̄-thang + *verb*

'do not *verb*'

你 毋通 啉 酒 駛車。

Lí m̄-thang lim chiú sái chhia.

你 別 喝 酒 開車。

Nǐ bié hē jiǔ kāichē.

Don't drink and drive.

佇 圖書館 毋通 講 話。

Tī tô·-su-kóan m̄-thang kóng ōe.

在 圖書館 別 說 話。

Zài túshūguǎn bié shuō huà.

Don't talk in the library.

Note that Mandarin modal verbs for prohibition **不要 bùyào** and **別 bié** are similar in tone and only differentiated in strength by one's speech volume.

12.6.3 Modal verb 毋好 m̄-hó 'do not'

The negative form of the adjective 好 **hó** 'good' using 毋 **m̄** can be used as a modal verb for prohibition 毋好 **m̄-hó** 'do not'. The other negative form **無好 bô hó** cannot serve as a modal verb *(see 6.4.3 Negation based on adjective desirability)*. Note that when contracted 毋好 **m̄-hó** may sometimes sound like '**m̄-mo**'. The overall tone of 毋好 **m̄-hó** is similar in strength to 毋通 **m̄-thang**.

毋好 + *verb*

m̄-hó + *verb*

'do not *verb*'

半暝 以後 <u>毋好</u> 出去。
Pòaⁿ-mê í-āu <u>m̄-hó</u> chhut--khì.
半夜 以後 <u>不要</u> 出去。
Bànyè yǐhòu <u>bùyào</u> chūqù.
<u>Don't</u> go out after midnight.

<u>毋好</u> 食 油 的 物件。
<u>M̄-hó</u> chia̍h iû ê mi̍h-kiāⁿ.
<u>別</u> 吃 油膩 的 食物。
<u>Bié</u> chī yóunì de shíwù.
<u>Don't</u> eat greasy foods.

12.7 Summary of modal verbs

	TAIWANESE		MANDARIN	
	AFFIRM	NEG	AFFIRM	NEG
POSSIBILITY *(FUTURE)*				
will	會 ē	袂 bē	會 huì	不會 búhuì
going to	欲 beh	未 bōe	要 yào	還沒 háiméi

DESIRE *(VOLITION)*				
want	欲 beh	毋 m̄, 無欲 bô beh	要 yào	不要 bùyào
	愛 ài	毋 m̄, 無愛 bô ài	要 yào	不要 bùyào
	欲愛 beh-ài	無欲愛 bô beh-ài	要 yào	不要 bùyào
	愛欲 ài-beh	無愛欲 bô ài-beh	要 yào	不要 bùyào
would like	想欲 siūⁿ-beh	無想欲 bô siūⁿ-beh	想要 xiǎngyào	不想要 bùxiǎngyào
	想愛 siūⁿ-ài	無想愛 bô siūⁿ-ài	想要 xiǎngyào	不想要 bùxiǎngyào
ABILITY				
SKILLS				
can	會曉 ē-hiáu	袂曉 bē-hiáu	會 huì	不會 bùhuì
	會 ē	袂 bē	會 huì	不會 bùhuì
CIRCUMSTANCES				
can	會當 ē-tàng	袂當 bē-tàng	能 néng	不能 bùnéng
PERMISSION				
GENERAL				
may	會使(得) ē-sái(-tit)	袂使(得) bē-sái(-tit)	可以 kěyǐ	不可以 bùkěyǐ
	會當 ē-tàng	袂當 bē-tàng	能 néng	不能 bùnéng
	會用得 ē-ēng-tit	袂用得 bē-ēng-tit	可以 kěyǐ	不可以 bùkěyǐ
POLITE				
may	通(好) thang(hó)	--	--	--
OBLIGATION				
GENERAL				
need	愛 ài	(毋)免 (m̄-)bián	要 yào	不用 bùyòng
	著愛 tio̍h-ài	(毋)免 (m̄-)bián	要 yào	不用 bùyòng
	著 tio̍h	(毋)免 (m̄-)bián	要 yào	不用 bùyòng
FORMAL				
need	需要 su-iàu	無需要 bô su-iàu	需要 xūyào	不需要 bùxūyào
ADVERBS				
should	應該 eng-kai	無應該 bô eng-kai	應該 yīnggāi	不應該 bùyīnggāi
must	一定 it-tēng	無一定 bô it-tēng	一定 yīdìng	不一定 bùyīdìng
PROHIBITION				
do not	--	莫 mài	--	別 bié, 不要 bùyào
	--	毋通 m̄-thang	--	別 bié, 不要 bùyào
	--	毋好 m̄-hó	--	別 bié, 不要 bùyào

13 Negation

Taiwanese has five common negatives: **毋 m̄**, **無 bô**, **免 bián**, **袂 bē**, and **未 bōe**. Their different usages are based on a combination of modality (possibility, desire, ability, permission, obligation, prohibition), aspect (perfective, continuous, experiential, anterior, habitual, tentative), and/or other attributes.

Additional negative forms in Taiwanese tend to be reserved for compound words or more formal terms such as with **不 put** (**不時 put-sî** 'frequently' or **不孝 put-hàu** 'unfilial').

Below is a table indicating the affirmative counterparts to the five negatives in Taiwanese. Note that the negative **毋 m̄** has two versions that will be explained further in this chapter.

NEGATIVE		AFFIRMATIVE	
毋 m̄	not want, not	欲 beh	want
毋 m̄	not	--	--
無 bô	not have	有 ū	have
袂 bē	will not	會 ē	will
免 bián	need not	著 tio̍h	must
未 bōe	not yet	了 le	have + *verb*

In contrast, Mandarin only uses two negatives for colloquial speech: **不 bù** and **沒 méi**. For the most part, **不 bù** is the general method of negation, while **沒 méi** applies to situations in which an action is not complete or has not occurred in the past. Additional negative forms in Mandarin such as **無 wú**, **非 fēi**, **勿 wù** tend to be reserved for written or more formal contexts. Note that the correspondence between Taiwanese and Mandarin negatives is not so easily mapped.

Additionally, for some speakers **袂 bē** and **未 bōe** are not differentiated in pronunciation. In other words, both are pronounced either **bē** or **bōe**. Or, an individual speaker may shift between both pronunciations freely without considering the distinction as meaningful. This is similar to how some speakers of English may pronounce the grammatical article 'a' both like the 'a' in 'sof<u>a</u>' and the 'a' in 'd<u>a</u>te' without intending a difference in meaning. Because written Taiwanese has not been common or widespread, some speakers may not consider **袂 bē** and **未 bōe** as distinct words. Nevertheless, some speakers do maintain a distinction. In effort to fully illustrate the context and usage for negative particles, this text distinguishes between the use of 袂 bē and 未 bōe throughout.

13.1 Negative 毋 m̄

毋 m̄ appears to have two distinct meanings in Taiwanese: one as a pure negative 'not', the other as a volitional negative for modal verbs of desire 'not want'. There is still debate among scholars whether there are actually two 毋 m̄'s or just one. This text will treat 毋 m̄ as having two distinct meanings.

PURE NEGATION
這 个 查埔人 毋是 阮 朋友。
Chit ê cha-po·-lâng m̄-sī gún pêng-iú.
這個 男人 不 是 我 的 朋友。
Zhège nánrén bù shì wǒ de péngyǒu.
This man is not my friend.

VOLITIONAL NEGATION
阮 阿姐 毋 洗 碗。
Gún a-chí m̄ sé óaⁿ.
我 姐姐 不 洗 碗。
Wǒ jiějiě bù xǐ wǎn.
My older sister does not want to wash dishes.

Below is a correspondence table between the usage of the Taiwanese 毋 m̄ and its Mandarin counterparts.

FUNCTION	TAIWANESE	MANDARIN
毋 M̄ (PURE NEGATIVE)		
Negation (word specific)	毋 m̄	不 bù
Affirmative-negative (question)	毋 -m̄-	不 -bu-
End-of-sentence tag (question)	毋 m̄	--
Experiential for 捌 bat (aspect)	毋捌 m̄-bat	不曾 bùcéng
毋 M̄ (VOLITIONAL NEGATIVE)		
Question particle (question)	毋 m̄	--
Desire (mood)	毋 m̄	不要 bùyào
Prohibition (mood)	莫 mài (毋愛 m̄-ài)	不要 bùyào

	TAIWANESE	MANDARIN
Prohibition (*mood*) (*cont'd*)	毋通 m̄-thang	不要 bùyào
	毋好 m̄-hó	不要 bùyào

13.1.1 Pure negative 毋 m̄ 'not'

In one sense, 毋 m̄ can function as a pure 'not' without any additional meaning. When used in this way, 毋 m̄ can only appear before a limited number of words.

Below is a table displaying some of the most common words that use 毋 m̄ in its negative form. Note that the list is made up of stative verbs, modal verbs, adjectives, adverb, and conjunctions. There are no action verbs negated by the pure 毋 m̄.

TAIWANESE	MANDARIN	MEANING
STATIVE VERBS		
毋是 m̄ sī	不是 bùshì	not be
毋驚 m̄-kiaⁿ	不怕 bùpà	not scared
毋捌 m̄ bat	不認識 bùrènshì	not recognize
毋知(影) m̄ chai(-iáⁿ)	不知道 bùzhīdào	not know
毋信 m̄ sìn	不相信 bùxiāngxìn	not believe
毋值 m̄-ta̍t	不如 bùrú	not equal to
MODAL VERBS		
毋免 m̄-bián	不用 bùyòng	no need
毋肯 m̄ khéng	不願意 bùyuànyì	not willing
毋願 m̄ goān	不希望 bùxīwàng	not wishing for
毋敢 m̄ káⁿ	不敢 bùgǎn	not dare
ADJECTIVES		
毋著 m̄-tio̍h	不對 bùduì	incorrect
毋值 m̄-ta̍t	不值得 bùzhídé	not worth it
毋好 m̄ hó	不好 bùhǎo	not good
毋(甘)願 m̄ (kam-)goān	不甘心 bùgānxīn	not resigned to

TAIWANESE	MANDARIN	MEANING
ADVERBS AND CONJUNCTIONS		
毋捌 m̄ bat	不曾 bùcéng	never
毋甘 m̄-kam	捨不得 shěbudé	reluctant
毋管 m̄-kóan	無論 wúlùn	regardless
毋爾 m̄-nā	不只是 bùzhǐshì	not only
毋過 m̄-koh	不過 bùguò	but, however
毋才 m̄-chiah	才 cái	because of that

Words that use the pure 毋 m̄ have a unique set of properties particularly in questions *(see 20.3 Particle questions)*.

13.1.2 Volitional 毋 m̄ 'not want'

The other sense of the negative 毋 m̄ is to 'not want', which is the negative form of the modal verb 欲 beh 'to want' *(see 12.2 Desire)*. Because there is only a limited number of words which use the pure 毋 m̄, the volitional sense of 毋 m̄ expressing 'not wanting' is much more common.

Additionally, note that because no action verbs can take the pure 毋 m̄ for the negative form, they can only be negated by the volitional 毋 m̄. Note that usage of 毋 m̄ is also synonymous with 無愛 bô ài and 無欲 bô-beh.

ADJECTIVE

伊 毋 乖。

I m̄ koai.

他 不 乖。

Tā bù guāi.

He will <u>not</u> behave himself.

STATIVE VERB

伊 毋 準備 明仔載 的 旅行。

I m̄ chún-pī bîn-á-chài ê lú-hêng.

她 不 準備 明天 的 旅行。

Tā bù zhǔnbèi míngtiān de lǚxíng.

She will <u>not</u> prepare for tomorrow's trip.

ACTION VERB

阮 毋 去。

Gún m̄ khì.

我們 不 (要) 去。

Wǒmen bù (yào) qù.

We do not want to go.

Note that in Mandarin, volition (*desire*) can often be bound in the interpretation of the verb. As a result, 要 **yào** is often omitted.

13.1.3 毋 m̄ in questions

Both the pure and volitional 毋 m̄ can be used in questions. However, there are slight differences in their usages.

13.1.3.1 Affirmative-negative questions (X-not-X format)

Only the pure negative 毋 m̄ can form affirmative-negative questions in the X-not-X format *(see 20.4.3 Affirmative-negative questions)*. Moreover, only the limited number of adjectives, stative, and modal verbs that are negated by the pure negative 毋 m̄ can use this construction for questions.

adjective / verb + 毋 + *adjective / verb*

adjective / verb + m̄ + *adjective / verb*

STATIVE VERB

伊 是毋是 你 的 學生？

I sī-m̄-sī lí ê ha̍k-seng?

他 是不是 你 的 學生？

Tā shìbùshì nǐ de xuéshēng?

Is he your student?

ADJECTIVE

我 下晡 焦 恁 去 遊樂園，<u>好毋好</u>？
Góa ē-poˈchhōa lín khì iû-lȯk-hn̂g, <u>hó-m̄-hó</u>?
我 下午 帶 你們 去 遊樂園，<u>好不好</u>？
Wǒ xiàwǔ dài nǐmen qù yóulèyuán, <u>hǎobùhǎo</u>?
<u>How about</u> I take you all to the amusement park this afternoon?

MODAL VERB

你 <u>敢毋敢</u> 坐 佇 上 頭前？
Lí <u>káⁿ-m̄-káⁿ</u> chē tī siōng thâu-chêng?
你 <u>敢不敢</u> 坐 在 最 前面？
Nǐ <u>gǎnbùgǎn</u> zuò zài zuì qiánmiàn?
<u>Do</u> you <u>dare</u> sit in the very front?

Note that in Mandarin the X-not-X question format is much more commonly used and accepts a large variety of verbs and adjectives.

In responses to X-not-X questions, the pure 毋 m̄ cannot stand alone. The main verb or adjective from the question must be restated with the negative 毋 m̄ in the response.

QUESTION

你 <u>信毋信</u> 伊 的 故事？
Lí <u>sìn-m̄-sìn</u> i ê kòˈsū?
你 <u>相不相信</u> 她 的 故事？
Nǐ <u>xiāngbùxiāngxìn</u> tā de gùshì?
<u>Do</u> you <u>believe</u> her story?

ANSWER

毋信。
M̄-sìn.
不 相信。
Bù xiāngxìn.
No *(I don't believe it)*.

13.1.3.2 Tag questions with negatives

Tags are short phrases seeking confirmation that can be attached to the end of a declarative sentence transforming the sentence into a question ('This seat is yours, right?') *(see 20.2*

Negation 303

Tag questions). The declarative sentence component preceding the tag can be referred to as the *proposition*.

While both the pure 毋 m̄ and volitional 毋 m̄ can form tag questions, there are some differences.

The pure 毋 m̄ can be used to form tag questions but must repeat the verb or adjective from the proposition in the tag. Additionally, the pure 毋 m̄ cannot stand independently and most always be bound to another verb or adjective.

PROPOSITION	TAG
verb / adjective…	*verb / adjective* + 毋?
verb / adjective…	*verb / adjective* + m̄?

PURE 毋 M̄

這碗麵是我的，是毋？

Chit óaⁿ mī sī góa--ê, <u>sī m̄</u>?

這碗麵<u>是不是</u>我的？

Zhè wǎn miàn <u>shìbùshì</u> wǒ de?

This bowl of noodles is mine, <u>isn't it</u>?

恁知我細漢的時陣規工攏咧包水餃，知毋？

Lín chai góa sè-hàn ê sî-chūn kui kang lóng teh pau chúi-kiáu, <u>chai m̄</u>?

你們<u>知不知道</u>我小的時候整天都在包水餃？

Nǐmen <u>zhībùzhīdào</u> wǒ xiǎo de shíhòu zhěngtiān dōu zài bāo shuǐjiǎo?

<u>Did</u> you <u>know</u> that when I was young I wrapped dumplings all day?

In contrast, the volitional 毋 m̄ can appear independently without attaching to another verb or adjective. Repeating the adjective or verb before the question particle is optional.

PROPOSITION	QUESTION PARTICLE
verb / adjective…	*(verb / adjective)* + 毋?
verb / adjective…	*(verb / adjective)* + m̄?

VOLITIONAL 毋 M̄

你欲參加婚禮，毋？

Lí beh chham-ka hun-lé, <u>m̄</u>?

你<u>要不要</u>參加婚禮？

Nǐ <u>yàobùyào</u> cānjiā hūnlǐ?

<u>Do</u> you <u>want</u> to attend the wedding?

你 欲 和 我 做伙 去 踅街，欲 毋？
Lí beh hām góa chò-hóe khì sèh-ke, <u>beh m̄</u>?
你 <u>要不要</u> 跟 我 一起 去 逛街？
Nǐ <u>yàobùyào</u> gēn wǒ yīqǐ qù guàngjiē?
<u>Do</u> you <u>want</u> to go shopping with me?

In responses to these questions, the pure **毋** m̄ cannot stand independently, while the volitional **毋** m̄ can.

PURE 毋 M̄

QUESTION

你 捌 食 王梨酥, 捌 毋？
Lí bat chiah ông-lâi-so͘, <u>bat m̄</u>?
你 吃過 鳳梨酥 嗎？
Nǐ <u>chīguò</u> fènglísū <u>ma</u>?
<u>Have</u> you eaten pineapple cake <u>before</u>?

ANSWER

毋 捌。
M̄ bat.
沒 吃過 (沒有)。
Méi chīguò (méiyǒu).
No *(I haven't)*.

Note that the Mandarin response **沒有** méiyǒu does not require repeating the verb from the question.

VOLITIONAL 毋 M̄

QUESTION

你 欲 食 冰, (欲) 毋？
Lí beh chiah peng, <u>(beh) m̄</u>?
你 <u>要不要</u> 吃 冰淇淋？
Nǐ <u>yàobùyào</u> chī bīngqílín?
<u>Do</u> you <u>want</u> to eat ice cream?

ANSWER

毋 (無愛)。

M̄ (bô-ài).

不要。

Bùyào.

No (*I don't want to eat it*).

Note that in the Mandarin response, the negative **不 bù** cannot stand alone but must include the modal verb **要 yào**.

In Taiwanese, **無愛 bô-ài** is an alternate form to negatively respond to a volitional **毋 m̄** question.

13.1.4 毋 m̄ in prohibitions

毋 m̄ is also used with prohibitions which warn or advise against an action *(see 12.6 Prohibition)*.

莫 mài (derived from the contraction of **毋愛 m̄-ai**) is used as a negative command to express 'don't'.

莫駛傷緊啦!

Mài sái siuⁿ kín--lah!

別開太快啦!

Bié kāi tài kuài la!

Don't drive too fast!

毋通 m̄-thang and **毋好 m̄-hó** (sometimes contracted to 'm̄-mo') are also often used in commands to strongly discourage behavior. However, the tone is less emphatic than that of **莫 mài**.

毋通食薰。

M̄-thang chia̍h hun

不要吸菸。

Bù yào xīyān

Don't smoke (*it's better not to do so*).

毋好 講 遐爾 大聲。

M̄-hó kóng hiah-nī tōa siaⁿ

不 要 講 那麼 大 聲。

Bù yào jiǎng nàme dà shēng

Don't talk so loud (*it's better not to do so*).

Note that the Mandarin modal verb for prohibition 不要 **bù yào** and its contraction 別 **bié** are similar in tone and only differentiated in strength by one's speech volume.

13.1.5 Negating the experiential aspect marker 捌 bat

毋 **m̄** appears in the negative form of the experiential aspect marker 捌 **bat**, which indicates that an action has been experienced at some unspecified point in the past. 毋捌 **m̄ bat** therefore indicates that the action has not been experienced. Often adverbs such as 從來 **chêng-lâi** 'since always' are added to convey the meaning of 'never' *(see 8.3.1 Experiential aspect with* 捌 *bat)*.

阮 翁 從來 毋 捌 送 我 珠寶。

Gún ang chêng-lâi m̄ bat sàng góa chu-pó.

我 先生 從來 沒 送 我過 飾品。

Wǒ xiānshēng cónglái méi sòngguò wǒ shìpǐn.

My husband has never given me jewelry.

Mandarin does not have an experiential aspect marker occurring before the verb. Instead, the experiential aspect is marked by placing the suffix 過 **-guò** after the verb.

Taiwanese can also mark the experiential aspect 過 **-kòe** after the verb or both 捌 **bat** and 過 **-kòe**. If only 過 **-kòe** appears, then 無 **bô** negates the verb phrase *(see 13.2.3* 無 *bô negating the experiential aspect suffix* 過 *-kòe)*. When both 捌 **bat** and 過 **-kòe** are used, 毋捌 **m̄ bat** is used to negate the verb phrase.

13.2 Negative 無 bô

The negative particle 無 **bô** has a multitude of roles within the language. Working both as a verb and a grammatical element, 無 **bô** can be used as a negative for possession, existence, perfective aspect, experiential aspect, habitual aspect, emphasis, potential verb complements, and before adjectives with desirable attributes.

Below is a correspondence table between the usage of the Taiwanese 無 **bô** and its Mandarin counterparts.

FUNCTION	TAIWANESE	MANDARIN
Possession (*verb*)	無 bô	沒有 měiyǒu
Existence (*verb*)	無 bô	沒有 měiyǒu
Perfective (*aspect*)	無 bô	沒有 měiyǒu
Experiential for 過 kòe (*aspect*)	無 bô	沒有 měiyǒu
Habitual (*aspect*)	無 bô	不 bù
Emphasis marker	無 bô	確實 不 quèshí bù
Potential verb complement	無 -bô-	不 -bu-
General-purpose tag (*question*)	無 --bô	對不對 duìbùduì
Perfective question particle (*question*)	無 --bô	了沒(有) le měi(yǒu)
Universal question particle (*question*)	無 --bô	嗎 ma
Adjectives (*desirable*)	無 bô	不 bù

13.2.1 無 bô negating possession and existence

As an independent verb, 無 **bô**, the negative form of the verb 有 **ū**, indicates both possession 'to not have' and existence 'there is/are not' (*see 10.2* 有 *ū*). In general, 無 **bô** functions as a verb when a noun immediately follows. When the subject is a location, the meaning shifts from possession to existence.

POSSESSION

張 小姐 無 顧客 的 名片。

Tiuⁿ sió-chiá <u>bô</u> kò͘-kheh ê bêng-phìⁿ.

張 小姐 沒有 顧客 的 名片。

Zhāng xiǎojiě <u>méiyǒu</u> gùkè de míngpiàn.

Ms. Tiunn <u>does not have</u> her client's business card.

EXISTENCE

這 个 市場 無 弓蕉。

Chit ê chhī-tiûⁿ <u>bô</u> keng-chio.

這個 市場 沒有 香蕉。

Zhège shìchǎng <u>méiyǒu</u> xiāngjiāo.

<u>There are no</u> bananas in this market.

13.2.2 無 bô in the perfective aspect

無 **bô** is the negative form of the aspect marker 有 **ū** that is used to indicate a completed action *(see 8.1.1 Perfective aspect with 有 ū, 10.2.3 有 ū as a perfective aspect maker)*. 無 **bô** in this context shows that an action did not take place or occur.

阮 昨暗 佇 舞會 無 跳舞。
Gún cha-àm tī bú-hōe <u>bô</u> thiàu-bú.
我們 昨晚 在 舞會 沒有 跳舞。
Wǒmen zuówǎn zài wǔhuì <u>méiyǒu</u> tiàowǔ.
We <u>didn't</u> dance at the party last night.

13.2.3 無 bô negating the experiential aspect suffix 過 -kòe

無 **bô** negates the experiential aspect marker 過 **-kòe**, which indicates an action that has been experienced at some unspecified point in the past *(see 8.3.2 Experiential aspect with 過 -kòe)*. Experiential aspect sentences in the negative often include adverbs such as 從來 **chêng-lâi** 'since always' to convey the meaning of 'never'.

這 个 查某 囝仔 從來 無 看過 雪。
Chit ê cha-bó͘ gín-á chêng-lâi <u>bô</u> khòaⁿ-<u>kòe</u> seh.
這個 女孩 從來 沒 看過 雪。
Zhège nǚhái cónglái <u>méi</u> kànguò xuě.
The girl <u>has never</u> seen snow <u>before</u>.

The experiential aspect may also be indicated in Taiwanese by the marker 捌 **bat**, which occurs before the verb, or a combination of both 捌 **bat** and 過 **kòe**. In both these cases, the negative form is 毋捌 **m̄ bat** *(see 13.1.5 Experiential aspect with 捌 bat)*.

Mandarin only has the single experiential aspect marker 過 **-guò**, which occurs after the verb.

13.2.4 無 bô in the habitual aspect

無 **bô** is the negative form of 有咧 **ū teh** when used in the habitual aspect. 無咧 **bô teh** is placed before the verb phrase to indicate that the subject does not regularly perform the action *(see 8.5 Habitual aspect, 10.2.5 有 ū as a habitual aspect marker)*.

伊 無 咧 食薰。
I bô teh chiȧh-hun.

她 不 抽煙。
Tā bù chōuyān.

She doesn't smoke.

In Mandarin, no special marker needs to be used for a reading in the habitual aspect.

13.2.5 無 bô as an emphasis marker

無 bô is the negative form of 有 ū when used to emphasize that an action did occur or is indeed happening. 無 bô in this context underscores that an action did not take place or is not occurring *(see 10.2.4 有 ū as an emphasis marker)*.

阮 這馬 無 咧 看 電視！
Gún chit-má bô teh khòaⁿ tiān-sī!

我們 現在 確實 沒有 在 看 電視 啊！
Wǒmen xiànzài quèshí méiyǒu zài kàn diànshì a!

We are not watching television right now!

Note that Mandarin does not have an exact equivalent to 無 bô as an emphasis marker, but can use adverbs such as 確實 quèshí 'indeed' and end-of-sentence particles such as 啊 a to show emphasis.

13.2.6 無 bô in verb complements

無 bô is the negative form of 有 ū when used as part of a verb complement. With phase complements, 無 bô indicates that a verb is unable to be completed successfully. In actualized potential complement constructions, 無 bô indicates that the main verb is unable to attain the outcome specified by the complement *(see 11.1.2 Phase complements indicating achievement, 11.4.1 Actualized potential complements)*.

PHASE COMPLEMENT ACHIEVEMENT

現做 的 麵包，伊 買 無。
Hiān-chò ê mī-pau, i bé bô.

他 買不到 現烤 的 麵包。
Tā mǎibùdào xiànkǎo de miànbāo.

He failed to buy fresh bread.

POTENTIAL COMPLEMENT

黃 先生 的 工課 做無了。

Ñg--sian-siⁿ ê khang-khòe chò-bô-liáu.

黃 先生 做不完 他 的 工作。

Huáng xiānshēng zuòbuwán tā de gōngzuò.

Mr. Ng was unable to finish his work.

13.2.7 無 --bô in questions

無 --bô appears in many question constructions both as part of a question tag and as an independent question particle.

13.2.7.1 無 --bô as a general-purpose question tag

無 --bô is part of the construction of the general-purpose tag 是著無 sī tio̍h--bô 'is that right?'. Because this tag only seeks a yes-no confirmation, it can be appended to most declarative sentences to change them into questions. Alternate forms of this tag include 著無 tio̍h--bô and 是無 sī--bô *(see 20.2.1 General-purpose tag 是著無 sī tio̍h--bô)*.

咱 應該 坐 下早 九點 的 班機,是著無?

Lán eng-kai chē e-chái káu tiám ê pan-ki, sī tio̍h--bô?

我們 應該 坐 早上 九 點 的 航班,對不對?

Wǒmen yīnggāi zuò zǎoshang jiǔ diǎn de hángbān, duìbùduì?

We are supposed to be on the 9 AM flight, right?

13.2.7.2 無 --bô as perfective aspect question particle

A declarative statement using 有 ū as a perfective aspect marker can be changed into a question by adding the negative particle 無 --bô. 有 ū can be repeated before the question particle 無 --bô or omitted *(see 20.3.1 Negative question particles)*.

你 有 開 窗仔,(有) 無?

Lí ū khui thang-á, (ū)--bô?

你 開了 窗戶 沒有?

Nǐ kāile chuānghù méiyǒu?

You opened the window, didn't you?

13.2.7.3 無 --bô as a universal question particle

For some speakers, 無 --bô is becoming a universal question particle that can be appended to any sentence as a question marker similar to the Mandarin question particle 嗎 ma *(see 20.3.2 無 --bô as a universal question particle)*. This linguistic change may be due to the continued influence from Mandarin.

伊 欲 去 德國 讀 冊 無?
I beh khì Tek-kok thàk chheh--bô?
她 要 去 德國 讀 書 嗎?
Tā yào qù Déguó dú shū ma?
Does she want to go study in Germany?

13.2.8 無 bô negating desirable adjectives

無 bô is the negative form of 有 ū when used before desirable adjectives. 無 bô in this context indicates that the object described does not possess a desirable quality or attribute *(see 6.4.3 Negation based on adjective desirability, 10.2.7 有 ū with desirable adjectives)*.

彼 塊 肉 無 軟。
Hit tè bah bô nńg.
那 塊 肉 不 嫩。
Nà kuài ròu bù nèn.
That piece of meat is not tender.

13.3 Negative 袂 bē

The negative particle 袂 bē can form negation for some modal verbs (possibility, ability, permission), undesirable adjectives, and unrealized potential complements.

FUNCTION	TAIWANESE	MANDARIN
Possibility *(mood)*	袂 bē	不會 bùhuì
Ability *(mood)*	袂 bē	不會 bùhuì
	袂曉 bē-hiáu	不會 bùhuì
	袂當 bē-tàng	不能 bùnéng

FUNCTION	TAIWANESE	MANDARIN
Permission *(mood)*	袂當 bē-tàng	不能 bùnéng
	袂使(得) bē-sái(-tit)	不可以 bùkěyǐ
	袂用得 bē-ēng-tit	不可以 bùkěyǐ
Question particle *(question)*	袂 --bē	--
Potential verb complement	袂 bē	不 -bu-
Adjectives *(undesirable)*	袂 bē	不 bù

13.3.1 袂 bē as a modal verb

袂 **bē** is the negative form of the modal verb 會 **ē** which is used in several compounds to express possibility, ability, and permission.

13.3.1.1 袂 bē negating possibility

袂 **bē** 'will not' is the negative form of the modal verb 會 **ē** 'will' which indicates a high likelihood that an event will occur *(see 12.1.1 Modal verb* 會 *ē 'will').*

阮 老師 袂 參加 舞會。
Gún lāu-su <u>bē</u> chham-ka bú-hōe.
我們 的 老師 不會 參加 舞會。
Wǒmen de lǎoshī <u>bù huì</u> cānjiā wǔhuì.
Our teacher <u>won't</u> come to the dance.

13.3.1.2 袂 bē negating ability

袂 **bē** 'cannot' is the negative form of 會 **ē** which forms compounds for modal verbs expressing ability. 袂 **bē** and 袂曉 **bē-hiáu** both indicate the lack of a learned ability or acquired skill, while 袂當 **bē-tàng** indicates an inability to complete a task due to physical or situational constraints *(see 12.3 Ability).*

阮 阿媽 袂曉 上網。
Gún a-má <u>bē-hiáu</u> chiū^n-bāng.
我 奶奶 不會 上網。
Wǒ nǎinǎi <u>bù huì</u> shàngwǎng.
My grandma <u>doesn't know how</u> to get online.

劉 先生 後 禮拜 袂當 去 北京。
Lâu--sian-si^n āu lé-pài bē-tàng khì Pak-kia^n.
劉 先生 下 禮拜 不 能 去 北京。
Liú xiānshēng xià lǐbài bù néng qù Běijīng.
Mr. Lau can't go to Beijing next week.

13.3.1.3 袂 bē negating permission

袂 **bē** 'may not' is the negative form of 會 **ē** which forms compounds for modal verbs expressing permission: 袂當 **bē-tàng**, 袂使(得) **bē-sái(-tit)**, and 袂用得 **bē-ēng-tit** *(see 12.4 Permission)*. Note that for some speakers the 得 **-tit** suffix is also pronounced **-eh** (e.g. 袂使得 **bē-sái-eh**, 袂用得 **bē-ēng-eh**).

周 先生 袂當 直接 敲 電話 予 顧客。
Chiu--sian-si^n bē-tàng tit-chiap khà tiān-ōe hō͘ kò͘-kheh.
周 先生 不 能 直接 打 電話 給 顧客。
Zhōu xiānshēng bù néng zhíjiē dǎ diànhuà gěi gùkè.
Mr. Chiu is not permitted to call clients directly.

阮 小妹 袂使得 家己 看 電影。
Gún sió-mōe bē-sài-tit ka-tī khòa^n tiān-iá^n.
我 妹妹 不 可以 自己 看 電影。
Wǒ mèimei bù kěyǐ zìjǐ kàn diànyǐng.
My younger sister isn't allowed to watch movies alone.

13.3.2 袂 bē as question particle

A declarative statement using the modal verb 會 **ē** (or any compounds constructed from 會 **ē** such as 會曉 **ē-hiáu**, 會當 **ē-tàng**, 會使 **ē-sái**, etc.) can be changed into a question by adding the negative particle 袂 **--bē** *(see 20.3.1 Negative question particles)*.

你 下晡 會 去 購物 中心 袂？
Lí ē-po͘ ē khì kò͘-bu̍t tiong-sim--bē?
你 下午 會不會 去 購物 中心？
Nǐ xiàwǔ huìbùhuì qù gòuwù zhòngxīn?
Will you go to the mall this afternoon?

阮 會使 看 電影 袂？

Gún ē-sái khòaⁿ tiān-iáⁿ--bē?

我們 可不可以 看 電影？

Wǒmen kěbùkěyǐ kàn diànyǐng?

May we watch a movie?

Note that some speakers will replace the question tag **袂 bē** with **無 bô** regardless of the verb used in the sentence.

13.3.3 袂 bē in verb complements

袂 -bē- appears as an infix in the negative form of the unrealized potential complement, which indicates the inability of the main verb to achieve the complement *(see 11.4.2 Unrealized potential complements)*. The action takes place either in the present or the future.

就 算 有 三 點鍾，伊 考券 嘛 寫袂了。

Chiū sǹg ū saⁿ tiám-cheng, i khó-kǹg mā siá-bē-liáu.

即使 有 三 個 小時，他 也 寫不完 考卷。

Jíshǐ yǒu sān gè xiǎoshí, tā yě xiěbuwán kǎojuàn.

Even if he has 3 hours, he can't finish this test.

連 游泳池 的 一 輾，我 嘛 泅袂了。

Liàn iû-éng-tî ê chit liàn, góa mā siû-bē-liáu.

連 游泳池 的 一 圈，我 也 游不完。

Lián yóuyǒngchí de yī quān, wǒ yě yóubùwán.

Even one lap in the pool, I can't swim.

Mandarin does not make a distinction between actualized or unrealized potential complements. All potential complements are negated with the infix **不 -bu-**.

13.3.4 袂 bē negating undesirable adjectives

袂 bē is the negative form of **會 ē** when used before adjectives describing undesirable qualities. **袂 bē** in this context indicates that the object described does not possess the undesirable quality or attribute *(see 6.4.3 Negating adjectives, 10.2.7 有 ū with desirable adjectives)*.

坐 踮 傘 的 下 跤 袂 熱。

Chē tàm sòaⁿ ê ē-kha bē joah.

坐在陽傘的下面不熱。

Zuò zài yángsǎn de xiàmiàn bù rè.

It <u>isn't hot</u> sitting beneath the umbrella.

Mandarin does not make a distinction in negation between desirable or undesirable adjectives. All adjectives are negated with **不 bù**.

13.4 Negative 未 bōe

The negative particle **未 bōe** serves as the negation for the anterior aspect and can function as a question particle.

FUNCTION	TAIWANESE	MANDARIN
Anterior *(aspect)*	(猶)未 (iáu-)bōe	還沒 háiměi
Question particle *(question)*	未 --bōe	了沒(有) le měi(yǒu)

13.4.1 未 bōe in the anterior aspect

未 bōe (also pronounced **bē**) 'not yet' is the negative form of the anterior aspect marker **矣 --ah**, which indicates that the clause or sentence has some relevance to the current situation *(see 8.4 Anterior aspect)*. **猶未 iáu-bōe** 'not yet' is the form when occurring before the verb, while **未 --bōe** only appears independently within a question tag.

我 猶未 買 票。

Góa <u>iáu-bōe</u> bé phiàu.

我 還沒 買 票。

Wǒ <u>hái méi</u> mǎi piào.

I <u>haven't</u> bought tickets <u>yet</u>.

13.4.2 未 bōe as question particle

A declarative statement can be changed into a question by adding the negative particle **未 --bōe** 'yet'. This puts the sentence into the anterior aspect *(see 8.4 Anterior aspect, 20.3.1 Negative question particles)*.

恁 食 飽 未?

Lín chiảh pá--bōe?

你們 吃 飽 了 沒?

Nǐmen chī bǎo le méi?

Have you eaten yet?

13.5 Negative 免 bián

The negative particle 免 bián serves as the negation for the modal verbs for necessity or obligation and can also function as a question particle.

FUNCTION	TAIWANESE	MANDARIN
Obligation (mood)	(毋)免 (m̄-)bián	不用 bùyòng
Question particle (question)	抑 免 iah bián	還是不用 háishì bùyòng

13.5.1 免 bián negating obligation

免 bián 'no need' is the negative form of the modal verbs for necessity or obligation: 著 tio̍h, 著愛 tio̍h-ài, and 愛 ài (see 12.5 Obligation). For emphasis, some speakers also include 毋 m̄ to form the compound 毋免 m̄-bián (often contracted to mián).

你 免 帶 你 的 護照。

Lí bián tòa lí ê hō·-chiàu.

你 不用 帶 你 的 護照。

Nǐ bù yòng dài nǐ de hùzhào.

You don't need to bring your passport.

(毋) 免啦!

(M̄-) Bián--lah!

不用 啦!

Bù yòng la!

There's no need!

13.5.2 免 bián as question particle

免 **bián** is less commonly used as a negative question particle but can be placed at the end of declarative sentences with obligation modal verbs to form a question *(see 12.5 Obligation, 20.3.1 Negative question particles)*. Generally, 免 **bián** is preceded by 抑 **iah** 'or'.

我 著愛 袋 錢,抑 免?
Góa tio̍h-ài tē chîⁿ, iah bián?
我 得 帶 錢, 還是 不用?
Wǒ děi dài qián, háishì bùyòng?
Do I need to take money?

13.6 Summary of negation

FUNCTION	TAIWANESE	MANDARIN
毋 M̄ *(PURE NEGATIVE)*		
Negation (*word specific*)	毋 m̄	不 bù
Affirmative-negative (*question*)	毋 -m̄-	不 -bu-
End-of-sentence tag (*question*)	毋 m̄	---
Experiential for 捌 bat (*aspect*)	毋捌 m̄-bat	沒有 méiyǒu
毋 M̄ *(VOLITIONAL NEGATIVE)*		
Question particle (*question*)	毋 m̄	---
Desire (*mood*)	毋 m̄	不要 bùyào
Prohibition (*mood*)	莫 mài (毋愛 m̄-ài)	不要 bùyào
	毋通 m̄-thang	不要 bùyào
	毋好 m̄-hó	不要 bùyào

FUNCTION	TAIWANESE	MANDARIN
無 *BÔ*		
Possession (*verb*)	無 bô	沒有 měiyǒu
Existence (*verb*)	無 bô	沒有 měiyǒu
Perfective (*aspect*)	無 bô	沒有 měiyǒu
Experiential for 過 kòe (*aspect*)	無 bô	沒有 měiyǒu
Habitual (*aspect*)	無 bô	不 bù
Emphasis marker	無 bô	不 (啊) bù (a)
Potential verb complement	無 -bô-	不 -bu-
General-purpose tag (*question*)	無 --bô	對不對 duìbùduì
Perfective question particle (*question*)	無 --bô	了沒(有) le měi(yǒu)
Universal question particle (*question*)	無 --bô	嗎 ma
Adjectives (*desirable*)	無 bô	不 bù
袂 *BĒ*		
Possibility (*mood*)	袂 bē	不會 bùhuì
Ability (*mood*)	袂 bē	不會 bùhuì
	袂曉 bē-hiáu	不會 bùhuì
	袂當 bē-tàng	不能 bùnéng
Permission (*mood*)	袂當 bē-tàng	不能 bùnéng
	袂使(得) bē-sái(-tit)	不可以 bùkěyǐ
	袂用得 bē-ēng-tit	不可以 bùkěyǐ
Question particle (*question*)	袂 --bē	--
Potential verb complement	袂 bē	不 -bu-
Adjectives (*undesirable*)	袂 bē	不 bù
未 *BŌE*		
Anterior (*aspect*)	(猶)未 (iáu-)bōe	還沒 háiměi
Question particle (*question*)	未 --bōe	了沒(有) le měi(yǒu)
免 *BIÁN*		
Obligation (*mood*)	(毋)免 (m̄-)bián	不用 bùyòng
Question particle (*question*)	抑 免 iah bián	還是不用 háishì bùyòng

14 Adverbs

Adverbs can modify verbs, adjectives, and even other adverbs. Not all, but many adverbs in English are words that end in '–ly'.

MODIFYING VERBS
The children walked <u>quietly</u> down the hall.
He <u>still</u> brings his teddy bear.

MODIFYING ADJECTIVES
It was such a <u>brightly</u> lit room.
We ate some <u>numbingly</u> spicy chicken.

MODIFYING OTHER ADVERBS
You ran <u>extremely</u> quickly.
She came <u>unusually</u> late.

In Taiwanese, adverbs can broadly be grouped into three types: intensifiers, sentence-level adverbs, and verb-level adverbs.

Intensifiers are a special type of adverb that specifies the degree (such as barely, very, extremely) or intensity of adjectives. These are given special treatment in the Adjectives chapter *(see 6.1 Intensifiers)*.

伊足肥。
I <u>chiok</u> pûi.
他非常胖。
Tā <u>fēicháng</u> pàng.
He is <u>very</u> fat.

Aside from intensifiers, there are two other main types of adverbs that will be discussed in this chapter: sentence-level adverbs and verb-level adverbs.

Sentence-level adverbs impact the entire sentence by providing both an overall temporal framework and an understanding of the speaker's attitude and confidence towards the main action/event in the sentence.

Verb-level adverbs focus more on modifying the verb phrase itself or relating elements within the sentence to the main verb.

14.1 Sentence-level adverbs

Sentence-level adverbs affect the entire sentence. As such, they all have the flexibility of being placed at the beginning of the sentence before the subject or immediately after the subject. In addition, sentence-level adverbs always precede negation and modal verbs.

ORDER 1

sentence-level adverbs *+ subject + negation + modal verbs + main verb*

ORDER 2

*subject + **sentence-level adverbs** + negation + modal verbs + main verb*

Sentence-level adverbs can be subdivided into three categories of adverbs:

- Attitude
- Time
- Confidence

14.1.1 Attitude adverbs

Attitude adverbs reflect the speaker's view of the statement that is made in the rest of the sentence. While these adverbs do not impact the truth of the statement, they help convey the mood or tone of the speaker towards what follows.

明明 伊 的 狗 比 你 的 走 較 緊。
<u>Bêng-bêng</u> i ê káu pí lí--ê cháu khah kín.
明明 她 的 狗 比 你 的 跑 得 快。
<u>Míngmíng</u> tā de gǒu bǐ nǐ de pǎo de kuài.
<u>Obviously</u>, her dog runs faster than yours.

In the above example, the truth of the statement 'her dog runs faster than yours' is not impacted by the attitude adverb. Rather, the adverb reveals that the speaker's attitude is that this fact is 'obvious'. Additionally, note that the attitude adverb does not necessarily describe the attitude of the subject of the sentence (which is 'her dog' in this example), but in fact describes the attitude of the speaker of the sentence. Below is a table of some common attitude adverbs loosely grouped by meaning.

TAIWANESE	MANDARIN	MEANING
TRUTH AND APPEARANCES		
老實講 láu-sit-kóng	老實說 lǎoshíshuō	frankly, honestly
明明 bêng-bêng	明明 míngmíng	obviously, clearly
其實 kî-sit	其實 qíshí	actually
(若)親像 (ná-)chhin-chhiūⁿ	好像 hǎoxiàng	to seem like, as if
袂輸 bē-su	好像 hǎoxiàng	to seem like, as if
敢若 káⁿ-ná	好像 hǎoxiàng	to seem like, as if
SURPRISE		
雄雄 hiông-hiông	忽然 hūrán	abruptly
竟然 kèng-jiân	竟然 jìngrán	unexpectedly
煞 soah	竟然 jìngrán	unexpectedly
顛倒 tian-tó	反而 fǎn'ér	on the contrary *(second clause only)*
ANYWAY		
橫直 hôaiⁿ-tit	反正 fǎnzhèng	anyway, in any case
反正 hóan-chèng	反正 fǎnzhèng	anyway, in any case
無彩 bô-chhái	枉費 wǎngfèi	What a waste!
LUCK		
拄好 tú-hó	剛好 gānghǎo	coincidentally
(好)佳哉 (hó-)ka-chài	幸虧 xìngkuī	luckily, fortunately
無拄好 bô-tú-hó	不巧 bù qiǎo	unfortunately
偏偏 phian-phian	不巧 bù qiǎo	unfortunately
IN THE END		
早慢 chá-bān	遲早 chízǎo	eventually
到底 tàu-tē	到底 dàodǐ	ultimately
不得已 put-tek-í	不得已 bùdéyǐ	reluctantly

老實講 你 的 手筆 真 歹讀。
Láu-sit-kóng lí ê chhiú-pit chin pháiⁿ-tha̍k.
老實說 你 的 筆跡 很 難看。
Lǎoshíshuō nǐ de bǐjī hěn nánkàn.
<u>Honestly</u>, your handwriting is hard to read.

伊 竟然 行過來，然後 共 我 抱。
I <u>kèng-jiân</u> kiâⁿ--kòe-lâi, jiân-āu kā góa phō.
她 竟然 跑過來，然後 給 我 抱。
Tā <u>jìngrán</u> zǒuguòlái, ránhòu gěi wǒ bào.
She <u>unexpectedly</u> walked over and gave me a big hug.

反正 你 猶閣 愛 趁錢。
<u>Hóan-chèng</u> lí iáu-koh ài thàn-chîⁿ.
反正 你 還 需要 賺錢。
<u>Fǎnzhèng</u> nǐ hái xūyào zhuànqián.
<u>In any case</u>, you still have to earn money.

好佳哉 我 有 袋 較 濟 錢。
<u>Hó-ka-chài</u> góa ū tē khah chē chîⁿ.
幸虧 我 帶 了 比較 多 錢。
<u>Xìngkuī</u> wǒ dàile bǐjiào duō qián.
<u>Luckily</u>, I brought extra money.

怹 到底 食 物仔，就 著愛 出 錢。
In <u>tàu-té</u> chia̍h mih-á, tō tio̍h-ài chhut chîⁿ.
他們 到底 吃 東西，就 需要 出 錢。
Tāmen <u>dàodǐ</u> chī dōngxī, jiù xūyào chū qián.
They <u>ultimately</u> will need to pay for the food they ate.

14.1.2 Time adverbs

Time adverbs and expressions are used to provide a temporal framework in which the action or event of the sentence occurs. Time expressions refer to a specific time (e.g. June 21, 8:00 in the morning, next weekend, etc.), while time adverbs refer to the present or a specific event (in the past, soon, next time, etc.). However, note that when discussing time in terms of duration or frequency, the placement is generally after the verb *(see 11.8*

Duration and absolute frequency complements).

Below is a table of some common time adverbs. They are roughly divided into two categories: time-based and event-based.

TAIWANESE	MANDARIN	MEANING
TIME-BASED		
從來 chiông-lâi (chêng-lâi)	從來 cónglái	from the beginning
從到今 chêng-kàu-ta^n	從來 cónglái	from the beginning
本底 pún-té	本來 běnlái	originally
本來 pún-lâi	本來 běnlái	originally
以前 í-chêng	以前 yǐqián	prior (*specified time*)
古早 kó·-chá	以前 yǐqián	earlier, in the past
較早 khah-chá	早一點 zǎoyīdiǎn	earlier, in the past
最近 chòe-kīn	最近 zuìjìn	recently
拄(仔) tú(-á)	剛才 gāngcái	to have just
拄才 tú-chiah	剛才 gāngcái	to have just
頭拄仔 thâu-tú-á	剛才 gāngcái	to have just
這馬 chit-má	現在 xiànzài	now
這陣 chit-chūn	現在 xiànzài	now
這站 chit-chām	現在 xiànzài	now
眼前 gán-chiân (-chêng)	目前 mùqián	currently, presently
目前 bo̍k-chiân (-chêng)	目前 mùqián	currently, presently
面前 bīn-chêng	目前 mùqián	currently, presently
連鞭 liâm-mi	馬上 mǎshàng	immediately
馬上 má-siōng	馬上 mǎshàng	immediately
咧欲 teh-beh (tih-beh)	快要 kuàiyào	just about to, soon
強欲 kiōng-beh (liong-beh)	快要 kuàiyào	just about to, soon
較停仔 khah-thêng-á	待會兒 dàihuì'er	a moment later
等一下 tán--chit-ē	等一下 děng yīxià	a little later
較晏 khah-òa^n	晚一點 wǎnyīdiǎn	later on
較暗 khah-àm	晚一點 wǎnyīdiǎn	later on
後日 āu-ji̍t	以後 yǐhòu	someday
另日 lēng-ji̍t	改天 gǎitiān	another day
別日(仔) pa̍t-ji̍t(-á)	改天 gǎitiān	another day

TAIWANESE	MANDARIN	MEANING
以後 í-āu	以後 yǐhòu	after (*specified time*)
將來 chiong-lâi	將來 jiānglái	in the future
未來 bī-lâi	未來 wèilái	in the future

TAIWANESE	MANDARIN	MEANING
EVENT-BASED		
頂擺 téng-pái	上次 shàngcì	last time
頂過 téng-kòe	上次 shàngcì	last time
頂改 téng-kái	上次 shàngcì	last time
進前 chìn-chêng	之前 zhīqián	prior (*specific event*)
先 seng	先 xiān	first, beforehand
上頭仔 siōng-thâu-á	一開始 yī kāishǐ	initially, at first
頭仔 thâu--á	一開始 yī kāishǐ	initially, at first
紲落去 sòa--lo̍h-khì	接下來 jiēxiàlái	next, following
然後 jiân-āu (lian-āu)	然後 ránhòu	and then
後來 āu--lâi	後來 hòulái	afterwards, later on
了後 liáu-āu	之後 zhīhòu	after (*specific event*)
路尾 lō͘-bóe	最後 zuìhòu	finally
已經 í-keng	已經 yǐjīng	already
後擺 āu-pái	下次 xiàcì	next time
下擺 ē-pái	下次 xiàcì	next time
下改 ē-kái	下次 xiàcì	next time

阮 查囝 較早 佇 市長 的 辦公室 上班。
Gún chá-kiáⁿ <u>khah-chá</u> tī chhī-tiúⁿ ê pān-kong-sek siōng-pan.
我 女兒 以前 在 市長 的 辦公室 上班。
Wǒ nǚ'ér <u>yǐqián</u> zài shìzhǎng de bàngōngshì shàngbān.
My daughter <u>previously</u> worked at the mayor's office.

我 頭拄仔 按 海邊 轉來。
Góa <u>thâu-tú-á</u> àn hái-piⁿ tńg--lâi.
我 剛剛 從 海灘 回來。
Wǒ <u>gānggāng</u> cóng hǎitān huílái.
I <u>just</u> returned from the beach.

將來 你的 頭家 應該 對 你 較 好。
<u>Chiong-lâi</u> lí ê thâu-ke eng-kai tùi lí khah hó.
未來 你的 老闆 應該 對 你 比較 好。
<u>Wèilái</u> nǐ de lǎobǎn yīnggāi duì nǐ bǐjiào hǎo.
<u>In the future</u>, your boss should treat you better.

阮 路尾 佇 樹仔頂 揣著 貓仔。
Gún <u>lō͘-bóe</u> tī chhiū-á-téng chhōe-tio̍h niau-á.
我們 最後 在 樹 上 找到 貓。
Wǒmen <u>zuìhòu</u> zài shù shàng zhǎodào māo.
We <u>finally</u> found the cat in the tree.

14.1.3 Confidence adverbs

Confidence adverbs refer to the speaker's confidence of how likely the statement made in the sentence is true. In other words, the confidence adverb expresses how certain the speaker is that the events of the sentence may or may not occur.

可能 張 先生 會 過來 食 飯。
<u>Khó-lêng</u> Tiuⁿ--sian-siⁿ ē kòe-lâi chia̍h pn̄g.
可能 張 先生 會 過來 吃 飯。
<u>Kěnéng</u> Zhāng xiānshēng huì guòlái chī fàn.
<u>Maybe</u> Mr. Tiunn will come over to eat.

Below is a table of some common confidence adverbs.

TAIWANESE	MANDARIN	MEANING
UNCERTAINTY		
可能 khó-lêng	可能 kěnéng	maybe, probably
無定著 bô-tiāⁿ-tio̍h	說不定 shuōbudìng	can't say for sure, maybe
無一定 bô-it-tēng	不一定 bùyīdìng	not necessarily, possibly
大概 tāi-khài	大概 dàgài	most likely, probably
CERTAINTY		
定著 tiāⁿ-tio̍h	一定 yīdìng	definitely, certainly
一定 it-tēng	一定 yīdìng	definitely, certainly
的確 tek-khak	確定 quèdìng	definitely, certainly

TAIWANESE	MANDARIN	MEANING
必然 pit-jiân	確定 quèdìng	definitely, certainly
絕對 choa̍t-tùi	絕對 juéduì	absolutely, definitely

無一定 服務生 偷提 你 的 信用卡。
Bô-it-tēng ho̍k-bū-seng thau-the̍h lí ê sìn-iōng-khah.
不一定 服務員 偷 拿 你 的 信用卡。
Bùyīdìng fúwùyuán tōu ná nǐ de xìnyòngkǎ.
The waiter <u>didn't necessarily</u> steal your credit card.

無定著 咱 會當 共 這 台 車 坐 六 个 人。
Bô-tiāⁿ-tio̍h lán ē-tàng kā chit tâi chhia chē la̍k ê lâng.
說不定 我們 能 把 這 台 車 坐 六 個 人。
Shuōbudìng wǒmen néng bǎ zhè tái chē zuò liù gè rén.
<u>It's not certain</u> if we can fit six people in this car.

伊 絕對 袂 行 到 車頭。
I <u>choa̍t-tùi</u> bē kiâⁿ kàu chhia-thâu.
她 絕對 不 會 走 到 車站。
Tā <u>juéduì</u> bù huì zǒu dào chēzhàn.
She <u>absolutely</u> won't walk to the train station.

這 家 的確 較 好 的 餐廳。
Chit ke <u>tek-khak</u> khah hó ê chhan-thiaⁿ.
這家 確定 的 比較 好 的 餐廳。
Zhè jiā <u>quèdìng</u> de bǐjiào hǎo de canting.
This one is <u>definitely</u> the better restaurant.

14.1.4 Co-occurring sentence-level adverbs

When sentence-level adverbs co-occur in the same sentence, attitude adverbs come first while the position of confidence and time adverbs are interchangeable. The subject may be placed in any position before, after, or in between adverbs.

ORDER 1

attitude + time + confidence

其實 後擺 可能 伊 會 去 東京。

Kî-sit āu-pái khó-lêng i ē khì Tang-kiaⁿ.

其實 下次 可能 她 會 去 東京。

Qíshí xiàcì kěnéng tā huì qù Dōngjīng.

Actually, next time maybe she will go to Tokyo.

ORDER 2

attitude + confidence + time

其實 可能 後擺 伊 會 去 東京。

Kî-sit khó-lêng āu-pái i ē khì Tang-kiaⁿ.

其實 可能 下次 她 會 去 東京。

Qíshí kěnéng xiàcì tā huì qù Dōngjīng.

Actually, maybe next time she will go to Tokyo.

14.2 Verb-level adverbs

Verb-level adverbs only affect the main verb or verb phrase in the sentence. They are placed in the space between the subject and the main verb.

subject + **verb-level adverb** *+ main verb*

In addition, this space can also contain other grammatical elements such as negatives, modal verbs, and prepositional phrases. The following sections will explain how the adverbs interact with these other elements.

Verb-level adverbs can be subdivided into three categories of adverbs:

- Reference
- Relative frequency
- Manner

14.2.1 Reference adverbs

Reference adverbs refer to another person, time, or thing that appears earlier or later in the sentence and relates it to the main verb. These adverbs generally indicate inclusion, repetition, continuation, exclusivity, or promptness.

Below is a table of some common reference adverbs.

TAIWANESE	MANDARIN	MEANING
INCLUSION		
攏 lóng	都 dōu	all, both
嘛 mā	也 yě	also
也 iā(ā)	也 yě	also
REPETITION		
閣 koh	再 zài, 又 yòu	again
又閣 iū-koh	再 zài, 又 yòu	again
閣再 koh-chài	再 zài, 又 yòu	again
才閣 chiah-koh	再 zài	again (*future*)
CONTINUATION		
猶 iáu (iah, ah, á, iá)	還 hái, 依然 yīrán	still, yet
猶閣 iáu-koh	還 hái, 依然 yīrán	still, yet
猶原 iû-gôan	仍然 réngrán	still, yet
EXCLUSIVITY		
干焦 kan-na	只 zhǐ, 只有 zhǐyǒu	only, only have
才 chiah (khah)	才 cái	only, only have
爾爾 niā-niā	而已 éryǐ	only (*end of sentence*)
PROMPTNESS		
就 tō (chiū, tioh)	就 jiù	just, then
都 to	已經 yǐjīng, 完全 wánquán	already, completely
才 chiah (khah)	才 cái	just, only then

The sections that follow provide additional notes on usage for a few reference adverbs.

14.2.1.1 Inclusion

14.2.1.1.1 All, both

The reference adverb **攏 lóng** refers to a plural subject or object that precedes it and indicates 'all, both' or 'each case, entirely'. If referring to a plural object, the object is generally topicalized at the beginning of the sentence or omitted altogether and implied.

阮 阿兄 佮 阿嫂 下昏暗 攏 欲 食 日本 料理。
Gún a-hiaⁿ kah a-só e-hng-àm lóng beh chiȧh Ji̍t-pún liāu-lí.
我 哥哥 和 嫂嫂 今晚 都 要 吃 日本 料理。
Wǒ gēgē hé sǎosǎo jīnwǎn dōu yào chī Rìběn liàolǐ.
My older brother and his wife both want to eat Japanese food tonight.

六 罐 麥仔酒，謝 先生 攏 啉 了 矣。
La̍k kòan be̍h-á-chiú, Siā--sian-siⁿ lóng lim liáu--ah.
六 罐 啤酒，謝 先生 都 喝 完 了。
Liù guàn píjiǔ, Xiè xiānshēng dōu hē wán le.
Mr. Sia finished drinking all six cans of beer.

我 攏 愛。
Góa lóng ài.
我 都 喜歡。
Wǒ dōu xǐhuān.
I like them all (*the object is implied*).

If there is both a plural subject and object, the sentence becomes ambiguous and can be interpreted in multiple ways.

遮的 柳丁，阮 攏 買起來。
Chia-ê liú-teng, gún lóng bé--khí-lâi.
這裡 的 柳丁，我們 都 買起來。
Zhèlǐ de liǔdīng, wǒmen dōu mǎiqǐlái.
We all bought up oranges.
We bought up all the oranges.
We all bought up all the oranges.

攏 **lóng** can also be used to refer to the 'whole part' or 'each/every case' of the preceding noun.

阮三頓攏食無肉的。
Gún saⁿ tǹg lóng chiảh bô bah--ê.
我們三餐都吃沒肉的。
Wǒmen sān cān dōu chī méi ròu de.
For <u>each</u> of our three meals, we didn't eat meat.

伊規日攏看電視。
I kui jit lóng khòaⁿ tiān-sī.
他整天都看電視。
Tā zhěngtiān dōu kàn diànshì.
He watched television the <u>entire</u> day.

Additionally, 攏 **lóng** can appear before or after negation but the meaning potentially changes depending on placement.

阮無攏愛恐怖片。
Gún bô lóng ài khióng-pò͘ phìⁿ.
我們不都喜歡恐怖片。
Wǒmen bù dōu xǐhuān kǒngbù piàn.
We <u>don't</u> <u>all</u> like horror movies (*only some of us like them*).

阮攏無愛恐怖片。
Gún lóng bô ài khióng-pò͘ phìⁿ.
我們都不喜歡恐怖片。
Wǒmen dōu bù xǐhuān kǒngbù piàn.
We <u>all</u> <u>don't</u> like horror movies (*everyone doesn't like them*).

14.2.1.1.2 Also

嘛 **mā** is used to express that the subject 'also' (in addition to another subject stated or implied) performs the action of the main verb.

阮 小弟 嘛 欲 參加 聚會。
Gún sió-tī má beh chham-ka chū-hōe.

我 弟弟 也 要 參加 聚會。
Wǒ dìdi yě yào cānjiā jùhuì.

My younger brother <u>also</u> wants to attend the party.

伊 嘛 算 羊。
I má sǹg iûⁿ.

她 也 屬 羊。
Tā yě shǔ yáng.

She is <u>also</u> born in the year of the goat.

14.2.1.1.3 Sentences with both 嘛 má and 攏 lóng

嘛 **má** 'also' can co-occur with 攏 **lóng** 'all, both'. The ordering is grammatically acceptable either way, but the emphasis changes slightly.

怹 攏 嘛 無 想欲 去 泅水。
In <u>lóng</u> <u>má</u> bô siuⁿ-beh khì siû chúi.

他們 都 也 不 想 去 游泳。
Tāmen <u>dōu</u> <u>yě</u> bù xiǎng qù yóuyǒng.

They <u>also</u> <u>don't</u> feel like going to swim (*all of this group in addition to other groups*).

怹 嘛 攏 無 想欲 去 泅水。
In <u>má</u> <u>lóng</u> bô siuⁿ-beh khì siû chúi.

他們 也 都 不 想 去 游泳。
Tāmen <u>yě</u> <u>dōu</u> bù xiǎng qù yóuyǒng.

They <u>also</u> <u>don't</u> feel like going to swim (*this group in addition to the speaker*).

14.2.1.2 Repetition

To express the idea of 'again' or 'to repeat', use 閣 **koh**, 又閣 **iū-koh**, 閣再 **koh-chài**. These three terms are generally interchangeable. 才閣 **chiah-koh**, on the other hand, tends to only occur in future contexts.

我 頂 禮拜 閣 打毋見 鎖匙!
Góa téng lé-pài koh phah-m̄-kìⁿ só-sî!
我 上 禮拜 又 不見了 鑰匙!
Wǒ shàng lǐbài yòu bùjiànle yàoshi!
Last week I lost my keys again!

明年 阮 會 閣再 去 韓國。
Mê-nî gún ē koh-chài khì Hân-kok.
明年 我們 會 再 去 韓國。
Míngnián wǒmen huì zài qù Hánguó.
Next year we will go again to Korea.

你 得 工課 了後, 才閣 講。
Lí tit khang-khòe liáu-āu, chiah-koh kóng.
你 獲得 工作 之後, 再 說。
Nǐ huòdé gōngzuò zhīhòu, zài shuō.
Let's talk about it again after you get a job.

Taiwanese differs from Mandarin in that **閣 koh**, **又閣 iū-koh**, **閣再 koh-chài** can be used for both the past and present, unlike the distinction between the Mandarin **再 zài** *(future)* and **又 yòu** *(past)*. In Taiwanese **才閣 chiah-koh** is an exception and is generally reserved for future contexts.

14.2.1.3 Continuation

猶 iáu (also pronounced **iah**, **ah**, **á**, **iá**) and **猶閣 iáu-koh** can be used to indicate continuation of an action by expressing 'still' or 'yet'. They are generally interchangeable.

伊 的 女朋友 猶閣 和 伊 受氣 矣。
I ê lú pêng-iú iáu-koh hām i siū-khì--ah.
他 的 女朋友 還 跟 他 生氣 了。
Tā de nǚ péngyǒu hái gēn tā shēngqì le.
His girlfriend is still angry with him.

政府 猶 提供 免錢 的 教育。
Chèng-hú iáu thê-kiong bián-chîⁿ ê kàu-io̍k.
政府 還 提供 免費 的 教育。
Zhèngfǔ hái tígōng miǎnfèi de jiàoyù.
The government still provides free education.

14.2.1.4 Exclusivity

The adverbs **干焦 kan-na**, **才 chiah**, **爾爾 niā-niā** can be used to indicate exclusivity or uniqueness in performing an action.

阮 干焦 看 阮 後生 的 比賽。
Gún kan-na khòaⁿ gún hāu-seⁿ ê pí-sài.
我們 只 看 我們 兒子 的 比賽。
Wǒmen zhǐ kàn wǒmen érzi de bǐsài.
We only watched our son's match.

我 佇 巴黎 才 有 三 工。
Góa tī Pa-lê chiah ū saⁿ kang.
我 在 巴黎 只 有 三 天。
Wǒ zài Bālí zhǐ yǒu sān tiān.
I only have three days in Paris.

爾爾 niā-niā 'nothing more' can only be placed at the end of the sentence and may co-occur with other adverbs expressing 'only'. Note that **爾爾 niā-niā** can only refer to quantities and not actions.

楊 小姐 有 兩 个 顧客 爾爾。
Iûⁿ sió-chiá ū nn̄g ê kò͘-kheh niā-niā.
楊 小姐 有 兩 個 顧客 而已。
Yáng xiǎojiě yǒu liǎng gè gùkè éryǐ.
Ms. Iunn only has two clients.

遮 干焦 有 三 个 位 爾爾。
Chia kan-na ū saⁿ ê ūi <u>niā-niā</u>.
這裡 只 有 三 個 位子 而已。
Zhèlǐ zhǐ yǒu sān gè wèizi <u>éryǐ</u>.
There are <u>only</u> three seats here.

14.2.1.5 Promptness

Both **才 chiah** and **就 tō** (also pronounced **chiū** or **tioh**) have multiple meanings depending on context and whether or not they belong to a one- or two-clause sentence.

	才 CHIAH	就 TŌ
ONE-CLAUSE SENTENCE	only, only after	precisely, just
	later than expected	earlier than expected
TWO-CLAUSE SENTENCE (SEQUENCE)	only then	then

14.2.1.5.1 Only, only after

When there is only one clause with a single verb or verb phrase, **才 chiah** takes on the meaning of 'only, just' expressing exclusivity. Along with this, is the additional connotation of not meeting expectations or a sense of lacking.

伊 才 有 一 領 褲。
I <u>chiah</u> ū chit niá khò͘.
他 只 有 一 件 褲子。
Tā <u>zhǐ</u> yǒu yī jiàn kùzi.
He <u>only</u> has one pair of pants (*he really should own more than just one*).

伊 才 讀 英文 一 年。
I <u>chiah</u> thak Eng-bûn chit nî.
她 才 讀 英文 一 年。
Tā <u>cái</u> dú Yīngwén yī nián.
She's <u>just</u> studied English for one year (*she should study much longer*).

Additionally, **才 chiah** signals that 'after some effort' a particular outcome was realized.

這馬 我 才 知影 百貨 公司 按怎 關起來 矣。
Chit-má góa <u>chiah</u> chai-iáⁿ pah-hòe kong-si án-chóaⁿ koaiⁿ--khí-lâi--ah.
現在 我 才 知道 百貨 公司 為何 倒閉 了。
Xiànzài wǒ <u>cái</u> zhīdào bǎihuò gōngsī wèihé dǎobì le.
Now I (*after some effort*) know why the department store closed down.

我 坐 公車，結果 九 點 才 轉來 矣。
Góa chē kong-chhia, kiat-kó káu tiám <u>chiah</u> tńg--lâi--ah.
我 坐 公車，結果 九點 才 回來 了。
Wǒ zuò gōngchē, jiéguǒ jiǔ diǎn <u>cái</u> huílái le.
I took the bus and (*finally*) got home at nine.

14.2.1.5.2 Precisely, just

When **就 tō** appears in a single clause, the meaning is 'precisely', 'just', or 'right' and reconfirms or offers certainty to whatever follows.

頭前 的 厝 就 是 阮 的。
Thâu-chêng ê chhù <u>tō</u> sī gún--ê.
前面 的 房子 就 是 我 的。
Qiánmiàn de fángzi <u>jiù</u> shì wǒ de.
The house in front (*precisely that one*) is mine.

停遮 就 好 矣。
Thêng chia <u>tō</u> hó--ah.
聽 這裡 就 好 了。
Tīng zhèlǐ <u>jiù</u> hǎo le.
Stopping here is (*just*) fine.

Note that unlike the Mandarin **就 jiù**, the Taiwanese **就 tō** cannot be used to express the meaning of 'only' (*exclusivity*).

14.2.1.5.3 Following time expressions

When following a time expression, 才 **chiah** and 就 **tō** indicate opposing expectations as to when the verb occurs. 才 **chiah** implies that the action takes place 'earlier than expected' while 就 **tō** implies that the action takes place 'later than expected'.

> 阮 七 點 就 起來 矣。
> Gún chhit tiám tō khí-lâi--ah.
> 我們 七 點 就 起床 了。
> Wǒmen qī diǎn jiù qǐchuáng le.
> We woke up at 7 o'clock (*earlier than expected*).

> 阮 七 點 才 起來 矣。
> Gún chhit tiám chiah khí-lâi--ah.
> 我們 七 點 才 起床 了。
> Wǒmen qī diǎn cái qǐchuáng le.
> We woke up at 7 o'clock (*later than expected*).

14.2.1.5.4 Two clauses (sequence)

Both 就 **tō** and 才 **chiah** are commonly used in sentences indicating a sequence of events. When there are two clauses present, 就 **tō** and 才 **chiah** can function as connectors to show the relationship between each clause (*see 32.1.3 Reference adverbs* 就 *tō and* 才 *chiah*).

In a sequence of events, 就 **tō** or 才 **chiah** is placed before the second action to underscore that one action happens after another.

> 食 十 碗 麵 了後，我 就 想欲 吐 矣。
> Chiah chap óaⁿ mī liáu-āu, góa tō siūⁿ-beh thò--ah.
> 吃 十 碗 麵 之後，我 就 想要 吐 了。
> Chī shí wǎn miàn zhīhòu, wǒ jiù xiǎngyào tǔ le.
> After eating ten bowls of noodles, I just wanted to throw up.

才 **chiah** similarly is used in a sequence of events but stresses that the second action will occur 'only after' the first action has already happened.

練琴幾年了後，才會當彈這條歌。
Liān khîm kúi nî liáu-āu, <u>chiah</u> ē-tàng tôaⁿ chit tiâu koa.
練琴幾年之後，才會彈這首歌。
Liàn qín jǐ nián zhīhòu, <u>cái</u> huì dàn zhè shǒu gē.
<u>Only after</u> you practice for years will you be able to play this song.

伊睏醒了後，咱才出去食早頓。
I khùn-chhéⁿ liáu-āu, lán <u>chiah</u> chhut-khì chiah chá-tǹg.
她睡醒之後，我們再出去吃早餐。
Tā shuìxǐng zhīhòu, wǒmen <u>zài</u> chūqù chī zǎocān.
<u>Once</u> she wakes up, let's (<u>then</u>) go out for breakfast.

Note that Mandarin often uses 再 **zài** in suggestions and requests to indicate a sequence that similarly emphasizes 'only after' a condition is fulfilled.

14.2.2 Relative frequency adverbs

Relative frequency adverbs describe how frequently an action occurs, not with exact numbers but in relative terms (e.g. often, sometimes, always). Absolute terms of frequency appear after the verb *(see 11.8 Duration and absolute frequency complements, 7.1.6 Including both objects and frequency)*.

Below is a table of some common relative frequency adverbs.

TAIWANESE	MANDARIN	MEANING
逐擺 ta̍k-pái	每次 měi cì	each/every time
逐改 ta̍k-kái	每次 měi cì	each/every time
逐遍 ta̍k-piàn	每次 měi cì	each/every time
每一擺 múi chit pái	每次 měi cì	each/every time
每一改 múi chit kái	每次 měi cì	each/every time
每一遍 múi chit piàn	每次 měi cì	each/every time
攏是 lóng sī	都是 dōu shì	always, in every case
直直 ti̍t-ti̍t	一直 yīzhí	always, continuously
一直 it-ti̍t	一直 yīzhí	always, continuously

TAIWANESE	MANDARIN	MEANING
定定 tiāⁿ-tiāⁿ	常常 chángcháng	constantly, frequently
常常 siông-siông	常常 chángcháng	constantly, frequently
不時 put-sî	經常 jīngcháng	constantly, frequently
四常 sù-siông	時常 shícháng	constantly, frequently
通常 thong-siông	通常 tōngcháng	usually, normally
普通 phó͘-thong	通常 tōngcháng	usually, normally
平常 pêng-siông	平常 píngcháng	ordinarily, occasionally
有時 ū-sî	有時候 yǒu shíhòu	sometimes, occasionally
有時仔 ū-sî-á	有時候 yǒu shíhòu	sometimes, occasionally
有時陣 ū-sî-chūn	有時候 yǒu shíhòu	sometimes, occasionally
有棠時(仔) ū-tang-sî(-á)	偶爾 ǒu'ěr	sometimes, occasionally
罕得 hán-tit	難得 nándé	rarely
難得 lân-tit	難得 nándé	rarely

頭家 逐擺 記得 我 的 名。
Thâu-ke ta̍k-pái kì-tit góa ê miâ.
老闆 每次 記得 我 的 名字。
Lǎobǎn měi cì jìdé wǒ de míngzì.
The shop owner remembers my name every time.

阮 阿爸 直直 叫 我 拍拚。
Gún a-pa tit-tit kiò góa phah-piàⁿ.
我 爸爸 一直 叫 我 努力 工作。
Wǒ bàba yīzhí jiào wǒ nǔlì gōngzuò.
My father always tells me to work hard.

許 小姐 不時 咧 換 頭路。
Khó͘ sió-chiá put-sî teh ōaⁿ thâu-lō͘.
許 小姐 經常 換 工作。
Xǔ xiǎojiě jīngcháng huàn gōngzuò.
Ms. Khou is constantly changing jobs.

公車 有當時仔 無 準時。

Kong-chhia ū-tang-sî-á bô chún-sî.

公車 有 的 時候 不 準時。

Gōngchē yǒu de shíhòu bù zhǔnshí.

Sometimes the bus is not on time.

伊 罕得 食薰。

I hán-tit chiảh-hun.

她 難得 抽煙。

Tā nándé chōuyān.

She rarely smokes cigarettes.

14.2.3 Manner adverbs

Manner adverbs describe how an action is performed by focusing on the bodily senses ('We loudly chatted', 'I firmly held') and intentions of the subject ('She secretly read', 'He slowly drank'). Many manner adverbs are derived from adjectives. Short one-syllable adjectives generally are duplicated before being used as manner adverbs. Multi-syllabic adjectives may but do not need to be reduplicated.

14.2.3.1 Short one-syllable adjectives

Manner adverbs can be constructed from reduplicated short one-syllable adjectives (**緊 kín** 'fast', **恬 tiām** 'quiet'). Often an optional particle **仔 -á** is added for euphony. Note that when given an adjective reading, reduplicated adjectives have a lesser intensity than the original adjective *(see 6.7 Repetition)*.

reduplicated adjective + (仔) + *verb*

reduplicated adjective + (-á) + *verb*

'*adjective* + -ly'

ADJECTIVE	REDUPLICATED ADJECTIVE	ADJECTIVE READING	ADVERB READING
緊 kín	緊緊 kín-kín	a little fast	fast
俗 siỏk	俗俗 siỏk-siỏk	a little cheap	cheaply
輕 khin	輕輕 khin-khin	a little light	lightly, carefully

ADJECTIVE	REDUPLICATED ADJECTIVE	ADJECTIVE READING	ADVERB READING
直 tit	直直 tit-tit	a little straight	continuously
短 té	短短 té-té	a little short	briefly
慢 bān	慢慢 bān-bān	a little slow	slowly
漸 chiām	漸漸 chiām-chiām	gradual	gradually
好 hó	好好 hó-hó	well	properly, carefully
勻 ûn	勻勻 ûn-ûn	——	cautiously

囡仔 恬恬 聽 阿公 講 故事。
Gín-á <u>tiām-tiām</u> thiaⁿ a-kong kóng kò·-sū.
孩子 靜靜地 聽 爺爺 說 故事。
Háizi <u>jìngjìng de</u> tīng yéyě shuō gùshì.
The children <u>quietly</u> listen to grandpa tell a story.

車禍 了後，伊 慢慢仔 行。
Chhia-hō liáu-āu, i <u>bān-bān-á</u> kiâⁿ.
車禍 之後，他 慢慢地 走。
Chēhuò zhīhòu, tā <u>mànman de</u> zǒu.
After the car accident, he walks <u>slowly</u>.

In Mandarin, manner adverbs generally are followed by the **地 de** particle except when used in commands or with adverbs beginning with **一 yī** (**一起 yīqǐ** 'together', **一味 yīwèi** 'blindly', etc.).

Additionally, note that manner adverbs, which occur before the verb, differ from manner complements, which occur after the verb. Manner adverbs tend to include more of the subject's attitude or intentions towards the action, while manner complements tend to be observations made by an outside party. Moreover, manner adverbs may be used in commands, while manner complements may not *(see 11.6 Manner complements)*.

MANNER ADVERB	MANNER COMPLEMENT
伊 慢慢 行。	伊 行著 真 慢。
I <u>bān-bān</u> kiâⁿ.	I <u>kiâⁿ-tio̍h</u> chin bān.
他 慢慢地 走。	他 走得很慢。
Tā <u>mànman de</u> zǒu.	Tā zǒu <u>de hěn màn</u>.
He walked <u>slowly</u> *(he doesn't want to slip)*.	He walked <u>slowly</u> *(appeared to walk slowly)*.

14.2.3.2 Multi-syllable adverbs

Some adjectives that are more than one syllable can also be reduplicated and used as adverbs.

TAIWANESE	MANDARIN	MEANING
歡歡喜喜 hoaⁿ-hoaⁿ-hí-hí	高高興興 gāogāoxìngxìng	happily
馬馬虎虎 má-má-hu-hu	馬馬虎虎 mǎmǎhǔhǔ	casually
輕輕鬆鬆 khin-khin-sang-sang	輕輕鬆鬆 qīngqīngsōngsōng	relaxed
清清楚楚 chheng-chheng-chhó-chhó	清清楚楚 qīngqīngchǔchǔ	clearly
時時刻刻 sî-sî-khik-khik	無時無刻 wúshíwúkè	incessantly

彼 个 查某 囝仔 歡歡喜喜仔 咧 騎 硈硈馬。
Hit ê cha-bó͘ gín-á <u>hoaⁿ-hoaⁿ-hí-hí-á</u> teh khiâ lo̍k-kho̍k-bé.
那個 女孩子 <u>高高興興 地</u> 騎 木馬。
Nàge nǚháizi <u>gāogāoxìngxìng de</u> qí mùmǎ.
That little girl is <u>happily</u> riding the rocking horse.

學生 考試 考 了 的 時陣，愬 攏 輕輕鬆鬆 開講。
Ha̍k-seng khó-chhì khó liáu ê sî-chūn, in lóng <u>khin-khin-sang-sang</u> khai-káng.
學生 考試 考了 的 時候，他們 都 <u>輕輕鬆鬆 地</u> 聊天。
Xuéshēng kǎoshì kǎole de shíhòu, tāmen dōu <u>qīngqīngsōngsōng de</u> liáotiān.
After the students finished their exams, they <u>casually</u> chatted.

Some multi-syllabic adverbs are not derived from adjectives.

TAIWANESE	MANDARIN	MEANING
強強 kiông-kiông	幾乎 jīhū	almost
大部分 tōa-pō͘-hūn	大部份 dàbùfèn	mostly
做伙 chò-hóe	一起 yīqǐ	together
烏白 o͘-pe̍h	亂來 luànlái	chaotically, randomly
另外 lēng-gōa	另外 lìngwài	separately
刁工 tiau-kang	專程 zhuānchéng	specifically, intentionally
無細膩 bô-sè-jī	不小心 bù xiǎoxīn	accidentally, inadvertently
直接 tit-chiap	直接 zhíjiē	directly
順紲 sūn-sòa	順便 shùnbiàn	in passing, conveniently

因為 阮 回收，你 愛 共 玻璃 <u>另外</u> 囥。
In-ūi gún hôe-siu, lí ài kā po-lê <u>lēng-gōa</u> khǹg.
因為 我們 回收，你 需要 把 玻璃 <u>另外</u> 放。
Yīnwèi wǒmen huíshōu, nǐ xūyào bǎ bōlí <u>lìngwài</u> fàng.
Because we recycle, you need to dispose of the glass <u>separately</u>.

這 个 櫃台 <u>暫時</u> 停止 服務。
Chit ê kūi-tai <u>chām-sî</u> thêng-chí ho̍k-bū.
這個 櫃台 <u>暫時</u> 停止 服務。
Zhège guìtái <u>zhànshí</u> tíngzhǐ fúwù.
This counter is <u>temporarily</u> closed.

14.2.3.3 Manner adverbs in commands

When occurring in commands *(see 21 Requests and commands)*, one-syllable adverbs are optionally reduplicated.

adverb + (adverb)

緊(緊) 過來！
<u>Kín(-kín)</u> kòe--lâi!
快(快) 過來！
<u>Kuài(-kuài)</u> guòlái!
<u>Hurry</u> come over!

慢(慢) 行。
<u>Bān(-bān)</u> kiâⁿ.
慢(慢) 走。
<u>Màn(-màn)</u> zǒu.
Walk <u>slowly</u>.

While both Mandarin and Taiwanese can double adverbs within commands, this is less commonly done in Taiwanese.

14.2.4 Co-occurring verb-level adverbs

When verb-level adverbs (reference, relative frequency, manner) co-occur in the same sentence, the manner adverbs generally come last while the position of the reference and relative frequency adverbs are interchangeable with little to no change in meaning.

ORDER 1

reference + relative frequency + manner

伊 嘛 定定 予 朋友 和 伊 做伙 免錢 入去。
I mā tiān-tiān hō͘ pêng-iú hām i chò-hóe bián-chîⁿ jip--khì.
他 也 常常 讓 朋友 和 他 一起 免費 進去。
Tā yě chángcháng ràng péngyǒu hé tā yīqǐ miǎnfèi jìnqù.
He also often lets his friend go in together with him for free.

ORDER 2

relative frequency + reference + manner

伊 定定 嘛 予 朋友 和 伊 做伙 免錢 入去。
I tiān-tiān mā hō͘ pêng-iú hām i chò-hóe bián-chîⁿ jip--khì.
他 常常 也 讓 朋友 和 他 一起 免費 進去。
Tā chángcháng yě ràng péngyǒu hé tā yīqǐ miǎnfèi jìnqù.
He often also lets his friend go in together with him for free.

14.3 Adverbs with other grammatical elements

While the subject may appear before or after sentence-level adverbs (attitude, time, confidence), all other grammatical elements (verb-level adverbs, negatives, modal verbs, prepositional phrases) generally follow sentence-level adverbs. Note that there are a few sentence-level confidence adverbs expressing uncertainty that have negatives built-in as part of the word such as **無一定 bô-it-tēng** or **無定著 bô-tiāⁿ-tio̍h**.

ORDER 1

subject + **sentence-level adverbs (attitude, confidence, time)** + *other elements*

ORDER 2

sentence-level adverbs (attitude, confidence, time) + *subject* + *other elements*

Verb-level adverbs (reference, relative frequency, and manner) must appear in the space *between* the subject and the main verb. However, there is some degree of flexibility with placement of the verb-level adverbs among negatives, modal verbs, and prepositional phrases. Often differing placements can give a slightly different meaning.

Among the non-adverb grammatical elements, the general order is:

subject + *negatives* + *modal verbs* + *prepositional phrases* + *main verb*

When including the verb-level adverbs, the general order is:

subject + **reference** + **relative frequency** + *negatives* + *modal verbs* + *prepositional phrases* + **manner** + *main verb*

Depending on the context, this ordering can be flexible. The following sections examine more closely the interaction between adverbs and other grammatical elements.

14.3.1 Negation and adverbs

Even if they occur after the subject, negatives cannot appear before sentence-level adverbs (attitude, time, confidence).

sentence-level adverb + **negative** + *verb*

ATTITUDE ADVERB

伊 親像 **毋敢** 家己 唱 歌。
I chhin-chhiūⁿ **m̄-káⁿ** ka-tī chhiùⁿ koa.
好像 他 **不 敢** 自己 唱 歌。
Hǎoxiàng tā **bù gǎn** zìjǐ chàng gē.

Seems like he **does not** dare sing by himself.

TIME ADVERB

阮 本底 無 想著 阮 會當 較早 離開。
Gún p̪ún-té **bô** siūⁿ-tio̍h gún ē-tàng khah-chá lī-khui.
我們 本來 沒 想到 我們 能 早 一點 離開。
Wǒmen běnlái **méi** xiǎngdào wǒmen néng zǎo yīdiǎn líkāi.
We originally **did not** think we could leave early.

CONFIDENCE ADVERB

你 絕對 毋通 家己 一 个 人 轉去！
Lí cho̍at-tùi **m̄-thang** ka-tī chit ê lâng tńg--khì!
你 絕對 不 要 自己 一 個 人 回家！
Nǐ juéduì **bù yào** zìjǐ yī gè rén huí jiā!
You absolutely **must not** go home by yourself!

However, when it comes to verb-level adverbs (reference, relative frequency, and manner), the position of the negative can come *before* or *after* the adverb. The negative negates whatever follows immediately afterwards, so the placement of the negative can change the meaning of the sentence as seen in the examples below. In general, negative sentence constructions more often negate the verb instead of the adverb. Additionally, many adverbs make less sense negated and are not considered acceptable. As a result, the more typical placement of the negative is *after* the verb-level adverb.

TYPICAL PLACEMENT

verb-level adverb + ***negative*** + *verb*

LESS COMMON PLACEMENT

negative + *verb-level adverb* + *verb*

MANNER ADVERB

恁 刁工 無 佇 伊 的 邊仔 坐咧。
In tiau-kang **bô** tī i ê piⁿ-á chē--leh.
她們 故意 不 在 她 的 旁邊 坐著。
Tāmen gùyì **bù** zài tā de pángbiān zuòzhe.
They deliberately **didn't** sit by her (*perhaps they didn't like her*).

恁 無 刁工 佇 伊 的 邊仔 坐咧。

In **bô** tiau-kang tī i ê piⁿ-á chē--leh.

她們 不 故意 在 她 的 旁邊 坐著。

Tāmen **bù** gùyì zài tā de pángbiān zuòzhe.

They **didn't** deliberately sit by her (*perhaps they didn't recognize her before sitting down, so they just happened to sit next to her*).

RELATIVE FREQUENCY ADVERB

蔡 小姐 定定 無 去 病院。

Chhòa sió-chiá tiāⁿ-tiāⁿ **bô** khì pēⁿ-īⁿ.

蔡 小姐 常常 不 去 醫院。

Cài xiǎojiě chángcháng **bù** qù yīyuàn.

Ms. Chhoa often **doesn't** go to the hospital (*implies she is supposed to go more often, perhaps to volunteer or to visit someone*).

蔡 小姐 無 定定 去 病院。

Chhòa sió-chiá **bô** tiāⁿ-tiāⁿ khì pēⁿ-īⁿ.

蔡 小姐 不 常常 去 醫院。

Cài xiǎojiě **bù** chángcháng qù yīyuàn.

Ms. Chhoa **doesn't** frequently go to the hospital (*implies she is healthy and does not need to go often*).

REFERENCE ADVERB

伊 閣 無 清 便所。

I koh **bô** chheng piān-só.

他 又 不 清 廁所。

Tā yòu **bù** qīng cèsuǒ.

Again he **didn't** clean the bathrooms.

伊 無 閣 清 便所。

I **bô** koh chheng piān-só.

他 不 再 清 廁所。

Tā **bù** zài qīng cèsuǒ.

He **doesn't** clean bathrooms anymore (*perhaps he has changed jobs*).

14.3.2 Modal verbs and adverbs

Some verb-level adverbs can appear before or after modal verbs, but placement sometimes may change the meaning or emphasis.

ORDER 1

*verb-level adverb + **modal verb** + verb*

ORDER 2

***modal verb** + verb-level adverb + verb*

MANNER

伊 直接 會 參 你 聯絡。

I <u>tit-chiap</u> **ē** chhām lí <u>liân-lo̍k</u>.

他 直接 會 跟 你 聯絡。

Tā zhíjiē **huì** gēn nǐ liánluò.

He **will** contact you directly.

伊 會 直接 參 你 連絡。

I **ē** <u>tit-chiap</u> chhām lí <u>liân-lo̍k</u>.

他 會 直接 跟 你 聯絡。

Tā **huì** zhíjiē gēn nǐ liánluò.

He **will** contact you directly.

In the examples above, there is no significant difference in meaning.

RELATIVE FREQUENCY

這 隻 狗 不時 會 吠。

Che chiah káu <u>put-sî</u> **ē** pūi.

這 隻 狗 隨時 會 吠。

Zhè zhī gǒu <u>suíshí</u> **huì** <u>fèi</u>.

This dog barks all the time (*emphasizing that the barking is frequent*).

這 隻 狗 會 不時 吠。
Che chiah káu **ē** put-sî pūi.
這 隻 狗 會 隨時 吠。
Zhè zhī gǒu **huì** suíshí fèi.
This dog **will** bark at any time (*emphasizing that barking can occur at any instant*).

REFERENCE

伊 干焦 會當 講 話。
I kan-na **ē-tàng** kóng ōe.
他 只 能 講 話。
Tā zhǐ **néng** jiǎng huà.
All he **can** do is talk.

伊 會當 干焦 講 話。
I **ē-tàng** kan-na kóng ōe.
他 能 只 講 話。
Tā **néng** zhǐ jiǎng huà.
It's acceptable that he only has to talk.

14.3.3 Prepositional phrases and adverbs

When prepositional phrases occur before the verb, they serve as a backdrop against which the main verb occurs. For the purpose of word order, prepositional phrases can be subdivided into *location expressions* ('in the tree', 'at the park', etc.) and *non-location expressions* ('with my sister', 'using a knife', etc.) *(see 15 Prepositions, 16 Location and directional expressions)*. If both types of prepositional phrases co-occur, the non-location expression comes before the location expression.

> *non-location expression* + *location expression*

伊 和 恁 大家 佇 露台 啉 茶。
I **hām in ta-ke** tī lō͘-tâi lim tê.
她 和 她 婆婆 在 陽台 喝 茶。
Tā **hé tā pópo** zài yángtái hē chá.
She drank tea **with her mother-in-law** on the balcony.

Reference and relative frequency adverbs generally appear *before* prepositional phrases. However, manner adverbs may occur *before* or *after* the prepositional phrases. It is also possible for manner adverbs to appear *in between* the non-location expression and location expression.

ORDER 1

reference + relative frequency + manner + **prepositional phrase(s)**

ORDER 2

reference + relative frequency + **prepositional phrase(s)** *+ manner*

ORDER 3

reference + relative frequency + **non-location expression** *+ manner +* **location expression**

If the manner adverb focuses more on the subject's feelings and intentions, then the manner adverb comes *before* the prepositional phrases.

manner (intention) + **prepositional phrases**

伊 恬恬 和 悠 大家 佇 露台 啉 茶。
I <u>tiām-tiām</u> **hām in ta-ke tī lō·-tâi** lim tê.
她 靜靜 地 和 她 婆婆 在 陽台 喝 茶。
Tā <u>jìngjìng de</u> **hé tā pópo zài yángtái** hē chá.
She <u>quietly</u> drank tea **with her mother-in-law on the balcony** (*perhaps she is nervous and shy*).

On the other hand, if the manner adverb focuses more on a physical description of the how the action is carried out, the manner adverb appears *after* the prepositional phrase(s) or *in between* a non-location expression and location expression.

prepositional phrases *+ manner adverb (physical description)*

伊 和 恁 大家 佇 露台 恬恬 啉 茶。
I hām in ta-ke tī lō͘-tâi tiām-tiām lim tê.
她 和 她 婆婆 在 陽台 靜靜地 喝 茶。
Tā hé tā pópo zài yángtái jìngjìng de hē chá.
She drank tea **with her mother-in-law** in silence **on the balcony**.

non-location expression + manner adverb + location expression

伊 和 恁 大家 恬恬 佇 露台 啉 茶。
I hām in ta-ke tiām-tiām tī lō͘-tâi lim tê.
她 和 她 婆婆 靜靜地 在 陽台 喝 茶。
Tā hé tā pópo jìngjìng de zài yángtái hē chá.
She drank tea **with her mother-in-law** in silence **on the balcony**.

For longer prepositional phrases or where emphasis is needed, the prepositional phrase can also appear at the beginning of the sentence.

佇 海邊 彼个 舊 的 細間 厝，我 有 揣著 一 檯 鋼琴。
<u>Tī hái-piⁿ hit ê kū ê sè keng chhù</u>, góa ū chhōe-tio̍h chi̍t tâi kǹg-khîm.
在 海邊 那個 舊 的 小 房子，我 找到了 一 檯 鋼琴。
<u>Zài hǎibiān nàge jiù de xiǎo fángzi</u>, wǒ zhǎodàole yī tái gāngqín.
<u>In that small, old house by the sea</u>, I found an old piano.

照 恁 阿爸 講 的 方向，咱 應該 已經 到 矣。
<u>Chiàu in a-pa kóng ê hong-hiòng</u>, lán eng-kai í-keng kàu--ah.
照 他 爸爸 講 的 方向，我們 應該 已經 到 了。
<u>Zhào tā bàba jiǎng de fāngxiàng</u>, wǒmen yīnggāi yǐjīng dào le.
<u>According to his father's directions</u>, we should already have arrived.

14.4 Summary of word order for adverbs

While word order of adverbs and other grammatical elements have some degree of flexibility according to emphasis and individual preference, the ordering presented below is the most neutral:

> subject + **attitude** + **confidence** / **time** + **reference** / **relative frequency** + negative + modal verb + preposition (non-location) + 共 **kā** construction / 予 hō˙ (benefactive marker) + prepositional phrase (location) + **manner** + verb + duration / absolute frequency complement

If a negative verb is used with a duration/absolute frequency complement, then the complement is moved to a position before the verb *(see 11.8.3 Duration and absolute frequency with negated verbs)*.

> subject + **attitude** + **confidence** / **time** + duration / absolute frequency complement (when used with negative verb) + **reference** / **relative frequency** + negative + modal verb + prepositional phrase (non-location) + 共 **kā** construction / 予 hō˙ (benefactive marker) + prepositional phrase (location) + **manner** + verb

Note that if a 共 **kā** construction or benefactive phrase is used, the placement occurs between the non-location and location prepositional phrases *(see 17.4 共 kā construction, 18.3 Benefactives)*.

15 Prepositions

Prepositions introduce a noun phrase and relate it to the main verb of the sentence explaining details such as for whom, with whom, how, when, and where.

I cooked dinner <u>for my mom</u> (*for whom*).

My sister went to dinner <u>with my aunt</u> (*with whom*).

The children ate spaghetti <u>with their hands</u> (*how*).

We have an appointment <u>at four o'clock</u> (*when*).

They are eating lunch <u>on the balcony</u> (*where*).

In general, prepositional phrases come before the main verb of the sentence helping to set the background context for the main verb.

陳小姐 和 伊 的 朋友 啉 茶。
Tân sió-chiá <u>hām i ê pêng-iú</u> lim tê.
陳小姐 和 她 的 朋友 喝 茶。
Chén xiǎojiě <u>hé tā de péngyǒu</u> hē chá.
Ms. Tan drank tea <u>with her friend</u>.

阮 小弟 愛 用 攕仔 食 麵。
Gún sió-tī ài <u>ēng chhiám-á</u> chiảh mī.
我 弟弟 喜歡 用 叉子 吃 麵。
Wǒ dìdì xǐhuān <u>yòng chāzi</u> chī miàn.
My younger brother likes <u>using a fork</u> to eat noodles.

When the prepositional phrase is not providing background information but rather a target destination or location, the placement of the prepositional phrase comes after the main verb.

佢 開 到 巴黎。

In khui kàu Pa-lê.

他們 開 到 巴黎。

Tāmen kāi dào Bālí.

They drove to Paris (*the driving had to occur before reaching Paris*).

這 个 查某 囡仔 共 雞卵糕 园 踮 伊 家己 的 面頂。

Chit ê cha-bó͘ gín-á kā ke-nn̄g-ko khǹg tàm i ka-tī ê bīn-téng.

這個 女孩子 把 蛋糕 放 在 她 自己 的 臉 上。

Zhège nǚháizi bǎ dàngāo fàng zài tā zìjǐ de liǎn shàng.

The little girl put the cake onto her face (*picking up the cake had to occur before placing it on her face*).

Prepositions concerning locations are discussed more in detail in the next chapter *(see 16 Location and directional expressions)*.

15.1 Prepositions of movement

Prepositions of movement clarify points along a trajectory from a start point to an end point. Those prepositions that introduce a destination are placed after the verb and form a *directional expression (see 16.4 Directional expressions)*.

TAIWANESE	MANDARIN	MEANING
按 àn	從 cóng	starting from
對…來 (t)ùi…lâi	從 cóng	coming from
對…去 (t)ùi…khì	向 xiàng	going towards (*after verb*)
順 sūn	順著 shùnzhe	following along
甲 kah	到 dào	up to a certain location
到 kàu	到 dào	arriving at

高鐵 按 高雄 開 到 台北。

Ko-thih àn Ko-hiông khui kàu Tâi-pak.

高鐵 行駛 高雄 到 臺北。

Gāotiě xíngshǐ Gāoxióng dào Táiběi.

The high-speed rail runs from Kaohsiung to Taipei.

你順彼條路行，就會看著藥房。

Lí sūn hit tiâu lōˈkiaⁿ, tō ē khòaⁿ-tiȯh iȯh-pâng.

你順著那條路走，就可以看到藥局。

Nǐ shùnzhe nà tiáo lù zǒu, jiù kěyǐ kàndào yàojú.

If you walk along that road, you will see a pharmacy.

阮爸母對東京來。

Gún pē-bú ùi Tang-kiaⁿ lâi.

我父母從東京來。

Wǒ fùmǔ cóng Dōngjīng lái.

My parents are coming from Tokyo.

恁阿兄開對機場去。

In a-hiaⁿ khui tùi ki-tiûⁿ khì.

他哥哥向機場方向開去。

Tā gēgē xiàng jīchǎng fāngxiàng kāi qù.

His older brother is driving towards the airport.

Note that when appearing before the main verb, the Taiwanese preposition **對 (t)ùi** means 'coming from' and is followed by the speaker perspective **來 lâi** (*towards the speaker*). However, the same preposition **對 (t)ùi** means 'towards' when occurring after the main verb and is followed by the speaker perspective **去 khì** (*away from the speaker*).

15.2 Prepositions of orientation

Prepositions of orientation offer more information about which direction a verb is facing.

TAIWANESE	MANDARIN	MEANING
對 (t)ùi	對 dùi / 向 xiàng	facing, towards, to
共 kā	對 dùi / 向 xiàng	facing, towards
當 tng	對 dùi	facing, in front of

伊對阿母咒誓後擺袂拍小弟。

I tùi a-bú chiù-chōa āu-pái bē phah sió-tī.

他對媽媽發誓下次不會打弟弟。

Tā duì māmā fāshì xià cì bù huì dǎ dìdì.

He swore to his mom that next time he would not hit his younger brother.

我 的 老師 <u>共</u> 我 講 我 的 毛筆 字 歹 讀。

Góa ê lāu-su <u>kā</u> góa kóng góa ê mô·-pit jī pháiⁿ-thák.

我 的 老師 <u>跟</u> 我 說 我 的 書法 難看。

Wǒ de lǎoshī <u>gēn</u> wǒ shuō wǒ de shūfǎ nánkàn.

My teacher said <u>to</u> me that my handwriting is hard to read.

15.3 Prepositions of location

Prepositions of location placed *before* the main verb introduce *location expressions*, prepositional phrases specifying where the action of the main verb occurs *(see 16.1 Prepositions for location expressions)*. Prepositions of location can also occur *after* the main verb when indicating a location resulting from an action *(see 16.3.3 Placement after the verb)* or when introducing *directional expressions*, prepositional phrases specifying a destination *(see 16.4 Directional expressions)*.

TAIWANESE	MANDARIN	MEANING
佇 tī	在 zài	at, on, in
踮 tàm	在 zài	at, on, in
蹛 tòa	在 zài	at, on, in
離 lī	離 lí	set apart from

大學 <u>離</u> 阮 厝 無 傷 遠。

Tāi-hȧk <u>lī</u> gún chhù bô siuⁿ hn̄g.

大學 <u>離</u> 我 家 不 太 遠。

Dàxué <u>lí</u> wǒ jiā bù tài yuǎn.

The university is not very <u>far from</u> my house.

阮 阿叔 <u>佇</u> 附近 的 湖 釣 魚。

Gún a-chek <u>tī</u> hù-kīn ê ô· tiò hî.

我 叔叔 <u>在</u> 附近 的 湖 釣 魚。

Wǒ shūshu <u>zài</u> fùjìn de hú diào yú.

My uncle is <u>at</u> a nearby lake fishing.

伊 踮 遐 坐咧 無 代誌 通 做。
I tàm hia chē--leh bô tāi-chì thang chò.
他 在 那裡 坐著 沒有 事 可以 做。
Tā zài nàlǐ zuòzhe méiyǒu shì kěyǐ zuò.
He is sitting there with nothing to do.

15.4 Prepositions of time

Prepositions of time specify either the endpoints of a time period or a precise point in time.

TAIWANESE	MANDARIN	MEANING
佇 tī	在 zài	at
按 àn	從 cóng	from
對 tùi	從 cóng	from
從 chêng	從 cóng	from, since (*time specified*)
到 kàu	到 dào	to, until a point in time
甲 kah	到 dào	to, until a point in time
至 chì	至 zhì	to (*time specified*)

咱 佇 兩 點 有 業務 會議。
Lán tī nn̄g tiám ū giap-bū hōe-gī.
我們 在 兩 點 有 銷售 會議。
Wǒmen zài liǎng diǎn yǒu xiāoshòu huìyì.
At 2 o'clock we have a sales meeting.

彼 齣 電影 按 暗時 八 點 搬 到 十 點。
Hit chhut tiān-iáⁿ àn àm-sî peh tiám poaⁿ kàu cha̍p tiám.
那 部 電影 從 晚上 八 點 演 到 十 點。
Nà bù diànyǐng cóng wǎnshàng bā diǎn yǎn dào shí diǎn.
That movie plays from 8pm to 10pm.

我 從 高中 時 開始 佇 外口 走。
Góa chêng ko-tiong sî khai-sí tī gōa-kháu cháu.
我 從 高中 時 開始 在 戶外 跑步。
Wǒ cóng gāozhōng shí kāishǐ zài hùwài pǎobù.
Since I was in high school, I have always run outside.

15.5 Prepositions of accompaniment and interaction

Prepositions of accompaniment and interaction introduce nouns as companions or involved parties.

TAIWANESE	MANDARIN	MEANING
佮 kah (kap)	跟 gēn / 和 hé	with, and, from *(source)*
和 hām	跟 gēn / 和 hé	with, and
參 chham	跟 gēn / 和 hé	with, and
共 kā	跟 gēn	to *(one-sided)*
綴 tòe (tè)	隨 suí	to follow along

阿公 佮 阿媽 做伙 行 去 公園。
A-kong <u>kah</u> a-má chò-hóe kiâⁿ khì kong-hn̂g.
爺爺 和 奶奶 一起 走 到 公園。
Yéyé <u>hé</u> nǎinai yīqǐ zǒu dào gōngyuán.
Grandpa <u>and</u> grandma walked to the park together.

伊 共 我 罵 一睏。
I <u>kā</u> góa mē chit-khùn.
他 跟 我 罵 一 頓。
Tā <u>gēn</u> wǒ mà yī dùn.
He gave me a scolding.

和 阮 阿姊 討論 週末 旅行。
<u>Hām</u> gún a-chí thó-lūn chiu-boa̍t lú-hêng.
跟 我 姐姐 討論 週末 旅行。
<u>Gēn</u> wǒ jiějiě tǎolùn zhōumò lǚxíng.
Discuss <u>with</u> my older sister about the weekend trip.

頭家 參 客戶 做伙 去 拍 網球。
Thâu-ke <u>chham</u> kheh-hō͘ chò-hóe khì phah bāng-kiû.
老闆 和 客戶 一起 去 打 網球。
Lǎobǎn <u>hé</u> kèhù yīqǐ qù dǎ wǎngqiú.
The boss went <u>with</u> the clients to play tennis.

15.6 Prepositions of manner

Prepositions of manner introduce nouns as instruments or vehicles that are used to accomplish the main verb.

TAIWANESE	MANDARIN	MEANING
坐 chē	坐 zuò	by means of *(a vehicle)*, via
閘 chảh	搭 dā, 攔 lán	by means of *(a vehicle)*, via
用 ēng	用 yòng	with *(an instrument or appliance)*

咱 欲 <u>坐</u> 火車 到 台東。
Lán beh <u>chē</u> hóe-chhia kàu Tâi-tang.
我們 要 <u>坐</u> 火車 到 台東。
Wǒmen yào <u>zuò</u> huǒchē dào Táidōng.
We will <u>take</u> the train to Taitung.

趕 時間 的 時, <u>閘</u> 計程車。
Kóaⁿ sî-kan ê sî, <u>chảh</u> kè-thêng-chhia.
趕 時間 的 時候, <u>搭</u> 計程車。
Gǎn shíjiān de shíhòu, <u>dā</u> jìchéngchē.
If you are in a rush, <u>take</u> a taxi.

<u>用</u> 鉛筆 寫 數學 考試單。
<u>Ēng</u> iân-pit siá sò͘-hảk khó-chhì-toaⁿ.
<u>用</u> 鉛筆 寫 數學 考試卷。
<u>Yòng</u> qiānbǐ xiě shùxué kǎoshìjuàn.
Write <u>with</u> a pencil on your math test.

15.7 Prepositions for benefactives

Benefactives are prepositional phrases that introduce nouns benefitting from the action of the main verb *(see 18.3 Benefactives)*.

TAIWANESE	MANDARIN	MEANING
共 kā	幫 bāng, 給 gěi	for *(to help do)*
替 thè	替 tì	to stand in for
為 ūi	為 wèi	because of, for

這 本 冊，你 敢 會當 共 我 包起來？
Che pún chheh, lí kám ē-tàng kā góa pau--khí-lâi?
這 本 書，你 能不能 幫 我 包起來？
Zhè běn shū, nǐ néngbùnéng bāng wǒ bāoqǐlái?
Can you wrap this book for me?

阮 查囝 欲 替 我 領受 獎品。
Gún cha-kiáⁿ beh thè góa niá-siū chióng-phín.
我 女兒 要 替 我 領 獎品。
Wǒ nǚ'ér yào tì wǒ lǐng jiǎngpǐn.
My daughter will accept the award for me.

我 欲 為 伊 做生日。
Góa beh ūi i chò-seⁿ-jit.
我 要 為 她 過 生日。
Wǒ yào wèi tā guò shēngrì.
I am going to throw a birthday party for her.

While not originally used as a preposition, the Taiwanese verb 幫 **pang** has recently expanded into a usage similar to its Mandarin counterpart 幫 **bāng**.

凡勢 彼 个 服務員 會當 幫 阮 翕相。
Hōan-sè hit ê ho̍k-bū-ôan ē-tàng pang lán hip-siòng.
也許 那個 服務員 能 幫 我們 拍照。
Yěxǔ nàgè fúwùyuán néng bāng wǒmen pāizhào.
Maybe that waiter can take a picture for us.

15.8 Prepositions with grammatical function

Some prepositions have specific grammatical functions.

15.8.1 予 hō˙ marking indirect objects

Unlike direct objects, which receive the action of the verb, indirect objects represent the 'goal' for which actions are done ('She blew a kiss to me', 'I sent a postcard to him'). Typically, indirect objects are people, animals, or institutions (universities, hospitals, etc.). In Taiwanese, the preposition 予 hō˙ is used to mark indirect objects. Note that some verbs do not require a preposition to mark indirect objects *(see 18.2 Dative verbs)*.

verb + 予 + *indirect object*

verb + hō˙ + *indirect object*

阮 阿爸 寫 這 張 批 予 我。
Gún a-pa siá chit tiuⁿ phoe hō˙ góa.
我 爸爸 寫 這 封 信 給 我。
Wǒ bàba xiě zhè fēng xìn gěi wǒ.
My father wrote this letter to me.

恁 提 雞卵糕 予 伊。
In theh ke-nn̄g-ko hō˙ i.
他們 拿 蛋糕 給 她。
Tāmen ná dàngāo gěi tā.
They brought a cake to her.

15.8.2 共 kā marking direct objects

Direct objects receive the action from the verb ('I threw the ball', 'She dropped her glasses'). In some instances, direct objects must be moved from the typical position after the verb to a position before the verb. The preposition 共 kā allows this to occur with the 共 kā construction *(see 17.4 共 kā construction)*. In some cases, a preposition is not required and the object is simply *pre-posed*, placed before the verb *(see 17.1 Pre-posed objects)*.

subject + 共 + *direct object* + *verb*

subject + kā + *direct object* + *verb*

伊 共 我 的 手機 擗 踮 水內。

I kā góa ê chhiú-ki khian tàm chúi-lāi.

他 把 我 的 手機 丟 在 水 裡。

Tā bǎ wǒ de shǒujī diū zài shuǐ lǐ.

He threw my mobile phone into the water.

㑩 共 果子 囥 佇 桌仔頂。

In kā kóe-chí khǹg tī toh-á-téng.

他們 把 水果 放 在 桌子 上。

Tāmen bǎ shuǐguǒ fàng zài zhuōzi shàng.

They put the fruit onto the table.

15.8.3 予 hō͘ marking passive voice constructions

In a passive sentence, the direct object (recipient of the action) becomes the subject of the sentence. The preposition 予 hō͘ is placed before the main verb to indicate the passive voice. Sometimes the passive marker 予 hō͘ is preceded by the verb 去 khì *(see 19 Passive voice)*.

direct object + (去) + 予 + *verb*

direct object + (khì) + hō͘ + *verb*

伊 予 伊 的 同學 笑。

I hō͘ i ê tông-ha̍k chhiò.

她 被 她 的 同學 笑。

Tā bèi tā de tóngxué xiào.

She was laughed at by her classmates.

我 的 朋友 予 球棒 摃著。

Góa ê pêng-iú hō͘ kiû-pāng kòng-tio̍h.

我 的 朋友 被 球棒 打 到。

Wǒ de péngyǒu bèi qiúbàng dǎ dào.

My friend was hit by a baseball bat.

15.9 Prepositions doubling as verbs

Some prepositions may also function as verbs. Because historically many prepositions in Chinese were derived from verbs, a few prepositions still retain capabilities as a verb.

	PREPOSITION	VERB
到 *KÀU*	TO (DESTINATION)	TO ARRIVE
	到 機場 愛 偌久？	阮 機場 到 矣。
	Kàu ki-tiûⁿ ài jōa-kú?	Gún ki-tiûⁿ kàu--ah.
	到 機場 要 多久？	我們 到 機場 了。
	Dào jīchǎng yào duōjiǔ?	Wǒmen dào jīchǎng le.
	How long is it to the airport?	We arrived at the airport.
佇 *TĪ*	AT, ON, IN	TO BE LOCATED AT
	阮 阿兄 佇 眠床 倒咧。	阮 阿兄 佇 眠床頂。
	Gún a-hiaⁿ tī bîn-chhn̂g tó--leh.	Gún a-hiaⁿ tī bîn-chhn̂g-téng.
	我 哥哥 在 床 上 躺著。	我 哥哥 在 床 上。
	Wǒ gēgē zài chuáng shàng tǎngzhe.	Wǒ gēgē zài chuáng shàng.
	My brother is lying on the bed.	My brother is on the bed.
坐 *CHĒ*	BY MEANS OF (A VEHICLE)	TO SIT
	我 坐 計程車 去 遐。	我 佇 計程車 坐咧。
	Góa chē kè-thêng-chhia khì hia.	Góa tī kè-thêng-chhia chē--leh.
	我 坐 計程車 去 那裡。	我 在 計程車 坐著。
	Wǒ zuò jìchéngchē qù nàlǐ.	wǒ zài jìchéngchē zuòzhe.
	I will take a taxi there.	I am sitting in a taxi.

16 Location and directional expressions

Location expressions are a type of prepositional phrase that specifies where the action of the main verb occurs *(see 15.3 Prepositions of location)*.

Directional expressions are a type of prepositional phrase that introduces a destination and are placed *after* the main verb.

16.1 Prepositions for location expressions

Location expressions typically begin with one of three prepositions: 佇 **tī**, 踮 **tàm**, or 蹛 **tòa** signifying 'on', 'at', or 'in'.

佇 **tī** is more general in purpose and can be used in both location and time expressions. An alternative form is 佇咧 **tī-leh**.

阮 佇 厝 的 頭前 拍 籃球。
Gún tī chhù ê thâu-chêng phah nâ-kiû.
我們 在 房子 的 前面 打 籃球。
Wǒmen zài fángzi de qiánmiàn dǎ lánqiú.
We played basketball in front of the house.

導遊 佇 兩 點 會 共 咱 接。
Tō-iû tī nn̄g tiám ē kā lán chiap.
導遊 在 兩 點 會 接 我們。
Dǎoyóu zài liǎng diǎn huì jiē wǒmen.
The tour guide will pick us up at 2 o'clock.

踮 **tàm** (also pronounced **tiàm**) is commonly used but limited to location expressions.

阮 敢 會使 跕 遮 奕 牌仔？

Gún kám ē-sái tàm chia ī pâi-á?

我們 可以 在 這裡 玩 牌？

Wǒmen kěyǐ zài zhèlǐ wán pái?

Can we play cards here?

蹛 **tòa** tends to be used more for situations in the future along with commands or requests. However, because 蹛 **tòa** also means 'to stay' or 'to live', some speakers prefer to use 佇 **tī** or 跕 **tàm**.

伊 明仔載 欲 蹛 灶跤 做 肉粽。

I bîn-á-chài beh tòa chàu-kha chò bah-chàng.

她 明天 要 在 廚房 做 粽子。

Tā míngtiān yào zài chúfáng zuò zòngzi.

Tomorrow she will make sticky rice dumplings in the kitchen.

莫 蹛 電視前 食 物件。

Mài tòa tiān-sī-chêng chiȧh mı̇h-kiāⁿ.

不要 在 電視 前 吃 東西。

Bùyào zài diànshì qián chī dōngxī.

Don't eat in front of the television.

16.2 Location participles

The most basic form of a location expression comprises a preposition and a noun / noun phrase. Together they indicate where the main verb occurs. However, often more specific location information is given by the addition of a location participle. The *location participle* (on top of, below, next to, etc.) further specifies a position that is relative to the noun itself.

    preposition + noun / noun phrase + (location participle)

弓蕉 佇 桌仔頂 咧 生菇。

Keng-chio tī toh-á-téng teh seⁿ-ko.

香蕉 在 桌子 上 在 發霉。

Xiāngjiāo zài zhuōzi shàng zài fāméi.

The bananas are rotting on the table.

伊 的 朋友 佇 公園內 睏。

I ê pêng-iú tī kong-hn̂g-lāi khùn.

他 的 朋友 在 公園 裡 睡覺。

Tā de péngyǒu zài gōngyuán lǐ shuìjiào.

His friend slept in the park.

16.2.1 Common location participles

There are five common location participles in Taiwanese that specify a position relative to the noun in the location expression. Note that the location participles are suffixed to the preceding noun.

TAIWANESE	MANDARIN	MEANING
頂 -téng	上 shàng	on top of
跤 -kha	下 xià	below of
外 -gōa	外 wài	outside of
內 -lāi	內 nèi, 裡 lǐ	inside of, within
前 -chêng	前 qián	in front of

囡仔 佇 厝內 咧 耍 迌迌物仔。

Gín-á tī chhù-lāi teh sńg chhit-thô-mih-á.

孩子 在 家 裡 在 玩 玩具。

Háizi zài jiā lǐ zài wán wánjù.

The children are playing with toys in the house.

我 踮 膨椅跤 揣著 一 雙 舊 鞋仔。

Góa tàm phòng-í-kha chhōe-tio̍h chit siang kū ê-á.

我 在 沙發 下 找到 一 雙 舊 鞋子。

Wǒ zài shāfā xià zhǎodào yī shuāng jiù xiézi.

I found an old pair of shoes under the sofa.

Note that Mandarin has a distinction between 內 **nèi** 'inside' and 裡 **lǐ** 'in, within'. In contrast, Taiwanese generally uses 內 **-lāi** for both cases. In a small number of expressions, 裡 **-lí (nih)** may be used although 內 **-lāi** is also considered acceptable.

阮 佇 厝裡 攏 講 台語。

Gún tī chhù-lí lóng kóng Tâi-gí.

我們 在 家裡 都 講 台語。

Wǒmen zài jiā lǐ dōu jiǎng Táiyǔ.

We always speak Taiwanese at home.

阮 佇 厝內 攏 講 台語。

Gún tī chhù-lāi lóng kóng Tâi-gí.

我們 在 家裡 都 講 台語。

Wǒmen zài jiā lǐ dōu jiǎng Táiyǔ.

We always speak Taiwanese at home.

16.2.2 Location participles with noun suffixes 面 -bīn and 頭 -thâu

Location participles themselves can be suffixed with 面 -bīn 'face' or 頭 -thâu 'head' to form nouns. However, not every combination is deemed acceptable for all speakers. By using the modifying particle 的 ê, this noun form of the location participle can also be used within location expressions. Note the modifying particle 的 ê can be omitted.

> noun or noun phrase + (的) + location participle + noun suffix
>
> noun or noun phrase + (ê) + location participle + noun suffix

貓仔 佇 桌仔 的 下面。

Niau-á tī toh-á ê ē-bīn.

貓 在 桌子 的 下面。

Māo zài zhuōzi de xiàmiàn.

The cats are underneath the table.

Below is a table exhibiting combinations of location particles with the noun suffixes **面 -bīn** 'face' and **頭 -thâu** 'head'. In addition, some common alternatives have been provided. Note that the order of the noun suffix and location particle is switched for the 'front, front side'.

面 -BĪN 'FACE'	頭 -THÂU 'HEAD'	ALTERNATIVES	MEANING
頂面 téng-bīn 上面 shàngmiàn	頂頭 téng-thâu 上頭 shàngtou	頂懸 téng-kôan	top
下面 ē-bīn 下面 xiàmiàn	下頭 ē-thâu 下頭 xiàtou	下跤 ē-kha, 下底 ē-té	underneath
外面 gōa-bīn 外面 wàimiàn	外頭 gōa-thâu 外頭 wàitou	外口 gōa-kháu	outside
內面 lāi-bīn 裡面 lǐmiàn	內頭 lāi-thâu 裡頭 lǐtou	內底 lāi-té	inside
後面 āu-bīn 後面 hòumiàn	後頭 āu-thâu 後頭 hòutou	後壁 āu-piah	back, back side
面前 bīn-chêng 面前 miànqián	頭前 thâu-chêng —	面頭前 bīn-thâu-chêng	front, front side

Below is a table of additional terms commonly used in location expressions.

TAIWANESE	MANDARIN	MEANING
對面 tùi-bīn	對面 duìmiàn	opposite side
邊(仔) piⁿ(-á)	邊 biān	side
中央 tiong-ng	中間 zhōngjiān	middle
正爿 chiàⁿ-pêng	右邊 yòubiān	right side
正手爿 chiàⁿ-chhiú-pêng	右手邊 yòushǒubiān	right-hand side
倒爿 tò-pêng	左邊 zuóbiān	left side
倒手爿 tò-chhiú-pêng	左手邊 zuóshǒubiān	left-hand side

16.2.3 Cardinal directions

Cardinal directions can also be used within location expressions. Generally, cardinal directions are given in the order 東 **tang** 'east', 西 **sai** 'west', 南 **lâm** 'south', 北 **pak** 'north' in more casual speech. However, in more poetic or formal speech, the order changes to 東 **tang** 'east', 南 **lâm** 'south', 西 **sai** 'west', 北 **pak** 'north'.

TAIWANESE	MANDARIN	MEANING
東 tang	東 dōng	east
南 lâm	南 nán	south
西 sai	西 xī	west
北 pak	北 běi	north

Intermediate (ordinal) directions are stated in the reverse order of their English counterparts (i.e. east or west is stated first).

TAIWANESE	MANDARIN	MEANING
東北 tang-pak	東北 dōngběi	northeast
東南 tang-lâm	東南 dōngnán	southeast
西北 sai-pak	西北 xīběi	northwest
西南 sai-lâm	西南 xīnán	southwest

When describing a geographic region in relationship to cardinal directions, the cardinal direction may be placed before 部 **pō** 'region' and 爿 **pêng** 'side'.

TAIWANESE	MANDARIN	MEANING
東部 tang-pō	東部 dōngbù	eastern region
南部 lâm-pō	南部 nánbù	southern region
西部 sai-pō	西部 xībù	western region
北部 pak-pō	北部 běibù	northern region
東爿 tang-pêng	東方 dōngfāng	east side
南爿 lâm-pêng	南方 nánfāng	south side
西爿 sai-pêng	西方 xīfāng	west side
北爿 pak-pêng	北方 běifāng	north side

我 是 佇 台灣 的 <u>南部</u> 大漢 矣。

Góa sī tī Tâi-ôan ê <u>lâm-pō</u> tōa-hàn--ah.

我 是 在 台灣 的 <u>南部</u> 長大 了。

Wǒ shì zài Táiwān de <u>nánbù</u> zhǎngdà le.

I grew up in the <u>southern part</u> of Taiwan.

In Taiwan, speakers sometimes use **頂港 téng-káng** 'northern port' or **下港 ē-káng** 'southern port' to refer to the northern and southern parts of the island. In Mandarin, only the terms **北部 běibù** 'northern part' and **南部 nánbù** 'southern part' are used to refer to these regions in Taiwan.

TAIWANESE	MANDARIN	MEANING
頂港 téng-káng	北部 běibù	northern part of Taiwan
下港 ē-káng	南部 nánbù	southern part of Taiwan

16.3 Placement of location expressions

While the general placement of location expressions is between the subject and verb of a sentence, there are also circumstances in which the location expression can appear before the subject or even after the verb.

16.3.1 Placement between the subject and verb

16.3.1.1 Single prepositional phrase

If the location expression is the only prepositional phrase, the typical placement is between the subject and the verb.

subject + location expression + verb

In this position, the location specifies the background setting for where the main verb occurs or happens.

同事 佇 公園 食 中晝頓。

Tông-sū tī kong-hn̂g chiȧh tiong-tàu-tǹg.

同事 在 公園 吃 午餐。

Tóngshì zài gōngyuán chī wǔcān.

The coworkers ate their lunches in the park.

姐妹 佇 塗跤 包 禮物。

Chí-mōe tī thô͘-kha pau lé-bu̇t.

姐妹 在 地上 包 禮物。

Jiěmèi zài dìshàng bāo lǐwù.

The sisters wrapped the gifts on the floor.

16.3.1.2 Location expressions with other prepositional phrases

Location expressions are just one type of prepositional phrase. Non-location prepositional phrases (with my friend, using a pencil, for my mother, etc.), which can explain other types of relationships between a noun and the main verb, also appear between the subject and verb of a sentence *(see 15 Prepositions)*. If both types of prepositional phrases co-occur within a sentence, the location expression is placed after the non-location prepositional phrase *(see 14.3.3 Prepositional phrases and adverbs)*.

subject + non-location prepositional phrase + location expression + verb

洪 先生 參 客戶 佇 高級 的 餐廳 咧 食 中晝頓。

Âng--sian-siⁿ chham kheh-hō͘ tī ko-kip ê chhan-thiaⁿ teh chiȧh tiong-tàu-tǹg.

洪 先生 跟 客戶 在 高級 的 餐廳 在 吃 午餐。

Hóng xiānshēng gēn kèhù zài gāojí de cāntīng zài chī wǔcān.

Mr. Ang is having lunch with his clients in a fancy restaurant.

阮 阿兄 為 阮 的 狗仔 佇 後花園 起厝。

Gún a-hiaⁿ ūi gún ê káu-á tī āu-hoe-hn̂g khí-chhù.

我 哥哥 為 我們 的 狗 在 後院 蓋 房子。

Wǒ gēgē wèi wǒmen de gǒu zài hòuyuàn gài fángzi.

My older brother is building a house in the backyard for our dog.

16.3.2 Placement before the subject

A location expression can occur before the subject if additional emphasis is placed on the location.

location expression + subject + verb

佇厝仔頂恁後生咧行！
Tī chhù-á-téng lín hāu-seⁿ teh kiâⁿ!
在屋頂你的兒子在走！
Zài wūdǐng nǐ de érzi zài zǒu!
Your son is walking <u>on the roof</u>!

佇機場恁會當予退稅。
Tī ki-tiûⁿ lín ē-tàng hō͘ thè-sòe.
在機場你們能退稅。
Zài jīchǎng nǐmen néng tuìshuì.
You can get a tax refund <u>at the airport</u>.

If the sentence is used to describe the existence of something with the verb **有 ū**, then the preposition **佇 tī** is generally omitted unless additional emphasis is desired.

(佇) + *location expression* + 有

(tī) + *location expression* + ū

佇桌仔頂有真濟蚼蟻！
Tī toh-á-téng ū chin chē káu-hiā!
在桌子上有很多螞蟻！
Zài zhuōzi shàng yǒu hěn duō mǎyǐ!
<u>On the table</u> <u>there are</u> lots of ants!

墓仔埔 有 鬼。
Bōng-á-po͘ ū kúi.
墓地 有 鬼。
Mùdì yǒu guǐ.
There are ghosts in the cemetery.

16.3.3 Placement after the verb

Location expressions generally appear before the verb. However, there are some verbs that allow for location expressions to occur after the verb. Most of these verbs indicate where the subject or object ends up as a result of the action of the verb. Typically, this involves changes in positioning, arranging, appearance, or posture.

This text loosely categorizes this group of verbs into four types: displacement, placement, appearance, and posture. Bear in mind that this categorization is not exhaustive, and that there may be some verbs that accept post-verb location expressions yet still do not fit neatly within these categories.

Additionally, some of these verbs accept placement of the location expression both *before* and *after* the verb.

In some contexts, the meaning can change depending on placement.

BEFORE THE VERB

恁 共 罐仔 佇 路邊 擲。
In kā kòan-á tī lō͘-piⁿ tàn.
他們 把 罐子 在 路邊 丟。
Tāmen bǎ guànzi zài lù biān diū.
They threw the can while on the road (*they are directly on the road itself, possibly walking on it*).

AFTER THE VERB

恁 共 罐仔 擲 佇 路邊。
In kā kòan-á tàn tī lō͘-piⁿ.
他們 把 罐子 丟 在 路邊。
Tāmen bǎ guànzi diū zài lù biān.
They threw the can onto the road (*they are not directly on the road, perhaps in a vehicle*).

While other contexts, the meaning remains the same regardless of placement.

BEFORE THE VERB

阮 老師 佇 車頭 後壁 蹛。

Gún láu-su tī chhia-thâu āu-piah tòa.

我 的 老師 在 車站 後面 住。

Wǒ de lǎoshī zài chēzhàn hòumiàn zhù.

My teacher lives <u>behind the train station</u>.

AFTER THE VERB

阮 老師 蹛 佇 車頭 後壁。

Gún láu-su tòa tī chhia-thâu āu-piah.

我 的 老師 住 在 車站 後面。

Wǒ de lǎoshī zhù zài chēzhàn hòumiàn.

My teacher lives <u>behind the train station</u>.

16.3.3.1 Displacement verbs

Verbs of displacement include actions that result in a local change in position. If the location expression is placed before the verb, there can be a difference in meaning.

BEFORE THE VERB

伊 佇 露台 落著 伊 的 鎖匙。

I tī lō-tâi lak-tio̍h i ê só-sî.

他 在 陽台 掉落 他 的 鑰匙。

Tā zài yángtái diàoluò tā de yàoshi.

He dropped his keys <u>on the balcony</u> (*he was standing on the balcony*).

AFTER THE VERB

伊 的 鎖匙 落著 佇 露台。

I ê só-sî lak-tio̍h tī lō-tâi.

他 的 鑰匙 掉落 在 陽台。

Tā de yàoshi diàoluò zài yángtái.

His keys dropped <u>onto the balcony</u> (*he was standing above the balcony, perhaps a higher floor*).

Below is a table of some common displacement verbs.

TAIWANESE	MANDARIN	MEANING
倒 tò	倒 dào	to pour out
落 lak	掉落 diàoluò	to drop
偃倒 ián-tó	推倒 tuīdǎo	to push over; knock over
跋倒 poa̍h-tó	跌倒 diédǎo	to stumble; to fall
摔倒 siak-tó	摔倒 shuāidǎo	to slip and fall
掔 khian	丟 diū	to throw
擲 tàn	丟 diū	to toss casually

阿媽 佇 塗跤 跋倒。
A-má tī thô͘-kha poa̍h-tó.
奶奶 在 地上 跌倒。
Nǎinǎi zài dìshàng diédǎo.
Grandma fell <u>on the floor</u>.

共 牛奶 倒 踮 碗仔內。
Kā gû-leng tò tàm óaⁿ-á-lāi.
把 牛奶 倒 在 碗 裡。
Bǎ niúnǎi dào zài wǎn lǐ.
Take the milk and pour it <u>into the bowl</u>.

Verbs that involve movement to a new destination (such as 'run' or 'swim') cannot use the preposition **佇 tī** to express this destination. Instead, the prepositions **到 kàu** 'until, to' is used to form a directional expression *(see 16.4 Directional expression)*.

伊 走 到 郵局。
I cháu kàu iû-kio̍k.
她 跑 到 郵局。
Tā pǎo dào yóujú.
She ran <u>to the post office</u>.

16.3.3.2 Placement verbs

Placement verbs are concerned with the putting, arranging, creating, and wearing of physical objects or images. The location expression may be placed before or after the verb without any change in meaning.

BEFORE THE VERB

伊 佇 椅仔腳 囥 淺拖仔。
I tī í-á-kha khǹg chhián-thoa-á.
她 在 椅子 下 放 拖鞋。
Tā zài yǐzi xià fàng tuōxié.
She put the sandals under the chair.

AFTER THE VERB

伊 囥 淺拖仔 佇 椅仔腳。
I khǹg chhián-thoa-á tī í-á-kha.
她 放 拖鞋 在 椅子 下。
Tā fàng tuōxié zài yǐzi xià.
She put the sandals under the chair.

Below is a table of some common placement verbs.

TAIWANESE	MANDARIN	MEANING
掛 kòa	掛 guà	to hang up
囥 khǹg	放 fàng	to put, to place
下 hē	放 fàng	to put, to place
寫 siá	寫 xiě	to write down
畫 ōe	畫 huà	to draw on
排 pâi	排 pái	to line up
穿 chhēng	穿 chuān	to put on (*below the neck*)
戴 tì	戴 dài	to put on (*above the neck*)

請 共 恁 澹 的 洗浴巾 囥 佇 籠仔。
Chhiáⁿ kā lín tâm ê sé-e̍k-kin khǹg tī láng-á.
請 把 你們 的 濕 浴巾 放 在 籠子。
Qǐng bǎ nǐmen de shī yùjīn fàng zài lóngzi.
Please put your wet towels in the basket.

希望，囡仔 共 怹 寫 踮 細張 的 紙頂。
Hi-bāng, gín-á kā in siá tàm sè tiuⁿ ê chóa-téng.
希望，小孩子 寫 在 小張 的 紙 上。
Xīwàng, xiǎo háizi xiě zài xiǎo zhāng de zhǐ shàng.
The children wrote their wishes on small pieces of paper.

16.3.3.3 Appearance verbs

Appearance verbs include actions that describe the appearance or disappearance of the subject. The location expression may be placed before or after the verb without any change in meaning.

BEFORE THE VERB

海龜 佇 動物園 死 矣。

Hái-ku tī tōng-bu̍t-hn̂g sí--ah.

海龜 在 動物園 死 了。

Hǎiguī zài dòngwùyuán sǐ le.

The sea turtles died in the zoo.

AFTER THE VERB

海龜 死 佇 動物園 矣。

Hái-ku sí tī tōng-bu̍t-hn̂g--ah.

海龜 死 在 動物園 了。

Hǎiguī sǐ zài dòngwùyuán le.

The sea turtles died in the zoo.

Below is a table of some common appearance verbs.

TAIWANESE	MANDARIN	MEANING
消失 siau-sit	消失 xiāoshī	to disappear
無去 bô--khì	不見 bù jiàn	to be missing, to disappear
死 sí	死 sǐ	to die
出世 chhut-sì	出生 chūshēng	to be born
大漢 tōa-hàn	長大 zhǎngdà	to grow up
發生 hoat-seng	發生 fāshēng	to occur, to happen

阮 囡仔 敢若 消失 佇 怹 迌迌 的 所在。

Gún gín-á kán-ná siau-sit tī in chhit-thô ê só͘-chāi.

我 孩子 好像 消失 在 他們 玩 的 地方。

Wǒ háizi hǎoxiàng xiāoshī zài tāmen wán de dìfāng.

My children always seem to disappear in play areas.

我 佇 澳洲 大漢。

Góa tī Ò-chiu tōa-hàn.

我 在 澳洲 長大。

Wǒ zài Àozhōu zhǎngdà.

I grew up in Australia.

16.3.3.4 Posture verbs

Posture verbs include actions that describe changes in pose or stance of the subject. The location expression may be placed before or after the verb without any change in meaning. However, when the location expression is placed before the verb, the verb often takes on the static continuative aspect marker 咧 --leh *(see 8.2.2.2 Describing a continued posture)*. When the location expression occurs after the verb, there are two choices: 1) the static continuative aspect marker 咧 -leh is omitted, or 2) the static continuative aspect marker 咧 -leh remains, but the preposition 佇 tī is omitted.

BEFORE THE VERB

location expression + verb + 咧

location expression + verb + --leh

彼 个 老阿伯 佇 路邊 跍 咧。

Hit ê láu-á-peh tī lō͘-piⁿ khû--leh.

那個 老 伯伯 在 路邊 蹲著。

Nàge lǎo bóbo zài lùbiān dūnzhe.

The old man is squatting by the side of the road.

AFTER THE VERB

METHOD 1

verb + 佇 + *noun or noun phrase*

verb + tī + *noun or noun phrase*

彼 个 老阿伯 跍 佇 路邊。

Hit ê láu-á-peh khû tī lō͘-piⁿ.

那個 老 伯伯 蹲 在 路邊。

Nàge lǎo bóbo dūn zài lùbiān.

The old man is squatting by the side of the road.

METHOD 2

verb + 咧 + *noun or noun phrase*

verb + --leh + *noun or noun phrase*

彼 个 老阿伯 跍咧 路邊。

Hit ê láu-á-peh khû--leh lō͘-piⁿ.

那個 老 伯伯 蹲 在 路邊。

Nàge lǎo bóbo dūn zài lùbiān.

The old man is squatting by the side of the road.

Below is a table of some common posture verbs.

TAIWANESE	MANDARIN	MEANING
坐 chē	坐 zuò	to sit
徛 khiā	站 zhàn	to stand
覆 phak	趴 pā	to lie face down
跍 khû	蹲 dūn	to squat
靠 khò	靠 kào	to lean on

伊 攏 覆咧 外口 曝日。

In lóng phak--leh gōa-kháu pha̍k-ji̍t.

她們 都 趴 在 外面 曬 太陽。

Tāmen dōu pā zài wàimiàn shài tàiyáng.

They are all lying outside sunbathing.

火車動的時陣莫靠踮門。

Hóe-chhia tāng ê sî-chūn mài khò tàm mn̂g.

火車動的時候不要靠門。

Huǒchē dòng de shíhòu bù yào kào mén.

Don't lean on the door when the train is moving.

16.4 Directional expressions

Directional expressions are prepositional phrases that introduce a destination.

Generally they begin with prepositions like 到 **kàu** 'until, to' and are followed by a location. In some cases, a speaker perspective complement 去 **khì** 'away from the speaker' or 來 **lâi** 'towards the speaker' is added after the location *(see 11.3.1 Directional complements indicating speaker perspective)*.

preposition + location + (speaker perspective complement 去 / 來)

preposition + location + (speaker perspective complement khì / lâi)

These directional expressions are only used with verbs that involve movement to a new destination (such as 'run' or 'swim'). Such *destination verbs* cannot use the preposition 佇 **tī** to express this destination as a location expression.

16.4.1 Destination verbs

Destination verbs are verbs involving movement that imply a destination not in the immediate vicinity of the subject *(see 16.3.3.1 Displacement verbs)*. The target location of these destination verbs can be specified through a directional expression. These directional expressions may only occur after the verb.

destination verb + directional expression

周先生行到郵局。

Chiu--sian-siⁿ kiâⁿ kàu iû-kiỏk.

周先生走到郵局。

Zhōu xiānshēng zǒu dào yóujú.

Mr. Chiu walked to the post office.

Below is a table of some common destination verbs.

TAIWANESE	MANDARIN	MEANING
行 kiâⁿ	走 zǒu	to walk
走 cháu	跑 pǎo	to run
騎 khiâ	騎 qí	to ride
飛 poe	飛 fēi	to fly
駛 sái	開 kāi	to drive
泅 siû	游泳 yóuyǒng	to swim
轉 tńg	回 huí	to return

我 下早 走 甲 廟寺 彼爿。
Góa e-chái cháu kah biō-sī hit-pêng.
我 早上 跑 到 寺廟 那邊。
Wǒ zǎoshang pǎo dào sìmiào nà biān.
This morning I ran over to the temple.

怹 騎 車 到 阮 兜。
In khiâ chhia kàu gún tau.
他們 騎 車 到 我們 家。
Tāmen qí chē dào wǒmen jiā.
They rode their bicycles to our house.

Note that Mandarin allows for directional expressions before the verb.

16.4.2 Speaker perspective with directional expressions

Directional expressions may also include the speaker perspective directional complements 來 -lâi 'come' and 去 -khì 'go', which refer to the direction of movement with reference to the speaker. These can co-occur with destination verbs and are optionally added after the location.

> *verb* + 到 + *location* + (*speaker perspective complement* 去 / 來)
> *verb* + kàu + *location* + (*speaker perspective complement* khì / lâi)

伊 騎 車 到 便利 商店 去。

I khiâ chhia kàu piān-lī siong-tiàm--khì.

他 騎 車 到 便利 商店 去。

Tā qí chē dào biànlì shāngdiàn qù.

He rode his scooter over to the convenience store.

伊 的 同事 會 飛 到 台北 來。

I ê tông-sū ē poe kàu Tâi-pak--lâi.

她 的 同事 會 飛 到 台北 來。

Tā de tóngshì huì fēi dào Táiběi lái.

Her colleague will fly to Taipei (*speaker is in Taipei*).

Note that destination verbs can still append speaker perspective complements without a directional expression *(see 11.3.1 Directional complements indicating speaker perspective)*. In this case, the target location is not introduced by a preposition.

verb + (*speaker perspective complement* 去 / 來) + *location*

verb + (*speaker perspective complement* khì / lâi) + *location*

林 先生 駛去 海邊。

Lîm--sian-si^n sái-khì hái-pi^n.

林 先生 開去 海邊。

Lín xiānshēng kāiqù hǎibiān.

Mr. Lim drove to the beach.

伊 轉去 韓國。

I tńg-khì Hân-kok.

他 回去 韓國。

Tā huíqù Hánguó.

He returned to Korea.

去 khì 'go' and **來 lâi** 'come' can also function as destination verbs themselves occurring with directional expressions. Unlike other destination verbs, the directional expression can be placed before or after **去 khì** 'go' or **來 lâi** 'come'.

BEFORE THE VERB

directional expression + 去 / 來

directional expression + khì / lâi

伊 的 學生 到 病院 去。
I ê ha̍k-seng kàu pēⁿ-īⁿ khì.
他 的 學生 到 醫院 去。
Tā de xuéshēng dào yīyuàn qù.
His student went to the hospital.

阮 所有 的 親成 攏 到 加州 來。
Gún só͘-ū ê chhin-chiâⁿ lóng kàu Ka-chiu lâi.
我們 所有 的 親戚 都 到 加州 來。
Wǒmen suǒyǒu de qīnqī dōu dào Jiāzhōu lái.
All of our relatives came to California.

AFTER THE VERB

去 / 來 + *directional expression*

khì / lâi + *directional expression*

伊 的 學生 去 到 病院。
I ê ha̍k-seng khì kàu pēⁿ-īⁿ.
他 的 學生 去 到 醫院。
Tā de xuéshēng qù dào yīyuàn.
His student went to the hospital.

阮 所有 的 親成 攏 來 到 加州。
Gún só͘-ū ê chhin-chiâⁿ lóng lâi kàu Ka-chiu.
我們 所有 的 親戚 都 來 到 加州。
Wǒmen suǒyǒu de qīnqī dōu lái dào Jiāzhōu.
All of our relatives came to California.

17 Direct objects

Direct objects are nouns or noun phrases that receive the action of a verb.

> She kicks the chair.

In the sentence above, 'the chair' is a direct object that receives the action from 'kicks'. In Taiwanese, the ordering for simple sentences is similar to English:

> *subject + verb + object*

> 伊 踢 <u>椅仔</u>。
> I that <u>í-á.</u>
> 她 踢 <u>椅子</u>。
> Tā tī <u>yǐzi</u>.
> She kicks <u>the chair</u>.

Typically, objects come after the main verb. However, in some cases due to emphasis or grammatical requirements, the object is placed before the verb or verb phrase. For example, in Taiwanese if the verb adds a complement (phase, resultative, directional, etc.) to form a more complex verb compound, there are some cases when the direct object must be moved to the front or placed in a repeated verb sentence pattern, also known as *verb copying (see 11 Verb complements)*.

There are four ways to move a direct object before the verb.

METHOD 1
PRE-POSE DIRECT OBJECT BEFORE THE VERB

伊 椅仔 踢倒去 矣。

I í-á that-tó--khì--ah.

她 椅子 踢倒 了。

Tā yǐzi tīdǎo le.

She kicked over the chair.

METHOD 2
TOPICALIZE THE OBJECT

椅仔，伊 踢倒去 矣。

Í-á, i that-tó--khì--ah.

椅子，她 踢倒 了。

Yǐzi, tā tīdǎo le.

She kicked over the chair.

METHOD 3
COPYING OF THE VERB PHRASE

伊 踢 椅仔 踢倒去 矣。

I that í-á that-tó--khì--ah.

她 踢 椅子 踢倒 了。

Tā tī yǐzi tīdǎo le.

She kicked over the chair.

METHOD 4
USE THE 共 KĀ CONSTRUCTION

伊 共 椅仔 踢倒去 矣。

I kā í-á that-tó--khì--ah.

她 把 椅子 踢倒 了。

Tā bǎ yǐzi tīdǎo le.

She kicked over the chair.

Mandarin differs with Taiwanese in that direct objects are permitted to follow verb compounds in more circumstances. As a result, Taiwanese tends to more frequently place objects before the verb than Mandarin. The above example can also be written in Mandarin with the direct object after the verb.

MANDARIN

她 踢倒 了 椅子。

Tā tīdǎo le yǐzi.

She kicked over the chair.

17.1 Pre-posed objects

A *pre-posed object* is a direct object placed before the verb but after the subject without the use of a preposition. Generally, pronouns are restricted from this repositioning and can only be moved before the verb with the **共 kā** construction *(see 17.4 共 kā construction)*.

subject + direct object + verb

阿公 狗仔 會 拍。

A-kong káu-á ē phah.

爺爺 狗 會 打。

Yěyě gǒu huì dǎ.

Grandpa will hit dogs.

彼 个 查埔 团仔 雞卵糕 攏 食了去 矣。

Hit ê cha-poˑ gín-á ke-nñg-ko lóng chiah-liáu--khì--ah.

那個 男孩子 蛋糕 都 吃完 了。

Nàge nánháizi dàngāo dōu chīwán le.

That boy ate the entire cake.

17.2 Topicalized objects

When direct objects are placed at the beginning of the sentence or immediately before the subject in the topic position, the direct objects are referred to as having been *topicalized*.

direct object + subject + verb

狗仔，阿公 會 拍。
Káu-á, a-kong ē phah.
狗，爺爺 會 打。
Gǒu, yěyě huì dǎ.
As for dogs, Grandpa will hit them.

雞卵糕，彼 个 查埔 囝仔 攏 食了去 矣。
Ke-nñg-ko, hit ê cha-poˑ gín-á lóng chiàh-liáu--khì--ah.
蛋糕，那個 男孩子 都 吃完 了。
Dàngāo, nàge nánháizi dōu chīwán le.
As for the cake, that boy ate all of it.

17.3 Verb copying

Direct objects can also be moved to a position before the verb by being placed in a verb copying sentence pattern. This method essentially repeats the verb with the first instance followed by the direct object, and the second instance followed by the verb complements.

subject + verb + direct object + verb + verb complements

阿公 會 拍 狗仔 拍 予 怹 走去。
A-kong ē phah káu-á phah hōˑ in cháu--khì.
爺爺 會 打 狗 打 到 它們 跑掉。
Yěyě huì dǎ gǒu dǎ dào tāmen pǎodiào.
Grandpa will hit dogs until they run away.

彼 个 查埔 囝仔 食 雞卵糕 攏 食了去 矣。
Hit ê cha-poˑ gín-á chiàh ke-nñg-ko lóng chiàh-liáu--khì--ah.
那個 男孩子 吃 蛋糕 都 吃完 了。
Nàge nánháizi chī dàngāo dōu chīwán le.
That boy ate the entire cake.

17.4 共 kā construction

While the preposition 共 **kā** has several uses, one particular usage, called the 共 *kā construction*, involves moving a direct object from the typical position after the verb to a position before the verb. The reason for moving a direct object to a position before the verb can arise from either a grammatical constraint on the number of elements after a verb or from a desire to emphasize the action that is performed on the object.

17.4.1 Setting up the 共 kā construction

By placing the preposition 共 **kā** in front of the direct object, the prepositional phrase can be moved before the main verb.

> *subject* + 共 + *direct object* + *verb*
> *subject* + kā + *direct object* + *verb*

阿公 會 共 狗仔 拍。
A-kong ē kā káu-á phah.
爺爺 會 把 狗 打。
Yéyé huì bǎ gǒu dǎ.
Grandpa will hit dogs.

彼 个 查埔 囡仔 共 雞卵糕 攏 食了去 矣。
Hit ê cha-po͘-gín-á kā ke-nn̄g-ko lóng chiah-liáu--khì--ah.
那個 男孩子 把 蛋糕 都 吃完 了。
Nàge nánháizi bǎ dàngāo dōu chīwán le.
That little boy ate the entire cake.

因為 伊 袂記得 掛 目鏡，所以 伊 就 共 我 撞著。
In-ūi i bē-kì-tit kòa ba̍k-kiàⁿ, só-í i tō kā góa lòng--tio̍h.
因為 他 忘記 戴 眼鏡，所以 他 就 撞到 我。
Yīnwèi tā wàngjì dài yǎnjìng, suǒyǐ tā jiù zhuàngdǎo wǒ.
Because he forgot to wear his glasses, he crashed into me.

Note that speakers of Taiwan Mandarin use 把 bǎ less frequently than do speakers in other Mandarin-speaking areas. The example above can also be written in Standard Mandarin as follows:

STANDARD MANDARIN

因為 他 忘記 戴 眼鏡，所以 他 就 把 我 撞到。

Yīnwèi tā wàngjì dài yǎnjìng, suǒyǐ tā jiù <u>bǎ wǒ</u> zhuàngdǎo.

Because he forgot to wear his glasses, he crashed into <u>me</u>.

17.4.2 Comparisons to the Mandarin 把 bǎ construction

The 共 kā construction is similar to the Mandarin 把 bǎ construction but is less restricted in its usage. While the Mandarin 把 bǎ and Taiwanese 共 kā function similarly in bringing forward a direct object to a position before the main verb, the Mandarin 把 bǎ is more restricted in the following ways:

The noun phrase that follows the Mandarin 把 bǎ generally must be *definite* (known to the listener) such as 'the car' or 'this girl' or *generic* (a class or category of items) such as 'cars' or 'girls' *(see 4.9 Definite and indefinite nouns)*.

An *indefinite* (not known to the listener) object such as 'a car' or 'three girls' is not acceptable in the Mandarin 把 bǎ construction. The Taiwanese 共 kā does not have this restriction.

老師 共 兩 的 學生 罵。

Lāu-su <u>kā nn̄g ê ha̍k-seng</u> mē.

老師 罵 兩 個 學生。

Lǎoshī mà <u>liǎng ge xuéshēng</u>.

The teacher scolded <u>two students</u>.

In the above example, a direct Mandarin translation of the Taiwanese sentence would be unacceptable.

UNACCEPTABLE MANDARIN USAGE

老師 把 兩個 學生 罵。

Lǎoshī <u>bǎ liǎng ge xuéshēng</u> mà.

The teacher scolded <u>two students</u>.

Additionally, the main verb within Mandarin 把 bǎ sentences must show completion. In other words, the 把 bǎ construction puts emphasis on the how the object was disposed or handled. In general, a perfective aspect marker, a verb complement, or duration/frequency quantity must be used to mark completion of the verb in Mandarin 把 bǎ constructions.

On the other hand, the Taiwanese 共 kā construction does not have this restriction.

伊 <u>共 門</u> 一直 挵。

I <u>kā mn̂g</u> it-tit lòng.

他 一直 <u>敲 門</u>。

Tā yīzhí <u>qiāo mén</u>.

He kept knocking on <u>the door</u>.

In the above example, a direct Mandarin translation of the Taiwanese sentence is not acceptable. The verb is in the continuative aspect and so is not a completed action. As a result, the Mandarin 把 bǎ construction is not permitted.

UNACCEPTABLE MANDARIN USAGE

他 <u>把 門</u> 一直 敲。

Tā <u>bǎ mén</u> yīzhí qiāo.

He kept knocking on <u>the door</u>.

17.4.3 Traditional usage of 共 kā and 將 chiong

Among more traditional speakers of Taiwanese, nouns and noun phrases after the preposition 共 kā are restricted to pronouns. As a result, non-pronoun direct objects are topicalized and then later echoed by a *trace pronoun* representing the topicalized direct object. Additionally, note that for some speakers, the preposition and trace pronoun combination 共伊 kā i is contracted to 共 kā.

direct object + *subject* + 共 + *trace pronoun* + *verb*

direct object + *subject* + kā + *trace pronoun* + *verb*

<u>我 的 衫褲</u>, 阮 阿母 攏 共 <u>(恁)</u> 洗 清氣 矣。

<u>Góa ê saⁿ-khò͘</u>, gún a-bú lóng kā <u>(in)</u> sé chheng-khì--ah.

<u>我 的 衣服</u>, 我 媽媽 都 洗 乾淨 了。

<u>Wǒ de yīfú</u>, wǒ māmā dōu xǐ gānjìng le.

<u>As for my clothes</u>, my mother has washed <u>them</u> all.

這隻狗，李小姐會 <u>共 (伊)</u> 飼 予 健康。
Chit chiah káu, Lí sió-chiá ē <u>kā (i)</u> chhī hōˈkiān-khong.

這隻狗，李小姐會養到健康。
<u>Zhè zhī gòu</u>, Lǐ xiǎojiě huì yǎng dào jiànkāng.

<u>As for this dog</u>, Ms. Li will raise <u>it</u> until it is healthy.

貓仔，伊 <u>共 (伊)</u> 趕出去。
Niau-á, i <u>kā (i)</u> kóaⁿ--chhut-khì.

貓，他 <u>把 它</u> 趕出去。
<u>Māo</u>, tā <u>bǎ tā</u> gǎnchūqù.

He shooed <u>the cat</u> away.

Because of the strong influence of the Mandarin **把 bǎ** construction, more recent generations of Taiwanese speakers do not restrict the nouns and noun phrases that follow **共 kā** to only pronouns. Rather, they allow all types of nouns to follow.

將 chiong is a preposition from the literary register of Taiwanese with a similar grammatical function to **共 kā**. While **將 chiong** is not restricted to pronouns, the usage tends to focus on inanimate objects. A distinction between **共 kā** for people and pronouns and **將 chiong** for objects was traditionally made. However, many speakers no longer strictly uphold this distinction.

王子 <u>將 花</u> 囥 佇 桌仔。
Ông-chú <u>chiong hoe</u> khǹg tī toh-á.

王子 <u>將 花</u> 放 在 桌子。
Wángzǐ <u>jiāng huā</u> fàng zài zhuōzi.

The prince put <u>the flowers</u> on the table.

The Mandarin cognate **將 jiāng** is generally reserved for more formal contexts.

17.4.4 Placement with other grammatical elements

With regards to positioning within a sentence, the **共 kā** construction has some restrictions when co-occurring with other grammatical elements. Modal verbs and negation must occur before the **共 kā** construction. However, if the **共 kā** construction is not used, a preposed object can appear before negation and modal verbs.

ORDER 1 WITH 共 KĀ CONSTRUCTION

negation + modal verbs + 共 kā *construction + verb*

伊 袂當 共 行李 關咧。
I bē-tàng kā hêng-lí koaiⁿ--leh.
她 不能 把 行李 關上。
Tā bùnéng bǎ xínglǐ guānshàng.
She cannot close her suitcase.

阮 小弟 袂曉 共 紅嬰仔 抱。
Gún sió-tī bē-hiáu kā âng-eⁿ-á phō.
我 弟弟 不 會 把 嬰兒 抱。
Wǒ dìdì bù huì bǎ yīng'ér bào.
My younger brother doesn't know how to hold a baby.

ORDER 2 WITH PRE-POSED OBJECT

pre-posed object + negation + modal verbs + verb

伊 行李 袂當 關咧。
I hêng-lí bē-tàng koaiⁿ--leh.
她 行李 不能 關著。
Tā xínglǐ bùnéng guānzhe.
She cannot close her suitcase.

阮 小弟 紅嬰仔 袂曉 抱。
Gún sió-tī âng-eⁿ-á bē-hiáu phō.
我 弟弟 不 會 抱 嬰兒。
Wǒ dìdì bù huì bào yīng'ér.
My younger brother doesn't know how to hold a baby.

Among adverbs and prepositions, the **共 kā** construction generally occurs before manner adverbs and location expressions but after non-location prepositional phrases and relative frequency / reference adverbs *(see 14.3 Adverbs with other grammatical elements)*.

*subject + reference + relative frequency + non-location expression + **共 kā construction** + manner + location expression + verb*

我 有當時仔 和 朋友 共 囡仔 <u>𤆬</u>去 遊樂園。
Góa ū-tang-sî-á hām pêng-iú <u>kā gín-á</u> chhōa-khì iû-lo̍k-hn̂g.
我 有 的 時候 和 朋友 <u>帶 孩子</u> 去 遊樂園。
Wǒ yǒu de shíhòu hé péngyǒu <u>dài háizi</u> qù yóulèyuán.
I occasionally go with my friend to take <u>the kids</u> to the amusement park.

伊 <u>共 篋仔</u> 直接 囥 踮 我 的 跤指頭仔。
I <u>kā kheh-á</u> tit-chiap khǹg tàm góa ê kha-chéng-thâu-á.
他 <u>把 盒子</u> 直接 放 在 我 的 腳指頭。
Tā <u>bǎ hézi</u> zhíjiē fàng zài wǒ de jiǎozhǐtou.
He put <u>the box</u> directly onto my toes.

17.4.5 共 kā construction in commands

With the emphasis on performing an action on an object, there is a natural tendency to use the **共 kā** construction in commands and requests *(see 21.9 Using the 共 kā construction in commands)*.

共 糞埽 提出去。
<u>Kā pùn-sò</u> the̍h--chhut-khì.
把 垃圾 拿出去。
<u>Bǎ lèsè</u> náchūqù.
Take out <u>the garbage</u>.

共 報紙 提 予 我。
<u>Kā pò-chóa</u> the̍h hō͘ góa.
把 報紙 拿 給 我。
<u>Bǎ bàozhǐ</u> ná gěi wǒ.
Hand me <u>the newspaper</u>.

共 門 關 咧!
<u>Kā mn̂g</u> koaiⁿ--leh!
把 門 關 了!
<u>Bǎ mén</u> guān le!
Shut <u>the door</u>!

18 Indirect objects

While direct objects receive the action from the verb, *indirect objects* can often be thought of as the 'goal' of the action. Typically, indirect objects are people, animals, or institutions (universities, hospitals, etc.).

    He throws the ball <u>to his brother</u>.

In the example above, the indirect object 'his brother' is the goal of the action 'throws'.

18.1 Using 予 hō͘ to mark indirect objects

While 予 hō͘ has several meanings in Taiwanese, one function is as a preposition to introduce indirect objects. These indirect object prepositional phrases occur after the main verb.

    verb + 予 + indirect object
    verb + hō͘ + indirect object

    伊 寫 <u>予 恁 阿爸</u>。
    I siá <u>hō͘ in a-pa</u>.
    他 寫 <u>給 他 爸爸</u>。
    Tā xiě <u>gěi tā bàba</u>.
    He wrote <u>to his dad</u>.

If both a direct object and an indirect object co-occur, then the ordering of the two objects depends on the context. The object that is the new piece of information to the listener is presented last.

    ORDER 1

    verb + indirect object + direct object (new to listener)

伊 寫 予 偲 老師 一 張 感謝 批。

I siá hō͘ in lāu-su chit tiuⁿ kám-siā phoe.

他 寫 給 他 的 老師 一 張 感謝 信。

Tā xiě gěi tā de lǎoshī yī zhāng gǎnxiè xìn.

He is writing a thank you letter to his teacher (*perhaps the listener knew he wanted to thank his teacher but didn't yet know how*).

ORDER 2

verb + direct object + indirect object (new to listener)

伊 寫 一 張 感謝 批 予 偲 老師。

I siá chit tiuⁿ kám-siā phoe hō͘ in lāu-su.

他 寫 一 張 感謝 信 給 他 的 老師。

Tā xiě yī zhāng gǎnxiè xìn gěi tā de lǎoshī.

He is writing a thank you letter to his teacher (*perhaps the listener could tell that he is writing a thank you letter but didn't know yet to whom*).

18.2 Dative verbs

Dative verbs are special verbs that can take both an indirect and direct object. These verbs inherently include the idea of transferring a direct object between parties (such as sending, giving, receiving, transporting, paying, returning, hitting, or throwing).

Some of these verbs require the preposition 予 **hō͘** to be placed before the indirect object, while other verbs including the 予 **hō͘** is optional. Still others are restricted from using 予 **hō͘** before the indirect object. Moreover, depending on these groupings, the ordering of indirect object and direct object may also be restricted.

18.2.1 Dative verbs that require 予 **hō͘**

For dative verbs that require the use of 予 **hō͘** before the indirect object, the ordering of the indirect object and direct object depends on which object is new information to the listener.

Indirect objects 395

ORDER 1

verb + 予 + ***indirect object*** + *direct object (new information)*

verb + **hō·**+ ***indirect object*** + *direct object (new information)*

伊 的 秘書 會 寄 予 我 文件。

I ê pì-su ē <u>kià</u> **hō·góa** bûn-kiāⁿ.

她 的 秘書 會 寄 給 我 文件。

Tā de mìshū huì <u>jì</u> **gěi wǒ** wénjiàn.

Her secretary will <u>send</u> **me** the documents (*perhaps the listener did not know what would be sent*).

ORDER 2

verb + *direct object* + 予 + ***indirect object (new information)***

verb + *direct object* + **hō·**+ ***indirect object (new information)***

伊 的 秘書 會 寄 文件 予 我。

I ê pì-su ē <u>kià</u> bûn-kiāⁿ **hō·góa**.

她 的 秘書 會 寄 文件 給 我。

Tā de mìshū huì <u>jì</u> wénjiàn **gěi wǒ**.

Her secretary will <u>send</u> the documents **to me** (*perhaps the listener did not know to whom the documents would be sent*).

Below is a table of some common dative verbs that require 予 **hō·**:

TAIWANESE	MANDARIN	MEANING
TRANSPORT		
提 theh	拿 ná	to take (*to someone*)
紮 chah	攜帶 xiédài	to carry (*to someone*)
帶 tòa	帶 dài	to carry (*to someone*)
交 kau	交 jiāo	to hand over (*to someone*)
搬 poaⁿ	搬 bān	to move (*to someone*)
擲 tàn	丟 diū	to throw (*to someone*)
寄 kià	寄 jì	to mail (*to someone*)

TAIWANESE	MANDARIN	MEANING
COMMUNICATION		
寫 siá	寫 xiě	to write (*to someone*)
解說 kái-soeh	解釋 jiěshì	to explain (*to someone*)
敲 khà	打 dǎ	to call (by telephone) (*to someone*)
TRANSACTION		
買 bé	買 mǎi	to buy (*for someone*)
PHYSICAL		
掔 khian	扔 rēng	to throw (*to someone*)
踢 that	踢 tī	to kick (*to someone*)
留 lâu	留 liú	to save, to keep behind (*for someone*)

伊 䖝 予 我 一 枝 雨傘。
I <u>chah</u> **hō góa** chit ki hō-sòaⁿ.
他 攜帶 給 我 一 枝 雨傘。
Tā <u>xiédài</u> **gěi wǒ** yī zhī yǔsǎn.
He <u>brought</u> an umbrella **to me**.

導遊 解說 予 阮 廟寺 的 歷史。
Tō-iû <u>kái-soeh</u> **hō͘ gún** biō-sī ê le̍k-sú.
導遊 解釋 給 我們 寺廟 的 歷史。
Dǎoyóu <u>jiěshì</u> **gěi wǒmen** sìmiào de lìshǐ.
The tour guide <u>explained</u> **to us** the history of the temple.

恁 小妹 踢 球 予 我。
In sió-mōe <u>that</u> kiû **hō͘ góa**.
她 妹妹 踢 球 給 我。
Tā mèimei <u>tī</u> qiú **gěi wǒ**.
His younger sister <u>kicked</u> the ball **to me**.

18.2.2 Dative verbs that optionally use 予 hō͘

For dative verbs that optionally use 予 hō͘ before the indirect object, the ordering of the indirect object and direct object also depends on which object is considered new information to the listener. However, if the indirect object comes after the direct object (i.e. the indirect object does not immediately follow the verb), then 予 **hō**˙ must be used.

ORDER 1

verb + (**予**) + ***indirect object*** + *direct object (new information)*

verb + (**hō**˙) + ***indirect object*** + *direct object (new information)*

阮 公司 欲 <u>送</u> **恁** 這 个 細 紀念品。

Gún kong-si beh <u>sàng</u> **lín** chit ê sè kì-liām-phín.

我們 的 公司 要 <u>送</u> **你們** 這個 小 紀念品。

Wǒmen de gōngsī yào <u>sòng</u> **nǐmen** zhège xiǎo jìniànpǐn.

Our company would like <u>to give</u> **you** a small souvenir (*perhaps the listeners did not know what was being offered to them*).

ORDER 2

verb + *direct object* + **予** + ***indirect object (new information)***

verb + *direct object* + **hō**˙ + ***indirect object (new information)***

阮 公司 欲 <u>送</u> 這 个 細 紀念品 **予 恁**。

Gún kong-si beh <u>sàng</u> chit ê sè kì-liām-phín **hō**˙ **lín**.

我們 的 公司 要 送 這個 小 紀念品 **給 你們**。

Wǒmen de gōngsī yào <u>sòng</u> zhège xiǎo jìniànpǐn **gěi nǐmen**.

Our company would like <u>to give</u> a small souvenir **to you** (*perhaps the listeners did not know for whom the souvenirs were intended*).

Additionally, some verbs that optionally use 予 **hō**˙ before the indirect object shift slightly in meaning depending on the inclusion or absence of 予 **hō**˙:

黃 先生 欲 <u>介紹</u> 恁 某 一 个 老 朋友。

Ñg--sian-siⁿ beh <u>kài-siāu</u> in bó˙ chit ê láu pêng-iú.

黃 先生 要 <u>介紹</u> 他 太太 一 個 老 朋友。

Huáng xiānshēng yào <u>jièshào</u> tā tàitai yī gè lǎo péngyǒu.

Mr. Ng wants <u>to introduce</u> an old friend of his wife (*to whom is unstated*).

黃 先生 欲 <u>介紹</u> **予** 您 某 一 个 老 朋友。
Ng--sian-siⁿ beh <u>kài-siāu</u> **hō͘ in bó͘** chit ê láu pêng-iú.
黃 先生 要 <u>介紹</u> 給 他 太太 一 個 老 朋友。
Huáng xiānshēng yào <u>jièshào</u> **gěi tā tàitài** yī gè lǎo péngyǒu.
Mr. Ng wants <u>to introduce</u> an old friend **to his wife**.

Below is a table of some common dative verbs that optionally use **予 hō͘**:

TAIWANESE	MANDARIN	MEANING
TRANSPORT		
送 sàng	送 sòng	to send (to someone), to give as a gift
COMMUNICATION		
教 kà	教 jiāo	to teach (to someone)
回覆 hôe-hok	回復 huífù	to respond, to reply (to someone)
答應 tah-èng	答應 dāyìng	to promise (to someone)
介紹 kài-siāu	介紹 jièshào	to give an introduction (to someone)
TRANSACTION		
賣 bē	賣 mài	to sell (to someone)
還 hêng	還 huán	to return (to someone), to give back (to someone)
賠 pôe	賠 péi	to compensate (to someone)

我 的 室友 袂 記得 還 鎖匙 **予 我**。
Góa ê sek-iú bē-kì-tit <u>hêng</u> só-sî **hō͘ góa**.
我 的 室友 忘記 還 鑰匙 **給 我**。
Wǒ de shìyǒu wàngjì <u>huán</u> yàoshi **gěi wǒ**.
My roommate forgot <u>to return</u> the keys **to me**.

恁 爸母 <u>教</u> **伊** 麻雀。
In pē-bú <u>kà</u> **i** môa-chhiok.
她 的 父母 <u>教</u> **她** 麻將。
Tā de fùmǔ <u>jiāo</u> **tā** májiàng.
Her parents <u>taught</u> **her** how to play mahjong.

伊 爸母 教 予 伊 𪜶 厝 的 招牌 醬。

In pē-bú kà **hō͘ i** in chhù ê chiau-pâi chiùⁿ.

她 的 父母 教 給 她 家庭 的 招牌 醬。

Tā de fùmǔ jiào gěi tā jiātíng de zhāopái jiàng.

Her parents taught **her** how to make the family's secret sauce.

In the examples above, **教 kà** and **教予 kà hō͘** differ slightly in meaning. While both mean 'to teach', **教予 kà hō͘** suggests passing down a tradition or secret to younger generations.

18.2.3 Dative verbs that cannot use 予 hō͘

For dative verbs that cannot use 予 hō͘ before the indirect object, the ordering of the indirect object and direct object is restricted. The indirect object must occur before the direct object.

*verb + **indirect object** + direct object*

你 明仔載 應該 收 我 兩 本 冊。

Lí bîn-á-chài eng-kai siu **góa** nn̄g pún chheh.

你 明天 應該 收 我 兩 本 書。

Nǐ míngtiān yīnggāi shōu wǒ liǎng běn shū.

Tomorrow you should receive two books **from me**.

Below is a table of some common dative verbs that cannot use 予 hō͘:

TAIWANESE	MANDARIN	MEANING
TRANSPORT		
予 hō͘	給 gěi	to give *(to someone)*
收 siu	收 shōu	to receive *(from someone)*
COMMUNICATION		
問 mn̄g	問 wèn	to ask
恭喜 kiong-hí	祝賀 zhùhè	to congratulate
TRANSACTION		
贏 iâⁿ	贏 yíng	to win *(from someone)*
搶 chhiúⁿ	搶 qiǎng	to rob *(from someone)*, to steal *(from someone)*

你 若 射著，會當 贏 我 五 百 箍。
Lí nā siā--tio̍h, ē-tàng iâⁿ **góa** gō˙pah kho˙.
如果 中的，你 能 贏 我 五 百 塊。
Rúguǒ zhòngdì, nǐ néng yíng **wǒ** wǔ bǎi kuài.
If you can hit the target, you can <u>win</u> 500 dollars **from me**.

伊 問 我 一寡 我 袂曉 的。
I mn̄g **góa** chi̍t-kóa góa bē-hiáu--ê.
他 問 我 一些 我 不 會 的。
Tā <u>wèn</u> **wǒ** yīxiē wǒ bù huì de.
He <u>asked</u> **me** a few questions I didn't know how to answer.

Note that some of these dative verbs can accept 予 hō˙ if the preposition is used to express 'on behalf of' someone else. This can offer a similar meaning to benefactive phrases *(see 18.3 Benefactives)*.

你 明仔載 敢 會當 收 予 我 兩 領 衫？
Lí bîn-á-chài kám ē-tàng <u>siu</u> **hō˙ góa** nn̄g niá saⁿ?
你 明天 能不能 收 給 我 兩 件 衣服？
Nǐ míngtiān néngbùnéng <u>shōu</u> **gěi wǒ** liǎng jiàn yīfú?
Can you <u>accept</u> two pieces of clothing **for me** tomorrow?

18.2.4 Dual-direction dative verbs

Two verbs 借 **chioh** 'to borrow / to lend' and 租 **cho˙** 'to rent to / to rent from' can be used to express movement of direct objects in both directions between parties. However, the distinction in direction must be made clear by the addition of the prepositions 予 **hō˙** 'to' or 共 **kā** to 'from'.

Without prepositions the meaning of these two verbs is ambiguous without proper context. The English word 'rent' is similarly ambiguous without context or prepositions to clarify.

伊 借 兩 百 箍。
I <u>chioh</u> nn̄g pah kho˙.
她 借 兩 百 塊。
Tā <u>jiè</u> liǎng bǎi kuài.
She <u>lent</u> two hundred dollars.
She <u>borrowed</u> two hundred dollars.

我這馬咧租房間。
Góa chit-má teh cho͘ pâng-keng.

我現在在租房間。
Wǒ xiànzài zài zū fángjiān.

I am renting a room right now (*renting to someone or renting from someone are both possible interpretations without context*).

With the addition of prepositions, the direction of transfer becomes much clearer.

To unambiguously express 'to lend' and 'to rent to' the preposition 予 hō͘ is placed before the indirect object (the recipient of the direct object). The ordering of the indirect object and direct object can still be switched according to whether the information is new to the listener.

ORDER 1

借 + 予 + *indirect object* + direct object (new information)

chioh + **hō͘** + *indirect object* + direct object (new information)

'to lend/rent **to** *indirect object* direct object'

伊昨昏借予悠阿姊一領膨紗衫。
I cha-hng chioh hō͘ in a-chí chit niá phòng-se-saⁿ.

她昨天借給她姐姐一件毛衣。
Tā zuótiān jiè gěi tā jiějiě yī jiàn máoyī.

She lent **to her older sister** a sweater yesterday (*perhaps the listener did not know what was lent to the sister*).

阮朋友熱天的時陣欲租予阮小弟一間房間。
Gún pêng-iú joah-thiⁿ ê sî-chūn beh cho͘ hō͘ gún sió-tī chit keng pâng-keng.

我的朋友夏天的時候要租給我弟弟一間房間。
Wǒ de péngyǒu xiàtiān de shíhòu yào zū gěi wǒ dìdi yī jiàn fángjiān.

My friend will rent **to my younger brother** a room over the summer (*perhaps the listener did not know what was being rented*).

ORDER 2

借 / 租 + *direct object* + 予 + *indirect object (new information)*

chioh / cho͘ + *direct object* + **hō͘** + *indirect object (new information)*

'to lend / rent *direct object* **to** *indirect object*'

伊 昨昏 借 一 領 膨紗衫 予 恁 阿姊。

I cha-hng <u>chioh</u> chit niá phòng-se-saⁿ **hō͘ in a-chí**.

她 昨天 借 一 件 毛衣 給 她 姐姐。

Tā zuótiān <u>jiè</u> yī jiàn máoyī **gěi tā jiějiě**.

She <u>lent</u> a sweater **to her older sister** yesterday (*perhaps the listener did not know to whom the sweater was lent*).

阮 朋友 熱天 的 時陣 欲 租 一 間 房間 阮 予 小弟。

Gún pêng-iú joah-thiⁿ ê sî-chūn beh <u>cho͘</u> chit keng pâng-keng **hō͘ gún sió-tī**.

我 的 朋友 夏天 的 時候 要 租 一 間 房間 給 我 弟弟。

Wǒ de péngyǒu xiàtiān de shíhòu yào <u>zū</u> yī jiān fángjiān **gěi wǒ dìdì**.

My friend will <u>rent</u> a room **to my younger brother** over the summer (*perhaps the listener did not know to whom the room was being rented*).

To express 'to borrow from' and 'to rent from', the preposition 共 **kā** is placed before the indirect object or source from whom the entity is transferred. Note that this prepositional phrase occurs before the verb.

共 + *indirect object* + 借 / 租 + *direct object*

kā + *indirect object* + chioh / cho͘ + *direct object*

'to borrow/rent *direct object* **from** *indirect object*'

伊 昨昏 共 恁 阿姊 借 一 領 膨紗衫。

I cha-hng **kā in a-chí** <u>chioh</u> chit niá phòng-se-saⁿ.

她 昨天 跟 她 姐姐 借 一 件 毛衣。

Tā zuótiān **gēn tā jiějiě** <u>jiè</u> yī jiàn máoyī.

She <u>borrowed</u> a sweater **from her older sister** yesterday.

阮 朋友 熱天 的 時陣 欲 **共 阮 小弟** 租 一 間 房間。
Gún pêng-iú joah-thiⁿ ê sî-chūn beh **kā gún sió-tī** cho͘ chit keng pâng-keng.
我 的 朋友 夏天 的 時候 **跟 我 弟弟** 要 租 一 間 房間。
Wǒ de péngyǒu xiàtiān de shíhòu **gēn wǒ dìdì** yào zū yī jiān fángjiān.
My friend will rent a room **from my younger brother** over the summer.

TAIWANESE	MANDARIN	MEANING
借 chioh	借 jiè	to lend / to borrow
租 cho͘	租 zū	to rent to / to rent from
借 予 chioh hō͘	借 給 jiè gěi	to lend
租 予 cho͘ hō͘	租 給 zū gěi	to rent to
共…借 kā…chioh	跟…借 gēn…jiè	to borrow
共…租 kā…cho͘	跟…租 gēn…zū	to rent from

18.3 Benefactives

Benefactives are prepositional phrases that indicate that the main verb is performed 'for the benefit of' or done 'on behalf of' someone or something.

In English, the preposition 'for' is typically used as a benefactive preposition.

My husband cooked dinner <u>for me</u>.

The doctor wrote a prescription <u>for the patient</u>.

18.3.1 Prepositions marking benefactives

In Taiwanese, there are a few prepositions (**共 kā**, **替 thè**, **為 ūi**) that may be used to begin a benefactive phrase. In contrast to indirect object phrases, benefactive phrases occur before the main verb and can be used with many types of verbs aside from dative verbs.

preposition + someone / something + verb

'*verb* for the benefit of *someone / something*'

阮 翁 <u>為 我</u> 做 暗頓。

Gún ang <u>ūi góa</u> chò àm-tǹg.

我 先生 <u>為 我</u> 做 晚飯。

Wǒ xiānshēng <u>wèi wǒ</u> zuò wǎnfàn.

My husband cooked dinner <u>for me</u>.

醫生 <u>共 病人</u> 開 藥單。

I-seng <u>kā pēⁿ-lâng</u> khui io̍h-toaⁿ.

醫生 <u>替 病人</u> 開 藥單。

Yīshēng <u>tì bìngrén</u> kāi yàodān.

The doctor wrote a prescription <u>for the patient</u>.

Below is a table of some common prepositions indicating benefactive phrases.

TAIWANESE	MANDARIN	MEANING
共 kā	幫 bāng, 給 gěi	for *(to help do)*
替 thè	替 tì	to stand in for
為 ūi	為 wèi	because of, for

我 <u>替 阮 阿媽</u> 佇 網頂 買 飛龍機 票。

Góa <u>thè gún a-má</u> tī bāng-téng bé hui-lêng-ki phiò.

我 <u>替 我 奶奶</u> 在 網上 買 飛機 票。

Wǒ <u>tì wǒ nǎinai</u> zài wǎngshàng mǎi fēijī piào.

I bought plane tickets online <u>for my grandma</u> *(on her behalf)*.

張 先生 想欲 <u>為 悠 某</u> 減肥。

Tiuⁿ--sian-siⁿ siūⁿ-beh <u>ūi in bó</u> kiám-puî.

張 先生 想要 <u>為 他 太太</u> 減肥。

Zhāng xiānshēng xiǎngyào <u>wèi tā tàitài</u> jiǎnféi.

Mr. Tiunn is thinking of losing weight <u>for his wife</u>.

While not originally used as a preposition, the Taiwanese verb 幫 **pang** has recently expanded into a usage similar to its Mandarin counterpart 幫 **bāng**.

我 幫 阮 阿媽 佇 網頂 買 飛行機 票。
Góa <u>pang gún a-má</u> tī bāng-téng bé hoe-lêng-ki phiò.
我 幫 我 奶奶 在 網上 買 飛機 票。
Wǒ <u>bāng wǒ nǎinai</u> zài wǎngshàng mǎi fēijī piào.
I helped <u>my grandma</u> buy plane tickets online.

In addition to a benefactive meaning, the preposition 共 **kā** can also express 'from'. As a result there may be ambiguity in some contexts.

伊 共 我 買 兩 張 票。
I <u>kā góa</u> bé nñg tiuⁿ phiò.

BENEFACTIVE INTERPRETATION
他 替 我 買 兩 張 票。
Tā <u>tì wǒ</u> mǎi liǎng zhāng piào.
He bought two tickets <u>for me</u>.

NON-BENEFACTIVE INTREPRETATION
他 跟 我 買 兩 張 票。
Tā <u>gēn wǒ</u> mǎi liǎng zhāng piào.
He bought two tickets <u>from me</u>.

Note that in Mandarin there is less ambiguity as different prepositions are used to distinguish between 'from' and 'for'. To be less ambiguous in Taiwanese, other prepositions can be used such as 按 **àn** 'from' or 替 **thè** 'for'.

18.3.2 Benefactive and indirect object phrases

Depending on the circumstances, a distinction can be made between benefactive and indirect object phrases. Benefactive phrases, which emphasize someone or something benefitting from an action, are always placed before the verb. In contrast, indirect object phrases, which emphasize the recipients of an action, occur after the verb.

BENEFACTIVE PHRASE

恁 阿母 共 伊 寄 一 張 批。

In a-bú kā i kià chit tiuⁿ phoe.

他 媽媽 幫 他 寄 一 封 信。

Tā māmā bāng tā jì yī fēng xìn.

His mother sent a letter <u>for him</u> (*perhaps he was unable to send it himself*).

INDIRECT OBJECT PHRASE

恁 阿母 寄 共 伊 一 張 批。

In a-bú kià hō͘ i chit tiuⁿ phoe.

他 媽媽 寄 給 他 一 封 信。

Tā māmā jì gěi tā yī fēng xìn.

His mother sent a letter <u>to him</u> (*he was the recipient of the letter*).

In some cases the benefactive interpretation and indirect object interpretation are, practically speaking, equivalent in meaning.

BENEFACTIVE INTEPRETATION

伊 个 服務員 共 我 畫 一 張 圖。

Hit ê hok-bū-ôan kā góa ōe chit tiuⁿ tô͘.

那個 服務員 給 我 畫 一 張 圖。

Nàge fúwùyuán gěi wǒ huà yī zhāng tú.

The waiter drew a map <u>for me</u> (*he drew it to help me*).

INDIRECT OBJECT INTERPRETATION

伊 个 服務員 畫 予 我 一 張 圖。

Hit ê hok-bū-ôan ōe hō͘ góa chit tiuⁿ tô͘.

那個 服務員 畫 給 我 一 張 圖。

Nàge fúwùyuán huà gěi wǒ yī zhāng tú.

The waiter drew a map <u>for me</u> (*he drew it to give to me*).

In the example above, the context makes the slight distinction in meaning between the two phrases negligible. For all intents and purposes, either phrase may be used to describe the situation.

Note that in Mandarin, **給 gěi** may serve as a preposition for both benefactive phrases (placed before the verb) and indirect object phrases (placed after the verb). However, a linguistic shift in contemporary Mandarin has allowed indirect object phrases to occur before the verb with a small number of verbs. As a result, **給 gěi** before a verb can be interpreted as either a benefactive phrase or indirect object phrase.

MANDARIN

林小姐 給 顧客 送 一 個 包裹。

Lín xiǎojiě gěi gùkè sòng yī gè bāoguǒ.

Ms. Lin sent a package on behalf of her clients (*benefactive reading*).

Ms. Lin set a package to her clients (*indirect object reading*).

19 Passive voice

Before discussing passive voice, it is perhaps helpful to examine a typical sentence that is described in the active voice.

A sentence in active voice has the *agent*, or performer of the action, as the subject of the sentence. In the example below, 'Ms. Tan' is the agent and also the subject of the sentence.

Ms. Tan	watered	the plants.
agent	*action*	*direct object (recipient of action)*

In the *passive voice* sentence, the direct object (recipient of action) becomes the subject of the sentence and the agent may or may not be included.

The plants	were watered	(by Ms. Tan).
direct object	*action*	*agent*

The passive voice helps focus attention on the object or describe actions in which the agent is unknown or not desired to be disclosed. However, the passive voice in Taiwanese is generally used in negative situations when facing adversity or hearing unfortunate news. As a result, the usage of the passive voice is less common than in English. Note that even neutral verbs will imply negative contexts.

植物 予 陳 小姐 沃著 水。
Sit-bu̍t hō͘ Tân sió-chiá ak-tio̍h chúi.
植物 被 陳 小姐 澆 水 了。
Zhíwù bèi Chén xiǎojiě jiāo shuǐ le.
The plants <u>were watered</u> by Ms. Tan (*they should not have been watered*).

To focus on the object or action in more positive situations, topicalization *(see 17.2 Topicalized object)* can be used instead of the passive voice.

TOPICALIZED OBJECT

植物，有 沃著 水。

Sit-bu̍t, ū ak-tio̍h chúi.

植物，澆 水 了。

Zhíwù, jiāo shuǐ le.

As for the plants, they were watered.

Additionally, some contexts which use the passive voice in English use the 是 **sī...**的 **--ê** focusing construction in Taiwanese *(see 10.1.2* 是 *sī in the focusing construction)*.

咱 的 課本 是 咱 的 老師 寫 的。

Lán ê khò-pún sī lán ê lāu-su siá--ê.

我們 的 課本 是 我們 的 老師 寫 的。

Wǒmen de kèběn shì wǒmen de lǎoshī xiě de.

Our textbook is written by our teacher.

19.1 Passive marker 予 hō·

In a passive sentence, the direct object (recipient of the action) becomes the subject of the sentence. The passive marker 予 **hō·** is placed before the agent *(see 19.1 Stating the agent)* and main verb to indicate the passive voice. Additionally, the verb 去 **khì** can optionally precede 予 **hō·**.

object + (去) + 予 + *agent* + *verb*

object + (khì) + hō· + *agent* + *verb*

'*object* to be *verb*-ed by *agent*'

咱 的 話 有 予 人 聽著 矣。

Lán ê ōe ū hō· lâng thiaⁿ--tio̍h--ah.

我們 的 話 被 聽到 了。

Wǒmen de huà bèi tīngdào le.

We've been overheard.

Note that phonetic contractions often occur with 予 **hō·** in the passive voice. In the preceding example, 予 人 **hō· lâng** is often pronounced as **hông**.

伊 的 錢 <u>去 予</u> 賊仔 <u>偷提去</u> 矣。

I ê chîⁿ <u>khì hō͘</u> chha̍t-á <u>thau-the̍h--khì</u>--ah.

他 的 錢 <u>被</u> 小偷 <u>偷走</u> 了。

Tā de qián <u>bèi</u> xiǎotōu <u>tōuzǒu</u> le.

His money <u>was</u> <u>stolen</u> by a thief.

Mandarin uses **被 bèi** as a general passive marker. However, informal contexts may also include the use of **讓 ràng**, **叫 jiào**, or **給 gěi** to mark the passive.

19.2 Stating the agent

The agent (the doer of the action) is placed directly after the passive marker **予 hō͘**. In English, the preposition 'by' is used to mark the agent. Note that the agent can be either an animate or inanimate object.

object + (去) + 予 + *agent* + *verb*

object + (khì) + hō͘ + *agent* + *verb*

'*object* to be *verb*-ed by *agent*'

植物	予	陳 小姐	沃著 水
sit-bu̍t	hō͘	Tân sió-chiá	ak-tio̍h chúi
植物	被	陳小姐	澆 水 了
zhíwù	bèi	Chén xiǎojiě	jiāo shuǐ le
object	*passive marker*	*agent*	*action*
The plants	were watered	by Ms. Tan	
object	*action*	*agent*	

植物 予 <u>陳 小姐</u> 沃著 水。

Sit-bu̍t hō͘ <u>Tân sió-chiá</u> ak-tio̍h chúi.

植物 被 <u>陳 小姐</u> 澆水 了。

Zhíwù bèi <u>Chén xiǎojiě</u> jiāo shuǐ le.

The plants were watered <u>by Ms. Tan</u>.

Note that unlike Mandarin, Taiwanese technically always requires an agent to be placed after the passive marker **予 hō͘**. However, when the agent is the third person singular pronoun 伊 i, phonetic contraction reduces the syllables to **hō·**. In effect, the sentence appears to have no explicit agent stated.

咱 的 話 有 予 (伊) 聽著 矣。
Lán ê ōe ū hō· (i) thiaⁿ--tio̍h--ah.
我們 的 話 被 聽到 了。
Wǒmen de huà bèi tīngdào le.
We've been overheard (<u>by him / her</u>).

In addition, generally passive sentences in Chinese describe events that have occurred and reflect a change in situation. As a result, the particle 矣 **--ah** marking the anterior aspect commonly appears at the end of the sentence *(see 8.4 Anterior aspect, 29.3.1 Indicating a change of state with adjectives and particle 矣 --ah)*.

19.3 The use of 共 kā in the passive voice

In passive sentences, the subject of the sentence is the direct object (recipient of the action). However, in some cases, only a part of the subject is affected by the action, and the affected part of the subject can be set off through the use of the 共 **kā** construction.

object (whole) + 予 + *agent* + 共 + *object (part)* + *verb*
object (whole) + hō· + *agent* + kā + *object (part)* + *verb*
'*object (whole)* to be *verb*-ed *object (part)* by *agent*'

<u>劉 先生</u> 予 賊仔 <u>共 錢</u> 偷提去 矣。
<u>Lâu--sian-siⁿ</u> hō· chha̍t-á <u>kā chîⁿ</u> thau-the̍h--khì--ah.
<u>劉 先生 的 錢</u> 被 小偷 偷走 了。
<u>Liú xiānshēng de qián</u> bèi xiǎotōu tōuzǒu le.
<u>Mr. Lau</u> had <u>his money</u> stolen by a thief *(money is a 'part' of Mr. Lau)*.

<u>阮 小妹</u> 予 邊仔人 <u>共 伊 的 跤</u> 撞著 矣。
<u>Gún sió-mōe</u> hō· piⁿ-á-lâng <u>kā i ê kha</u> tōng--tio̍h--ah.
<u>我 妹妹 的 腳</u> 被 旁邊人 撞到 了。
<u>Wǒ mèimei de jiǎo</u> bèi pángbiānrén zhuàngdào le.
The person next to us bumped into <u>my younger sister's leg</u>.

李先生 予 薰枝 共 手 燒著 矣。

Lí--sian-si^n hō͘ hun-ki kā chhiú sio--tio̍h--ah.

李先生 的 手 被 香菸 燒到 了。

Lǐ xiānshēng de shǒu bèi xiāngyān shāodào le.

Mr. Li was burned on his hand by a cigarette.

In the sentence above, 'Mr. Li' and 'his hand' have a whole-to-part relationship in which only 'his hand' is directly affected by the main action. Note that Taiwan Mandarin speakers are more likely to omit the use of the 把 **bǎ** construction in passive voice sentences and instead join 'Mr. Li' and 'his hand' with the modifying particle 的 **de**. In contrast, in other Mandarin-speaking areas, the 把 **bǎ** construction is more likely to be used.

STANDARD MANDARIN

李先生 被 香菸 把 手 燒到 了。

Lǐ xiānshēng bèi xiāngyān bǎ shǒu shāodào le.

Mr. Li was burned on his hand by a cigarette.

劉先生 被 小偷 把 錢 偷走 了。

Liú xiānshēng bèi xiǎotōu bǎ qián tōuzǒu le.

Mr. Lau had his money stolen by a thief (*money is a 'part' of Mr. Lau*).

我 妹妹 被 旁邊人 把 她 的 腳 撞到 了。

Wǒ mèimei bèi pángbiānrén bǎ tā de jiǎo zhuàngdào le.

The person next to us bumped into my younger sister's leg.

19.4 Causative verbs

Causative verbs indicate that the subject of the sentence causes, makes, or allows someone to perform an action.

I made my younger brother vacuum the floor.

My mom allowed me to watch the horror film.

The police requested that I not park here.

As opposed to passive sentences, the subject of the sentence is understood to have been the initiator of the action in the sentence.

Because in Taiwanese 予 **hō͘** can function as both a passive marker and a causative verb 'to allow', in some cases, the only difference between a causative and passive sentence is interpretation.

劉先生 予 賊仔 共 錢 偷提去 矣。
Lâu--sian-siⁿ hō͘ chha̍t-á kā chîⁿ thau-the̍h--khì--ah.

PASSIVE VOICE READING
劉先生 被 小偷 把 錢 偷走 了。
Liú xiānshēng bèi xiǎotōu bǎ qián tōuzǒu le.
Mr. Lau had his money stolen by a thief.

CAUSATIVE READING
劉先生 讓 小偷 把 錢 偷走 了。
Liú xiānshēng ràng xiǎotōu bǎ qián tōuzǒu le.
Mr. Lau allowed his money to be stolen by a thief.

While **被 bèi** in Mandarin is the general passive marker, **讓 ràng** and **叫 jiào** can both have causative and passive interpretations.

In Taiwanese, there is a range of causative verbs in addition to **予 hō͘** 'to allow'.

Below is a table of some common causative verbs.

TAIWANESE	MANDARIN	MEANING
予 hō͘	讓 ràng	to allow
叫 kiò	叫 jiào	to ask or request
請 chhiáⁿ	請 qīng	to request (*polite*)
討 thó	要求 yàoqiú	to beg or request
逼 pek	逼 bì	to compel or force
勞煩 lô-hôan	麻煩 máfán	to bother someone to do
派 phài	派 pai	to dispatch someone to do

subject + causative verb + subject (recipient) + verb ('caused')

我 逼 阮 小弟 欶 塗跤。
Góa pek gún sió-tī suh thô͘-kha.
我 逼 我 弟弟 吸 地板。
Wǒ bī wǒ dìdi xī dìbǎn.
I made my younger brother vacuum the floor.

阮 阿母 予 我 看 恐怖 片。

Gún a-bú hō͘ góa khòaⁿ khióng-pò͘ phìⁿ.

我 媽媽 讓 我 看 恐怖 片。

Wǒ māmā ràng wǒ kàn kǒngbù piàn.

My mom <u>allowed</u> me to watch the horror film.

警察 叫 咱 停 車 佇 遐。

Kéng-chhat kiò lán thêng chhia tī hia.

警察 叫 我們 把 車 停 在 那裡。

Jǐngchá jiào wǒmen bǎ chē tíng zài nàlǐ.

The police <u>asked</u> that we park over there.

20 Questions

In English, questions can be formed by raising the intonation at the end of a sentence, inverting the subject and verb word order, or adding a question word.

DECLARATIVE	QUESTION FORMAT	TYPE
She went home.	She went home?	Rising intonation
They are students.	Are they students?	Inverted subject-verb
The hotel is here.	Where is the hotel?	Question word

Unlike English, Taiwanese does not invert the order of the subject and verb to create a question from a statement. However, in shorter utterances, it is possible to ask a question with just a change in intonation. The final syllable is lighter, higher in pitch, and slightly drawn out. Typically, this is used for confirmation.

DECLARATIVE	QUESTION
你 食飽。	你 食飽?
Lí chia̍h-pá.	Lí chia̍h-pá?
You are full (*from eating*).	You are full?

In the example above, **飽 pá** 'full' is the final syllable and is higher in pitch, lighter, and slightly drawn out.

In addition to using question words, Taiwanese has a few other grammatical elements and sentence patterns to formulate a question. The following chapter will discuss five basic methods of formulating questions in Taiwanese:

- 敢 kám question marker questions

- Tag questions

- Particle questions

- Disjunctive questions

- Content questions

Note that while there are several ways to ask a question, some speakers prefer some methods to others.

20.1 敢 kám question marker

The use of the 敢 **kám** (also pronounced **kaⁿ**) question marker is a neutral and fairly common method of transforming a declarative statement into a question.

A question is formed by inserting the question marker 敢 **kám** directly before the word in question.

DECLARATIVE STATEMENT

伊 明仔載 欲 炁 囝仔 去 公園。
I bîn-á-chài beh chhōa gín-á khì kong-hn̂g.
她 明天 要 帶 孩子 去 公園。
Tā míngtiān yào dài háizi qù gōngyuán.
She will take the children to the park tomorrow.

QUESTIONS WITH DIFFERING FOCUS

敢 伊 明仔載 欲 炁 囝仔 去 公園？
Kám i bîn-á-chài beh chhōa gín-á khì kong-hn̂g?
是 她 明天 要 帶 孩子 去 公園 嗎？
Shì tā míngtiān yào dài háizi qù gōngyuán ma?
Is it she who will take the children to the park tomorrow?

伊 敢 明仔載 欲 炁 囝仔 去 公園？
I kám bîn-á-chài beh chhōa gín-á khì kong-hn̂g?
她 是 明天 要 帶 孩子 去 公園 嗎？
Tā shì míngtiān yào dài háizi qù gōngyuán ma?
Is it tomorrow when she will take the children to the park?

伊 明仔載 敢 欲 炁 囝仔 去 公園？
I bîn-á-chài kám beh chhōa gín-á khì kong-hn̂g?
她 明天 是 要 帶 孩子 去 公園 嗎？
Tā míngtiān shì yào dài háizi qù gōngyuán ma?
Will she be taking the children to the park tomorrow?

Note that Mandarin does not have a direct equivalent with the Taiwanese question marker 敢 **kám**. As 敢 **kám** is fairly neutral, corresponding translations into Mandarin often make use of the 嗎 **ma** question marker. In order to shift emphasis within a question, Mandarin can use the 是 **shì** …(的 **de**) focusing construction.

20.1.1 敢 kám placement restrictions

While 敢 **kám** can be placed in several positions, there are some restrictions. 敢 **kám** must come before the verb phrase including those with negation. Negative particles cannot appear before 敢 **kám**.

> 敢 + *negation* + *verb phrase*
>
> kám + *negation* + *verb phrase*

> 伊 敢 毋捌 咱 老師？
> I <u>kám</u> m̄-bat lán lāu-su?
> 他 不 認識 我們 的 老師 嗎？
> Tā bù rènshí wǒmen de lǎoshī <u>ma</u>?
> Doesn't he know our teacher?

In addition, 敢 **kám** must also come before the 是 **sī** in the focusing construction 是 **sī** … (的 **--ē**). Note the end-of-sentence particle 的 **--ê** is in the neutral tone and may be omitted *(see 10.1.2 是 sī in the focusing construction)*.

> 敢 + 是 + *item of focus* + (的)
>
> kám + sī + *item of focus* + (--ē)

> 敢 是 伊 欲 載 咱 去 機場 (的)？
> <u>Kám sī</u> i beh chài lán khì ki-tiûⁿ (--ē)?
> 是 他 要 載 我們 去 機場 (的)？
> <u>Shì</u> tā yào zài wǒmen qù jīchǎng (<u>de</u>)?
> <u>Is it</u> he who will drive us to the airport?

20.1.2 敢 kám in verb compounds

敢 **kám** on occasion can appear inside verb compounds between the main verb and the complement. The emphasis of the question asks whether the complement has succeeded given that the action from the main verb has already begun.

> *main verb* + 敢 + *complement*
> *main verb* + kám + *complement*

伊 做 敢 好 矣？
I chò kám hó--ah?
他 做 好 了 嗎？
Tā zuò hǎo le ma?
Did he finish making it?

紅嬰仔 坐敢起來 未？
Âng-eⁿ-á chē-kám-khí-lâi--bōe?
嬰兒 還沒 坐得起來 嗎？
Yīng'ér háiméi zuòdeqǐlái ma?
Isn't the baby able to sit up yet?

20.1.3 Responding to 敢 kám questions

Because 敢 **kám** questions are essentially yes-no questions, the general response in the affirmative can be 是 **sī** or 嘿 **hèⁿ**. For a negative response, the response is 無 **bô**.

QUESTION
敢 是 佇 遮 排隊？
Kám sī tī chia pâi-tūi?
是 這裡 排隊 嗎？
Shì zhèlǐ páiduì ma?
Is this where we stand in line?

RESPONSE	
AFFIRMATIVE	NEGATIVE
是 / 嘿。	無。
Sī / Hèⁿ.	Bô.
是。	不是。
Shì.	Bù shì.
Yes.	No.

20.2 Tag questions

Tag questions are a type of question formed by attaching a *question tag*, a short phrase or word seeking confirmation, to the end of a declarative sentence. The tag transforms the statement into a question. The component of the question that precedes the tag can be referred to as the *proposition*.

In English, a tag is often constructed by taking the main verb and posing the opposite form whether positive or negative followed by the subject.

> This bag is yours, <u>isn't it</u>?
>
> They don't have a television, <u>do they</u>?

Another method is to attach a single word seeking confirmation.

> We can sit here, <u>right</u>?
>
> I should sign my name here, <u>correct</u>?

Taiwanese uses three types of tag questions to seek confirmation of the proposition:

- General-purpose tag 是著無 **sī tiȯh--bô**
- Affirmative tags
- Pure negative 毋 **m̄** tag

Mandarin similarly has question tags, but tends to use an affirmative-negative (X-not-X) format to confirm the proposition (such as 對不對 **duìbùduì** 'right?', 好不好 **hǎobùhǎo** 'okay?', 是不是 **shìbùshì** 'is it?', or 行不行 **xíngbùxíng** 'does that work?').

20.2.1 General-purpose tag 是著無 sī tio̍h--bô 'is that right?'

The general-purpose tag 是著無 sī tio̍h--bô 'is that right?' can be appended to most declarative statements. With this tag, the speaker assumes that the proposition made is true and searches for confirmation. Because the tag is only looking for a yes-no confirmation, the tag does not need to match the verb in the proposition. 是著無 sī tio̍h--bô is usually abbreviated to either 是無 sī--bô '…isn't it' or 著無 tio̍h--bô '…right?'.

proposition + 是著無?

proposition + sī tio̍h--bô?

'*proposition*, isn't it? / is that right?'

你 明仔載 八 點 愛 上班，是 著 無?
Lí bîn-á-chài peh tiám ài siōng-pan, <u>sī tio̍h--bô</u>?
你 明天 八 點 得 上班，<u>對不對</u>?
Nǐ míngtiān bā diǎn děi shàngbān, <u>duìbùduì</u>?
You have to go to work tomorrow at 8 o'clock, <u>is that right</u>?

伊 㤅 伊 的 男 朋友，是 無?
I chhōa i ê lâm pêng-iú, <u>sī--bô</u>?
她 帶 她 的 男 朋友，<u>是不是</u>?
Tā dài tā de nán péngyǒu, <u>shìbùshì</u>?
She is bringing her boyfriend, <u>isn't she</u>?

林 先生 捌 去過 德國，著 無?
Lîm--sian-siⁿ bat khì-kòe Tek-kok, <u>tio̍h--bô</u>?
林 先生 去過 德國，<u>對不對</u>?
Lín xiānshēng qùguò Déguó, <u>duìbùduì</u>?
Mr. Lim has already been to Germany, <u>right</u>?

20.2.2 Responding to the general-purpose tag 是著無 sī tio̍h--bô?

The response to a question using the general-purpose tag 是著無 sī tio̍h--bô tag depends on which form is used. Affirmative responses require either a corresponding 是 sī 'yes' or

著 tiȯh 'correct', while negative responses use the negative forms 毋是 m̄-sī 'no' or 毋著 m̄-tiȯh 'incorrect'.

PATTERN 1

咱 拜五 下早 有 考試，是 著 無？
Lán pài-gō͘ ê-chái ū khó-chhì, sī tiȯh--bô?
我們 禮拜五 早上 有 考試，是不是？
Wǒmen lǐbàiwǔ zǎoshang yǒu kǎoshì, shìbùshì?
We have an exam Friday morning, is that right?

AFFIRMATIVE RESPONSE	NEGATIVE RESPONSE
是 / 著。	毋是 / 毋著。
Sī / Tiȯh.	M̄-sī / M̄-tiȯh.
是 / 對。	不是 / 不對。
Shì / Duì.	Bù shì / Bù duì.
Yes / Right.	No / Incorrect.

PATTERN 2

咱 拜五 下早 有 考試，是 無？
Lán pài-gō͘ ê-chái ū khó-chhì, sī--bô?
我們 禮拜五 早上 有 考試，是不是？
Wǒmen lǐbàiwǔ zǎoshang yǒu kǎoshì, shìbùshì?
We have an exam Friday morning, don't we?

AFFIRMATIVE RESPONSE	NEGATIVE RESPONSE
是。	毋是。
Sī.	M̄-sī.
是。	不是。
Shì.	Bù shì.
Yes.	No.

PATTERN 3

咱 拜五 下早 有 考試，著 無？
Lán pài-gō͘ ê-chái ū khó-chhì, tiȯh--bô?
我們 禮拜五 早上 有 考試，對不對？
Wǒmen lǐbàiwǔ zǎoshang yǒu kǎoshì, duìbùduì?
We have an exam Friday morning, right?

AFFIRMATIVE RESPONSE	NEGATIVE RESPONSE
著。	毋著。
Tio̍h.	M̄-tio̍h.
對。	不對。
Duì.	Bù duì.
Right.	Incorrect.

20.2.3 Affirmative tags

Affirmative tags, formed with particles indicating affirmation (乎 --hoⁿh, 呢 --nih), can also be used to form questions seeking confirmation of statements made in the proposition These tags appear at the end of a sentence and express a meaning similar to 'right?'. Because the tag is only looking for a yes-no confirmation, the tag does not need to match the verb in the proposition. Note that usage of these tags varies by region and individual preference.

proposition + 乎 / 呢 ?

proposition + --hoⁿh / --nih ?

'*proposition*, right?'

咱 欲 做伙 食 暗飯 乎?
Lán beh chò-hóe chia̍h àm-pn̄g--hoⁿh?
我們 要 一起 吃 晚飯 吧?
Wǒmen yào yīqǐ chī wǎnfàn ba?
We're going to have dinner together, right?

你 後 禮拜 會 敲 電話 予 我 呢?
Lí āu lé-pài ē khà tiān-ōe hō͘ góa--nih?
你 下 禮拜 會 打 電話 給 我, 對 吧?
Nǐ xià lǐbài huì dǎ diànhuà gěi wǒ, duì ba?
You will call me next week, right?

20.2.4 Pure negative 毋 m̄ tags

The negative 毋 m̄ has two meanings as both a pure negative 'not' and as a volitional *(desire)* negative 'not want' *(see 13.1 Negative 毋 m̄)*. Only the pure negative 毋 m̄ can be included as part of a question tag. The volitional 毋 m̄ functions instead as an end-of-sentence particle *(see 20.3 Particle questions)*.

Pure 毋 m̄

Only a limited number of verbs and adjectives can accept the pure 毋 m̄ for negation *(see 13.1.1 Pure negative 毋 m̄ 'not')*. These few verbs and adjectives can form a question tag when followed by 毋 m̄. The verb or adjective used in the proposition does not need to match the verb or adjective used in the tag. Like other tag questions, the tags formed with the pure 毋 m̄ seek confirmation of the proposition made.

QUESTION TAG

pure 毋 m̄ verb / adjective + 毋

pure 毋 m̄ verb / adjective + --m̄

陳 小姐 愛 去 海邊, <u>是 毋</u>?
Tân sió-chiá ài khì hái-piⁿ, <u>sī--m̄</u>?
陳 小姐 喜歡 去 海邊, <u>是不是</u>?
Chén xiǎojiě xǐhuān qù hǎibiān, <u>shìbùshì</u>?
Ms. Tan likes to go to the seaside, <u>doesn't she</u>?

我 無 愛 閣 駛 車, <u>好 毋</u>?
Góa bô ài koh sái chhia, <u>hó--m̄</u>?
我 不 要 繼續 開 車, <u>好不好</u>?
Wǒ bù yào jìxù kāi chē, <u>hǎobùhǎo</u>?
I don't want to drive anymore, <u>okay</u>?

咱 著愛 佇 遮 斡 倒爿, <u>著 毋</u>?
Lán tio̍h-ài tī chia oat tò-pêng, <u>tio̍h--m̄</u>?
我們 需要 在 這裡 左 轉, <u>對不對</u>?
Wǒmen xūyào zài zhèlǐ zuǒ zhuǎn, <u>duìbùduì</u>?
We have to turn left here, <u>right</u>?

下昏暗 毋通 啉 酒, <u>知 毋</u>?
E-hng-àm m̄-thang lim chiú, <u>chai--m̄</u>?
今晚 不要 喝 酒, <u>知不知道</u>?
Jīnwǎn bù yào hē jiǔ, <u>zhībùzhīdào</u>?
There must be no drinking alcohol tonight, <u>understand</u>?

Volitional 毋 m̄

The volitional 毋 m̄ is the negative form of the modal verb 欲 **beh**. In contrast to the pure negative 毋 m̄, the volitional 毋 m̄ can only function as an end-of-sentence particle *(see 20.3 Particle questions)*. If the modal verb 欲 **beh** is part of the proposition, only then can the volitional 毋 m̄ be used as a question particle to change the declarative sentence into a question. The modal verb 欲 **beh** does not need to be repeated before the particle 毋 m̄. Rather than seeking confirmation, particle questions are more neutral in tone.

proposition with modal verb 欲 + 毋

proposition with modal verb beh + --m̄

你 欲 食 日本 料理 毋？
Lí beh chia̍h Ji̍t-pún liāu-lí--m̄?
你 要不要 吃 日本 料理？
Nǐ yàobùyào chī Rìběn liàolǐ?
Do you want to eat Japanese food?

恁 欲 和 阮 做伙 去 唱 歌 毋？
Lín beh hām gún chò-hóe khì chhiùⁿ koa--m̄?
你們 要不要 和 我們 一起 去 唱 歌？
Nǐmen yàobùyào hé wǒmen yīqǐ qù chàng gē?
Do you want to go singing with us?

20.3 Particle questions

Particle questions make use of end-of-sentence grammatical particles to indicate that the sentence is a question. The usage of some particles relies on which verb or adjective is part of the proposition. Taiwanese can form particle questions from the five negative particles. Note that the tone is generally neutral.

20.3.1 Negative question particles

The five negative particles in Taiwanese 毋 --m̄, 無 --bô, 袂 --bē, 未--bōe, and 免 --bián can be used to form particle questions. Because negatives in Taiwanese are differentiated according to a mixture of aspect and mood, the choice of negative particle for questions also depends on the aspect and mood of the proposition *(see 13 Negation, 12 Modal verbs, 8 Aspect)*.

Below is a summary table of the five negatives in Taiwanese along with their affirmative counterparts and aspect/mood categorization.

ASPECT/MOOD	NEGATIVE	AFFIRMATIVE
Volition (*mood*)	毋 m̄ 'not want'	欲 beh 'want'
Perfective (*aspect*)	無 bô 'not have'	有 ū 'have'
Possibility (*mood*)	袂 bē 'will not'	會 ē 'will'
Obligation (*mood*)	免 bián 'need not'	著愛 tio̍h-ài 'must'
Anterior (*aspect*)	未 bōe 'not yet'	了 le 'have + *verb*'

Particle questions are formed by adding the negative particle that matches the aspect and mood of the proposition.

proposition + negative particle?

Note that the pure negative 毋 m̄ cannot be used as a question particle but only as a question tag *(see 20.2.4 Pure negative 毋 m̄ tags)*.

ASPECT/MOOD	EXAMPLE
VOLITION (MOOD)	
毋 --m̄	伊 欲 泅 水 毋？
	I beh siû chúi--m̄?
	他 <u>要不要</u> 游泳？
	Tā <u>yàobùyào</u> yóuyǒng?
	<u>Does</u> he <u>want</u> to swim?
PERFECTIVE (ASPECT)	
無 --bô	伊 有 泅 水 <u>無</u>？
	I ū siû chúi--<u>bô</u>?
	他 游泳 <u>了 沒有</u>？
	Tā yóuyǒng <u>le méiyǒu</u>?
	<u>Did</u> he swim?

POSSIBILITY (MOOD)

袂 --bē

伊 會 泅 水 袂?
I ē siû chúi--bē?
他 會不會 游泳?
Tā huìbùhuì yóuyǒng?
Will he swim?

ANTERIOR (ASPECT)

未--bōe

伊 泅 水 矣 未?
I siû chúi--ah--bōe?
他 游泳 了 嗎?
Tā yóuyǒng le ma?
Has he swum yet?

OBLIGATION (MOOD)

免 bián

伊 愛 泅 水 抑 免?
I ài siû chúi iȧh bián?
他 需要 游泳 還是 不 用?
Tā xūyào yóuyǒng háishì bù yòng?
Does he need to swim (or not)?

免 bián is often preceded by **抑 iȧh** 'or' but is less commonly used as a question particle.

你 欲 看 電影 毋?
Lí beh khòaⁿ tiān-iáⁿ--m̄?
你 要不要 看 電影?
Nǐ yàobùyào kàn diànyǐng?
Do you want to watch a movie?

咱 有 關 車庫 無?
Lán ū koaiⁿ chhia-khò͘--bô?
我們 關了 車庫 沒有?
Wǒmen guānle chēkù méiyǒu?
Did we close the garage?

伊 會 讀 大學 袂?
I ē thảk tāi-hảk--bē?
他 會不會 讀 大學?
Tā huìbùhuì dú dàxué?
Will he attend university?

怹 開 冷氣 矣 未?
In khui léng-khì--ah--bōe?
他們 開 冷氣機 了 嗎?
Tāmen kāi lěngqìjī le ma?
Have they turned on the air conditioner yet?

咱 愛 買 較 濟 飲料 抑 免?
Lán ài bé khah chē ím-liāu iȧh bián?
我們 需要 買 多一點 飲料 還是 不用?
Wǒmen xūyāo mǎi duō yī diǎn yǐnliào háishì bù yòng?
Do we need to buy extra drinks (or not)?

20.3.2 無 --bô as a universal question particle

For some speakers 無 --**bô** can be used as a question particle regardless of the mood or aspect in the proposition. This appears to be a contemporary linguistic change within Taiwanese in which 無 --**bô** is becoming a universal question particle similar to the Mandarin 嗎 **ma**. Additionally, some younger speakers are beginning to use 嘛 **mah** as a phonetic and functional analog to the Mandarin 嗎 **ma**.

In the examples below, the corresponding negative question particle to verbs in the proposition has been replaced in all cases by 無 --**bô** including sentences using the pure negative 毋 **m̄**.

VOLITION (MOOD)
怹 欲 去 高雄 無?
In beh khì Ko-hiông--bô?
他們 要 去 高雄 嗎?
Tāmen yào qù Gāoxióng ma?
Do they want to go to Kaohsiung?

PERFECTIVE (ASPECT)

恁 有 去 高雄 無？

In ū khì Ko-hiông--bô?

他們 去了 高雄 嗎？

Tāmen qùle Gāoxióng ma?

Did they go to Kaohsiung?

POSSIBILITY (MOOD)

恁 會 去 高雄 無？

In ē khì Ko-hiông--bô?

他們 會 去 高雄 嗎？

Tāmen huì qù Gāoxióng ma?

Will they go to Kaohsiung?

ANTERIOR (ASPECT)

恁 已經 去 高雄 矣 無？

In í-keng khì Ko-hiông--ah--bô?

他們 已經 去 高雄 了 嗎？

Tāmen yǐjīng qù Gāoxióng le ma?

Have they gone to Kaohsiung yet?

OBLIGATION (MOOD)

恁 著愛 去 高雄 無？

In tio̍h-ài khì Ko-hiông--bô?

他們 需要 去 高雄 嗎？

Tāmen xūyào qù Gāoxióng ma?

Did they need to go to Kaohsiung?

PURE 毋 M̄

恁 捌 去 高雄 無？

In bat khì Ko-hiông--bô?

他們 去過 高雄 嗎？

Tāmen qùguò Gāoxióng ma?

Have they gone to Kaohsiung before?

20.4 Disjunctive questions

Disjunctive questions provide two options that are joined by the conjunction 'or'. Each argument on either side of 'or' is occupied by the same parts of speech.

Would you like to drink tea or coffee? (*nouns*)

Can we swim or jog in the park? (*verbs*)

Should I read a book or watch television? (*verbs with objects*)

Is it better to write quickly or precisely? (*adverbs*)

20.4.1 The conjunction 抑是 iȧh-sī 'or'

Taiwanese uses **抑是 iȧh-sī** (alternate pronunciations include **iah-sī, ȧh-sī, ah-sī**) to express the conjunction 'or'. Note that **抑是 iȧh-sī** is commonly abbreviated to **抑 iȧh**. Nouns, verbs, or adjectives can all serve as arguments for the disjunctive question.

noun/verb/adjective + 抑(是) + *noun/verb/adjective*

noun/verb/adjective + iȧh(-sī) + *noun/verb/adjective*

'*noun/verb/adjective* or *noun/verb/adjective*'

NOUNS
你 想欲 食 梨仔 抑是 弓蕉？
Lí siuⁿ-beh chiȧh lâi-á iȧh-sī keng-chio?
你 想要 吃 梨子 還是 香蕉？
Nǐ xiǎngyào chī lízi háishì xiāngjiāo?
Would you like to eat a pear or banana?

VERBS
你 想欲 看 冊 抑 看 報紙？
Lí siuⁿ-beh khòaⁿ chheh iȧh khòaⁿ pò-chóa？
你 想要 看 書 還是 看 報紙？
Nǐ xiǎngyào kàn shū háishì kàn bàozhǐ?
Would you like to read a book or newspaper?

ADJECTIVES

這領裙有好看抑是會歹看？

Chit niá kûn ū hó-khòaⁿ iah-sī ē pháiⁿ-khòaⁿ?

這件裙子好看還是難看？

Zhè jiàn qúnzi hǎokàn háishì nánkàn?

Is this skirt pretty or ugly?

20.4.2 Affirmative-negative disjunctive question (X-or-not-X)

In contrast to disjunctive questions that offer two distinct choices, the affirmative-negative disjunctive question (X-or-not-X) focuses on whether a single choice is true or not. While it is more common to use the 敢 **kám** question method for yes/no questions, affirmative-negative disjunctive questions are often used for emphasis or rhetorical effect.

The affirmative-negative disjunctive question uses the format X-or-not-X, which is formed with a verb or adjective followed by the conjunction 抑是 **iah-sī** 'or' and then the negative form of the initial verb or adjective. If an object follows the verb as part of a verb phrase, the object is not repeated after the negated verb/adjective.

verb/adjective + *(object)* + 抑(是) + *negative* + *verb/adjective*

verb/adjective + *(object)* + iah(-sī) + *negative* + *verb/adjective*

VERB

伊哭抑是無哭？

I khàu iah-sī bô khàu?

他有沒有哭？

Tā yǒuméiyǒu kū?

Did he cry (or not)?

VERB PHRASE (OBJECT)

你下早食飯抑無食？

Lí e-chái chiah pn̄g iah-sī bô chiah?

你早上吃飯了沒有？

Nǐ zǎoshang chī fàn le méiyǒu?

Did you eat this morning (or not)?

ADJECTIVE

這 塊 柳丁 甜 抑 無 甜？

Chit tè liú-teng tiⁿ iah bô tiⁿ?

這 塊 柳丁 甜不甜？

Zhè kuài liǔdīng tiánbùtián?

Is this orange sweet (or not)?

This question format can be further abbreviated by omitting the repeated verb or adjective after the negative.

verb/adjective + 抑(是) + *negative*

verb/adjective + iah(-sī) + *negative*

VERB

伊 哭 抑是 無？

I khàu iah-sī bô?

他 有沒有 哭？

Tā yǒuméiyǒu kū?

Did he cry (or not)?

VERB PHRASE (OBJECT)

你 下早 食 飯 抑是 無？

Lí e-chái chiah pñg iah-sī bô?

你 早上 吃 飯 了 沒有？

Nǐ zǎoshang chī fàn le méiyǒu?

Did you eat this morning (or not)?

ADJECTIVE

這 塊 柳丁 甜 抑 無？

Chit tè liú-teng tiⁿ iah bô?

這 塊 柳丁 甜不甜？

Zhè kuài liǔdīng tiánbùtián?

Is this orange sweet (or not)?

20.4.3 Affirmative-negative questions (X-not-X)

Affirmative-negative questions (X-not-X) are essentially disjunctive questions without the conjunction 'or'. In this format, the affirmative verb or adjective is immediately followed by the negated verb or adjective.

Taiwanese only permits the X-not-X format for the limited verbs and adjectives that can be negated by the pure negative 毋 m̄ *(see 13.1.1 Pure negative 毋 m̄ 'not')*. Note that for some speakers only the verb 是 sī 'to be' is acceptable in this construction.

> *verb/adjective* + 毋 + *verb/adjective*
> *verb/adjective* + -m̄- + *verb/adjective*

伊 是毋是 你 的 狗仔？
I sī-m̄-sī lí ê káu-á?
牠 是不是 你 的 狗？
Tā shìbùshì nǐ de gǒu?
Is it (or isn't it) your dog?

我 是毋是 後日 愛 加班？
Góa sī-m̄-sī āu-jit ài ka-pan?
我 是不是 後天 得 加班？
Wǒ shìbùshì hòutiān děi jiābān?
Is it (or isn't it) the day after tomorrow that I have to work overtime?

恁 捌毋捌 去過 中國？
In bat-m̄-bat khì-kòe Tiong-kok?
他們 有沒有 去過 中國？
Tāmen yǒuméiyǒu qùguò Zhōngguó?
Have (or haven't) they ever gone to China?

你 驚毋驚 鬼？
Lí kiaⁿ-m̄-kiaⁿ kúi?
你 怕不怕 鬼？
Nǐ pàbùpà guǐ?
Are you scared (or not) of ghosts?

Note that Mandarin is less restrictive with the affirmative-negative question (X-not-X) format than Taiwanese and allows many types of verbs and adjectives to serve as arguments in the construction.

20.5 Question words

For questions seeking content instead of a yes/no response, question words such as 'who', 'what', 'when', 'why', 'how', and 'which' can be used.

<u>Where</u> are the bathrooms?

<u>When</u> is dinner?

<u>Who</u> is the man in the yellow hat?

In general, the word order for declarative sentences and content questions remain the same in Taiwanese.

DECLARATIVE SENTENCE

便所佇<u>一樓</u>。
Piān-só͘ tī <u>it lâu</u>.
廁所在<u>一樓</u>。
Cèsuǒ zài <u>yī lóu</u>.
The bathrooms are on <u>the 1st floor</u>.

暗飯是<u>六點</u>。
Àm-pn̄g sī <u>la̍k tiám</u>.
晚餐是<u>六點</u>。
Wǎncān shì <u>liù diǎn</u>.
Dinner is at <u>six o'clock</u>.

戴黃帽仔是<u>吳先生</u>。
Tì n̂g bō-á sī <u>Gô͘-sian-siⁿ</u>.
戴黃帽子是<u>吳先生</u>。
Dài huáng màozi shì <u>Wú xiānshēng</u>.
<u>Mr. Gou</u> is the man in the yellow hat.

QUESTION

便所佇<u>佗位</u>？
Piān-só͘ tī <u>tó-ūi</u>?
廁所在<u>哪裡</u>？
Cèsuǒ zài <u>nǎlǐ</u>?
<u>Where</u> are the bathrooms?

暗飯是<u>幾點</u>？
Àm-pn̄g sī <u>kúi tiám</u>?
晚餐是<u>幾點</u>？
Wǎncān shì <u>jǐ diǎn</u>?
<u>When</u> is dinner?

戴黃帽仔是<u>啥人</u>？
Tì n̂g bō-á sī <u>siáⁿ-lâng</u>?
戴黃帽子是<u>誰</u>？
Dài huáng màozi shì <u>shéi</u>?
<u>Who</u> is the man in the yellow hat?

20.5.1 What

In Taiwanese, the single character 啥 siáⁿ can serve as the interrogative pronoun 'what'.

彼 是 啥？
He sī <u>siáⁿ</u>?
那 是 甚麼？
Nà shì <u>shénme</u>?
<u>What</u> is that?

共 我 講 你 欲 啥。
Kā góa kóng lí beh <u>siáⁿ</u>.
跟 我 講 你 要 什麼。
Gēn wǒ jiǎng nǐ yào <u>shénme</u>.
Tell me <u>what</u> you want.

啥 遐爾仔 芳？
<u>Siáⁿ</u> hia-nī-á phang?
什麼 那麼 香？
<u>Shénme</u> nàme xiāng?
<u>What</u> smells so good?

However, 啥 siáⁿ is often paired with 物 mih 'thing' or 貨 hòe 'product' to form a two-syllable version of 'what'. Despite the component characters, these versions of 'what' are not limited to concrete objects. Abstract ideas can also be replaced by both of these two-syllable versions. Another alternate form is 甚物 sīm-mih.

VERSION 1
彼 是 啥物？
He sī <u>siáⁿ-mih</u>?

VERSION 2
彼 是 啥貨？
He sī <u>siáⁿ-hòe</u>?

VERSION 3

彼 是 甚物？
He sī sīm-mih?

那 是 甚麼？
Nà shì shénme?
What is that?

When 啥 siáⁿ appears before a noun, it can function as an adjective indicating 'what kind'.

這 是 啥物 狗 仔？
Che sī siáⁿ-mih káu-á?
這 是 什麼 狗？
Zhè shì shénme gǒu?
What kind of dog is this?

20.5.2 Who

For questions inquiring about identity, the question word 啥 siáⁿ 'what' is placed before 人 lâng 'person' to form the interrogative pronoun 啥人 siáⁿ-lâng 'who, whom', or literally 'what person'. Often 啥人 siáⁿ-lâng is contracted and pronounced as a single syllable 啥人 siâng.

佇 門口 是 啥人？
Tī mn̂g-kháu sī siáⁿ-lâng (siâng)?
在 門口 是 誰？
Zài ménkǒu shì shéi?
Who is outside the door?

In Taiwanese, there is no distinction in case. As a result, 啥人 siáⁿ-lâng can appear both as subject or object within a sentence.

這 張 批，啥人 欲 共 你 寄？
Chit tiuⁿ phoe, siáⁿ-lâng beh kā lí kià?
這 封 信，誰 要 幫 你 寄？
Zhè fēng xìn, shéi yào bāng nǐ jì?
Who is going to send this letter for you?

這張批,我應該寄予<u>啥人</u>?
Chit tiuⁿ phoe, góa eng-kai kià hō <u>siáⁿ-lâng</u>?

這封信,我應該寄到<u>誰</u>?
Zhè fēng xìn, wǒ yīnggāi jì dào <u>shéi</u>?

To <u>whom</u> should I send this letter?

The two-syllable 啥物 **siáⁿ-mıh** 'what' can also be paired with 人 **lâng** 'person' to form 啥物人 **siáⁿ-mıh lâng**. While 甚物人 **sīm-mıh lâng** is also acceptable, 啥貨人 **siáⁿ-hòe lâng** cannot be used to form 'who, whom'.

佇門口是<u>啥物人</u>?
Tī mn̂g-kháu sī <u>siáⁿ-mıh lâng</u>?

在門口是<u>誰</u>?
Zài ménkǒu shì <u>shéi</u>?

<u>Who</u> is outside the door?

20.5.3 Where

For questions inquiring about location, the question word 啥物 **siáⁿ-mıh** 'what' is placed before 所在 **só·-chāi** 'place' to form the interrogative pronoun 啥物所在 **siáⁿ-mıh só·-chāi** 'where', or literally 'what place'.

你上愛的餐廳佇<u>啥物所在</u>?
Lí siōng ài ê chhan-thiaⁿ tī <u>siáⁿ-mıh só·-chāi</u>?

你最愛的餐廳在<u>什麼地方</u>?
Nǐ zuì ài de cāntīng zài <u>shénme dìfāng</u>?

<u>Where</u> is your favorite restaurant?

Additionally, Taiwanese uses another term for the question word 'where', 佗位 **tó-ūi**, which literally means 'which position'. 佗位 **tó-ūi** is also commonly contracted to 佗 **toeh** and **toh** (note the slight changes in pronunciation).

阮的行李佇<u>佗位</u>?
Gún ê hêng-lí tī <u>tó-ūi</u>?

我們的行李在<u>哪裡</u>?
Wǒmen de xínglǐ zài <u>nǎlǐ</u>?

<u>Where</u> is our luggage?

20.5.4 When

For questions inquiring about the time, the question word 啥物 siáⁿ-mih 'what' is placed before 時間 sî-kan 'time' to form the interrogative pronouns 啥物 時間 siáⁿ-mih sî-kan 'when', or literally 'what time'. 啥物 時間 siáⁿ-mih sî-kan can also be abbreviated to 啥物 時 siáⁿ-mih sî. Additionally, alternate forms can be constructed by combining 啥物 siáⁿ-mih 'what' with other words for 'time' including 時陣 sî-chūn and 時後 sî-hāu.

伊 啥物 時間 欲 去 馬來西亞？
I siáⁿ-mih sî-kan beh khì Má-lâi-se-a?
他 什麼 時間 要 去 馬來西亞？
Tā shénme shíjiān yào qù Mǎláixīyà?
<u>When</u> is he going to Malaysia?

你 啥物 時陣 和 朋友 講 話？
Lí siáⁿ-mih sî-chūn hām pêng-iú kóng ōe?
你 什麼 時候 跟 朋友 講 話？
Nǐ shénme shíhòu gēn péngyǒu jiǎng huà?
<u>When</u> do you talk to your friends?

Moreover, other words for 'when' include 當時 tang-sî (also pronounced tiang-sî) and 底時 tī-sî.

恁 爸母 當時 欲 來？
Lín pē-bú tang-sî beh lâi?
你們 父母 何時 要來？
Nǐmen fùmǔ héshí yào lái?
<u>When</u> are your parents coming?

For questions inquiring about the time on the clock, the expression 幾點 kúi tiám 'what time *(clock)*' can be used.

你 訂 幾 點 的 位？
Lí teng kúi tiám ê ūi?
你 訂 幾 點 的 位子？
Nǐ dìng jǐ diǎn de wèizi?
<u>What time</u> did you make a reservation?

Note the Mandarin equivalent to ask the time 幾點鐘 jǐ diǎn zhōng 'What time is it?' asks a different question in Taiwanese, 幾點鐘 kúi tiám-cheng, 'How many hours?'.

請問，這馬 幾 點？
Chhiáⁿ-mñg, chit-má kúi tiám?
請問，現在 幾 點(鐘)？
Qǐngwèn, xiànzài jǐ diǎn(zhōng)?
Excuse me, may I ask what time it is?

猶閣 幾 點鍾 才 會 到？
Iáu-koh kúi tiám-cheng chiah ē kàu?
還有 幾 個 小時 才 會 到？
Háiyǒu jǐ gè xiǎoshí cái huì dào?
How many hours are left before we arrive?

20.5.5 Which

When inquiring about a selection out of a larger set of items, the question word 佗 tó is followed by a number and measure word to form the expression for 'which'.

佗 + *number* + *measure word*

tó + *number* + *measure word*

'which'

佗 一 个 眠床 是 我 的？
Tó chit ê bîn-chhñg sī góa--ê?
哪 (一) 張 床 是 我 的？
Nǎ (yī) zhāng chuáng shì wǒ de?
Which is my bed?

佗 三 本 冊 是 你 的？
Tó saⁿ pún chheh sī lí--ê?
哪 三 本 書 是 你 的？
Nǎ sān běn shū shì nǐ de?
Which three books are yours?

Note that in Mandarin if the selection is a single item, 一 **yī** can be left out of the expression 哪(一) **nǎ(yī)** + *measure word*. However, in Taiwanese a number must always form part of the expression.

For an indeterminate plural number of items in the selection, the plural measure word 寡 **kóa** 'some' can be used in the 'which' expression.

佗 一 寡 是 熟 的？
<u>Tó chit kóa</u> sī se̍k--ê?
哪 (一) 些 是 熟 的？
<u>Nǎ (yī) xiē</u> shì shóu de?
<u>Which ones</u> are ripe?

20.5.6 Why

For questons inquiring about a reason, the question word 哪 **ná** 'why' generally appears after the subject but before the verb.

subject + 哪 + *verb*

subject + <u>ná</u> + *verb*

你 哪 欲 去 病院？
Lí <u>ná</u> beh khì pēⁿ-īⁿ?
你 為甚麼 要 去 醫院？
Nǐ <u>wèishènme</u> yào qù yīyuàn?
<u>Why</u> are you going to the hospital?

Alternate forms to express 'why' include 是按怎 **sī-án-chóaⁿ** (also pronounced **sī-án-noá** and **sī-án-ná**), 為甚物 **ūi-sīm-mih**, and 為啥物 **ūi-siáⁿ-mih**. These question words can be placed either before or after the subject but must occur before the verb. In other contexts, note that 按怎 **án-chóaⁿ** can also mean 'how' *(see 20.5.7 How)*.

ORDER 1

是按怎 + *subject* + *verb*

sī-án-chóaⁿ + *subject* + *verb*

你 是按怎 愛 共 伊 拍？
Lí sī-án-chóaⁿ ài kā i phah?
你 為甚麼 要 打 他？
Nǐ wèishènme yào dǎ tā?
Why did you need to hit him?

ORDER 2

是按怎 + *subject* + *verb*

sī-án-chóaⁿ + *subject* + *verb*

是按怎 你 愛 共 伊 拍？
Sī-án-chóaⁿ lí ài kā i phah?
為甚麼 你 要 打 他？
Wèishènme nǐ yào dǎ tā?
Why did you need to hit him?

In addition, there is a difference in the usage for the character 哪 **ná** 'why' in Taiwanese and 哪 **nǎ** 'where' in Mandarin. In Taiwanese, 哪 **ná** has a broader latitude of uses and meanings. In some expressions, it still retains the idea of 'location'.

哪 有？
Ná ū?
哪 有？
Nǎ yǒu?
Please, you are too kind (*lit. Where is there any? — A phrase used to deflect praise*).

Beyond asking for a simple reason, 哪 **ná** can also convey a strong sense of doubt. In these cases, it is often paired with additional words.

TAIWANESE	MANDARIN	MEANING
哪會 ná-ē	怎麼 會 zěnme huì	Why would?
哪毋 ná-m̄	為什麼 不 wèishéme bù	Why wouldn't?
哪未 ná-bōe	為何 還沒 wèihé háiméi	Why haven't?
哪著 ná-tioh	何須 héxū	Why should?

伊 哪毋 提 錢？

I ná-m̄ theh chîⁿ?

他 為甚麼 不 拿 錢？

Tā wèishènme bù ná qián?

Why wouldn't he take the money?

你 哪未 共 我 敲 電話？

Lí ná-bōe kā góa khà tiān-ōe?

你 為何 還沒 打 電話 給我？

Nǐ wèihé háiméi dǎ diànhuà gěi wǒ?

Why haven't you called me?

For an even stronger sense of disbelief, the word **盍 khah** 'Why would... / How could it be?' may be used in questions seeking a reason.

伊 盍 會 按呢？

I khah ē án-ne?

他 怎麼 會 這樣？

Tā zěnme huì zhèyàng?

Why would he do that? How could it be this way?

20.5.7 How

For questions inquiring about the manner in which an event occurs, the question word **按怎 án-chóaⁿ** (also pronounced **án-nóa** or **án-ná**) 'how' can be used. Alternate forms include **按怎樣 án-chóaⁿ-iūⁿ** and **怎樣 chóaⁿ-iūⁿ**.

你 按怎 做 餅？

Lí án-chóaⁿ chò piáⁿ?

你 怎麼 做 餅乾？

Nǐ zěnme zuò bǐnggān?

How do you make cookies?

你 今仔日 上班 按怎樣？
Lí kin-á-jit sióng-pan án-chóaⁿ-iūⁿ?
你 今天 上班 怎麼樣？
Nǐ jīntiān shàngbān zěnme yàng?
How was work today?

電影 怎樣？
Tiān-iáⁿ chóaⁿ-iūⁿ?
電影 怎樣？
Diànyǐng zěnyàng?
How was the movie?

20.5.8 How much / how many

For questions inquiring about quantity, the question word **偌濟 gōa-chē** (also pronounced **lōa-chē** and **jōa-chē**) 'how much, how many' is used for non-countable items and countable items in larger numbers.

彼 台 電視 偌濟 錢？
Hit tâi tiān-sī gōa-chē chîⁿ?
那 台 電視 多少 錢？
Nà tái diànshì duōshǎo qián?
How much money is that television set?

台北 有 偌濟 人？
Tâi-pak ū gōa-chē lâng?
台北 有 多少 人？
Táiběi yǒu duōshǎo rén?
How many people does Taipei have?

For countable items and smaller quantities (generally under ten) or within an ordered and fixed range of numbers, **幾 kúi** is used with an appropriate measure word.

幾 + *measure word*

kúi + *measure word*

你有幾枝筆?
Lí ū kúi ki pit?
你有幾枝筆?
Nǐ yǒu jǐ zhī bǐ?
How many pens do you have?

這馬幾點?
Chit-má kúi tiám?
現在幾點?
Xiànzài jǐ diǎn?
What time is it?

20.5.9 How long / how big

For questions inquiring about the duration of time, the question word 偌久 gōa-kú (also pronounced lōa-kú and jōa-kú) 'how long *(time)*' is used.

愛偌久才到後一站?
Ài gōa-kú chiah kàu āu chit chām?
要多久才到下一站?
Yào duōjiǔ cái dào xià yī zhàn?
How long until we reach the next station?

For questions inquiring about the physical length of an object, the question word 偌長 gōa-tn̂g (also pronounced lōa-tn̂g and jōa-tn̂g) 'how long *(length)*' is used.

這塊膨椅偌長?
Chit tè phòng-í gōa-tn̂g?
這張沙發多長?
Zhè zhāng shāfā duō cháng?
How long is this sofa?

For questions inquiring about the overall physical size of an object, the question word 偌大 gōa-tōa (also pronounced lōa-tōa and jōa-tōa) 'how big' is used.

恁 厝 偌大?
Lín chhù gōa-tōa?
你 房子 多 大?
Nǐ fángzi duō dà?
How big is your house?

20.5.10 Whose

To change any of the question words for 'who' into the possessive form 'whose', the possessive marker **的 ê** can be added to form **啥人的 siá^n-lâng (siâng) ê** or **啥物人的 siá^n-mı̍h lâng ê**.

啥人 的 翕相機 佇 遮?
Siá^n-lâng (siâng) ê hip-siōng-ki tī chia?
誰 的 照相機 在 這裡?
Shéi de zhàoxiàngjī zài zhèlǐ?
Whose camera is this?

彼 塊 雞卵糕 是 啥物人 的?
Hit tè ke-nn̄g-ko sī siá^n-mı̍h lâng--ê?
這 塊 蛋糕 是 誰 的?
Zhè kuài dàngāo shì shéi de?
Whose piece of cake is this?

20.5.11 Summary of question words

TAIWANESE	MANDARIN
WHAT	
啥 siá^n	甚麼 shénme
啥物 siá^n-mih	甚麼 shénme
啥貨 siá^n-hòe	甚麼 shénme
甚物 sīm-mih	甚麼 shénme
WHO / WHOM	
啥人 siá^n-lâng (siâng)	誰 shéi
啥物人 siá^n-mih lâng	誰 shéi
甚物人 sím-mih lâng	誰 shéi
WHERE	
啥物所在 siá^n-mih só·-chāi	什麼地方 shénme dìfāng
甚物所在 sím-mih só·-chāi	什麼地方 shénme dìfāng
佗位 tó-ūi	哪裡 nǎlǐ
佗 toeh / toh	哪裡 nǎlǐ
WHEN (GENERAL)	
啥物時(間) siá^n-mih sî(-kan)	什麼時候 shénme shíhòu
甚物時(間) sím-mih sî(-kan)	什麼時候 shénme shíhòu
啥物時(陣) siá^n-mih sî(-chūn)	什麼時候 shénme shíhòu
甚物時(陣) sím-mih sî(-chūn)	什麼時候 shénme shíhòu
啥物時(後) siá^n-mih sî(-hāu)	什麼時候 shénme shíhòu
甚物時(後) sím-mih sî(-hāu)	什麼時候 shénme shíhòu
當時 tang-sî	何時 héshí
底時 tī-sî	何時 héshí
WHEN (CLOCK TIME)	
幾點 kúi tiám	幾點 jǐ diǎn

TAIWANESE	MANDARIN
WHICH ONE	
佗 tó + *number* + *measure word*	哪 nǎ + *number* + *measure word*
WHICH ONES	
佗一寡 tó chit-kóa	哪些 nǎxiē
WHY (REASON)	
哪 ná	為甚麼 wèishènme
是按怎 sī-án-chóaⁿ (sī-án-noá, sī-án-ná)	為甚麼 wèishènme
為甚物 ūi-sīm-mih	為甚麼 wèishènme
為啥物 ūi-siáⁿ-mih	為甚麼 wèishènme
WHY (DISBELIEF)	
哪會 ná-ē	怎麼會 zěnme huì
哪毋 ná m̄	為什麼不 wèishéme bù
哪未 ná-bōe	為何還沒 wèihé háiméi
哪著 ná-tioh	何須 héxū
盍 khah	怎麼 zěnme
HOW (MANNER)	
按怎 án-chóaⁿ (án-nóa, án-ná)	怎麼 zěnme
按怎樣 án-chóaⁿ-iūⁿ	怎麼樣 zěnme yàng
怎樣 chóaⁿ-iūⁿ	怎樣 zěnyàng
HOW MUCH / MANY	
偌濟 gōa-chē (lōa-chē, jōa-chē)	多少 duōshǎo
幾 kúi + *measure word*	幾 jǐ + *measure word*
HOW LONG (TIME)	
偌久 gōa-kú (lōa-kú, jōa-kú)	多久 duōjiǔ
HOW LONG (LENGTH)	
偌長 gōa-tn̂g (lōa-tn̂g, jōa-tn̂g)	多長 duōcháng
HOW BIG (SIZE)	
偌大 gōa-tōa (lōa-tōa, jōa-tōa)	多大 duōdà

21 Requests and commands

Requests and commands in Taiwanese can be constructed in a number of ways using particles, aspect markers, modal verbs, polite phrases, and special grammatical constructions.

21.1 Particle 咧 --leh

The static continuous aspect marker 咧 **--leh** can be suffixed to verbs in commands in which the listener is requested to maintain a current or imminent state *(see 8.2.2 Static continuous aspect)*. When used within commands, the particle 咧 **--leh** does not need to occur at the end of a clause or sentence.

verb + 咧

verb + --leh

共 我 手 牽咧。
Kā góa chhiú khan--leh.
把 我 手 握著。
Bǎ wǒ shǒu wòzhe.
Take my hand.

遮 囥咧 就 好。
Chia khǹg--leh tō hó.
這裡 放著 就 好。
Zhèlǐ fàngzhe jiù hǎo.
Just put it here.

乖咧！
Koai--leh!
你 乖乖！
Nǐ guāiguāi!
Be good!

Note that Mandarin similarly uses the particle 著 -zhe in commands.

For adjectives, 較 **khah** 'more' is often added before the adjective to express 'be a little more *adjective*'.

較 + *adjective* + 咧

khah + *adjective* + --leh

'be a little more *adjective*'

較 細聲咧！
Khah sè-sian--leh!
小聲 一點！
Xiǎo shēng yīdiǎn!
Be a little quieter!

較 清氣咧！
Khah chheng-khì--leh!
乾淨 一點！
Gānjìng yīdiǎn!
Be a little cleaner!

Note that in Mandarin, the equivalent expression places 一點 yīdiǎn 'a little bit' after the adjective.

21.2 Using 去 khì 'to go' in commands

The verb 去 **khì** 'to go' can be placed before action or active stative verbs to command or suggest doing an action *(see 7 Action verbs, 9.3 Stative verbs and continuous aspect)*. Adjectives and passive stative verbs cannot be made into commands with this form.

去 + *action / stative (active) verb*

khì + *action / stative (active) verb*

'go *action / stative (active) verb*'

你看起來真忝,緊去睏。

Lí khòaⁿ-khí-lâi chin thiám, kín <u>khì</u> khùn.

你看起來很累,快去睡。

Nǐ kànqǐlái hěn lèi, kuài <u>qù</u> shuì.

You look very tired. <u>Go</u> to sleep now.

去想著別的辦法。

<u>Khì</u> siūⁿ-tio̍h pa̍t ê pān-hoat.

去想到別的辦法。

<u>Qù</u> xiǎngdào bié de bànfǎ.

<u>Go</u> think of another way to do it.

21.3 Using the tentative aspect

The tentative aspect can describe actions that are done 'for a little while' or 'to try out and see' *(see 8.6 Tentative aspect)*. As a result, the tentative aspect is often used as a polite way to make commands. Two of the methods for indicating the tentative aspect are often employed in commands: reduplicating the verb and adding the phrase 一下 **--chi̍t-ē** 'a little bit'.

21.3.1 Verb reduplication

Reduplication has the effect of putting a verb into the tentative aspect, which can indicate that a verb is performed for a short period of time. Note that when verbs are repeated in a command, the second verb is put in the neutral tone.

verb + verb

'doing *verb* for a while'

你 的 手 <u>洗洗</u> 予 清氣！

Lí ê chhiú <u>sé--sé</u> hō͘ chheng-khì!

你 的 手 <u>洗洗</u> 乾淨！

Nǐ de shǒu <u>xǐxǐ</u> gānjìng!

<u>Wash</u> your hands until they're clean!

先 <u>哺哺</u> 才 吞落去。

Seng <u>pō͘--pō͘</u> chiah thun--lȯh-khì.

先 <u>咬咬</u> 才 吞下去。

Xiān <u>yǎoyǎo</u> cái tūnxiàqù.

First <u>chew</u>, and then swallow.

The particle 咧 **--leh** may also be added to reduplicated verbs for additional emphasis.

verb + *verb* + 咧

verb + *verb* + --leh

青菜 食食 咧！

Chheⁿ-chhài chiȧh--chiȧh--leh!

青菜 吃吃 吧！

Qīngcài chīchī ba!

Eat up the vegetables!

咱 先 遮 坐坐 咧。

Lán seng chia chē--chē--leh.

我們 先 這裡 坐坐 吧。

Wǒmen xiān zhèlǐ zuòzuò ba.

Let's sit here first.

Note that in Mandarin if the verb is reduplicated for a command, the particle 吧 **ba** is used instead of the suffix 著 **-zhe**.

21.3.2 Adding the phrase 一下 --chit-ē 'a little bit'

The phrase 一下 --chit-ē 'a little bit' is used as a softener for commands and may be placed after a verb. The phrase 一下 --chit-ē is put in the neutral tone.

> verb + 一下
>
> verb + --chit-ē
>
> '*verb* a little bit'

> 等 一下。
>
> Tán--chit-ē.
>
> 等 一下。
>
> Děng yīxià.
>
> Wait a little bit.

> 看 一下！
>
> Khòaⁿ--chit-ē!
>
> 看 一下！
>
> Kàn yīxià!
>
> Take a quick look!

小 sió 'small' may be added before the verb to further diminish the size of the request.

> 小 + verb + 一下
>
> sió + verb + --chit-ē

> 小 等 一下。
>
> Sió tán--chit-ē.
>
> 稍 等 一下。
>
> Shāo děng yīxià.
>
> Please wait briefly.

恁 小 歇睏 一下。

Lín sió hioh-khùn--chi̍t-ē.

你們 稍 休息 一下。

Nǐmen shāo xiūxí yīxià.

You should all rest a bit.

21.4 Polite words and phrases

Additional words and phrases may be added to make requests more polite.

21.4.1 請 chhiá^n 'please'

請 chhiá^n 'please' can be placed at the beginning of the sentence. A second person pronoun may also be used or omitted when making a request.

請 + *(second person pronoun)* + *verb*

chhiá^n + *(second person pronoun)* + *verb*

'Please *verb*'

請 坐 踮 遮 等 一下。

Chhiá^n chē tàm chia tán--chi̍t-ē.

請 坐 在 這裡 等 一下。

Qǐng zuò zài zhèlǐ děng yīxià.

Please sit here for a moment.

請 大家 排隊。

Chhiá^n ta-ke pâi-tūi.

請 大家 排隊。

Qǐng dàjiā páiduì.

Everyone please make a line.

請問 **chhiá^n-mn̄g** 'May I ask' is a common phrase to begin an inquiry.

> 請問 便所 佇 佗位?
> Chhiá^n-mn̄g piān-só͘ tī tó-ūi?
> 請問 廁所 在 哪裡?
> Qǐngwèn cèsuǒ zài nǎlǐ?
> May I ask where the bathrooms are?

Note that 請 **chhiá^n** can be used to mean 'to invite', 'to pay for (someone else)', or 'to ask someone to do something'. When used with these meanings, 請 **chhiá^n** often appears in the middle of the sentence.

> 恁 請 阮 食 飯 佇 真 高級 的 餐廳。
> In chhiá^n gún chia̍h pn̄g tī chin ko-kip ê chhan-thia^n.
> 他們 請 我們 吃 飯 在 很 高級 的 餐廳。
> Tāmen qǐng wǒmen chī fàn zài hěn gāojí de canting.
> They invited us to eat at a very fancy restaurant.

> 你 敢 會當 請 恁 小妹 共 我 提 便當?
> Lí kám ē-tàng chhiá^n lín sió-mōe kā góa the̍h piān-tong?
> 你 能 請 你的 妹妹 幫 我 拿 便當 嗎?
> Nǐ néng qǐng nǐ de mèimei bāng wǒ ná biàndāng ma?
> Can you ask your younger sister to bring a lunchbox for me?

請教 **chhéng-kàu** 'May I ask (for your advice)?' is another polite expression used to inquire about advice, suggestions, comments, or directions.

> 請教 一下, 阮 按怎 去 博物館?
> Chhéng-kàu chit-ē, gún án-chóa^n khì phok-bu̍t-kóan?
> 請教 一下, 我們 怎麼 去 博物館?
> Qǐngjiào yīxià, wǒmen zěnme qù bówùguǎn?
> May I ask how we can get to the museum?

21.4.2 麻煩你 Mâ-hôan lí 'May I trouble you'

麻煩 **mâ-hôan** 'troublesome' can be placed before a second person pronoun to create the phrase 麻煩你 **Mâ-hôan lí** 'May I trouble you'. This phrase is used in situations where the speaker requests the listener to do something that benefits someone other than the listener. An alternate form is 勞煩 **lô-hôan**.

麻煩 + *second person pronoun* + *verb*

mâ-hôan + *second person pronoun* + *verb*

'May I trouble you to *verb*'

麻煩 你 去 郵局 寄 這 張 批？

Mâ-hôan lí khì iû-kiók kià chit tiu^n phoe?

麻煩 你 去 郵局 寄 這 封 信？

Máfan nǐ qù yóujú jì zhè fēng xìn?

May I trouble you to go to the post office to mail this letter?

麻煩 恁 㤉 阮 後生 去 學校？

Mâ-hôan lín chhōa gún hāu-se^n khì ha̍k-hāu?

麻煩 你們 帶 我 兒子 去 學校？

Máfan nǐmen dài wǒ érzi qù xuéxiào?

May I trouble you to take my son to school?

21.4.3 拜託 pài-thok 'please'

拜託 **pài-thok** 'please' is a polite way to begin a request similar to 請 **chhiá^n** 'please'. However, 拜託 **pài-thok** at times can have a slightly stronger sense of urgency.

拜託 + *(second person pronoun)* + *verb*

pài-thok + *(second person pronoun)* + *verb*

'Please, *verb*'

拜託 你 共 阮 鬥 搬厝。

Pài-thok lí kā gún tàu poa^n-chhù.

拜託 你 幫 我們 搬家。

Bàituō nǐ bāng wǒmen bānjiā.

Please help us move.

拜託你共你的車借予我。

Pài-thok lí kā lí ê chhia chioh hō͘ góa.

拜託你借給我你的車。

Bàituō nǐ jiè gěi wǒ nǐ de chē.

<u>Please</u> lend me your car.

Additionally, **拜託 pài-thok** can appear independently. In this case, the meaning is more akin to pleading, 'I'm begging you' or 'Please!'. At times this can be done in a sarcastic tone as in, 'Come on!' or 'Please!'.

我的錢包拍毋見,你敢會當予我上車? 拜托!

Góa ê chîⁿ-pau phah-m̄-kìⁿ, lí kám ē-tàng hō͘ góa chiūⁿ-chhia? <u>Pài-thok</u>!

我的錢包不見了,你能不能讓我上車? 拜託!

Wǒ de qiánbāo bùjiàn le, nǐ néngbùnéng ràng wǒ shàngchē? <u>Bàituō</u>!

I lost my wallet. Can you just let me ride the bus? <u>Please</u>!

拜托! 你敢真正想我會信這个藉口?

<u>Pài-thok</u>! Lí kám chin-chiàⁿ siūⁿ góa ē sìn chit ê chioh-kháu?

拜託! 你真是想我會相信這個藉口嗎?

<u>Bàituō</u>! Nǐ zhēnshi xiǎng wǒ huì xiāngxìn zhège jièkǒu ma?

<u>Please</u>! Do you really expect me to believe this excuse?

21.4.4 歹勢 pháiⁿ-sè 'apologies'

歹勢 pháiⁿ-sè which means 'sorry' and 'my apologies' indicates embarrassment and remorse. However, **歹勢 pháiⁿ-sè** can be used to politely make a request by asking to be excused beforehand.

歹勢 + *verb*

pháiⁿ-sè + *verb*

'I'm sorry to ask you to *verb*'

歹勢 叫 你 和 我 換 位。
Pháiⁿ-sè kiò lí hām góa ōaⁿ ūi.
不好意思 叫 你 和 我 換 位子。
Bùhǎoyìsi jiào nǐ hé wǒ huàn wèizi.
I'm sorry to ask you to switch seats with me.

歹勢 叫 你 替 我 用 中文 共 文件 寫好。
Pháiⁿ-sè kiò lí theh góa ēng Tiong-bûn kā bûn-kiāⁿ siá-hó.
不好意思 叫 你 幫 我 用 中文 把 文件 寫好。
Bùhǎoyìsi jiào nǐ bāng wǒ yòng Zhōngwén bǎ wénjiàn xiěhǎo.
Excuse me. I'm embarrassed to ask you to help me fill out this form in Chinese.

歹勢 **pháiⁿ-sè** does not have an exact Mandarin equivalent but can be used in contexts where 不好意思 **bùhǎoyìsi**, 對不起 **duìbùqǐ**, and 抱歉 **bàoqiàn** are often used.

21.5 Modal verbs in requests

The modal verbs expressing 'permission' (會當 **ē-tàng**, 會使(得) **ē-sái(-tit)**, 會用得 **ē-ēng-tit**) can be used in questions to make polite requests *(see 12.4. Permission)*.

我 敢 會使 系 一 个 朋友 來 和 咱 食 飯？
Góa kám ē-sài chhōa chi̍t ê pêng-iú lâi hām lán chia̍h pn̄g?
我 可不可以 帶 一 個 朋友 來 跟 我們 一起 吃 飯？
Wǒ kěbùkěyǐ dài yī gè péngyǒu lái gēn wǒmen yīqǐ chī fàn?
May I bring a friend to dinner with us?

你 敢 會當 紮 你 的 翕相機？
Lí kám ē-tàng chah lí ê hip-siōng-ki?
你 能不能 帶 你 的 照相機？
Nǐ néngbùnéng dài nǐ de zhàoxiàngjī?
Can you take your camera with you?

阮 拜五 會用得 去 游泳池 無？
Gún pài-gō͘ ē-ēng-tit khì iû-éng-tî--bô?
我們 禮拜五 能 去 游泳池 嗎？
Wǒmen lǐbàiwǔ néng qù yóuyǒngchí ma?
Can we go to the pool on Friday?

21.6 Group proposals

For proposals to a group including the speaker, the phrase 咱來(去) **lán lâi(-khì)** 'Let's…..' can be placed before the verb.

咱來(去) + *verb*

lán lâi(-khì) + *verb*

'Let's *verb*'

咱 下晡 來去 動物園！
Lán ē-po͘ lâi-khì tōng-bu̍t-hn̂g!
我們 下午 去 動物園 吧！
Wǒmen xiàwǔ qù dòngwùyuán ba!
Let's go to the zoo this afternoon!

咱 來 歇睏。
Lán lâi hioh-khùn.
我們 來 休息 吧。
Wǒmen lái xiūxí ba.
Let's take a break.

Mandarin only needs to use the end-of-sentence particle 吧 **ba** to make a group suggestion. Taiwanese does not have an exact equivalent particle to 吧 **ba** when used in this manner. At the same time, Mandarin does have an equivalent to the Taiwanese phrase and can also use 我們來 **wǒmen lái** to convey the group suggestion 'Let's…'

21.7 Negative commands

Negative modal verbs are often used in negative commands, which demand or request an action not to happen. Taiwanese has three modal verbs that can be used to prohibit an action *(see 12.6 Prohibition)*.

The combination of the negative 毋 **m̄** and 愛 **ài** produces a phonetic blend 莫 **mài** with only the prohibitive meaning 'do not'. 莫 **mài** can only be used in the second person to prohibit or advise against an action.

莫 + *verb*

mài + *verb*

'do not *verb*'

莫 拍 狗!

<u>Mài</u> phah káu!

別 打 狗!

<u>Bié</u> dǎ gǒu!

<u>Don't</u> hit the dog!

毋通 m̄-thang is the negative form of the polite permission modal verb **通 thang** 'may'. However, when used in the negative the modal verb can only function as a negative command. Note that **毋通 m̄-thang** is less emphatic in tone than **莫 mài**.

毋通 + *verb*

m̄-thang + *verb*

'do not *verb*'

你 毋通 卦 電話!

Lí <u>m̄-thang</u> kòa tiān-ōe!

你 別 掛 電話!

Nǐ <u>bié</u> guà diànhuà!

<u>Don't</u> hang up the phone!

毋好 m̄-hó also means 'do not' and is generally interchangeable with **毋通 m̄-thang**. Sometimes contracted **毋好 m̄-hó** may sound like **'m̄-mo'**.

毋好 + *verb*

m̄-hó + *verb*

'do not *verb*'

毋好 啉 酒。
M̄-hó lim chiú.
不要 喝 酒。
Bùyào hē jiǔ.
Don't drink alcohol.

Note that Mandarin modal verbs for prohibition **不要 bùyào** and **別 bié** are similar in tone and only differentiated in strength by one's speech volume.

21.8 Using causative verbs in commands

Because causative verbs cause (by request, command, or allowance) someone to perform an action, causative verbs naturally lend themselves to be used in commands *(see 19.4 Causative verbs)*. In English, the verbs 'make' or 'have' are commonly used to convey that an action was 'caused' to happen ('My mom made me clean my room' or 'We had the bellboy take the luggage to our room'). In Taiwanese, the verb 予 hō͘ 'to give' or 'to allow' is a causative verb that can be used as a command. With this usage, 予 hō͘ precedes an outcome or extent that is desired and roughly conveys 'such that...' or 'to the point of'. Note that 予 hō͘ can also be used in non-commands for extent complements *(see 11.7.2 Extent complements with 予 hō͘)*.

verb + 予 + *desired outcome*

verb + hō͘ + *desired outcome*

'*verb* such that *desired outcome*'

功課 寫 予 了!
Kong-khò siá hō͘ liáu!
功課 寫完!
Gōngkè xiěwán!
Finish your homework!

窗仔 拭 予 清氣!
Thang-á chhit hō͘ chheng-khì!
窗戶 擦 乾淨!
Chuānghù cā gānjìng!
Wipe the windows clean!

Note that Mandarin tends to use a resultative complement to indicate an outcome or extent.

21.9 Using the 共 kā construction in commands

The 共 **kā** construction can be used to indicate how an object is handled or manipulated *(see 17.4 共 kā construction)*. As a result, this construction is often used in commands.

共 + *object* + *verb*

kā + *object* + *verb*

'take the *object* and *verb*'

共 遮的 冊 還 圖書館。
Kā chia-ê chheh hêng tô·-su-kóan.
把這些書還圖書館。
Bǎ zhè xiē shū huán túshūguǎn.
Take these books back to the library.

共 雞卵 囥 踮 冰箱內。
Kā ke-nn̄g khǹg tàm peng-siun-lāi.
把雞蛋放在冰箱裡。
Bǎ jīdàn fàng zài bīngxiāng lǐ.
Put the eggs in the refrigerator.

22 Particles

Some particles help to convey the speaker's attitude or tone, while other particles have grammatical functions such as marking aspect or question type.

Particles can also be subdivided according to their placement within a sentence. End-of-sentence particles can indicate tone, aspect, and question type. On the other hand, exclamatory particles occur at the beginning of sentences or as stand-alone exclamations. These particles tend to only indicate the speaker's attitude or tone.

Moreover, a few particles can function both as an end-of-sentence particle and exclamatory particle. However, note that the meaning conveyed may differ depending on the position within the sentence.

22.1 End-of-sentence particles

End-of-sentence particles appear at the end of a clause or sentence and can convey the speaker's tone, mark aspect, or indicate question type.

Generally, these particles are placed in the neutral tone. Additionally, note that it is possible to have several particles in succession at the end of a sentence—all in the neutral tone.

22.1.1 Single particles

Below is a table of some common end-of-sentence particles. Particles in this table have been subcategorized into those used primarily to mark tone, aspect, or question type *(see 8 Aspect, 20 Questions)*.

TAIWANESE	MANDARIN	MEANING	EXAMPLE
矣 --ah	了 le	new or relevant situation *(anterior aspect)*	我 看著 矣。 Góa khòaⁿ--tio̍h--ah. 我 感冒 了。 Wǒ gǎnmào le. I've caught a cold.
啊 --ah	啊 a	affirmation, approval *(tone)*	揀上細的就好阿。 Kéng siōng sè--ê tō hó--ah. 挑最小的就好啊。 Tiāo zuì xiǎo de jiù hǎo a. Picking the smallest one will be fine.
袂 --bē	會不會 huìbùhuì	possible or future action *(question)*	阿爸會去買菜袂? A-pa ē khì bé chhài--bē? 爸爸會不會去買菜? Bàba huìbùhuì qù mǎi cài? Will dad go buy the vegetables?
(抑)免 (iah-)bián	還是不用 háishì bùyòng	obligation *(question)*	咱愛加油抑免? Lán ài ka-iû iah-bián? 我們需要加油還是不用? Wǒmen xūyào jiāyóu háishì bùyòng? Do we need to fill gas or not?

TAIWANESE	MANDARIN	MEANING	EXAMPLE
無 --bô	了沒有 le méiyǒu	completed action (*perfective aspect*)	伊有食藥仔無？ I ū chiảh ioh-á--bô? 他吃了藥沒有？ Tā chīle yào méiyǒu? Did he take his medicine?
	嗎 ma	neutral (*question*)	你啉酒無？ Lí lim chiú--bô? 你喝酒嗎？ Nǐ hē jiǔ ma? Do you drink alcohol?
未 --bōe (bē)	了嗎 le ma	relevant situation (*anterior aspect*)	彼間新餐廳開門未？ Hit keng sin chhan-thiaⁿ khui-mน̂g--bōe? 那間新餐廳開門了嗎？ Nà jiān xīn cāntīng kāimén le ma? Has that new restaurant opened yet?
乎 --hoⁿh	吧 ba	seeking confirmation (*question*)	你講欲草莓乎？ Lí kóng beh chháu-m̂--hoⁿh? 你說要草莓吧？ Nǐ shuō yào cǎoméi ba? You said you wanted strawberries, right?
啦 --lah	啦 la	contentment or impatience (*tone*)	停遮就好啦！ Thêng chia tō hó--lah! 停這裡就好啦！ Tíng zhèlǐ jiù hǎo la! Stopping here is good enough!

TAIWANESE	MANDARIN	MEANING	EXAMPLE
咧 --leh	呢 ne	'What about....' (question)	恁 小妹 咧? Lín sió-mōe--leh? 你 妹妹 呢? Nǐ mèimei ne? What about your younger sister?
	著 zhe	holding a posture (continuous aspect)	伊 佇 遐 坐咧。 I tī hia chē--leh. 她 在 那裡 坐著。 Tā zài nàlǐ zuòzhe. She's sitting over there.
囉 --loh	囉 luo	affirmation, obviousness (tone)	伊 做完 囉。 I chò-ôan--loh. 她 做完 囉。 Tā zuòwán luō. She's done.
毋 --m̄	要不要 yàobùyào	volition (question)	伊 啉 果汁 毋? I lim kó-chiap--m̄? 她 喝不喝 果汁? Tā hēbùhē guǒzhī? Does she want to drink juice?
嘛 --mah	嘛 ma	exasperation, impatience (tone)	伊 袂 接, 你 莫 閣 敲 嘛! I bē chiap, lí mài koh khà--mah! 他 不會 接, 你 不要 再 打 嘛! Tā bù huì jiē, nǐ bù yào zài dǎ ma! He won't answer, stop calling!

TAIWANESE	MANDARIN	MEANING	EXAMPLE
嘛 --mah *(cont.)*	嗎 ma	neutral *(question)*	你 啉 酒 嘛？ Lí lim chiú--mah? 你 喝 酒 嗎？ Nǐ hē jiǔ ma? <u>Do</u> you drink alcohol?
呢 --neh	耶 ye	enthusiasm, praise, encouragement *(tone)*	伊 足 媠 呢！ I chiok súi--neh! 她 非常 漂亮 耶！ Tā fēicháng piàoliang ye! She's so pretty!
--nih	對吧 duì ba	confirmation *(question)*	恁 蹛 遮 呢？ In tòa chia--nih? 他們 住 這裡 對 吧？ Tāmen zhù zhèlǐ duì ba? They live here, right?
喔 --oh	喔 wō	reminding, urging *(tone)*	恁 較 早 轉來 喔。 Lín khah chá tńg--lâi--oh. 你們 早 一 點 回來 喔。 Nǐmen zǎo yīdiǎn huílái wō. You should come home earlier.

22.1.2 Double particles

In some cases, it is possible to have two end-of-sentence particles appended to the end of a clause or sentence. For this to occur, the first particle is generally an aspect marker (矣 --ah, 咧 --leh), while the second particle is a tone or question particle. Note that both particles are placed in the neutral tone.

aspect particle + tone/question particle

較緊咧啦!
Khah kín--leh--lah!
快一點啦!
Kuài yīdiǎn la!
Hurry up!

好矣啦!
Hó--ah--lah!
好了啦!
Hǎo le la!
That's enough!

22.2 Exclamatory particles

Some particles can appear as an exclamation at the beginning of the sentence or as a stand-alone exclamation. In general, exclamatory particles only convey the speaker's tone or attitude.

TAIWANESE	MANDARIN	MEANING	EXAMPLE
啊 ah	啊 ā	surprise ('Ah!' 'Oh!')	啊!你贏錢! Ah! Lí iâⁿ chîⁿ! 啊!你贏錢! Ā! Nǐ yíng qián! Oh! You won money!
	啊 à	recognition ('Oh, it's you!'), reluctance ('Oh, okay')	啊!是你寫的! Ah! Sī lí siá--ê! 啊!是你寫的! Ā! Shì nǐ xiě de! Oh, you wrote it!
噯 aih	哎 āi	sadness, regret, (sigh)	噯,團隊閣輸去。 Aih, thôan-tūi koh su--khì. 哎,團隊又輸了。 Āi, tuánduì yòu shūle. Ah, the team lost again.

TAIWANESE	MANDARIN	MEANING	EXAMPLE
哎唷 aih-ioh	哎唷 āi yō	pain or surprise ('Oh no!')	哎唷! 我 的 錢 拍毋見 矣! Aih-ioh! Góa ê chîⁿ phah-m̄-kìⁿ--ah! 哎唷!我 的 錢 不見 了! Āi yō! Wǒ de qián bùjiàn le! Oh no! My money is missing!
欸 eh	咦 yí	contrary to expectation ('Huh?')	欸？是按怎 愛 做 按呢？ Eh? Sī-án-chóaⁿ ài chò án-ne? 咦？為甚麼 要 做 這樣？ Yí? Wèishènme yào zuò zhèyàng? Huh? Why is it done like this?
喂 eh (oeh)	喂 wèi	calling attention ('Hey!')	喂! 過來! Eh! Kòe--lâi! 喂! 過來! Wèi! Guòlái! Hey! Come over!
唉 haih	哎 āi	sadness, regret, (gasp)	唉，團隊 閣 輸去! Haih, thôan-tūi koh su--khì! 哎，團隊 又 輸了! Āi, tuánduì yòu shūle! Ah, the team lost again!
哈 haⁿh	啊 a	surprise ('What?', 'Huh?')	哈？伊 和 總統 講話？ Haⁿh? I hām chóng-thóng kóng ōe? 啊？她 跟 總統 講話？ A? Tā gēn zǒngtǒng jiǎng huà? What? She spoke to the president?

TAIWANESE	MANDARIN	MEANING	EXAMPLE
嘿 he^{n}h (heh)	是 shì	acknowledgement	嘿，嘿，嘿，我 知影 啦。 He^{n}h, he^{n}h, he^{n}h, góa chai-iá^n-lah. 是，是，是，我 知道 啦。 Shì, shì, shì, wǒ zhīdào la. Yes, yes, yes, I know, I know.
諾 hioh	哦 ò	realization, understanding ('Oh')	諾，是 按呢 才 會當 拍開。 Hioh, sī án-ne chiah ē-tàng phah-khui. 哦，是 這樣 才 能 打開。 Ò, shì zhèyàng cái néng dǎkāi. Oh, it needs to be like this to open.
哼 hngh (hmh)	哼 hēng	disdain, contempt ('Hmph!')	哼！遮 我 袂 閣 來。 Hngh! Chia góa bē koh lâi. 哼！這裡 我 不 會 再 來。 Hēng! Zhèlǐ wǒ bù huì zài lái. Hmph! I will never come here again.
	哼 hēng	surprise ('Huh?')	哼？是按怎 愛 做 按呢？ Hngh? Sī-án-chóa^n ài chò án-ne? 哼？為甚麼 要 做 這樣？ Hēng? Wèishènme yào zuò zhèyàng? Huh? Why is it done like this?
乎 ho^{n}h	哦 ò	realization, understanding ('Oh')	乎，是 按呢 才 會當 拍開。 Ho^{n}h, sī án-ne chiah ē-tàng phah-khui. 哦，是 這樣 才 能 打開。 Ò, shì zhèyàng cái néng dǎkāi. Oh, it needs to be like this to open.

TAIWANESE	MANDARIN	MEANING	EXAMPLE
謼 hoʽh	喔 ō	resentment	謼，袂使 超過 一 點鐘。 <u>Hoʽh</u>, bē-sái chhiau-kòe chit tiám-cheng. 喔，不 可以 超過 一 個 小時。 <u>Ō</u>, bù kěyǐ chāoguò yī gè xiǎoshí. <u>Fine</u>, no more than one hour.
	喔 ō	astonishment	謼，伊 食 遐爾 濟！ <u>Hoʽh</u>, i chiảh hiah-nī chē! 喔，他 吃 那麼 多！ <u>Ō</u>, tā chī nàme duō! <u>Oh</u>, he ate that much!
喂 oeh	喂 wéi	answering phone ('Hello?')	喂？你 好。 <u>Oeh</u>? Lí hó. 喂？你 好。 <u>Wéi</u>? Nǐ hǎo. <u>Hello</u>? How are you?
喔 oʽh	喔 ō	reluctance ('Ugh!')	喔，莫 叫 我 食 菜！ <u>Oʽh</u>, mài kiò góa chiảh chhài! 喔，不 要 叫 我 吃 菜！ <u>Ō</u>, bù yào jiào wǒ chī cài! <u>Ugh</u>, don't make me eat vegetables!
	哦 ò	surprise, realization ('Oh')	喔，是 按呢 才 會當 拍開。 <u>Oʽh</u>, sī án-ne chiah ē-tàng phah-khui. 哦，是 這樣 才 能 打開。 <u>Ò</u>, shì zhèyàng cái néng dǎkāi. <u>Oh</u>, it needs to be like this to open.

23 Terms of address

Terms of address vary according to degree of familiarity and level of respect. Through the use of a combination of title, kinship term, surname, and/or given name, terms of address can be adjusted to reflect the appropriate degree of formality and familiarity.

23.1 Social niceties

23.1.1 Greetings

The general greeting 你好 **Lí hó** 'Hello' can be used with both strangers and acquaintances and is either stated with a slight bow or repeated with multiple quick nods of the head. A more polite method of greeting can be formed with an appropriate term of address followed by 好 **hó**.

> term of address + 好
> term of address + hó
> 'Hello, term of address'

老師 好。
Lāu-su hó.
老师 好。
Lǎoshī hǎo.
Hello, Teacher.

王 小姐 好。
Ông sió-chiá hó.
王 小姐 好。
Wáng xiǎojiě hǎo.
Hello, Ms. Ong.

大叔 好。
Tōa chek hó.
大叔 好。
Dàshū hǎo.
Hello, Uncle.

The phrase 食飽未? **Chia̍h-pá--bōe?** 'Have you eaten yet?' is a traditional way of greeting a guest. This greeting originates from the cultural tradition of a host ensuring that his or her guests are well-fed and looked after. Other variations on the question can be used such as '你敢食飽? **Lí kám chia̍h-pá?**' or '你食好未? **Lí chia̍h-hó--bōe?**' Similar to the greeting in English, 'How are you?', the question generally is asked out of politeness and custom rather than truly inquiring about one's state of hunger. Typically, a response to the question is a simple affirmation of having already eaten such as **'有矣' 食飽 ū--ah, chia̍h-pá'**.

歡迎 Hoan-gêng 'Welcome' is the general expression to welcome a guest. The two traditional expressions **失敬 Sit-kèng** and **失迎 Sit-gêng** now find limited usage in more formal contexts.

TAIWANESE	MANDARIN	MEANING
你好。Lí hó.	你好。Nǐ hǎo.	Hello.
喂？Oeh?	喂？Wéi?	Hello? (*telephone*).
你好無？Lí hó--bô?	你好？Nǐ hǎo ma?	How are you?
食飽未？Chia̍h-pá--bōe?	吃飽了嗎？Chībǎo le ma?	How are you? (*lit. Have you eaten?*)
歡迎。Hoan-gêng.	歡迎。Huānyíng.	Welcome.
失敬。Sit-kèng.	失敬。Shī jìng.	Welcome (*polite*) (*lit. Excuse me for being disrespectful*).
失迎。Sit-gêng.	失迎。Shī yíng.	Welcome (*polite*) (*lit. Excuse me for not greeting you personally*).
賢早。Gâu-chá.	早安。Zǎo ān.	Good morning.
午安。Ngó͘-an.	午安。Wǔ ān.	Good afternoon.

Note that Taiwanese does not have a direct equivalent of the Mandarin polite form of the singular second person pronoun 您 **nín** 'you (*polite*)' to form the expression 您好 **Nín hǎo** 'Hello (*polite*)'.

23.1.2 Giving thanks

多謝 to-siā 'Thank you' is the most common form of expressing gratitude, while **感恩 kám-un** and **感謝 kám-siā** are slightly more formal in tone. These terms can be used independently or followed by the reason for offering thanks.

非常 感謝 你 來 機場 共 我 接。
Hui-siông kám-siā lí lâi ki-tiûⁿ kā góa chiap.
非常 感謝 你 來 機場 接 我。
Fēicháng gǎnxiè nǐ lái jīchǎng jiē wǒ.
Thank you very much for picking me up at the airport.

Responses to offerings of thanks play down the importance or magnitude of the gesture generally with meanings like 免客氣 **Bián-kheh-khì** 'Don't be polite,' or 無啥物 **Bô-siá^n-mih** 'It's nothing'.

TAIWANESE	MANDARIN	MEANING
SHOWING APPRECIATION		
多謝。To-siā.	謝謝。Xièxiè.	Thank you.
感謝。Kám-siā.	謝謝。Xièxiè.	Thank you.
感恩。Kám-un.	感謝。Gǎnxiè.	I'm very grateful.
ACKNOWLEDGEMENT		
免客氣。Bián-kheh-khì.	不客氣。Bù kèqì.	You're welcome *(lit. Don't be polite)*.
無啥物。Bô-siá^n-mih.	沒什麼。Méishénme.	It's nothing.
無代誌。Bô-tāi-chì.	沒事。Méishì.	It's nothing.

23.1.3 Apologies

The expression 失禮 **sit-lé** 'excuse me, sorry' is generally used in instances where one unintentionally wrongs or disrespects another party. 歹勢 **pháі^n-sè**, which conveys both embarrassment and awkwardness, is more often used for situations in which a mistake or error has knowingly been made. However, note that many speakers disregard this distinction and use them interchangeably.

對不住 **Tùi-put-chū** comes from the literary register, and its usage is limited to more formal contexts.

Responses to apologies vary but generally play down the importance or magnitude of the offense.

TAIWANESE	MANDARIN	MEANING
APOLOGIZING		
失禮。Sit-lé.	對不起。Duìbùqǐ.	Sorry *(disrespect)*. Excuse me.
歹勢。Pháі^n-sè.	不好意思。Bùhǎo yìsi.	Sorry *(embarrassment, mistake)*. Apologies.
對不住。Tùi-put-chū.	抱歉。Bàoqiàn.	Sorry *(formal)*. Apologies.
FORGIVING		
無要緊。Bô-iàu-kín.	不要緊。Bùyàojǐn.	It's not important.
無打緊。Bô-tá^n-kín.	不要緊。Bùyàojǐn.	It's not important.

TAIWANESE	MANDARIN	MEANING
無關係。Bô-koan-hē.	沒關係。Méiguānxì.	It doesn't matter.
無啥物。Bô-siáⁿ-mih.	沒什麼。Méishénme.	It's nothing.
無代誌。Bô-tāi-chì.	沒事。Méishì.	It's nothing.
無代無誌。Bô-tāi-bô-chì.	沒事。Méishì.	It's nothing.

23.1.4 Salutations

再見 **Chài-kiàn** and 再會 **Chài-hòe**, both meaning 'Goodbye', may be used by either party. However, 閣再來 **koh-chài-lâi** 'Come again' and 順行 **sūn-kiâⁿ** 'Take care' are stated by the host sending off a guest.

一路平安 **Chi̍t-lō͘ pêng-an** and 一路順風 **Chi̍t-lō͘ sūn-hong** 'Have a good trip!' are two proverbs offering well wishes to anyone about to embark on a journey.

TAIWANESE	MANDARIN	MEANING
再見。Chài-kiàn.	再見。Zàijiàn.	Goodbye.
再會。Chài-hòe.	再見。Zàijiàn.	Goodbye.
閣再來。Koh-chài-lâi.	再來。Zàilái.	Come again.
失陪。Sit-pôe.	先走了。Xiān zǒu le.	Excuse me for leaving early.
順行。Sūn-kiâⁿ.	慢走。Mànzǒu.	Take care.
暗安。Àm-an.	晚安。Wǎn ān.	Good evening/night.
晚安。Bóan-an.	晚安。Wǎn ān.	Good evening/night.
一路平安。Chi̍t-lō͘ pêng-an.	一路平安。Yīlù píng'ān.	Have a good trip!
一路順風。Chi̍t-lō͘ sūn-hong.	一路順風。Yīlù shùnfēng.	Have a good trip!

23.2 Introductions

23.2.1 Surnames

When meeting someone for the first time, it is customary to inquire about his or her surname. Once the surname has been established, a title relating to gender, marital status, or profession can be used to form a direct term of address *(see 23.2.3 Titles)*.

surname + title

SURNAME	TITLE	TERM OF ADDRESS
劉	先生	劉 先生
Lâu	sian-si^n	Lâu--sian-si^n
劉	先生	劉 先生
Liú	xiānshēng	Liú xiānshēng
Lau	Mr.	Mr. Lau
蔡	醫師	蔡 醫師
Chhòa	i-su	Chhòa i-su
蔡	醫師	蔡 醫師
Cài	yīshī	Cài yīshī
Chhoa	Dr.	Dr. Chhoa
洪	太太	洪 太太
Âng	thài-thài	Âng thài-thài
洪	太太	洪 太太
Hóng	tàitài	Hóng tàitài
Ang	Mrs.	Mrs. Ang

To politely ask for someone's surname, the polite term 貴 **kùi** 'honorable' can be used. Additionally, a response can include 小 **sió** 'lowly' to suggest humility.

你 貴 姓？
Lí kùi sè^n?
您 貴 姓？
Nín guì xìng?
What is your surname *(polite)*?

我 小 姓 林。
Góa sió sè^n Lîm.
我 敝 姓 林。
Wǒ bì xìng Lín.
My surname is Lim *(polite)*.

Note that Taiwanese does not have an equivalent polite form of the second person pronoun 您 **nín** 'you *(polite)*'. However, another polite way to ask someone's surname is to include the first person plural-inclusive pronoun 咱 **lán** 'we *(inclusive)*' suggesting a more friendly tone.

咱 貴 姓？

Lán kùi sèⁿ?

What is your surname *(polite)*?

(lit. What are we surnamed?)

In less formal settings, the question and response can be more direct.

你 姓 啥物？

Lí sèⁿ siáⁿ-mih?

你 姓 什麼？

Nǐ xìng shénme?

What is your surname?

我 姓 張。

Góa sèⁿ Tiuⁿ.

我 姓 張。

Wǒ xìng Zhāng.

My surname is Tiunn.

23.2.2 Given names

In circumstances where additional interaction may not be expected or in more respectful contexts, a surname followed by the appropriate title suffices for a term of address. In other formal contexts, the full name, which includes both the surname and given name, can be used. Note that the surname always precedes the given name.

surname + given name

SURNAME	GIVEN NAME	TERM OF ADDRESS
陳	嘉明	陳 嘉明
Tân	Ka-bêng	Tân Ka-bêng
陳	嘉明	陳 嘉明
Chén	Jiāmíng	Chén Jiāmíng
Tan	Ka-beng	Ka-beng Tan

楊	玫黎	楊 玫黎
Iûⁿ	Mûi-lê	Iûⁿ Mûi-lê
楊	玫黎	楊 玫黎
Yáng	Méilí	Yáng Méilí
Iunn	Mui-le	Mui-le Iunn

If asking about the full name or just the given name, the verbs **叫(做) kiò(-chò)** or **號(做) hō(-chò)**, both meaning 'to be called by', can be used. Note that **做 -chò** may be omitted.

你 號做 / 叫做 啥物 名?

Lí hō-chò / kiò-chò siáⁿ-mih miâ?

What is your name *(full or given name)*?

Depending on whether the surname has already been established or on the preference of the person addressed, the response can include the full name or just the given name.

Below are variations on how to respond with the full name or just the given name.

VARIATION 1

我 姓 楊,叫 玫黎。

Góa sèⁿ Iûⁿ, kiò Mûi-lê.

我 姓 楊,叫 玫黎。

Wǒ xìng Yáng, jiào Méilí.

My surname is Iunn, and my given name is Mui-le.

VARIATION 2

我 是 楊 玫黎。

Góa sī Iûⁿ Mûi-lê.

我 是 楊 玫黎。

Wǒ shì Yáng Méilí.

I am Mui-le Iunn.

VARIATION 3

我 的 名 是 玫黎。

Góa ê miâ sī Mûi-lê.

我 的 名字 是 玫黎。

Wǒ de míngzì shì Méilí.

My name is Mui-le.

VARIATION 4

我 叫(做) 玫黎。

Góa kiò(-chò) Mûi-lê.

我 叫 玫黎。

Wǒ jiào Méilí.

I am called Mui-le.

In more informal contexts among peers, a person may introduce himself or herself by only a given name or nickname *(see 23.2.7 Adding the prefix 阿 A- to mark endearment)*.

我 叫 嘉明 / 我 叫 阿明。

Góa kiò Ka-bêng / Góa kiò A-bêng.

我 叫 嘉明 / 我 叫 阿明。

Wǒ jiào Jiāmíng / Wǒ jiào Amíng.

I am called Ka-beng (*given name*) / I am called A-beng (*nickname*).

23.2.3 Titles

Titles can be given based on gender/marital status or profession. Both in direct address and in reference to a person, the surname is first given followed by the title.

SURNAME	TITLE	TERM OF ADDRESS
林	先生	林 先生
Lîm	sian-si^n	Lîm--sian-si^n
林	先生	林 先生
Lín	xiānshēng	Lín xiānshēng
Lim	Mr.	Mr. Lim
黃	經理	黃 經理
N̂g	keng-lí	N̂g keng-lí
黃	經理	黃 經理
Huáng	jīnglǐ	Huáng jīnglǐ
Ng	Manager	Manager Ng

When the surname is not known, the title can be used on its own in direct address.

先生，小 等 一下。
Sian-si^n, sió tán--chi̍t-ē.
先生，稍 等 一下。
Xiānshēng, shāo děng yīxià.
Sir, please wait a moment.

For a more polite form of address without the surname, the professional title can be followed by the gender/marital status title.

title (professional) + *title (gender/marital status)*

TITLE (PROFESSION)	TITLE (GENDER/MARITAL STATUS)	TERM OF ADDRESS
總統	小姐	總統 小姐
chóng-thóng	sió-chiá	chóng-thóng sió-chiá
總統	小姐	總統 小姐
Zǒngtǒng	xiǎojiě	Zǒngtǒng xiǎojiě
President	Ms. / Madam	Madam President

Married women generally use their maiden names when giving full names or addressed with the title 小姐 sió-chiá 'Ms.'. Only when addressed with the title 太太 thài-thài 'Mrs.' do women use their husbands' surnames.

Note that the title 先生 sian-si^n 'Mr.' is placed in the neutral tone when following a surname.

TAIWANESE	MANDARIN	MEANING
GENDER/MARITAL STATUS		
先生 sian-si^n (sian-se^n)	先生 xiānshēng	Mr., Sir
小姐 sió-chiá	小姐 xiǎojiě	Ms., Miss, Madam
太太 thài-thài	太太 tàitài	Mrs., Madam
PROFESSION		
醫師 i-su	醫師 yīshī	Dr. *(medical)*
護士 hō·-sū	護士 hùshì	nurse
律師 lu̍t-su	律師 lǜshī	lawyer
法官 hoat-koa^n	法官 fǎguān	judge
老師 lāu-su	老師 lǎoshī	teacher

TAIWANESE	MANDARIN	MEANING
教授 kàu-siū	教授 jiàoshòu	professor
博士 phok-sū	博士 bóshì	Dr. *(PhD)*
校長 hāu-tiúⁿ	校長 xiàozhǎng	principal
秘書 pì-su	秘書 mìshū	secretary
經理 keng-lí	經理 jīnglǐ	manager
主任 chú-jīm (chú-līm)	主任 zhǔrèn	director
總經理 chóng-keng-lí	總經理 zǒngjīnglǐ	general manager (CEO)
董事長 táng-sū-tiúⁿ	董事長 dǒngshìzhǎng	chairman
市長 chhī-tiúⁿ	市長 shìzhǎng	mayor
總統 chóng-thóng	總統 zǒngtǒng	president
師傅 sai-hū	師傅 shīfu	master craftsman, expert
師父 su-hū	師父 shīfu	mentor, teacher, monk

23.2.4 Adding the suffix 姓 --sèⁿ to a surname

The suffix 姓 --sèⁿ can be added to a surname as a polite way to both directly address or refer to a man. This appellation is acceptable to use with strangers as well as with those one has already acquainted. Note that the suffix 姓 --sèⁿ is placed in the neutral tone.

surname + 姓

surname + --sèⁿ

SURNAME	PREFIX/TITLE	SUFFIX	TERM OF ADDRESS
李	-	姓	張姓
Lí	-	--sèⁿ	Lí--sèⁿ
李	老	-	老李
Lì	lǎo	-	Lǎo Lì
Li	Mr.	-	Mr. Li

This is similar to the Mandarin practice of adding the prefix 老 lǎo- before a surname to politely refer to a man.

23.2.5 Adding the suffix 的 --ê to a surname

The suffix 的 --ê can be added to a surname as a polite way to both directly address or refer to a man with whom one is already familiar. A few professional titles (such as 董事長 táng-sū-tiúⁿ 'chairman' and 總經理 chóng-keng-lí 'CEO') can also be abbreviated by the suffix. Note that the suffix 的 --ê is in the neutral tone.

surname + 的

surname + --ê

SURNAME	PREFIX/TITLE	SUFFIX	TERM OF ADDRESS
吳	-	的	吳的
Ngôʼ	-	--ê	Ngôʼ--ê
吳	老	-	老吳
Wú	lǎo	-	Lǎo Wú
Ngou	Mr.	-	Mr. Ngou
曾	董事長	的	曾 董的
Chan	Táng-sū-tiúⁿ	--ê	Chan táng--ê
曾	董事長	-	曾 董事長
Zēng	dǒngshìzhǎng	-	Zēng dǒngshìzhǎng
Chan	Chairman	-	Chairman Chan

This is similar to the Mandarin practice of adding the prefix 老 lǎo- before a man's surname.

23.2.6 Adding the suffix 仔 --á to a surname

The suffix 仔 --á can be added to a surname as a polite way to both directly address or refer to a man with whom one is already familiar. Note that the suffix 仔 --á is placed in the neutral tone.

surname + 仔

surname + --á

SURNAME	PREFIX/TITLE	SUFFIX	TERM OF ADDRESS
張	-	仔	張仔
Tiu^n	-	--á	Tiu^n--á
張	老	-	老張
Zhāng	lǎo	-	Lǎo Zhāng
Tiunn	Mr.	-	Mr. Tiunn

This is similar to the Mandarin practice of adding the prefix 老 **lǎo**- before a man's surname.

23.2.7 Adding the prefix 阿 A- to mark endearment

The prefix 阿 **A-** is often paired with one character from the given name to suggest familiarity and as a term of endearment. This nickname is often used among friends and to refer to family members by name.

SURNAME	GIVEN NAME	NICKNAME 1	NICKNAME 2
陳	嘉明	阿嘉	阿明
Tân	Ka-bêng	A-ka	A-bêng

Moreover, this prefix has also been incorporated as part of many kinship terms.

TAIWANESE	MANDARIN	MEANING
阿母 a-bú	媽媽 māmā	mother
阿兄 a-hia^n	哥哥 gēgē	older brother
阿姊 a-chí	姊姊 jiějiě	older sister

23.2.8 Referencing a family with the suffix 家 --ka

The suffix 家 **--ka** can be added to a surname to refer to a family collectively. Note that the suffix 家 **--ka** is placed in the neutral tone.

surname + 家

surname + --ka

'the *surname* family'

SURNAME	SUFFIX	TERM OF REFERENCE
王	家	王家
Ông	--ka	Ông--ka
王	家	王家
Wáng	jiā	Wáng jiā
Ong	family	the Ong family / the Ongs

悠 劉家 攏 對 咱 足 好。

In Lâu--ka lóng tùi lán chiok hó.

他們 劉 家 都 對 我們 非常 好。

Tāmen Liú jiā dōu duì wǒmen fēicháng hǎo.

The Laus always treat us very well.

23.3 Kinship terms

Kinship terms are special terms used to either directly address or indirectly refer to another family member. The kinship term system is quite extensive in Chinese culture and specifies what type of familial relationship exists between two individuals.

Generally relatives who are of the same generation address each other by his or her given name. Relatives who belong to a younger generation are also addressed by their given name, while relatives who are of an older generation are addressed by a kinship term denoting the relationship.

Differentiation within the kinship term system is based on lineage (blood relation), gender, relative age, and generation. While there is some degree of variance in usage, a few principles guide the system of nomenclature.

The Chinese kinship term system is patrilineal and privileges relations along the paternal side. Traditionally, only males with a blood relation through the father could continue the familial line. Once a woman marries, she is considered part of her husband's family. Some kinship terms have prefixes such as **外 gōe, gōa** 'outside' or **表 piáu** 'via female relations' to explicitly indicate that the relation is non-patrilineal.

There is also a strong emphasis placed on relative age and generation. More respect is accorded to relatives older than oneself in the same generation. Additionally, this level of respect based on relative age carries across generations. For example, more respect should be given to one's father's older brother than one's father's younger brother.

Note that there is quite a degree of variance among families in the usage of kinship terms. Due to its complexity and traditional nature, some families are less strict in adhering to the proper terminology. Moreover, with contemporary Taiwanese families smaller and more dispersed, younger generations may not be as familiar with the terms for more distant relatives.

Finally, note that in less formal contexts, the same term used in direct address can also be casually used to refer to one's family member.

23.3.1 Immediate family

There is significant variety in how one can address immediate family members. Note that younger siblings and children are generally addressed by their given names.

TAIWANESE REFERENCE	DIRECT ADDRESS	MANDARIN REFERENCE	DIRECT ADDRESS
FATHER			
老爸 lāu-pē	阿爸 a-pa	父親 fùqīn	爸爸 bàba
	爸爸 pa-pa (pá-pah)		爸 bà
	爸 pâ*		
MOTHER			
老母 lāu-bú	阿母 a-bú (a-bó)	母親 mǔqīn	媽媽 māmā
	媽媽 ma-ma (má-mah)	媽 mā	
	媽 mâ*		
OLDER BROTHER			
兄哥 hiaⁿ-ko	阿兄 a-hiaⁿ	哥哥 gēgē	哥哥 gēgē
	哥哥 ko-ko	兄 xiōng	哥 gē
	哥 kô*		
OLDER SISTER			
阿姊 a-chí (a-ché)	阿姊 a-chí (a-ché)	姊姊 jiějie	*same as reference*
	姊姊 ché-ché	姊 jiě	
	姊 chî*		
YOUNGER BROTHER			
小弟 sió-tī	*given name*	弟(弟) dì(dì)	*given name*

TAIWANESE		MANDARIN	
REFERENCE	DIRECT ADDRESS	REFERENCE	DIRECT ADDRESS
YOUNGER SISTER			
小妹 sió-mōe (sió-bē)	given name	妹(妹) mèi(mèi)	given name
HUSBAND			
翁 ang	given name	丈夫 zhàngfū	given name
頭家 thâu-ke	翁的 ang--ê	先生 xiānshēng	老公 lǎogōng
先生 sian-si^n			
WIFE			
某 bó͘	given name	妻子 qīzi	given name
太太 thài-thài	某的 bó͘--ê	太太 tàitài	老婆 lǎopó
牽手 khan-chhiú			
家後 ke-āu			
SON			
後生 hāu-se^n	given name	兒子 érzi	given name
囝 kiá^n	後生 hāu-se^n		兒子 érzi
DAUGHTER			
查某囝 cha-bó͘-kiá^n	given name	女兒 nüér	given name
查囝 cha-kiá^n	查囝 cha-kiá^n		女兒 nüér

*Some Taiwanese speakers informally address immediate family members with a one-syllable term that is quickly but smoothly drawn out over two tones. The sound is somewhat like a rising fifth tone that is then followed by a short falling third tone.

STANDARD TERM	INFORMAL TERM	MEANING
阿爸 a-pa	爸 pa* (pâ → à)	father
阿母 a-bú	媽 ma* (mâ → à)	mother
阿兄 a-hia^n	哥 ko* (kô → ò)	older brother
阿姊 a-chí	姊 chi* (chî → ì)	older sister

23.3.2 Paternal side

On the paternal side, uncles are differentiated by relative age to one's father while no distinction is made for aunts. The spouses of paternal uncles and aunts have special terms as well. Cousins who are children of paternal uncles are prefixed with **叔伯 chek-peh** 'via male relations' before adding the proper sibling term according to one's relative age. On the other hand, the cousins who are children of aunts follow the same appellation as all cousins on one's maternal side, which are prefixed **表 piáu** 'via female relations' before adding the appropriate sibling term relative to one's age. For cousins, **叔伯 chek-peh** and **表 piáu** are typically used only in reference and not direct address. Instead, the terms for 'older brother' and 'older sister' are used to directly address older cousins.

TAIWANESE		MANDARIN	
REFERENCE	DIRECT ADDRESS	REFERENCE	DIRECT ADDRESS
GRANDFATHER | FATHER'S FATHER			
阿公 a-kong	阿公 a-kong	祖父 zǔfù	爺爺 yéyé
內公 lāi-kong			
GRANDMOTHER | FATHER'S MOTHER			
阿媽 a-má	阿媽 a-má	祖母 zǔmǔ	奶奶 nǎinai
內媽 lāi-má			
UNCLE | FATHER'S OLDER BROTHER			
阿伯 a-peh	same as reference	伯父 bófù	伯伯 bóbo
伯仔 peh-á			
AUNT | FATHER'S OLDER BROTHER'S WIFE			
阿姆 a-ḿ	same as reference	伯母 bómǔ	伯母 bómǔ
姆仔 ḿ--á		伯娘 bóniáng	
UNCLE | FATHER'S YOUNGER BROTHER			
阿叔 a-chek	same as reference	叔父 shūfù	叔叔 shūshu
AUNT | FATHER'S YOUNGER BROTHER'S WIFE			
阿嬸 a-chím	same as reference	嬸嬸 shěnshen	嬸嬸 shěnshen
		嬸母 shěnmǔ	
		叔母 shūmǔ	

TAIWANESE		MANDARIN	
REFERENCE	DIRECT ADDRESS	REFERENCE	DIRECT ADDRESS
AUNT | FATHER'S OLDER/YOUNGER SISTER			
阿姑 a-ko˙	阿姑 a-ko˙ 姑姑 ko˙-ko˙	姑媽 gūmā 姑母 gūmǔ	姑媽 gūmā 姑姑 gūgū
UNCLE | FATHER'S OLDER/YOUNGER SISTER'S HUSBAND			
姑丈 ko-tiūⁿ	same as reference	姑丈 gūzhàng 姑夫 gūfū	姑丈 gūzhàng
COUSIN | FATHER'S BROTHER'S SON OLDER THAN ONESELF			
叔伯阿兄 chek-peh-a-hiaⁿ 叔伯大兄 chek-peh-tōa-hiaⁿ	阿兄 a-hiaⁿ	堂兄 tángxiōng 堂哥 tánggē	哥哥 gēgē 堂哥 tánggē
COUSIN | FATHER'S BROTHER'S DAUGHTER OLDER THAN ONESELF			
叔伯大姊 chek-peh-tōa-chí	阿姊 a-chí	堂姊 tángjiě	姊姊 jiějiě
COUSIN | FATHER'S BROTHER'S SON YOUNGER THAN ONESELF			
叔伯小弟 chek-peh-sió-tī	given name	堂弟 tángdì	given name
COUSIN | FATHER'S BROTHER'S DAUGHTER YOUNGER THAN ONESELF			
叔伯小妹 chek-peh-sió-mōe	given name	堂妹 tángmèi	given name
COUSIN | FATHER'S SISTER'S SON OLDER THAN ONESELF			
表兄 piáu-hiaⁿ	阿兄 a-hiaⁿ	表哥 biǎogē	哥哥 gēgē
COUSIN | FATHER'S SISTER'S DAUGHTER OLDER THAN ONESELF			
表姊 piáu-chí	阿姊 a-chí	表姊 biǎojiě	姊姊 jiějiě
COUSIN | FATHER'S SISTER'S SON YOUNGER THAN ONESELF			
表小弟 piáu-sió-tī	given name	表弟 biǎodì	given name
COUSIN | FATHER'S SISTER'S DAUGHTER YOUNGER THAN ONESELF			
表妹 piáu-mōe (piáu-bē)	given name	表妹 biǎomèi	given name

23.3.3 Maternal side

On the maternal side, grandparents are prefixed by **外 gōa-** 'outside' in indirect address but in direct address follow the same terms as those on the paternal side. Additionally, on the maternal side neither uncles nor aunts are differentiated by relative age to one's mother. All cousins on the maternal side are prefixed by **表 piáu** followed by the appropriate sibling term relative to one's age.

TAIWANESE		MANDARIN	
REFERENCE	DIRECT ADDRESS	REFERENCE	DIRECT ADDRESS
GRANDFATHER | MOTHER'S FATHER			
外公 gōa-kong	阿公 a-kong	外祖父 wàizǔfù	姥爺 lǎoyé
		外租公 wàizǔgōng	外公 wàigōng
		外父 wàifù	
GRANDMOTHER | MOTHER'S MOTHER			
外媽 gōa-má	阿媽 a-má	外祖母 wàizǔmǔ	姥姥 lǎolǎo
		外婆 wàipó	外婆 wàipó
UNCLE | MOTHER'S OLDER/YOUNGER BROTHER			
阿舅 a-kū	阿舅 a-kū	舅舅 jiùjiu	舅舅 jiùjiu
母舅 bú-kū (bó-kū)		舅父 jiùfù	
UNCLE | MOTHER'S OLDER/YOUNGER BROTHER'S WIFE			
阿妗 a-kīm	阿妗 a-kīm	舅媽 jiùmā	舅媽 jiùmā
母妗 bú-kīm (bó-kīm)		舅母 jiùmǔ	妗母 jìnmǔ
			妗子 jìnzi
AUNT | MOTHER'S OLDER/YOUNGER SISTER			
阿姨 a-î	same as reference	姨媽 yímā	姨媽 yímā
		姨母 yímǔ	阿姨 āyí
UNCLE | MOTHER'S OLDER/YOUNGER SISTER'S HUSBAND			
姨丈 î-tiūⁿ	same as reference	姨丈 yízhàng	姨丈 yízhàng
		姨夫 yífū	
COUSIN | MOTHER'S BROTHER/SISTER'S SON OLDER THAN ONESELF			
表兄 piáu-hiaⁿ	阿兄 a-hiaⁿ	表哥 biǎogē	哥哥 gēgē

TAIWANESE		MANDARIN	
REFERENCE	DIRECT ADDRESS	REFERENCE	DIRECT ADDRESS
COUSIN | MOTHER'S BROTHER/SISTER'S DAUGHTER OLDER THAN ONESELF			
表姊 piáu-chí	阿姊 a-chí	表姊 biǎojiě	姊姊 jiějiě
COUSIN | MOTHER'S BROTHER/SISTER'S SON YOUNGER THAN ONESELF			
表小弟 piáu-sió-tī	given name	表弟 biǎodì	given name
COUSIN | MOTHER'S BROTHER/SISTER'S DAUGHTER YOUNGER THAN ONESELF			
表妹 piáu-mōe (piáu-bē)	given name	表妹 biǎomèi	given name

Note that Mandarin uses different terms for direct address between maternal and paternal grandparents.

23.3.4 In-laws

While English adds '-in-law' to a kinship term to refer to family through marriage, Taiwanese has specific kinship terms for each spouse depending on relative age, gender, and bloodline. Note the kinship terms for the siblings of one's spouse resemble closely the terms that one's children would use to address them.

TAIWANESE		MANDARIN	
REFERENCE	DIRECT	REFERENCE	DIRECT
IMMEDIATE FAMILY (SPOUSE OF A BLOOD RELATION)			
SISTER-IN-LAW | OLDER BROTHER'S WIFE			
阿嫂 a-só	same as reference	嫂 sǎo	嫂嫂 sǎosǎo 嫂子 sǎozi
SISTER-IN-LAW | YOUNGER BROTHER'S WIFE			
弟婦仔 tē-hū-á 小嬸 sió-chím 妗仔 kīm-á	same as reference	弟媳 dìxí	弟妹 dìmèi 弟婦 dìfù
BROTHER-IN-LAW | OLDER SISTER'S HUSBAND			
姊夫 chí-hu	same as reference	姊夫 jiěfū	same as reference
BROTHER-IN-LAW | YOUNGER SISTER'S HUSBAND			
妹婿 mōe-sài (bē-sài)	same as reference	妹夫 mèifū	same as reference

Terms of address 489

TAIWANESE		MANDARIN	
REFERENCE	DIRECT	REFERENCE	DIRECT

SON-IN-LAW

囝婿 kiáⁿ-sài	same as reference	女婿 nǚxù	same as reference

DAUGHTER-IN-LAW

新婦 sin-pū	same as reference	兒媳 érxí	媳婦 xífù

HUSBAND'S SIDE

FATHER-IN-LAW | HUSBAND'S FATHER

大官 ta-koaⁿ	same as reference	公公 gōnggōng	same as reference

MOTHER-IN-LAW | HUSBAND'S MOTHER

大家 ta-ke	same as reference	婆婆 pópo	same as reference

BROTHER-IN-LAW | HUSBAND'S OLDER BROTHER

大伯(仔) tōa-peh(-á)	same as reference	大伯 dàbó	大伯(子) dàbó(zi)

SISTER-IN-LAW | HUSBAND'S OLDER BROTHER'S WIFE

大嫂 tōa-só	same as reference	大嫂 dàsǎo	大嫂 dàsǎo
大姆 tōa-ḿ			嫂嫂 sǎosao

BROTHER-IN-LAW | HUSBAND'S YOUNGER BROTHER

細叔 sè-chek	same as reference	小叔 xiǎoshū	same as reference
小叔 sió-chek			
阿叔仔 a-chek-á			

SISTER-IN-LAW | HUSBAND'S YOUNGER BROTHER'S WIFE

小嬸 sió-chím	same as reference	小嬸 xiǎoshěn	same as reference
弟妹 dìmèi			

SISTER-IN-LAW | HUSBAND'S OLDER SISTER

大娘姑 tōa-niû-ko͘	same as reference	大姑 dàgū	大姑(子) dàgū(zi)

BROTHER-IN-LAW | HUSBAND'S OLDER SISTER'S HUSBAND

姉夫 chí-hu	same as reference	姊夫 jiěfū	same as reference

SISTER-IN-LAW | HUSBAND'S YOUNGER SISTER

小姑 sió-ko͘	same as reference	小姑 xiǎogū	小姑(子) xiàogū(zi)

TAIWANESE		MANDARIN	
REFERENCE	DIRECT	REFERENCE	DIRECT

BROTHER-IN-LAW | HUSBAND'S YOUNGER SISTER'S HUSBAND

妹婿 mōe-sài (bē-sài)	same as reference	妹夫 mèifū	same as reference

WIFE'S SIDE
FATHER-IN-LAW | WIFE'S FATHER

丈人(爸) tiūⁿ-lâng(-pâ)	same as reference	岳父 yuèfù	岳丈 yuèzhàng

MOTHER-IN-LAW | WIFE'S MOTHER

丈姆(婆) tiūⁿ-ḿ(-pô)	same as reference	岳母 yuèmǔ	丈母(娘) zhàngmǔ(niáng)

BROTHER-IN-LAW | WIFE'S OLDER BROTHER

大舅(仔) tōa-kū(-á)	same as reference	內兄 nèixiōng	大舅(子) dàjiù(zi)

SISTER-IN-LAW | WIFE'S OLDER BROTHER'S WIFE

兄嫂 hiaⁿ-só	same as reference	大舅嫂 dàjiùsǎo	大舅嫂 dàjiùsǎo
阿嫂 a-só			嫂嫂 sǎosǎo

BROTHER-IN-LAW | WIFE'S YOUNGER BROTHER

舅仔 kū-á	same as reference	內娣 nèidì	小舅(子) xiǎojiù(zi)

SISTER-IN-LAW | WIFE'S YOUNGER BROTHER'S WIFE

妗仔 kīm-á	same as reference	小舅嫂 xiǎojiùsǎo	小舅嫂 xiǎojiùsǎo
			內娣婦 nèidìfù

SISTER-IN-LAW | WIFE'S OLDER/YOUNGER SISTER

姨仔 î-á	same as reference	姨姐 yíjiě (older)	大姨(子) dàyí(zi) (older)
		姨妹 yímèi (younger)	小姨(子) xiǎoyí(zi) (younger)

BROTHER-IN-LAW | WIFE'S OLDER/YOUNGER SISTER'S HUSBAND

大細仙 tōa-sòe-sian	same as reference	襟兄 jīnxiōng (older)	same as reference
大細丈 tōa-sòe-tiūⁿ		襟第 jīndì (younger)	
同門的 tâng-mn̂g--ê		連襟 liánjīn	

23.3.5 Children of relatives

Note that the character 孫 **sun** 'descendant' is used in varying combinations of terms to represent not only grandchildren but also nephews and nieces.

Additionally, the terms that are used to refer to one's sister's children depends on one's own gender. Because the kinship term system is patrilineal, children of one's sister are outside of the family and prefixed with 外 **gōe-** if the speaker is male. If the speaker is female, the children of one's sister are prefixed with 姨 **î** 'aunt' indicating sisterhood on the maternal side.

TAIWANESE REFERENCE	DIRECT ADDRESS	MANDARIN REFERENCE	DIRECT ADDRESS
IMMEDIATE FAMILY			
*NEPHEW	BROTHER'S SON*			
孫仔 sun-á	given name	姪子 zhízi	given name
姪仔 tit-á		姪兒 zhí'ér	
*NIECE	BROTHER'S DAUGHTER*			
查某孫仔 cha-bó͘-sun-á	given name	姪女 zhínǚ	given name
姪女 tit-lú			
*NEPHEW	SISTER'S SON AND ONE IS MALE*			
外甥(仔) gōe-seng(-á)	given name	外甥 wàishēng	given name
*NIECE	SISTER'S DAUGHTER AND ONE IS MALE*			
外甥女(仔) gōe-seng-lí(-á)	given name	外姪女 wàizhínǚ	given name
*NEPHEW	SISTER'S SON AND ONE IS FEMALE*			
姨甥 î-seng	given name	姨甥 yísheng	given name
*NIECE	SISTER'S DAUGHTER AND ONE IS FEMALE*			
姨甥女 î-seng-lú	given name	姨甥女 yíshēngnǚ	given name
HUSBAND'S SIDE			
*NEPHEW	HUSBAND'S BROTHER'S SON*			
姪仔 tit-á	given name	姪兒 zhí'ér	given name
孫仔 sun-á		姪子 zhízi	

TAIWANESE		MANDARIN	
REFERENCE	DIRECT ADDRESS	REFERENCE	DIRECT ADDRESS
*NIECE	HUSBAND'S BROTHER'S DAUGHTER*			
查某孫仔 cha-bó-sun-á	given name	姪女 zhínǚ	given name
*NEPHEW	HUSBAND'S SISTER'S SON*			
外甥(仔) gōe-seng(-á)	given name	外甥 wàishēng	given name
*NIECE	HUSBAND'S SISTER'S DAUGHTER*			
外甥女(仔) gōe-seng-lí(-á)	given name	外姪女 wàizhínǚ	given name
WIFE'S SIDE			
*NEPHEW	WIFE'S BROTHER/SISTER'S SON*			
外甥(仔) gōe-seng(-á)	given name	外甥 wàishēng	given name
*NIECE	WIFE'S BROTHER/SISTER'S DAUGHTER*			
外甥女(仔) gōe-seng-lí(-á)	given name	外姪女 wàizhínǚ	given name
GRANDCHILDREN			
*GRANDSON	SON'S SON*			
孫 sun	given name	孫兒 sūnér	given name
內孫 lāi-sun		內孫 nèisūn	
		孫子 sūnzi	
*GRANDDAUGHTER	SON'S DAUGHTER*			
查某孫 cha-bó-sun	given name	孫女 sūnnǚ	given name
		內孫女 nèisūnnǚ	
*GRANDSON	DAUGHTER'S SON*			
外孫 gōa-sun	given name	外孫(兒) wàisūn(ér)	given name
*GRANDDAUGHTER	DAUGHTER'S DAUGHTER*			
外查某孫 gōa-cha-bó-sun	given name	外孫女 wàisūnnǚ	given name

23.3.6 Multiple siblings

If there are multiple siblings, a number representing the order of birth is often appended before the proper kinship term. The oldest generally has the prefix **大 tōa** 'eldest'.

大叔	tōa chek	<u>eldest</u> uncle *(paternal side)*
二叔	jī chek	<u>2nd</u> oldest uncle *(paternal side)*
三叔	saⁿ chek	<u>3rd</u> oldest uncle *(paternal side)*
:	:	:
<u>number</u> 叔	<u>number</u> chek	<u>order of birth</u> oldest uncle *(paternal side)*

23.3.7 Group kinship terms

Group kinship terms generally are formed by stating the constituent members (**爸母 pē-bú** 'parents' or lit. 'father-mother') or adding a suffix indicating familial relations (**表親 piáu-chhin** 'mother's and father's sisters' families).

TAIWANESE	MANDARIN	MEANING
爸母 pē-bú	父母 fùmǔ	parents
囝 kiáⁿ	孩子 háizi	children
兄弟 hiaⁿ-tī	兄弟 xiōngdì	brothers
姊妹 chí-mōe (chí-bē)	姐妹 jiěmèi	sisters
兄弟姊妹 hiaⁿ-tī-chí-mōe (hiaⁿ-tī-chí-bē)	兄弟姐妹 xiōngdìjiěmèi	siblings
阿公(佮)阿媽 a-kong (kah) a-má	祖父母 zǔfùmǔ	grandparents
阿祖 a-chó͘	曾祖父母 zēngzǔfùmǔ	great-grandparents
叔伯的 chek-peh--ê	堂兄弟姐妹 tángxiōngdìjiěmèi	cousins (father's brothers' children)
親堂 chhin-tông	堂兄弟姐妹 tángxiōngdìjiěmèi	cousins (father's brothers' children)
表親 piáu-chhin	表親 biǎoqīn	mother's and father's sisters' families
親情 chhin-chiâⁿ	親戚 qīnqi	relatives

Note that Taiwanese does not have a collective term to represent both grandparents. Instead, each grandparent kinship term can be read in succession or joined by a conjunction.

Additionally, note that the Taiwanese use of the character 祖 in **阿祖 a-chó͘** indicates 'great-grandparents', while the same character in the Mandarin **祖父母 zǔfùmǔ** refers to 'grandparents'.

Taiwanese uses two terms to refer to children, **囝 kiáⁿ** and **囝仔 gín-á**. Generally, **囝 kiáⁿ** refers to one's own blood relation, while **囝仔 gín-á** refers to any child of a young age. However, this distinction is not strictly upheld. One may also hear **囝仔囝 gín-á-kiáⁿ** or **囝仔人 gín-á-lâng** to refer to small children. Mandarin does not make a distinction and uses the term 孩子 háizi in both cases.

23.3.8 Friends and colleagues within the same generation

Among friends and colleagues within the same generation, the sibling kinship terms 哥 --**ko** 'older brother' and 姊 ---**chí** (--**ché**) 'older sister', can be suffixed to a given name to show respect. Additionally, the prefix 阿 **a**-- may be added to suggest familiarity.

TAIWANESE	MEANING
嘉明哥 Ka-bêng--ko	'Brother Ka-beng'
阿明哥 A-bêng--ko	'Brother A-beng'
美珍姊 Bí-tin--chí	'Sister Bi-tin'
阿珍哥 A-tin--chí	'Sister A-tin'

姊仔 **chí--á** is a term generally used for friends and colleagues who are older females but not familial relatives.

24 Time

24.1 Duration

24.1.1 Exact duration

When discussing length of time, use the following measure words to represent duration.

	TAIWANESE	MANDARIN
hour	點鐘 tiám-cheng	小時 xiǎoshí
minute	分(鐘) hun(-cheng)	分(鐘) fēn(zhōng)
second	秒(鐘) bió(-cheng)	秒(鐘) miǎo(zhōng)

Note that the measure word 點 **tiám** 'hour' requires 鐘 **cheng** 'clock' to be placed after it whenever expressing duration. For the measure words 分 **hun** 'minute' and 秒 **bió** 'second' the inclusion of 鐘 **cheng** 'clock' is optional.

我 今仔下早 走 的 時間 是 一 點鐘，十八 分，三十五 秒。
Góa kin-á-e-chái cháu ê sî-kan sī chit <u>tiám-cheng</u>, cha̍p-peh <u>hun</u>, saⁿ-cha̍p-gō͘ <u>bió</u>.
我 今天 早上 跑步 的 時間 是 一 個 小時，十八 分，三十五 秒。
Wǒ jīntiān zǎoshang pǎobù de shíjiān shì yī gè <u>xiǎoshí</u>, shíbā <u>fēn</u>, sānshíwǔ <u>miǎo</u>.
My run this morning was 1 <u>hour</u>, 18 <u>minutes</u>, and 35 <u>seconds</u>.

When stating only half an increment, use 半 **pòaⁿ** 'half' *before* the measure word.

半 + *measure word*

pòaⁿ + *measure word*

	TAIWANESE	MANDARIN
half an hour	半點鐘 pòaⁿ tiám-cheng	半(個)小時 bàn (gè) xiǎoshí
half a minute	半分(鐘) pòaⁿ hun(-cheng)	半分(鐘) bàn fēn(zhōng)
half a second	半秒(鐘) pòaⁿ bió(-cheng)	半秒(鐘) bàn miǎo(zhōng)

When discussing duration with mixed whole and half units of time, place the 半 **pòaⁿ** 'half' *after* the measure word.

whole number + measure word + 半

whole number + measure word + pòaⁿ

	TAIWANESE	MANDARIN
2.5 hours	兩點半鐘 nñg tiám-pòaⁿ-cheng	兩個半小時 liǎng gè bàn xiǎoshí
5.5 minutes	五分半(鐘) gō˙ hun pòaⁿ(-cheng)	五分半(鐘) wǔ fēn bàn (zhōng)
10.5 seconds	十秒半(鐘) chȧp bió pòaⁿ (-cheng)	十秒半(鐘) shí miǎo bàn (zhōng)

24.1.2 Approximate duration

There are several ways to express approximate duration.

24.1.2.1 More than

Placing 以上 **í-siōng** after the measure word and noun indicates that the duration is 'equal to or greater than' the stated number.

number + measure word + noun + 以上

number + measure word + noun + í-siōng

'greater than or equal to *number*'

十 分(鐘) 以上
chàp hun(-cheng) í-siōng
十 分(鐘) 以上
shí fēn(zhōng) yǐshàng
ten minutes or more

半 點鐘 以上
pòaⁿ tiám-cheng í-siōng
半 個 小時 以上
bàn gè xiǎoshí yǐshàng
at least a half hour

On the other hand, if 外 gōa 'more than' is placed directly after the measure word but before the noun, this indicates a duration that is 'more than' the stated number.

> *number* + *measure word* + 外 + *noun*
>
> *number* + *measure word* + -gōa- + *noun*
>
> 'more than *number*'

兩 點外鐘
nn̄g tiám-gōa-cheng
兩 個 多 小時
liǎng gè duō xiǎoshí
more than two hours

五 分外(鐘)
gō˙ hun gōa(-cheng)
五 分 多 (鐘)
wǔ fēn duō (zhōng)
more than five minutes

24.1.2.2 Less than

Placing 以下 í-hā after the measure word and noun indicates that the duration is 'equal to or less than' the stated number.

number + *measure word* + *noun* + 以下

number + *measure word* + *noun* + í-hā

'less than or equal to *number*'

十 秒(鐘) 以下
chảp bió(-cheng) í-hā
十秒 以下
shí miǎo yǐxià
ten seconds or less

四十五 分(鐘) 以下
sì-chảp-gō˙hun(-cheng) í-hā
四十五 分(鐘) 以下
Sìshíwǔ fēn(zhōng) yǐxià
45 minutes or less

Alternatively, **無到 bô kàu** 'not even' can be placed directly before the number expression to indicate that the stated duration has not yet been reached.

無到 + *number* + *measure word* + *noun*

bô kàu + *number* + *measure word* + *noun*

'less than *number*'

無 到 一 點鐘
bô kàu chit tiám-cheng
不 到 一 個 小時
bù dào yī gè xiǎoshí
not even an hour

無 到 二十 秒(鐘)
bô kàu jī-chảp bió(-cheng)
不 到 二十秒
bù dào èrshí miǎo
less than 20 seconds

24.1.2.3 Within and between

Placing **(以)內 (í)-lāi** after the measure word and noun indicates that the duration is 'within' the duration given by the stated number.

> *number* + *measure word* + *noun* + (以)內
> *number* + *measure word* + *noun* + (í-)lāi
> 'within *number*'

一點鐘 (以)內
chit tiám-cheng (í)-lāi
一個小時 (以)內
yī gè xiǎoshí (yǐ)nèi
within an hour

一工 (以)內
chit kang (í)-lāi
一天 (以)內
yī tiān (yǐ)nèi
during a day

If providing a duration within a given range, place **至 chì** 'between' the extents of the range.

> *X number* + 至 + *Y number* + *measure word* + *noun*
> *X number* + chì + *Y number* + *measure word* + *noun*
> 'between *X number* to *Y number*'

五 至 七 分鐘
gō͘ chì chhit hun-cheng
五 至 七 分鐘
wǔ zhì qī fēnzhōng
between 5-7 minutes

兩 至 三 點鐘

nn̄g chì saⁿ tiám-cheng

兩 至 三 個 小時

liǎng zhì sān gè xiǎo shí

within 2-3 hours

24.2 Clock time

24.2.1 Telling time

When referring to time on the clock, the word for 'hour' 點 **tiám** is used to express 'o'clock'. However, when talking about time on the clock and not duration 鐘 **cheng** is not used. To emphasize that the time is exactly a specific time, place 正 **chiàⁿ** after the hour.

hour + 點

hour + tiám

'hour o' clock'

	TAIWANESE	MANDARIN
1 o'clock	一點 chit tiám	一點 yī diǎn
2 o'clock	兩點 nn̄g tiám	兩點 liǎng diǎn
3 o'clock	三點 saⁿ tiám	三點 sān diǎn
:	:	:
11 o'clock	十一點 cha̍p-it tiám	十一點 shíyī diǎn
12 o'clock	十二點 cha̍p-jī tiám	十二點 shí'èr diǎn
7 o'clock exactly	七點正 chhit tiám chiàⁿ	七點整 qī diǎn zhěng
on the hour	正點 chiàⁿ tiám	整點 zhěng diǎn
half past	半點 pòaⁿ tiám	半點 bàn diǎn

Note that Taiwanese uses the character 正 **chiàⁿ** to mean 'exactly, on the dot' or 'on the hour' while Mandarin uses 整 **zhěng**.

Time 501

When including minutes in telling the time, **分 hun** can optionally be placed after the number of minutes.

hour + 點 + *minutes* + (分)

hour + tiám + *minutes* + (hun)

TIME
1:18   一點十八 (分)   chit tiám cha̍p-peh (hun)
        一點十八 (分)   yī diǎn shíbā (fēn)

2:40   兩點四十 (分)   nn̄g tiám sì-cha̍p (hun)
        兩點四十 (分)   liǎng diǎn sìshí (fēn)

Minutes that are less than **10 minutes** past the hour can optionally include **空 khòng** '0' before the number of minutes.

TIME
7:05   七點(空)五分   chhit tiám (khòng) gō͘ hun
        七點(〇)五分   qī diǎn (líng) wǔ fēn

10:02   十點(空)二分   cha̍p tiám (khòng) jī hun
        十點(〇)二分   shí diǎn (líng) èr fēn

24.2.2 Clock-time expressions

24.2.2.1 Half-hour increments

When indicating 'half past the hour', **半 pòaⁿ** 'half' is added after the specified hour. Note that the hour 一 **chi̍t** 'one' is often left off in this expression.

hour + 半

hour + pòaⁿ

'half past the hour'

TIME		TAIWANESE	MANDARIN
half past one	1:30	(一)點半 (chit-)tiám-pòaⁿ	一點半 yīdiǎn bàn
half past two	2:30	兩點半 nn̄g-tiám-pòaⁿ	兩點半 liǎng diǎn bàn
half past four	4:30	四點半 sì-tiám-pòaⁿ	四點半 sì diǎn bàn

24.2.2.2 Past the hour

To express a number of minutes 'past the hour', it is possible to place 過 **kòe** 'past' after the hour followed by 分 **hun** 'minute'. However, generally this expression is not used beyond 30 minutes past the hour.

hour + 過 + *minute*

hour + -kòe- + *minute*

'*minutes* past the hour'

TIME		TAIWANESE	MANDARIN
seven past one	1:07	一點過七分 chit-tiám-kòe-chhit-hun	一點過七分 yī diǎn guò qī fēn
quarter past two	2:15	兩點過十五分 nn̄g-tiám-kòe-cha̍p-gō͘-hun	兩點一刻 liǎng diǎn yī kè

Note that, unlike the Mandarin 刻 **kè** 'quarter', Taiwanese does not use a special term for fifteen minute increments.

Taiwan Mandarin speakers tend not to use 'past the hour' expressions and instead prefer the '*hour* 點 **tiám** *minute*' format.

TIME		TAIWAN MANDARIN
seven past one	1:07	一點(〇)七分 yī diǎn (líng) qī fēn
quarter past two	2:15	兩點十五分 liǎng diǎn shíwǔ fēn

24.2.2.3 Before the hour

In Taiwanese, when 差 **chha** 'difference' is placed *before* the specified hour, it indicates a number of minutes 'before the hour'.

差 + *minute* + *hour*

chha + *minute* + *hour*

'*minutes* before the hour'

TIME		TAIWANESE	MANDARIN
twenty to two	1:40	差二十分兩點 chha-jī-cha̍p-hun-nn̄g-tiám	差二十分兩點 chā èrshí fēn liǎng diǎn
ten to six	5:50	差十分六點 chha-cha̍p-hun-la̍k-tiám	差十分六點 chà shífēn liù diǎn
five to eleven	10:55	差五分十一點 chha-gō͘-hun-cha̍p-it-tiám	差五分十一點 chà wǔ fēn shíyī diǎn

24.3 Parts of the day

Taiwanese has many terms that refer to different parts of the day as opposed to a strict separation between AM or PM. The table in the following section offers an hourly mapping of when particular terms are commonly used. However, note that even within a specific region there are a wide variety of options and individual preferences for these terms. Additionally, there are some terms tied to the rising and setting of the sun. As a result, the appropriate time for these terms fluctuates throughout the year.

24.3.1 Period of the day

When indicating the time using a 12-hour clock, the term for which 'period of day' comes before stating the 'clock time'. Note that **中晝 tiong-tàu** or **午時 gō͘-sî** 'noon' includes the full hour between 12pm-1pm and for some speakers may even begin around 11am.

period of day + clock time

8:30 AM	下早(仔) 八點半	e-chái(-á) peh-tiám-pòaⁿ
	早上 八點半	zǎoshàng bā diǎn bàn
12:30 PM	中晝 十二點半	tiong-tàu cha̍p-jī-tiám-pòaⁿ
	中午 十二點半	zhōngwǔ shí'èr diǎn bàn
2:00 PM	下晡 兩點	e-po͘ nn̄g-tiám
	下午 兩點	xiàwǔ liǎng diǎn
9:30 PM	暗時(仔) 九點半	àm-sî(-á) káu-tiám-pòaⁿ
	晚上 九點半	wǎnshàng jiǔ diǎn bàn
12:00 AM	半暝(仔) 十二點	pòaⁿ-mê(-á) cha̍p-jī-tiám
	半夜 十二點	bànyè shí'èr diǎn

TIME	TAIWANESE		MANDARIN	
6 (*dawn*)	早起(時)	chái-khí(-sî)	早上	zǎoshàng
	下早(仔)	e-chái(-á)		
	透早	thàu-chá		
	早時(仔)	chái-sî(-á)		
7	:	:	:	:
8	:	:	:	:
9	:	:	上午	shàngwǔ
10	:	:	:	:
11	午時	gō͘-sî	:	:
12 (*noon*)	午時	gō͘-sî	中午	zhōngwǔ
	中晝	tiong-tàu		
1	下晝	e-tàu	下午	xiàwǔ
	下晡	e-po͘		
2	:	:	:	:
3	:	:	:	:
4	:	:	:	:
5	:	:	:	:

TIME	TAIWANESE		MANDARIN	
6 (dusk)	欲暗仔	beh-àm-á (before sunset)	傍晚	bàngwǎn
7	暗時(仔) 下昏(暗) 暗頭仔	àm-sî(-á) e-hng(-àm) àm-thâu-á	:	:
8	:	:	:	:
9	:	:	晚上	wǎnshàng
10	:	:	:	:
11	:	:	:	:
12 (midnight)	半暝(仔)	pòa^n-mê(-á)	半夜	bànyè
1	:	:	半夜 凌晨	bànyè língchén
2	:	:	:	:
3	:	:	凌晨	língchén
4	早起(時) 下早(仔) 透早 早時(仔)	chái-khí(-sî) e-chái(-á) thàu-chá chái-sî(-á)	:	:
5	:	:	:	:

24.3.2 Parts of the day relative to the present

When referring to approximate times of the day relative to the present, the specified day (yesterday, today, tomorrow) is followed by the 'period of the day'. If the specified time is on the same day (this morning, this afternoon, this evening), **今仔日 kin-á-jit** 'today' may be omitted.

	TAIWANESE	MANDARIN
yesterday afternoon	昨昏 下晝 cha-hng e-tàu	昨天下午 zuótiān xiàwǔ
this morning	(今仔日) 早起 (kin-á-jit) chái-khí	(今天) 早上 (jīntiān) zǎoshang
tomorrow afternoon	明仔載下晝 bîn-á-chài e-tàu	明天下午 míngtiān xiàwǔ

Abbreviated forms exist for 'last night', 'tonight', 'tomorrow morning', and 'tomorrow night'.

	TAIWANESE	MANDARIN
last night	昨暗 cha-àm 昨暝 cha-mê	昨晚 zuó wǎn
tonight	下暗 e-àm 下昏 e-hng 下昏暗 e-hng-àm	今晚 jīn wǎn
tomorrow morning	明仔早起 bîn-á-chái-khí	明天早上 míngtiān zǎoshang
tomorrow evening	明仔暗 bîn-á-àm 明仔下昏 bîn-á e-hng	明天晚上 míngtiān wǎnshàng

24.3.3 Referring to habitual occurrences

When expressing a habitual or regular occurrence, add 時 -sî 'time' after the period of day.

	TAIWANESE	MANDARIN
in the mornings	早起時 chá-khí-sî	早上時 zǎoshang shí
	下早時 e-chái-sî	
in the afternoons	下晡時 e-po͘-sî	下午時 xiàwǔ shí
in the evenings	暗時 àm-sî	晚上時 wǎnshàng shí

25 Calendar

25.1 Years

The word 年 **nî** 'year' itself is a measure word and requires no additional measure word. An alternative term for 'year' when referring to the duration is 冬 **tang**.

	TAIWANESE	MANDARIN
one year	一年 chit nî	一年 yī nián
	一冬 chit tang	
two years	兩年 nn̄g nî	兩年 liǎng nián
	兩冬 nn̄g tang	
10 years	十年 cha̍p nî	十年 shí nián
	十冬 cha̍p tang	
every year	逐年 ta̍k nî	每年 měinián
	逐冬 ta̍k tang	
	每一年 múi chit nî	
	每一冬 múi chit tang	
within/during a year	一冬內 chit tang lāi	一年以內 yī nián yǐnèi
	一冬中 chit tang tiong	一年中 yī nián zhōng

25.1.1 Relative references to a year

To refer to a year relative to the present or a specific point in time, use the expressions in the following table.

	TAIWANESE	MANDARIN
this year	今年 kin-nî	今年 jīnnián
last year	舊年 kū-nî	去年 qùnián
two years ago	前年 chûn-nî	前年 qiánnián
three years ago	大前年 tōa-chûn--nî	大前年 dà qiánnián
four years ago	四年前 sì nî chêng	四年前 sì nián qián
next year	明年 mê-nî (môa-nî)	明年 míngnián
the following year	隔年 keh-nî	翌年 yìnián
two years from now	後年 āu-nî	後年 hòunián
three years from now	大後年 tōa-āu-nî	大後年 dà hòunián
four years from now	四年以後 sì-nî í-āu	四年以後 sì nián yǐhòu
beginning of the year	年頭 nî-thâu	年頭 niántóu
end of the year	年底 nî-té	年底 niándǐ
	年尾 nî-bóe	年尾 niánwěi
	冬尾 tang-bóe	

25.1.2 Specifying a year

To specify a year, read aloud each numeral of the year in sequence followed by **年 nî** 'year'. Numerals for years are read using the literary reading of numbers *(see 3.1.2 Literary reading for numbers)*.

	TAIWANESE	MANDARIN
1960	一九六空年 it kiú lio̍k khòng nî	一九六〇年 yī jiǔ liù líng nián
2005	二空空五年 jī khòng khòng ngó͘ nî	二〇〇五年 èr líng líng wǔ nián

25.2 Months

The word for 'month' **月 goe̍h** is preceded by the measure word **個 kò** when describing a number of months. Without the measure word, the pairing of a number with **月 goe̍h** 'month' refers to a specific calendar month. Naturally, because 'one' and 'two' have different counting and measure word versions, the distinction is even clearer. When referring to the duration of a month rather than the calendar month, an alternative but more traditional form of 'month' can also be used 月日 **goeh-jit**. Note that the term 月日 **goeh-jit** itself is a measure word and requires no additional measure word.

	TAIWANESE	MANDARIN
one month	一個月 chit kò goeh	一個月 yī gè yuè
	一月日 chit goeh-jit	
January	一月 it-goeh	一月 yī yuè
two months	兩個月 nn̄g kò goeh	兩個月 liǎng gè yuè
	兩月日 nn̄g goeh-jit	
February	二月 jī-goeh	二月 èr yuè
three months	三個月 saⁿ kò goeh	三個月 sān gè yuè
	三月日 saⁿ goeh-jit	
March	三月 saⁿ-goeh	三月 sān yuè
every month	逐個月 tak kò goeh	每個月 měi gè yuè
	逐月日 tak goeh-jit	
	每(一)個月 múi (chit) kò goeh	
	每(一)月日 múi (chit) goeh-jit	

25.2.1 Relative references to a month

To refer to a month relative to the present, use the following expressions in the table below.

	TAIWANESE	MANDARIN
this month	這個月 chit kò goeh	這個月 zhège yuè
	這月日 chit goeh-jit	
last month	頂個月 téng kò goeh	上個月 shàng gè yuè
	頂月日 téng goeh-jit	
next month	後個月 āu kò goeh	下個月 xià gè yuè
	後月日 āu goeh-jit	

25.2.2 Approximate duration

To refer to an approximate period of time or duration related to a month, use the expressions in the table below.

	TAIWANESE	MANDARIN
first third of the month	月初 goeh-chhe	月初 yuèchū
	月頭 goeh-thâu	
middle third of the month	月中 goeh-tiong	月中 yuè zhōng
last third of the month	月短 goeh-té	月底 yuèdǐ
	月尾 goeh-bóe	
more than a month	一個外月 chit kò-gōa-goeh	一個多月 yī gè duō yuè
15th of the month (lunar)	月半 goeh-pòaⁿ	月半 yuè bàn
within/during a month	一個月的中間 chit kò goeh ê tiong-kan	一個月之間 yī gè yuè zhī jiān
	一個月中 chit kò goeh-tiong	一個月中 yī gè yuè zhōng

25.2.3 Months of the year

	TAIWANESE	MANDARIN
January	一月 it-goeh	一月 yī yuè
	正月 chiaⁿ-goeh	
February	二月 jī-goeh	二月 èr yuè
March	三月 saⁿ-goeh	三月 sān yuè
April	四月 sì-goeh	四月 sì yuè
May	五月 gō·-goeh	五月 wǔ yuè
June	六月 lak-goeh	六月 liù yuè
July	七月 chhit-goeh	七月 qī yuè
August	八月 peh-goeh	八月 bā yuè
September	九月 káu-goeh	九月 jiǔ yuè
October	十月 chap-goeh	十月 shí yuè
November	十一月 chap-it-goeh	十一月 shíyī yuè
December	十二月 chap-jī-goeh	十二月 shí'èr yuè

The alternative form for 'January' 正月 **chiaⁿ-goeh** originally comes from the name for the first month in the lunar calendar. However, it is now used interchangeably with 一月 **it-goeh**. In Mandarin, 正月 **zhēngyuè** is only used when referring to the lunar calendar.

25.3 Weeks

The word 禮拜 **lé-pài** 'week' itself is a measure word and requires no additional measure word. Note that this differs from Mandarin in that both words 'week' 星期 **xīngqí** and 禮拜 **lǐbài** require the additional measure word 個 **gè**.

	TAIWANESE	MANDARIN
one week	一禮拜 chit lé-pài	一個禮拜 yī gè lǐbài
two weeks	兩禮拜 nn̄g lé-pài	兩個禮拜 liǎng gè lǐbài
10 weeks	十禮拜 cha̍p lé-pài	十個禮拜 shí gè lǐbài
every week	逐禮拜 ta̍k lé-pài	每個禮拜 měi gè lǐbài
	每禮拜 múi lé-pài	
within/during a week	一禮拜的中間 chit lé-pài ê tiong-kan	一個禮拜之間 yī gè lǐbài zhī jiān
	一禮拜中 chit lé-pài-tiong	一個禮拜中 yī gè lǐbài zhōng

Additionally, 禮拜 **lé-pài** can mean 'Sunday'. The addition of the measure word 个 **ê** before 禮拜 **lé-pài** as well as context generally helps to make clear which meaning is intended.

阮 這 禮拜 欲 去 日本。
Gún chit lé-pài beh khì Ji̍t-pún.
我們 這個 禮拜 要 去 日本。
Wǒmen zhège lǐbài yào qù Rìběn.
This week we are going to Japan.

阮 這 个 禮拜 欲 去 日本。
Gún chit ê lé-pài beh khì Ji̍t-pún.
我們 這個 禮拜天 要 去 日本。
Wǒmen zhège lǐbàitiān yào qù Rìběn.
This Sunday we are going to Japan.

To refer to a week relative to the present, use the expressions in the table below.

	TAIWANESE	MANDARIN
this week	這禮拜 chit lé-pài	這(個)禮拜 zhè(ge) lǐbài
last week	頂禮拜 téng lé-pài	上(個)禮拜 shàng (gè) lǐbài
next week	後禮拜 āu lé-pài	下(個)禮拜 xià (gè) lǐbài
two weeks, fortnight	半個月 pòaⁿ-kò-goėh	半(個)月 bàn (gè) yuè
	半月日 pòaⁿ goėh-jit	

25.4 Days

The word 日 jit (also pronounced lit) 'day' is also a measure word and requires no additional measure word. An alternative term 工 kang 'day' is often preferred when counting or referring to the duration.

	TAIWANESE	MANDARIN
one day	一工 chit kang	一天 yī tiān
	一日 chit jit	
two days	兩工 nñg kang	兩天 liǎng tiān
	兩日 nñg jit	
10 days	十工 chȧp kang	十天 shí tiān
	十日 chȧp jit	
everyday	逐工 tȧk-kang	每天 měitiān
	每(一)工 múi(chit)-kang	
	逐日 tȧk-jit	
	每日 múi-jit	
within/during a day	一工內 chit kang lāi	一天內 yī tiān nèi
	一工中 chit kang-tiong	一天中 yī tiān zhōng

In Mandarin, 天 tiān 'day' is more commonly used, while 日 rì 'day' is reserved for more formal uses. Taiwanese tends to reserve 天 thiⁿ to signify the weather, seasons, or for use in set expressions.

25.4.1 Relative references to a day

To refer to a day relative to the present, use the expressions in the following table.

	TAIWANESE	MANDARIN
today	今仔日 kin-á-jit	今天 jīntiān
yesterday	昨昏 cha-hng (châng)	昨天 zuótiān
two days ago	頂日(仔) téng-jit(-á)	前天 qiántiān
	昨日 choh--jit	
three days ago	落昨日 loh-choh--jit	大前天 dàqiántiān
	大昨日 tōa-choh--jit	
four days ago	四日前 sì-jit-chêng	四天前 sì tiān qián
tomorrow	明仔載 bîn-á-chài	明天 míngtiān
	明仔日 bîn-á-jit	
two days from now	後日 āu--jit	後天 hòutiān
three days from now	大後日 tōa-āu--jit	大後天 dàhòutiān
four days from now	四日(以)後 sì-jit (í-)āu	四天以後 sì tiān yǐhòu

Note that 後日 **āu-jit** without the neutral tone has the meaning of 'someday' or 'some unspecified time in the future'.

25.4.2 Days of the week

The days of the week are presented in the table below. The days of the week 'Monday' through 'Saturday' optionally may be prefixed by 禮 **lé-**.

	TAIWANESE	MANDARIN
Sunday	禮拜 lé-pài	禮拜天 lǐbài tiān
	禮拜日 lé-pài-jit	禮拜日 lǐbài rì
Monday	(禮)拜一 (lé-)pài-it	禮拜一 lǐbài yī
Tuesday	(禮)拜二 (lé-)pài-jī	禮拜二 lǐbài èr
Wednesday	(禮)拜三 (lé-)pài-san	禮拜三 lǐbài sān
Thursday	(禮)拜四 (lé-)pài-sì	禮拜四 lǐbài sì
Friday	(禮)拜五 (lé-)pài-gō͘	禮拜五 lǐbài wǔ
Saturday	(禮)拜六 (lé-)pài-la̍k	禮拜六 lǐbài liù

Note that if referring to a preceding or subsequent day of the week, 禮 **lé-** cannot be omitted from the expression.

	TAIWANESE	MANDARIN
next Monday	後禮拜一 āu lé-pài-it	下禮拜一 xià lǐbài yī
last Monday	頂禮拜一 téng lé-pài-it	上禮拜一 shàng lǐbài yī

25.4.3 Days of the month

Sometimes the first 10 days of the month follow a practice used with the lunar calendar. Each day is preceded by 初 **chhe** 'beginning'.

	TAIWANESE	MANDARIN
first of the month	初一 chhe-it	初一 chū yī
second of the month	初二 chhe-jī	初二 chū èr
third of the month	初三 chhe-saⁿ	初三 chū sān
:	:	:
tenth of the month	初十 chhe-cha̍p	初十 chū shí

25.5 Specifying dates

In Taiwanese, dates are specified from the largest increment of time to the smallest (i.e. year, month, day). Note that numerals for years are read using the literary reading of numbers *(see 3.1.2 Literary reading for numbers)*.

June 21, 2013

YEAR	MONTH	DAY
二空一三年	六月	二十一號
jī khòng it sam nî	la̍k goe̍h	jī-cha̍p-it hō
二〇一三年	六月	二十一號
èr líng yī sān nián	liù yuè	èrshíyī hào

November 7, 1950

YEAR	MONTH	DAY
一九五空年	十一月	七號
it kiú ngó͘ khòng nî	cha̍p-it goe̍h	chhit hō
一九五〇年	十一月	七號
yī jiǔ wǔ líng nián	shíyī yuè	qī hào

Note that for days up to the tenth of the month, the lunar calendar system of reading days may be used *(see 25.4.3 Days of the month)*.

25.6 Seasons

	TAIWANESE	MANDARIN
Spring	春天 chhun-thiⁿ	春天 chūntiān
Summer	夏天 hā-thiⁿ	夏天 xiàtiān
	熱天 joa̍h-thiⁿ	
Autumn	秋天 chhiu-thiⁿ	秋天 qiūtiān
Winter	冬天 tang-thiⁿ	冬天 dōngtiān
	寒天 kôaⁿ-thiⁿ	

26 Present

In English, the present tense can be used to indicate actions that are in progress or habitual.

IN PROGRESS

She is writing a long letter.

HABITUAL

She writes long letters.

Taiwanese does not inflect or change the form of the verb to reflect tense (past, present, or future). However, time-specific phrases and grammatical elements can be used to help clarify when context is insufficient.

26.1 Present tense from context

Generally, context will indicate when an action has occurred. However, if more clarification is required, a time expression ('January 24', 'today', 'this week') or time adverb ('now', 'currently') can be provided *(see 14.1.2 Time adverbs)*.

The sentence below can be set in any point in time given the proper context.

伊 寫 批。
I siá phoe.
她 寫 信。
Tā xiě xìn.
She wrote / is writing / will write a letter.

26.2 Time expressions and time adverbs indicating the present

If the tense has not yet been established, a specific time expression or time adverb can be used to indicate or to underscore the time of the action. Time expressions and adverbs are generally placed after the subject but may be placed before the subject in the topic position for emphasis.

TAIWANESE	MANDARIN	MEANING
這馬 chit-má	現在 xiànzài	now
今仔日 kin-á-jit	今天 jīntiān	today
目前 bȯk-chiân	目前 mùqián	currently, presently
這禮拜 chit lé-pài	這(個)禮拜 zhè (gè) lǐbài	this week
這個月 chit kò gȯeh	這個月 zhè gè yuè	this month
今年 kín-nî	今年 jīnnián	this year

伊 這馬 佇 大 間 的 報社 食 頭路。
I <u>chit-má</u> tī tōa keng ê pò-siā chia̍h thâu-lō͘.
他 現在 在 大 的 報社 工作。
Tā <u>xiànzài</u> zài dà de bàoshè gōngzuò.
He <u>now</u> works for a large newspaper.

劉 小姐 今仔日 干焦 招待 新 的 人客。
Lâu sió-chiá <u>kin-á-jit</u> kan-na chiau-tāi sin ê lâng-kheh.
劉 小姐 今天 只 接待 新 的 客人。
Liú xiǎojiě <u>jīntiān</u> zhǐ jiēdài xīn de kèrén.
Ms. Lau is only seeing new clients <u>today</u>.

目前 阮 替 你 定位 愛 受 服務 費。
<u>Bȯk-chiân</u> gún thè lí tēng-ūi ài siu ho̍k-bū hùi.
目前 我們 替 你 定位 要 收 服務 費。
<u>Mùqián</u> wǒmen tì nǐ dìngwèi yào shōu fúwù fèi.
<u>Currently</u>, we charge a service fee for helping you make a reservation.

這禮拜 公車 無 停 佇 市政府。
Chit lé-pài kong-chhia bô thêng tī chhī-chèng-hú.
這禮拜 公車 不 停 在 市政府。
Zhè lǐbài gōngchē bù tíng zài shìzhèngfǔ.
This week the bus does not stop at city hall.

今年 阮 的 棒球隊 逐 場 比賽 攏 輸。
Kin-nî gún ê pāng-kiû-tūi ta̍k tiûⁿ pí-sài lóng su.
今年 我們 的 棒球隊 每 場 比賽 都 輸。
Jīnnián wǒmen de bàngqiúduì měi chǎng bǐsài dōu shū.
This year our baseball team is losing every game.

26.3 Ongoing actions

26.3.1 Emphasizing that an action is in progress using 咧 teh

In English, to describe an action that is ongoing the '-ing' suffix is added to the verb along with a form of 'to be' as a helping verb ('She is talking').

Taiwanese conveys this ongoing action by placing the dynamic continuous aspect marker **咧 teh** before an action verb *(see 8.2.1 Dynamic continuous aspect)*. This emphasizes that the action is already in progress.

咧 + *verb*

teh + *verb*

'to be *verb*-ing'

伊 咧 行 路。
I teh kiâⁿ lō͘.
他 在 走路。
Tā zài zǒu lù.
He is walking.

吳小姐和朋友咧講話。

Ngô˙ sió-chiá hām pêng-iú teh kóng ōe.

吳小姐跟朋友在講話。

Wú xiǎojiě gēn péngyǒu zài jiǎng huà.

Ms. Ngou is talking to her friend.

The particle **咧 teh** can only be placed before action verbs *(see 7 Action verbs)*. Stative verbs, modal verbs, and adjectives used as verbs can only emphasize the present by using time expressions *(see 9 Stative verbs, 12 Modal verbs, 6 Adjectives)*.

STATIVE VERB

我這陣想欲眠一下。

Góa chit-chūn siuⁿ-beh bîn--chit-ê.

我現在想要睡一下。

Wǒ xiànzài xiǎngyào shuì yīxià.

Right now I am thinking of taking a nap.

ADJECTIVE

湯這馬真燒。

Thng chit-má chin sio.

湯現在很熱。

Tāng xiànzài hěn rè.

The soup is hot right now.

MODAL

伊這馬欲走。

I chit-má beh cháu.

他現在要走。

Tā xiànzài yào zǒu.

He wants to go now.

26.3.2 Emphasizing the immediacy of an action in progress

While the use of the particle **咧 teh** before an action verb states that an action is already in progress, the immediacy can be further emphasized by placing **佇 tī-** before **咧 teh** to form **佇咧 tī-leh** (note the slight change in pronunciation), conveying 'in the middle of' doing something. Alternate forms include **當咧 tng-teh** and **拄咧 tú-teh** *(see 8.2.1.2 Emphasizing the immediacy of an action)*.

佇咧 + *verb*

tī-leh + *verb*

'in the middle of *verb* + -ing'

我 袂當 和 你 講 話，因為 我 這馬 佇咧 讀 冊。
Góa bē-tàng hām lí kóng ōe, in-ūi góa chit-má tī-leh thȧk chheh.
我 不能 跟你 講 話，因為 我 現在 正在 讀 書。
Wǒ bùnéng gēn nǐ jiǎng huà, yīnwèi wǒ xiànzài zhèngzài dú shū.
I can't talk to you because I am in the middle of studying.

阮 這馬 當咧 整理 桌仔，所以 請 小等 一下。
Gún chit-má tǹg-teh chéng-lí toh-á, só-í chhiáⁿ sió-tán--chit-ē.
我們 現在 正在 整理 桌子，所以 請 稍 等 一下。
Wǒmen xiànzài zhèngzài zhěnglǐ zhuōzi, suǒyǐ qǐng shāo děng yīxià.
We are setting up your table right now, so please wait a moment.

彼 个 老歲仔 拄咧 和 鳥仔 講 話。
Hit ê láu-hòe-á tú-teh hām chiáu-á kóng ōe.
那個 老人家 正在 和 鳥 講 話。
Nàge lǎorénjiā zhèngzài hé niǎo jiǎng huà.
That old man right now is talking to the birds.

In Mandarin, the equivalent emphasis can be expressed by placing **正在 zhèngzài** before the verb phrase.

26.3.3 Including manner with ongoing actions

The particle **咧 teh** is separable from the verb, so adverbs of manner can be placed in between *(see 14.2.3 Manner adverbs)*.

咧 + *manner adverb* + *verb*

teh + *manner adverb* + *verb*

恁囝足乖，恁攏咧恬恬耍。

Lín kiáⁿ chiok koai, in lóng teh tiām-tiām sńg.

你的孩子非常乖，他們都在靜靜地玩。

Nǐ de háizi fēicháng guāi, tāmen dōu zài jìngjìng de wán.

Your children are so well behaved. They are all playing so quietly.

阮小弟這馬佇塗跤咧慢慢趖。

Gún sió-tī chit-má tī thô·-kha teh bān-bān sô.

我的弟弟現在在地上在慢慢地爬行。

Wǒ dìdì xiànzài zài dìshàng zài mànman de páxíng.

My little brother is now slowly crawling on the floor.

26.3.4 Describing an ongoing state using verb suffix 咧 --leh

The static continuous aspect marker **咧 --leh** can be used as a suffix to change-of-state action verbs to emphasize an action that is in a persistent state or condition *(see 8.2.2 Static continuous aspect, 7.2 Change-of-state action verbs)*. The verb can be describing a posture (e.g. sitting down), manner of existence (e.g. picture hanging on the wall), or repetitive motion (e.g. chewing gum).

verb + 咧

verb + --leh

伊佇車頭前徛咧。

I tī chhia thâu-chêng khiā--leh.

她在車前面站著。

Tā zài chē qiánmiàn zhànzhe.

She is standing in front of the car.

學生冊提咧。

Ha̍k-seng chheh the̍h--leh.

學生拿著書。

Xuéshēng názhe shū.

The students are holding their books.

水晶燈 按 厝頂 吊咧。

Chúi-chiⁿ-teng àn chhù-téng <u>tiàu--leh</u>.

水晶燈 在 天花板 吊著。

Shuǐjīngdēng zài tiānhuābǎn <u>diàozhe</u>.

Crystal lights <u>are hanging</u> from the ceiling.

門 攏 關咧。

Mn̂g lóng <u>koaiⁿ--leh</u>.

門 都 關著 呢。

Mén dōu <u>guānzhe</u> ne.

All the doors <u>are closed</u>.

阮 車 停咧 佇 外口。

Gún chhia <u>thêng--leh</u> tī gōa-kháu.

我們 的 車 停 在 外面。

Wǒmen de chē <u>tíng</u> zài wàimiàn.

Our car <u>is parked</u> outside.

Note that Taiwanese does not have an end-of-sentence particle equivalent to the Mandarin 呢 **ne** for emphasizing ongoing actions in the present. Additionally, in some contexts, the Mandarin phrasing sounds more natural without an explicit suffix marking an ongoing state.

26.4 Habitual actions in the present

26.4.1 Expressing habitual actions with 有 ū

To emphasize a habitual action in the present, place 有 **ū** followed by the dynamic aspect marker 咧 **teh** before the verb *(see 8.5 Habitual aspect)*. Note that if a time expression is provided, the addition of 有咧 **ū teh** before the verb is optional.

有 + 咧 + *verb*

ū + teh + *verb*

暗頓 食 了，我 有 咧 啉 茶。
Àm-tǹg chia̍h liáu, góa ū teh lim tê.

晚餐 吃 完，我 經常 喝 茶。
Wǎncān chī wán, wǒ jīngcháng hē chá.

I drink tea after dinner.

廖 小姐 拜五 暗時 佇 廟寺 的 戲台 搬戲。
Liāu sió-chiá pài-gō͘ àm-sî tī biō-sī ê hì-tâi poaⁿ-hì.

廖 小姐 禮拜五 晚上 在 寺廟 的 舞台 表演。
Liào xiǎojiě lǐbàiwǔ wǎnshàng zài sìmiào de wǔtái biǎoyǎn.

Ms. Liau performs on the temple stage on Friday nights.

阮 有 咧 檢查 身份證。
Gún ū teh kiám-cha sin-hūn-chèng.

我們 經常 檢查 身份證。
Wǒmen jīngcháng jiǎnchá shēnfènzhèng.

We do check identification.

Note that in Standard Mandarin habitual action is generally understood through context, with a time expression, or emphasized through an adverb such as **經常 jīngcháng** 'regularly'. Taiwan Mandarin can also use **有在 yǒu zài** before the verb for habitual action.

TAIWANESE

伊 有 咧 行路。

I ū teh kiâⁿ lō͘.

He does go for walks.

STANDARD MANDARIN

他 經常 走路。

Tā jīngcháng zǒu lù.

He does go for walks.

TAIWAN MANDARIN

他 有 在 走路。

Tā yǒu zài zǒu lù.

He does go for walks.

26.4.2 Using time adverbs to indicate habitual actions

逐 ta̍k 'each, every' paired with a period of time may be used to create a time adverb that indicates habitual actions. An alternate form is 每 múi.

TAIWANESE	MANDARIN	MEANING
逐點鍾 ta̍k tiám-cheng	每個小時 měi gè xiǎoshí	each/every hour
逐日 ta̍k ji̍t	每天 měitiān	each/every day
逐工 ta̍k kang	每天 měitiān	each/every day
逐禮拜 ta̍k lé-pài	每(個)禮拜 měi (gè) lǐbài	each/every week
逐個月 ta̍k kò go̍eh	每個月 měi gè yuè	each/every month
逐冬 ta̍k tang	每年 měinián	each/every year

Note that in Taiwanese 點鍾 tiám-cheng 'hour' does not use a measure word like its Mandarin counterpart.

學生 逐 點鐘 換 課。
Ha̍k-seng ta̍k tiám-cheng ōaⁿ khò.
學生 每 個 小時 換 課。
Xuéshēng měi gè xiǎoshí huàn kè.
The students change classes <u>each hour</u>.

我 每 禮拜 拍 排球。
Góa múi lé-pài phah pâi-kiû.
我 每 禮拜 打 排球。
Wǒ měi lǐbài dǎ páiqiú.
<u>Every week</u> I play volleyball.

26.4.3 Using relative frequency adverbs to indicate habitual actions

Relative frequency adverbs can be used to describe habitual actions. Below is a selection of some common adverbs used *(see 14.2.2 Relative frequency adverbs)*.

TAIWANESE	MANDARIN	MEANING
直直 tit-tit	一直 yīzhí	always, continuously
不時 put-sî	經常 jīngcháng	regularly
定定 tiāⁿ-tiāⁿ	常常 chángcháng	constantly, frequently

TAIWANESE	MANDARIN	MEANING
有棠時仔 ū-tang-sî-á	偶爾 ǒu'ěr	sometimes, occasionally
罕得 hán-tit	難得 nándé	rarely

伊 <u>直直</u> 袂記得 紮 伊 的 身份證。
I <u>tit-tit</u> bē-kì-tit chah i ê sin-hūn-chèng.
她 <u>一直</u> 忘記 帶 她 的 身分證。
Tā <u>yīzhí</u> wàngjì dài tā de shēnfènzhèng.
She <u>always</u> forgets to bring her ID card.

隔壁 的 狗仔 <u>定定</u> 咧 吠。
Keh-piah ê káu-á <u>tiāⁿ-tiāⁿ</u> teh pūi.
隔壁 的 狗 <u>常常</u> 在 吠。
Gébì de gǒu <u>chángcháng</u> zài fèi.
The neighbor's dog is <u>constantly</u> barking.

<u>有當時仔</u> 我 用 行 的 去 上班。
<u>Ū-tang-sî-á</u> góa ēng kiâⁿ--ê khì siōng-pan.
<u>有 的 時候</u> 我 用 走 的 去 上班。
<u>Yǒu de shíhòu</u> wǒ yòng zǒu de qù shàngbān.
<u>Sometimes</u> I walk to work.

伊 <u>罕得</u> 共 功課 做 予 了。
I <u>hán-tit</u> kā kong-khò chò hōˈliáu.
他 <u>難得</u> 把 功課 做完。
Tā <u>nándé</u> bǎ gōngkè zuòwán.
He <u>rarely</u> finishes his homework.

26.5 Indicating past events relevant to the present using 矣 --ah

When an action occurs in the past but continues to have relevance in the present, the anterior aspect marker **矣 --ah** is placed at the end of the sentence *(see 8.4 Anterior aspect)*. This often occurs in situations where English uses the present perfect tense ('I <u>have eaten</u>, so I'm not hungry now').

sentence + 矣

sentence + --ah

阮 蹛 踮 這 鄰 三 年 矣。
Gún tòa tàm chit lîn saⁿ nî--ah.
我們 住 在 這 鄰 三 年 了。
Wǒmen zhù zài zhè lín sān nián le.
We have lived in this neighborhood for 3 years.

你 已經 共 咱 煮 中晝頓 矣。
Lí í-keng kā lán chú tiong-tàu-tǹg--ah.
你 已經 幫 我們 做 午餐 了。
Nǐ yǐjīng bāng wǒmen zuò wǔcān le.
You have already cooked us lunch.

楊 先生 已經 共 阮 買 電影 票 矣。
Iûⁿ--sian-siⁿ í-keng kā gún bé tiān-iáⁿ phiò--ah.
楊 先生 已經 幫 我們 買 電影 票 了。
Yáng xiānshēng yǐjīng bāng wǒmen mǎi diànyǐng piào le.
Mr. Iunn has already bought our theater tickets.

27 Past

Taiwanese does not inflect or change the form of the verb to reflect the past tense. Instead, the past tense is understood from context, specified by time expressions, or indicated through aspect markers.

27.1 Time expressions and time adverbs indicating the past

Time expressions ('yesterday', 'last year') and time adverbs ('in the past', 'previously') can provide a temporal context for the verb. Generally, time expressions or adverbs are placed after the subject but may be placed before the subject in the topic position for emphasis.

TAIWANESE	MANDARIN	MEANING
昨昏 cha-hng (châng)	昨天 zuótiān	yesterday
頂禮拜 téng lé-pài	上(個)禮拜 shàng (gè) lǐbài	last week
頂個月 téng kò gòeh	上個月 shàng gè yuè	last month
頂月日 téng gòeh-jit	上個月 shàng gè yuè	last month
舊年 kū-nî	去年 qùnián	last year
過去 kòe-khì	過去 guòqù	in the past
以前 í-chêng	以前 yǐqián	previously

我 <u>昨昏</u> 申請 護照。
Góa <u>cha-hng</u> sin-chhéng hō͘-chiàu.
我 <u>昨天</u> 申請 護照。
Wǒ <u>zuótiān</u> shēnqǐng hùzhào.
I applied for a passport <u>yesterday</u>.

頂個月你應該收著退稅。

Téng kò goeh lí eng-kai siu-tioh thè-sòe.

上個月你應該受到退稅。

Shàng gè yuè nǐ yīnggāi shōudào tuìshuì.

<u>Last month</u> you should have gotten a tax refund.

阮舊年去美國旅行。

Gún <u>kū-nî</u> khì Bí-kok lú-hêng.

我們去年去美國旅行。

Wǒmen <u>qùnián</u> qù Měiguó lǚxíng.

We traveled to the United States <u>last year</u>.

以前動物園予阮用翕相機。

<u>Í-chêng</u> tōng-but-hng hō gún ēng hip-siōng-ki.

以前動物園讓我們用照相機。

<u>Yǐqián</u> dòngwùyuán ràng wǒmen yòng zhàoxiàngjī.

<u>Previously</u>, the zoo let us use cameras.

27.2 Completed actions in the past

To express that an action was completed in the past, the verb is placed in the perfective aspect *(see 8.1 Perfective aspect)*. In Taiwanese, there are two types of perfective aspect markers: **有 ū** and phase complements.

27.2.1 Expressing a completed action with 有 ū

To indicate that an action verb is completed, place **有 ū** before the verb. Stative verbs, modal verbs, and adjectives used as verbs can only express the past by using time expressions.

有 + *verb*

ū + *verb*

伊 有 來。

I ū lâi.

他 來了。

Tā láile.

He came.

曾 太太 有 帶 餅 來。

Chan thài-thài ū tòa piáⁿ lâi.

曾 太太 帶了 餅乾 來。

Zēng tàitài dàile bǐnggān lái.

Mrs. Chan brought cookies.

Note that Mandarin uses the verb suffix **了** -le to indicate a completed action and does not have a direct equivalent to the Taiwanese use of **有 ū** for marking the perfective aspect. However, Taiwan Mandarin has adopted the use of placing **有 yǒu** before a verb, reflecting the grammar of Taiwanese.

STANDARD MANDARIN

你 吃 飯 了 嗎？

Nǐ chī fàn le ma?

Did you eat?

TAIWAN MANDARIN

你 有 吃 飯 嗎？

Nǐ yǒu chī fàn ma?

Did you eat?

TAIWANESE

你 有 食 飯 無?

Lí ū chia̍h pn̄g--bô?

Did you eat?

27.2.2 Expressing a completed action with a phase complement

Another method to indicate that an action is completed in the past is by adding a phase complement *(see 11.1.1 Phase complements indicating completion)*. Phase complements indicating completion (了 **liáu**, 完 **ôan**, 好 **hó**, 煞 **soah**) signal that the action of the verb has ended. Placed immediately after the verb, phase complements must be the final element in a clause or sentence.

> *verb + phase complement (completion)*

> 阮 昨昏 共 文章 寫 完。
> Gún cha-hng kā bûn-chiong siá ôan.
> 我們 昨天 寫了 文章。
> Wǒmen zuótiān xiěle wénzhāng.
> Yesterday we wrote our essays.

> 恁 阿媽 佮 阿母 做 好 遐爾 濟 菜。
> Lín a-má kah a-bú chò hó hiah-nī chē chhài.
> 你們 的 奶奶 和 媽媽 做了 那麼 多 菜。
> Nǐmen de nǎinai hé māmā zuòle nàme duō cài.
> Your grandma and mother cooked so many dishes.

Note that Mandarin marks the perfective aspect on the verb by adding the suffix 了 **-le**. Additionally, Mandarin does not require the perfective aspect marker 了 **-le** to be the final element of a clause or sentence.

27.2.3 Emphasizing a completed action in the past with 有 ū

有 **ū** can also be used as an emphasis marker. To emphasize that an action did indeed occur, place 有 **ū** before the verb *(see 10.2.4 有 ū as a marker for emphasis)*. Additional vocal stress or a pause can help distinguish 有 **ū** as an emphasis marker from a completed action marker. By optionally adding a phase complement after the verb to mark completion, the emphasis function of 有 **ū** becomes unambiguous *(see 11.1.1 Phase complements indicating completion, 27.2.2 Expressing a completed action with a phase complement)*.

> 有 + *verb* + *(phase complement)*
> ū + *verb* + *(phase complement)*

咱 離開 辦公室 進前，我 有 共 報告 寫 了 矣。
Lán lî-khui pān-kong-sek chìn-chêng, góa ū kā pò-kò siá liáu--ah.
我們 離開 辦公室 之前，我 有 把 報告 寫完 啦。
Wǒmen líkāi bàngōngshì zhīqián, wǒ yǒu bǎ bàogào xiěwán la.
Before we left the office, I *did* finish writing the report.

恁 爸母 有 共 你 的 學費 納 了。
Lín pē-bú ū kā lí ê ha̍k-hùi la̍p liáu.
你 父母 有 幫 你 繳了 學費 啊。
Nǐ fùmǔ yǒu bāng nǐ jiǎole xuéfèi a.
Your parents *did* pay for your tuition.

有 ū as an emphasis marker in the past can also be used with the experiential aspect markers **捌 bat** and **過 -kòe** (see 8.3 Experiential aspect, 27.6 Talking about past experience using 捌 bat and 過 -kòe).

我 有 捌 食過 印尼 料理。
Góa ū bat chia̍h-kòe Ìn-nî liāu-lí.
我 有 吃過 印尼 料理。
Wǒ yǒu chīguò Yìnní liàolǐ.
I *have* had Indonesian cuisine before.

恁 已經 有 來過 亞洲。
In í-keng ū lâi-kòe A-chiu.
他們 有 已經 來過 亞洲。
Tāmen yǒu yǐjīng láiguò Yàzhōu.
They *have* come to Asia before.

27.2.4 Expressing an action that did not occur

If an action did not occur in the past, use the appropriate negative form of the verb. While most verbs use **無 bô** for the negative form, a few verbs use the negative **毋 m̄** (see 13.1.1 Pure negative 毋 m̄ 'not'). Without context or a time expression, the action that did not occur could refer to the past or present.

WITHOUT TIME EXPRESSIONS

彼 兩 的 查埔 囡仔 無 去 上課。
Hit nn̄g ê cha-po͘ gín-á bô khì siōng-khò.

PAST INTERPRETATION

那 兩 個 男孩子 沒有 上課。

Nà liǎng gè nánháizi méiyǒu shàngkè.

Those two boys didn't go to class.

PRESENT INTERPRETATION

那 兩 個 男孩子 不 上課。

Nà liǎng gè nánháizi bù shàngkè.

Those two boys don't go to class (*they don't attend classes*).

Note that in Mandarin, the difference in negation indicates if an action verb has not occurred in the past (**沒有 měiyǒu**) or does not occur in the present (**不 bù**).

With stative verbs, modal verbs, or adjectives, Mandarin can only use **不 bù** for negation. In this case, the Mandarin is ambiguous like Taiwanese and requires a time expression for clarification.

我 講 的 話，伊 無 相信。
Góa kóng ê ōe, i bô siong-sìn.
我 說 的 話，她 不 相信。
Wǒ shuō de huà, tā bù xiāngxìn.
She didn't believe what I had said (*past interpretation*).
She doesn't believe what I said (*present interpretation*).

With explicit time expressions, the ambiguity for both action and stative verbs is removed.

WITH TIME EXPRESSIONS

彼 兩 的 查埔 囡仔 昨昏 無 去 上課。
Hit nñg ê cha-po˙ gín-á cha-hng bô khì siōng-khò.
那 兩 個 男孩子 昨天 沒有 上課。
Nà liǎng gè nánháizi zuótiān méiyǒu shàngkè.
Those two boys didn't go to class yesterday.

我 講 的 話，伊 彼陣 無 相信。
Góa kóng ê ōe, i hit-chūn bô siong-sìn.
我 說 的 話，她 那 時 不 相信。
Wǒ shuō de huà, tā nà shí bù xiāngxìn.
That time she didn't believe what I had said.

27.2.5 Expressing actions that have not yet occurred using 猶未 iáu-bōe

For actions that still have not occurred, place the negative 猶未 **iáu-bōe** 'not yet' before the verb.

猶未 + *verb*

iáu-bōe + *verb*

明仔載 的 考試,伊 猶未 讀 好。
Bîn-á-chài ê khó-chhì, i iáu-bōe thak hó.
明天 的 考試,她 還沒 讀 好。
Míngtiān de kǎoshì, tā háiméi dú hǎo.
She hasn't studied for tomorrow's test yet.

阮 猶未 拍算 阮 的 暑假。
Gún iáu-bōe phah-sǹg gún ê sú-ká.
我們 還沒 打算 我們 的 暑假。
Wǒmen háiméi dǎsuàn wǒmen de shǔjià.
We haven't planned our summer break yet.

27.3 Habitual actions in the past

For habitual actions that occurred in the past ('We used to jog' or 'He used to play guitar'), place a time expression before the habitual action markers 有咧 **ū teh** *(see 8.5 Habitual aspect, 10.2.5 有 ū in the habitual aspect, 26.4 Habitual actions)*.

time expression (past) + 有 + 咧 + *verb*

time expression (past) + ū + teh + *verb*

'used to *verb*'

我 過去 跿 這 條 溪仔 有 咧 泅水。
Góa kòe-khì tàm chit tiâu khe-á ū teh siû chúi.

我 過去 在 這 條 溪 經常 有 游泳。
Wǒ guòqù zài zhè tiáo xī jīngcháng yǒu yóuyǒng.

I used to swim in this creek.

Note that Standard Mandarin generally uses an adverb or time expression to indicate the habitual action. However, Taiwan Mandarin can also use **有在 yǒu zài** before the phrase to indicate the habitual aspect.

TAIWAN MANDARIN

我 過去 在 這 條 溪 有 在 游泳。
Wǒ guòqù zài zhè tiáo xī yǒu zài yóuyǒng.

I used to swim in this creek.

An alternative method to express the habitual past is to use a time expression along with a relative frequency adverb and the reference adverb **攏 lóng** 'always'.

time expression (past) + relative frequency adverb + 攏 + verb

time expression (past) + relative frequency adverb + lóng + verb

'*time expression (past)* always *verb*'

學生 以前 通常 攏 聽 老師 的 話。
Ha̍k-seng í-chêng thong-siông lóng thiaⁿ láu-su ê ōe.

學生 以前 通常 都 聽 老師 的 話。
Xuéshēng yǐqián tōngcháng dōu tīng lǎoshī de huà.

In the past the students usually listened to the teacher.

伊 以前 逐 日 攏 佇 樹仔跤 食 中晝頓。
I í-chêng ta̍k ji̍t lóng tī chhiū-á-kha chia̍h tiong-tàu-tǹg.

她 以前 每天 都 在 樹下 吃 午餐。
Tā yǐqián měitiān dōu zài shùxià chī wǔcān.

She used to eat lunch under the tree every day.

27.4 Expressing a repeated event in the past with 閣(再) koh(-chài)

For an event that happened 'again' in the past, place the adverb 閣(再) koh(-chài) before the verb. If there is a prepositional phrase, it must come between the adverb 閣(再) koh(-chài) and the verb.

閣(再) + *(prepositional phrase)* + *verb*

koh(-chài) + *(prepositional phrase)* + *verb*

鳥鼠仔 閣 按 籠仔 偷 走出去。
Niáu-chhí-á <u>koh</u> àn láng-á thau cháu--chhut-khì.
老鼠 又 從 籠子 偷 跑出去。
Lǎoshǔ <u>yòu</u> cóng lóngzi tōu pǎochūqù.
The mouse escaped from its cage <u>again</u>.

伊 閣再 袂記得 帶 伊 的 錢袋仔 矣。
I <u>koh-chài</u> bē-kì-tit tòa i ê chîⁿ-tē-á--ah.
他 又 忘記 帶 他 的 錢包 了。
Tā <u>yòu</u> wàngjì dài tā de qiánbāo le.
He forgot to bring his wallet <u>again</u>.

Note that in Mandarin 又 **yòu** 'again' is used for past occurrences while 再 **zài** is reserved for the future. Taiwanese, has no such restrictions and may use 閣(再) **koh(-chài)** for both the past and present.

27.5 Expressing the recent past with 頭拄仔 thâu-tú-á

To describe an event that has occurred in the recent past, place the adverb 頭拄仔 **thâu-tú-á** before the verb to express 'to have just done' some action *(see 14.1.2 Time adverbs)*. Some alternate forms include 拄才 **tú-chiah** or 拄(仔) **tú(-á)**.

頭拄仔 + *verb*

thâu-tú-á + *verb*

'to have just *verb*'

劉 小姐 <u>頭拄仔</u> 離開 辦公室 矣。
Lâu sió-chiá <u>thâu-tú-á</u> lī-khui pán-kong-sek--ah.
劉 小姐 <u>剛剛</u> 離開 辦公室 了。
Liú xiǎojiě <u>gānggāng</u> líkāi bàngōngshì le.
Ms. Lau <u>just</u> left the office.

我 <u>拄才</u> 袂紀得 帶 鎖匙。
Góa <u>tú-chiah</u> bē-kí-tit tòa só-sî.
我 <u>剛才</u> 忘記 帶 鑰匙。
Wǒ <u>gāngcái</u> wàngjì dài yàoshi.
I <u>just</u> forgot to bring my keys.

伊 <u>拄</u> 走 去。
I <u>tú</u> cháu--khì.
他 <u>才</u> 走 了。
Tā <u>cái</u> zǒu le.
He <u>just</u> left.

我 <u>拄仔</u> 咧 看 報紙。
Góa <u>tú-á</u> teh khòaⁿ pò-chóa.
我 <u>剛剛</u> 在 看 報紙。
Wǒ <u>gānggāng</u> zài kàn bàozhǐ.
I was <u>just</u> reading the newspaper.

27.6 Past experiences

27.6.1 Expressing past experiences using 捌 bat and 過 -kòe

To talk about a past experience, use the experiential aspect markers by placing **捌 bat** before the verb, **過 -kòe** after the verb, or use both **捌 bat** and **過 -kòe**. Note that the past experience must be a repeatable event *(see 8.3 Experiential aspect)*. Often the adverb **已經 í-keng** 'already' is added for emphasis.

METHOD 1

(已經) + 捌 + *verb*

(í-keng) + bat + *verb*

我 捌 去 印度。
Góa bat khì Ìn-tō͘.
我 去過 印度。
Wǒ qùguò Yìndù.
I have gone to India before.

蔡 先生 已經 捌 去 予 醫生 看著 頭疼。
Chhài--sian-siⁿ í-keng bat khì hō͘ i-seng khòaⁿ-tiȯh thâu-thiàⁿ.
蔡 先生 已經 給 醫生 看過 頭痛。
Cài xiānshēng yǐjīng gěi yīshēng kànguò tóutòng.
Mr. Chhai has already seen the doctor for his headache.

METHOD 2

(已經) + *verb* + 過

(í-keng) + *verb* + -kòe

我 去過 印度。
Góa khì-kòe Ìn-tō͘.
我 去過 印度。
Wǒ qùguò Yìndù.
I have gone to India before.

蔡 先生 已經 去過 予 醫生 看著 頭疼。
Chhài--sian-siⁿ í-keng khì-kòe hō͘ i-seng khòaⁿ-tiȯh thâu-thiàⁿ.
蔡 先生 已經 給 醫生 看過 頭痛。
Cài xiānshēng yǐjīng gěi yīshēng kànguò tóutòng.
Mr. Chhai has already seen the doctor for his headache.

METHOD 3

(已經) ＋ 捌 ＋ *verb* ＋ 過

(í-keng) ＋ bat ＋ *verb* ＋ -kòe

我 捌 去過 印度。
Góa bat khì-kòe Ìn-tō͘.
我 去過 印度。
Wǒ qùguò Yìndù.
I have gone to India before.

蔡 先生 已經 捌 去過 予 醫生 看著 頭疼。
Chhài--sian-siⁿ í-keng bat khì-kòe hō͘ i-seng khòaⁿ-tio̍h thâu-thiàⁿ.
蔡 先生 已經 給 醫生 看過 頭痛。
Cài xiānshēng yǐjīng gěi yīshēng kànguò tóutòng.
Mr. Chhai has already seen the doctor for his headache.

Note that in Mandarin only the suffix 過 **-guò** is used to indicate past experience.

27.6.2 Expressing not having had an experience

To indicate that an event has not been experienced before, use 毋 m̄ to negate 捌 **bat**, if present. If only the suffix 過 **-kòe** marks the experiential aspect, use the proper negation for the main verb. To provide additional emphasis on 'never' having had an experience, the adverb 從來 **chiông-lâi** 'since before' or 到今 **kàu-taⁿ** 'until now' may be used.

METHOD 1

毋 ＋ 捌 ＋ *verb* ＋ (過)

m̄ ＋ bat ＋ *verb* ＋ (-kòe)

伊 毋 捌 食 臭豆腐。
I m̄ bat chia̍h chhàu-tāu-hū.
她 沒 吃過 臭豆腐。
Tā méi chīguò chòu dòufu.
She has not eaten stinky tofu before.

伊 到今 <u>毋 捌</u> 駛過 車。

I kàu-taⁿ <u>m̄ bat</u> sái-<u>kòe</u> chhia.

她 從來 <u>沒</u> 開過 車。

Tā cónglái <u>méi</u> kāiguò chē.

She <u>has never</u> driven a car <u>before</u>.

賴 先生 從來 <u>毋 捌</u> 看 京戲。

Lōa--sian-siⁿ chiông-lâi <u>m̄ bat</u> khòaⁿ Kiaⁿ-hì.

賴 先生 從來 <u>沒</u> 看過 京劇。

Lài xiānshēng cónglái <u>méi</u> kànguò Jīngjù.

Mr. Loa <u>has never</u> seen Peking Opera <u>before</u>.

METHOD 2

negation + *verb* + 過

negation + *verb* + -kòe

伊 <u>無</u> 食<u>過</u> 臭豆腐。

I <u>bô</u> chiảh-<u>kòe</u> chhàu-tāu-hū.

她 <u>沒</u> 吃過 臭豆腐。

Tā <u>méi</u> chīguò chòu dòufu.

She <u>has not</u> eaten stinky tofu <u>before</u>.

伊 到今 <u>無</u> 駛<u>過</u> 車。

I kàu-taⁿ <u>bô</u> sái-<u>kòe</u> chhia.

她 從來 <u>沒</u> 開過 車。

Tā cónglái <u>méi</u> kāiguò chē.

She <u>has never</u> driven a car <u>before</u>.

賴 先生 從來 <u>無</u> 看<u>過</u> 京戲。

Lōa--sian-siⁿ chiông-lâi <u>bô</u> khòaⁿ-<u>kòe</u> Kiaⁿ-hì.

賴 先生 從來 <u>沒</u> 看過 京劇。

Lài xiānshēng cónglái <u>méi</u> kànguò Jīngjù.

Mr. Loa <u>has never</u> seen Peking Opera <u>before</u>.

28 Future

In English, the future tense is generally marked by placing the modal verb 'will' before the main verb.

He will watch television.

While Taiwanese does not inflect or change the form of the verb to reflect tense (past, present, or future), future actions often include a modal verb functioning similarly to the English 'will'.

伊 會 看 電視。
I ē khòaⁿ tiān-sī.
他 會 看 電視。
Tā huì kàn diànshì.
He will watch television.

Additionally, time-specific phrases can be used to help clarify the tense when insufficient context is provided.

28.1 Time expressions and time adverbs indicating the future

Time expressions ('tomorrow', 'next Thursday') and time adverbs ('in the future', 'next time') can provide a temporal context for the verb. Generally, time expressions or adverbs are placed after the subject but may be placed before the subject in the topic position for emphasis.

Following is a table of common time adverbs used to discuss the future.

TAIWANESE	MANDARIN	MEANING
下昏暗 e-hng-àm	今晚 jīnwǎn	tonight
明仔載 bîn-á-chài	明天 míngtiān	tomorrow
後禮拜 āu lé-pài	下(個)禮拜 xià (gè) lǐbài	next week

TAIWANESE	MANDARIN	MEANING
後個月 āu kò góeh	下個月 xià gè yuè	next month
明年 mê-nî	明天 míngtiān	next year
將來 chiong-lâi	將來 jiānglái	in the future
咧欲 teh-beh	快要 kuàiyào	just about to
後擺 āu-pái	下次 xià cì	next time

下昏暗 阮 欲 看 恐怖片。
E-hng-àm gún beh khòaⁿ khióng-pò͘-phìⁿ.
今晚 我們 要 看 恐怖片。
Jīnwǎn wǒmen yào kàn kǒngbùpiàn.
<u>Tonight</u> we will watch a horror film.

阮 查囝 明年 會 按 高中 畢業。
Gún cha-kiáⁿ <u>mê-nî</u> ē àn ko-tiong pit-gia̍p.
我 女兒 明年 會 從 高中 畢業。
Wǒ nǚ'ér <u>míngnián</u> huì cóng gāozhōng bìyè.
<u>Next year</u> my daughter will graduate from high school.

伊 咧欲 到 矣。
I <u>teh-beh</u> kàu--ah.
他 快要 到 了。
Tā <u>kuàiyào</u> dào le.
He's <u>just about to</u> arrive.

28.2 Indicating the future with possibility modal verbs

To express the events that will occur in the future, Taiwanese generally makes use of modal verbs to express the possibility or desire for an action to occur.

28.2.1 Expressing possibility using 會 ē

To indicate a strong possibility of an event occurring, place the modal verb 會 ē 'will' before a verb. Generally, the feeling is one of inevitability and not necessarily intention *(see 12.1.1 Modal verb 會 ē 'will').*

會 + *verb*

ē + *verb*

'will *verb*'

後 禮拜五 阮 會 為 總統 投票。

Āu lé-pài-gō͘ gún ē ūi chóng-thóng tâu-phiò.

下 禮拜五 我們 會 為 總統 投票。

Xià lǐbàiwǔ wǒmen huì wèi zǒngtǒng tóupiào.

Next Friday we will vote for the president.

咱 去 曼谷 的 飛行機 明仔早仔 會 起飛。

Lán khì Bān-kok ê hoe-lêng-ki bîn-á-chái-á ē khí-poe.

我們 去 曼谷 的 飛機 明早 會 起飛。

Wǒmen qù Màngǔ de fēijī míngzǎo huì qǐfēi.

Our flight to Bangkok will take off tomorrow morning.

28.2.2 Expressing possibility using 欲 beh

To stress the possibility that an event will likely occur in the immediate future, place the modal verb **欲 beh** (also pronounced **boeh**) 'going to' before a verb *(see 12.1.2 Modal verb 欲 beh 'to be going to')*. Note that because **欲 beh** also has the meaning 'to want', when the subject is an animate being (person or animal), the future action may also be interpreted to include intention. If the subject is inanimate (objects, non-living things), **欲 beh** only conveys future possibility.

欲 + *verb*

beh + *verb*

'to be going to *verb*'

謝 先生 下昏暗 欲 請 阮 食 飯。

Siā--sian-siⁿ e-hng-àm beh chhiáⁿ gún chiȧh pn̄g.

謝 先生 今晚 要 請 我們 吃飯。

Xiè xiānshēng jīnwǎn yào qǐng wǒmen chī fàn.

Mr. Sia is going to treat us to dinner tonight.

政府 欲 予 人 獎學金。

Chèng-hú beh hō͘ lâng chióng-ha̍k-kim.

政府 要 給 人 獎學金。

Zhèngfǔ yào gěi rén jiǎngxuéjīn.

The government is going to award scholarships.

28.3 Describing events that are just about to happen

To indicate that an event is just about to happen, place the adverb **咧欲 teh-beh** 'just about to' before the verb. Additionally, the end-of-sentence particle **矣 --ah**, which can be used to indicate a change in situation, is also commonly used with imminent events *(see 8.4 Anterior aspect)*. An alternate version is **強欲 kiōng-beh**.

咧欲 + *verb* + (矣)

teh-beh + *verb* + (--ah)

'just about to *verb*'

緊 抱 紅嬰仔，伊 咧欲 哭 矣。

Kín phō âng-eⁿ-á, i teh-beh khàu--ah.

快 抱抱 嬰兒，他 快要 哭 了。

Kuài bàobào yīng'ér, tā kuàiyào kū le.

Hurry and hold the baby. He's just about to cry.

天 看起來 強欲 落 雨 矣。

Thiⁿ khòaⁿ-khí-lâi kiōng-beh lo̍h hō͘--ah.

天空 看起來 快要 下 雨 了。

Tiānkōng kànqǐlái kuàiyào xià yǔ le.

The sky looks like it's just about to rain.

28.4 Indicating the future with desire modal verbs

Actions in the future can also be described in terms of desire (wanting, wishing, hoping, thinking of doing).

28.4.1 'Wanting to' perform an action

To express desiring to perform an action in the future, place the modal verb 欲 **beh** or 愛 **ài** before a verb *(see 12.2.1 Modal verb 欲 beh 'to want', 12.2.2 Modal verb 愛 ài 'to want')*. Note that 愛 **ài** is generally preferred over 欲 **beh** when there are different subjects or when used before an adjective. In some contexts the desire to perform an action can include translations of 'hoping' or 'wishing'.

欲 / 愛 + *verb*

beh / ài + *verb*

'to want to *verb*'

我 愛 伊 會當 讀 台大。
Góa <u>ài</u> i ē-tàng tha̍k Tâi-tāi.
我 要 她 能 讀 台大。
Wǒ <u>yào</u> tā néng dú Táidà.
I <u>hope</u> that she can study at National Taiwan University.

阮 欲 坐 船 去。
Gún <u>beh</u> chē chûn khì.
我們 要 坐 船 去。
Wǒmen <u>yào</u> zuò chuán qù.
We <u>wish</u> to travel by boat.

阮 欲/愛 踮 遐 坐 咧。
Gún <u>beh/ài</u> tàm hia che--leh.
我們 要 在 那裡 坐著。
Wǒmen <u>yào</u> zài nàlǐ zuòzhe.
We <u>want</u> to sit over there.

28.4.2 'Would like to' perform an action

To express an early interest in an action or to politely convey a desire, place **想欲 siuⁿ-beh** 'would like to' before a verb *(see 12.2.3 Modal verbs* 想欲 *siūⁿ-beh and* 想愛 *siūⁿ-ài 'would like, thinking of')*. An alternate form is **想愛 siuⁿ-ài**.

想欲 + *verb*

siuⁿ-beh + *verb*

'would like to *verb*'

伊 想欲 共 他 囝 送 去 補習班。
I siūⁿ-beh kā in kiáⁿ sàng khì pó͘-sip-pan.
他 想要 把 他 兒子 送 去 補習班。
Tā xiǎngyào bǎ tā érzi sòng qù bǔxíbān.
He would like to put his son in cram school.

邱 小姐 想愛 開店。
Khu sió-chiá siūⁿ-ài khui-tiàm.
邱 小姐 想要 開店。
Qiū xiǎojiě xiǎngyào kāidiàn.
Ms. Khu is thinking of opening a new business.

29 Changes

29.1 Words expressing change

The English word 'change' can occur in quite a variety of contexts that sometimes requires a more precise term in Taiwanese. This section broadly divides the terms for 'change' with regards to *intransitive* actions, the subject undergoes the action itself ('The dog smells like flowers'), and *transitive* actions, the subject performs an action on another object ('That dog smells every fire hydrant').

29.1.1 Changes that occur with no object

These verbs for 'change' can be used to express changes that are *intransitive* (there is no object), the subject itself undergoes the change.

29.1.1.1 Changes in characteristics

The verb 變 **pìⁿ** can be used when describing how one characteristic or aspect of the subject changes. The literary register pronunciation 變 **piàn** is also commonly used but is more often found in compound words such as 改變 **kái-piàn** 'to transform' or 變做 **piàn-chó** 'to become'.

> 變 Pìⁿ
> 你 應該 等 到 弓蕉 變 黃色 才 食。
> Lí eng-kai tán kàu keng-chio pìⁿ n̂g-sek chiah chia̍h.
> 你 應該 等 到 香蕉 變 黃色 才 吃。
> Nǐ yīnggāi děng dào xiāngjiāo biàn huángsè cái chī.
> You should wait for the banana to change yellow before you eat it.

伊 驚 伊 若 留 踮 這 个 空 課 伊 會 變。
I kiaⁿ i nā lâu tàm chit ê khang-khòe i ē piⁿ.
他 怕 如果 他 留 在 這個 工作 他 會 變。
Tā pà rúguǒ tā liú zài zhège gōngzuò tā huì biàn.
He's afraid he will change if he stays at this job.

變 PIÀN

我 逐 擺 看 著 伊，伊 的 頭 毛 閣 變 矣。
Góa ta̍k pái khòaⁿ-tio̍h i, i ê thâu-mo͘ koh piàn--ah.
我 每 次 看 到 她，她 的 髮型 又 變 了。
Wǒ měi cì kàndào tā, tā de fàxíng yòu biàn le.
Every time I see her, her hairstyle has changed again.

29.1.1.2 To transform

The terms 改變 kái-piàn and 轉變 chóan-piàn generally refer to a more substantial change that 'transforms' or 'alters' the entirety of the subject into something significantly different.

改變 KÁI-PIÀN

你 的 文章 已經 改變 真 濟。
Lí ê bûn-chiong í-keng kái-piàn chin chē.
你 的 文章 已經 改變 很 多。
Nǐ de wénzhāng yǐjīng gǎibiàn hěnduō.
Your essay has already changed a lot.

轉變 CHÓAN-PIÀN

對 長輩 來 講，社會 最近 轉變 傷 濟。
Tùi tióng-pòe lâi kóng, siā-hōe chòe-kīn chóan-piàn siuⁿ chē.
對 長輩 來 說，社會 最近 改變 太 多。
Duì zhǎngbèi lái shuō, shèhuì zuìjìn gǎibiàn tài duō.
For the older generations, society has changed too much recently.

29.1.1.3 To become something

The term **成為 sêng-ūi** is often used to stress the result of a change or what a subject has become.

> 成為 SÊNG-ŪI
> 伊 細漢 時 想講 我 會 成為 台灣 的 總統。
> Góa sè-hàn sî siūⁿ-kóng góa ē sêng-ūi Tâi-ôan ê chóng-thóng.
> 我 小 的 時候 以為 我 會 成為 台灣 的 總統。
> Wǒ xiǎo de shíhòu yǐwéi wǒ huì chéngwéi Táiwān de zǒngtǒng.
> When I was young, I thought I would become Taiwan's president.

29.1.2 Changing an object

The verbs for 'change' in this section can be used to express changes that are *transitive*, the subject performs an action on an object.

29.1.2.1 To correct, edit, or fix

The terms **改 kái** and **修改 siu-kái** below generally refer to changes made through small adjustments to correct, edit, or fix an object.

> 改 KÁI
> 我 下昏暗 會 共 恁 的 考試 攏 改 好。
> Góa e-hng-àm ē kā lín ê khó-chhì lóng kái hó.
> 我 今晚 會 把 你們 的 考試 都 改 好。
> Wǒ jīnwǎn huì bǎ nǐmen de kǎoshì dōu gǎi hǎo.
> I will correct all of your tests tonight.

> 修改 SIU-KÁI
> 手䘼 若 傷 長，我 會當 替 你 修改。
> Chhiú-ńg nā siuⁿ tn̂g, góa ē-tàng theh lí siu-kái.
> 如果 袖子 太 長，我 能 幫 你 修改。
> Rúguǒ xiùzi tài cháng, wǒ néng bāng nǐ xiūgǎi.
> If the sleeves are too long, I can help you change them.

29.1.2.2 To exchange, switch

The terms 換 ōaⁿ and 改換 kái-ōaⁿ generally refer to changes made through a switch or exchange of objects.

換 ŌAⁿ

咱 來 換 位 去 窗仔 邊 遐。

Lán lâi ōaⁿ ūi khì thang-á piⁿ hia.

我們 換 位子 到 靠 窗戶 那 邊 吧。

Wǒmen huàn wèizi dào kào chuānghù nà biān ba.

Let's change our seats to the ones by the window.

改換 KÁI-ŌAⁿ

改換 較 輕鬆 的 音樂。

Kái-ōaⁿ khah khin-sang ê im-ga̍k.

改換 比較 輕鬆 的 音樂。

Gǎihuàn bǐjiào fàngsōng de yīnyuè.

Change the music to something more relaxing.

29.1.2.3 To improve

The terms 改良 kái-liông, 改善 kái-siān, and 改進 kái-chìn generally refer to changes that 'improve' or make an object better.

改良 KÁI-LIÔNG

作穡的 改良 番麥 品種。

Chò-sit--ê kái-liông hoan-be̍h phín-chéng.

農夫 改良 玉米 品種。

Nóngfū gǎiliáng yùmǐ pǐnzhǒng.

The farmer improved this variety of corn.

改善 KÁI-SIĀN

伊 的 成績 若 無 改善，伊 袂當 畢業。

I ê sêng-chek nā bô kái-siān, i bē-tàng pit-gia̍p.

她 的 成績 如果 不 改善，她 不 能 畢業。

Tā de chéngjī rúguǒ bù gǎishàn, tā bù néng bìyè.

If her grades don't change, she won't be able to graduate.

改進 KÁI-CHÌN

你 若 和 計程車 司機 講話，就 會 真 緊 改進 你 的 台語。
Lí nā hām kè-thêng-chhia su-ki kóng ōe, tō ē chin kín kái-chìn lí ê Tâi-gí.

如果 你 和 計程車 司機 講話，就 會 很 快 改進 你 的 台語。
Rúguǒ nǐ hé jìchéngchē sījī jiǎng huà, jiù huì hěn kuài gǎijìn nǐ de Táiyǔ.

You will <u>improve</u> your Taiwanese quickly by speaking with taxi drivers.

29.1.3 Unchanging

To indicate that no change occurs, the negative **無 bô** can be used for events in the past and **袂 bē** for events in the present or future. **不變 put-piàn** 'unchanging' is a word compound that can be used in all time periods.

無變 BÔ PIÀN

雖然 伊 變做 有名，但是 伊 的 個性 無 變。
Sui-jiân i piàn-chó ū-miâ, tān-sī i ê kò-sèng bô piàn.

雖然 她 變成 有名，但是 她 的 個性 沒有 變。
Suīrán tā biànchéng yǒumíng, dànshì tā de gèxìng méiyǒu biàn.

Even though she became famous, her personality <u>did not change</u>.

袂變 BĒ PIÀN

無論 我 幾 擺 佮 伊 問，伊 的 回答 攏 袂 變。
Bô-lūn góa kúi pái kah i mn̄g, i ê hôe-tap lóng bē piàn.

不管 我 幾 次 問 她，她 的 回答 都 不變。
Bùguǎn wǒ jǐ cì wèn tā, tā de huídá dōu bù biàn.

Regardless of how many times I ask her, her answer <u>doesn't change</u>.

不變 PUT-PIÀN

雖然 伊 失業 矣，但是 伊 堅持 的 態度 不變。
Sui-jiân i sit-gia̍p--ah, tān-sī i kian-chhî ê thài-tō put-piàn.

雖然 他 失業 了，但是 他 堅持 的 態度 不變。
Suīrán tā shīyè le, dànshì tā jiānchí de tàidù bù biàn.

Even though he has lost his job, his attitude is <u>unchanging</u>.

Unlike the Mandarin negative **不 bù**, the Taiwanese **不 put** only appears within word compounds and cannot be used to freely negate any verb or adjective.

29.2 Resultative complements indicating change

Resultative complements can also be used to indicate change *(see 11.2 Resultative complements)*. In some cases, they are used together with other words signifying change.

29.2.1 Changing into with resultative 做 -chò

The resultative complement 做 -chò can be paired with some verbs to reflect a 'change into' a different form or 'to become'.

> *verb* + 做
> *verb* + chò
> 'change into *verb*'

換做 ŌAⁿ-CHÒ
你 敢 會當 共 這 寡 英鎊 換做 美金？
Lí kám ē-tàng kā chit kóa Ing-pōng ōaⁿ-chò Bí-kim?
你 能不能 把 這 些 英鎊 換成 美金 嗎？
Nǐ néngbùnéng bǎ zhè xiē Yīngbàng huànchéng Měijīn ma?
Can you change these British pounds into American dollars?

變做 PIÀN-CHÒ
阮 阿爸 變做 我 的 頭家，我 就 袂堪得。
Gún a-pah piàn-chò góa ê thâu-ke, góa tō bē-kham-tit.
我 爸爸 變成 我 的 老闆，我 就 受不了。
Wǒ bàba biànchéng wǒ de lǎobǎn, wǒ jiù shòubùliǎo.
When my father became my boss, I couldn't stand it.

咱 的 乖乖 後生 按怎 變做 遮爾仔 歹？
Lán ê koai-koai hāu-seⁿ án-chóaⁿ piàn-chò chiah-nī-á pháiⁿ?
我們 的 乖乖 兒子 怎麼 成為 這麼 懷？
Wǒmen de guāiguāi érzi zěnme chéngwéi zhème huái?
How did our well-behaved boy become so bad?

In some contexts, the resultative complement 做 -chò is used to indicate that one has misinterpreted an action.

你 拄才 講「買」我 聽做「賣」。
Lí tú-chiah kóng 'bé' góa thiaⁿ-chò 'bē'.
你 剛才 說「買」我 聽成「賣」。
Nǐ gāngcái shuō 'mǎi' wǒ tīngchéng 'mài'.
When you just said 'buy', I (*mistakenly*) thought I heard you say 'sell'.

29.2.2 Successfully achieving with resultative 成 -sêng

The resultative complement 成 -sêng can be attached to verbs to signal that a goal has been successfully achieved. This is often used to emphasize that a change has moved from incompletion to successful completion.

> *verb* + 成
>
> *verb* + sêng
>
> 'successfully become *verb*'

> 變成 PIÀN-SÊNG
> 政府 欲 遮的 查埔 囡仔 變成 好 公民。
> Chèng-hú beh chia-ê cha-po͘ gín-á piàn-sêng hó kong-bîn.
> 政府 要 這 些 男孩子 變成 好 公民。
> Zhèngfǔ yào zhè xiē nánháizi biànchéng hǎo gōngmín.
> The government wants these boys to become good citizens.

> 完成 ÔAN-SÊNG
> 我 今仔日 的 功課 已經 完成 矣。
> Góa kin-á-jit ê kong-khò í-keng ôan-sêng--ah.
> 我 今天 的 功課 已經 完成 了。
> Wǒ jīntiān de gōngkè yǐjīng wánchéng le.
> I've already finished today's homework.

養成 IÓNG-SÊNG

囝仔 愛 按 細漢 開始 才 會當 養成 好 習慣。
Gín-á ài àn sè-hàn khai-sí chiah ē-tàng <u>ióng-sêng</u> hó sip-kòan.
孩子 要 從 小 開始 才 能 養成 好 習慣。
Háizi yào cóng xiǎo kāishǐ cái néng <u>yǎngchéng</u> hǎo xíguàn.
<u>Successfully raising</u> children with good habits must begin when they are young.

29.3 Expressing a new situation with end-of-sentence particles

29.3.1 Indicating a change of state with adjectives and particle 矣 --ah

When an adjective functions like a verb and signals a new state or situation, the anterior aspect marker **矣 --ah** is added to the end of the clause or sentence *(see 8.4 Anterior aspect, 6.5.1 Change-of-state particle 矣 --ah).*

changed situation + 矣

changed situation + --ah

掃地 了後，塗跤 清氣 矣。
Sàu-tè liáu-āu, thô͘-kha chheng-khì<u>--ah</u>.
掃地 以後，地板 乾淨 了。
Sǎodì yǐhòu, dìbǎn gānjìng <u>le</u>.
After sweeping, the floor <u>is now</u> clean.

伊 這馬 無 咧 讀 俄文 矣。
I chit-má <u>bô</u> teh tha̍k Gô-bûn<u>--ah</u>.
他 現在 不 念 俄文 了。
Tā xiànzài <u>bù</u> niàn Éwén <u>le</u>.
He <u>is no longer</u> studying Russian.

這 條 椅仔 的 跤 斷 去 矣。
Chit liâu í-á ê kha tn̄g--khì--ah.
這 把 椅子 的 腳 斷掉 了。
Zhè bǎ yǐzi de jiǎo duàndiào le.
This chair's leg is broken now.

29.3.2 Emphasizing a new situation with the end-of-sentence particle --啦 lah

The end-of-sentence particle 啦 --lah can follow the anterior aspect marker 矣 --ah to give further emphasis that the situation has changed *(see 8.4 Anterior aspect, 22.1 End-of-sentence particles)*.

> *changed situation* + 矣 + 啦
>
> *changed situation* + --ah + --lah

攏 無 物仔 通 食 因為 予 伊 食了 矣 啦！
Lóng bô mi̍h-á thang chia̍h in-ūi hō͘ i chia̍h-liáu--ah--lah!
都 沒有 吃 的 東西 因為 被 他 吃完 啦！
Dōu méiyǒu chī de dōngxī yīnwèi bèi tā chīwán la!
There's no food left because he ate it all!

因為 你 袂記得 共 牛奶 囥 踮 冰箱內，所以 歹 去 啦。
In-ūi lí bē-kì-tit kā gû-leng khǹg tàm peng-siuⁿ-lāi, só-í pháiⁿ--khì--lah.
因為 你 忘了 把 牛奶 放 在 冰箱 裡，所以 壞掉 啦。
Yīnwèi nǐ wàngle bǎ niúnǎi fàng zài bīngxiāng lǐ, suǒyǐ huàidiào la.
Because you forgot to put it in the fridge, the milk has gone bad.

Note that in Mandarin 啦 **la** is considered a combination of the Mandarin anterior aspect marker 了 **le** and end-of-sentence particle 啊 **a**.

29.4 Describing a condition that has gotten worse using 去 --khì

The suffix **去 --khì** can be attached to some adjectives to indicate that a condition has become worse *(see 6.5.2 Describing conditions that have worsened 去 --khì)*. The end-of-sentence particle **矣 --ah** may optionally be added to emphasize the change in situation.

adjective + 去 + (矣)

adjective + --khì + (--ah)

緊來食,若無,菜會冷去。
Kín lâi chiảh, nā bô, chhài ē léng--khì.
快來吃,要不然菜會冷了。
Kuài lái chī, yàobùrán cài huì lěng le.
Eat soon or the food will become cold.

我袂記得共衫按洗衫機提出來,所以臭去矣。
Góa bē-kì-tit kā saⁿ àn sé-saⁿ-ki thẻh--chhut-lâi, só-í chhàu--khì--ah.
我忘記把衣服從洗衣機拿出來,所以臭了。
Wǒ wàngjì bǎ yīfú cóng xǐyījī náchūlái, suǒyǐ chòu le.
I forgot to take the clothes out of the washer, so they stink now.

One exception to this construction is **好去 hó--khì** which conveys that a situation has improved.

歇睏幾工了後,感冒攏好去矣。
Hioh-khùn kúi kang liáu-āu, kám-mō˙ lóng hó--khì--ah.
休息幾天之後,感冒都好了。
Xiūxí jǐ tiān zhīhòu, gǎnmào dōu hǎo le.
After resting a few days, my cold has completely gotten better.

29.5 Emphasizing a change in the immediate future

To indicate a change brought on by an action about to happen, place 咧欲 **teh-beh** (also pronounced **tih-beh**) before the verb. 強欲 **kiōng-beh** is an alternate form.

咧欲 + *verb*

teh-beh + *verb*

'just about to + *verb*'

毋免 佮 洪 先生 敲 電話，因為 伊 咧欲 到位 矣。
M̄-bián kah Âng--sian-siⁿ khà tiān-ōe, in-ūi i teh-beh kàu-ūi--ah.
不用 給 洪 先生 打 電話，因為 他 快要 抵達 了。
Bùyòng gěi Hóng xiānshēng dǎ diànhuà, yīnwèi tā kuàiyào dǐdá le.
There is no need to call Mr. Ang because he is just about to arrive.

阮 強欲 離開 停車場。
Gún kiông-beh lî-khui thêng-chhia-tiûⁿ.
我們 快要 離開 停車場。
Wǒmen kuàiyào líkāi tíngchēchǎng.
We are just about to leave the parking lot.

彼 欉 樹仔 強欲 倒落去。
Hit châng chhiū-á kiōng-beh tó--lȯh-khì.
那 棵 樹 快要 倒下去。
Nà kē shù kuàiyào dàoxiàqù.
That tree is about to fall down.

29.6 Expressing changes over time

29.6.1 Changes over time 'more and more'

To express that an adjective, stative verb, or modal verb is becoming 'more and more' over time, place 愈來愈 jú lâi jú 'more and more' (also pronounced **lú lâi lú**) before the adjective, stative verb, or modal verb *(see 6.8.1 Changes over time)*. An alternate form is 那來那 **ná lâi ná**.

愈來愈 + *adjective/stative verb/modal verb*

jú lâi jú + *adjective/stative verb/modal verb*

'more and more + *adjective/stative verb/modal verb*'

ADJECTIVE

最近 汽油 愈 來 愈 貴。

Chòe-kīn khì-iû jú lâi jú kùi.

最近 汽油 越 來 越 貴。

Zuìjìn qìyóu yuè lái yuè guì.

Recently gasoline is getting more and more expensive.

STATIVE VERB

我 愈 來 愈 佮意 你 的 朋友。

Góa jú lâi jú kah-ì lí ê pêng-iú.

我 越 來 越 喜歡 你 的 朋友。

Wǒ yuè lái yuè xǐhuān nǐ de péngyǒu.

I like your friend more and more.

MODAL VERB

彼 齣 電影 我 愈 來 愈 想欲 看。

Hit chhut tiān-iáⁿ góa jú lâi jú siuⁿ-beh khòaⁿ.

那 部 電影 我 越 來 越 想要 看。

Nà bù diànyǐng wǒ yuè lái yuè xiǎngyào kàn.

More and more I would like to see that movie.

29.6.2 Changes over time 'less and less'

To express that an adjective, stative verb, or modal verb is becoming 'less and less' over time, use **愈來愈 jú lâi jú** before the negative form of an adjective, stative verb, or modal verb *(see 6.8.1 Changes over time)*. An alternate form is **那來那 ná lâi ná**.

愈 來 愈 + *negative* + *adjective/stative verb/modal verb*

jú lâi jú + *negative* + *adjective/stative verb/modal verb*

'less and less + *adjective/stative verb/modal verb*'

這 個 故事 愈 來 愈 無 趣味。
Chit ê kò͘-sū jú lâi jú bô chhù-bī.
這個 故事 越 來 越 沒 興趣。
Zhège gùshì yuè lái yuè méi xìngqù.
This story is getting less and less interesting.

這 个 工作，我 愈 來 愈 無 考慮。
Chit ê kang-chok, góa jú lâi jú bô khó-lī.
這個 工作，我 越 來 越 不 考慮。
Zhège gōngzuò, wǒ yuè lái yuè bù kǎolù.
I'm considering this job less and less.

伊 那 來 那 袂當 記得 伊 細漢 的 時陣。
I ná lâi ná bē-tàng kì-tit i sè-hàn ê sî-chūn.
他 越 來 越 不 能 記得 他 小 的 時候。
Tā yuè lái yuè bù néng jìdé tā xiǎo de shíhòu.
He is less and less able to remember his childhood.

29.6.3 Changes caused by another action

To express that the increase of one action influences another action, place 愈 **jú** or 那 **ná** before both the action verb and the adjective, stative verb, or modal verb *(see 6.8.2 Changes that cause other changes)*.

愈 + *action verb* + 愈 + *adjective/stative verb/modal verb*

jú + *action verb* + jú + *adjective/stative verb/modal verb*

'the more *action verb*, the more *adjective/stative verb/modal verb*'

伊愈走愈瘦。
I jú cháu jú sán.
她越跑越瘦。
Tā yuè pǎo yuè shòu.
The more she runs, the thinner she becomes.

伊駛車愈緊我會愈驚。
I sái chhia jú kín góa ē jú kiaⁿ.
他開車越快我會越怕。
Tā kāi chē yuè kuài wǒ huì yuè pà.
The faster he drives, the more scared I get.

伊那大我那愛照顧伊。
I ná tōa góa ná ài chiàu-kò͘ i.
他越大我越得照顧他。
Tā yuè dà wǒ yuè děi zhàogù tā.
The bigger he gets, the more I have to watch over him.

30 Additions

30.1 Expanding the subject or object

The preposition 佮 **kah** (also pronounced **kap**) 'with, and' can be used to join together nouns whether as part of a multiple subject or multiple object *(see 15.5 Prepositions of accompaniment and interaction)*. Alternate forms include 和 **hām** and 參 **chham**.

noun 1 + 佮 + noun 2

noun 1 + kah + noun 2

阮 阿母、阿兄 佮 小妹,恁 夜市 已經 去 了。
Gún a-bú, a-hiaⁿ kah sió-mōe, in iā-chhī í-keng khì liáu.
我 媽媽、哥哥 和 妹妹,他們 已經 去 了 夜市。
Wǒ māmā, gēgē hé mèimei, tāmen yǐjīng qùle yèshì.
My mother, older brother, and younger sister already went to the night market.

請 你 共 牛奶 和 雞卵 囥 踮 冰箱。
Chhiáⁿ lí kā gû-leng hām ke-nñg khǹg tàm peng-siuⁿ.
請 你 把 牛奶 跟 雞蛋 放 在 冰箱。
Qǐng nǐ bǎ niúnǎi gēn jīdàn fàng zài bīngxiāng.
Please put the milk and eggs in the refrigerator.

醫生 參 護士 佇 急診 等 病人。
I-seng chham hō·-sū tī kip-chín tán pēⁿ-lâng.
醫生 和 護士 在 急診 等 病人。
Yīshēng hé hùshì zài jízhěn děng bìngrén.
The doctor and nurse are waiting for the patient in the emergency room.

If there are more than two nouns, then a special backwards slanting comma 頓號 **tǹg-hō** ' 、 ' is used to mark a series and placed between the nouns. The conjunction 佮 **kah** 'with, and' is used before the last item in the series.

noun 1 、 noun 2 、 noun 3 + 佮 + noun 4

noun 1 、 noun 2 、 noun 3 + kah + noun 4

還 我 的 冊、膨紗衫、牛仔褲 佮 耳鉤。
Hêng góa ê chheh, phòng-se-saⁿ, gû-á-khò ͘ kah hīⁿ-kau.
還 我 的 書、毛衣、牛仔褲 和 耳環。
Huán wǒ de shū, máoyī, niúzǎikù hé ěrhuán.
Give back my books, sweater, jeans, <u>and</u> earrings.

30.2 Providing additional information about the subject

30.2.1 Adding descriptions in a subsequent sentence

To indicate that a subject possesses an additional quality in subsequent sentences, place 嘛 **mā** 'also' before the adjective or stative verb. An alternate form is 也 **iā**.

subject + 嘛 + adjective / stative verb

subject + mā + adjective / stative verb

邱 小姐 足 專門。伊 嘛 真 巧。
Khu sió-chiá chiok choan-bûn. I <u>mā</u> chin khiáu.
邱 小姐 非常 專業。她 也 很 聰明。
Qiū xiǎojiě fēicháng zhuānyè. Tā <u>yě</u> hěn cōngmíng.
Ms. Khu is very professional. She is <u>also</u> smart.

彼 隻 馬仔 真 緊。伊 也 真 少年。
Hit chiah bé-á chin kín. I iā chin siàu-liân.

那 隻 馬 很 快。牠 也 很 年輕。
Nà zhī mǎ hěn kuài. Tā yě hěn niánqīng.

That horse is fast. It is also very young.

30.2.2 Describing two qualities within a sentence

又閣 iū-koh can be used to express a subject possessing two qualities which are both positive or both negative. Place 又閣 iū-koh before the first adjective and then repeat 又閣 iū-koh before the second adjective. Depending on individual preference, the leading 又閣 iū-koh may be omitted.

(又閣) + *adjective* + 又閣 + *adjective*

(iū-koh) + *adjective* + iū-koh + *adjective*

作穡人 的 生活 (又閣) 歹做 又閣 艱苦。
Choh-sit-lâng ê seng-oáh (iū-koh) pháiⁿ-chò iū-koh kan-khó͘.

農人 的 生活 又 難做 又 辛苦。
Nóngrén de shēnghuó yòu nánzuò yòu xīnkǔ.

A farmer's life is difficult as well as tiring.

Note that while in Mandarin the leading 又 yòu can be omitted, it is more commonly included.

An alternate form of describing two qualities is to omit the 又 iū- component altogether.

(閣) + *adjective* + 閣 + *adjective*

(koh) + *adjective* + koh + *adjective*

你 的 紅嬰仔 (閣) 乖 閣 古錐。
Lí ê âng-eⁿ-á (koh) koai koh kó͘-chui.

你 的 嬰兒 也 乖 也 可愛。
Nǐ de yīng'ér yě guāi yě kě'ài.

Your baby is both well-behaved and cute.

30.2.3 Expressing surprise at having two qualities

To convey surprise that a subject possesses two qualities, place **毋但 m̄-nā** 'not only' before the first quality and **閣 koh** 'but also' before the second quality. Adjectives, verbs, verb phrases, and clauses may all be placed in this sentence pattern. Note that **毋但 m̄-nā** 'not only' can appear before or after the subject/topic. However, **閣 koh** 'but also' must appear at the beginning of the second clause.

1ST CLAUSE	2ND CLAUSE
毋但 + *quality 1*	閣 + *quality 2*
m̄-nā + *quality 1*	koh + *quality 2*
'Not only...*quality 1*	but also...*quality 2*'

暗頓 *毋但* 歹食，*閣* 真 貴。
Àm-tǹg m̄-nā pháiⁿ-chia̍h, koh chin kùi.
晚餐 不但 難吃，而且 很 貴。
Wǎncān bùdàn nánchī, érqiě hěn guì.
Dinner not only did not taste good but also was expensive.

Alternate forms include **不但 put-tān** to express 'not only' and **甚至 sīm-chì**, **也 iá-sī**, **嘛是 mā-sī**, and **猶閣 iáu-koh** to express 'but also'.

1ST CLAUSE	2ND CLAUSE
不但 put-tān	甚至 sīm-chì
	也 iá-sī
	嘛是 mā-sī
	猶閣 iáu-koh
'Not only...	but also...'

伊 *不但* 著傷，*甚至* 予 控告著。
I put-tān tio̍h-siong, sīm-chì hō͘ khòng-kò--tio̍h.
他 不但 受傷，而且 被 控告 了。
Tā bùdàn shòushāng, érqiě bèi kònggào le.
Not only did he get injured, but also he was sued.

我 的 好 朋友 <u>毋但</u> 緣投，<u>嘛是</u> 好額。

Góa ê hó pêng-iú <u>m̄-nā</u> iân-tâu, <u>mā-sī</u> hó-giáh.

我 的 好 朋友 <u>不但</u> 帥，<u>也是</u> 富有。

Wǒ de hǎo péngyǒu <u>bùdàn</u> shuài, <u>yěshì</u> fùyǒu.

My good friend is <u>not only</u> good-looking <u>but also</u> wealthy.

30.3 Describing a subject performing multiple actions

30.3.1 Multiple actions of equal standing

To indicate that a subject performs more than one action of more or less equal standing, place 也 **iā** before the additional verb. Alternate forms include 嘛 **mā** or 另外 **lēng-gōa**.

1ST CLAUSE	2ND CLAUSE
subject + verb 1	也 + verb 2
	iā + verb 2

賴 先生 負責 訓練 新 的 員工，<u>嘛</u> 負責 管理 秘書。

Lōa--sian-siⁿ hū-chek hùn-liān sin ê ôan-kang, <u>mā</u> hū-chek kóan-lí pì-su.

賴 先生 負責 連訓新 的 員工，<u>還</u> 負責 管理 秘書。

Lài xiānshēng fùzé liánxùn xīn de yuángōng, <u>hái</u> fùzé guǎnlǐ mìshū.

Mr. Loa's responsibilities are to train new employees <u>and</u> to manage the secretaries.

我 清 洗浴間，<u>另外</u> 共 糞埽 提出去。

Góa chheng sé-ėk-keng, <u>lēng-gōa</u> kā pùn-sò theh--chhut-khì.

我 清 浴室，<u>另外</u> 把 垃圾 拿出去。

Wǒ qīng yùshì, <u>lìngwài</u> bǎ lèsè náchūqù.

I cleaned the bathroom <u>and</u> took out the garbage.

30.3.2 Multiple actions contrary to expectation

To convey that the subject performs another action contrary to expectation, place 猶閣 **iáu-koh** 'still, yet' before the second verb (also pronounced **iah-koh, ah-koh, á-koh, iá-koh**) (see 34 Simultaneous actions). Additionally, 閣 **-koh** can be omitted.

1ST CLAUSE	2ND CLAUSE
verb 1	猶(閣) + *verb 2*
	iáu(-koh) + *verb 2*

恁 查某囝 拍 籃球，猶閣 拍 排球。
In cha-bó͘-kiáⁿ phah nâ-kiû, <u>iáu-koh</u> phah pâi-kiû.
他 的 女兒 打 籃球，還 打 排球。
Tā de nǚ'ér dǎ lánqiú, <u>hái</u> dǎ páiqiú.
Her daughter plays basketball *and* even volleyball, too.

阮 著愛 先 轉去 窮 行李，猶 較 早 睏。
Gún tio̍h-ài seng tńg-khì khêng hêng-lí, <u>iáu</u> khah chá khùn.
我們 需要 先 回 家 整理 行李，還有 早 一點 睡覺。
Wǒmen xūyào xiān huí jiā zhěnglǐ xínglǐ, <u>háiyǒu</u> zǎo yīdiǎn shuìjiào.
We have to go home first to pack bags, *and* we need to sleep early.

30.4 Introducing related information to the previous statement

To introduce more information to a statement, use the following expressions to begin a new clause or sentence.

30.4.1 Moreover, furthermore

The terms below expressing 'moreover' or 'furthermore' can be used to introduce substantially new information that supports the preceding statement.

1ST CLAUSE/SENTENCE	2ND CLAUSE/SENTENCE
statement	並且 pēng-chhiáⁿ
	而且 jî-chhiáⁿ
	又閣 iū-koh
	'moreover, furthermore'

並且 PĒNG-CHHIÁⁿ

我 忝 甲 行袂去 矣。並且 我 腹肚 枵。
Góa thiám kah kiâⁿ-bē-khì--ah. Pēng-chhiáⁿ góa pak-tó ʼiau.

我 累 得 走不動 了。並且 我 很 餓。
Wǒ lèi de zǒubudòng le. Bìngqiě wǒ hěn è.

I am too tired to walk anymore. Moreover, I'm hungry.

而且 JÎ-CHHIÁⁿ

這馬 俄國 傷 寒。而且 機票 會 真 貴。
Chit-má Ngô-kok siuⁿ kôaⁿ. Jî-chhiáⁿ ki-phiò ē chin kùi.

現在 俄國 太 冷。而且 機票 會 很 貴。
Xiànzài Éguó tài lěng. Érqiě jīpiào huì hěn guì.

Right now Russia is too cold. Moreover, the flight ticket will be expensive.

又閣 IŪ-KOH

伊 定定 坐 佇 我 的 位，又閣 伊 的 糞埽 攏 擲 佇 遐。
I tiāⁿ-tiāⁿ chē tī góa ê ūi, iū-koh i ê pùn-sò lóng tàn tī hia.

她 常常 坐 在 我 的 位子，而且 她 的 垃圾 都 丟 在 那裡。
Tā chángcháng zuò zài wǒ de wèizi, érqiě tā de lèsè dōu diū zài nàlǐ.

She frequently takes my seat. Furthermore, she leaves all her trash there.

30.4.2 In addition, also, one other thing

The terms below expressing 'also', 'in addition', or 'one other thing' can be used to offer additional or supplemental information to the preceding statement.

1ST CLAUSE/SENTENCE	2ND CLAUSE/SENTENCE
statement	另外 lēng-gōa
	猶有 iáu-ū
	'also, in addition, one other thing'

另外 LĒNG-GŌA

這 个 報告 的 期限 是 後日。另外 你 下昏暗 愛 敲 予 客戶。

Chit ê pò-kò ê kî-hān sī āu--jit. Leng-gōa lí e-hng-àm ài khà hō ̇kheh-hō. ̇

這個 報告 的 期限 是 後天。另外 你 今晚 得 打 給 客戶。

Zhège bàogào de qíxiàn shì hòutiān. Lìngwài nǐ jīnwǎn děi dǎ gěi kèhù.

The deadline for this report is the day after tomorrow. Also, you need to call the client tonight.

猶有 IÁU-Ū

公園 佇 咱 的 飯店 附近。猶有 咱 會當 行 去 博物館。

Kong-hn̂g tī lán ê pn̄g-tiàm hù-kīn. Iáu-ū lán ē-tàng kiâⁿ khì phok-bu̇t-kóan.

公園 在 我們 的 飯店 附近。還有 我們 能 走 去 博物館。

Gōngyuán zài wǒmen de fàndiàn fùjìn. Háiyǒu wǒmen néng zǒu qù bówùguǎn

The park is close to our hotel. Also, we will be able to go the museum.

30.4.3 Besides, except for

除了 tû-liáu can mean either to include ('besides, in addition to') or exclude ('except for, not including') the item specified in the first clause. Generally context helps to clarify which meaning is desired.

30.4.3.1 Inclusive 除了 tû-liáu

除了 **tû-liáu** 'besides' can be used at the beginning of the first clause to indicate that including the argument in the first clause, there is a second argument in the second clause. The arguments can be nouns, adjectives, or verbs. To clarify an inclusive reading, place 閣 **koh** 'also' in the second clause. Note that 以外 **i-góa** 'apart from' can optionally be added to the end of the first clause but does not imply either an inclusive or exclusive reading.

1ST CLAUSE	2ND CLAUSE
除了 + *argument 1* + (以外)	(閣) + *argument 2*
tû-liáu + *argument 1* + (i-góa)	(koh) + *argument 2*
'besides + *argument 1*	(also) + *argument 2*'

除了 拍 網球 以外，你 閣 愛 創 啥物？
Tû-liáu phah bāng-kiû i-góa, lí koh ài chhòng siáⁿ-mih?
除了 打 網球 以外，你 還 喜歡 做 什麼？
Chúle dǎ wǎngqiú yǐwài, nǐ hái xǐhuān zuò shénme?
Besides playing tennis, what else do you like to do?

除了 印尼，我 閣 捌 去 泰國 佮 印度。
Tû-liáu Ìn-nî, góa koh bat khì Thài-kok kah Ìn-tō.
除了 印尼，我 還 去過 泰國 和 印度。
Chúle Yìnní, wǒ hái qùguò Tàiguó hé Yìndù.
In addition to Indonesia, I have also been to Thailand and India.

30.4.3.2 Exclusive 除了 tû-liáu

除了 tû-liáu 'except for' or 'not including' can also be used at the beginning of the first clause to indicate that excluding the argument in the first clause, there is another argument that holds in the second clause. The arguments can be nouns, adjectives, or verbs. Note that 以外 i-góa 'apart from' can optionally be added to the end of the first clause, but does not imply either an inclusive or exclusive reading.

1ST CLAUSE	2ND CLAUSE
除了 + *argument 1* + (以外)	*argument 2*
tû-liáu + *argument 1* + (i-góa)	*argument 2*
'besides + *argument 1*	*argument 2*'

除了 海鮮 以外，我 無 食 肉。
Tû-liáu hái-sian i-góa, góa bô chiah bah.
除了 海鮮 以外，我 不 吃 肉。
Chúle hǎixiān yǐwài, wǒ bù chī ròu.
Except for seafood, I do not eat meat.

除了 拍 網球，其他 的 運動 伊 攏 真 愛。
Tû-liáu phah bāng-kiû, kî-thaⁿ ê ūn-tōng i lóng chin ài.
除了 打 網球，其他 的 運動 他 都 喜歡。
Chúle dǎ wǎngqiú, qítā de yùndòng tā dōu xǐhuān.
Not including tennis, he loves to play all sports.

31 Contrasts

31.1 Conjunctions indicating contrast

31.1.1 Simple contrasts

Some conjunctions such as **毋過 m̄-koh** (also pronounced as **m̄-kò** or **m̄-kù**) 'but' or 'however' can be placed in the beginning of the second clause to change the direction of a statement made in the first clause. The conjunction, a word used to join clauses, appears in the beginning of the second clause. If the subject is included in the second clause, then it follows the conjunction. Alternate forms include **但是 tān-sī** and **總是 chóng--sī**. The expression **猶毋過 iáu-m̄-koh** can be used to convey 'but still'.

1ST CLAUSE	2ND CLAUSE
statement	毋過 m̄-koh
	但是 tān-sī
	總是 chóng--sī
	'but, however'

BU過 M̄-KOH

我 穿 罩衫 佮 戴 帽仔，<u>毋過</u> 我 猶閣 寒。
Góa chhēng tà-saⁿ kah tì bō-á, <u>m̄-koh</u> góa iáu-koh kôaⁿ.
我 穿 外套 也 戴 帽子，<u>不過</u> 我 還 會 冷。
Wǒ chuān wàitào yě dài màozi, <u>bùguò</u> wǒ hái huì lěng.
I'm wearing a coat and hat, <u>but</u> I'm still cold.

但是 TĀN-SĪ

伊 愛 來 參加 酒會，<u>但是</u> 伊 工作 著愛 先 做 予 了。
I ài lâi chham-ka chiú-hōe, <u>tān-sī</u> i kang-chok tio̍h-ài seng chò hō͘ liáu.
她 要 來 參加 酒會，<u>但是</u> 她 得 先 做完 工作。
Tā yào lái cānjiā jiǔhuì, <u>dànshì</u> tā děi xiān zuòwán gōngzuò.
She wants to come to the cocktail party, <u>but</u> she has to first finish her work.

總是 CHÓNG--SĪ

恁 有 夠 錢 通 請 暗頓，<u>總是</u> 恁 真 凍酸。
In ū káu chîⁿ thang chhiáⁿ àm-tǹg, <u>chóng--sī</u> in chin tàng-sng.
他們 有 錢 可 請 晚餐，<u>可是</u> 他們 很 吝嗇。
Tāmen yǒu qián kě qǐng wǎncān, <u>kěshì</u> tāmen hěn lìnsè.
They have the money to pay for dinner, <u>but</u> they are stingy.

猶毋過 IÁU-M̄-KOH

食 魚 會 予 伊 袂 爽快，<u>猶毋過</u> 伊 也是 會 食。
Chia̍h hî ē hō͘ i bē sóng-khòai, <u>iáu-m̄-koh</u> i iā-sī ē chia̍h.
吃 魚 會 讓 他 不 舒服，<u>不過</u> 他 還是 會 吃。
Chī yú huì ràng tā bú shūfú, <u>búguò</u> tā háishì huì chī.
Eating fish makes him sick, <u>but</u> still he eats it.

31.1.2 Emphasizing contrasts

To further emphasize the contrast between clauses, stronger contrast conjunctions expressing 'on the contrary' (such as 卻是 **khiok-sī**) can be placed before or after the subject in the second clause. The subject is often omitted in the second clause if there is no change in subject. Alternate forms include 顛倒 **tian-tò** and 反倒轉 **hóan-tò-tńg**.

1ST CLAUSE	2ND CLAUSE
statement	卻是 khiok-sī
	顛倒 tian-tò
	反倒轉 hóan-tò-tńg
	'on the contrary, nevertheless'

卻是 KHIOK-SĪ

佇 咱 兜 犯法 袂使得，卻是 阮 猶原 愛 你。

Tī lán tau hōan-hoat bē-sái--tit, <u>khiok-sī</u> gún iû-ôan ài lí.

在 我們 家 犯法 是 不 被 允許 的，但是 我們 仍然 愛 你。

Zài wǒmen jiā fànfǎ shì bù bèi yǔnxǔ de, <u>dànshì</u> wǒmen réngrán ài nǐ.

Breaking the law is not acceptable in this family. <u>Nevertheless</u>, we still love you.

顛倒 TIAN-TÒ

伊 拄仔 贏 獎學金，伊 顛倒 無 歡喜。

I tú-á iâⁿ chióng-ha̍k-kim, i <u>tian-tò</u> bô hoaⁿ-hí.

他 剛 贏得 獎學金，他 反而 不 開心。

Tā gāng yíngdé jiǎngxuéjīn, tā <u>fǎn'ér</u> bù kāixīn.

He just won a scholarship, but <u>surprisingly</u> he isn't happy.

反倒轉 HÓAN-TÒ-TŃG

彼 个 查埔 囡仔 干焦 行 一下 就 跋落去，反到轉 伊 開始 笑。

Hit ê cha-poˈ gín-á kan-na kiâⁿ chit-ê tō po̍ah--lo̍h-khì, <u>hóan-tò-tńg</u> i khai-sí chhiò.

那個 男孩子 才 走 一下 就 跌到，反而 他 開始 笑。

Nàge nánháizi cái zǒu yīxià jiù diēdào, <u>fǎn'ér</u> tā kāishǐ xiào.

That little boy only walked a few steps before he fell. <u>Contrary to what you would expect</u>, he started to laugh.

31.2 Offering a concession in an argument

To offer a concession in an argument, 雖然 sui-jiân, which expresses 'although' or 'despite', can introduce the concession in the first clause. The second clause begins with a contrast conjunction such as 但是 tān-sī 'but' or a reference adverb such as 嘛 mā 'yet, still' to reinforce the contrast. Note that in English the second clause does not begin with a contrast conjunction.

31.2.1 Concessions with simple contrasts

For a simple contrast to the concession given by the first clause beginning with 雖然 sui-jiân 'although', place a contrast conjunction such as 但是 tān-sī 'but' or 毋過 m̄-koh 'however' at the beginning of the second clause.

1ST CLAUSE	2ND CLAUSE
雖然 + subject	但是
sui-jiân + subject	tān-sī
'Although subject…'	

雖然 落 雨, 但是 伊 欲 去 外口 迌迌。
Sui-jiân lȯh hō͘, tān-sī i beh khì gōa-kháu chhit-thô.
雖然 下 雨, 但是 她 要 去 外面 玩。
Suīrán xià yǔ, dànshì tā yào qù wàimiàn wán.
Although it is raining, she wants to go outside to play.

雖然 伊 會曉 讀 字, 但是 伊 袂曉 寫。
Sui-jiân i ē-hiáu thȧk jī, tān-sī i bē-hiáu siá.
雖然 他 會 看 字, 但是 他 不 會 寫。
Suīrán tā huì kàn zì, dànshì tā bù huì xiě.
Although he knows how to read characters, he cannot write them.

雖然 阮 足 想欲 去, 但是 阮 無 狗 人 通 訂 行程。
Sui-jiân gún chiok siuⁿ-beh khì, tān-sī gún bô káu lâng thang tèng hêng-têng.
雖然 我們 很 想要 去, 但是 我們 不 夠 人 可以 預訂 行程。
Suīrán wǒmen hěn xiǎngyào qù, dànshì wǒmen bù gòu rén kěyǐ yùdìng xíngchéng.
Despite the fact we are excited to go, we don't have enough people to book the trip.

雖然 弟一 車 較 袂 擠，毋過 干焦 予 查某 坐。
Sui-jiân tē-it chhia khah bē kheh, m̄-koh kan-na hō͘ cha-bó͘ chē.
雖然 第一 車 比較 不 會 擠，不過 只 讓 女生 搭乘。
Suīrán dìyī chē bǐjiào bù huì jǐ, bùguò zhǐ ràng nǚshēng dāchéng.
Even though the first train car is less crowded, it is only for women.

31.2.2 Emphasizing contrasts between clauses with a concession

To further emphasize the contrast between clauses with a concession, place a reference adverb expressing 'yet, still' (such as 也 iā or 嘛 mā) in the second clause. If the subject is stated in the second clause, the reference adverb appears after the subject.

1ST CLAUSE	2ND CLAUSE
雖然 + subject	(subject) + 嘛
sui-jiân + subject	(subject) + mā
'Although subject…'	

雖然 伊 愛 動物，伊 嘛 真 愛 食 肉。
Sui-jiân i ài tōng-bu̍t, i mā chin ài chia̍h bah.
雖然 她 喜歡 動物，她 還是 很 喜歡 吃 肉。
Suīrán tā xǐhuān dòngwù, tā háishì hěn xǐhuān chī ròu.
Although she likes animals, she still loves to eat meat.

雖然 怹 逐 日 練習，怹 猶 袂當 贏 比賽。
Sui-jiân in ta̍k ji̍t liān-si̍p, in iáu bē-tàng iâⁿ pí-sài.
雖然 他們 每天 練習，他們 還 不能 贏 比賽。
Suīrán tāmen měitiān liànxí, tāmen hái bùnéng yíng bǐsài.
Despite the fact they practice everyday, they still can't win a competition.

32 Sequence

32.1 Chronological sequence

32.1.1 Expressing sequence through consecutive verbs

Taiwanese generally follows the principle of presenting verbs in the order of which they would chronologically occur. This principle also allows a sequence of events to be indicated solely through the ordering of verbs within a sentence. No additional words are required.

我寫一張批寄予伊。
Góa siá chit tiuⁿ phoe kià hō͘ i.
我寫一封信寄給她。
Wǒ xiě yī fēng xìn jì gěi tā.
I wrote a letter and then sent it to her.

32.1.2 Adverbs in sequences

Besides the use of consecutive verbs, a sequence of events can be indicated through two-clause sentence patterns using time adverbs *(see 14.1.2 Time adverbs)*.

32.1.2.1 Describing an event occurring prior to another event

To indicate that *event 1* occurs prior to *event 2*, the time adverb 進前 **chìn-chêng** 'previous to' may be used. Generally, *event 2*, which occurs later chronologically, is placed in the first clause followed by 進前 **chìn-chêng** 'prior to' or 'before'. Note that this is an exception to the general principle of chronological order of verb placement.

1ST CLAUSE	2ND CLAUSE
event 2 + 進前	*event 1*
event 2 + chìn-chêng	*event 1*
'before *event 2*	, *event 1* occurs'

上 飛行機 進前，我 想欲 買 一 杯 咖啡。
Chiūⁿ hoe-lêng-ki <u>chìn-chêng</u>, góa siuⁿ-beh bé chit poe ka-pi.
上 飛機 之前，我 想要 買 一 杯 咖啡。
Shàng fēijī <u>zhīqián</u>, wǒ xiǎngyāo mǎi yī bēi kāfēi.
<u>Before</u> getting on the plane, I want to buy a cup of coffee.

寫 這 篇 文章 進前，我 需要 較 濟 研究。
Siá chit phiⁿ bûn-chiong <u>chìn-chêng</u>, góa su-iàu khah chē gián-kiù.
寫 這 篇 文章 之前，我 需要 多 一點 研究。
Xiě zhè piān wénzhāng <u>zhīqián</u>, wǒ xūyào duō yīdiǎn yánjiū.
<u>Before</u> writing this essay, I need to do more research.

Note that the adverb **以前 í-chêng** can be placed before the verb in the first clause to mean 'previously' or 'in the past'.

我 以前 驚 狗，但是 這馬 有 三 隻 矣。
Góa <u>í-chêng</u> kiaⁿ káu, tān-sī chit-má ū saⁿ chiah--ah.
我 以前 怕 狗，但是 現在 有 三 隻 了。
Wǒ <u>yǐqián</u> pà gǒu, dànshì xiànzài yǒu sān zhī le.
I was afraid of dogs <u>before</u>, but I have three of them now.

32.1.2.2 Describing an event occurring after another event

To indicate that *event 2* occurs after *event 1*, the time adverb **了(後) liáu(-āu)** 'after' may be used. Place *event 1* in the first clause followed by **了(後) liáu(-āu)** 'after', then put *event 2* in the second clause. Note that **了(後) liáu(-āu)** 'after' must follow an action or event, not a time period.

1ST CLAUSE	2ND CLAUSE
event 1 + 了(後)	*event 2*
event 1 + liáu(-āu)	*event 2*
'after *event 1*	, *event 2* occurs'

伊 關門 <u>了後</u>，紅嬰仔 就 開始 吼 矣。

I koaiⁿ mn̂g <u>liáu-āu</u>, âng-eⁿ-á tō khai-sí háu--ah.

他 關門 <u>之後</u>，嬰兒 就 開始 哭 了。

Tā guān mén <u>zhīhòu</u>, yīng'ér jiù kāishǐ kū le.

<u>After</u> he closed the door, the baby started to cry.

提 行李 <u>了</u>，去 換 錢 咧。

Théh hêng-lí <u>liáu</u>, khì ōaⁿ chîⁿ--leh.

拿 行李 <u>之後</u>，去 換 錢 吧。

Ná xínglǐ <u>zhīhòu</u>, qù huàn qián ba.

<u>After</u> picking up your luggage, go exchange money.

To express that an event occurs after a certain amount of time, use the expression **以後 í-āu** 'after' instead of **了(後) liáu(-āu)**.

1ST CLAUSE	2ND CLAUSE
period of time + 以後	*event*
period of time + í-āu	*event*
'after *period of time*	, *event* occurs'

五 年 <u>以後</u>，我 才 會當 做 永久 居民。

Gō˙nî <u>í-āu</u>, góa chiah ē-tàng chò éng-kiú ku-bîn.

五 年 <u>以後</u>，我 才 能 當 永久 居民。

Wǔ nián <u>yǐhòu</u>, wǒ cái néng dāng yǒngjiǔ jūmín.

<u>After</u> 5 years, I can become a permanent resident.

四十五 分鐘 <u>以後</u>，你 的 雞卵糕 才 烘了。

Sì-cha̍p-gō˙ hun-cheng <u>í-āu</u>, lí ê ke-nn̄g-ko chiah ē hang-liáu.

四十五 分鐘 <u>以後</u>，你 的 蛋糕 才 會 考完。

Sìshíwǔ fēnzhōng <u>yǐhòu</u>, nǐ de dàngāo cái huì kǎowán.

Your cake will be finished baking <u>after</u> 45 minutes.

以後 í-āu can also appear at the beginning of the second clause to introduce the next part of a sequence. In this context, 以後 í-āu means 'later'.

1ST CLAUSE	2ND CLAUSE
event 1	以後 + event 2
event 1	í-āu + event 2
'event 1 occurs	, later event 2 occurs'

你的後生真好笑，以後伊應該會當做藝人。
Lí ê hāu-seⁿ chin hó-chhiò, í-āu i eng-kai ē-tàng chò gē-jîn.
你的兒子很好笑，以後他應該能當藝人。
Nǐ de érzi hěn hǎoxiào, yǐhòu tā yīnggāi néng dāng yìrén.
Your son is very funny. He should be an entertainer <u>later on</u>.

然後 jiân-āu 'afterwards' similarly can begin a second clause to introduce the next part of a sequence. Generally, the events occur closely in time.

1ST CLAUSE	2ND CLAUSE
event 1	然後 + event 2
event 1	jiân-āu + event 2
'event 1 occurs	, afterwards event 2 occurs'

黃先生載恁囝去學效，然後伊去上班。
Ńg--sian-siⁿ chài in kiáⁿ khì ha̍k-hāu, jiân-āu i khì siōng-pan.
黃先生載他的孩子去學校，然後他去上班。
Huáng xiānshēng zài tā de háizi qù xuéxiào, ránhòu tā qù shàngbān.
Mr. Ng drove his children to school. <u>Afterwards</u>, he went to work.

明仔載阮欲參觀藝術館，然後做伙食中晝頓。
Bîn-á-chài gún beh chham-koan gē-su̍t-kóan, jiân-āu chò-hóe chia̍h tiong-tàu-tǹg.
明天我們要參觀藝術館，然後一起吃午餐。
Míngtiān wǒmen yào cānguān yìshùguǎn, ránhòu yīqǐ chī wǔcān.
Tomorrow we are going to the art museum. <u>Afterwards</u>, we will have lunch together.

後來 āu-lâi 'afterwards' is only used when referring to past events.

1ST CLAUSE	2ND CLAUSE
event 1	後來 + event 2
event 1	āu-lâi + event 2
'event 1 occurred	, afterwards event 2 occurred'

阮 阿姊 搬 去 溫哥華，<u>後來</u> 伊 嫁 予 一 个 加拿大 人。
Gún a-chí poan khì Un-ko-hôa, <u>āu-lâi</u> i kè hō˙chit ê Ka-ná-tāi lâng.
我 姐姐 搬 去 溫哥華，<u>後來</u> 她 嫁 給 一 個 加拿大 人。
Wǒ jiějiě bān qù Wēngēhuá, <u>hòulái</u> tā jià gěi yī gè Jiānádà rén.
My older sister moved to Vancouver. <u>Afterwards</u>, she married a Canadian.

有 一 擺 細漢 時，我 按 樹仔 跋落來，<u>後來</u> 救護車 來 矣。
Ū chit pái sè-hàn sî, góa àn chhiū-á poah--lo̍h-lâi, <u>āu-lâi</u> kiù-hō˙-chhia lâi--ah.
有 一 次 小 的 時候，我 從 樹 掉下來，<u>後來</u> 救護車 來 了。
Yǒu yī cì xiǎo de shíhòu, wǒ cóng shù diàoxiàlái, <u>hòulái</u> jiùhùchē lái le.
Once when I was young, I fell from a tree. <u>Afterwards</u>, the ambulance came.

32.1.3 Reference adverbs 就 tō and 才 chiah

Besides time adverbs, two reference adverbs 就 **tō** (also pronounced **chiū**) and 才 **chiah** are often used in two-clause sentence patterns to emphasize the sequence *(see 14.2.1.5 Promptness)*.

32.1.3.1 就 tō 'then'

In a sequence of events, the reference adverb 就 **tō** 'then' is placed just before the second action to underscore the order of events

1ST CLAUSE	2ND CLAUSE
event 1	就 + event 2
event 1	tō + event 2
'event 1 occurs	, then event 2 occurs'

共 碗 洗 了 了後，阮 就 去 客廳 看 電視。
Kā óaⁿ sé liau liáu-āu, gún tō khì kheh-thiaⁿ khòaⁿ tiān-sī.
把 碗 洗 完 之後，我們 就 去 客廳 看 電視。
Bǎ wǎn xǐ wán zhīhòu, wǒmen jiù qù kètīng kàn diànshì.
After washing the dishes, we *(directly)* went to the living room to watch television.

十 碗 麵 食 了 了後，我 就 想欲 吐 矣。
Cha̍p óaⁿ mī chiah liáu liáu-āu, góa tō siūⁿ-beh thò͘--ah.
吃 了 十 碗 麵 之後，我 就 想要 吐 了。
Chīle shí wǎn miàn zhīhòu, wǒ jiù xiǎngyào tǔ le.
After eating ten bowls of noodles, I *just* wanted to vomit.

32.1.3.2 才 chiah 'then'

In a sequence of events, the reference adverb **才 chiah** 'then' can also be placed just before the second action to underscore the order of events.

1ST CLAUSE	2ND CLAUSE
event 1	才 + *event 2*
event 1	chiah + *event 2*
'*event 1* occurs	, then *event 2* occurs'

阮 食 暗頓 了後，才 去 散步。
Gún chiah àm-tǹg liáu-āu, chiah khì sàm-pō͘.
我們 吃 晚餐 之後，再 去 散步。
Wǒmen chī wǎncān zhīhòu, zài qù sànbù.
After we finish eating dinner, we will *(then)* go take a walk.

先 洗浴，才 洗喙。
Seng sé-e̍k, chiah sé-chhùi.
先 洗澡，再 刷牙。
Xiān xǐzǎo, zài shuāyá.
First take a shower, then brush your teeth.

32.1.3.3 才 chiah 'only then'

In other contexts 才 chiah is used in a sequence of events but stresses that the second action will only occur if the first action has already happened.

1ST CLAUSE	2ND CLAUSE
event 1	才 + event 2
event 1	chiah + event 2
'After event 1 occurs	, only then does event 2 occur'

訓練你的狗了後，伊才會乖。
Hún-liān lí ê káu liáu-āu, i <u>chiah</u> ē koai.
訓練你的狗之後，牠才會乖。
Xùnliàn nǐ de gǒu zhīhòu, tā <u>cái</u> huì guāi.
<u>Only after</u> training your dog will it know how to behave.
After training your dog, <u>only then</u> will it know how to behave.

押金了後，你才會使得手機仔。
Ah kim liáu-āu, lí <u>chiah</u> ē-sài tit chhiú-ki-á.
押金之後，你才可以得到手機。
Yā jīn zhīhòu, nǐ <u>cái</u> kěyǐ dédào shǒujī.
<u>Only after</u> paying a deposit will you be allowed to get a mobile phone.
After paying a deposit, <u>only then</u> will you be allowed to get a mobile phone.

32.1.4 Describing an event occurring as soon as another event occurs

To express an event occurs as soon as another event occurs, place the phrase 一(下) chit(-ē) before the verb in event 1. Often, the second clause includes the reference adverb 就 tō before the verb in event 2.

1ST CLAUSE	2ND CLAUSE
一 (下) + event 1	(就) + event 2
chit(-ē) + event 1	(tō) + event 2
'As soon as event 1 occurs	, then event 2 occurs'

你 <u>一(下)</u> 洗 手 了 後, <u>就</u> 會使 食 飯。
Lí <u>chit(-ē)</u> sé chhiú liáu-āu, <u>tō</u> ē-sái chiảh pn̄g.
你 一 洗完 手, 就 可以 吃 飯。
Nǐ yī xǐwán shǒu, jiù kěyǐ chī fàn.
<u>As soon as</u> you wash your hands, *(then)* you may eat.

你 <u>一(下)</u> 到 遮, 餐廳 會 予 咱 坐咧。
Lí <u>chit(-ē)</u> kàu chia, chhann-thiaⁿ ē hō͘ lán chē--leh.
你 一 到 這裡, 餐廳 就 會 讓 我們 坐者。
Nǐ yī dào zhèlǐ, cāntīng jiù huì ràng wǒmen zuòzhě.
<u>As soon as</u> you arrive here, *(then)* the restaurant will allow us to sit down.

32.2 Cause and effect

32.2.1 Using 因為 in-ūi 'because' and 所以 só-í 'therefore' for cause and effect

The general sentence construction to indicate cause and effect uses **因為 in-ūi** 'because' in the first clause and **所以 só-í** 'therefore' at the beginning of the second clause.

1ST CLAUSE	2ND CLAUSE
因為 + *cause*	所以 + *effect*
in-ūi + *cause*	só-í + *effect*
'Because *cause*	, therefore *effect*'

<u>因為</u> 天氣 遐爾 熱, <u>所以</u> 伊 毋 出去 外口 耍。
<u>In-ūi</u> thiⁿ-khì hiah-nī joảh, <u>só-í</u> i m̄ chhut-khì gōa-kháu sńg.
<u>因為</u> 天氣 那麼 熱, <u>所以</u> 她 不 要 出去 外面 玩。
<u>Yīnwèi</u> tiānqì nàme rè, <u>suǒyǐ</u> tā bù yào chūqù wàimiàn wán.
<u>Because</u> the weather is so hot, *(so)* she doesn't want to go outside and play.

因為 吳 小姐 對 蝦仔 過敏，所以 予 伊 食 雞腿飯。
In-ūi Gô·sió-chiá tùi hê-á kòe-bín, só-í hō·i chiảh ke-thúi-pn̄g.
因為 吳 小姐 對 蝦子 過敏，所以 讓 她 吃 雞腿飯。
Yīnwèi Wú xiǎojiě duì xiāzi guòmǐn, suǒyǐ ràng tā chī jītuǐfàn.
Because Ms. Gou is allergic to shrimp, *(so)* let her eat the chicken rice.

因為 **in-ūi** 'because' may be used independently and appear in either the first clause or second clause. If the subject is the same for both clauses, the subject may be left out of either clause.

ORDER 1	
1ST CLAUSE	2ND CLAUSE
因為 + *cause*	*effect*
in-ūi + *cause*	*effect*
'Because *cause*	, therefore *effect*'

因為 塞 車，伊 會 袂赴 開會。
In-ūi that chhia, i ē bē-hù khui-hōe.
因為 塞 車，他 會議 會 遲到。
Yīnwèi sāi chē, tā huìyì huì chídào.
Because there is traffic, he will be late to the meeting.

ORDER 2	
1ST CLAUSE	2ND CLAUSE
effect	因為 + *cause*
effect	in-ūi + *cause*
'*effect*	because *cause*'

伊 會 袂赴 開會，因為 塞 車。
i ē bē-hù khui-hōe, in-ūi that chhia.
他 會議 會 遲到，因為 塞 車。
Tā huìyì huì chídào, yīnwèi sāi chē.
He will be late to the meeting because of traffic.

所以 **só-í** 'therefore' can also be used independently but can only occur in the second clause.

1ST CLAUSE	2ND CLAUSE
cause	所以 + *effect*
cause	só-í + *effect*
'*cause*	, therefore *effect*'

老師 受氣 矣，所以 咱 應該 恬恬 坐咧。
Lāu-su siu-khì--ah, <u>só-í</u> lán eng-kai tiām-tiām chē--leh.
老師 生氣 了，所以 我們 應該 安靜 坐著。
Lǎoshī shēngqì le, <u>suǒyǐ</u> wǒmen yīnggāi ānjìng zuòzhe.
The teacher is angry; <u>therefore</u>, we should all sit quietly.

我 真 忝，所以 咱 來 轉去。
Góa chin thiám, <u>só-í</u> lán lâi tńg--khì.
我 很 累，所以 我們 回家 吧。
Wǒ hěn lèi, <u>suǒyǐ</u> wǒmen huíjiā ba.
I'm tired, <u>so</u> let's go home.

32.2.2 Using 既然 kì-jiân 'since' to express cause

既然 **kì-jiân** 'since' can be used to express cause. However 既然 **kì-jiân** is less common and can only be used in the first clause. An alternate form is 甲 **kah**.

1ST CLAUSE	2ND CLAUSE
既然 + *cause*	*effect*
kì-jiân + *cause*	*effect*
'Since *cause*	, then *effect*'

既然 頭家 受氣 矣，咱 下昏暗 愛 加班。
<u>Kì-jiân</u> thâu-ke siu-khì--ah, lán e-hng-àm ài ka-pan.
既然 老闆 生氣 了，我們 今晚 要 加班。
<u>Jìrán</u> lǎobǎn shēngqì le, wǒmen jīnwǎn yào jiābān.
<u>Since</u> the boss got angry, we have to work late tonight.

既然 外口 有 蠓仔，咱 就 佇 內底 食 飯。
Kì-jiân gōa-kháu ū báng-á, lán tō tī lāi-té chia̍h pn̄g.
既然 戶外 有 蚊子，我們 就 在 裏面 吃 飯 吧。
Jìrán hùwài yǒu wénzi, wǒmen jiù zài lǐmiàn chī fàn ba.
<u>Since</u> there are mosquitos outside, let's eat inside.

伊 甲 毋 納錢，阮 只好 揣 㑹 某 討。
I <u>kah</u> m̄ la̍p-chîⁿ, gún chí-hó chhōe in bó͘ thó.
既然 他 不 要 繳 錢，我們 只好 找 他 的 妻子 索取。
Jìrán tā bù yào jiǎo qián, wǒmen zhǐhǎo zhǎo tā de qīzi suǒqǔ.
<u>Since</u> he won't pay, we have no other choice than to ask his wife.

32.2.3 Using 毋才 m̄-chiah 'therefore' to express effect

The conjunction 毋才 m̄-chiah 'therefore' or 'as a result' can also be used to express effect. Place 毋才 m̄-chiah at the beginning of the second clause.

1ST CLAUSE	2ND CLAUSE
cause	毋才 *effect*
cause	m̄-chiah *effect*
'*cause*	, therefore *effect*'

因為 你 佮 伊 講 伊 貧惰，伊 毋才 做 較 濟 矣。
In-ūi lí kah i kóng i pîn-tōaⁿ, i <u>m̄-chiah</u> chò khah chē--ah.
因為 你 告訴 他 他 很 懶惰，<u>所以</u> 他 才 做 比較 多 了。
Yīnwèi nǐ gàosu tā tā hěn lǎnduò, <u>suǒyǐ</u> tā cái zuò bǐjiào duō le.
You told him he was lazy; <u>as a result</u>, he works even more.

導遊 破病 矣，遊覽 毋才 取消 矣。
Tō-iû phòa-pēⁿ--ah, iû-lám <u>m̄-chiah</u> chhú-siau--ah.
導遊 病 了，<u>所以</u> 旅遊 取消 了。
Dǎoyóu bìng le, <u>suǒyǐ</u> lǚyóu qǔxiāo le.
The guide got sick; <u>as a result</u>, the tour was cancelled.

33 Purpose

33.1 Expressing purpose through consecutive verbs

Taiwanese generally follows the principle of presenting verbs in the order in which they would chronologically occur. This principle also allows a sequence of events to be indicated solely through the ordering of verbs within a sentence. No additional words are required. Depending on the meaning of the verbs, a relationship of purpose can be established suggesting the first verb was performed in order to accomplish the second verb.

verb 1 + verb 2

'*verb 1* performed in order to *verb 2*'

伊 提 皮包仔 出來 納錢。
I thėh phôe-pau-á chhut-lâi lap-chîⁿ.
他 拿 皮包 出來 繳 費。
Tā ná píbāo chūlái jiǎo fèi.
He took out his wallet to pay.

彼 工 阮 阿兄 早 起來 坐 第一 班 火車。
Hit kang gún a-hiaⁿ chá khí-lâi chē tē-it pan hóe-chhia.
那天 我 哥哥 早 起 坐 第一 班 火車。
Nèitiān wǒ gēgē zǎo qǐ zuò dìyī bān huǒchē.
That day, my older brother got up early to catch the first train.

33.2 Using 來 lâi 'come' and 去 khì 'go' to indicate purpose

To indicate that the purpose of the first verb is to perform the second verb, place the verb **來 lâi** or **去 khì** before the second verb. The choice of direction reflects whether the direction of movement is towards the speaker (**來 lâi**) or away from the speaker (**去 khì**). When there is no actual physical movement in a particular direction towards the speaker, either verb may be used.

verb 1 + 來 / 去 + *verb 2*

verb 1 + lâi / khì + *verb 2*

'*verb 1* performed in order to *verb 2*'

貓仔 跳 來 佇 桌仔頂 來 食 阮 的 菜。
Niau-á thiau lâi tī toh-á-téng lâi chiảh gún ê chhài.
貓 跳 到 桌子 上 來 吃 我們 的 菜。
Māo tiào dào zhuōzi shàng lái chī wǒmen de cài.
The cat jumped onto the table to eat our food.

阮 坐 佇 窗仔邊 來 看 山。
Gún chē tī thang-á-piⁿ lâi khòaⁿ soaⁿ.
我們 坐 在 窗戶 邊 來 看 山。
Wǒmen zuò zài chuānghù biān lái kàn shān.
We sat by the windows to see the mountains.

彼 个 查埔 囡仔 用 哭 去 討 較 濟 餅。
Hit ê cha-po͘ gín-á ēng khàu khì thó khah chē piáⁿ.
那個 小 男孩 用 哭 去 要 更 多 的 餅乾。
Nàge xiǎo nánhái yòng kū qù yào gèng duō de bǐnggān.
That little boy used crying to get more cookies.

阮 阿母 拍手 去 驚走 鬼。
Gún a-bú phah-chhiú khì kiaⁿ-cháu kúi.
我 媽 拍手 去 嚇跑 鬼。
Wǒ mā pāishǒu qù xiàpǎo guǐ.
My mother clapped her hands to scare away the ghosts.

33.3 Expressing a goal or purpose of action with 為著 ūi-tio̍h

To express that an action is performed for a certain goal or purpose, place **為著 ūi-tio̍h** before the desired goal or purpose.

為著 + *desired result*

ūi-tio̍h + *desired result*

為著 贏 比賽,棒球隊 逐 日 練球。
Ūi-tio̍h iâⁿ pí-sài, pāng-kiû-tūi ta̍k ji̍t liān-kiû.
為了 贏 比賽,棒球隊 每天 練球。
Wèile yíng bǐsài, bàngqiúduì měitiān liàn qiú.
To win the tournament, the baseball team practiced every day.

阮 的 商店 為著 提供 上 方便 的 服務,逐 日 攏 有 開。
Gún ê siong-tiàm ūi-tio̍h thê-kiong siōng hong-piān ê ho̍k-bū, ta̍k ji̍t lóng ū khui.
為了 提供 最 方便 的 服務 給 客人,我們 的 商店 每天 都 有 開。
Wèile tígōng zuì fāngbiàn de fúwù gěi kèrén, wǒmen de shāngdiàn měitiān dōu yǒu kāi.
To offer the most convenience to our customers, our store is open every day.

我 食 兩 个 頭路 就 是 為著 繳 學費。
Góa chia̍h nn̄g ê thâu-lō͘ tō sī ūi-tio̍h kiáu ha̍k-hùi.
我 有 兩個 工作 就 是 為了 繳 學費。
Wǒ yǒu liǎng gè gōngzuò jiù shì wèile jiǎo xuéfèi.
I have two jobs in order to pay for tuition.

33.4 Expressing actions taken to avoid an outcome

To indicate an action that was performed to avoid an outcome, place **較免 khah bián** before the unwanted outcome.

較免 + *unwanted outcome*

khah bián + *unwanted outcome*

家己 帶 餅 較免 踮 遐 買 物食。
Ka-ti tòa piáⁿ <u>khah bián</u> tàm hia bé mih-chiah.

自己 帶 零食 免得 在 那裡 買 吃 的 東西。
Zìjǐ dài língshí <u>miǎndé</u> zài nàlǐ mǎi chī de dōngxī.

Bring a snack so you <u>won't have to</u> buy food there.

伊 佇 學校 共 功課 做 了，所以 較免 紮 課本 轉去。
I tī ha̍k-hāu kā kong-khò chò liáu, só-í <u>khah bián</u> chah khò-pún tńg--khì.

他 在 學校 做 了 功課，所以 免 帶 課本 回去。
Tā zài xuéxiào zuòle gōngkè, suǒyǐ <u>miǎn</u> dài kèběn huíqù.

He did his homework at school, so he <u>didn't have to</u> take his textbooks home.

33.5 Expressing for whom an action is performed

When an action is performed on someone else's behalf, the person who benefits can be introduced by prepositions known as benefactives *(see 15.7 Prepositions for benefactives)*. The prepositions **替 thè**, **共 kā**, and **為 ūi** in this context can often be translated into English as 'for'. However, note that several of these prepositions have other meanings as well.

替 THÈ

我 替 阿母 洗 衫。
Góa <u>thè</u> a-bú sé saⁿ.

我 替 媽媽 洗 衣服。
Wǒ <u>tì</u> māmā xǐ yīfú.

I washed the clothes <u>for</u> my mom.

共 KĀ

李小姐 共 伊 的 狗仔 買 衫。
Lí sió-chiá kā i ê káu-á bé saⁿ.
李小姐 給 她 的 狗 買 衣服。
Lǐ xiǎojiě gěi tā de gǒu mǎi yīfú.
Ms. Li bought clothes for her dog.

為 ŪI

遮 的 職員 為 經理 拍拚。
Chia ê chit-ôan ūi keng-lí phah-piàⁿ.
這裡 的 職員 為 經理 努力 工作。
Zhèlǐ de zhíyuán wèi jīnglǐ nǔlì gōngzuò.
The employees here work hard for their manager.

34 Simultaneous actions

34.1 Describing two actions occurring at the same time

34.1.1 When each activity receives attention independently

To indicate that two activities occur during the same time period but require a shift in attention, place 一面 **chit-bīn** 'on one side' before each verb phrase. An alternate form is to place 那 **ná** before each verb phrase.

> 一面 + *verb phrase* + 一面 + *verb phrase*
> chit-bīn + *verb phrase* + chit-bīn + *verb phrase*

歇熱 時，我 拍算 <u>一面</u> 上課 <u>一面</u> 食 頭路。
Hioh-joah sî, góa phah-sǹg <u>chit-bīn</u> siōng-khò <u>chit-bīn</u> chiah thâu-lō͘.
暑假 的 時候，我 計劃 <u>一邊</u> 上課 <u>一邊</u> 工作。
Shǔjià de shíhòu, wǒ jìhuà <u>yībiān</u> shàngkè <u>yībiān</u> gōngzuò.
This summer break I plan on taking classes <u>and</u> working.

阮 下昏暗 <u>那</u> 奕 牌仔 <u>那</u> 看 電視。
Gún e-hng-àm <u>ná</u> ī pâi-á <u>ná</u> khòaⁿ tiān-sī.
我們 今晚 <u>一邊</u> 玩 牌 <u>一邊</u> 看 電視。
Wǒmen jīnwǎn <u>yībiān</u> wán pái <u>yībiān</u> kàn diànshì.
Tonight we are going to play cards <u>and</u> watch television.

34.1.2 When two activities are performed at once 像時 siāng-sî

To indicate that two activities are conducted at the same time, place **像時 siāng-sî** before the verb phrase. The conjunction **也 iā** 'also' can optionally be used to connect the two verb phrases.

MULTIPLE ACTIONS

像時 + *verb phrase 1* + (也) + *verb phrase 2*

siāng-sî + *verb phrase 1* + (iā) + *verb phrase 2*

我 真 愛 像時 騎 跤踏車 也 聽 音樂。
Góa chin ài siāng-sî khiâ kha-tah-chhia iā thiaⁿ im-ga̍k.
我 很 喜歡 同時 騎 腳踏車 也 聽 音樂。
Wǒ hěn xǐhuān tóngshí qí jiǎotàchē yě tīng yīnyuè.
I really enjoy cycling and listening to music at the same time.

莫 像時 食 物 講 話。
Mái siāng-sî chia̍h mi̍h kóng ōe.
不要 同時 吃 東西 說 話。
Bùyào tóngshí chī dōngxī shuō huà.
Don't chew and talk at the same time.

像時 siāng-sî can also be used when multiple subjects perform a single action simultaneously.

MULTIPLE SUBJECTS

subject(s) + 像時 + *verb phrase*

subject(s) + siāng-sî + *verb phrase*

學生 像時 寫了 考券。
Ha̍k-seng siāng-sî siá-liáu khó-kǹg.
學生 同時 寫完 考卷。
Xuéshēng tóngshí xiěwán kǎojuàn.
The students simultaneously completed their tests.

李 先生 佮 洪 先生 攏 像時 予 辭 頭路 矣。
Lí--sian-siⁿ kah Âng--sian-siⁿ lóng siāng-sî hō˙sî thâu-lō͘--ah.
李 先生 和 洪 先生 都 同時 被 炒魷魚 了。
Lǐ xiānshēng hé Hóng xiānshēng dōu tóngshí bèi chǎoyóuyú le.
Mr. Li and Mr. Ang were fired at the same time.

34.1.3 When multiple subjects perform an activity together at once

To indicate that multiple subjects do a single activity together, place **同齊 tâng-chê** before the verb phrase. While the multiple subjects are performing an activity together, it is possible for each subject to independently perform different actions.

multiple subjects or *plural subject* + 同齊 + *verb phrase*

multiple subjects or *plural subject* + tâng-chê + *verb phrase*

咱 下昏暗 來 同齊 包 水餃!
Lán e-hng-àm lâi tâng-chê pau chúi-kiáu!
我們 今晚 一起 包 水餃 吧!
Wǒmen jīnwǎn yīqǐ bāo shuǐjiǎo ba!
Let's make dumplings (together) tonight!

謝 小姐 佮 恁 小妹 欲 同齊 種 一 欉 樹仔。
Siā sió-chiá kah in sió-mōe beh tâng-chê chéng chit châng chhiū-á.
謝 小姐 和 她的 妹妹 要 一起 種 一 棵 樹。
Xiè xiǎojiě hé tā de mèimei yào yīqǐ zhǒng yī kē shù.
Ms. Sia and her younger sister are going to plant a tree together.

34.1.4 Performing actions together

To more generally indicate that an activity is performed with others, use the adverb **做伙 chò-hóe** 'together'. Place this manner adverb before the verb or verb phrase. Alternate forms include **做陣 chò-tīn**, **相佮 saⁿ-kap**, or **鬥陣 tàu-tīn**.

做伙 + *verb*

chò-hóe + *verb*

'do *verb* together'

咱 做伙 來 去 看 電影。
Lán chò-hóe lâi khì khòaⁿ tiān-iáⁿ.
我們 一起 去 看 電影 吧。
Wǒmen yīqǐ qù kàn diànyǐng ba.
Let's go to the movies together.

咱的 頭家 著愛 做陳 解決 這 个 問題。
Lán ê thâu-ke tio̍h-ài chò-tīn kái-koat chit ê būn-tê.
我們 的 老闆 必須 一起 解決 這個 問題。
Wǒmen de lǎobǎn bìxū yīqǐ jiějué zhège wèntí.
Our bosses will have to solve this problem together.

阮 兜 的 規定 其中 一 个 是 愛 相佮 食 飯。
Gún tau ê kui-tēng kî-tiong chit ê sī ài saⁿ-kap chia̍h pn̄g.
我們 家 的 規定 其中 之 一 是 得 一起 吃 飯。
Wǒmen jiā de guīdìng qízhōng zhī yī shì děi yīqǐ chī fàn.
One of our family rules is to always eat together.

恁 若 鬥陣 工作，明仔載 以前 恁 一定 做 予 了。
Lín nā tàu-tīn kang-chok, bîn-á-chài í-chêng lín it-tēng chò hō͘ liáu.
你們 如果 一起 工作，明天 前 你們 一定 會 做完。
Nǐmen rúguǒ yīqǐ gōngzuò, míngtiān qián nǐmen yīdìng huì zuòwán.
You will finish by morning if you work together.

34.2 Giving priority to one action over another

To give priority of attention to one action over another, place one verb into the background.

34.2.1 Indicating a constant state with verb suffix 咧 --leh

The verb suffix 咧 **--leh** can be added to verbs to indicate a constant state. This pertains to verbs used to describe a manner of existence (a picture hanging on the wall), a persistent posture (crouching on the ground), or repetitive motions without an implied ending (cutting with scissors) *(see 8.2.2 Static continuous aspect)*. Placing a suffixed verb into the background allows a second more active verb to occur in the foreground. The more active verb in the foreground follows immediately after the 咧 **--leh** suffixed verb in the background

background verb + 咧 + *foreground verb*

background verb + --leh + *foreground verb*

查某 囡仔 佇 眠床頂 坐咧 笑。
Cha-bó͘ gín-á tī bîn-chhn̂g-téng chē--leh chhiò.
女孩子 在 床上 坐著 笑。
Nǚháizi zài chuángshàng zuò<u>zhe</u> xiào.
The little girl <u>is</u> sitt<u>ing</u> on the bed smiling.

阮 後生 佇 溪仔墘 跍咧 揣 水雞。
Gún hāu-seⁿ tī khe-á-kîⁿ khû--leh chhōe chúi-ke.
我 兒子 在 河岸 蹲著 找 青蛙。
Wǒ érzi zài hé'àn dūn<u>zhe</u> zhǎo qīngwā.
My son <u>is</u> crouch<u>ing</u> by the river looking for frogs.

34.2.2 Indicating a state or action already occurring in the background

To indicate that an action or state is already occurring in the background before another more active verb occurs in the foreground, place 的 時陣 **ê sî-chūn** 'during that time, when' after the action or state that sits in the background. Note that either or both 的 **ê** and 陣 **-chūn** may be omitted in this expression.

background verb + (的)時(陣) + *foreground verb*

background verb + (ê) sî(-chūn) + *foreground verb*

阮 睏 的 時陣，阮 狗仔 偷 走去。
Gún khùn ê sî-chūn, gún káu-á thau cháu--khì.
我們 睡覺 的 時候，我們 的 狗 偷 跑出去。
Wǒmen shuìjiào de shíhòu, wǒmen de gǒu tōu pǎochūqù.
When we were sleeping, our dog ran away.

阮 阿姊 細漢 時，較 媠。
Gún a-chí sè-hàn sî, khah súi.
我 姐姐 小 的 時候，比較 漂亮。
Wǒ jiějiě xiǎo de shíhòu, bǐjiào piàoliang.
When my older sister was younger, she was much prettier.

34.2.3 Habitual occurrences

The expression 的 時陣 ê sî-chūn 'whenever' can also be used to describe habitual occurrences. The action that initiates or co-occurs with the second action is followed by 的 時陣 ê sî-chūn 'whenever'. Note that either or both 的 ê and 陣 -chūn may be omitted in this expression.

verb 1 + (的) 時(陣) + *verb 2*
verb 1 + (ê) sî(-chūn) + *verb 2*

伊 啉 酒 的 時陣，講 話 真 大 聲。
I lim chiú ê sî-chūn, kóng ōe chin tōa sia^n.
他 喝 酒 時，說話 很 大 聲。
Tā hē jiǔ shí, shuō huà hěn dà shēng.
Whenever he drinks, he talks very loudly.

我 運動 時，我 流 真 濟 汗。
Góa ūn-tōng sî, góa lâu chin chē kōa^n.
我 運動 時，我 流 很 多 汗。
Wǒ yùndòng shí, wǒ liú hěn duō hàn.
Whenever I exercise, I sweat a lot.

35 Conditionals

Conditional sentences are made up of two main components: the *condition* and the *result*. The *condition* describes a hypothetical set of circumstances that generally must happen in order for the *result* to occur. In English, the condition is often placed within an 'if' clause and set apart by a comma.

    If <u>she comes here</u>, then <u>I will leave</u>.

CONDITION	RESULT
'she comes here'	'I will leave'

The order may be switched even though the 'if' clause must occur first chronologically in order for the result to happen.

    I will leave if she comes.

In Taiwanese, the condition set up by the 'if' clause generally comes before the result.

伊 若 來, 我 就 離開。
I nā lâi, góa tō lī-khui.
如果 她 來, 我 就 離開。
Rúguǒ tā lái, wǒ jiù líkāi.
If she comes here, then I will leave.

CONDITION	RESULT
(伊) 來	我 就 離開
(i) lâi	góa tō lī-khui
'she comes here'	'I will leave'

If the subject is the same in both clauses, the subject may appear in both clauses or omitted from one of the clauses.

35.1 Conditionals without special conjunctions

Conditional sentences can be formed without the use of special conjunctions signifying 'if' or 'then'. Simply stating the condition to be fulfilled in the first clause followed by the result or consequence in the second clause can produce a conditional sentence. A comma or pause in spoken speech is made in between clauses. Additionally, the second clause often will have a potential or future marker by using the modal verbs 會 ē 'will' or 袂 bē 'will not' with the verb *(see 12.1.1 Modal verb 會 ē 'will')*.

1ST CLAUSE	2ND CLAUSE
condition	*result*

無 清 房間，袂使 出去。
Bô chheng pâng-keng, bē-sài chhut-khì.
不 清 房間，不 可以 出去。
Bù qīng fángjiān, bù kěyǐ chūqù.
If you don't clean your room, you will not be allowed to go out.

35.2 If-then clauses

An if-then clause is a two-part conditional sentence which first states a necessary condition ('if' clause) for a result ('then' clause) to occur.

若 nā 'if' can be placed before or after the subject. However, the placement of 若 nā 'if' can influence the meaning. Whatever follows 若 nā becomes part of the condition. 就 tō 'then' may optionally appear before the verb in the second clause to emphasize the causal relation between the 'if' clause and 'then' clause.

1ST CLAUSE	2ND CLAUSE
subject + 若	(就) + *verb*
subject + nā	(tō) + *verb*
'If *condition*	, then *result*'

AFTER THE SUBJECT (SUBJECT IS EXCLUDED FROM THE CONDITION)

伊 若 去，我 會 受氣 矣。

I nā khì, góa ē siū-khì--ah.

他 要是 去，我 會 生氣 了。

Tā yàoshi qù, wǒ huì shēngqì le.

If he *goes*, I will become angry (*the act of 'going' causes the anger*).

1ST CLAUSE	2ND CLAUSE
若 + *subject*	(就) + *verb*
nā + *subject*	(tō) + *verb*
'If *condition*	, then *result*'

BEFORE THE SUBJECT (SUBJECT IS INCLUDED IN THE CONDITION)

若 伊 去，我 會 受氣 矣。

Nā i khì, góa ē siū-khì--ah.

要是 他 去，我 會 生氣 了。

Yàoshi tā qù, wǒ huì shēngqì le.

If *he* goes, I will become angry (*the fact that 'he' goes causes the anger*).

Alternate terms for 'if' include 若準 **nā-chún**, 若是 **nā-sī**, 假使(-若) **ká-sú (-nā)**, and 如果 **jû-kó**. 假使 **ká-sú** must come before the subject.

若是 NĀ-SĪ

若是 阮 阿兄，伊 這馬 就 買 票。

Nā-sī gún a-hiaⁿ, i chit-má tō bé phiàu.

要是 我 哥哥，他 現在 就 買 票。

Yàoshi wǒ gēgē, tā xiànzài jiù mǎi piào.

If it were my older brother, then he would buy the tickets now.

若準 NĀ-CHÚN

伊 若準 啉 咖啡，就 會 睏袂去。

I nā-chún lim ka-pi, tō ē khùn-bē--khì.

她 如果 喝 咖啡，就 會 睡不著。

Tā rúguǒ hē kāfēi, jiù huì shuìbuzháo.

If she drinks coffee, she will not be able to sleep.

如果 JÛ-KÓ

伊 如果 無 聽 你 的 話，就 敲 電話 予 恁 阿母。
I jû-kó bô thiaⁿ lí ê ōe, tō khà tiān-ōe hō ˈin a-bú.
他 如果 不 聽 你 的 話，就 打 電話 給 他 媽媽。
Tā rúguǒ bù tīng nǐ de huà, jiù dǎ diànhuà gěi tā māmā.
If he doesn't listen to you, then call his mother.

假使(若) KÁ-SÚ (NĀ)

假使 若 鞋仔 傷 細 的，你 就 予 小弟。
Ká-sú nā ê-á siuⁿ sè ê, lí tō hō ˈsió-tī.
如果 鞋子 太 小 的，你 就 給 弟弟。
Rúguǒ xiézi tài xiǎo de, nǐ jiù gěi dìdì.
If the shoes are too small, then give them to your younger brother.

35.3 Other types of conditional clauses

35.3.1 In the event, just in case

To emphasize that the condition is not expected or not likely to occur, use **萬一 bān-it** to express 'in the event' or 'just in case' in the condition. Alternate versions include **一旦 it-tàn** and **毋拄好 m̄-tú-hó**. Generally, **毋拄好 m̄-tú-hó** is used before an event that is considered unwanted or unlucky. Note that 'in the event' conditional clauses may occur in the second clause.

萬一 BĀN-IT

萬一 若 落 雨，阮 會 共 婚禮 改做 後 禮拜。
Bān-it nā lȯh hō˙, gún ē kā hun-lé kái-chò āu lé-pài.
萬一 如果 下 雨，我們 會 把 婚禮 改成 下 禮拜。
Wànyī rúguǒ xià yǔ, wǒmen huì bǎ hūnlǐ gǎichéng xià lǐbài.
In the event that it rains, we will change the wedding to next week.

毋拄好 M̄-TÚ-HÓ

伊 有 紮 一寡 電池，毋拄好 手電 的 電 用了 矣。

I ū chah chit-kóa tiān-tî, m̄-tú-hó chhiú-tiān ê tiān ēng-liáu--ah.

他 帶 一些 電池，萬一 手電筒 的 電 用完 了。

Tā dài yīxiē diànchí, wànyī shǒudiàntǒng de diàn yòngwán le.

He brought some batteries just in case the flashlight runs out of power.

一旦 IT-TÀN

一旦 我 揣著 頭路，我 會 真 歡喜。

It-tàn góa chhōe-tiȯh thâu-lō͘, góa ē chin hoaⁿ-hí.

一旦 我 找到 工作，我 會 很 高興。

Yīdàn wǒ zhǎodào gōngzuò, wǒ huì hěn gāoxìng.

If one day I find a job, I will be very happy.

35.3.2 Unless, only if

To emphasize a more restricted condition, **除非 tû-hui** 'unless' can be placed before the subject of the first clause. **除非 tû-hui** 'unless' is often paired with **若無 nā-bô** 'otherwise' in the second clause. This underscores the result that will occur if the condition in the first clause fails to happen.

1ST CLAUSE	2ND CLAUSE
除非 + *subject*	(若無) + *verb*
tû-hui + *subject*	(nā-bô) + *verb*
'Unless *condition*	, otherwise *result*'

除非 你 的 車 會當 飛，(若無) 咱 會 袂赴 矣。

Tû-hui lí ê chhia ē-tàng poe, (nā-bô) lán ē bē-hù--ah.

除非 你 的 車 能 飛，(要不然) 我們 會 來不及 了。

Chúfēi nǐ de chē néng fēi, (yàobùrán) wǒmen huì láibují le.

Unless your car can fly, *(otherwise)* we will be late.

However, when **除非 tû-hui** is paired with **才 chiah** in the second clause, the meaning of **除非 tû-hui** shifts to 'only if'. With this construction, the second clause describes a result that can only occur if the condition in the first clause is fulfilled.

1ST CLAUSE	2ND CLAUSE
除非 + *subject*	才 + *verb*
tû-hui + *subject*	chiah + *verb*
'Only if *condition*	, then *result*'

除非 你 會當 泅 1500 公尺，你 才 會使 參加 團隊。
Tû-hui lí ē-tàng siû chit chheng go˙kong-chhioh, lí chiah ē-sài chham-ka thôan-tūi.
除非 你 能 游泳 1500 公尺，你 才 可以 參加 團隊。
Chúfēi nǐ néng yóuyǒng 1500 gōngchǐ, nǐ cái kěyǐ cānjiā tuánduì.
Only if you can swim 1500 meters will you *(then)* be allowed to join the team.

35.3.3 Even if

To emphasize that a result will occur even if the condition occurs, place 準做 **chún-chò** 'even if' before the subject in the first clause. An alternate form is 就算是 **chiū-sǹg sī**. The result often begins with an adverb expressing 'still' such as 嘛 **mā**, 猶 **iáu**, or 猶原 **iû-gôan**.

1ST CLAUSE	2ND CLAUSE
準做 + *subject*	(嘛) + *verb*
chún-chò + *subject*	(mā) + *verb*
'Even if *condition*	, still *result*'

準做 CHÚN-CHÒ
準做 我 好額，我 猶原 袂 買 車。
Chún-chò góa hó-giȧh, góa iû-gôan bē bé chhia.
即使 我 富有，我 仍然 不 會 買 車。
Jíshǐ wǒ fùyǒu, wǒ réngrán bù huì mǎi chē.
Even if I were wealthy, I still would not buy a car.

就算是 CHIŪ-SǸG SĪ
就算 是 伊 請 所有 恁 親情，新娘 的 人客 嘛 會 較 濟。
Chiū-sǹg sī i chhiáⁿ só˙-ū in chhin-chiâⁿ, sin-niû ê lâng-kheh mā ē khah chē.
就算 是 他 請了 所有 他 的 親戚，新娘 的 客人 也 比較 多。
Jiùsuàn shì tā qǐngle suǒyǒu tā de qīnqī, xīnniáng de kèrén yě bǐjiào duō.
Even if he invited all his relatives, there would still be more guests from the bride's side.

35.3.4 If not for, if it weren't for

To emphasize that without a condition having occurred, the result would not have happened, place 若無 **nā-bô** 'if not for' before the condition. An alternate version is 若毋是 **nā-m̄-sī** 'if it weren't for'.

若無 NĀ-BÔ

若無 恁 鬥相共，我 共 這 塊 桌仔 搬袂去。
Nā-bô in tàu-saⁿ-kāng, góa kā chit tè toh-á poan-bē--khì.
要不是 他 的 幫忙，我 這 張 桌子 搬不動。
Yàobùshì tā de bāngmáng, wǒ zhè zhāng zhuōzi bānbùdòng.
If not for his help, I would not have been able to move this table.

若毋是 NĀ-M̄-SĪ

若毋是 狗仔 咧 吠，阮 共 賊仔 掠袂著。
Nā-m̄-sī káu-á teh pūi, gún kā chha̍t-á lia̍h-bē-tio̍h.
要不是 狗 在 吠叫，我們 抓不到 小偷。
Yàobùshì gǒu zài fèijiào, wǒmen zhuābùdào xiǎotōu.
If it weren't for the dog's barking, we wouldn't have been able to catch the burglar.

35.3.5 As long as, provided that, if only

To emphasize that only a single condition needs to be met in order for the result to occur, place 只要 **chí-iàu** 'as long as' before the condition. Other translations include 'provided that' and 'if only'.

只要 押 身份證，你 會使 借 藍球。
Chí-iàu ah sin-hūn-chèng, lí ē-sài chioh nâ-kiû.
只要 押 身分證，你 可以 借 籃球。
Zhǐyào yā shēnfènzhèng, nǐ kěyǐ jiè lánqiú.
As long as you leave your ID, you may borrow the basketball.

只要 無 落 雨，咱 會 佇 外口 舉行 婚禮。
Chí-iau bô lo̍h hōʼ, lán ē tī gōa-kháu kí-hêng hun-lé.
只要 不 下 雨，我們 會 在 外面 舉行 婚禮。
Zhǐyào bù xià yǔ, wǒmen huì zài wàimiàn jǔxíng hūnlǐ.
Provided that it doesn't rain, we will have the wedding outside.

35.3.6 Regardless, no matter, whether or not, in any case

To emphasize that regardless if a condition occurs the same result will occur, place 無論 **bô-lūn** before the condition. An alternate version is 毋管 **m̄-kóan**. Other translations include 'regardless if', 'no matter if', and 'whether or not'.

無論 BÔ-LŪN

無論 你 有 請 我 食 飯，無，我 袂 和 你 做伙 去 彼 間 餐廳。
<u>Bô-lūn</u> lí ū chhiáⁿ góa chiảh pn̄g, bô, góa bē hām lí chò-hóe khì hit keng chhan-thiaⁿ.
不管 你 有沒有 請 我 吃飯，我 還是 不 會 跟 你 一起 去 那家 餐廳。
<u>Bùguǎn</u> nǐ yǒuméiyǒu qǐng wǒ chī fàn, wǒ háishì bù huì gēn nǐ yīqǐ qù nà jiā canting.
<u>Whether or not</u> you buy me dinner, I will not go with you to that restaurant.

毋管 M̄-KÓAN

毋管 李 小姐 加班，伊 錢 趁袂夠。
<u>M̄-kóan</u> Lí sió-chiá ka-pan, i chîⁿ thàn-bē-kàu.
不管 李 小姐 是否 加班，她 錢 仍然 賺不夠。
<u>Bùguǎn</u> Lǐ xiǎojiě shìfǒu jiābān, tā qián réngrán zhuànbùgòu.
<u>Regardless if</u> Ms. Li works overtime, she won't earn enough money.

較講 **khah-kóng** and 總是 **chóng--sī** can be added to sentences without providing a specific condition. These expressions are commonly translated to 'in any case', 'no matter what', and 'regardless'.

較講 KHAH-KÓNG

較講 你 嘛 愛 趁 錢。
<u>Khah-kóng</u> lí mā ài thàn chîⁿ.
無論 如何 你 總是 要 賺錢。
<u>Wúlùn rúhé</u> nǐ zǒngshì yào zhuànqián.
<u>In any case</u>, you still have to earn money.

總是 CHÓNG--SĪ

咱 總是 應該 揣著 下昏暗 會當 蹛 的 所在。
Lán <u>chóng--sī</u> eng-kai chhōe-tioh e-hng-àm ē-tàng tòa ê só͘-chāi.
無論 如何 我們 應該 找到 今晚 能 住 的 地方。
<u>Wúlùn rúhé</u> wǒmen yīnggāi zhǎodào jīnwǎn néng zhù de dìfāng.
<u>No matter what</u>, we should find a place to stay tonight.

35.4 Implying possible consequences 'otherwise, or else, if not'

To emphasize that possible consequences will occur if action is not taken, place the adverb **若無 nā-bô** 'otherwise' before the implied consequence. An alternate version is **無 bô** set aside by a comma. These expressions are also commonly translated as 'or else' or 'if not'.

若無 NĀ-BÔ

若無，你 按怎 欲 去？
Nā-bô, lí án-chóaⁿ beh khì?
不然，你 怎麼 要 去？
Bùrán, nǐ zěnme yào qù?
If not, how will you get there?

無 BÔ

共 文件 緊 傳過來 咧，無，客戶 會 受氣 矣。
Kā bûn-kiāⁿ kìn thôan--kòe-lâi--leh, bô, kheh-hō͘ ē siū-khì--ah.
把 文件 快 傳過來 吧，不然，客戶 會 生氣 了。
Bǎ wénjiàn kuài chuánguòlái ba, bùrán, kèhù huì shēngqì le.
Send me the document right away; otherwise, the client will be angry.

References

Blust, Robert. (1999). Subgrouping, circularity and extinction: some issues in Austronesian comparative linguistics. In E. Zeitoun & P.J.K Li (Eds.) *Selected papers from the Eighth International Conference on Austronesian Linguistics*, 31–94. Taipei: Academia Sinica.

Chang, Miao-Hsia. (2009). Metaphorization and Metonymization: Diachronic Development of Verbs of Volition in Southern Min. *Taiwan Journal of Linguistics*, 7(1), 53-84. Taipei: Crane Publishing Co.

Chao, Yuen-ren. (1968). *A Grammar of Spoken Chinese*. Berkeley and Los Angeles: University of California Press.

Chappell, Hilary. (1982). Towards a typology of aspect in Sinitic languages. *Zhōngguó Jìngnèi Yǔyán jì Yǔyánxué: Hànyǔ Fāngyán* 中國境內語言暨語言學:漢語方言 [Chinese Languages and Linguistics: Chinese dialects], 1(1), 67–106. Taipei: Academia Sinica.

———. (1989). The grammatical category of aspect in Southern Min: preverbal coding of aspect in Min-Xiamen. *La Trobe working papers in linguistics*, (2), 113-126.

———. (2001). The experiential perfect as an evidential marker in Sinitic Languages. *A typology of evidential markers in Sinitic languages*. In H. Chappell (ed.), *Sinitic Grammar: Synchronic and diachronic perspectives*, 56-84. Oxford: Oxford University Press.

Chen, Ping. (2004). *Modern Chinese: History and Sociolinguistics*. Cambridge: Cambridge University Press.

Cheng, Lisa L.S., Huang, C.T. James, Li, Y.H. Audrey, & Tang, C.C. Jane. (1999). Hoo, hoo, hoo: syntax of the causative, dative, and passive constructions in Taiwanese. In Pang-Hsin Ting (Ed.), *Contemporary Studies on the Min Dialects* [Journal of Chinese Linguistics Monograph 14], 146-203. Berkeley: University of California.

Cheng, Lisa L.S. & Sybesma, Rint. (2005). Classifiers in four varieties of Chinese. In Giglielmo Cinque and Richard S. Kayne (Eds.). *The Oxford Handbook of Comparative Syntax*, 259-291. Oxford: Oxford University Press.

Cheng, Robert L. (鄭良偉). (1968). Tone Sandhi in Taiwanese. *Linguistics*, 41, 19-42.

——. (1985). A Comparison of Taiwanese, Taiwan Mandarin, and Peking Mandarin. *Language* 61(2), 352-377. Washington, DC: The Linguistic Society of America.

——. (1990). *Yǎnbiàn zhōng de Táiwān shèhuì yǔwén: Duō yǔ shèhuì jí shuāngyǔ jiàoyù* (演變中的台灣社會語文 ： 多語社會及雙語教育) [Essays on sociolinguistic problems of Taiwan]. Taipei: *Zìlì wǎnbào shè wénhuà chūbǎn bù* (自立晚報社文化出版部).

Chiung, Wi-vun Taiffalo. (2000). Peh-oe-ji, Childish writing? *Paper presented at the 6th Annual North American Taiwan Studies Conference*. Cambridge: Harvard University.

Ethnologue. (2009). Chinese, Min Nan. Retrieved from: http://www.ethnologue.com/language/nan

Huang, C.-T. James. (1999). Chinese Passives in Comparative Perspective. *Tsing Hua Journal of Chinese Studies 29*, 423-509. Hsinchu: National Tsing Hua University.

Klöter, Henning. (2004). Language Policy in the KMT and DPP Eras. *China Perspectives* 56. Retrieved from: http://chinaperspectives.revues.org/442

——. (2005). Written Taiwanese. Wiesbaden: Otto Harrassowitz.

Kurpaska, Maria. (2010). Chinese Language(s): a Look through the Prism of The Great Dictionary of Modern Chinese Dialects. In Volker Gast (Ed.), *Trends in Linguistics Studies and Monographs (215)*. Berlin and New York: De Gruyter Mouton.

Lâu, Sêng-hiân (劉承賢). (2010a). *Syntax of Kám Questions in Taiwanese*. Masters thesis. Taipei: National Taiwan Normal University.

——. (2010b). Excising Tags: Distinguishing Between Interrogative SFPs And Tag Questions In Taiwanese. *Taiwan Journal of Linguistics 8*(1), 1-28. Taipei: National Cheng Chi University.

Li, Charles N. & Thompson, Sandra A. (1981). *Mandarin Chinese—A Functional Reference Grammar*. Berkeley: University of California Press.

Li, Chin-An, Yeh, Chieh-Ting & Lee, Marian. (2005). *Harvard Taiwanese 101*. Tainan: King-an Publishing.

Li, Hui-chi. (2008). Obligatory Object Shift in Taiwan Southern Min. In Shin-mei Kao and Shelley Ching-yu Hsieh (Eds.). *NCKU FLLD Monograph Series Vol.1.* : Languages across Cultures, 151-170. Tainan: National Cheng Kung University.

——. (2012). Passives and Causatives in a Specific Taiwanese Construction. *Tsing Hua Journal of Chinese Studies, New Series 42*(1), 169-189. Hsinchu: National Tsing Hua University.

Li, Hui-chi & Hsieh, Ching-yu. (2009). The reference of the third person pronoun i in the ka… hoo construction. *Journal of Taiwanese Vernacular 1*(1), 62-79. Tainan: National Cheng Kung University.

Li, Paul Jen-kuei. (2000). *Formosan languages: The state of the art.* In David Blundell(Ed.), 45-67.

Lien, Chin-fa. (1994). The Order of 'Verb-Complement' Constructions in Taiwan Southern Min.*The Tsing Hua Journal of Chinese Studies, New Series 24*(3), 345-369. Hsinchu: National Tsing Hua University.

——. (2003). In search of covert grammatical categories in Taiwanese Southern Min: a cognitive approach to verb semantics. *Language and Linguistics*(4), 379-402. Taipei: Academia Sinica.

——. (2011). Interface of Modality and the tit4 得 Constructions in Southern Min: A CaseStudy of Their Developments from Earlier Southern Min in the Ming and Qing to Modern Taiwanese Southern Min. *Language and Linguistics 12*(4), 723-752. Taipei: Academia Sinica.

Lin, Alvin. (1999). Writing Taiwanese: The Development of Modern Written Taiwanese.*Sino-Platonic Papers (89)*. Philadelphia: Department of Asian and Middle Eastern Studies, University of Pennsylvania.

Lin, Huei-Ling. (2002). The Interface between Syntax and Morphology: Taiwanese Verbal Complexes. *Proceedings of the 16th Pacific Asia Conference on Language, Information and Computation*, 308-319. Jeju: The Korean Society for Language and Information.

——. (2003). Postverbal Secondary Predicates In Taiwanese. *Taiwan Journal of Linguistics 1*(2), 65-94. Taipei: National Cheng Chi University.

——. (2004). Lexical vs. Syntactic Negation in Taiwanese. *Concentric: Studies in Linguistics (30)*, 107-128. Taipei: National Taipei Normal University.

——. (2012). Preverbal Objects in Taiwan Southern Min: Topic or Focus? *Studies in Chinese Linguistics 33*(3), 165-182. Hong Kong: Chinese University of Hong Kong.

Lin, Yenchun. (2011). Superlatives in Taiwanese. In Zhuo Jing-Schmidt (Ed.), *Proceedings of the 23rd North American Conference on Chinese Lingusitics ()NACCL-23) Volume 2*, 164-174. Eugene: University of Oregon.

Maryknoll Language Service Center. (2001). *Taiwanese-English Dictionary*. Taichung, Taiwan. Retrieved from: http://www.taiwanesedictionary.org/

——. (2013). *English-Taiwanese Dictionary*. Taichung, Taiwan. Retrieved from: http://www.taiwanesedictionary.org/

Norman, Jerry. (1979). Chronological strata in the Min dialects. *Fāngyán* 方言. 4, 268-273.

——. (1991). The Mǐn dialects in historical perspective. In William S.Y. Wang (Ed.). *Languages and dialects of China. Journal of Chinese Linguistics Monograph Series 3*, 325-360. Berkeley: Universiy of California.

Ota, Katsuhiro J. (2005). *An Investigation of Written Taiwanese*. Masters thesis. University of Hawaii at Manoa. Retrieved from ScholarSpace: http://scholarspace.manoa.hawaii.edu/

Ross, Claudia & Ma, Jing-heng Sheng. (2006). *Modern Mandarin Chinese grammar: a practical guide*. New York: Routledge.

Shī Yǒngshēng (施永生). (1990). *Taiwanese Book 2* (2nd ed.). Taichung: Maryknoll Language Service Center.

——. (1997). *Taiwanese Book 1* (2nd ed.). Taichung: Maryknoll Language Service Center.

Symonds, Martin & Seiboth, David. (1998). *Taiwanese Survival Course*. Taipei: Taipei Language Institute Press.

Teng, Shou-Hsin. (1995). Objects and verb-complexes in Taiwanese. In Tsao Fengfu and Tsai Meihuei (Eds.). *Papers from the 1994 Conference on Language Teaching and Linguistics in Taiwan*, 1-22. Taipei: Crane Publishing Co.

Yang, Hui-lang. (2012). *The Interaction of Negatives with Modality, Aspect, and Interrogatives*. Doctoral dissertation. Arizona State University. Retrieved from Arizona State University Digital Repository: http://repository.asu.edu/attachments/93660/content/tmp/package-x7LZKb/Yang_asu_0010E_11800.pdf

Yip, Po-Ching & Rimmington, Don. (2004). *Chinese: a Comprehensive Grammar*. London and New York: Routledge.

Yu, Szu-I Sylvia. (2011). Post-Verbal Markers in Taiwanese Southern Min and Fuzhounese.*Concentric: Studies in Linguistics 37*(2), 241-258. Taipei: National Taipei Normal University.

Zhōnghuá Mínguó Jiàoyùbù 中華民國教育部 [ROC Ministry of Education]. (2011). Retrieved from: http://twblg.dict.edu.tw/holodict_new/index.html

Index

a- 阿 23.2.7
-á 仔 noun suffix 4.1
    tone change rules 2.6.4.1
--á 仔 23.2.6
ability
    expressing ability with modal verbs 12.3
action verbs *see* verbs
additions 30
adjectives 6
    absolute adjectives 6.2
    desirable adjectives 6.4, 10.2.7, 13.2.8
    reduplication 6.7, 14.2.3.1
    tone change rules 2.6.3.10
    undesirable adjectives 6.4, 13.3.4
addressing others *see* names
adverbs 14
    attitude adverbs 14.1.1
    confidence adverbs 14.1.3
    manner adverbs 14.2.3, 26.3.3
    reference adverbs 14.2.1
    relative frequency adverbs 14.2.2, 26.4.3
    time adverbs 14.1.2, 26.2, 26.4.2, 27.1, 28.1, 32.1.2
    tone change rules 2.6.3.6
    word order 14.1.4, 14.2.4, 14.3
after 14.1.2, 32.1.2.2
ah 啊 22.2
--ah 矣 6.5.1, 8.4.1, 12.1.2, 22.1.1, 26.5, 29.3.1
ài 愛
    to need 12.5.1, 13.5.1
    to want 12.2.2, 28.4.1
    to like 12.2.4
all 14.2.1.1.1
although 31.2
aih-ioh 哎唷 22.2
àn 按
    from (time) 15.4

from (place) 15.1
án-chóaⁿ 按怎 *how* 20.5.7
án-chóaⁿ-iūⁿ 按怎樣 *how* 20.5.7
and 15.5, 30.1, 30.2.2
anterior aspect *see* aspect
any
    anyone 5.5.1
    anything 5.5.1
    anywhere 5.5.1
apologies 21.4.4, 23.1.3
appearance verbs *see* verbs
approximations 3.4
arithmetic *see* numbers
as long as 35.3.5
as soon as 32.1.4
aspect 8
    anterior aspect 8.4
    continuous aspect
        dynamic continuous aspect 8.2.1, 9.3, 10.3.3, 26.3.1
        static continuous aspect 7.2.1, 8.2.2, 10.3.3, 26.3.4
    experiential aspect 8.3
    habitual aspect 8.5, 10.2.5, 13.2.4
    perfective aspect 8.1
        with phase complements 8.1.2
    tentative aspect 8.6, 21.3
    tone change rules 2.6.3.4
aspiration 2.1.1, 2.1.4
at 15.3, 15.4, 16.1
āu-lâi 後來 *afterwards (past)* 32.1.2.2
auxiliary verbs *see* modal verbs
bān-it 萬一 *in the event, just in case* 35.3.1
bat 捌 1.2.2.3, 8.3.1, 8.3.3, 13.1.5, 27.6.1
bē 袂 13.3
    as question particle 13.3.2, 22.1.1
    negating ability 13.3.1.2
    negating permission 13.3.1.3
    negating possibility 13.3.1.1
    negating potential complements (unrealized) 13.3.3
    negating undesirable adjectives 6.4.2, 13.3.4
because 32.2.1
before the hour 24.2.2.3
beforehand 14.1.2
beh 欲
    to be going to 12.1.2, 28.2.2
    to want 12.2.1, 28.4.1

beh-ài 欲愛 *to want (noun)* 12.2.4
benefactives 15.7, 18.3
besides 30.4.3.1
between 6.3.2, 24.1.2.3
bián 免 12.5.1
    as question particle 13.5.2, 22.1.1
    negating obligation 13.5.1
bô 無 13.2
    as a general-purpose question tag 13.2.7.1
    as a universal question particle 12.2.7.3, 20.3.2, 22.1.1
    as an emphasis marker 13.2.5
    if not, or else 35.4
    negating desirable adjectives 6.4.2, 13.2.8
    negating existence 13.2.1
    negating experiential aspect 13.2.3
    negating habitual aspect 13.2.4
    negating perfective aspect 8.1.1, 13.2.2, 13.2.7.2, 22.1.1
    negating phase complements 13.2.6
    negating possession 13.2.1
    negating potential complements (actualized) 13.2.6
bô kàu 無到 *not even* 3.4.4
bô-lūn 無論 *regardless, no matter, whether or not* 35.3.6
bōe 未 see **iáu-bōe** 猶未
    negating anterior aspect 8.4, 13.4.1
    as question particle 13.4.2, 22.1.1
both 14.2.1.1.1, 30.2.2
but 31.1.1, 31.2.1
but also 30.2.3
calendar time 25
can 12.3.1, 12.3.2, 13.3.1.2
cardinal directions 16.2.3
cause and effect 32.2
causative verbs *see* verbs
chah 閘 *by means of (a vehicle), via* 15.6
change 29
    change-of-state action verbs 7.2
    change-of-state particle 6.5.1
    changes over time 6.8.1, 29.6
    intransitive changes 29.1.1
    transitive changes 29.1.2
characters 1.4.1
che 這 *this* 5.4.3
chē 坐
    by means of (a vehicle), via 15.6
    posture verbs 16.3.3.4

prepositions doubling as verbs 15.9
chêng 從 *from, since (time specified)* 15.4
chêng-lâi 從來 *from the beginning* 8.3.1
chha 差 *before the hour* 24.2.2.3
chha-put-to 差不多 *almost, nearly* 3.4.2
chham 參 *with, and* 15.5, 30.1
chhì 試 *to try* 8.6.4
chhiáⁿ 請 *please* 21.4.1
chhiáⁿ-kàu 請教 *may I ask (for your advice)* 21.4.1
chhiáⁿ-mn̄g 請問 *may I ask* 21.4.1
chì 至
    to (time specified) 15.4
    to (range) 24.1.2.3
chí-iàu 只要 *as long as, provided that, if only* 35.3.5
chia 遮 *here* 2.6.4.3
chia-ê 遮的 *these* 4.6.3
chia--ê 遮的 *these (ones)* 5.4.2
chiah 才
    only, only have exclusivity 14.2.1.4
    just, only then promptness 14.2.1.5, 32.1.3.2
chiah-nī-á 遮爾仔 *so, as much as* 6.3.7
chiâⁿ 成 *almost, nearly* 3.4.2
chìn-chêng 進前 *previous to* 32.1.2.1
chîⁿ 錢 *money* 3.5
chioh 借 *to borrow/to lend* 18.2.4
chiong 將 17.4.3
chit 這 *this* 4.6.1
chit 這 *these* 4.6.2
chit-bīn...chit-bīn... 一面...一面... 34.1.1
chit-ē 一下 *a little bit*
    tentative aspect 8.6.2, 21.3.2
    as soon as 32.1.4
chiū-sǹg sī 就算是 *even if* 35.3.3
-chò 做 *to change into* 29.2.1
chò-hóe 做伙 *together* 34.1.3
chó-iū 左右 *more or less* 3.4.2
chò-tīn 做陣 *together* 34.1.3
chóaⁿ-iūⁿ 怎樣 *how* 20.5.7
chóng--sī 總是
    but, however 31.1.1
    regardless, no matter what, in any case 35.3.6
cho͘ 租 *to rent* 18.2.4
chún-chò 準做 *even if* 35.3.3
clock time *see* time
colloquial reading 1.2.2.2

commands 21
    causative verbs in commands 21.8
    group proposals 21.6
    manner adverbs in commands 14.2.3.3
    modal verbs in commands 21.5
    negative commands 21.7
    with kā 共 construction 17.4.5, 21.9
comparisons 6.3
    comparative degree 6.3.9
    superlative degree 6.3.10
complements *see* verb complements
conditionals 35
conjunctions 31.1.1
    tone change rules 2.6.3.10
continuous aspect *see* aspect
contractions 2.3.1
contrasts 31
dates 25.5
dative verbs *see* verbs
days 25.4
decimals *see* numbers
default objects *see* objects
definite nouns *see* nouns
definite objects *see* objects
demonstratives 4.6
    demonstrative adjectives 4.6.1, 4.6.2, 4.6.3
    demonstrative pronouns 4.6.3, 5.4
despite 31.2
destination verbs *see* verbs
direct objects *see* objects
directional complements *see* complements
directional expresssions 16.4
discounts *see* numbers
displacement verbs *see* verbs
duration
    approximate duration 24.1.2, 25.2.2
    duration complements 11.8
    duration for action verbs 7.1.1
    exact duration 24.1.1
    including duration and objects 7.1.5
ê 的
    as modifying particle 6.6
    as possessive marker 4.8.1
--ê 的 23.2.5
ē 會

desirable adjectives 6.4.2, 13.3.4
    will 12.1.1, 13.3.1.1, 28.2.1
    can 12.3.1, 13.3.1.2
-ē- 會
    potential complements (unrealized) 11.4.2, 13.3.3
ē-ēng-tit 會用得 *may* 12.4.1, 13.3.1.3, 21.5
ē-hiáu 會曉 *can* 12.3.1, 13.3.1.2
ē-sái(-tit) 會使(得) *may* 12.4.1, 13.3.1.3, 21.5
ē-tàng 會當
    can 12.3.2, 13.3.1.2
    may 12.4.1, 13.3.1.3, 21.5
eh 欸 22.2
eh 喂 22.2
emphasis 10.2.4, 13.2.5, 27.2.3
end-of-sentence particles *see* particles
eng-kai 應該 *should* 12.5.2
ēng 用 *with (an instrument or appliance)* 15.6
estimates numbers
except for 30.4.3.2
exclamatory particles 22.2
existence 10.1.4, 10.2.2, 10.3.1, 13.2.1
experiential aspect *see* aspect
extent complements *see* verb complements
even if 35.3.3
even more 6.1.1, 6.3.9
even though see although
every
    everyone 5.5.1
    everything 5.5.1
    everywhere 5.5.1
family names *see* names
finals 2.2
focusing construction *see* **sī** 是
fractions *see* numbers
frequency
    absolute frequency complements 11.8
    absolute frequency for action verbs 7.1.2
    including objects and frequency 7.1.6
furthermore 30.4.1
future time 28
    change in the immediate future 29.4
    imminent actions 12.1.3, 28.3
    time expressions and adverbs for the future 28.1
given names *see* names
goodbyes *see* salutations

gratitude 23.1.2
greetings 23.1.1
-gōa 外 *more than* 3.4.3, 24.1.2.1
gōa-chē 偌濟 *how much, how many* 20.5.8
gōa-kú 偌久 *how long (time)* 20.5.9
gōa-tn̂g 偌長 *how long (length)* 20.5.9
gōa-tōa 偌大 *how big* 20.5.9
habitual actions
    in the past 8.5.1, 10.2.5, 27.3
    in the present 8.5.2, 26.4
        manner complement indicating habitual actions 11.6.1
        specifying time of habitual occurrences 24.3.3, 34.2.3
habitual aspect *see* aspect
haih 唉 22.2
half 3.3.1
    multiples 3.3.6
        time (duration) 24.1.1
        time (clock) 24.2.2.1
hām 和 *with, and* 15.5, 30.1
haⁿh 哈 22.2
he 彼 *that* 5.4.3
heⁿh 嘿 22.2
hia 遐 *there* 2.6.4.3
hia-ê 遐的 *those* 4.6.3
hia--ê 遐的 *those (ones)* 5.4.2
hiah-nī-á 遐爾仔 *so, as much as* 6.3.7
hioh 諾 22.2
hit 彼 *that* 4.6.1
hit 彼 *those* 4.6.2
hngh 哼 22.2
hó 好
    easy to + action verb 6.4.1
    as phase complement 8.1.2, 11.1.1, 27.2.2
-hó 好
    as resultative complement 11.2
    greetings 23.1.1
hóan-tò-tńg 反倒轉 *nevertheless, on the contrary* 31.2
--hoⁿh 乎 20.2.3, 22.1.1, 22.2
hour 24.1, 24.2
how 20.5.7
how big 20.5.9
how long 20.5.9
how much/many 20.5.8
however 31.1.1, 31.2.1
hō· 予

    as a causative verb 19.4, 21.8
    extent complements 11.7.2
    indicating indirect objects 15.8.1, 18.1
    indicating passive voice 15.8.3, 19.1
hoh 謼 22.2
hun-chi 分之 3.3.1, 3.3.3
í-āu 以後 *after (time), later* 32.1.2.2
í-chêng 以前 *previously, in the past* 32.1.2.1
i-góa 以外 *apart from* 30.4.3
í-hā 以下 *less than* 3.4.4, 24.1.2.2
í-lāi 以內 *within* 24.1.2.3
í-siōng 以上 *more than* 3.4.3, 24.1.2.1
iā 也
    also 14.2.1, 30.2.1
    and 30.3.1
iā-sī 也是 *but also...* 30.2.3
iah-sī 抑是 *or* 20.4.1
iáu-bōe 猶未 *not yet*
    negating anterior aspect 8.4, 13.4.1, 27.2.5
    negating possibility modal verb **beh** 欲 12.1.2
iáu-koh 猶閣
    but also... 30.2.3
    still more 6.3.9, 14.2.1.3
    still yet 30.3.2
iáu-m̄-koh 猶毋過 *but still* 31.1.1
iáu-ū 猶有 *in addition, also* 30.4.2
if not 35.4
if not for 35.3.4
if only 35.3.5
if-then clauses 35.2
imperatives *see* comands
in 15.3, 16.1
in any case 35.3.6
in the event 35.3.1
in-ūi 因為 *because* 32.2.1
indefinite objects *see* objects
indefinite pronouns *see* pronouns
indirect objects *see* objects
initials 2.1
intensifiers 6.1, 9.2
interjections *see* exclamatory particles
intransitive verbs 29.1.1
introductions 23.2
it-tàn 一旦 *in the event, just in case* 35.3.1
it-tēng 一定 *definitely* 12.5.2, 14.1.3

iū-koh 又閣
>   *both...and...* 30.2.2
>   *moreover, furthermore* 30.4.1

jî-chhiáⁿ 而且 *moreover, furthermore* 30.4.1

jiân-āu 然後 *afterwards* 32.1.2.2

jú lâi jú 愈來愈
>   *more and more* 6.8.1, 29.6.1
>   *less and less* 29.6.2

jú-khah 愈較 *even more* 6.3.9

jû-kó 如果 *if* 35.2

just in case 35.3.1

--ka 家 23.2.8

kā 共
>   *benefactive* 15.7, 18.3, 33.5
>   *facing, towards* 15.2
>   in the passive voice 19.3
>   kā 共 construction 4.9, 15.8.2, 17.4, 21.9
>   *to* 15.5

ká-sú-nā 假使若 *if* 35.2

ka-tī 家己 *oneself* 5.2

kah 甲
>   *extent* 11.7.1
>   *to* 15.1

kah 佮 *with, from (source)* 15.5, 30.1

kak 角 *dime* 3.5

kám 敢 1.2.2.3, 11.5, 20.1

kan-na 干焦 *only, only have* 14.2.1.4

kāng-khóan 仝款 *same, equally* 6.3.8

kàu 到 *to, arrive*
>   in directional expresssions 16.4
>   indicating endpoint to duration 7.1.3, 15.1
>   prepositions doubling as verbs 15.9

khah 盍 *why, how could it be* 20.5.6

khah 較 *comparatively, more* 6.3, 21.1

khah-bián 較免 33.4

khah-kóng 較講 *regardless, no matter what, in any case* 35.3.6

khàu 扣 *to deduct* 3.3.4

khì 去
>   in the passive voice 15.8.3
>   in commands 21.1
>   indicating purpose 33.2

-khì 去 *away from (speaker perspective)* 7.1.3, 11.3.1, 15.1, 16.4, 16.4.2

--khì 去 *indicating a worsening condition* 6.5.2, 29.3

khiok-sī 卻是 *nevertheless, on the contrary* 31.2

khòaⁿ-māi 看覓 *to check out* 8.6.3

kho͘ 箍 *dollar* 3.5
kì-jiân 既然 *since* 32.2.2
kinship terms 23.3
kiōng-beh 強欲 *just about to* 12.1.3, 14.1.2, 28.3
kóa 寡 *some* 4.4, 20.5.5
-kòe 過 experiential aspect 8.3.2, 8.3.3, 13.2.3, 27.6.1
koh 閣
    again 14.2.1.2, 27.4
    both...and... 30.2.2
    but also... 30.2.3
koh-khah 閣較 *even more* 6.3.9
kú 久
    question word 20.5.9
    with duration *long (time)* 7.1.1
kúi 幾 *several* 3.4.3, 4.5
kúi 幾 *how many* 4.5, 20.5.8
kùi 貴 *honorable* 23.2.1
kúi tiám 幾點 *what time (clock)* 20.5.4
--lah 啦 22.1.1, 29.3.2
lâi 來 indicating purpose 33.2
-lâi 來 *towards (speaker perspective)* 7.1.3, 11.3.1, 15.1, 16.4, 16.4.2
last 14.1.2
--leh 咧 7.2.1, 8.2.2, 10.3.3, 21.1, 21.3.1, 22.1.1, 26.3.4, 34.2.1
lēng-gōa 另外
    and 30.3.1
    in addition, also 30.4.2
less and less 29.6.2
lī 離 *set apart from* 15.3
liaison 2.3.2, 4.1
liáu 了
    as manner complement 11.6.2
    as phase complement 8.1.2, 11.1.1, 27.2.2
-liáu 了 as resultative complement 11.2
liáu-āu 了後 *after (events)* 32.1.2.2
literary reading 1.2.2.2
    numbers 3.1.2
loanwords 1.2.2.2
location expressions 16
location participles 16.2
    tone change rules 2.6.3.8
--loh 囉 22.1.1
lóng 攏 *both, all* 5.5.1, 5.5.2, 14.2.1.1.1, 14.2.1.1.3
m̄ 毋 13.1
    as question particle 20.3.1, 22.1.1
    as question tag 20.2.4

Index 621

    not 13.1.1, 20.2.4
    not want 13.1.2, 20.3.1
m̄-bián 毋免 *see* **bián** 免
m̄-chiah 毋才 *therefore, as a result* 32.2.3
m̄-hó 毋好 *do not* 6.4.3, 12.6.3, 13.1.4, 21.7
m̄-kóan 毋管 *regardless, no matter, whether or not* 35.3.6
m̄-koh 毋過 *but, however* 31.1.1, 31.2.1
m̄-nā 毋但 *not only...* 30.2.3
m̄-thang 毋通 *do not* 12.4.2, 12.6.2, 13.1.4, 21.7
m̄-tú-hó 毋拄好 *in the event, just in case* 35.3.1
mā 嘛
    also 5.5.1, 5.5.2, 14.2.1.1.2, 14.2.1.1.3, 30.2.1
    and 30.3.1
mâ-hôan lí 麻煩你 *may I trouble you* 21.4.2
mā-sī 嘛是 *but also...* 30.2.3
--mah 嘛 22.1.1
mài 莫 *do not* 12.6.1, 13.1.4, 21.7
manner complements *see* verb complements
may 12.4.1, 12.4.2, 13.3.1.3, 21.5
may I ask 21.4.1
may I ask (for your advice) 21.4.1
may I trouble you 21.4.2
measure words 4.3
    group measure words 4.4
    tone change rules 2.6.3.10
minute 24.1, 24.2
modal verbs *see* verbs
money 3.5
months 25.2
more and more 6.8.1, 29.6.1
more or less 3.4.2
more than 3.4.3, 24.1.2.1
moreover 30.4.1
múi 每 *each, every* 26.4.2
multiples *see* numbers
must 12.5
ná 哪 *why* 20.5.6
nā 若 *if* 35.2
nā-bô 若無
    if not for 35.3.4
    if not 35.4
ná-bōe 哪未 *why haven't* 20.5.6
nā-chún 若準 *if* 35.2
ná-ē 哪會 *why would* 20.5.6
ná lâi ná 那來那

more and more 29.6.1
less and less 29.6.2
ná-m̄ 哪毋 *why wouldn't* 20.5.6
nā-m̄-sī 若毋是 *if it weren't for* 35.3.4
ná...ná... 那...那... 34.1.1
nā-sī 若是 *if* 35.2
ná-tióh 哪著 *why should* 20.5.6
names 23.2
    given names 23.2.2
    surnames 23.2.1
    titles 23.2.3
    tone change rules 2.6.4.2
nasals 1.2.2.1, 2.2.1
nearly 3.4.2
need 12.5.1, 13.5.1
negation 1.2.2.3, 13
    negative question particles 20.3.1
    tone change rules 2.6.3.10
    with duration complements 11.8.3
    with frequency complements 11.8.3
--neh 呢 22.1.1
never 13.1.1, 13.2.3
nevertheless 31.2
next 14.1.2, 28.1
niā-niā 爾爾 *nothing more* 14.2.1.4
--nih 呢 20.2.3, 22.1.1
no matter 35.3.6
no one 5.5.2
nobody 5.5.2
none 5.5.2
not any 5.5.2
nothing 5.5.2
nouns 4
    decimals 3.3.5
    definite 4.9, 11.3.3.2
    discounts 3.3.4
    indefinite 4.9, 11.2.2,
    modifying without 的 ê 6.6.3
    noun phrases and modifying particle 的 ê 6.6
    omitting the noun 4.7, 6.6.4
    plural with group measure words 4.4
    tone change rules 2.6.3.1
nowhere 5.5.2
numbers 3
    arithmetic 3.3.7

Index   623

        counting numbers 3.1
        estimates 3.4.2
        fractions 3.3.1
        literary reading for numbers 3.1.2
        multiples 3.3.6
        numbers with measure word forms 4.3.1
        ordinal numbers 3.2
        percentages 3.3.3
        range 3.4.1
        rates 3.3.2
        tone change rules 2.6.3.9
o'clock 24.2.1
ôan 完 as phase complement 8.1.2, 11.1.1, 27.2.2
-ôan 完 as resultative complement 11.2
objects
        default objects 7.1.4
        definite objects 11.2.2.2, 11.3.3
        direct objects 1.2.2.3, 17
        indefinite objects 11.3.3
        indirect objects 18
        kā 共 construction 11.3.3.1
        objects and duration 7.1.5
        objects and frequency 7.1.6
        pre-posed objects 17.1
        topicalized objects 11.3.3.1, 17.2
        with directional complements 11.3.3
        with duration complements 11.8.2
        with extent complements 11.7.3
        with frequency complements 11.8.2
        with manner complements 11.6.3
        with phase complements 11.1.4
        with potential complements 11.4.4
        with resultative complements 11.2.2
oeh 喂 22.2, 23.1.1
on 15.3, 16.1
or disjunctive questions 20.4
or else 35.4
otherwise 35.4
--oh 喔 22.1.1, 22.2
pài-thok 拜托 *please* 21.4.3
palatalization 2.1.3, 2.1.4
particles 22
        double particles 22.1.2
        end-of-sentence particles 22.1
        exclamatory particles 22.1.2

negative question particles 20.3.1
passive voice 19
past the hour 24.2.2.2
past time 27
    completed actions 27.2
    past experiences 27.6
    recent past 27.5
    repeated events in the past 27.4
    stative verbs 9.4
    time expressions and adverbs for the past 27.1
pēng-chhiáⁿ 並且 *moreover, furthermore* 30.4.1
pêⁿ 平 *equally* 6.3.8
percentages *see* numbers
perfective aspect *see* aspect
permission 12.4
phah chiat 拍折 *to discount* 3.3.4
pháiⁿ 歹 *difficult to* 6.4.1
pháiⁿ-sè 歹勢 *apologies* 21.4.4, 23.1.3
phase complements *see* verb complements
please 21.4.1
pí 比 *compared with* 6.3
pí-kàu 比較 *to compare* 6.3.2
placement verbs *see* verbs
pòaⁿ 半 *half* 3.3.1
    multiples 3.3.6
    time (duration) 24.1.1
    time (clock) 24.2.2.1
pōe 倍 *-fold* 3.3.6
possessive 4.8
    implied possessive 4.8.2, 4.8.3
    possession with demonstrative adjectives 5.3.3
    possession with plural personal pronouns 5.3.2
    possessive pronouns 5.3
possibility
    expressing possibility with modal verbs 12.1
posture verbs *see* verbs
potential complements 10.2.6.2, 11.4
    potential complements (actualized) 11.4.1, 13.2.6
    potential complements (unrealized) 11.4.2
    versus modal verbs 11.4.2
pre-posed objects *see* objects
prepositions 15
    doubling as verbs 15.9
    in directional expresssions 16.4
    in location expressions 16.1

    of accompaniment and interaction 15.5
    of location 15.3, 16.1
    of manner 15.6, 16.4
    of movement 15.1
    of orientation 15.2
    of time 15.4
    tone change rules 2.6.3.10
present time 26
    time expressions and adverbs for the present 26.2
prices 3.5
prohibition 12.6, 13.1.4, 21.7
pronouns 5
    demonstrative pronouns 4.6.3, 5.4
    indefinite pronouns 5.5
    personal pronouns 5.1, 11.2.2.2, 11.4.4
    plural pronoun suffix 5.1.3
    possessive pronouns 5.3
    reflexive pronouns 5.2
    tone change rules 2.6.3.2
pronunciation 2
    regional variation 2.4
provided that 35.3.5
purpose 33
put-tān 不但 *not only...* 20.2.3
questions 20
    affirmative-negative questions 13.1.3.1, 20.4.3
    disjunctive questions 20.4
    particle questions 13.2.7.2, 13.2.7.3, 20.3
    question words 20.5
    tag questions 13.1.3.2, 20.2
    tone change rules 2.6.3.7
range *see* numbers
rates *see* numbers
regardless 35.3.6
relatives *see* kinship terms
repetition
    repetitive movements 8.2.2.3
    tentative aspect 8.6.1, 21.3.1
requests *see* commands
resultative complements *see* verb complements
Romanization 1.4.2
salutations 23.1.4
saⁿ-kap 相佮 *together* 34.1.3
seasons 25.6
second (time) 24.1

second (ordinal) 3.2
--**sêng** 成 *to successfully become* 29.2.2
--**sèⁿ** 姓 23.2.4
sequence 32
should 12.5.2
sī 是
    existence 10.1.4
    focusing construction 10.1.2, 19
    linking verb 10.1.1
    passive voice 10.1.3
sī-án-chóaⁿ 是按怎 *why* 20.5.6
sī--bô 是無 *is that right?* 20.2.1
sī tio̍h--bô 是著無 *is that right?* 20.2.1
sián 仙 *cent* 3.5
siāng-sî 像時 *at the same time* 34.1.2
siáⁿ 啥 *what* 20.5.1
siáⁿ-lâng 啥人 *who, whom* 20.5.2
siáⁿ-lâng ê 啥人的 *whose* 20.5.10
siáⁿ-mi̍h 啥物 *what* 20.5.1
siáⁿ-mi̍h lâng 啥物人 *who, whom* 20.5.2
siáⁿ-mi̍h lâng ê 啥物人的 *whose* 20.5.10
siáⁿ-mi̍h sî-hāu 啥物時後 *when* 20.5.4
siáⁿ-mi̍h sî-kan 啥物時間 *when* 20.5.4
siáⁿ-mi̍h sî-chūn 啥物時陣 *when* 20.5.4
siáⁿ-mi̍h só͘-chāi 啥物所在 *where* 20.5.3
sīm-chì 甚至 *but also...* 30.2.3
sīm-mi̍h 甚物 *what* 20.5.1
sīm-mi̍h lâng 甚物人 *who, whom* 20.5.2
sīm-mi̍h lâng ê 甚物人的 *whose* 20.5.10
sīm-mi̍h sî-hāu 甚物時後 *when* 20.5.4
sīm-mi̍h sî-kan 甚物時間 *when* 20.5.4
sīm-mi̍h sî-chūn 甚物時陣 *when* 20.5.4
sīm-mi̍h só͘-chāi 甚物所在 *where* 20.5.3
simultaneous actions 34
since 32.2.2
sió 小 *small* 21.3.2, 23.2.1
sio-kāng 相仝 *same, identical* 6.3.8
siōng 上 *most* 6.3.10
siūⁿ-ài 想愛 *would like, thinking of* 12.2.3, 28.4.2
siūⁿ-beh 想欲 *would like, thinking of* 12.2.3, 28.4.2
soah 煞
    as adverb 14.1.1
    as phase complement 8.1.2, 11.1.1, 27.2.2
someone 5.5.3
something 5.5.3

sometimes 14.2.2
somewhere 5.5.3
sorry see apologies
só-í 所以 *therefore* 32.2.1
special verbs *see* verbs
stative verbs *see* verbs
still 14.2.1
still more 6.3.9, 14.2.1.3
still yet 30.3.2
stops 1.2.2.1, 2.2.2
su-iàu 需要 *to need* 12.5.1
sui-jiân 雖然 *although* 31.2
sūn 順 *following along* 15.1
surnames *see* names
tȧk 逐 *each, every* 26.4.2
tàm 跮 *at, on in* 15.3, 16.1
tān-sī 但是 *but, however* 31.1.1, 31.2.1
tâng-chê 同齊 *together* 34.1.3
tang-sî 當時 *when* 20.5.4
tàu-tīn 鬥陣 *together* 34.1.3
tē- 第 3.2
teh 咧 8.2.1.1, 8.5.1, 10.2.4, 10.2.5, 26.3.2
teh-beh 咧欲 *just about to* 12.1.3, 14.1.2, 28.3
telling time 24.2.1
tentative aspect *see* aspect
terms of address 23
thang(-hó) 通(好) *may* 12.4.2
thank you see gratitude
that 4.6.1, 5.4.3
thâu-tú-á 頭拄仔 *to have just* 27.5
thè 替 *to stand in for* 15.7, 18.3, 33.5
there 2.6.4.3
there is see existence
therefore 32.2.1, 32.2.3
those 4.6.2, 4.6.3
those (ones) 5.4.2
tī 佇 10.3
existence 10.3.1
on, at (time) 15.4
on, at, in (place) 10.2.2, 15.3, 16.1
prepositions doubling as verbs 15.9
tī-leh 佇咧 8.2.1.2, 26.3.2, 10.3.3
tī-sî 底時 *when* 20.5.4
tiám 點 *point* 3.3.5
tian-tò 顛倒 *nevertheless, on the contrary* 31.2

tih 挃 *to want to have* 12.2.2
time 24
    time adverbs 14.1.2, 26.2, 26.4.2, 27.1, 28.1, 32.1.2
    time expressions 26.2, 27.1, 28.1
-tio̍h 著
    manner complement indicating habitual actions 11.6.1
    phase complement indicating achievement 11.1.2
tio̍h-ài 著愛 *to need* 12.5.1, 13.5.1
tio̍h--bô 著無 *is that right?* 20.2.1
-tit 得 potential complements (unrealized) 11.4.3
titles 23.2.3
tng 當 *facing, in front of* 15.2
tng-teh 當咧 8.2.1.2, 26.3.2
to
    destination 15.1, 16.4
    indicating indirect objects 15.8.1, 18
    interaction 15.5
    orientation 15.2
    time 15.4, 24.2.2.3
tó 佗 *which* 20.5.5
tō 就 *just, then* 14.2.1.5, 32.1.3.1
tó-ūi 佗位 *where* 20.5.3
tòa 蹛 *at, on, in* 15.3, 16.1
toeh 佗 *where* 20.5.3
together 34.1.3
toh 佗 *where* 20.5.3
tones 2.5
    comparison to Mandarin 1.2.2
    neutral tone 2.6.2
    tone changes 1.2.2.1, 2.5.3
    tone change rules 2.6
    tone diacritics 2.5.2
topicalized objects *see* objects
transitive verbs 29.1.2
tû-hui 除非 *unless, only if* 35.3.2
tû-liáu 除了
    besides, in addition to 30.4.3.1
    except for, not including 30.4.3.2
tú-teh 拄咧 8.2.1.2, 26.3.2
tùi 對
    coming from, going towards (movement) 15.1
    facing, towards, to (orientation) 15.2
    from (time) 15.4
    with, and (interaction) 15.5
ū 有

Index   629

    desirable adjectives 6.4.2, 10.2.7
    emphasis 10.2.4, 27.2.3
    existence 10.1.4, 10.2.2
    expressing *some-* 5.5.3
    habitual aspect 8.5.1, 10.2.5, 26.4.1
    perfective aspect 1.2.2.3, 8.1.1, 10.2.3, 27.2
    phase complement indicating achievement 11.1.2
    phase complement indicating potential 11.1.3
    possession 10.2.1
    potential complements (actualized) 10.2.6.2, 11.4.1
ùi 對 *see* tùi 對 preposition of movement
ūi 為
    benefactive 15.7, 18.3, 33.5
ūi-siáⁿ-mih 為啥物 *why* 20.5.6
ūi-sīm-mih 為甚物 *why* 20.5.6
ūi-tio̍h 為著 indicating purpose 33.3
unless, only if 35.3.2
verbs
    action verbs 7
        open-ended action verbs 7.1
        change-of-state action verbs 7.2
    appearance verbs 16.3.3.3
    causative verbs 19.4, 21.8
    dative verbs 18.2
    destination verbs 16.4.1
    displacement verbs 16.3.3.1
    modal verbs 12
        of ability 12.3
        of desire 12.2, 28.4
        of obligation 12.5
        of permission 12.4
        of possibility 12.1, 28.2.1
        of prohibition 12.6
        versus potential complements 11.4.2
    placement verbs 16.3.3.2
    posture verbs 16.3.3.4
    special verbs 10
    stative verbs 9
        doubling as change-of-state verbs 7.2.2
    tone change rules 2.6.3.3
verb complements 11
    directional complements 11.3
        indicating speaker perspective 7.1.3, 11.3.1
        double-directional complements 11.3.2
    duration complements 11.8

      extent complements 1.2.2.3, 11.7
      frequency complements 11.8
      manner complements 1.2.2.3, 11.6
           versus manner adverbs 11.6.2
      phase complements 10.2.6.1, 11.1
           indicating perfective aspect 8.1.2, 10.2.4, 13.2.6, 27.2.2
           indicating achievement 11.1.2, 13.2.6
           indicating potential 11.1.3, 13.2.6
      potential complements 1.2.2.3, 10.2.6.2, 11.4
      resultative complements 11.2, 29.2
      tone change rules 2.6.3.5
verb copying 7.1.5, 7.1.6, 17.3
voicing 2.1.2, 2.1.4
welcome 23.1.1
weeks 25.3
what 20.5.1
whatever 5.5.1
when 20.5.4
whenever 5.5.1
where 20.5.3
wherever 5.5.1
whether or not 35.3.6
which 20.5.5
whichever 5.5.1
who/whom 20.5.2
whoever/whomever 5.5.1
whose 20.5.10
why 20.5.6
with
      accompaniment 15.5, 30.1
      by means of 15.6
within 16.2.1, 24.1.2.3
years 25.1